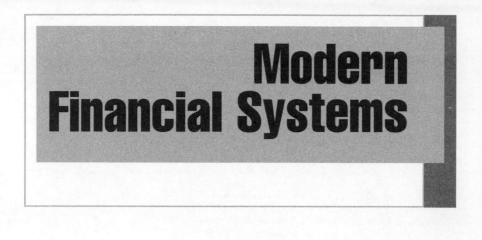

Modern Financial Systems

The Frank J. Fabozzi Series

Modern Financial Systems

Theory and Applications

EDWIN H. NEAVE

WILEY

John Wiley & Sons, Inc.

Published by John Wiley & Sons, Inc., Hoboken, New Jersey.
Published simultaneously in Canada.

For general information on our other products and services or for technical support, please contact our Customer Care Department within the United States at (800) 762-2974, outside the United States at (317) 572-3993 or fax (317) 572-4002.

Wiley also publishes its books in a variety of electronic formats. Some content that appears in print may not be available in electronic formats. For more information about Wiley products, visit our Web site at www.wiley.com.

Library of Congress Cataloging-in-Publication Data

Neave, Edwin H.
  Modern financial systems : theory and applications / Edwin H. Neave.
      p.   cm. – (The Frank J. Fabozzi series)
  Includes index.
  ISBN 978-0-470-41973-1 (cloth)
  1. Finance.   2. Financial institutions.   I. Title.
  HG173.N334 2010
  332–dc22

                                                           2009014325

Printed in the United States of America.

10 9 8 7 6 5 4 3 2 1

This book is for Liz.

Contents

Preface

This book is a theoretical survey of financial system activity illustrated with the way the theory applies in practice. The theoretical sections outline the economic principles underlying the organization of financial systems and show how a system's component institutions and markets complement each other. The applications sections illustrate how the principles affect financial transactions as well as the institutions and markets that carry them out.

It is argued here that financial markets and institutions with differing capabilities are aligned against groups of transactions with differing attribute combinations in a process that aims to achieve cost-effective forms of financial governance. The alignments within a financial system evolve over time. The book identifies the forces driving change and illustrates how they do so. Especially, the book focuses on why financial system organization has been changing so rapidly since the beginning of the 1970s and how those changes present the analyst with profit opportunities.

The focus on principles permits a more integrated analysis and a more concise description of financial systems than is found in other texts. For example, many texts describing financial activities do not analyze how markets and intermediaries complement each other. Yet *complementarity* is one of the financial system's main organizing principles, and by recognizing the interactions between different parts of the system, we can solve such puzzles as:

- Why have banks focused much less heavily on savings deposits and much more heavily on mutual funds since the 1980s?
- Why do some corporate borrowings use market issues of securities while others use bank loans?
- Why did most, but not all, forms of swaps evolve from negotiated arrangements into standardized market transactions?
- What explains the growth of credit default swaps and how have they contributed to the financial system turmoil of 2007–2008?

The capstone survey is aimed at students who are already familiar with the basic ideas of financial theory and financial practice. Its main purpose is to explain financial activity within an integrated, coherent framework. It does so by showing how financial organizations are shaped by the economics of setting up and governing financial transactions or deals. For example, the book explains the principles underlying securitization and how these principles have been applied to different markets at different times. It shows that securitization does not indicate the demise of banking activity (as has been conjectured), explains why securitization of standard mortgages worked so well, and why securitization of subprime mortgages worked so badly. As a second example, the book illustrates the main ideas used in designing and valuing risk management instruments rather than merely describing their detail.

The book aims to strengthen readers' understanding of the economic forces shaping modern financial systems and how the markets and institutions in these systems interact with each other. Whether the readers of this book are undergraduate or graduate students, whether they are in economics or in business, is not as important as whether they are familiar with the principles of finance. Earlier versions of this book have been used both with students and with financial system professionals continuing their education. Members of these audiences can use the material most productively if they are already familiar with the principal concepts underlying financial practice.

The unified perspective on financial system activity here is drawn on a selection of literature, but it is not intended as a definitive survey. Its approach is closest in spirit to Allen and Gale's *Comparing Financial Systems* (2000), but the present work discusses financial governance at greater length than do Allen and Gale and also contains more applications material. The book surveys existing theories of banking, but it does not cover them in the same depth as Freixas and Rochet (1997, 2008) or Lewis (1995). Similarly, its analysis of markets is much less detailed than the work of O'Hara (1995). In yet another comparison, the present book relies on Crane et al. (1995) to identify financial functions, but emphasizes financial governance to a greater extent than do Crane and his colleagues. It recognizes the Bodie-Merton (2005) view that financial systems tend toward the forms explained by the neoclassical paradigm, while arguing further that the economics of governance profoundly and permanently affect the types of organizations present within a financial system. Finally, the book's focus on economic principles means it offers less institutional detail than such other texts as Johnson (2000) or Mishkin (2007).

Many readers have provided constructive commentary during the preparation of this material. Their willingness to question some of the ideas here have contributed substantially to improving the material. While it is not possible to recognize all contributions individually, I cannot omit telling

Rosaire Couturier, Mike Durland, Bulat Gainullin, Lew Johnson, Popon Kangpenkae, Mike McIntyre, Mike Ross, Serge Slavinsky, and Brishen Viaud how much I have benefited from their commentary.

The series editor, Frank J. Fabozzi, suggested important improvements to this manuscript. He consistently urged rewrites that introduced substantial distinctions to the material, and I am deeply grateful for his advice. Our working relationship has been both productive and highly enjoyable. Equally importantly, in cases of interpretive differences, Frank has been especially tolerant of author independence. Accordingly, the conclusions here are solely my responsibility.

EDWIN H. NEAVE
Queen's University
January 2009

Theoretical Overview

This part outlines how individual financial transactions are governed. The process is one in which financiers and their clients jointly strive to find cost-effective alignments of governance mechanisms' capabilities with transaction attributes. Classes of similar transactions are governed by financial firms that have specialized capabilities, thus explaining system organization at the level of institutions and the markets in which they trade.

Customary alignments evolve as transaction attributes change and as governance mechanisms' capabilities evolve, meaning that the details of transaction governance can change over time. As the operating economics of financial institutions and markets change, alignments also change at the aggregate level, thus explaining changes in financial system structure.

CHAPTER 1

Introduction

After introducing the book's aims and approach, this chapter stresses the importance of financial system analysis. Financial and economic activities are mutually interrelated, with the consequence that financial activity can affect the rate of economic growth, the types of projects funded, and the well-being of economic agents. The chapter argues further that, while financial systems exhibit wide-ranging differences in appearance, their structure and activities have greater commonality than is customarily realized. Indeed, the apparent complexity and uniqueness of financial system organization can be explained in terms of a relatively small number of concepts. First, all financial systems perform the same, relatively small set of functions, and differ mainly in the ways the functions are organized within financial firms and financial markets. Second, transactions differ in the combinations of attributes[1] they present, but the taxonomy of attributes is essentially fixed and the attributes themselves relatively few in number. Similarly, the governance methods used in firms and in markets differ in the combinations of capabilities they exercise, but the taxonomy of capabilities is also fixed and the capabilities are few in number. Finally, the alignments of attributes and capabilities can also be classified using only a small number of principal categories.

This book explains how financial systems are organized, why they assume those forms, and why the systems evolve over time. Even though financial systems initially appear to be complicated entities, financial economics can provide a straightforward analytical and descriptive picture of how such systems work and how they change over time. The book begins with the view that a financial system

---

[1]Technical terms are italicized when first introduced and defined at the end of the chapter.

performs an unchanging set of tasks or functions. The same functions are performed in all financial systems, but the organizations performing them differ according to the operating economics of financial institutions and markets, the capabilities of financiers, and the attributes of the transactions that financiers agree on. The book examines the matches reached between financiers and their clients in a process called alignment. These alignments are studied in the context of financial deals that principally involve commitments of financial resources over time and those that principally involve reallocation of risks.

At any point in time, the attributes of financial deals, the organizations funding them, and the capabilities of the organizations' governance methods jointly determine the financial system's organization. Analyzing the workings of a financial system thus involves identifying the major attributes of proposed deals, the capabilities of the financiers who fund and govern them, and cost-effective ways of aligning deal attributes with governance capabilities. Since financiers and their clients both strive to arrange cost-effective forms of financing, a financial system's static organization is determined principally by economic considerations. Although not every type of deal is governed cost-effectively from the outset, governance choices typically evolve toward greater efficiency as agents learn. As a result, both a system's static organization and its evolution are largely determined by the changing economics of performing different financial functions and by learning how to exploit the economic changes.

AIMS AND APPROACH

This book presents the foregoing theory of financial system organization and shows how the theory explains observed practice. All economies' financial systems perform similar functions, but differ in the relative importance of three major financing mechanisms: markets, intermediaries, and internally provided financing.[2] In comparing financial systems, it becomes evident that since each of the three major financing mechanisms complements the other two, explaining how financial resources are allocated can be greatly aided

---

[2]"Markets" refers to both capital and money markets, while "intermediaries" refers to financial institutions that raise funds for the purposes of relending or reinvesting them. "Internally provided financing" refers to financing provided by one part of a business organization to finance activity in another part. All three terms are more fully defined in Chapter 3.

by examining these complementary roles. For example, in some economies financial markets are not very important, and most financial resources are allocated through intermediaries. In these economies, an analysis of financial markets would give a very incomplete picture of how the financial system works. As a second example, studying the financial intermediaries in a financial system does not show how intermediaries complement both market and internally provided forms of finance. Even for developed economies like those of the United States or the United Kingdom, a comprehensive understanding of the financial system requires examining the complementary roles played by the principal types of external finance—market and intermediated transactions—as well as the complementarities between external and internal finance.

To analyze financial systems requires a theoretical road map. This book uses a framework, initially developed by Oliver Williamson (1975) and elaborated in Neave (1991, 1998), to structure its investigation. It uses the framework to classify currently available theoretical models and to identify where the theoretical models' predictions need to be qualified. It also considers where there are open questions resulting from gaps in current theoretical knowledge, and what all these features mean for the practice of finance.

IMPORTANCE OF FINANCIAL SYSTEM ANALYSIS

The impression that a financial system encompasses an enormous variety of deals is correct in a descriptive sense, but an analytic approach helps to simplify the picture. Just as it is possible to define a few basic financial system functions, it is also possible to describe financial deals, whether they are entered principally for raising funds or for exchanging risks, in terms of a few distinguishing economic attributes. There is a taxonomy of attributes from which individual deals' attributes are drawn. Moreover, some members of the taxonomy are much more important than others in characterizing the essence of a given deal.

Thus, while deal attributes may appear in different combinations, this does not mean that deals with a few novel features will necessarily differ fundamentally from more familiar deals. Indeed, many of the arrangements characterized as new by the financial press actually turn out to be variants of familiar deals. The rapidity with which apparently new deals appear is evidence that the same attributes are being recombined, often in only slightly different ways. For example, in a later chapter an interest rate swap will be shown to be the theoretical equivalent of several forward contracts, meaning both instruments can be viewed as risk management tools that employ similar ideas in similar ways.[3]

The study of financial systems is worthwhile both for its own sake and because financial activity contributes importantly to economic well-being. Yet these beneficial effects are rarely apparent to casual observers. Indeed, some readers of the financial press may have the misleading impression that a financial system is principally a set of markets in which shares and exotic instruments such as financial derivatives are traded. But in fact, financial activity generates a significant share of national income in many economies, and most of this income is generated by performing everyday functions, such as transferring funds between agents, investing accumulated wealth, funding viable new projects, and managing risks.[4]

At the same time, a financial system's economic importance extends well beyond performing everyday functions. Macroeconomic theory explains that while consumption, investment, and government spending are the major determinants of economic activity over the near term, changes in the rate of investment (capital formation) importantly affect the rate of economic growth. Moreover, different amounts and types of capital formation can affect both an economy's productivity growth and its international competitiveness. A financial system plays an important role in determining these effects, since capital formation is affected by conditions for obtaining financing. For example, if financiers favor some types of projects over others, they can discourage the types of capital formation they do not favor.[5] The influences can be positive as well: In economies with underdeveloped financial markets intermediaries can help overcome financing constraints that would otherwise impede development.

Financiers are a scarce resource, partly because they must be capable of looking at innovative projects both constructively and critically. Some economies have many creative financiers, others relatively few. Countries with creative financiers and a supportive financial infrastructure foster more completed deals, and more diverse forms of deal arrangements. If the regulatory climate encourages responsible experimentation, financing will be still further encouraged. The more diverse a financial system's capabilities,

---

[3]Financial engineers like to emphasize the differences between instruments used for risk management. However, for explanatory purposes it is more important to recognize the instruments' similarities.

[4]A risky financial deal is one whose earnings cannot be determined exactly in advance. Rather, they are known only in terms of a probability distribution.

[5]Financiers may exhibit these preferences even after adjusting returns for differences in risk. Chapters 15 and 16 show how specialized financial intermediaries can play important roles in assessing particular deals.

the more likely the economy will be able to enhance international competitiveness through investing in new productive capacity. Finally, steady provision of financing is important for reducing fluctuations in economic growth: Financial systems under stress can experience severe economic cycles, as illustrated for example by the Southeast Asian economies in the late 1990s and the turbulence in world financial markets that first emerged in U.S. markets in 2007.

DIFFERENCES AMONG FINANCIAL SYSTEMS: OVERVIEW

The world's economies exhibit a wide range of financial systems whose evolution appears to be dependent on both the economies' histories and their legal and institutional frameworks. The elements common to financial systems are institutions and markets, but the mixes of these components differ quite considerably among countries. The United States and United Kingdom are examples of (principally) market-oriented systems, while Japan, France, and Germany are examples of (principally) intermediary-oriented systems. Households in the United States and United Kingdom hold significant proportions of equity; but this is not as true of households in Japan, France, and Germany. In the United States and United Kingdom, individuals directly invest proportionately large amounts of funds, while in Japan, France, and Germany, they mainly invest indirectly. In all of the five economies, firms rely about equally on internal and external finance, and this appears to hold true for most developed economies. The picture is somewhat more mixed in developing economies: In some, firms rely quite heavily on external finance while in others external finance is much less readily available.

Allen and Gale (2000) compare the financial systems of the United States, United Kingdom, Japan, France, and Germany along several dimensions. They view the U.S. and U.K. financial systems as offering the greatest emphasis on financial markets, while those of Japan, France, and Germany offer a greater emphasis on financial intermediaries. The United States, United Kingdom also stress competition and efficiency more heavily than the other three countries, whose emphases are on insurance and stability. The United States, United Kingdom are distinguished by greater use of public information. The other three countries also recognize the importance of financial information, but use it privately to a much greater extent. Firms and financiers are subject to greater external control in the United States, United Kingdom; exhibit greater autonomy in the remaining three countries.

Yet the differences among financial systems are not as stark or as profound as the foregoing might suggest. As already mentioned, in many developed countries about half the funds required to finance new business investment are raised internally, through business operations. Moreover, "when businesses go looking for funds to finance their activities, they usually obtain them indirectly from financial intermediaries and not directly from securities markets. Even in the United States...loans from financial intermediaries are far more important than securities markets are. (In Germany and Japan) financing from financial intermediaries has been almost ten times greater than that from securities markets, although (in Japan) the share...has been declining (in recent years)" (Mishkin 2007, 36).

Demirgüç-Kunt and Maksimovic (1998) contend that a greater proportion of firms use long-term external financing in countries whose legal systems score high on an efficiency index. An active, although not necessarily large stock market and a large banking sector are also associated with financing external growth. At the same time, greater proportions of external financing may also be demanded because established firms in countries with well-functioning institutions typically have lower profit rates and, therefore, fewer opportunities to finance projects internally.

Financiers cannot directly stimulate capital formation by making funds available for projects, but they can constrain proposed projects by deciding not to fund them. A lack of financial availability can pose particular difficulties in less developed countries, where both private and public sector capital formation can be at relatively low levels. Even if underdeveloped economies can obtain capital offshore, the kinds of projects adopted will likely be influenced by the preferences of foreign investors, and the most highly productive projects from a domestic point of view will not always be first in line to obtain whatever funds are available from the offshore sources.

Differences in financier capability can affect the cost as well as the availability of finance. Hubbard and Palia (1999, 1,150) suggest that as "emerging markets develop, large diversified firms (which are usually affiliated into a group or into a large family concern) may use their capital to help finance target companies.... As capital markets develop in emerging [financial systems], many firms can provide company-specific information to the capital markets directly, and more easily bypass firm internal capital markets for investment funds." Nevertheless, even in developed financial systems internal capital market transactions such as conglomerate mergers can play an important role in overcoming informational asymmetries that could otherwise impede investment activity. Hubbard and Palia regard overcoming informational asymmetries as providing a partial explanation for a boom in conglomerate mergers that occurred in the United States during the 1960s.

While financial system performance can affect economic growth, the reverse is also true: There can be feedback effects from successful industrial growth to financial development. As the nonfinancial sector of an economy grows, the financial sector usually evolves to meet the economy's emerging demands for new financial services. Indeed, over time financial system development is largely driven by attempts to realize profits through overcoming existing forms of financial system imperfection (see Bodie and Merton 2005). For example, and as will later be explained in detail, during the 1970s a worldwide increase in the demand for risk management services was met by corresponding supply increases that took the forms of both increased trading activity and the development of many new risk management products.

Both high financing costs (relative to market-required returns for similarly risky projects) and limited availability of funds can signal financial underdevelopment. The interests of an economy are served by overcoming financial underdevelopment, but doing so is not an easy task. Enhancing financial capabilities requires that the financial system build up greater skills in screening and governing financial deals. This type of development is most likely to occur in a sophisticated financial system, because that is where innovation is least costly and most likely to be profitable. As a result, encouraging financial system development is relatively difficult in underdeveloped countries, placing those countries at disadvantages that can only be overcome by patiently building up the elements of a sound financial system over time.

FUNCTIONS AND GOVERNANCE

Functional analysis describes the principal and unchanging functions performed by all financial systems. These functions include clearing and settling payments, pooling resources, acting as a store of value, transferring financial resources across regions and through time, managing and transferring risks, developing transaction information, and managing incentives. Crane, Froot, Mason, Perold, Merton, Bodie, Sirri, and Tufano (1995), as well as Bodie and Merton (2005), regard functions rather than institutions as the basic elements of their financial system analyses. Bodie and Merton (2005) further argue that a synthesis of neoclassical,[6] institutional, and behavioral perspectives is needed to explain the structure of financial systems and to predict how they are likely to evolve. They begin with a neoclassical model of financial markets and propose that the emergence of institutional forms is influenced by behavioral and institutional as well as by economic considerations. Chapter 2 examines this functional approach in greater detail.

---

[6]"Neoclassical economics" refers to the formal economic analysis discussed in many economics textbooks. It is characterized by assumptions of individual rationality, homogeneously distributed information, absence of transactions costs, and focuses heavily on the kinds of equilibria attained under these assumptions.

Some financial system functions—pooling resources, transferring resources, and managing risks—require special attention because they involve either the commitment of financial resources over relatively long periods of time, significant transfers of risks, or both. The book's analysis of these functions begins at the level of individual financial deals. If deals are to work out profitably, they need appropriate forms of *governance*, where governance refers to the process of looking after deals with a view to suitably contracting the arrangement at the beginning and with a further view to ensuring, as far as possible, their profitable conclusion. As the book will argue, the most effective governance methods depend on both the capabilities of accommodating financiers and the attributes of the deals themselves. Once an alignment of deal attributes and governance capabilities has been reached, the actual tasks of governance typically involve developing transaction information and managing incentives. However, these tasks will receive different emphases according to the deal's attributes, as Chapter 3 shows.

FINANCIAL SYSTEM ORGANIZATION

Financial system organization is influenced by the economics of performing basic functions, the economics of governing deals, and by the operating economics of the institutions that group deals together. Both the functional and the governance approaches contend that deals of particular types are governed as cost-effectively as possible, subject to the limitations imposed by current financial technology. Financial firms with particular governance capabilities usually specialize in deals with particular attributes, because that is how the firms can utilize their resources most effectively. Moreover, the sizes of financial firms are determined by their cost and profitability characteristics. For example, financial firms will grow if they can add business of a given type and reduce their unit costs while doing so—that is, if they realize scale economies. Financial firms will also grow if they enter businesses of different types and reduce overall costs—again, if they realize scope economies. Even if a new product line does not yield scale or scope economies, financial firms will add it so long as the new line creates incremental profits.

Financiers have sharply varying capabilities for funding projects that are backed by uncertain earnings, illiquid assets, or both. Especially, financiers show marked variation in their capability and willingness to assess and fund unfamiliar projects. These capability differences are partially due to familiarity with specific kinds of business. Capabilities develop as a result of learning, and financiers' experientially acquired knowledge varies according to differing patterns of trade, differing entrepreneurial skills, and differing governmental environments. Acquired capabilities are also affected by differences in the cost and difficulty of producing financial information. The latter is in turn affected both by deal attributes and by the details of an economy's financial infrastructure, such as its legal framework and its accounting standards.

FINANCIAL SYSTEM CHANGE

Today's financial managers find it more urgent than ever to understand the basic forces driving financial system change. As the world's financial markets become increasingly more competitive and more closely integrated, new profit opportunities need to be exploited quickly if they are to be retained in the face of competition. In a rapidly changing environment, the manager without an understanding of how and why change occurs is a manager who will quickly become outdated and, therefore, find it difficult to prosper.

Adding to the difficulties of coping with change, various forms of financial business experience cyclical expansions and contractions. For example, during the 1980s, management personnel in some of the larger securities firms earned much of their companies' revenue by arranging mergers and acquisitions. During the later 1980s and early 1990s, the pace of this activity tailed off, and earnings declined commensurately. During the later 1990s, interest in merger activity again increased. During the early 1990s, subprime mortgage lending expanded at a very rapid rate in the United States, and this expansion was later followed by losses and retrenchment that by 2008 were affecting large parts of the world economy. This book will examine further details of these kinds of cycles in later chapters.

Understanding how and why change occurs is not simply a matter of describing what is currently happening: Description is not explanation. Explanation demands drawing an organized picture of the forces driving change, and of how those forces influence financial activity. This book's analysis will help to develop such a picture. Economics will be used to explain why financial systems take their manifest forms, and why these forms change over time. For example, readers of this book will learn why there was a virtual explosion in derivatives trading over the 1970s and 1980s, and will therefore come to understand the reasons for this immense increase in derivatives' popularity. While some press accounts suggest that the growth of derivatives trading is largely due to a willingness to speculate, more fundamental reasons are to be found in the changing risks within the financial system and the corresponding changes in the economics of their management. Both the demand for and the supply of risk management instruments were affected by economic and technological change, including the development of option pricing theory.

REFERENCES

Allen, Franklin D., and Douglas Gale. 2000. *Comparing financial systems*. Cambridge, MA: MIT Press.

Bodie, Zvi, and Robert C. Merton. 2005. Design of financial systems: Towards a synthesis of function and structure. *Journal of Investment Management* 3: 1–23.

Crane, Dwight B., Kenneth A. Froot, Scott P. Mason, Andre E. Perold, Robert C. Merton, Zvi Bodie, Erik R. Sirri, and Peter Tufano. 1995. *The global financial system: A functional perspective*. Boston: Harvard Business School Press.

Demirguc-Kunt, Asli and V. Maksimovic. 1998. "Law, finance, and firm growth." *Journal of Finance* 53: 2107–2137.

Hubbard, R. Glenn, and Darius Palia. 1999. A reexamination of the conglomerate merger wave in the 1960s: An internal capital markets view. *Journal of Finance* 54: 1,131–1,152.

Mishkin, Frederic S. 2007. *The economics of money, banking, and financial markets*, 8th ed. Boston: Pearson Addison-Wesley.

Neave, Edwin H. 1991. *The economic organisation of a financial system*. London: Routledge.

Neave, Edwin H. 1998. *Financial systems: Principles and organisation*. London: Routledge.

Williamson, Oliver E. 1975. *Markets and hierarchies: Analysis and antitrust implications*. New York: Free Press.

TERMS

alignment   The matching up of the administrative methods used by a financier, and the kind of deal the client presents. The process of alignment is discussed in Chapter 3.

attributes   The qualities of a deal, such as whether it is backed by liquid or illiquid assets, whether its environment can be described as risky or uncertain. Attributes are further discussed in Chapter 3.

capabilities   The qualities of governance possessed by a financier. For example, a market agent (i.e., a financier who facilitates market transactions) may have highly developed capabilities for assessing market risk, while a financial intermediary may have highly developed capabilities for assessing default or credit risk. Financier capabilities are further discussed in Chapter 3.

deal   A financial arrangement between a client and a financier. The deals discussed in this book represent either allocations of financial resources through time, trading of risks, or both. For example, the purchase of a U.S. Treasury bond is one form of deal, the provision of venture financing, and the purchase of default insurance are all examples of deals.

governance (governance methods)   The process of looking after deals with a
view to suitably contracting the arrangement at the beginning and with
a further view to ensuring, as far as possible, their profitable conclusion.
For example, an exchange-traded risk instrument is usually governed
with a focus on to the properties of a liquid security, whereas a venture
capital investment is usually governed with a focus on a highly illiquid
investment whose returns are likely subject to considerable uncertainty.
Different governance methods are further discussed in Chapter 3.

CHAPTER 2

Financial System Functions

*The unchanging functions performed by every financial system in-
clude clearing and settling payments, pooling resources, transferring resources, managing risks, producing information, and managing incentives. Although every financial system performs these
functions, the organizations carrying them out are determined endogenously, in response to the characteristics of the local economic
environment and currently available transactions technology. Thus
the observed structures of financial systems can differ, both at any
point in time and also over time.*

*Chapter 1 observed that in every financial system, markets, inter-
mediaries, and internal finance complement each other. However,
the proportions of funds raised internally differ across systems, as do
the proportions of external funds raised in markets and through intermediaries. This book's principal purpose is to explain why these
variations occur and, as a first step, the present chapter reviews
the functional approach due to Crane et al. (1995). The chapter
also sketches how the original functional approach has evolved
into Bodie and Merton's functional-structural views (2005) arguing
that the organizations carrying out financial system functions tend
toward, but do not necessarily attain, a structure predicted by neoclassical economics. Along with market imperfections due to such
features as informational asymmetries and transactions costs, Bodie
and Merton stress that behavioral and institutional considerations
can inhibit the tendencies of a financial system to evolve toward the
form predicted by neoclassical economics.*

*Beginning with the next chapter, this book combines the per-
spectives of the functional-structural approach with the study of
financial activity at the level of individual deals. After outlining the
ideas of deal attributes and financing capabilities, it is proposed that
agents strive to negotiate cost-effective alignments and that financial*

structure represents groupings of alignment activities. The varying proportions of market and intermediary activity are determined endogenously, in that the capabilities financiers have historically developed are aligned with the particular attributes of financial deals that a given economy presents.

Over longer periods, economic forces affect the structure of the organizations carrying out and financing the deals. This evolution of the financial system takes the form of a search for economic efficiency that is constrained both by behavioral considerations and by current institutional practice. These matters are considered further here and in Chapter 3.

INTRODUCTION

Following Crane et al. (1995), this chapter examines six financial functions that comprise relatively permanent features of any financial system. Identifying the unchanging features of financial activity is a useful exercise for several reasons. First, the variety of financial activities is so great that if analysis is to be of lasting relevance it must go beyond transient differences to focus on longer-lasting phenomena. It is not nearly as informative to use a reporter's approach and describe current events. Second, when the present discussion of relatively permanent functions is combined with the next chapter's analysis of deals and their governance, we will be able to describe financial activity comprehensively, using differing combinations of a few basic deal attributes and a few basic governance capabilities. Third, identifying these basic dimensions helps understand how the financial system organization emerges endogenously from the economics of governing deals, as well as indicating how it is likely to evolve in the future.

CLEARING AND SETTLING PAYMENTS

One principal financial function involves clearing and settling payments, both domestic and international. In essence, clearing and settling payments means that a payment order requiring one agent to pay another is executed by a third party who effects a transfer of funds from the payer's to the payee's institution. Although settlement has been a traditional financial system function throughout history, the financial system now makes it easy and cheap to transfer funds quickly between almost any two points in the world, and usually in whatever currency the payer desires.

For example, at the retail level, many persons now use automated banking machines (ABMs), and an increasing number of individuals use debit cards. In most countries, both ABM and debit card transactions are effected by privately owned computer and communications networks. The client gets the funds from the ABM; her bank account or credit card is eventually charged with the transaction. The paying bank collects its funds, possibly through a series of intermediaries, from the bank operating the account or issuing the credit card. The traveler appreciates the convenience of this type of arrangement most acutely when communications are disrupted and the banking machine on which she is relying for her weekend expenditures in a foreign country does not dispense the cash she expected.

Most ABM networks have been developed privately by associations of financial institutions. At present these networks are becoming so widely used that network access is an important competitive consideration, both for the original developers and for other institutions. For example, some banks offer highly popular savings accounts that can be accessed both over the telephone and using local ABMs. Sellers of insurance products and mutual funds would benefit competitively if they could offer similar access. At the time of this writing, most countries would find it economic to modernize their payments system operations further, but in order to realize the benefits of scale economies, securing these improvements may involve ensuring that new players can obtain access to existing networks.

The increasing use of credit cards, debit cards, and cards that function as electronic purses all contribute to an important form of change in the retail payments system. The number of credit and debit card transactions is massive, and large cost savings can be realized by running those operations as efficiently as possible. Currently, the most efficient providers of credit card services are U.S.-based monoline financial institutions such as MBNA Corporation or BancOne of Ohio. Even a large multiproduct bank cannot currently match the monolines' cost performance. Similarly, debit card networks are usually operated by associations of banks rather than by individual banks themselves. The apparent economies of scale to both credit and debit card operations suggest that at some future date the monolines may actually operate both businesses, and that banks might end up acting as agents using monoline services. The eventual number of monoline providers will thus depend on whether the scale economies now being enjoyed are exhausted as existing providers continue to increase in size.

The rapidity of ongoing technological change means that the most important organizational issues of today may change completely within a few years' time. Access to an ABM network is currently an important issue, but it might not remain so for many years to come. For example, since it has recently become possible to transfer balances to a smart card through a home telephone and, in some cases, by cellular telephone, the networks' present importance is likely to diminish as land-line access becomes less important.

Similarly, Internet payments are becoming increasingly popular as Internet usage spreads and the security problems of transferring funds are resolved. Eventually card payments are likely to be supplanted by wireless transactions using cell phones or other access devices. In some lesser-developed countries, where the developed world's payments technologies are not available, wireless technologies are reducing the need to build up the kinds of infrastructures with which the developed world has become familiar.

At the wholesale level, clearing and settlement functions are becoming integrated worldwide. As one example, U.S. financial institutions are improving the efficiency and lowering the cost of transfers from the United States to Latin America. Within the European community, similar integration of payment and settlement systems is taking place. The principal organizational issues involved in each of these developments include taking advantage of scale and scope economies by ensuring the compatibility of different systems in different parts of the world.[1]

POOLING RESOURCES

Resource pooling is a second financial system function. Some of the ways in which savings are pooled at the retail level are through bank deposits, mutual fund and other stock investments, and insurance policies. Mutual funds pool savings and invest the funds in marketable securities, principally shares. In North America this form of savings has shown remarkable growth over the 1980s and 1990s, particularly from 1995 until the end of 2000. Growth diminished during the early 2000s, resumed in the mid-2000s, and again diminished following on the market turmoil of 2007–2008.[2] Mutual funds present an important competitive threat to savings deposits, and exchange-traded funds represent an important competitive threat to the more conventional kinds of mutual funds. For competitive reasons, mutual fund operators would like to offer more active participation in payment networks, but in most countries this kind of access has yet to be arranged.

While savers are concerned with the expected return on their funds, most want to ensure their wealth is invested relatively safely. A developed financial system acts to store wealth, not without any risk, but at a risk commensurate with the expected rate of return on the investment. Since investors are usually

---

[1]Similarly, worldwide mergers of stock and derivatives exchanges are partly being driven by the economics of integrating clearing and settlement functions.

[2]Mutual funds usually show diminished growth rates, and sometimes negative growth, following on stock market declines. In the past, growth has recovered once the stock markets again begin to advance.

risk-averse, they normally demand that asset returns increase as the perceived risk of an investment increases. As is well confirmed by empirical research, informed savers profit from one of the most important conclusions of modern financial theory: The expected return on an asset normally increases with the risk of realizing that return. For example, if investors regard long-maturity assets as riskier than short-maturity assets, the former will carry a higher rate of return. As pooling activities become increasingly computerized, the emergence of such securities as exchange-traded funds is attracting proportionately large amounts of funds from mutual fund investments.

Despite the ease with which retail investors can now diversify, it is still possible to find exceptional cases in which savers take relatively big risks with their wealth. Such persons may expect great rewards, but fail to recognize that great rewards are almost always associated with taking great risks. The next time you read that some financial institution, somewhere in the world, is paying extremely high rates of return to depositors, and that it is growing extremely quickly, you will probably be witness to an example of savers taking very great risks. Some of the savers you will be reading about will likely lose most or all of their capital when the scheme eventually goes bankrupt. Similarly, if you read that a new investment vehicle is offering extraordinarily attractive returns, consider carefully the possibility that the vehicle might be riskier than the lower-return investments with which it is being compared.

Funds are also pooled at the wholesale and commercial level in transactions known as *securitization*. For example, mortgage lenders raise funds from investors by forming pools of mortgages and issuing mortgage-backed securities against the pools. Since the 1970s, bank loans to corporate borrowers have also been pooled and securities issued against the pools. In both activities, the securities issued are sold mainly to institutional investors. Institutions such as insurance companies, pension funds, and hedge funds are willing to invest in the mortgage- or loan-backed securities because they can rely on the security of the particular loan portfolio[3] rather than on the creditworthiness of the originating lender. Sometimes securities issued against loan pools are enhanced by default insurance, and issues may also be quality-rated by independent rating agencies.[4]

---

[3]The effects of diversification are only obtained when the loans in the pool retain a degree of statistical independence. If, as in the case of some subprime mortgage securities, many were likely to default simultaneously, say, because of a change in the macroeconomic climate, risk reduction through diversification would be sharply reduced.

[4]Although even some early forms of securitization involved a transfer of risk to securities purchasers, the practice of risk transfers burgeoned in the 1980s and grew

Pooling activities will be discussed further in the next chapter as well as in several later sections on asset securitization, mortgage pools, mutual funds, and hedge funds. The discussions recognize that the previous rapid growth of pooling practices turned sharply negative as investors experienced losses following the stock market declines of late summer and early fall of 2008.

TRANSFERRING RESOURCES

A third basic function is to transfer resources, not only from one geographical region to another, but more importantly from one time period to another. Resource transfers through time channel funds from savers to borrowers, thus implementing lending or investing transactions. In open economies, the funds used to finance new investment are typically raised from both domestic and foreign sources. However, projects will only get funded if they win the favor of financial managers, and the decisions of those financial managers depend on both their skills and their preferences.

Not all financiers are equally good at evaluating viable projects, and not all potential projects present the same kinds of risks. Accordingly, different types of projects receive complementary forms of financing from differently specialized institutions. For example, banks are good at lending short-term to provide small businesses with operating credit, but they are not usually skilled at providing startup risk capital to fund a new business over the longer term. Indeed, startup financing can be quite difficult to obtain, and when available it is usually through specialized venture capital companies or private investors.[5]

Relatively new financial companies emerge frequently, sometimes changing the ways funds are channeled between asset pools. For example, leasing companies provide competition in corporate finance by arranging a transaction between, say, a pension fund and an equipment lessee. Sometimes a leasing company will place part of the transaction on its own books, at other times it acts as an agent. In either case, the novel forms of financing that leasing companies provide present banks with new competitive challenges in corporate finance. Similarly, the 1990s and subsequent growth of

------

even more sharply in the 2000s, as discussed in Chapter 5. The 2007–2008 difficulties with risk transfer arrangements are examined in Chapter 15.

[5]Many, if not most, venture capital companies concentrate on expansion financing rather than on start-ups.

the subprime mortgage markets represented a channeling of funds to a new type of business.[6]

MANAGING RISKS

Risk management, a fourth basic financial system function, includes everything from retail transactions such as selling car insurance to wholesale transactions such as trading derivatives in international markets. Almost every aspect of economic life is subject to various forms of either risk or uncertainty, and Arrow (1974) notes that pooling, sharing, and shifting risks are pervasive forms of economic activity. The ability of an individual or business enterprise to shift risks of losses from fire or theft to specialized insurance companies provides an obvious example of a retail transaction. The stock markets, futures markets, and forward exchange markets can all be seen as providing certain forms of wholesale risk management.

Historically, a series of institutions and arrangements has evolved to carry out risk management activities, and the arrangements continue to evolve. Although risk management is often discussed as if it began to emerge in the 1970s and 1980s, that view mainly stems from the observation that derivatives trading has grown very rapidly since the 1970s. In that period risk management expanded greatly in volume and importance, first in the United States, then soon after in the United Kingdom, Japan, and other countries. The explosive growth of derivatives trading was due both to shifts in the demand for risk management and to changes in the supply of instruments suitable for risk management, as discussed in Chapters 9 and 12. The growth of *credit derivatives* in the 1990s and into the beginning of the 2000s represents a further evolution of risk management practices. Credit derivatives known as credit *default swaps* were introduced at the beginning of the 2000s and grew at an explosive pace until the financial turmoil of 2007 and 2008. The instruments, which facilitate the market trading of risks, are discussed further in Chapter 5. The instruments' relations to the 2007–2008 market turmoil are discussed in Chapter 15.

Despite its recent spectacular growth and even more recent decline, the concept of managing and exchanging risks has been familiar to financiers for a very long time. For example, insuring some of the risks of trade began when camel caravans followed the silk routes to the Far East. From this historical beginning, insurance companies were formed principally to assume risks that

---

[6]The difficulties to which growth of the subprime market led are discussed at later points in the book.

others wished to sell.[7] Other risk instruments such as commodities futures have also been traded actively for a long time. The commodities futures markets were originally set up by securities traders who were both familiar and comfortable with secondary market trading, and who used such trading to transfer risks from one agent to another. For example, growers have sold commodities futures to hedge against the risks of fluctuating crop prices, while speculators have purchased the same contracts to assume the risks.

As the discussion suggests, risk trading is better thought of as a kind of insurance activity rather than as a form of gambling in which financiers make money at the expense of uninformed players. Indeed, the growth of risk trading represents a valuable economic function aimed at spreading rather than at increasing risk.[8] Probably most people would agree that buying fire insurance can be a good idea, but fewer observers realize that such forms of financial engineering as using derivative securities to hedge portfolio risk are conceptually similar. Buying fire insurance is a familiar transaction, but hedging portfolio risk seems exotic and strange until one gets to know it better.

The demand for risk management services has shifted outward a number of times since the 1970s. The introduction of floating exchange rates in the early 1970s, the increases in interest rate volatility during the 1970s and 1980s, and the increasing internationalization of business have all meant increased demand for managing interest rate and currency risks. As one example, the increasing strength of the Japanese yen in the late 1970s and early 1980s meant Japanese investors suffered large capital losses on their U.S. dollar denominated investments, many of which took the form of U.S. government securities. These losses were a major impetus in stimulating the Japanese to develop their current high-volume, sophisticated risk trading activities. The late 1990s and early 2000s increases in demand for credit derivatives, and the still more recent proliferation of the specialized forms of credit derivatives—that is, credit default swaps—represent other outward shifts in the demand functions.[9]

---

[7]Many of the risks underwritten held by insurance companies remain on the insurance company's books as liabilities that do not trade. Later chapters will discuss how and why insurance companies trade only some of their underwriting liabilities.

[8]Risks may be reduced for the agent selling them off, but the same risks are then borne by another party. Financial activity that divides up and trades risks does not alter the underlying physical or economic realities that present the risks in the first place.

[9]Increased risk trading can mean that risks are spread differently. However, while trading may reduce the risks assumed by a given agent, it does so by transferring the risk to another agent. In the aggregate, risk trading reallocates but does not eliminate

The supply of risk management services has also shifted outward. Market trading of derivatives is actually based on the same ideas as the exchanges of futures instruments carried out by the first commodities traders. Market trading of derivatives is also an outgrowth of the ideas underlying policies issued by the first insurance companies. However, two important technological changes have greatly increased the supply of risk management services since the 1970s. First, the terms of instruments traded were standardized, lowering the costs of negotiation and of trading. Second, market agents learned to guarantee contract performance,[10] obviating the need for traders to investigate each others' creditworthiness. Such guarantees lower both screening cost and the probability of default, and thus make the instruments attractive to more potential buyers. The creation and supply of credit derivatives and credit default swaps represent further supply increases.

Market trading of risk instruments does not represent the only supply side change. Over-the-counter trading[11] of nonstandardized risk instruments has also increased substantially, especially since the later 1980s. During this period, standardized instruments proved inadequate to meet the demands of clients becoming increasingly familiar with the importance of risk management, and the number of intermediaries engaged in over-the-counter risk trading increased in response, as further discussed in Chapters 15 and 18.

The financial system provides facilities for both privately negotiated and exchange trading of risks, and exchange trading of risk instruments produces public information in a fashion similar to the information produced by securities market activity. Trading in the primary and secondary securities markets determines securities prices and, therefore, values the firms whose securities are traded. Securities prices are largely based on expectations of firms' future earnings generation capabilities. Since expectations are based on current information, they can change as new or additional information becomes available. Secondary market trading further increases the liquidity of financial assets, and greater liquidity may also increase total investment by making primary securities easier to sell.

Similarly, risk trading produces information about the economic value of different kinds of risk. Moreover, risk trading on the secondary markets facilitates the primary undertaking of risky projects, just as secondary markets for securities improve the functioning of primary markets for raising

---

risk. Indeed, it is possible for risk trading to increase some forms of risks because trading can obscure exactly where the risks are being borne, and this can in turn reduce incentives to manage the origins of the risks.

[10] Usually the clearing house of the exchange on which the instruments are traded.

[11] Over-the-counter markets are discussed in Chapters 11 and 12.

funds. An economy with access to cheap and easy risk trading will undertake more viable risky projects because the parties originally undertaking the risk find it easy to divide the risk into different components that can readily be tailored to the demands of specialized purchasers.

There have been and will continue to be abuses of risk trading, and the conditions that foster those abuses should be corrected as far as it is possible to do so. In the 2000s, the corrective activity required presents challenges for both private sector financial managers and for regulators. For example, use of collateralized debt obligations in the U.S. subprime mortgage markets seems to have stimulated the parties involved to exercise less due diligence than previously. At the time of this writing, more prudent management of risk trading is needed worldwide, and if the private sector continues to permit abuses, then regulators will likely decide to exercise closer supervision than they have done until now. At the same time, the need to correct abuses does not imply that risk trading should necessarily be restricted. Indeed, risk trading should grow further in some areas. For example, despite the increased participation in risk management by financial businesses, many types of nonfinancial business still do not take full advantage of financial engineering techniques.

INFORMATION PRODUCTION

The fifth basic function of a financial system is information production. As pointed out in the previous section, well functioning markets foster information production. The *Efficient Markets Hypothesis*, to be discussed further in Chapter 8, holds that when markets are perfectly competitive and trading is not impeded by transactions costs or institutional practices, securities will have equilibrium prices that fully reflect all publicly available information. The differences between instruments traded in efficient markets are captured in their risk–return characteristics.

Exchange trading in derivatives offers a second example of information production, and many derivatives markets are also efficient information producers. Derivatives trading was not originally thought of as an information producing activity, but option pricing theory (see Chapter 9) has made it evident that the prices of traded options can be used to obtain estimates of underlying asset volatilities. Volatility information can be used to interpret the degree of earnings uncertainty a given asset presents, and this information can prove valuable for making investment decisions. It is currently helping observers to understand, for example, why cycles in commercial real estate development may actually contribute to the orderly expansion of office space in a growing city.

Financial intermediaries also produce information, but do not usually disseminate it publicly. For example, financial intermediaries develop information when they evaluate loan applications, but this information is normally used privately by the intermediaries to decide whether credit will be extended to given clients. Nevertheless, skillful production of this information is also essential to economic well-being—without it institutions would be less discriminating in their lending and investment activities, and fewer good projects would be able to obtain funding.

MANAGING INCENTIVES

Still another form of financial system function involves managing incentives, especially incentives arising from informational differences. Informational differences can create situations in which, say, a client has private information that can put her financier at a disadvantage. Managing the likely effects of informational differences is the essence of everyday financial activity. For example, banks' credit departments investigate borrowers before loans are made, and subsequently monitor the activities of the borrowers to ensure that the terms of the contract are observed. Insurance companies investigate risks before they underwrite them. They also limit the kinds of activities or assets they will underwrite, thus affecting the incentives of the insured. Chapter 6 will examine in detail how the terms of deals can be set to manage incentives.

Incentive considerations affect both lender and borrower. A borrower providing information to a potential lender risks giving away a knowledge advantage. The borrower and the lender both need protection against exploitation by the other, and in recognition of this possibility, some financiers try to develop reputations for helping rather than exploiting borrowers. In recent years, as banks have increasingly come to originate and then sell loans to others, some transactions have made it less clear which party or parties bear loan default risks. If the originating banks come to believe they can sell off default risks, those banks face reduced incentives to assess default risks in the first place. This issue of changing incentives will arise at several points in the succeeding development.

FUNCTIONAL–STRUCTURAL APPROACH

Financial activity can involve a number of different financial system functions. For example, every loan or investment transaction involves making one or more payments, and thus involves funds transfers as well as clearing and settling functions. As a second example, risk-trading usually represents the reallocation of risks rather than lending or investment, but the transactions also involve payments requiring to be settled. Moreover, public information is developed as a by-product of both the securities trading and the derivatives trading carried out in public markets.[12] Finally, the way a financial transaction is set up creates a particular set of incentives for the parties involved, an issue that can be of considerable significance in loan or investment transactions agreed under conditions of informational asymmetries.

Bodie and Merton (2005) observe that existing prices of financial instruments and allocations of financial resources will not necessarily conform to the predictions of neoclassical economics. They attribute observable deviations to institutional rigidities, technological inadequacies, or behavioral dysfunctions that, at a given time, inhibit the financial system's tendency to adjust as economics would predict. Nevertheless, the neoclassical paradigm can help predict the kinds of institutional changes to expect over the longer run, partly because institutional redesign can and does help to mitigate the effects of deviations from the paradigm.

Financial transactions require detailed governance over time, and the type of governance required will depend on the attributes of the individual deal and the capabilities of the financiers involved with its governance. The principal concerns of all governance technologies are managing deal information and the incentives facing the contracting parties. The reader who learns to understand the combination of functions and governance methods involved in different transactions will understand the basic features of the large numbers of apparently different transactions occurring in any financial system.

REFERENCES

Arrow, Kenneth J. 1974. *Essays in the Theory of Risk-Bearing*. Amsterdam: North-Holland.

Blanco, Roberto, Simon Brennan, and Ian W. Marsh. 2005. An empirical analysis of the dynamic relationship between investment grade bonds and credit default swaps. Bank of England Working Paper No. 211, Cass Business School Research Paper.

Bodie, Zvi, and Robert C. Merton. 2005. Design of financial systems: Towards a synthesis of function and structure. *Journal of Investment Management* 3: 1–23.

---

[12] Negotiated or over-the-counter transactions also develop information, but in these cases the information is typically not disseminated publicly.

Crane, Dwight B., Kenneth A. Froot, Scott P. Mason, Andre E. Perold, Robert C. Merton, Zvi Bodie, Erik R. Sirri, and Peter Tufano. 1995. *The global financial system: A functional perspective*. Boston: Harvard Business School Press.

Fabozzi, Frank J., and Vinod Kothari. 2007. Securitization: The tools of financial transformation," *Journal of Financial Transformation* 20: 34–44.

TERMS

credit default swaps   A form of credit derivative (see next entry) designed to transfer the default risk on debt obligations (loans and bonds). A bondholder will pay to transfer the risks of a credit event, such as a default, to the issuer of a swap. If the credit event does not occur, the issuer of the swap retains the original payment. If it does occur, the bondholder is paid a specified sum by the issuer of the swap. A single-name CDS is a contract that provides protection against the risk of a credit event experienced by a particular company or country. Single-name CDSs have been the most liquid type of credit derivative traded, and form the basic building blocks for more complex structured credit products. (See Blanco, Brennan, and Marsh 2005.)

credit derivatives   Financial instruments that can be used to buy and sell credit protection. The buyer of protection makes period payments to the protection seller until the maturity of the contract or the occurrence of a credit event, whichever comes first.

efficient markets hypothesis   The notion that trading financial instruments results in the production and exchange of information to such an extent that the market prices of (actively traded) instruments fully reflect the value of available information.

securitization   A process of pooling securities such as bank loans or mortgages and selling new instruments against the security of the portfolio. Usually the new securities are sold to institutional investors. "In today's capital markets, ... securitization is understood to mean a process by which an entity pools together its interest in identifiable cash flows, transfers the claims on those future cash flows to another entity that is specifically created for the sole purpose of holding those financial claims, and then utilizes those future cash flows to pay off investors over time." (Fabozzi and Kothari, 2007).

CHAPTER 3

Financial System Governance

Although all financial transactions require governance, this book focuses on two main types—transactions aimed primarily at raising funds, and those aimed primarily at managing risks. Both types are referred to generically as deals. (In practice, deals often combine fund raising and risk management, but for discussion purposes it helps to distinguish the two.) Appropriate governance capabilities are particularly important to securing deals' expected profits. If funds are being raised, financiers commit resources over time and must subsequently recover the funds, with interest commensurate to the risk involved, if the financiers are to prosper. Similarly, financiers entering risk management deals must price and govern the risks appropriately. Deals that are well governed can be expected on average to reward financiers for assuming risks, while ineffectively governed deals have substantially greater probabilities of making losses.

The mechanisms for governing deals are variations of market, intermediary, and internal arrangements. Cost-effective alignments of deals and mechanisms depend on both particular deal attributes and particular governance capabilities. While each alignment of a deal and a mechanism is likely to have some distinctive features, financial system analysis is simplified by recognizing that deals can be grouped according to their combinations of attributes, and the economics of governance usually leads financiers to select a particular form of governance mechanism.

Chapter 2 discussed the main functions carried out by the financial system and sketched how functional analysis is evolving into a functional-structural explanation of financial system activity. The functional-structural approach postulates that financial system structure is largely determined by the economics of financial activity, although the economics can also be affected by institutional and behavioral factors. Financial-structural analysis is thus a top-down form of study that begins with an overall economic perspective and adds institutional and behavioral detail.

This chapter presents a complementary, bottom-up analysis that begins at the level of the individual transaction, referred to as the deal. Once the processes of agreeing and governing individual transactions have been examined, this chapter then considers how financiers aggregate deals, and how the aggregations of deal types endogenously determine the kinds of institutions and markets present in a financial system. The discussions of later chapters combine both approaches, depending on neoclassical economics to sketch the broad outlines of financial activity and on transaction analysis to supplement the application discussions.

The deals considered in this chapter involve the allocation of financial resources over time, the dividing up and trading of risks,[1] or both. In order to increase the likelihood that resources committed to a deal can profitably be recovered, financiers employ a variety of governance methods, beginning with an initial screening and a proposal of financing terms. This proposal is then negotiated, albeit sometimes briefly, with a client. A given choice of governance methods is intended to strengthen a deal's expected profitability. During the course of the deal, financiers may further adjust financing terms and, in some cases, may require changes in the firm's technical operations as well. As and when they are implemented, these subsequent changes are intended to strengthen further the possibilities that the financier will profit from a deal.

INTRODUCTION

Financial governance can be regarded as utilizing a few capabilities drawn from a fixed taxonomy, and financial deals can be described in terms of a few critical attributes, drawn from a second fixed taxonomy. Financiers with given capabilities enter deals with particular attribute combinations. In addition, financial firms choose a form of business organization that is intended to facilitate cost-effective governance. At the aggregate level, financiers' organizational choices are determined endogenously by the attributes of available details and the economies of governing those attributes. Therefore, the structure of a financial system—that is, the combination of

---

[1]Of course, lending or investing normally involves both a transfer of risks and a commitment of funds, but the distinction is useful to indicate the principal purpose of a given deal.

markets, intermediaries, and internal governance that it represents—is also determined endogenously by economics of governance and the operating economics of the organizations implementing the governance methods.

External finance is provided to financial system clients by both markets and intermediaries, and clients' choices among alternative financing forms depend on both the cost and the perceived stringency of the financing conditions. Differences in financing terms stem from differences in market structure, from differences in client and financier information, and from the incentives the informational conditions create.

In particular, information differences can create problems of moral hazard and adverse selection[2] that increase the costs of any deals that are actually agreed. If the problems caused by informational asymmetries are severe enough, external finance may not be obtainable even at a very high interest rate.[3] Even in an economy with a highly developed financial system, a considerable proportion of business financing is provided internally from business' own resources. Decisions to finance internally rather than externally will usually depend on the perceived *risk* or *uncertainty* inherent in the proposal, the cost of the external funding, and the perceived stringency of the funding conditions.

Some financial systems (those of the United States and the United Kingdom, for example) channel a relatively large proportion of external financing through financial markets, while others (those of France, Germany, and Japan, for example) channel a greater proportion through financial intermediaries. These differences in the proportional importance of different financing sources are reflected in the terms "market-oriented" and "intermediary-oriented" systems. For example, it is customary to describe the financial systems of the United States and the United Kingdom as "market-oriented," and those of France, Germany, and Japan as "intermediary-oriented." However, the book will argue at several points later that the differences between market-oriented and intermediary-oriented systems are to some extent a function of historical development and that, as the global financial system continues to evolve, the search for efficient forms of financing continues to reduce the differences between the classifications.

---

[2]"Moral hazard" refers to a client's (occasionally a financier's) failing to observe the agreed terms of a deal, while "adverse selection" refers to taking advantage of a financier's inability to discriminate among clients. Adverse selection is discussed fully in Chapter 6; moral hazard in Chapter 7.

[3]As described later, the term "interest rate" as charged by a financier is intended to cover both explicit interest rate payments and any extra charges such as fees or commission, converted to an effective rate basis. The issues of cost and availability are discussed in later chapters.

Markets and intermediaries utilize different capabilities and are, there-fore, not equally well suited to governing the same types of deals: In a static and efficiently organized financial system the types of financings arranged in markets will differ from the types arranged with intermediaries.[4] Thus, at the system level, a strongly intermediary-oriented system could exhibit a greater proportion of intermediary financings, partly because the expertise to provide market financings was not as well developed. As a result, the system could exhibit different aggregate performance characteristics than a strongly market-oriented system.

Similar differences can also be observed in practice, although at the applied level one type of system might be adjusting toward another over a sufficiently long period of time.[5] Nevertheless, at any particular point in time the differences can be quite important. As an example, two of the major functions performed in any financial system involve helping firms and individuals to smooth temporal fluctuations in income and expenditures, and sharing the risks of gains or losses in wealth. The ability to hedge against long-term risks is important to both businesses and households. "Since markets are incomplete, there is a demand for risk-sharing that can be provided by long-lived institutions" (Allen and Gale 2000, 11). However, at any given time managers of the long-lived institutions in an economy may not possess the capabilities needed, or face the appropriate incentives, to provide the desired types of risk-sharing. Equally, not all forms of insurance or hedging can be obtained through financial market transactions. In other words, at different points in time financial system performance encompasses the possibilities of both market and institutional failure. At later points the book will explain how these failures can arise and assess some possibilities for mitigating them.

Market-oriented and intermediary-oriented systems develop public and private information in different proportions. Through trading, markets ag-gregate the impact of widely diverse forms of public information. Portfolios composed largely of securities that trade actively in financial markets have readily established values that are frequently described as transparent. On the other hand, intermediaries offer greater potential for in-depth, private development of credit information. Since intermediaries acquire relatively

---

[4]In any observed situation, the economics of governance may not have been fully worked out. What might evolve to be a market form of financing may first be arranged as an intermediated form. We distinguish these situations using the terms static and dynamic complementarity.

[5]The rhythms of any such adjustment may not only be long, but also highly variable, depending on the context of a particular transaction (see Merton 1989).

TABLE 3.1 Mechanisms and Governance Capabilities

→ Markets → Intermediaries → Internal Organization
→ Allocation by price → Allocation by command and control
Greater screening (ex ante) capabilities
Greater monitoring (ex post) capabilities
Greater control capabilities (auditing, replacement of key personnel)
Greater adjustment capabilities (ability to alter contracts on an ex post basis)

large proportions of nontradable assets, their portfolios have less easily established values that are often referred to as opaque (Ross, 1989).

GOVERNANCE MECHANISMS

The three principal mechanisms for governing the allocation of financial resources are markets, intermediaries, and internal organization.[6] Each type of mechanism utilizes a mix of capabilities drawn from a fixed taxonomy. This chapter explores the differential capabilities of the three main mechanisms, and later chapters analyze each in greater detail. Table 3.1 presents a schematic representation of the differences between governance mechanisms and their capabilities. As the table shows, the type of allocation mechanism ranges along a continuum indicating that markets typically allocate financial resources using the price mechanism, intermediaries combine allocation by price with some forms of command and control,[7] while financial conglomerates provide internal governance primarily using command and control mechanisms. The capabilities of the mechanisms increase, in both effectiveness and cost, along a continuum having market governance at one extreme, internal organization at the other. The ideas underlying the table are examined in the next sections.

Market Finance

Markets allocate financial resources by price, which in the context of a financial transaction refers to the deal's effective interest rate. Market governance works best when a deal's essential attributes can be captured in the

---

[6]Some authors use the term "hierarchies" to refer to internal organization (see, for example, Williamson 1975).
[7]That is, to say, using governance capabilities additional to allocating resources by interest rate alone.

interest rate it bears. Such deals' essentials can be reflected by terms that are fully specified at the outset, meaning that the deals consummated by *market agents* can usually be regarded as *complete contracts*. Most of the deals that market agents entertain require relatively little *monitoring* after being struck, often because market deals finance the acquisition of assets with a ready resale value in secondary markets.

Typically, market agents effect trades between parties who do not necessarily know each other. Moreover, market agents often have well-developed research and information processing capabilities regarding readily observable short-term changes in each deal's likely profitability. For example, market trading of a firm's shares values the firm's underlying assets. As a second example, trading derivatives price volatility,[8] and thereby produce economic information about how different risks are valued in the marketplace. As Allen and Gale (2000) observe, markets are especially well-suited to assessing the economic impact of a variety of disparate forms of information.[9]

Market agents attempt to realize scale economies by standardizing the terms of the deals they take on, and thereby reducing the deals' transactions costs. Market agents can also realize scope economics if the same specialized information processing techniques can be used for numbers of similar deals. The most active markets usually deal primarily in standardized contracts, a category that includes the public share issues of widely traded companies. On the other hand, less active markets deal principally in contracts that can be more varied in their terms.

Within the markets category, distinctions can be made on the basis of differences in agent capabilities. For example private markets, in which securities are sold to one or a small group of investors, typically permit more detailed ex ante screening and more detailed negotiation of a deal's terms than do public markets in which securities are sold to a relatively large number of investors on standard terms. As a second example, financiers acting as principals for very short periods of time specialize in using market instruments. They have less developed capabilities for governing portfolios of illiquid assets than do other investors. The trader in government Treasury bills and the real estate developer both act as principals, but the widely differing time scales over which they hold assets, and the equally widely differing degrees of liquidity to these assets, mean the two types of agents use very different forms of governance.

---

[8]The relations between derivatives' prices and asset price volatility are examined in Chapter 9.
[9]Markets can perform this task well under relatively stable conditions. Their capabilities to do so are much more sharply limited in times of uncertainty.

Intermediary Finance

Financial intermediaries have historically been described[10] as enterprises that raise funds from depositors, mainly householders and, to a lesser extent, businesses. They relend the funds to business and personal borrowing customers, and in most developed economies provide the largest proportion of loan funds obtained by those ultimate users. The public normally views intermediary deposits as highly liquid, and expect to be able to withdraw the nominal amounts of their deposits on short notice. On the other hand, most of the loans granted by financial intermediaries are illiquid, typically being repaid in installments over months or years. Hence financial intermediaries must manage a portfolio of relatively illiquid assets that are funded by relatively short-term liabilities.[11]

Loans granted by financial intermediaries specify an interest rate, and therefore utilize a form of allocation by price, but the arrangements also incorporate a greater use of command and control mechanisms than is typically found in market transactions. As a result, intermediaries exercise certain kinds of governance capabilities that are not customarily utilized by market agents. The additional capabilities that intermediaries utilize include more intensive ex ante screening capabilities, more extensive capabilities for monitoring, control, and subsequent adjustment of deal terms. Intermediaries use these combinations of capabilities because they are cost-effective ways of governing the deals they enter. Intermediaries produce private information by screening loan applications ex ante, as well as by ex post monitoring of deals they have already entered. Information produced by financial intermediaries remains private because intermediaries do not normally trade their financial assets.[12] The contracts drawn up for intermediated deals are usually incomplete in comparison to the contracts drawn up for market deals. In particular, they may have implicit terms that not actively

---

[10] As later chapters will show, financial intermediaries have evolved from their historical business mix to become complex international businesses conducting a variety of fund-raising, lending, trading, and risk management businesses. For present purposes, we are addressing the questions of why even the simpler historical forms of intermediaries could raise funds, relend them, and create value. The economics of additional forms of contemporary intermediary business will be discussed at later points.

[11] This aspect of intermediary structure can create stability problems, as will be discussed in Chapter 20.

[12] Securitization involves selling beneficial interests in a portfolio and is different from selling the assets themselves, not least because the original lender usually collects the loan repayments and bears some responsibility for defaults.

invoked unless the originally agreed deal appears to be in some danger of producing less revenue for the financier than was first contemplated.

Not all intermediaries have all capabilities to the same degree,[13] and differential capabilities help to explain why intermediaries are likely to specialize. For example, some intermediaries can offer automated screening of credit card and consumer loan applications, thereby enjoying scale economies not available to those with smaller volumes of the same business. As a second example, expert systems and credit scoring techniques are coming to play an increasingly important role in assessing many types of deals, including business lending. Such systems exhibit declining average costs, chiefly because they require a large initial investment, but have relatively small marginal operating costs. As a result, expert systems will most likely be installed by a relatively small number of large firms. If they can negotiate profitable terms, smaller firms may purchase the services from their larger counterparts.

Internal Governance

Internal governance represents financial resource allocation using command and control capabilities to a still greater extent than those used by intermediaries. Internal governance offers the greatest potential for intensive ex ante screening, ex post monitoring, control over operations, and adjustment of deal terms. Internal governance mechanisms typically focus less on the nature of a financial contract and more on the command and control they can use to effect ex post adjustment of financing terms. Since internal governance mechanisms muster the greatest governance capabilities, their resource costs are likely to be greater than those incurred by market or intermediary mechanisms. As a result internal mechanisms will normally be used to govern deals with relatively large profit potential, but also deals whose uncertainties are greater than those acceptable to intermediaries.

For example, internal capital market transactions may be the only feasible way of governing financial transactions whose problems of *incomplete contracting* are relatively severe. Internal governance provides highly developed capabilities for auditing project performance, for changing operating management and for adjusting financing terms if conditions change. On all these counts, internal financing arrangements employ different governance

---

[13] For example, while investment bankers have highly developed capabilities for assessing market risk, they have lesser capabilities for assessing credit risk, and the reverse is usually true for commercial banks. This difference has implications for the treatment of securitized assets and is discussed at several later points in the book.

capabilities from those of either market agents or intermediaries, but also at higher administrative costs than those of the former two. Of course, in order to be viable such deals must offer a potential for both covering higher governance costs and for returning greater rewards.

As one example of the differences, Cai, Cheung, and Goyal (1999) show that bank lending creates positive externalities by improving the contracting environment for other public debt providers, and also that keiretsu firms do so to an even greater extent. Keiretsu firms are members of a sort of hierarchy with lower agency costs of debt than similar independent firms. In such cases, the advantages of belonging to a keiretsu outweigh the additional administrative costs, and this form of internal governance is chosen as a result.

TYPES OF DEALS

Financiers are faced with proposals for what appear to be many different types of deals. Indeed, on the surface deals differ so much that it might seem necessary to describe each one separately. However, for analytical purposes differences among financial deals can be described as different combinations of a few basic attributes.

Deal Attributes

Some deals are so familiar to financiers that their successful conclusion depends primarily on the results of an initial screening followed by using a standard form of governance. These simple forms of financings arise either when clients acquire relatively liquid[14] assets, or when collateral with a readily established market value can be used for security. Such kinds of financings are relatively easy to arrange because in the event of difficulty the underlying asset values can be used to repay most or all of the funding. The simplest kinds of risk management deals are similarly standardized. Such deals present risks rather than uncertainties, can be formalized using rule-based, complete contracts, are relatively easy to price, and can usually be agreed after only relatively cursory investigation.[15]

---

[14] Williamson (1987) stresses the importance of asset specificity as a deal attribute. This book uses the related (but not identical) concept of asset liquidity because financiers are often concerned with the likelihood that an asset can quickly be sold at or near its secondary market value.

[15] Since it can be investigated in a relatively cursory fashion, it will not present large fixed information processing costs.

TABLE 3.2 Attributes and Governance Implications

→ Changes in attributes →
→ Informational conditions →
Risk is perceived as increasing
Risk shades into uncertainty
Uncertainty is perceived as increasing
→ Decreasing liquidity of underlying assets →
→ Governance costs increase
→ Recovery of fund commitments more difficult

Other deals may be unfamiliar to financiers. These more complex kinds of deals often involve financing the purchase of illiquid assets when there is no collateral to serve as security. Additionally, they may have unusual terms or present greater uncertainty regarding the likelihood of repayment. For example, venture investments whose success rests on the talent and commitment of given individuals are deals in which financiers' rewards will depend on highly uncertain future earnings. There will usually be little in the way of marketable assets available to provide security.

Table 3.2 indicates that increasing information differences, decreasing asset liquidity, or both make deals more difficult to govern. In addition governance costs increase, partly because greater informational differences present possibilities of both adverse selection and moral hazard. The effects of such phenomena can be partially offset by exercising additional governance capabilities, but acquiring such capabilities is also costly, as is discussed further in the next sections.

Asset Liquidity

Asset liquidity makes a considerable difference as to whether a deal can be classified as simple or complex. If the underlying assets can readily be traded in secondary markets, financiers have two potential sources of repayment. They can recoup their investment with interest if the project or firm being financed turns out well and generates a sufficiently large cash flow. If project cash flows do not materialize, liquid assets can still be sold to recover at least some of the funds initially put up. However, if the assets are project-specific and, therefore, illiquid, the less the financier can rely on them as a source of repayment. Financiers can only expect to recover a return on their investment by working to ensure that the project will operate profitably.

The situation is further complicated by the possibility that asset liquidity will not necessarily remain constant over time. Indeed, liquidity depends primarily on the presence of both buyers and sellers: both a demand for and a supply of the asset are needed for trading to take place. In addition, illiquidity becomes more problematic in markets where asset values can be affected by the uncertainties of third-party actions. In such cases it is difficult for a potential buyer and a potential seller may not be able to agree on the nature of third-party influences, and consequently may find it difficult to agree on a suitable price at which to exchange the asset.

Risk versus Uncertainty

A second important deal attribute is whether its payoffs can usefully be described quantitatively using a probability distribution. If a deal's expected earnings can usefully be described in probabilistic terms the deal can be called risky. For example, estimating the returns on a typical small business working capital loan is a relatively straightforward task, even after allowing for likely write-offs of the accounts receivable or inventories customarily taken as security.

Risky deals are the kinds usually described in finance textbooks. They can present profitability risk, default risk, or both. Although profitability risk and default risk can be closely related, it is useful to distinguish them for descriptive purposes. *Profitability risk* refers to the probability of earning a relatively low return on an investment, whether it takes the form of debt, equity, or a more complex financial instrument. Profitability risk depends mainly on such deal features as the possible magnitude of fluctuations in realized earnings, the maturity of the deal, whether the interest rate on it is fixed or floating, and the currency in which the deal is expressed. *Default risk* refers to the possibility that a lender or investor faces the risk of not recovering an investment, either because the underlying firm goes bankrupt or because debt issued by the firm is not repaid as originally stipulated. Insofar as debt is concerned, default risk depends mainly on the probability that cash flows, including any cash that might be raised from selling assets, will be too small to permit making contracted repayments. Deals financing the purchase of liquid assets are less likely to pose default risk because liquid assets can be seized and sold to repay at least part, and perhaps all, of a loan or investment.

Uncertainty means that an agent cannot regard himself as understanding a deal well. Deals most likely to present uncertainty are those involving either a strategic change in business operations, or those financing a technological innovation. A start-up investment in a new, high technology business offers an example. It is often observed that such projects are particularly difficult to finance, mainly because agents find it difficult to make quantitative analyses of their likely payoffs. First, neither clients nor financiers may be able to determine a proposed deal's key profitability features. Second, the possible reactions of competitors may be difficult to predict. Despite these difficulties, deals presenting uncertainties are the essence of both business and financial innovation, and analyzing how financiers overcome the difficulties is profoundly important to studying financial activity.

Consider, for example, the press reports of profitability estimates for the Channel Tunnel project connecting England and France, begun in 1988 and commencing operations in 1994. The project's expected profitability changed considerably both during the construction phase and after construction was completed. Profitability estimates, and changes in them, depended on forecasting such variables as the demand for tunnel services, the reactions of competitors, world interest rates, and the like. Even sophisticated profitability models are not very helpful in such cases, since they depend critically on assumptions that are extremely difficult to render precisely. Moreover, the tunnel's assets are illiquid, and therefore provide little in the way of security against default. For all these reasons, the Channel Tunnel's financing essentially represented a deal struck under conditions of uncertainty.

Deals presenting uncertainties require different governance capabilities than do their merely risky counterparts. First, their successful governance requires greater adaptability to circumstances that are not easy to see when the deals are first entered. Deals entered under uncertainty will require relatively more monitoring, especially if relevant information is likely to be revealed gradually with the passage of time. Moreover if monitoring indicates that contract adjustments would be in order, the deal needs to provide for adjustment of terms or even control of underlying operations as and when such needs for change are revealed.[16] As a result, financiers often have to use incomplete contracts when entering deals under uncertainty.

Informational Differences

Financiers and clients do not always have the same deal information, even when they are only facing risk. The differences can arise either because the two parties do not have access to the same data, or because they interpret the same data differently. Differences in interpretation can stem from differing levels of competence, or because differing experiences color the parties' respective views. In addition to views of the deal itself, agents may form views of how counterparties regard the deal, complicating the picture further. Thus a deal's informational attributes can be classified according to whether agents perceive the risks or uncertainties symmetrically or asymmetrically. Moreover, the information differences between the two may change significantly during the life of a deal. Unless otherwise indicated specifically,

---

[16] The necessary changes may be in the client's operations, the terms of the financing, or both.

the rest of this book assumes the client's information is at least as precise as that of any financier.

Informational differences usually occur in deals that do not receive intensive study by a number of agents. Even in routine public market transactions, not all parties obtain the same information at the same time. Informational differences can even impede large public market transactions if the corporation involved is changing the nature of its business. In both the United States and Canada, stock market trading activity by corporate officers and market specialists based on inside information has been shown to yield abnormal risk-adjusted returns. Whatever the likelihood of informational differences in public market transactions, they are even more likely to occur in private markets or in intermediated transactions. For example, financiers are well aware that some clients will provide biased information in attempts to improve financing terms.

Whenever informational asymmetries are perceived to have economically important consequences for a financier, he will attempt to obtain more information, at least if the information's value is expected to be greater than the cost of gathering it. Cost-benefit analysis of information acquisition can be a challenging task under risk, and is even more so under uncertainty. In the latter case, financiers may not even know how to frame relevant questions regarding any benefits to gathering more information.[17]

Complete versus Incomplete Contracting

In risky deals the financier's main function is to determine the market price of the securities involved, mainly by using information publicly available to market participants. Such deals normally require only a minimal degree of subsequent monitoring, since their terms can be specified relatively completely at the time when funds are first advanced. Deals of this type are said to use complete contracting.

Only some financial deals can be formalized using complete contracts. Complete contracting is a situation under risk in which all important outcomes can be described fully, and a situation in which actions to be taken can also be described fully. Some market deals can be described as complete contracts because they have little need of ex post monitoring. In some other market deals ex post has little value because the monitor has no real capability to effect any necessary changes.

Deals under uncertainty are often characterized by incomplete contracting, which refers to situations in which not all important outcomes can

---

[17] If financiers decide that they cannot learn enough about a given deal to assess its profitability even roughly, they may decline to enter the deal.

usefully be described in terms of a probability distribution. Aghion and Bolton (1992) provide an example of incomplete contracting that arises from a conflict of interest between entrepreneurs and outside investors. The authors consider a situation in which the nature of the conflict cannot satisfactorily be resolved by specifying entrepreneurial effort and reward. To complicate the Aghion-Bolton situation further, entrepreneurial effort cannot always be modeled satisfactorily in quantitative terms.[18] Nor can entrepreneurial effort always be motivated by an incentive scheme: In some cases it can only be motivated by financiers' threat to liquidate the arrangement. When earnings prospects are good, the entrepreneur decides whether the profits from expansion are worth the effort she must supply. At the same time, if outside investors perceive the earnings prospects as bad, they may sometimes want to liquidate the company when the entrepreneur perceives expansion possibilities to be attractive. Such situations reflect some of the complexities of incomplete contracting.

ALIGNMENT

Financiers have specialized capabilities and accept deals whose attributes they can govern effectively. Relatively simple[19] deals are usually agreed with market agents while more complex deals are usually agreed either with intermediaries or, in extreme cases, internally to the funding organization. Over time, financiers align their capabilities with the deal attributes presented by their clients on the basis of cost-effectiveness. In the aggregate, the specialized capabilities of financiers and the deals they agree determine the mix of a given financier's business. Further, the numbers and kinds of business organizations formed to carry out financial deals ultimately determine the nature of financial system organization.

Principles

The alignment reached by an accommodating financier and a client depend importantly on whether the financier has the kinds of specialized capabilities

---

[18] Readers of Savage (1951) may object that if behavior conforms to certain axioms, a quantitative probability distribution can always be said to exist. But the Savage axioms provide no way of ensuring that the resulting quantitative probability distribution provides sufficiently precise information to make it useful for decision making purposes.

[19] In the specific sense of this chapter; that is, under risk, involving liquid assets, and not being subject to severe informational asymmetries.

needed to govern the deal's attributes cost-effectively. Information about some kinds of deals may be fully available when the deals are first prepared, but in other cases pertinent deal information may also be gained during the time the deal remains in force. Moreover, in unfamiliar deals, financiers may learn how better to govern a deal over the time it remains in force. Deals for which learning is important are usually agreed, either with financial intermediaries or internally to the business firm, because in these cases it can be easier to adapt the terms of the deal as learning takes place. The incomplete contracts created in evidence of such deals are not usually traded, but are retained by the original lender until the funds advanced have been repaid.

Jensen and Meckling (1998) help illuminate choices among different forms of financial governance. They refer to knowledge that is costly to transfer among agents as specific knowledge, and knowledge that is cheap to transfer as general knowledge. Deals whose governance requires specific knowledge are more difficult to exchange than are deals whose governance requires only general knowledge. For example, a deal whose governance requires specific knowledge is more likely to be held by the originating financial institution rather than being traded in the marketplace, partially because the skills of the personnel originating the deal are more likely to be used in its continuing administration.

Securitization is one financial technology that helps deal with the difficulties of transmitting specific knowledge. Securitization involves issuing new instruments against portfolios of the original, nontradable deals. The original loans have idiosyncratic characteristics that represent specific knowledge, but the instruments used in securitization are tradable instruments because investors in the new instruments need only general knowledge about portfolio characteristics when they decide whether to invest. Making sure the portfolio retains its value is usually a job for the original lender, who has specific knowledge of the transaction details involved.[20] The details of securitization are discussed further in Chapter 15. Some forms of loan syndication provide similar examples, as discussed in Chapter 17.

Decision makers are constantly assembling new knowledge, and Jensen and Meckling argue that the more specific the assembled knowledge becomes, the more costly its transfer and the greater the likelihood it will be retained within the producing organization. Jensen and Meckling also point out that the initial costs of acquiring idiosyncratic knowledge (learning) can

---

[20] If the incentives for the original lender to preserve value are weak, difficulties are likely to result. The sub-prime mortgage market difficulties and the difficulties of the asset-backed commercial paper market are both partially attributable to attenuated incentives, as discussed at later points in the book.

be modest, but the costs of transferring it can high relative to the benefits. Uncertainty about what pieces of idiosyncratic knowledge might prove valuable ex post can actually present high ex ante transfer costs in part because uncertainty implies a need to transfer knowledge that might never turn out to be useful. Thus idiosyncratic knowledge is also likely to be retained within the producing organization.

To enhance a deal's safety and profitability, financiers typically exercise more intensive governance capabilities if a project has uncertain rather than risky returns. When facing uncertainty, financiers (if they agree to put up any funds at all) will try to discover and manage a deal's key profitability features. But since they cannot specify exactly what might be required in advance, financiers can only formalize their loan agreements to the extent of citing principles that allow them to respond flexibly to changing conditions. That is, financiers use incomplete contracts to govern the uncertainties with which they grapple. If relatively precise specifications were possible, financiers could write complete contracts when the deals were agreed.

Contrast a public issue of stock with the arrangements a conglomerate headquarters might strike with one of its subsidiaries. In the first case information is widely shared by many parties; in the second it is not. Moreover, in the second case there are much greater opportunities for continuing supervision after financing has initially been provided. Finally, in contrast to a public securities issue whose features are explained in a publicly distributed prospectus, internal governance may be used to keep information about development plans from being revealed to competitors.

Process

Table 3.3 shows how alignments can be regarded as the results of an interplay between clients presenting deal attributes and financiers' possessing governance capabilities. The financing costs that clients face and the governance costs that financiers incur are determined as a result of the interplay. The first section of Table 3.3 arranges the three basic governance mechanisms—markets, financial intermediaries, and internal financing, in increasing order of command and control capability. For example, public markets are recorded to the left of private markets because private market agents can muster certain governance capabilities not possessed by public market agents. Private market agents usually have greater investigative capability and, in some cases, greater freedom to negotiate terms than do public market agents. Similarly, even though commercial banks and

TABLE 3.3 Governance Capabilities, Deal Attributes, and Alignment

	Governance	
Market Agents	Intermediaries	Internal Financing

Public Markets
    Private Markets
        Securities Firms
            Commercial Banks
                Venture Capital Companies
                    Universal Banks
                        Keiretsu
                            Financial Conglomerates

Governance Capabilities

→ Direction of change →

Greater monitoring capabilities
    (particularly on a continuing basis)
Greater control capabilities
    (auditing, replacement of key personnel)
Greater adjustment capabilities
    (ability to alter contracts as circumstances change)

Governance Costs

→ Increasing

Deals' Attributes

→ Direction of change →

Increasing information differences
Perceived greater risk; uncertainty rather than risk
Decreased asset liquidity
Greater need for continued monitoring
Greater need for subsequent adjustment
Increasing cost of default

venture capital firms are both intermediaries, commercial banks usually have less highly developed screening and monitoring capabilities than do venture capital firms. In particular, venture capital firms make greater use of discretionary arrangements, which usually include obtaining a seat on the board of any company to which they extend funds. Finally, internal governance means governance within a given organization or group. Western financial conglomerates sometimes offer examples of internal governance, as do the

Japanese keiretsu.[21] Similarly, the universal banks[22] found in Germany use something closer to internal governance when they both purchase the shares of, and make long-term loans to, the same clients.

Table 3.3's second section indicates that different governance mechanisms assemble differing degrees of capabilities. For example, internal financing arrangements have greater monitoring and control capabilities than market arrangements. The table's governance cost section is a reminder that greater capabilities cannot be acquired without incurring additional costs.

Reading from left to right in Table 3.3's attributes section shows that deals characterized by greater informational differences between the two parties (the financiers typically having less information) are viewed by financiers as involving higher degrees of risk or as presenting uncertainty instead of risk. Higher-risk deals, and deals whose prospects are uncertain, pose greater needs for continuing governance than do lower-risk deals. Similarly greater uncertainty, a lower degree of asset liquidity or both make it more difficult to establish market values for the underlying assets,[23] and hence to determine the breakup value of a firm in financial difficulty. If financiers cannot readily establish a breakup value for the firm, they do not know what they might be able to recover from a sale of assets if the firm should fail. Therefore, deals with such firms appear riskier than, say, deals that finance purchases of liquid assets with readily established market values.

Financings under uncertainty present the most difficult governance problems, and are therefore likely to be subjected to forms of governance with relatively sophisticated capabilities. Of course, greater capabilities are acquired at greater costs, and these governance costs must be recovered from gross returns on the investment. For example, administering a portfolio of short-term liquid securities principally requires market governance, while administering the financing of conglomerate subsidiaries that are entering new ventures can require a much more intensive, higher capability form of governance. As a result, the second kind of deal must offer higher gross returns if it is to be regarded as capable of generating expected net profits.

---

[21] Keiretsu are groups of firms with interrelated shareholdings. The firms within the keiretsu typically give business preference to other keiretsu members, and the keiretsu's main bank often takes a seat on the board of client companies experiencing financial difficulties.

[22] A universal bank is a bank that also performs such other functions as underwriting or selling securities. In Germany, universal banks own share positions in some of their larger client companies.

[23] The problem of determining asset values is particularly apparent in deals involving the privatization of former public sector firms.

Cost-Effectiveness

Financiers accept a deal on the basis of whether they regard themselves as having the capabilities to govern the deal profitably and reject deals that do not meet an expected profitability criterion. Expected profits depend both on the revenue from the deal and the cost of its governance. Financiers strive to control costs by only taking on those deals they can govern cost-effectively, as illustrated by the arrangements in the different parts of Table 3.3. For example, in comparison to intermediary or internally governed deals, market deals tend to be more standardized, and to exhibit less important informational differences between client and financier. As a result, market governance uses relatively few monitoring and control capabilities, and market-governed deals typically present lower administration costs than do internally governed deals. A market agent will not usually take on deals that require the specialized governance capabilities of a financial intermediary.

Market governance is generally cheaper than internal governance (see Williamson 1987, Jensen and Meckling 1976). In governing standard deals arranged under competitive conditions, there is little room to cover the extra resource costs of internal governance, and risk reduction has little importance for assessing profitability. It follows that the profitability[24] of doing a standard deal using market governance usually exceeds the profitability of doing a standard deal using, say, intermediary governance. If intermediaries were to take on such deals, they would do so primarily because they could exercise additional governance capabilities. In such cases, their loan administration costs would be higher than the administration costs of market agents, and the intermediaries would have to charge a higher interest rate to cover the costs.

A form of nonarm's-length governance can be a cost-effective alternative to market governance if the benefits of additional monitoring, control, and adjustment capabilities exceed the extra information and monitoring costs involved. Internal governance is especially likely to be cost-effective when the financing environment is uncertain. The reduced risk or increased return from internal governance more than compensates for the greater cost of acquiring the extra governance capabilities.

On the demand side, clients attempt to seek out a financier who offers the most attractive terms available. Clients strive to minimize their costs of obtaining funds, but they will not always find the best available deal terms. For example, a client will not willingly pay a higher fee to an intermediary

---

[24] Profitability is defined as expected future net earnings, discounted at a rate adjusted to reflect the risk or uncertainties involved.

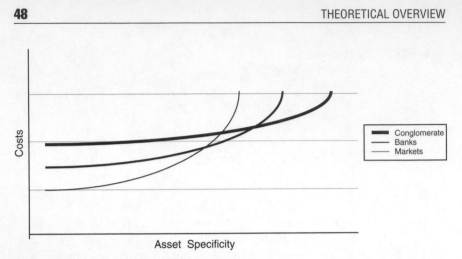

FIGURE 3.1   Comparative Costs of Governance
Source: Adapted from Williamson (2002)

than she would have to pay to a market agent performing the same services. Yet if search costs are high, a client will quite often accept one of the first few feasible arrangements he can find, maybe even the very first. That is, high search costs bias clients toward exploring familiar sources of funding.

Nevertheless, a client may be able to secure several offers of financing. For example, a client will consider, perhaps in consultation with one or more financiers, whether to offer securities in a public market place or through private negotiations. The client's eventual choice will depend on the offers' terms, including interest costs, the amount of information requiring to be provided, the parties who will become privy to the information, and the effects of information release on his competitive position.

Asset Specificity

Williamson (2002) models the complementarities of governance structures as a function of asset specificity.[25] Figure 3.1 shows the transactions cost consequences of organizing financings through markets, through banks, and through financial conglomerates when the transactions vary by asset specificity. Increasing asset specificity is plotted toward the right of the horizontal axis, and costs are plotted on the vertical axis. When assets have a low degree of specificity, the bureaucratic costs of financial conglomerates place them at a serious disadvantage relative to markets. Similarly, the bureaucratic costs of banks place them at a disadvantage relative to markets, albeit a

---

[25] Although the two concepts are not identical, for most purposes asset specificity can conveniently be thought of as similar to asset illiquidity.

lesser one than conglomerates. However, the cost differences narrow and are eventually reversed as asset specificity increases. Intermediaries are therefore viewed as a hybrid form of governance structure that possesses capabilities somewhere between those of markets and those of conglomerates. With an increase in asset specificity intermediaries come to offer a cost advantage relative to markets, and as asset specificity increases further still, conglomerates come to offer a cost advantage relative to intermediaries. Because added governance costs accrue on taking a transaction out of the market and supervising it with an intermediary or conglomerate organization, the three are usefully viewed as complements, the more expensive to be substituted for the less expensive as the degree of asset specificity increases. Cost-effective governance choices mean the effective form of cost curve in the circumstances displayed is the envelope reflecting the minimum of the three cost curves displayed.

Deal Terms

Financiers propose varied deal terms, both in attempts to ensure profitability and to fine-tune governance arrangements. The terms of a deal include repayment arrangements, the collateral taken, the currency used, and its maturity (fixed or variable). Along with the amount advanced, these terms also determine the effective interest rate. The effective interest rate on a deal increases with its risk, and will be higher for uncertainty than for risk, because financiers require larger returns to compensate for greater risks or for assuming uncertainty rather than risk.[26]

Terms can alter the nature of a deal's original attributes. For example, a deal offering uncertain payoffs can be much easier to finance if the client can offer marketable securities as collateral. In this case a loan can be made against the value of the securities, and the financier, who can rely on the securities' market value as collateral for the loan, will likely view the deal as merely risky rather than uncertain. Chapter 6 provides further details of how terms are set.

FINANCIAL SYSTEM ORGANIZATION

There will usually be a least cost form of governance for each type of deal. Over time, competitive pressures will create a tendency for a least-cost form of governance to emerge for deals of a given type. Both markets and intermediaries are mechanisms for governing deals, and the financial

---

[26]The tax status of a deal can also affect both the financier's return and the client's cost of funds.

system will contain both markets whose organization is intended to benefit their organizers and profit-seeking financial firms. A financial firm's size and organizational structure is determined mainly by the economics of the deals it takes on, and by its operating economics. The organization of the financial system is then determined principally by the aggregate activities of the markets and the firms thus formed.

Markets, Intermediaries, and Internal Finance

The alignment of deal attributes and governance capabilities, and the consequent assembly of portfolios to take advantage of the associated firms' operating economies, explain the static organization of the financial services industry. If there were no intermediaries, potential borrowers would individually have to seek out willing lenders. Similarly, lenders would individually have to screen borrowers, design financial contracts, and monitor borrower behavior. When intermediaries perform the same functions, they may be able to do so more economically by realizing scale and scope economies in their operations. Carey, Post, and Sharpe (1998) argue that (1) markets and intermediaries make different types of corporate loans; and that (2) within the class of intermediaries differently specialized firms make different types of corporate loans. "The evidence implies that it is not enough to understand the public-private debt mix; the mix of varieties of private debt also matters" (1998, 876).

Boot and Thakor (1993) model private banking markets as being less competitive than public securities markets. In their model greater interbank competition reduces banking rents, makes banks more like each other, and less likely to specialize. Increased capital market competition tends both to reduce banking rents and entry to the banking industry (1993). Boot and Thakor see the distinctions between banks and capital markets becoming increasingly blurred, but the analytical perspectives of this book suggest there will continue to be differences between different types of deals and, therefore, different kinds of governance mechanisms will continue to be needed for their administration. Static complementarity is likely to remain a reality. At the same time, the governance of some types of deals can evolve in what Merton and Bodie (2005) term the innovation spiral. Deals formerly handled as nonarm's-length deals may become more familiar, less costly to govern, and, therefore, capable of being handled as arm's-length deals in the market place.

In the aggregate, the organization of a financial system reflects a mix of alignments among the types of deals agreed and the capabilities of the economy's financiers. The size of an individual firm is determined by its operating economics. In addition, there is a natural evolution of any particular deal type from the right to the left in Table 3.3 that is due to financier learning, increasing volume of deals, standardization of deals over time, more nearly precise and cheaper information production. At the same time, a continual infusion of new deals means that high capability governance continues to be needed, even in advanced economies. The proportions of deals governed as market arrangements may change relative to the proportions governed by intermediaries or internally, but all three types of governance will continue to be needed.

Financial Firms

Financial firms assemble agreed deals into portfolios whose size and composition are determined by the firms' operating economics. Financiers specialize in particular types of deals as a means of realizing scale economies in screening, and information production. They realize additional *scale economies* by increasing the numbers of deals in their portfolios, and *scope economies* by taking on related types of deals. In other words, these actions reduce unit costs and, if unit revenue remains the same, profitability is improved.

Limits to the size of a financial firm depend mainly on the costs of coordinating the governance of different deal types, and on the limits to expansion of product lines due resulting from limited market size. When coordination costs begin to rise on a unit basis, taking on more business generating the same unit revenue means that the profitability of additional business begins to fall. When incremental profitability falls to zero, it does not pay the firm to take on still further business: Firms can only be expected to grow until coordination costs become large enough to impair the profitability of taking on more deals.

There are several economic reasons for specializing. First, specialized skills and experience may be required in order to be able to do deals profitably, and only a few intermediaries can justify incurring these expenses. For example, some banks specialize in foreign exchange transactions involving their home currencies, while other banks trade in most major foreign currencies. Second, certain types of deals can only be done in relatively small volumes, so that only a few firms can profitably service that market. Venture capital investments offer a case in point. Third, regulation may restrict intermediaries to only certain types of transactions. For example, North American trust companies have been restricted by legislation to having only a small proportion of their assets in consumer or commercial loans.

On the other hand, there can also be advantages to diversification. When a firm assumes a greater number of deals, as well as when it assumes additional types of deals, it can usually diversify portfolio risks.[27] Since

---

[27] Diversification is only effective if the different deals are not perfectly positively correlated. This topic is examined in Chapter 14.

diversifying portfolio risk reduces earnings risk relative to the expected level of earnings, the firm's performance is thereby improved.

Combinations of Mechanisms

There are many instances of governance mechanisms being combined. For example, an intermediary can partially diversify its asset portfolio by issuing securities against some of its loans (securitization) and using the proceeds to purchase other, unrelated securities. Usually, intermediaries use the funds raised from asset securitization to fund more of the same type of lending. Nevertheless, some potential for unbundling remains: A bank may have a competitive advantage in screening and monitoring, but an insurance company or pension fund may have a competitive advantage in raising funds for investment purposes.

Banks can complement the workings of the securities markets in other ways as well. For example, certifying the creditworthiness of borrowing customers makes it easier for those borrowing customers to avail themselves of additional capital market financing[28] (Fama 1985). Banks also assist their customers to obtain less costly capital market financing by providing guarantees, particularly in circumstances where a bank might have a competitive advantage in determining a client's creditworthiness.

Intermediaries also provide services that are not reflected on their balance sheets. Traditionally, off-balance sheet activities included providing letters of credit, and now include such other activities as arranging risk management services using such instruments as options, interest, currency swaps, credit derivatives, and default swaps.[29] In some risk management transactions, corporations can use exchange-traded instruments; but in others, they deal with intermediaries that trade the instruments on an over-the-counter basis. The difference in the types of transactions depends on whether it is securities markets or intermediaries that offer a competitive advantage; this in turn depends on the type of instrument, its complexities, and the creditworthiness of the parties involved.

---

[28] James (1987) argues that depositors availing themselves of CDs seem to pay the implicit tax of reserve requirements. He argues further that borrowing customers would willingly accept this cost if it meant that their access either to loan financing or to capital market financing was improved. James also provides evidence that granting bank credit can reduce the cost of capital market financing obtained by publicly quoted companies.

[29] The early- to mid-2000s growth in off-balance sheet activities is largely explained by differences in capital charges (see Chapter 22).

Implications for Aggregate System Performance

Both financial intermediaries and markets facilitate the flows of funds through the system. As they borrow to relend, financial intermediaries help create additional liquidity while simultaneously creating agency problems because their asset portfolios are relatively opaque to external valuation. As funds flow through financial markets, the markets also help create liquidity and, at the same time, produce a good deal of public information that is useful for valuation purposes. As these processes are carried out, one of the main issues in assessing performance characteristics is whether economically viable projects can be financed at competitive market rates of interest when taking their risks into account. A second issue is whether the system exhibits cycles—that is, alternating periods of overlending and credit crunches. The interactive roles of institutions and markets in contributing to both the funding and the cyclical phenomena will be examined in later chapters.

REFERENCES

Aghion, Philippe, and Patrick Bolton. 1992. An incomplete contracts approach to financial contracting. *Review of Economic Studies* 59: 473–494.

Allen, Franklin D., and Douglas Gale. 2000. *Comparing Financial Systems*. Cambridge, MA: MIT Press.

Bodie, Zvi and Robert C. Merton. 2005. "Design of financial systems: towards a synthesis of function and structure." *Journal of Investment Management* 3: 1–23.

Boot, Arnoud, and Anjan Thakor. 1993. Security design. *Journal of Finance* 48: 1,349–1,378.

Cai, Jun, Stephen Cheung, and Vidhan K. Goyal. 1999. "Bank monitoring and the maturity structure of Japanese debt issues." *Pacific-Basin Finance Journal* 7: 229–250.

Carey, Mark, Mitch Post, and Steven A. Sharpe. 1998. Does corporate lending by banks and finance companies differ? Evidence on specialization in private debt contracting. *Journal of Finance* 53: 845–878.

Fama, Eugene F. 1985: What's different about banks? *Journal of Monetary Economics* 15: 29–39.

James, Christopher. 1987 "Some Evidence on the Uniqueness of Bank Loans," *Journal of Financial Economics* 19: 217–235.

Jensen, Michael C., and Meckling, William. 1976. Theory of the firm: Managerial behavior, agency costs and ownership structure. *Journal of Financial Economics* 3: 305–360.

Savage, Leonard J. 1954. *The Foundations of Statistics*. New York: Wiley.

Williamson, Oliver E. 1985. *The Economic Institutions of Capitalism*. New York: Free Press.

Williamson, Oliver E. 1987. Transaction cost economics: The comparative contracting perspective. *Journal of Economic Behavior and Organization* 8: 617–625.

Williamson, Oliver E. 2002. "The Theory of the Firm as Governance Structure: From Choice to Contract" *Journal of Economic Perspectives* 16 (3), 171–195.

Williamson, Oliver E. 1975. *Markets and Hierarchies: Analysis and Antitrust Implications.* New York: Free Press.

TERMS

complete contracting   A situation in which the relevant terms of a deal can be fully specified at the outset. Complete contracting is possible only if a deal is risky rather than uncertain.

default risk   The risk that a loan or investment will not be repaid. In the case of debt, inability to repay usually results from the client having no funds with which to make repayment.

incomplete contracting   A situation in which the relevant terms of a deal cannot fully be specified at the outset. One of the main reasons complete contracting may not be possible is the uncertainty under which the deal is arranged.

internal financing (use of internal capital market)   Arranging financings between divisions of a firm, such as financing by conglomerate headquarters of a particular subdivision.

financial intermediaries   Firms whose business involves raising funds for relending. In most contemporary financial systems, these intermediary activities are combined with several other forms of business, as discussed in Chapters 16 through 18.

market agents   Economic agents who arrange or consummate deals in financial markets. For example, if you buy a U.S. Treasury bond from a bond dealer, then, in that transaction, the bond dealer acts as a market agent.

markets (financial markets)   Venues in which financial instruments are traded principally on the basis of their price. For example, in many countries there are public markets for many listed stocks, and there are many markets in which options and other derivative instruments are traded. This chapter defines and discusses a number of the most prominent forms of specialized financial markets.

monitoring   Supervising the evolution of a financial detail after it has first been struck.

profitability risk   The risk that a loan or investment will not yield its rate of return with certainty.

risk The returns to a business venture can only be specified probabilistically.

scale economies The ability to produce additional units of output at a decreasing average cost per unit and frequently arise from spreading fixed production costs over a larger number of units of output.

scope economies The ability to obtain combinations of goods or services at a lower average cost per unit than can be achieved if the goods or services are produced individually. Scope economies, sometimes called cost complementarities or synergies, frequently result from the ability to share common inputs.

screening The initial assessment of the risks and other details of a proposed deal.

uncertainty When an agent cannot regard himself as understanding a deal well. Information about uncertain payoffs is so variable or so diffuse that it cannot usefully be specified in terms of a probability distribution.

CHAPTER 4.

Financial System Organization and Change

Understanding the alignment of attributes with capabilities is key to understanding financial system organization. Some deals can profitably be governed as market transactions, while others require the capabilities provided by nonmarket governance. Most nonmarket governance is provided by intermediaries, but for some deals internal governance is the most cost-effective way of ensuring the expectation of a satisfactory conclusion. In sum, the three governance methods jointly complement each other, and the alignments they mutually reach endogenously determine financial system organization.

While there is a fixed and unchanging set of available governance capabilities, as well as a fixed and unchanging set of deal attributes, the capability mix utilized by a given governance mechanism can evolve over time, as can the attribute mixes of typical deals. Understanding the evolution of both is crucial to analyzing how deal governance can evolve over time, and equally crucial to understanding how financial systems themselves evolve.

This chapter examines financial system change. Change is driven principally by economics; financiers search for improved profitability, and clients search for lower-cost deals. Financiers seek to generate additional revenues by offering new products or entering new markets; they seek to decrease costs by achieving efficiency improvements in operations, in governance, or both. Changes in customary governance methods that promise greater cost-effectiveness are said to reflect dynamic complementarity. For example, many corporate financing deals currently use marketable securities, whereas in the past many of the same deals would have involved bank loans. In other words, market-provided corporate finance has become dynamically complementary to previously established forms of bank financing.

In contrast, static complementarity reflects competitive advantages to attribute-capability alignments at a given point in time. For example, a growing corporation that utilizes both venture financing and bank loans is treating the two sources of financing as statically complementary. If at some later point in time the corporation replaces the venture financing with a new equity issue, at that time the equity financing will be dynamically complementary to the venture financing. Then, if the corporation's debt-equity ratio remains constant for some subsequent period, during that period debt and equity financing will be statically complementary forms of finance.

TRENDS IN PROVIDING FINANCIAL SERVICES

The financial services industry is increasingly a global industry, and its member firms continue to increase both their absolute size and the diversity of their business lines. Many of the most important industry changes involve mergers, both domestic and international. The combinations are not just combinations of banks: Mergers of banks and investment banks have been commonplace for some time, and mergers of banks and insurance firms are becoming increasingly frequent. Throughout the world, mergers of exchanges, both exchanges from different countries and exchanges of different types, have become relatively common. For example, several stock and derivatives exchanges have merged in the 2000s.

Today's financial service providers (FSPs) are innovative developers. Innovation has improved both the FSPs' operating efficiency and the effectiveness with which clients can search for products, services, and prices. Some product and services markets are competitive, and in them transactions charges decrease as efficiency improvements are obtained. Consumers benefit from new and lower-priced products and services, while small businesses benefit from improved access to loans provided through credit scoring techniques. Large businesses benefit from increased availability of syndicated loans, market forms of financing, and improvements in risk management. Investors benefit from faster execution of securities trades, better and easier price comparisons, and thinner trading margins. Nevertheless, change does not bring unalloyed benefits. As shown in this chapter, various types of cost increases and other problems partly offset (but do not eliminate) the benefits just cited.

Globalization

Globalization of financial services has stimulated international integration of FSPs: Throughout the world, financial systems are witness to increasing convergence and increasing asset concentration. As the information processing aspects of financial activity have come to be better understood, many formerly specialized financial intermediaries have merged. The mergers are intended both to take advantage of the scale economies inherent in combining information processing functions and to realize both scale and scope economies by offering services based on the same information processing platform. New products have proliferated in the rapidly changing computing and communications environment, as financial institutions strive to retain or even increase their market shares through exploiting technological advances.

In the United States, more than 9,500 commercial and savings banks were taken over between 1987 and 2005, leaving fewer than 7,500 remaining. In the European Union, the number of credit institutions decreased from 12,250 to 9,285 between 1985 and 1997 (Schenk 2001). Globally, mergers and acquisitions in financial services rose from $85 billion in 1991 to $534 billion in 1998. Cross-border capital flows have also increased dramatically and continuously since the 1980s. The picture is not one of uniform growth in all sectors, but on the whole the world's financial system is becoming more international and more integrated.

Increasing internationalization has been accompanied by more permissive regulation. Constraints on foreign institutions' ability to enter formerly closed domestic markets have been relaxed in many countries, and some of the world's largest financial institutions now face few regulatory barriers to entry. On the other hand, some institutions face higher entry barriers from competitors as financial business becomes increasingly technology-intensive and firms incur increasingly greater setup costs.

Technological Change

The financial services industry exhibits nearly continuous technological change. Beginning in about 1980 and continuing to the present time, financial institutions have spent massive amounts on automating data processing, developing internationally connected networks of automated banking machines, expanding their Internet accessibility, and implementing various forms of wireless access. Nonfinancial companies also entered the financial business, particularly as service providers. All these changes enhance client access to financial services from many different locations and using a variety of technologies.

Financial services are changing contemporaneously. At the wholesale level, banks have become much more active in providing risk management services to their business clients. They have also become more active in trading risk instruments and securities, for both their clients' and their own accounts. Loan sales, the use of credit derivatives and of credit default swaps all mean that banks can now disperse lending risks to a greater degree than previously. At the level of small business, credit is becoming more widely available through the services of aggregators and the advent of credit scoring. At the retail level, banks are combining with insurance companies to offer a spectrum of banking and insurance products along with a variety of wealth management services. Finally, many of the services traditionally offered by banks are now being provided by both financial and nonfinancial entities, especially over the Internet.

Technological change is having profound impacts on access to the financial system. Less visibly, technological change also affects financial system infrastructure. As just one example, financial institutions are going to know more about their customers, and consequently be able to service them better, through developing a corporate memory. As information systems become increasingly better integrated, each transaction will be available to all the personnel of the institution, and as a result clients will enjoy more highly informed levels of service.

Financial markets are changing equally rapidly and profoundly. Communication costs are no longer distance-dependent, computer systems have lowered trading costs, and financial activity is moving to new forms and locations of electronic trading facilities. Electronic exchanges offer a variety of Internet-based trading services that present serious competition for traditional exchanges. Trading systems for equities, fixed income securities, and foreign exchange are all consolidating and becoming global operations. As securities and derivatives exchanges become more international and less specialized in the products they trade, they have become critically dependent on computer-based trading, and the traditional exchanges' open-outcry trading pits will soon be a vestige of the past. Increasingly, cheap access to information and greater information interchange is improving price determination, while simultaneously presenting fragmentation problems that require new forms of management attention, as discussed next.

Impacts of Trends

Internet and wireless communication technologies are not just new distribution channels: They offer new and different ways of providing financial services. In particular, the new technologies permit financial products to be simultaneously commoditized and tailored to individual consumer needs.[1] The now numerous forms of access devices, including ABMs, personal computers, personal digital assistants, televisions with Internet access, and cellular phones are becoming consumers' first points of contact with FSPs.

Advances in information and communications technology facilitate the delivery of a broad array of financial services through single providers. The new providers include online banks and brokerages, as well as aggregators and portals—facilities that allow consumers to compare financial services such as mortgage loans or insurance policies offered by suppliers of financial services. Indeed, in some countries (United States, Latin America, South Korea) portals are becoming a critical link between access devices and FSPs. Portal operators personalize information in their attempts to attract and retain consumers, then earn revenue by referring their customers to appropriate FSPs. Other institutions, known as enabling companies, both support the technology of traditional FSPs and set up their own virtual banks as well.

Entry has been particularly strong in financial services that initially offered attractive margins, especially margins that could be realized through unbundling and commoditization. These services include brokerage, trading systems, some retail banking products, bill presentment, and payment gateways for business-to-business commerce. Once established, the new entrants have moved toward more highly regulated services. For example E*TRADE, a company offering securities trading facilities, has recently acquired a bank to provide a full range of financial services to its customers, and now offers Web access to its clients.

Barriers between markets have been reduced as commercial paper and corporate bonds have been substituted for bank loans to larger and better-known corporations.[2] Similarly, but on the retail level, mutual funds and other forms of jointly owned securities portfolios have been substituted for bank deposits. These forces for disintermediation stimulate banks to expand other financial services in compensation. Banks and insurance companies are consolidating around recognized brand names to position themselves in the new environment of increased commoditization and electronic delivery. Although development of deposit-taking and payment services has

---

[1]Examples of commoditization and tailoring familiar to many readers are electronic systems for booking airline tickets, hotel accommodation, and entertainment. One might expect that these ways of temporarily leasing space (on an airplane, in a hotel, theater, or arena) will become more closely integrated with payment facilities than is now the case.

[2]In some cases, such as the growth of the asset-backed commercial paper market, the developments have been carried to inappropriate extremes. These issues are discussed at several later points in the book.

sometimes been slowed by regulatory and industry obstacles, new forms of online banks, along with new forms of credit and debit cards, including smart cards, are helping to foster further development.

The Internet and other technological advances have reduced economies of scale in the production of financial services that can easily be unbundled and commoditized—payment and brokerage services, mortgage loans, insurance, and some forms of trade finance. The reduced scale economies have in turn reduced barriers to entry and consequently increased competition among those kinds of financial services. The main financial service that still exhibits increasing returns to scale is the medium-size loan market, mainly because large databases of credit history are required to build a credit-scoring model for medium-size clients. For most other forms of credit economies of scale have become small as the fixed costs of screening small borrowers (say clients with loans of under $100,000) have dropped significantly.

Markets characterized by sunk costs and low commoditization potential have seen much less new entry. Examples are markets for underwriting, for facilitating mergers and acquisitions, and for providing advice to corporate clients. In order to compete effectively for these types of business, the FSP must have a certain size and a brand name, and the markets for these businesses are increasingly subject to global competition. In sufficiently large markets, global competition may lead to market contestability, even if only a few providers are active in the market.

Commercial borrowers using business-to-business transactions benefit from lower transaction and search costs and from greater access to financial services. New online companies[3] provide a full array of services to start-up companies, including legal services, Web design, accounting services, branding and advertisement, and advice regarding investor relations. Venture capital firms and other investors can use these companies to screen potential start-up ideas. Internet use of data gathering may enhance lending outreach to the point where it can eventually reach even very small companies.

PROFIT OPPORTUNITIES AND CHANGE

Financiers continually seek to improve their profit positions, both by looking to increase margins on the types of deals they are already doing and by finding new forms of profitable deals. In a competitive environment, financiers may be so anxious to find new profit opportunities that they will

---

[3]Such as Garage.com and TechPacific.com.

even take on deals whose profitability is suggested rather than confirmed. Profitability is affected by deal attributes, available governance methods, the possible presence of externalities, and the nature of the economic environment. Clearly, profitability can differ among types of deals, and even among deals of a given type. For example, if a new product is not easily imitated, at least in the near term, an innovator can gain market power that may allow her to extract rents, either through charging prices that exceed production costs or possibly through gaining market share. On the other hand, if a product can easily be imitated, free-rider problems posed by imitators may work to reduce the degree of innovation.

Changes in profitability can stem from changes either in the demand for or in the supply of deals. Demand changes derive both from the environmental conditions clients face and the fortunes of the clients' businesses, and can occur in two forms: a shift in the demand curve for deals of a given type or emergence of a demand for deals of a new type. As an example of environmental change, both increases in international trade and increases in foreign exchange volatility have greatly increased demands for foreign currency hedging over a period beginning in the 1970s and extending into the 2000s.

Changes in the terms on which financiers supply new products or services arise mainly from utilizing new technologies that render a new approach profitable. Changes in technology can change deals' risk-return ratios, usually by making their governance cheaper. As one example, computers permit supervising a credit card portfolio on a management-by-exception basis, thereby creating a new source of scale economies in governing credit card debt. Before computers became widely available, records were reviewed manually to identify slow payers or other clients whose accounts needed personal attention. As a second example, automating the process of approving mortgage loan applications reduced processing costs by several hundred dollars, and was a particularly important factor in contributing to the late 1990s to mid-2000s growth of the subprime mortgage market in the United States.[4]

Changes in financial technology can also affect the well-being of certain types of borrowers. As one example, before the mid-1980s loans were rarely made to small private borrowers in developing countries because it was then thought the credit risks of this type of business were too great. However, during the 1980s, the International Finance Corporation began extending loans to villages rather than to individual borrowers, and it was found

---

[4]Computer-based methods also made screening sub-prime mortgages much cheaper, but perverse incentives created additional negative effects in this market, as examined later.

that the default risk of these loans was much less than had been expected. More or less contemporaneously, the Grameen Bank pioneered the use of microcredit: loans of very small amounts to individual entrepreneurs. These technical changes in the supply of financing both led to the emergence of new forms of financial business and improved the well-being of clients able to obtain the new forms of credit.

Despite the many and varied responses to adopting new technologies, financiers do not always respond to demands for new or expanded forms of financing. In some markets, a failure to respond may be temporary, in others it will be persistent. One reason for this difference is that not all proposed deals look to financiers as though they will generate a profit sufficient to compensate for the deal's perceived risk or uncertainty. In addition, financiers will not always be willing to entertain types of deals whose profit potentials are not well understood, say because the deals are new and unfamiliar. A third reason is that financiers may not have an appropriate technology to entertain the new deals. The examples of development financing discussed in the previous paragraph offer cases in point: The financings were not provided until technological change made it possible to overcome the early difficulties.

Processes of Change

The organization of the world's major financial systems is changing rapidly, but the systems continue to perform the same basic functions described in Chapter 2. Understanding the processes of financial system change involves understanding how the same financial functions continue to be performed while the organizations performing the functions continue to evolve. New products using new technologies may be developed to perform the traditional basic functions, as is illustrated by using debit cards to make retail payments. In this case, a change in payments technology affects both system clients and the ways financial firms organize themselves, the latter because electronic payment systems reduce transactions costs through realizing new forms of scale economies.

The adaptation of institutions to changing economics is a relatively complex phenomenon with outcomes that differ according to the circumstances. Bodie and Merton (2005) characterize financial system change as a process of gravitating toward the predictions of the neoclassical paradigm. However, while change is an adaptive process driven by economics, it is also constrained by institutional rigidities and behavioral considerations. In addition, the types of financial governance described in Chapter 3 remain stable over relatively long periods of time, but the ways particular deals are governed can change quite rapidly as the economics of their governance changes.

Searching for New Profit Opportunities

The pace of financial innovation implies that not all profit opportunities will persist for long periods. Most financial markets are highly competitive and a newly developed advantage cannot usually be retained for long. Moreover, few financial innovations can be patented. On the other hand, the designers of a new product may develop skills that are difficult to replicate in the short run, giving the innovators a profit advantage so long as it gains the acceptance of a sufficiently large number of financiers. As a counter-example, if a certain contract is widely used to hedge a given type of risk, a new instrument may not succeed in replacing the old one even if the former has superior features.

Thus, even though it has become increasingly important to exploit new profit opportunities quickly, supply-side changes are not always instantaneous. Since both innovation and learning are costly, adapting established routines to new circumstances can be a lengthy process: Innovative deals and innovative governance structures usually evolve slowly from well-established technologies. Some viable new deals may be avoided, at least for a time, either because their gross returns are underestimated or because their governance costs are overestimated. Financiers can be less likely to innovate under competition than under monopoly because, under competition, the innovative financier may have less opportunity to recover unanticipated cost increases.

Temporary advantages to innovation may not always be exploited in the form of economic rents reaped through monopoly pricing. Tufano (1989) argues that even when investment banks create new products, they do not always charge monopoly prices. Rather, some innovative firms reduce their prices below monopoly levels to capture larger shares of business over a longer time horizon. By so doing, the innovator may be able to realize economies of scale and of scope. Innovative firms can thus enjoy lower costs of trading, underwriting, and marketing, and earn economic rents through cost reduction rather than through price increases. Finally, innovators may become skilled at learning by doing, and can thus develop new products more cheaply than their imitative rivals. Taking all the foregoing factors into account, a financial system's innovativeness can be said to depend on a delicate and shifting balance of the forces favoring and impeding innovation.

In contrast to product innovation, competition between exchanges for certain kinds of trading business may be subject to first mover advantages that can be exploited profitably for a relatively long period. Similarly, a merger of exchanges may capture network externalities that are profitable for a long time. In Europe, competition between exchanges increased after the adoption of the Euro in 1999. By the 2000s, international mergers and alliances between exchanges had become common, partly because of growing competition to list securities and to attract members. Moreover, technological change and electronic trading systems obviate the need for many different exchange floors, and the cost of electronic trading is substantially lower (Domowitz and Steil 1999). At the same time investment banks' margins are declining, forcing them to cut costs by measures which include reducing the number of exchanges to which they belong.

Experimentation

Financiers differ in their readiness to adapt to change. Whether a financier is willing to experiment or not can be regarded as a rational conclusion drawn from the financier's assessments of deal attributes, her ability to administer those attributes profitably, and her risk preferences. For example, during past merger waves some merchant bankers actively sought to arrange leveraged buyouts, even arranging bridging finance in order to capture additional merger and acquisition business. These innovative merchant bankers hoped to be able to earn new profits from attracting additional merger clients, but since they were experimenting with unfamiliar new forms of business, they could not always describe their expected returns quantitatively. Other merchant bankers avoided making the same choices, also because they had difficulties in describing their expected earnings quantitatively.

Financial system change represents intended rational action, but it is very often taken in an atmosphere of uncertainty. When they experiment, financiers understand that they are facing uncertainties. They may feel uncomfortable with having to face the uncertainties, but regard the potential profits as making the effort worthwhile nevertheless. That is, decisions to enter new businesses are based on anticipated net benefits of some kind, but at the time the decisions are being taken it may not be possible to describe the benefits in very precise terms.

When innovative deals are entered, experienced financiers employ forms of governance designed to cope with the uncertainties the deals present, forms that recognize the difficulty of describing returns in quantitative terms. Rather, governance of an uncertain deal mainly involves trying to identify key profitability factors and trying to limit the impacts of unfavorable developments. For example, the banks and securities firms that tried to take advantage of London's Big Bang (1986) through rapid expansion into new areas of business could not always justify their moves in profitability terms.[5] Yet, many felt they had to make such moves simply to keep even with the competition. The late 1980s and early 1990s retrenchments of international banks and securities firms are examples of further adjustments reflecting the same banks' learning that the originally perceived market opportunities were not large enough to sustain all the new entrants.

Product Innovation

Product innovation is another important driver of financial system change. While many innovations are introduced in the hope of generating new revenue sources, cost reductions stemming from technological change can also have significant impacts on product development. For example, automated processing of subprime mortgage loans was credited with reducing the costs of each mortgage approval by several hundred dollars, and the resultant new profit opportunities contributed importantly to the very rapid growth of the sub-prime market in the late 1990s and early 2000s. New product developments, along with innovations in fund raising and in risk transfer, are discussed in Chapter 5 and also in several later sections. Many innovations have contributed to growth spurts that were later followed by losses and rapid declines of business, as will also be discussed.

REFERENCES

Bodie, Zvi, and Robert C. Merton. 2005. Design of financial systems: Towards a synthesis of function and structure. *Journal of Investment Management* 3: 1–23.
Domowitz, Ian, and Benn Steil. 1999. Automation, trading costs, and the structure of the trading services industry. Brookings-Wharton Papers on Financial Services.
Schenk, Hans. 2001. "Mergers and the Economy: Theory and Policy Implications." Presentation to the workshop on European Integration, Financial Systems and Corporate Performance, Maastricht, February 17.
Tufano, Peter. 1989. Financial innovation and first-mover advantages. *Journal of Financial Economics* 25 (December): 213–240.

---

[5]The "Big Bang" was an important deregulatory move in which (1) computerized trading was established; (2) securities firms that traded in the United States and Japan were permitted for the first time to trade on the London Stock Exchange; and (3) fixed minimum commissions on stock trades were eliminated. In one of the most significant features of the Big Bang, investment firms that had previously traded only in New York and Tokyo were able to create a nearly 24-hour operation by trading in London as well.

Two

Market versus Nonmarket Governance

This part examines the main governance mechanisms—markets, intermediaries, and internal finance. It elaborates the capabilities of each governance type and the principal transaction attributes each is best equipped to govern. It explains how market and nonmarket methods are complementary both at any given point in time (static complementarity) and also through time (dynamic complementarity).

CHAPTER 5

Market Governance

Market performance is usually assessed in terms of market efficiency, liquidity, and information production. Marketplaces are usually organized in attempts to enhance these performance characteristics, and examining the principal capabilities of different market types shows how combinations of performance characteristics are used. For example public versus private markets, primary versus secondary markets, dealer versus broker markets, and wholesale versus retail markets all display different combinations of capabilities, and as a result align cost-effectively with classes of deals presenting different attribute combinations. The chapter also introduces the nature of securitization markets, whose principal purpose is to enhance the funding of portfolios composed of illiquid investments.

Casual observers of financial systems often describe many different specialized kinds of markets. However, expanding on the view of Chapter 3, financial markets can be distinguished analytically using just a few characteristics. These characteristics include the markets' cost and revenue functions, the economics of producing information about market-traded assets, and the economics of trading firms. Economic considerations determine the operating and allocative efficiency of any given market, the type and number of agents trading in it, the liquidity of the instruments traded in it,[1] and the extent to which price information is revealed by trading. The picture sketched here will be applied throughout the rest of the book.

---

[1]The liquidity of instruments traded in a given market may also vary considerably over time, as examined in this chapter.

FUNCTIONS OF MARKETS

The principal function of any financial market is to create a central location where buyers and sellers (or their agents) can meet to trade. In the past, markets were usually described by their physical locations, but as Internet access and trading have increased in importance, markets are now frequently described in terms of electronic access, which continues to become increasingly available. Both market agents and investors now trade mainly from their homes or offices, and the physical location of the computers processing the trades is less important than the kind of Internet access available to prospective traders.

Finding counterparties in a highly active marketplace is less time consuming and less costly than in a relatively inactive market. The more actively that instruments trade in the market, the greater their liquidity. Moreover the lower the market's trading costs, the greater trading volumes are likely to be. Thus a market in which it is cheap and easy to find counterparties is also likely to be a market in which the assets exchanged are relatively liquid, as Chapter 10 shows in greater theoretical detail. Markets also differ in the degree to which the parties to a deal either have or will be able to acquire the same information about the instruments they trade.

Two of the most prominent dimensions of marketplace activity are the volume and frequency of trading.[2] In some of the larger public stock markets, at least some shares[3] trade in large volumes on an almost minute-by-minute basis. On the other hand, there are markets that handle only relatively small transactions, and infrequently at that. The types of instruments traded constitute another dimension. Markets trade instruments such as bonds and equities issued principally to raise capital, as well as other instruments, such as derivatives, whose principal function is to exchange risks.

As already mentioned, the organizers of a market strive to enhance its profitability by increasing its trading volume. Thus market organizers work to reduce unit trading costs through standardizing the instruments traded, through processing trades efficiently, through executing trades quickly and as near to ruling market prices as possible. The charges market organizers collect take the forms of trading commissions, bid-ask spreads,[4] or both.

A market's total operating costs usually have a fixed component so that unit trading costs fall as trading volume increases. These scale economics to market operations mean that larger and more active markets can typically

---

[2]As will be shown later, these two dimensions are closely related to market liquidity.
[3]Even on a very active market, such as the New York Stock Exchange, some of the listed shares will trade relatively infrequently.
[4]That is, by purchasing instruments at lower prices than the market is currently selling them.

offer lower trading costs than their smaller, less active counterparts. Thus established markets strive both to attract large volumes of trades in individual instruments, and to expand the number of instruments in which they deal. In the past many markets specialized, say in either securities or derivatives. However, recent mergers of different types of markets, and mergers of markets in different jurisdictions, both suggest the presence of scope economies to trading many different types of instruments on the same facility.

Historically, markets have been organized as associations of traders who share market revenues and costs, usually in proportion to the amounts of business done. The goals of marketplaces organized in this way have not always been easy to specify, and in some cases controversy hindered the ability of the marketplace to grow and to adopt new practices. During the first decade of the 2000s, many of the larger stock and derivatives markets were reorganized as for-profit businesses accountable to their shareholders. A profit-oriented marketplace has clearly defined profitability criteria that can be used to resolve such issues as whether the market should specialize or combine different forms of trading, the amount and kinds of technology it should acquire, and other similar operating questions.

Technological change offers potentials for cost reduction that can both stimulate the creation of new markets and enhance access to existing markets. The rapid growth of Internet trading means that electronic marketplaces can and now do provide strong competition for organized stock exchanges. Parties who assemble bid and ask information from potential buyers and sellers can sometimes complete exchanges quickly at or near market prices, even if the computer network on which they trade has no established dealers[5] in the instrument.

Markets are less likely to emerge for instruments issued in small volumes, or for deals that require individual attention.[6] On a per unit basis trade in small volumes is more costly, and the trading that does take place is most likely to be completed on a negotiated rather than a standardized basis. At the extreme, some types of transactions cannot be completed at all. This phenomenon, known as market failure, can occur when the demand for trading an instrument is not sufficiently large to induce agents to take a position in it. Market failure is discussed further in Chapter 10.

---

[5]Markets such as Nasdaq have market-makers who act as both dealers and brokers. Dealers take positions in instruments, while brokers arrange transactions between counterparties. The economic differences of these functions are discussed in the "Market Agents" section of this chapter.

[6]Markets for these kinds of trades may be less costly to organize using the Internet, but in some cases even Internet trading may not prove profitable. The auction services provided by e-Bay offer one example of how such markets can successfully be set up.

DESCRIPTIVE AND ECONOMIC CHARACTERISTICS

This section relates descriptive market classifications to the principal underlying economics of marketplace operations.

Public versus Private Markets

The term public market refers to any member of a class of securities markets in which issues are both initially sold to[7] and subsequently traded by the public at large. Information about the nature of public market securities is usually widely and relatively evenly distributed, and regulations attempt to ensure that agents potentially have access to new or evolving information. The New York Stock Exchange,[8] the London Stock Exchange,[9] and Nasdaq are examples of public markets.

The term private market refers to any member of a class of markets in which instruments are traded among a small number of parties on a negotiated basis. Information about private market transactions is usually less widely distributed than it is for public market transactions. A negotiated sale of company debt to a pension fund that buys the whole issue is an example of a private market transaction.

Public and private markets differ mainly in the types of screening that market agents use, and in the ways information is distributed among participants. Assessing the underwriting risks of a public market issue usually involves determining whether a sufficient number of securities purchasers can be attracted to the new issue, and then setting a price at which they are likely to be attracted. For example, if a high-quality bond issuer is widely known to a large prospective group of purchasers, it is quite likely that a public issue will prove successful in raising the needed funds at or near market rates of interest.

On the other hand, the underwriter of a private market issue needs to find clients who will be willing to buy and hold the securities. Thus private issues can require more lengthy negotiations than their public market counterparts, but the smaller number of purchasers will also afford them an

---

[7]In some jurisdictions, particularly in the United States, initial offerings are floated off-exchange, and only outstanding shares are exchange traded. The principal reason for this separation is to separate new-issue price effects from other trading effects. Nevertheless, in many countries both initial and secondary trades are carried out on exchanges.

[8]Since a 2007 merger of the NYSE and Euronext, the parent company of the exchanges is now called NYSE-Euronext.

[9]The London Stock Exchange and the Borsa Italiana were merged in 2008.

opportunity for more intensive screening. For example, a less well-known firm is more likely to use a private rather than a public issue because the deal can be examined in detail by one or a few prospective buyers. Moreover, if the trade is between sophisticated parties, regulations do not usually require public disclosure of the information necessary to assess the trade, thus reducing issue costs.

Primary versus Secondary Markets

Primary market transactions involve selling new issues of securities. Primary public market issues of securities are sold to large numbers of purchasers who have potentially equal access to public information regarding an issuing firm.[10] In order for both to comply with disclosure regulations and to attract investors, underwriters usually distribute information about new public issues as widely as possible.

In contrast, primary private market issues are sold to a smaller number of possible investors. The information produced for analyzing and selling private issues is not usually required to be released to the public at large, because the issue is intended to be sold to a relatively small number of sophisticated parties. Primary market agents are concerned mainly with raising new funds, and depend on an effective distribution network to do so successfully. Firms that can successfully capture the business of floating primary issues are also usually skilled at reselling the securities to investors.

Trades in outstanding instruments are called secondary transactions. Most secondary market transactions involve rearrangements of outstanding securities or derivatives. Secondary transactions are used both to invest surplus funds and to raise cash, and are usually finalized in the stock markets, the bond markets, or the money markets. Instruments representing individual bank loans are not often resold in the market place, but securities issued against portfolios of individual loans are very often resold.[11]

---

[10] Primary transactions are particularly important to financing new capital formation and, therefore, for contributing to economic growth. If a domestic financial system does not finance certain kinds of deals, capital formation will be inhibited unless the necessary funds can be raised offshore. If neither domestic nor foreign financing is available, the proposed capital formation will either be postponed until it can be financed from retained earnings or even abandoned. In either case, economic growth is likely to be affected adversely (see King and Levine 1993).

[11] Banks securitize a loan portfolio (or a part of one) by selling new securities that normally use the whole portfolio (or the relevant part), and not individual loans in it, as collateral.

Secondary market agents are concerned mainly with carrying out trades at or near existing market prices. Successful performance of these functions depends largely on the agents' ability to find counterparties quickly and relatively cheaply, and to keep their trading costs as low as those of their competitors. Secondary transactions help evaluate new information about firms that issue publicly traded securities and also improve the liquidity of primary securities issues, in the latter case by making it easier to trade outstanding securities.

Dealer versus Broker Markets

Traders act as dealers by taking instruments into inventory, and as brokers when they arrange transactions between counterparties without taking a position themselves. The existence of dealers, and consequently the degree to which the market provides liquidity, depends in part on the inventory risk-trading reward ratio for a typical transaction, as discussed in Chapter 10. The specialists on exchanges like the New York Stock Exchange function as dealers, as do the market makers on exchanges[12] such as Nasdaq.

Wholesale versus Retail Markets

Some wholesale markets, such as the upstairs (institutional) market on the NYSE, operate in tandem with an exchange's regular trading. Other wholesale markets are operated separately by institutions that conduct their own trading entirely off-exchange. Securities are usually traded in large volumes in these wholesale markets, and large-volume trades may not always take place at the ruling market price, for at least two reasons. First, the counterparty to a large trade may be concerned about possible adverse selection. He might, for example, ask why the seller is willing to dispose of a large amount of securities. If he does not know the reasons, he may only be willing to buy the large amount at a discount from the prevailing market price. The second reason large trades can affect the price is that the demand curve for large amounts of a given security is usually thought to be downward-sloping—that is, to exhibit a degree of price inelasticity that is in part attributable to difficulty that might be encountered in reselling them. Similarly, the supply of a large amount of a given security is usually thought to be upward sloping.

---

[12] Although Nasdaq originated as an over-the-counter market, it is now frequently referred to as an exchange mainly because of the numbers of shares and the volumes it trades.

In contrast, retail market transactions are usually completed at or near the current market price (after allowing for agents' fees such as commissions and bid-ask spreads). Retail trades are not usually thought to be subject to a significant degree of adverse selection, partly because they occur much more frequently than wholesale trades, and the number of agents carrying out retail trades is usually large.

Types of Securities Firms

Securities firms act as market agents and, in so doing, exhibit two dominant forms of organization: (1) either large and multipurpose, or (2) small and specialized. The nature and size of these firms both depend on functions of the firms' operating economics. Large firms emerge because they can realize scale and scope economies through the activities they conduct. For example, large firms can realize scale economies in their sales activities, their research functions, and in their data processing and accounting activities. They can realize scope economies through combining such activities as underwriting on the one hand, arranging mergers and acquisitions on the other. Large firms can also obtain benefits from diversification. For example, by combining retail and corporate sales, large firms may be able to improve the return-risk ratio of their earnings. Small, specialized firms are set up primarily to exploit niche markets, usually by assembling particular combinations of skills that are not possessed by larger firms. In part, smaller firms may be able to provide more attractive incentives to their employees and, as a result, operate a highly productive specialized business.

MARKET EFFICIENCY

A perfectly competitive financial market is both allocatively and operationally efficient. Consider each in turn. Allocative efficiency means that equally risky proposals can be funded at the same interest rate. If an allocatively efficient system is not in equilibrium, atypical interest rate differentials signal that profit opportunities are available. As the Chapter 8 and 9 discussions of arbitrage show, if atypical interest differentials emerge they will stimulate trading that continues until the differentials have been eliminated. Theoretically, arbitrage opportunities can be eliminated in perfectly competitive markets because transactions costs or other impediments to arbitraging are assumed away.

The Efficient Markets Hypothesis maintains that when markets are perfectly competitive and trading is not impeded by transactions costs or institutional practices, the markets will be allocatively efficient in the sense that securities' equilibrium prices fully reflect all publicly available information. The only real difference between instruments traded in allocatively efficient markets is in their risk-return characteristics: On average riskier securities command relatively higher rates of interest than their less risky counterparts.

Market trading is most active, and consequently markets most nearly approach allocative efficiency, when deal terms are standardized and when agents have ready access to the same information. As Chapters 8 and 9 show, the prices (or the effective rates of interest) on securities that are close substitutes are likely to be kept aligned through active trading. In such cases the markets are said to be linked by arbitrage. If such markets display persistent price differences between instruments that are apparently close substitutes, the differences are likely attributable either to differences in their risk or in the details of the instruments' terms. For example, if interest earnings on some instruments receive different tax treatments than on other instruments of similar risk and maturity, there will be a price differential reflecting the different interest rate treatment.

The larger and more active secondary securities markets are usually regarded as allocatively efficient, and indeed they can conduct both small retail trades and large institutional trades at very nearly the same market prices. For example, large institutions' trading does not appear to influence stock price variability; compare Gemmill (1996). However since about 1960, financial institutions have accounted for increasingly larger proportions of securities trading, and from time to time observers have expressed concern as to whether the larger individual trades of institutions are fully compatible with retail trading in the same market.

Turning now to operational efficiency, a financial system is said to be operationally efficient if it can perform services at the lowest possible cost, given existing technology and use of best practices. A perfectly competitive market is operationally efficient by definition because the definition assumes that all deals can be completed without payment of transactions costs.[13] However, perfect competition is also operationally efficient in the deeper sense that agents trading in perfectly competitive markets must either deal at lowest feasible cost or be driven out of business. Under competition, any deal whose costs were above the minimum would also have to yield above-market returns in order to cover the higher costs. But, the only way to earn returns over and above their competitive levels is to buy securities at less than their market prices, and this is not possible at a competitive equilibrium. If a market agent does not have costs as low as other market agents, then she will earn less than competitive returns. But then, unless she

---

[13] In such a market all deals have to pay, or earn, the ruling market interest rate appropriate for the deal's risk.

can find ways of reducing her costs to below competitive levels, the business will not survive. Similarly, if a firm cannot operate at the lowest possible cost, any securities it sells would have to be overpriced to cover the higher costs. But then none would buy the securities from such a firm. In order to survive, the firm would have to trim its costs back to the same levels as those of other firms.

Research suggests that most developed countries have allocatively and operationally efficient markets in government securities, albeit to varying degrees in different economies and in markets for different governments' securities, even within the same economy. The public securities markets in many advanced economies exhibit a high degree of operating efficiency, partly because of scale economies to market operations (Tinic and West 1974). Moreover, transactions costs are typically lower in national markets with greater volumes of activity, a finding that indirectly confirms smaller exchanges have higher unit operating costs. For example, the transactions costs on a U.S. $500,000 trade in the Australian national market have been measured at 0.80%, while at the same time in the U.K. and U.S. national markets they were respectively 0.50% and 0.20% (Brinson and Carr 1989).

INFORMATION PRODUCTION

Securities firms develop research information both for their own trading purposes and for their clients' uses. If the cost of producing research information has a fixed component, the activity is subject to scale economies. The more deals of the same type for which information is produced, the lower the unit cost of producing the information. At the same time, it may be possible to sell the information to more than one client, increasing the revenue obtained from its production.

Research information affects the market value of securities, but not all traded securities receive the same degree of research attention. The amount of research conducted depends on the kinds of securities traded and the clientele who would likely use the information. Information regarding traded instruments is only produced if its value in use at least equals its cost. Value will be greater than cost in markets where securities information has a degree of heterogeneity and a number of trading agents will benefit from reducing the heterogeneity.[14] On the other hand, the value of producing some information may not equal its cost, either because the cost is relatively high or the information cannot be used to produce much revenue.

---

[14] Allen and Gale (2000) argue that securities markets are good at reconciling diverse forms of information, while intermediaries can be better at producing information that is less diverse.

Most economically worthwhile research in the public securities markets seems to be aimed at developing information about actively traded securities whose value is subject to some controversy. In some other markets there may be insufficient controversy to make research valuable. For example, the instruments traded on money markets are very close substitutes, meaning there is little uncertainty regarding the value of a particular instrument and additional research is unlikely to produce enough revenue to make its production profitable. In still other markets research information can be relatively valuable, but the information producers cannot recover their costs. For example, the instruments traded in the primary mortgage markets are likely to differ greatly in quality and in maturity, but they do not usually trade actively. In such markets, information might have large potential value for a few purchasers, but with just a few sales it is not always possible to recover the cost of producing the information.

LIQUIDITY

Market-traded instruments can differ substantially in their liquidity, and these differences depend on such factors as differences in market structure as well as in the nature of the instruments traded.[15] In particular, research reported in Chapter 10 shows that the economics of market making creates important differences in liquidity. In essence, highly liquid markets are markets in which there are competing dealers willing to take positions in the instruments traded. Dealers are likely to operate in markets where they can generate trading profit commensurate with the risks of taking inventory positions in traded assets. Thus most economies have dealers in short-term government securities, but few if any economies have secondary market dealers in residential housing. The risk-return ratios for taking positions in these two types of markets differ radically, as explained further in Chapter 10.

SECURITIZATION OF ILLIQUID ASSET PORTFOLIOS

As first mentioned in Chapter 2, financial intermediaries have securitized mortgages for a very long time, and corporate loans have been securitized

---

[15] The Bank of England has recently devised a liquidity measure that is a weighted average of bid-ask spreads, estimates of how prices change with volumes traded, and the spread of corporate over government bonds. (Source: *The Economist*, April 28, 2007.)

since the 1970s.[16] Originally, asset securitization involved selling new securities representing claims against a specialized portfolio of illiquid loans.[17] The practice releases funds that would otherwise be tied up in illiquid assets, permitting intermediaries to continue lending rapidly even if traditional forms of deposit growth have tailed off. Securitization also attracts additional capital from institutional investors, channeling it such activities as residential mortgage lending. The typical buyers of the new securities are financial institutions such as pension funds, insurance companies, and hedge funds with demands for specialized investments.

Securitization continued to grow steadily from its inception until the credit market turmoil of 2007–2008, when new securitizations declined sharply. While many of the early securitizations were based on portfolios of mortgages conforming to federal standards, mortgage-based issues were followed in the 1970s by securitization of corporate loans. During the early 2000s securitization techniques were further expanded to fund very rapid growth in commercial and residential mortgage operations, particularly subprime mortgages. Portfolios funded by asset-backed commercial paper also grew very rapidly from the early 2000s to 2007–2008.

As securitization practices continued to spread they evolved considerably, both in the process of raising funds and in transferring risk.[18] In current forms of securitization, a lending institution pools some of its loans and sells them on to a special purpose entity (SPE).[19] The SPE in turn funds its operations by selling new securities backed by the SPE's assets. Interest and principal payments on SPE-issued securities are funded by cash flows generated by the original loan pool. While the original lending institution usually retains some of the credit risk associated with the pool of loans, credit risk is also transferred to the holders of the securities issued by the SPE,[20] with

---

[16] There are actually two practices referred to as asset securitization. The first refers to the corporate practice of raising funds in financial markets rather than borrowing from banks; the second refers to intermediaries' practice of funding asset portfolios through selling securities to financial institutions.

[17] Historically, the practice of selling claims against illiquid assets was more common than actual sales of loans. Again historically, when claims against illiquid assets were sold, the default risk on the loans mainly continued to be borne by the originating intermediary.

[18] The succeeding discussion is greatly indebted to Fabozzi and Kothari (2007) and to Lucas, Goodman, and Fabozzi (2007).

[19] SPEs are also referred to as special purpose vehicles (SPVs) or as "conduits."

[20] When in some 2008 cases investor losses mounted to unexpected levels, for reputational reasons, some banks purchased the securities and thus reassumed the credit risk.

the extent and type of the transfers depending on the nature of the securities issued.[21]

Current forms of risk transfer can be implemented either independently through credit derivatives, as introduced in Chapter 2, or through securitizations. Credit default swaps (CDSs), specialized forms of credit derivatives, have been one of the most popular independent forms, at least up until the market turmoil of 2007–2008. A CDS is an insurance contract linked to underlying debt that protects the buyer in case of default, and is designed to transfer the credit exposure of fixed income products between parties.[22] The buyer of a CDS receives credit protection, whereas the seller underwrites the default risks. For example, a CDS could entitle its buyer to the par value of an underlying bond. In the event, the bond defaults on its coupon or principal payments, the shortfall is made up by the seller of the swap.[23]

Some CDS products are linked to an individual issuer and are akin to selling a bond short, while others consist of bundles of CDS indexes divided into *tranches* that specify the losses on an underlying asset portfolio to which a given security is exposed. The lowest and riskiest tranches expose the holder to the first few percentage points of losses, and in compensation promise higher returns to investors. The higher tranches offer lower risk and also lower returns. The spreads on CDS indexes provide benchmarks for the cost of default protection and for market evaluation of changes in credit quality.

Collateralized mortgage obligations (CMOs) and *collateralized debt obligations* (CDOs) are forms of securitization that both raise funds and transfer risks at the same time. As discussed further in Chapters 11 and 15, CMOs sell new debt and equity issues backed by a portfolio of mortgages. CDOs sell new debt and equity issues that were initially backed by corporate debt obligations.[24] Both CMOs and CDOs distribute the cash

---

[21] The 1988 Basel agreements did not impose capital charges on bank loans sold to conduits. This requirement was changed when Basel II began coming into effect in 2008. See Chapter 22 for further details.

[22] Transactions in credit default swaps do not require ownership of the underlying instrument. While some observers regard this feature as a detriment, it should be remembered that transactions in other forms of derivatives do not require ownership either. Chapter 9 presents a simple example of valuing a credit default swap. As discussed in Chapter 22, the difficulties with CDSs are principally related to transaction size, to counterparty risk in an OTC market, to the rapid growth of the market, and to the absence of a clearing house to help manage counterparty risk in this form of OTC market.

[23] See Chapter 9 for a simple example.

[24] The types and structures of CDOs are discussed extensively in Lucas, Goodman, and Fabozzi (2007).

flows from asset portfolios to investors in their securities according to terms specified by the securities' tranches. In a typical issue tranches may be specified as, for example, 0%–3%, 3%–7%, 7%–10%, 10%–15%, 15%–30%, and 30%–100%, with the divisions indicating the nature of the losses to which the particular tranche is exposed. Losses on the underlying portfolio amounting to less than 3% are borne solely by the 0%–3% tranche, losses from 3% and up to 7% are the responsibility of investors in the second tranche security, and so on. The 30%–100% tranche is only responsible for losses exceeding 30% of the value of the underlying securities.[25]

As CDO growth continued, the underlying assets came to encompass loans, credit-card receivables, mortgage-backed securities, and even recording royalties. CDO prices provide valuable information respecting market expectations regarding default risks on the different underlying assets. For example, the prices of CDOs convey information about how corporate defaults cluster, and can also be used to estimate the proportion of spread that market expectations assign to each of firm-specific, industry, and systemic default risks (Longstaff and Rajan 2008).

Synthetic CDOs are a still further development.[26] A synthetic CDO does not actually own the asset portfolio whose credit risk it bears, but instead incurs credit risk exposure by selling credit default swaps, instruments described above. In turn, the synthetic CDO buys protection from investors via the tranches defining its securities issues. The tranches are responsible for credit losses in the reference portfolio that rise above a particular point called an attachment point. A given tranche's liabilities end at a specified detachment or exhaustion point (Lucas, Goodman, and Fabozzi 2007).

The funding and risk transfer practices described above help intermediaries to raise funds, to manage their portfolio risks, to separate credit risk from credit obligations, and distribute each to particular clienteles. However, along with their advantages, the same funding and risk management practices have also brought difficulties, both to investors and to the originating intermediaries. In particular, as credit risks were increasingly transferred through the use of credit derivatives and CDOs, the originating lenders' incentives to screen and subsequently monitor the credit risks were attenuated.

As screening and monitoring procedures became less rigorous, the quality of accepted loans decreased. Loan quality decreased even more as banks and other lenders competed by easing lending standards during periods of rapid growth. Bank asset portfolios have always been opaque, but with declining loan quality and redistribution of loan risks it became substantially

---

[25] See Longstaff and Rajan (2008).
[26] In terms of the functions they perform, synthetic CDOs are a form of credit derivative. See Chapter 12 for further discussion.

more difficult for investors to assess the credit risks underlying the securitization instruments they had purchased, just as it became more difficult for analysts to rate the instruments.

Moreover, some of the risk redistribution turned out to be illusory in retrospect. The originating banks sometimes found themselves facing at least moral if not legal payout obligations following on a wave of defaults in the assets underlying their securitization issues. Therefore, even though they had originally transferred risk to other parties, the originating lenders sometimes found themselves reassuming risks for reputational reasons. These matters are discussed further in Chapter 22.

REFERENCES

Brinson, Gary P., and Richard C. Carr. 1989. International equities and bonds. Chapter 19 in *Portfolio and Investment Analysis: State-of-the-art Research, Analysis and Strategies*, edited by Frank J. Fabozzi. Chicago: Probus Publishing.

Fabozzi, Frank J., and Vinod Kothari. 2007. Securitization: The tool of financial transformation. *Journal of Financial Transformation* 20: 34–44.

Gemmill, Gordon. 1996. Transparency and liquidity: A study of block trades on the London stock exchange under different publication rules. *Journal of Finance* 51: 1765–1790.

King, Robert G., and Ross Levine. 1993. "Financial intermediation and economic development," in Colin Mayer and Xavier Vives, eds. *Financial intermediation in the construction of Europe*, London: Centre for Economic Policy Research, 156–189.

Longstaff, Francis A., and Arvind Rajan. 2008. An empirical analysis of the pricing of collateralized debt obligations. *Journal of Finance* 63: 529–563.

Lucas, Douglas J., Laurie Goodman, and Frank J. Fabozzi. 2007. Collateralized debt obligations and credit risk transfer. *Journal of Financial Transformation*, 20: 47–59.

Tinic, Seha M., and Richard R. West. 1974. Marketability of common stocks in Canada and the USA: A comparison of agent versus dealer dominated markets. *Journal of Finance* 29: 729–749.

TERMS

collateralized debt obligations (CDOs)   Financial claims to cash flows generated by a portfolio of debt securities or a basket of credit default swaps. The securities are typically issued in tranches bearing different proportions of losses on the asset portfolio, and are usually sold to institutional and other investors.

collateralized mortgage obligations (CMOs)   Financial claims to cash flows generated by a portfolio of mortgages. Like CDOs, the securities are typically issued in tranches bearing different proportions of losses on the asset portfolio, and are usually sold to institutional and other investors.

credit default swap (CDS)   A specialized form of credit derivative. A CDS takes the form of an insurance contract linked to underlying debt that protects the buyer in case of default, and is designed to transfer the credit exposure of fixed income products between parties. As with other derivatives, transactions in CDSs do not necessarily imply ownership of the underlying asset.

tranches   Ranges specifying the losses on an underlying asset portfolio to which an investor in a tranche security is exposed.

CHAPTER 6

Intermediation and Internal Governance

This chapter examines the capabilities of intermediary and internal governance mechanisms and the deal attributes each is best equipped to govern. Since early financial system theories do not explain how both intermediaries and financial markets can coexist, the chapter first examines how intermediaries can and do create value. Current explanations hold that, as banks raise deposit funds for subsequent relending, they create value through providing liquidity services, delegated monitoring, and information production.

Historically, bank loans have been governed on the books of the originating banks, using capabilities chosen primarily according to the attributes of the loans. As will be shown later, bank governance capabilities are more interactive, and less arm's-length, than the capabilities of financial markets. Starting in the 1990s, banks increased their "originate and distribute" activities (essentially securitization as introduced in Chapter 5). Along with these new functions banks have also become much more active in risk trading, both by hedging loan default risks and by assuming new kinds of risks in response to client demand. The nature of intermediation has been profoundly transformed by these changes, and at times the importance of governance has been underemphasized as the transformations occurred. At later points the book reviews these developments further and reiterate the importance of governance even when new forms of instruments are used. To provide an appropriate perspective for these views, the book examines the value and importance of governance activities in this chapter, and explores the more recent transformations at later points.

The values created by nonarm's-length governance can be realized to their fullest extent using the internal capital markets *of corporations. This chapter shows that the values of internal governance derive principally from using command and control processes not normally available to intermediaries. It also shows that internal governance processes are capable of affecting both the risk and return to certain classes of deals.*

This book argues that financial markets, financial intermediaries, and internal finance play complementary financial system roles. Chapter 3 surveyed the complementarities, while Chapter 5 examined the circumstances under which financial markets are the most cost-effective way of allocating financial resources. This chapter details circumstances in which financial intermediaries and internal capital allocations can provide more cost-effective governance than market agents.

Intermediaries, and internal capital markets, have competitive advantages when market arrangements cannot provide cost-effective governance of a deal's complexities. As one example, financial intermediaries aggregate information differently than do market agents. For example, the aggregate liquidity demands of a group of clients can be important to banks involved in certain kinds of portfolio planning, and market agents are not always able to assemble this kind of information. Second, ex ante deal information can be asymmetrically distributed, and offsetting the effects of asymmetric information is more easily arranged in nonmarket transactions. Finally, in circumstances such as capital rationing, command and control allocation through the internal capital markets of organizations such as financial conglomerates can prove more cost-effective than either market or intermediary allocations.

INTERMEDIARIES AND VALUE CREATION

Markets can offer competitive advantages for some types of deals, while intermediaries can do so for others. To provide a point of departure for understanding where and how intermediaries' competitive advantages can arise, it is useful to begin by outlining circumstances in which intermediaries do not possess competitive advantages.

When and Why Intermediaries Cannot Create Value

Financial governance is comparatively simple under the assumptions of the neoclassical paradigm. Neoclassical economic analysis often assumes that markets are perfectly competitive, that all transaction information is homogeneously distributed, and that transacting is costless. In striving to maximize their trading profits, the numerous agents in the market establish equilibrium securities prices that fully reflect all publicly available information.

In such an efficient market equilibrium, funds are supplied at a market rate of interest commensurate with a given deal's risk, and clients can only obtain funds by agreeing to pay that market interest rate. Moreover, only the most cost-effective forms of governance can remain viable at equilibrium. No financier's governance costs can be persistently greater than those of the most efficient competitor because inefficient financiers will be driven out of the market by competition. Hence each deal must be governed efficiently.

If all of the market's deals are of the same type, intermediaries cannot create value by doing things differently than market agents. One of the theories implying this no-value-creation result is the Capital Asset Pricing Theory (CAPT, outlined more fully in Chapter 14). The CAPT assumes a perfectly competitive market in which deals differ only in terms of their risk, and in which all investors have the same information about securities. The CAPT assumes further that any security's risk can be measured by its contribution to the variance of return on a portfolio held by all investors. Under these circumstances all investors will choose the same (best available) combination of risky securities, a combination referred to as the market portfolio. Given the further assumption that a riskless security exists, investors with different preferences combine the market portfolio and the riskless security in differing proportions to reflect their individual attitudes toward risk.

The CAPT establishes that securities bear equilibrium rates of interest reflecting each security's contribution to the risk of the market portfolio. If two securities make the same contribution to the risk of the market portfolio, they bear the same equilibrium interest rate; whereas if one security contributes more risk than another, it bears a higher equilibrium rate. The result means that all traders, individuals, and intermediaries, face the same portfolio diversification possibilities. Since individuals are assumed to incur no transaction costs while doing so, intermediaries cannot create value because they only perform services that investors could duplicate on their own.

The CAPT's conclusions imply indirectly that financial intermediaries might be able to create value if the CAPT assumptions were to be relaxed. The rest of the chapter will show there are several such sets of circumstances, including possibilities for providing nonmarket diversification, for reducing transactions costs, for taking positions in illiquid assets, and for performing certain kinds of information processing activities.

When and Why Intermediaries Can Create Value

Different types of governance are employed in practice because deals differ in several ways not recognized in the CAPT.[1] For example, some deals are consummated under conditions of asymmetrically distributed information. Governing such deals cost-effectively requires the use of screening and monitoring techniques different from those used when all parties have the same information. Moreover as Chapter 3 showed, different governance techniques employ different combinations of resources, acquired at different costs. Indeed, when the full complexities of financial arrangements are recognized, markets, intermediaries and internal financing can be viewed as offering complementary forms of governance.[2]

One of the most common ways that intermediaries create value is through using nonarm's-length transactions to govern their loan portfolios.[3] In carrying out nonarm's-length governance, intermediaries utilize both ex ante screening and ex post monitoring of individual deals. Exercising these capabilities means intermediaries produce different kinds of information than financial market agents, and use it differently as well.

Intermediaries can also coordinate liquidity services differently than can market agents. First, intermediaries may transact with entire groups of clients, and use features of the group's transactions to offer clients more satisfactory services than are available through market agents not possessing the same aggregate information. Intermediaries can usually issue liquid claims in amounts greater than the liquid assets they need to redeem those claims, because not all clients wish to redeem their deposits at the same time. As a result, intermediaries can use some of their deposit funds (usually most of them) to finance illiquid loans.

The rest of this chapter expands on the concepts just outlined. It begins by examining the major types of intermediaries in a financial system, and offers theoretical explanations for the advantages different intermediaries can offer. The chapter concludes by comparing intermediary activity and internal governance.

---

[1]For certain purposes the descriptions of reality conveyed by the CAPT may be perfectly adequate. But those descriptions do not fulfill our present purpose of explaining how a financial system with intermediaries and internal capital markets can arise.

[2]Most of the complementarities examined in this chapter are static in nature and co-exist on a continuing basis. The first treatments of functional analysis only recognized dynamic complementarities.

[3]Similarly, conglomerates create value by governing financial allocations even more intensively than intermediaries.

Successful Intermediaries

While this book will mention a relatively large variety of intermediaries, for the present it suffices to identify three major types – insurance companies, banks, and venture capital firms—and their principal distinguishing characteristics. Insurance companies collect premiums from purchasers of insurance policies, and invest the collected funds in asset portfolios covering the insurance companies' liabilities. Much of this work involves developing investment portfolios to fund the insurance companies' long-term (policy) liabilities.

Historically, banks have collected deposits from individual clients, gathered these deposits together, and lent them to business and householders. Such banks' liabilities are relatively liquid, but their loan portfolios are mostly illiquid, meaning the banks are essentially short-term borrowers and longer-term lenders. Much of the work done by banks consists of screening loan applications and subsequently governing the loans on their books. In recent years, the asset management tasks of banks have shifted as they have learned to securitize their loan portfolios and to sell off some of their default risks through credit derivatives and credit default swaps.[4]

Venture capital firms principally acquire long-term, high-risk investments in new or growing ventures, and fund their operations through equity issues that are often sold privately to institutions such as pension funds and insurance companies. Even less liquid than banks, venture capital firms principally recover their investments through taking their client companies public.

The foregoing sketch of intermediary types demonstrates that all intermediaries face asset-liability management challenges, but that the nature of the challenges varies considerably from one type of specialized business to another. Even in today's world of financial mergers, firms continue to specialize largely because the challenges of running many different kinds of combined businesses can prove more complex than the firms' managements find it profitable to meet.[5]

Bond (2004) examines financial conglomerates, banks, and trade credit arrangements as three different instances of financial intermediation. In the

---

[4]The reader should bear in mind that the more recent originate-and-distribute model of banking will be discussed later in the book.

[5]As one example, Citigroup was formed to combine the banking business of Citibank with the insurance businesses of Travellers Insurance. The principal arguments favoring the merger focused on the ability to conduct international business and to realize scale economies. Since the merger took place in 1997, the combined company has sold off, in separate transactions, two types of its insurance business.

language of this book, Bond analyzes discriminating alignments of project attributes with financier capabilities. To Bond, intermediaries differ in the types of projects they fund, the types of claims they issue to investors, and the costs of transmitting information between parties to the arrangement. Bond also emphasizes a link between the fate of a project's financing and the possibility that the intermediary itself can run into financial trouble.

Bond describes how different types of intermediaries emerge from the kinds of asset and liability portfolios they hold and the costs of information sharing.[6] One class of intermediaries, financial conglomerates, finances high-risk/low-quality projects and raises funds through offering investors high-risk securities. Investors attempt to guard their interests in a conglomerate through risk sharing: borrowers from the conglomerate partially absorb each others' losses. In essence, this risk sharing among borrowers will permit the conglomerate to manage better some of the moral hazard and adverse selection problems that might otherwise arise.

Banks and near banks form a second class of intermediaries. These operations fund low-risk/high-quality projects. Banks issue low-risk liabilities and borrowers from banks do not gain from absorbing each others' risks. Rather, it is efficient for bank investors to absorb project financing losses. If low-risk intermediaries are funded by many depositors, it will be economic for the intermediaries to specialize in information processing.

INTERMEDIARIES AND LIQUIDITY[7]

Intermediaries also differ from market agents in their ability to create certain forms of liquidity. They both create liquidity for their borrowing clients, and provide a different form of liquidity for their depositors. Consider each in turn.

Edgeworth Model

Intermediaries can provide liquidity to borrowing customers by taking advantage of the probability that depositors will not all use their deposit balances at the same time. Edgeworth (1886) showed that since deposit inflows and outflows could tend to offset each other, a bank could use its demand

---

[6]Bond implements the costs of information sharing by assuming an agent's output is private information unless a verification cost is incurred to disclose it to another agent.
[7]This section and the next are based on Freixas and Rochet (1997).

deposit liabilities to finance the acquisition of a relatively substantial proportion of illiquid loans. So long as depositors' actions have a degree of statistical independence, the amount of cash reserves needed by a bank to ensure a high probability of its being able to meet all depositors' demands can be much less than the total amount of deposits, thus enabling the loans to be made. The loans enhance the liquidity of the intermediary's borrowing customers, and the analysis also demonstrates how a fractional reserve banking system can operate.

Edgeworth's model assumes independent,[8] identically and normally distributed changes in deposit accounts. Under these assumptions a bank can realize scale economies in the amount of reserves it holds for liquidity purposes. To illustrate, suppose there are many potential clients, each of whom would hold an average balance of $100.00. At time 0, immediately before making a deposit or withdrawal, each client is assumed to hold exactly $100.00. The time 1 balance, after the transaction, is described from the perspective of time 0 by an independently and normally distributed random variable with a mean of $100.00 and standard deviation of 4. If the bank has only one client, it must hold approximately $12.00 in reserves to ensure that it will have enough reserves to meet withdrawals from the deposit account[9] 99.87% of the time. (For example, if the depositor reduced her balance by three standard deviations, she would withdraw $12.00 to leave a new balance of $88.00). However, if the bank has two such clients, the total balance is normally distributed with a mean of $200.00 and a standard deviation of

$$(4.00^2 + 4.00^2)^{0.5} = (32.00)^{0.5}$$

This means the bank should hold approximately $17.00 in reserves to provide against a reduction of the total balance by three standard deviations (i.e., a z-score of 3) since $(200.00 - 183.00)/(32.00)^{0.5} \approx 3$. This $17.00 in reserves would be sufficient to offset withdrawals that did not exceed three standard deviations, which given the model's assumptions would be 99.87% of the time. Additional values are shown in Table 6.1 next.

---

[8]The assumptions are convenient, but not strictly necessary. For example, similar results can be established if changes are not highly positively correlated independent rather than independent.

[9]The $12.00 represents a z-score of 3, where the score of 3 corresponds to a one-tail probability of approximately 0.13%. A z-score is defined by $(\mu - x)/\sigma = z$, where μ is the mean, σ the standard deviation, and x a value of the normally distributed variable in question. The present example requires finding a solution x to $(100.00 - x)/4.00 = 3$.

TABLE 6.1   Reserves Needed to Meet Withdrawals 99.87% of the Time

Number of Depositors	Standard Deviation of Cash Flows	Total Reserve Requirement	Reserve Requirement per Depositor
1	$(16.00)^{0.5} = 4.00$	12.00	12.00
2	$(32.00)^{0.5} = 5.66$	17.00	8.50
4	$(64.00)^{0.5} = 8.00$	24.00	6.00
8	$(128.00)^{0.5} = 11.31$	34.00	4.25
16	$(256.00)^{0.5} = 16.00$	48.00	3.00

Table 6.1 verifies that the reserves are subject to scale economies in the sense that the number of dollars needed to maintain the assumed 99.87% probability of meeting all withdrawals declines relative to total deposits as the number of depositors increases. In other words, a large bank with many depositors can rely on the law of large numbers to determine its reserve position, just as an insurance company can statistically calculate its liabilities to a pool of clients.

The safety of the reserve position in the example depends on the assumption that depositors' holdings are statistically independent. If the depositors' holdings were instead perfectly positively correlated, as might be the case when all a bank's depositors simultaneously lose confidence in the bank, the expected changes in balances would not be likely to remain small.[10] However, the present chapter is concerned primarily with reasons for intermediaries' existence rather than their stability,[11] and the Edgeworth model provides one such explanation whenever its assumptions are justified.

Individuals Provide Their Own Liquidity[12]

If an intermediary's depositors face liquidity risk, but cannot be certain if or when the risk will occur, an intermediary need only know the proportion of depositors with liquidity needs in order to make group investment decisions

---

[10] This is precisely what happened with some CDOs issued against a portfolio of many small subprime mortgages. While the defaults on the individual mortgages might have had little correlation in a buoyant economy, many individuals began to default simultaneously in 2007–2008 as economic conditions deteriorated. Apparently CDO issuers, their investors, and possibly some rating agencies, did not always recognize this possibility.

[11] Stability questions will be taken up in Chapter 20.

[12] This section utilizes arguments developed in Freixas and Rochet (1997).

TABLE 6.2 Time 0 Wealth Allocation

Cash	$1 - D$
Long-term asset	D
Value of endowment at time 0	1

on their behalf. Since individual members of the group do not know whether they will face liquidity demands or not, market agents who deal only with individual depositors cannot learn the aggregate liquidity risk presented by the group. However, an intermediary dealing with all depositors as a group can view the risks actuarially, and thus act like an association of depositors, in a role that can also be interpreted as providing an insurance scheme.

To see how banks can offer an advantage over markets with respect to liquidity provision, it is useful to present a second model. Suppose first that individuals try to provide for their own liquidity needs without benefit of either market or intermediary. Assume there are N individuals, each of whom has a \$1.00 endowment at time 0. The \$1.00 can either be held in cash for possible use at time 1, or it can be invested in an illiquid asset D, which yields $DR > D$ if it can be held until time 2. In an emergency the illiquid asset can be liquidated at time 1, but at a penalty value such that only $DL < D$ is realized.

At time 0, each agent must allocate her endowment between cash and the long-term investment. However, she will not obtain information about her liquidity needs until time 1. If she needs liquidity at time 1, she will have to cash in her illiquid asset, but if she faces no liquidity needs at time 1, she can continue holding the illiquid asset until time 2. Suppose she elects to hold $1 - D$ in cash, and D in the long-term asset,[13] as shown in Table 6.2.

At time 1 the agent learns whether she needs all her available funds immediately or whether she can wait until period 2. If she needs all her funds immediately, she liquidates her long-term asset for DL, and can thus spend a total of $1 - D + DL < 1$. (See Table 6.3.)

TABLE 6.3 If Agent Must Spend Her Wealth at Time 1

Cash	$1 - D$	$(0 < D < 1)$
Realizable value of long-term asset	DL	$(DL < D)$
Total assets of each agent at time 1	$1 - D + DL$	$(1 - D + DL < 1)$

---

[13] The quantities $1 - D$ and D are assumed to be chosen to maximize the expected utility of her future expenditures, as will be shown formally later in the chapter.

However, if she can wait until time 2 her assets will be worth $1 - D + DR > 1$.

If Agent Can Wait Until Time 2 to Spend

Cash	$1 - D$	$(0 < D < 1)$
Maturity value of long-term asset	DR	$(DR > D)$
Total assets of each agent at time	$1 - D + DR$	$(1 - D + DR > 1)$

Assuming the agent maximizes the expected utility of these allocations, she chooses D at time 0 to maximize

$$pu_1(1 - D + DL) + (1 - p)u_2(1 - D + DR)$$

which can be rewritten

$$pu_1[1 - D(1 - L)] + (1 - p)u_2[1 + D(R - 1)] \qquad (6.1)$$

where p is the probability of facing liquidity needs at time 1, $(1 - p)$ is the probability that expenditures can be deferred until time 2, and u_t is the utility function for time t expenditures, $t = 1, 2$.

For ease of analysis, assume that all depositors have identical functions $u_t = u$; $t = 1, 2$. Then if the probability of facing liquidity demands is roughly equal to the probability of being able to defer spending until time 2, the agent would likely place the greater proportion of her wealth in the long-term investment. The observation follows from differentiating equation (6.1) with respect to D, setting the derivative equal to zero, and rewriting the resulting equation as

$$pu'(c_1)/(1 - p)u'(c_2) = (R - 1)/(1 - L) \qquad (6.2)$$

where $c_1 = 1 - D(1 - L)$ is the time 1 optimal expenditure if the agent must consume to meet liquidity needs and $c_2 = 1 + D(R - 1)$ is the time 2 optimal expenditure in the absence of liquidity needs.[14] Equation (6.2) says the optimum is defined by an expenditure pattern for which the ratio of the expected marginal utilities equals the ratio of return differences. If p and $(1 - p)$ are roughly equal, equation (6.2) will be satisfied by setting $c_1 < c_2$, since marginal utility decreases as a given period's expenditure increases.

---

[14]It is assumed the solution satisfies the original wealth constraint, that is, $0 < D < 1$.

A Market for Liquidity

The discussion next shows that the agent's expected utility (6.1) can be increased by setting up a financial market. Then, it shows that an even greater increase can be obtained if the agent can use an intermediary.

Suppose an agent can buy a bond with any surplus cash she might have at time 1. The bond market is assumed to open, and bonds to become available, at time 1. Assume further that, once the bond market has opened, both lending and borrowing are possible. Suppose the bond is designed to pay off 1 unit at time 2, and hence its time 1 discounted price is $P_1 < 1$. If the market is in equilibrium an agent can borrow P_1 at time 1 in exchange for a promise to repay 1 at time 2. Equivalently if she borrows 1 at time 1, she must repay $1/P_1$ at time 2. These possibilities allow her to arrange the cash flows shown in Table 6.4.

TABLE 6.4 If Agent Must Spend All Wealth at Time 1

Cash	$1 - D$	$(0 < D < 1)$
Time 1 value of long-term asset	$P_1 DR$	
Available for spending at time 1	$1 - D + P_1 DR$	

If Agent Can Wait Until Time 2 to Spend

Time 2 value of bond purchased with cash available at time 1	$(1 - D)/P_1$
Time 2 value of long-term asset	DR
Available for spending at time 2	$(1 - D)/P_1 + DR = (1 - D + P_1 DR)/P_1$

Table 6.4 indicates that the agent's position might be improved by opening the market, at least so long as $P_1 = 1/R$, which implies $P_1 R > L$. Moreover, this last equality is easily established. Suppose, for example, that equality did not hold in the sense that $P_1 > 1/R$, or $P_1 DR > D$. Then it is apparent from Table 6.5 that the agent would have more than 1 to spend at time 1, and would buy as many bonds as she could. By a similar logic, if the condition $P_1 < 1/R$ were to obtain, the agent would never use bond transactions for spending at time 1. Putting the two results together means the quantity of bonds demanded at time 1 will only equal the quantity supplied if the equilibrium price $P_1 = 1/R$.

Now using the equilibrium bond price $P_1 = 1/R$, the agent's positions are as shown in Table 6.6. If she must spend her funds at time 1, the amount she will have available is 1, greater than the former $1 - D(1 - L)$.

TABLE 6.5 If Agent Must Spend All Wealth at Time 1

Cash	$1 - D$
Long-term asset's value at time 1	$(P_1 DR) > D$ if $P_1 > 1/R$
Available for spending at time 1	$(1 - D) + (P1DR) > 1$ if $P_1 > 1/R$

If she can wait until time 2, the amount she will have is R, greater than the former $1 + D(R - 1)$.

When the bond market is open, the agent can satisfy emergency liquidity needs by borrowing against the time 2 value of invested assets, and this transaction leaves her better off than when she has to meet liquidity requirements without recourse to borrowing.

Intermediary Provided Liquidity

Setting up an intermediary, such as a bank, can make the agent still better off. As suggested earlier, the improvement stems from the fact that an intermediary's liquidity needs depend on the total number of depositors facing liquidity demands, but not on the depositors' identities. Suppose each bank client can purchase a deposit contract promising to pay either C_1 at time 1 or C_2 at time 2. Depositors who find that they are facing liquidity needs at time 1 must take C_1, but all other depositors are required to wait until time 2 and receive C_2. Once she has determined whether she faces liquidity needs, a depositor cannot alter the contract terms and ask for payment at a different time. Suppose moreover that the bond market set up in the previous subsection "A Market for Liquidity" continues to operate. Since this subsection showed that depositors have wealth with a present worth of 1

TABLE 6.6 Agent's Positions

A. Must Spend All Wealth at Time 1		
Cash	$1 - D$	
Long-term asset's value at time 1	$(P_1 DR) = D$	(if $P_1 = 1/R$)
Available for spending at time 1	1	(if $P_1 = 1/R$)
B. Agent Can Wait Until Time 2 to Spend		
Time 2 value of bond purchased at time 1	$(1 - D)/P_1 = (1 - D)R$	(if $P_1 = 1/R$)
Time 2 value of long-term asset	DR	
Available for spending at time 2	R	(if $P_1 = 1/R$)

at time 1, the time 1 expected value of the two payments under the deposit contract must also equal 1. That is,

$$pC_1 + (1 - p)C_2/R = 1 \qquad (6.3)$$

where R is used to discount the time 2 payment as in "A Market for Liquidity."

Equation (6.4) shows that the market solution—the depositor spends 1 at time 1 if she faces liquidity needs, R if she can wait until time 2—satisfies equation (6.3).

$$p + (1 - p)R/R = 1 \qquad (6.4)$$

However, with the intermediary contract the depositor can also select any other spending combination that satisfies the budget constraint (6.3). Unless it just happens that depositors attain a maximum expected utility when $C_1 = 1$ and $C_2 = R$, a new contract that has different values of C_1 and C_2 and still satisfies (6.3) would yield greater satisfaction.

An intermediary can implement a solution that satisfies equation (6.3) so long as every depositor honors her contract as arranged. That is, if a depositor needs to meet liquidity needs at time 1, she must cash in her deposit as arranged; but if she does not need to spend until time 2, she cannot cash in her deposit at time 1. Since the intermediary knows what proportion p of depositors will consume at time 1, it must hold pC_1 in cash for use at time 1, and invest $(1 - p)C_2/R$ to finance the time 2 spending.

INFORMATION SHARING

Intermediaries can also create value by managing the effects of informational asymmetries. An ex ante asymmetry exists when the entrepreneur knows more than the lender about the probability distribution of future returns from a project. An ex post asymmetry arises when a lender or investor is unable to observe an entrepreneur's choice of investment project or the effort the entrepreneur might expend in attempting to make the project a success. The impacts created by asymmetries may stem either from adverse selection, an aggregate phenomenon, or from moral hazard, a difficulty affecting individual deals. It may be possible to resolve an asymmetry— sometimes partially, sometimes wholly—by screening.[15] This chapter

---

[15] A profit-maximizing lender will only incur screening costs if they produce at least commensurate improvements to the profitability of the deal.

examines managing the aggregate effects of adverse selection while Chapter 7, which discusses the terms of individual deals, considers moral hazard.

Informational Asymmetries and Adverse Selection

Adverse selection involves relations between a financier and a group of clients whose quality is indistinguishable to the financier. It can affect a financier's profitability by discouraging the best credit risks while at the same time attracting lower quality ones. For example, suppose financiers announce a set of terms on which they will deal with potentially indistinguishable clients whose proposals represent a range of different risks. If the terms are unattractive to the lowest risks in the client pool, those clients will turn to other financing sources and the average risk of the pool of clients who continue to be attracted to the intermediary's terms will increase.[16]

An intermediary can sometimes mitigate the impact of adverse selection by creating incentives for clients truthfully to signal their otherwise undistinguishable qualities. It is convenient to illustrate the issues with a model from Freixas and Rochet[17] (1997). Suppose risk-averse entrepreneurs would prefer to obtain outside financing rather than use their own resources to fund a risky project. However, they will not do so at any cost: Rather, they will only use outside financing if they can obtain it on sufficiently favorable terms. Suppose that different entrepreneurs seek financing for projects that have different means, and that all have the same variance. Suppose also that entrepreneurs value projects using the preference function

$$\theta - \rho\sigma^2/2 \tag{6.5}$$

where θ is the project mean, σ^2 its variance, and $\rho > 0$ is a coefficient reflecting the entrepreneur's attitude toward risk.[18] When considering whether to self-finance, the entrepreneur determines whether she would be better off retaining her shares or selling them to financiers.

Suppose that interest rates are zero, and that risk neutral financiers can set the price $S_0{}^*$ at which they will buy a firm's shares. The assumptions

---

[16] The adverse selection effect could be exacerbated if the announced terms attracted more high risk clients to the pool.

[17] One of the classic signaling models is due to Leland and Pyle (1977).

[18] One frequently used set of assumptions leading to this valuation is that the random prospect is normally distributed and that the investor has a negative exponential utility function.

imply that projects are valued at the financiers' estimate of project means—a quantity denoted $E(\theta)$—and the price of securities is set accordingly. That is,

$$S_0^* = E(\theta)$$

Since financiers cannot distinguish good firms from bad ones, they will offer S_0^* to all firms.

If S_0^* were an equilibrium price at which all firms sold their shares, financiers purchasing the shares for S_0^* would earn an expected return of zero (equal to the assumed interest rate). But S_0^* is not an equilibrium price because the reasoning to this point has not recognized the effects of adverse selection. The certainty equivalent value of the firm to the entrepreneur under self-financing is given by (6.5). The entrepreneur will choose the better of two deals—the price S_0^* or the certainty equivalent value of the firm

$$\theta - \rho\sigma^2/2$$

whichever is greater. That is, the entrepreneur will only sell her shares to the financiers if

$$S_0^* \geq \theta - \rho\sigma^2/2 \tag{6.6}$$

Inequality (6.6) implies that only the owners of lower quality firms will offer their shares for sale. Let θ_0^* be the value for which equation (6.6) holds with equality. Then firms with expected return $\theta \leq \theta_0^*$ will sell their shares to financiers but other, higher quality firms will regard S_0^* as too low and will choose not to sell. In other words, the financiers offer a form of insurance against downside risk, but high quality entrepreneurs regard the insurance as too costly to be worth purchasing.

Understanding these reactions, financiers will set the equilibrium price S_0^{**} at

$$S_0^{**} = E[\theta | \theta \leq \theta_0^*] \tag{6.7}$$

where θ_0^* is the value for which equation (6.6) holds with equality when the left-hand side of (6.6) is equal to S_0^{**}. This is the meaning of adverse selection: Since the price that financiers offer to a pool of indistinguishable risks will discourage some of the higher quality firms in the pool, the equilibrium price they offer must take this into account.

Signaling

The effects of adverse selection can be mitigated if potential clients can credibly signal their quality. Suppose there are only two types of firms, high and low quality, indicated by H and L, respectively. Let the firms' mean returns be indicated by θ_H and θ_L. Assume that H firms signal their quality by retaining a proportion α of the shares while selling off the remaining $(1 - \alpha)$. Assume further that L firms signal their low quality by selling all of their shares. In order for both signals to be credible, L firms must not be able to benefit by misrepresenting themselves as H firms. Therefore, the price received by L firms that retain no shares must be a price $S_L = \theta_L$ such that

$$\theta_L \geq (1 - \alpha)\theta_H + \alpha\theta_L - \rho\sigma^2\alpha^2/2 \qquad (6.8)$$

where the utility of wealth function takes the same form as in equation (6.5). Inequality (6.8), called the no-mimicking condition, means it is better for a low-quality firm to classify itself truthfully and to sell all its equity for S_L rather than receive the proceeds $S_H(1 - \alpha)$ through misrepresentation. If a low-quality firm were to retain proportion α of its shares, thereby representing itself as a high-quality firm, it would get the high quality firm price $S_H = \theta_H$, but only for proportion $(1 - \alpha)$ of the shares. Inequality (6.8) states that this outcome would leave the low-quality firm less well off than if it had represented itself as a low-quality firm and sold all its shares.

Since equation (6.8) provides no incentive for L firms to retain any proportion of their equity, any firms that do retain α will be H firms. High-quality firms get

$$(1 - \alpha)S_H = (1 - \alpha)\theta_H > (1 - \alpha)\theta_L$$

However the certainty equivalent value of H firms' wealth is only

$$\theta_H - \rho\sigma^2\alpha^2/2 \qquad (6.9)$$

because they have to retain proportion α of their shares in order to signal their higher quality. The minimum proportion α that high quality entrepreneurs must retain is defined by the no-mimicking condition (6.8), which can be rewritten as

$$\alpha^2/(1 - \alpha) = 2(\theta_H - \theta_L)/\rho\sigma^2 \qquad (6.10)$$

So long as equation (6.10) is satisfied, then at equilibrium, the low-quality firms get full outside financing, at price S_L. High-quality firms get $(1 - \alpha)S_H$.

A Cooperative Lending Association

To see how an intermediary could improve the present situation, it is first necessary to determine how α varies with σ^2. From equation (6.9), the certainty equivalent value of the loss to high-quality entrepreneurs can be measured by

$$\rho\sigma^2\alpha^2/2 \tag{6.11}$$

Combining equations (6.9) and (6.11) gives

$$\rho\sigma^2\alpha^2/2 = (\theta_H - \theta_L)(1 - \alpha) \tag{6.12}$$

To see how α varies with σ^2, note that the right-hand side of equation (6.10) increases as σ^2 decreases. By evaluating the left-hand side of equation (6.10) for α near zero, finding that it is higher for α near one, then checking to make sure the left-hand side increases everywhere on the interval between zero and one, we see the left-hand side increases in α. Thus we conclude that α increases as σ^2 decreases. Moreover, the right-hand side of equation (6.12) decreases as α increases, at least assuming that $0 < \alpha < 1$, as we do throughout. But since α increases as σ^2 decreases, this also means that the cost, that is, the left-hand side of equation (6.12), decreases as σ^2 decreases.

The foregoing results can now be used to examine what would happen if borrowers formed a coalition, that is, combined to form a financial intermediary. Assume the coalition members combine statistically independent projects with the same mean,[19] so that the combination of projects has a lower variance than does any single project. Since α increases as σ^2 decreases, the coalition can credibly signal that it has a lower standard deviation and hence a lower variance of return than any individual firm. As a result of this signal, the coalition's cost of raising external finance is lower than that of any individual firm. The importance of this conclusion is not just that a portfolio of loans can have a lower variance than any individual

---

[19] The same result could be obtained if the projects were only imperfectly correlated: It is simpler but not necessary to assume they are independent. Although it is applied in a different context, the argument is formally identical to Edgeworth's, as presented in the section "Intermediaries and Value Creation."

loan, but that the credit cooperative can credibly signal that its portfolio risks are lower than those of the individual borrowers in the cooperative. Thus setting up the credit cooperative, that is, setting up an intermediary can create value so long as the reduction in interest costs covers the cooperative's operating expenses.

DELEGATED MONITORING

Diamond (1984) argues that lenders may be able to realize scale economies by delegating some of their governance functions, implying that delegated monitoring can be a factor explaining intermediary existence. In the following model, the monitor verifies realized earnings to determine whether borrowers can repay the loan, either fully or to the extent permitted by realized earnings. Each lender could monitor earnings individually, but to do so would incur greater cost than delegating the responsibility to a central authority, here thought of as a bank. However delegating the monitoring function presents a new set of incentive problems since the lenders must be able to satisfy themselves that the monitor acts properly on their behalf.

Suppose that any lender who monitors a borrowing account incurs a unit cost K. Suppose in addition that borrowing accounts are large, so that to finance the demands of a given borrower requires m lenders, each of whom advances an equal fraction of the funds. Assuming there is a total of n borrowers, if each lender monitors accounts individually, the total cost of monitoring is nmK. (See Table 6.7.)

If the lenders delegate the monitoring to a bank, the bank will spend K per individual borrower, plus some other costs C_n, which depend on the number of borrowers. If the reduction in monitoring costs more than offsets the increase in operating costs, it will be worthwhile to have the bank monitor on behalf of the former individual lenders. In this setting bank depositors are regarded as the parties who would otherwise have been the individual lenders. (See Table 6.8.)

TABLE 6.7 Direct Finance: Each Lender Monitors Its Own Borrower—Total Cost nmK

Borrower 1	Lender 1
	Lender m
Borrower n	Lender $(n-1)m+1$
	Lender nm

TABLE 6.8 Intermediated Finance: Lenders Delegate Monitoring to Bank Lender—Total Cost $nK + C_n$.

Borrower 1		Lender 1 ... Lender m
	Bank	
Borrower n		Lender $(n-1)m + 1$ ... Lender nm

One issue remains. How do the depositors know the bank will monitor as arranged and will report its earnings truthfully to the depositors? Clearly, the depositors must employ some kind of contract that provides penalties if the bank fails to report accurately. Sometimes the literature proposes nonpecuniary penalties to ensure the bank will monitor in a manner consistent with depositor interests. Diamond shows that each depositor's monitoring costs can grow arbitrarily small as the institution's assets grow sufficiently large. Moreover, using the law of large numbers it is possible to define the likely fraction of loan defaults with increasing accuracy, and so long as the bank does not deviate from this proportion the depositors need do no further monitoring. In such cases, default losses are lowered by ex ante screening and ex post monitoring, and in addition the intermediary exploits the advantages of diversification.

INTERMEDIARY INFORMATION PROCESSING

Intermediary differences in information processing have long been recognized. DeLong (1991) and Ramirez (1995) argue that the U.S. banking firms of the later nineteenth and earlier twentieth century resolved external financing problems by mitigating principal-agent problems, including those arising from asymmetric information. Similarly, Gorton, and Kahn (2000) argue that bank loans have features quite distinct from those of bonds sold in the marketplace, features that arise from the ways banks govern their outstanding loans. They argue that banks perform important functions between the time they extend a loan and collect the repayments on it. In particular, banks have the ability, not possessed by market agents, to renegotiate credit terms with borrowers, and to create a link between renegotiation and monitoring.

The rest of this section models information processing to show how banks can coexist with securities markets at equilibrium, even in the absence of other frictions. The section shows that banks with different information processing technologies than markets can create differences in investor returns, even on projects with the same physical returns distribution. That is, differences in information processing are sufficient to create different kinds of financial governance, and consequently information processing differences are a factor that helps explain the existence of intermediaries.

Introduction

The analysis compares three different model economies. One economy has only a market technology, one an intermediary technology, and the third has both. Implementing either or both technologies involves paying a set-up cost, different in each case. Assume throughout that the intermediary technology conveys governance capabilities not available to market agents. These capabilities arise from intermediaries' exercising close supervision of their loan accounts and thereby generating private information about their clients' earnings distributions. In addition, intermediaries can reduce the risk of loan default by requiring operating changes that market agents cannot successfully demand. These differential capabilities are reflected through different return distributions to investors. Security returns depend on whether the nonfinancial firm obtains its funds in a market transaction or from an intermediary. If the former, investors directly purchase the securities of the nonfinancial firm in the marketplace. If the latter, investors purchase securities issued by the intermediary, which in turn holds the securities of the firm being financed.

Securities prices are determined competitively in each economy. There are many nonfinancial firms offering primary securities, and they all take market prices as given. There are no technological differences within the group of market financiers, and they all take prices as given also. For convenience, envision a single intermediary that takes securities prices as given.[20] The intermediary issues and sells securities to investors. These securities' returns depend on the performance of the intermediary's loans, and are sold at a price yielding the intermediary a zero profit.[21] Finally, assume there are no agency costs, an assumption intended but to highlight starkly the equilibrium impacts of using different financial technologies.[22]

Any investor can costlessly invest in the single riskless security, but investing in a risky security requires that a financial technology be available. Whichever technology or combination of technologies is set up, investors

---

[20] It would complicate the analysis, but would not otherwise change the essential nature of the results, to assume many competing intermediaries.

[21] The transaction envisioned is very much like an asset securitization transaction.

[22] Further research may well combine agency and technological factors. This more general view would likely encompass an interaction between (1) the costs and benefits to using different financial technologies and (2) the impact of agency costs on the financiers choosing among them.

pay an equal share of the relevant fixed costs. Intermediary operations also incur a positive marginal cost, borne by the purchasers of the intermediary's securities in proportion to their purchase amounts.

Each economy has many identical nonfinancial firms of unit size. All are seeking funds, and each such firm's operations generate the same payoff distribution. For simplicity, assume that the realized returns on primary securities are determined by a common underlying factor. A second common factor drives a noise term faced by the market agents, reflecting that they differ from the intermediary in signal extraction, monitoring, and control capabilities. The common factor assumption means that any realization of the investor returns distribution is identical for all firms financed by market agents, and that diversification within this class of securities yields no additional benefit to investors. The investor returns distribution is similarly identical for all firms financed by the intermediary, and again diversification within this class of securities yields no benefit to investors. However, in this case investor returns depend on how the payoff distribution from firm operations is modified by the intermediary governance technology. As a result, diversification between securities purchased in the marketplace and securities sold by intermediaries can create investor benefits.

An economy with only a securities market is called a type M economy. In a type M economy investors, pay a fixed cost λ_M to set up the financial market, which then operates at a marginal cost of zero. In the type M economy nonfinancial firms can only raise funds by selling securities in the marketplace. Securities are valued using homogeneously distributed public information regarding the investors' returns distribution, defined as the sum of a physical returns distribution and a noise distribution.

An economy with only an intermediary is called a type H (hierarchical) economy. Its investors are required to pay λ_H to set up the intermediary, and the intermediary also incurs a marginal cost α per dollar of project financing. All new financing in a type H economy is obtained from the intermediary. As already mentioned and as detailed later, the intermediary modifies the returns distribution, and then sells new securities with that modified distribution to investors. The sale of new securities is subject to a zero profit condition.

Let an economy with both a market and an intermediary be termed an MH economy. In the MH economy investors' set-up costs[23] are $\lambda_M + \lambda_H$, and nonfinancial firms can obtain financing from either market agents or the intermediary. In an MH economy, the intermediary and market agents

---

[23] Our static analyses compare different economies at the same point in time, thus avoiding any need to consider effects of differently timed expenses.

are competitive suppliers of funds to business and, therefore, must buy securities from firms at the same price. Whatever net benefits accrue to the signal extraction capabilities of the intermediary are, by the zero profits assumption, passed on the investors via the return distribution they receive.

Apppendix 6A and 6B show how to find equilibrium securities prices in the MH economy, and in the type M and type H economies. The next section compares and contrasts the three economies' equilibriums.

Comparisons of Equilibriums

To compare the three model economies' equilibriums, first consider differences between the type M and type H economies, then differences among the type M, H, and MH economies. The subsection first examines securities prices, then critical values for adoption of the different technologies.

Securities prices in the two single technology economies are related by

$$[S_M{}^0 - S_H{}^0](1 + r) = \alpha - K\beta\sigma^2(\varepsilon)/N \qquad (6.13)$$

where: $S_M{}^0$ = equilibrium security price in the type M economy
$S_H{}^0$ = equilibrium security price in the type H economy
α = marginal cost of screening
K = fixed number of projects seeking financing
β = coefficient of risk aversion
$\sigma^2(\varepsilon)$ = variance of noise distribution
N = number of securities purchasers

The equilibrium price in the type M economy exceeds the price in the type H economy if and only if the marginal cost of the type H technology exceeds the certainty equivalent effect (price is reduced as this effect increases) of purchasing the risky security in the type M economy.

The MH economy's price difference is

$$\begin{aligned}
[S_M{}^* - S_H{}^*](1 + r) &= \alpha - (1 - \delta)(\beta K/N)\sigma^2(\varepsilon) \\
&= [S_M{}^0 - S_H{}^0](1 + r) + \delta(\beta K/N)\sigma^2(\varepsilon)
\end{aligned} \qquad (6.14)$$

where, except for the following newly introduced variables, all the terms are as defined in (6.13):

$S_M{}^*$ = equilibrium price of market instruments in combined economy
$S_H{}^*$ = equilibrium price of bank-purchased instruments in combined economy
δ = proportion of shares purchased by intermediary in combined economy

The difference between the two sets of prices depends on the marginal cost of operating the intermediary technology, on the effects of taking greater perceived risk when market financing is used, and on the proportion of shares purchased by the intermediary in the MH economy. Comparing the first and third lines of equation (6.14) shows that intraeconomy price differences can, in the absence of competitive supplies of capital, exceed the price differences between the single technology economies.

Intermediaries and markets can exist together at equilibrium even in the absence of agency costs. Different equilibriums can result from different technology choices even though nonfinancial investment opportunities do not change, and even if the intermediary provides no public information about firms' operations. In our model with constant risk-averse investors, optimal technology choice depends on the costs and benefits offered by alternative technologies. In contrast to a Modigliani-Miller world, costly technological choice means that a nonfinancial firm's value to investors can depend on the nature of the project, on the available financial technology, and on the kind of capital market in which financiers compete for business.

Postulating different financial technologies allows qualifying some of the assumptions employed in the literature. For example, Freixas and Rochet (2008) assume direct finance is less expensive than intermediated finance, apparently drawing their conclusion from a partial equilibrium analysis. In our general equilibrium comparisons of economies intermediated finance can be either higher or lower cost than market finance. The price difference depends on a comparison between (1) the type H technology's marginal cost and (2) the risk premium associated with the less discerning type M signal extraction technology. Additionally, if the suppliers of funds vie for business in the same competitive market, they have somehow to strike a balance between the benefits of greater signal extraction capability and its costs. In a competitive market, the benefits and cost should adjust until they are equal at the margin, in which case available financing alternatives would be equally costly from the viewpoint of productive firms.

As already noted, the previous results assume a price inelastic supply of securities. However, since prices can be either higher or lower between single technology economies with inelastic securities supplies, they can also be either higher or lower between single technology economies if securities supplies exhibit a degree of price elasticity.

The framework also suggests why the securities purchased by intermediaries are usually nonmarketable. Intermediaries with a distinctive signal extraction technology normally use their information privately. If securities prices are determined in markets on the basis of public information, intermediaries cannot individually resell the securities for more than their market value, even if the intermediaries' private information indicates the securities' worth is actually greater. Notwithstanding the former, intermediaries may be able to sell new securities that represent claims against a portfolio of nonmarketable securities, and to obtain prices for the new securities that are valued, in part, on the intermediary's using its financial technology (see Stein 1997).[24]

INTERNAL GOVERNANCE

Stein (1997) shows how an internal capital market can add value to certain kinds of deals when the amount of available financing is limited. If it has the authority and the incentive to reallocate scarce funds across projects, a corporate headquarters operation can create value in a credit-constrained setting where not all positive NPV projects can be financed. The internal capital market created by the headquarters division can create value when credit constraints imposed by uninformed outsiders do not permit the optimal size of project to be adopted, as shown later.

Stein's model provides both an economic rationale for setting up an internal capital market and determines the optimal size of the conglomerate's capital budget.[25] Assume the scale of the projects is defined by their initial investment, which can be either 1 or 2 units of capital. The projects are one-period ventures with two possible payoffs—a high payoff in state G, and a lower payoff in state B. The state G payoff is θy_i and the state B payoff is $y_i; i = 1, 2$. The states obtain with probabilities p and $(1 - p)$, respectively and $\theta > 1$. Project managers observe the actual state; outside investors know only the probabilities with which the states obtain. Interest rates are assumed to be zero. Investments and investment returns are shown in Table 6.9.

Assume that $y_1 > 1$, so that even in state B the project yields a positive return to an investment of 1. As a result, there would never be any difficulty in obtaining external funding for an investment of 1. However, Stein also assumes that project returns are diminishing, and that the net present value of earnings in state B is no longer positive if the investment is equal to 2:

$$1 < y_1 < y_2 < 2 \tag{6.15}$$

---

[24] Investors who purchase intermediary-issued securities will not necessarily have access to the intermediary's technology, partly because it may yield increasing returns and partly because particular skills may be required to employ it. Indeed, it can be argued that securitization is based on exactly such considerations.

[25] Stein also addresses the determinants of the internal capital market's optimal scope.

TABLE 6.9 Investments and Investment Returns

Investment	State G (probability p)	State B (probability $1 - p$)
1	θy_1	Y_1
2	θy_2	Y_2

In the example that is continued for the rest of this section, we set $y_1 = 1.0100$, $y_2 = 1.9400$, and $\theta = 1.1000$.

Returning to the more general setting, we also assume

$$\theta(y_2 - y_1) > 1 \qquad (6.16)$$

so the optimal investment in state G is 2, as may be seen from the fact that equation (6.16) implies $\theta y_2 > \theta y_1 + 1$ or $\theta(y_2 - y_1) > 1$. Note that condition (6.16) is satisfied for the example data just given: $1.1000(1.9400 - 1.0100) = 1.0230$.

Suppose that in the absence of setting up a corporate headquarters each project has its own project manager. Project managers have an incentive to over-invest because projects yield private benefits as well as benefits to the firm. The private benefits, determined by a coefficient s, have the realizations displayed in Table 6.10. We assume neither the incomes nor the private benefits are verifiable by outsiders. Moreover, they present a moral hazard problem (see Chapter 7), since the private benefits mean that project managers have an incentive to misrepresent a project as being in state G when it is not.

To begin the analysis, suppose project managers' information is not revealed, either to outside investors or to other parties within the corporation. If a project receives one unit of financing, its expected net cash flow is

$$[p\theta + (1 - p)]y_1 - 1 \qquad (6.17)$$

TABLE 6.10 Private Benefits

Investment/ Private Benefit	State G (Probability p)	State B (Probability $1 - p$)
1	$s\theta y_1$	sy_1
2	$s\theta y_2$	sy_2

and, as already mentioned, financing of 1 can always be obtained from outside financiers as shown in equation (6.15). To continue the example just given, let $p = 0.3000$ and $1 - p = 0.7000$. Using these data along with the previous values, equation (6.17) becomes

$$1.0100 \times [0.3000(1.1000) + 0.7000] - 1.0000 = 0.0403$$

However, suppose the project manager desired to invest 2. Then the expected net return is

$$[p\theta + (1 - p)]y_2 - 2 \qquad (6.18)$$

For a given value θ, equation (6.18) can be less than equation (6.17) if p is sufficiently small, as is henceforth assumed. Indeed, if

$$[p\theta + (1 - p)] \times [y_2 - y_1] < 1 \qquad (6.19)$$

then outside financing for the greater size of project will not be obtainable, since equation (6.19) implies

$$\{[p\theta + (1 - p)]y_2 - 2\} - \{[p\theta + (1 - p)]y_1 - 1\}$$
$$= [p\theta + (1 - p)] \times [y_2 - y_1] < 1$$

Again in terms of the example data, equation (6.18) becomes

$$1.9400 \times [0.3000(1.1000) + 0.7000] - 2.0000 = -0.0018$$

Suppose headquarters can screen and therefore obtain (possibly noisy) information about project success. Then the presence of a headquarters division can improve the situation both with respect to financing individual projects and to obtaining funds from outside financiers. Assume headquarters has no financial resources of its own, but has an incentive to monitor because it can capture a fraction of the private benefits that project managers get. If publicly verifiable cash flows are y, and total private benefits are sy, assume that headquarters can appropriate ϕsy, leaving $(1 - \phi)sy$ to be retained by project managers. Headquarters' ability to expropriate private benefits reduces the incentives affecting project managers, as reflected by a factor $k < 1$ that reduces cash flows in all states of the world and at either level of initial investment. In other words, the existence of headquarters absorbs $(1 - k)$ of any realized cash flow.

Since a headquarters operation reduces cash flows as well as private benefits, it is always value reducing in a one-project setting. Moreover, because headquarters realizes private benefits from projects, its operation presents the same moral hazard problems as do the individual project managers. Despite these costs, however, headquarters can create value on a net basis if there are two or more projects.

Headquarters' span of control allows it to derive private benefits from several projects simultaneously, and it therefore has an incentive to channel funds toward the more productive investments. Assume that headquarters is entitled to redistribute investments across projects. If headquarters is controlling n projects and can therefore raise n units of financing, it can reallocate the n units across projects in any way it likes. Some projects may be allocated 2, others 1, and still others zero units of capital. Headquarters, therefore, differs from a bank that only has the authority to accept or reject individual financing proposals without making any reallocations.

Suppose there are two projects i and j whose states are realized independently, and suppose in addition that headquarters can observe the state perfectly by screening the projects. Since there are two projects, headquarters can raise 2 units of capital from outside financiers. Suppose the marginal returns to investing the second dollar in, say, project i, are greater than the marginal returns to investing one dollar in each of projects i and j when i is in the good state and j is in the bad state. That is, $\theta y_2 > (\theta + 1)y_1$, from which it follows that

$$\theta(y_2 - y_1) > y_1 \tag{6.20}$$

To assess the benefits of operating an internal capital market, note first that expected returns to external market investors are

$$EM = 2[y_1(p\theta + (1 - p)) - 1] \tag{6.21}$$

Again reverting to the example data, the calculation following equation (6.17) can be used to show that for these data $EM = 2(0.0403) = 0.0806$.

Since headquarters can reallocate funds to the more productive project, internal market returns are

$$IM = 2(1 - p)^2 k y_1 + 2p^2 k\theta y_1 + 2p(1 - p)k\theta y_2 - 2 \tag{6.22}$$

The term $2p(1 - p)k\theta y_2$ in equation (6.22) means that when the two projects are in different states, whichever project is in state G receives both units of financing. (Recall that establishing a headquarters operation means that proportion $(1 - k)$ of any realized cash flow is absorbed by that operation.) Continuing to use the example data previously given, along with $k = 0.9999$, equation (6.22) becomes

$$2(0.7000)^2(0.9999)(1.0100) + 2(0.3000)^2(1.1000)(1.0100)$$
$$+ 2(0.7000)(0.3000)(0.9999)(1.9400) - 2 = 0.0859$$

verifying that for the data in question the internal market solution generates greater value than the external market solution.

It is also possible to determine the optimal size of the capital budget that headquarters should allocate. Suppose that headquarters' ability to monitor decreases with the number of projects, and for simplicity suppose further that the projects are statistically independent. Let $M(n)$ be the probability that monitoring is successful, and suppose that $M(n)$ is a decreasing function of n. To calculate the optimal number of projects, begin by picking an arbitrary value of n, from which a value $M(n)$ can be determined. For an arbitrary level of funding F the ex ante expected profit is

$$\pi(n, F) = M(n)\pi^M(n, F) + [1 - M(n)]\pi^N(n, F) \tag{6.23}$$

where $\pi^M(n, F)$ is the per project profits if monitoring is successful and $\pi^N(n, F)$ is the per project profits if monitoring is unsuccessful and headquarters learns nothing. For each fixed value of n, optimize equation (6.23) over F to obtain $F^*(n)$. Finally, pick the value of n that maximizes

$$\pi(n, F^*(n)) \tag{6.24}$$

Improvements to the monitoring technology will not always imply an increase in the optimal size of the internal capital market, mainly because the calculation involves two offsetting effects: the increased profits from using a better monitoring technology, versus the increased profits that come from having more money to invest. When the monitoring technology improves, it may be possible to generate a substantial easing of credit constraints with a smaller number of projects. In such a case it becomes less important to add projects in an effort to boost the level of individual projects' funding.

In another paper, Stein (2002) discusses how different organizational structures generate different forms of information about investment projects. A decentralized approach—with small, single-manager firms—is most likely to be attractive when project information is difficult to transmit credibly. In contrast, large hierarchies perform better when information can be cheaply and easily transmitted within the firm. Stein argues that the model helps to think about the consequences of consolidation in the banking industry, particularly the documented tendency for mergers to lead to declines in small-business lending. Since information regarding small-business lending is difficult to transmit, it can be relatively more expensive for larger hierarchical organizations to process.

REFERENCES

Bond, Philip. 2004. Bank and nonbank financial intermediation. *Journal of Finance* 59: 2,489–2,529.

DeLong, Bradford. 1991. Did J. P. Morgan's men add value? An economist's perspective on financial capitalism. In *Inside the Business Enterprise: Historical Perspectives on the Use of Information*, edited by Peter Temin. Chicago: University of Chicago Press.

Diamond, Douglas. 1984. Financial intermediation and delegated monitoring. *Review of Economic Studies* 51: 393–414.

Edgeworth, F. Y. [1886] 1995. The mathematical theory of banking. Read to the British Association, September 1886. In *Financial Intermediaries*, by Mervyn K. Lewis. Aldershot, U.K.: Elgar, 1995.

Freixas, Xavier, and Jean-Charles Rochet. 1997. *Microeconomics of Banking*. Cambridge, MA: MIT Press.

Freixas, Xavier, and Jean-Charles Rochet. 2008. *Microeconomics of Banking*, 2nd ed. Cambridge, Mass.: MIT Press.

Gorton, G., and J. Kahn. 1993. The design of bank loan contracts, collateral, and renegotiation. Working Paper 1–93, Rodney L. White Center for Financial Research, Wharton School, University of Pennsylvania.

Leland, Hayne, and David H. Pyle. 1977. Informational asymmetries, Financial structure, and financial intermediation. *Journal of Finance* 32: 371–387.

Marschak, Jakob, and Roy A. Radner. 1972. *Economic Theory of Teams*. New Haven: Yale University Press.

Ramirez, Carlos D. 1995. Did J. P. Morgan's men add liquidity? Corporate investment, cash flow, and financial structure at the turn of the century. *Journal of Finance* 50: 661–678.

Stein, Jeremy C. 1997. Internal capital markets and the competition for corporate resources. *Journal of Finance* 52: 111–133.

Stein, Jeremy C. 2002. Information production and capital allocation: Decentralized versus hierarchical firms. *Journal of Finance* 57: 1,899–2,002.

APPENDIX 6A: INTERMEDIARY INFORMATION PROCESSING: RESULT DERIVATIONS

This appendix provides formal derivations of the results stated in the section "Intermediary Information Processing."

Governance and Earnings Distributions

At time 1, a riskless investment with a time 0 value of 1 pays $1 + r$ to an investor. If the market is set up, investor payoffs to an investment of 1 are

$M \equiv X + \varepsilon$. The distribution M reflects both the physical earnings distribution X of the firms financed, and a noise distribution ε. Both X and ε are assumed to be normally distributed, and $E(X) > 0$, $E(\varepsilon) = 0$. A time 1 realization of X is determined by a single common factor; that is, $X \equiv X(f_1)$, and a time 1 realization of ε is determined by a second and independent common factor, that is, $\varepsilon \equiv \varepsilon(f_2)$. The effect of the common factor assumptions is to remove any incentives for diversifying either among the individual firms' securities or the securities sold by market agents. This and a similar assumption for intermediary financing focus the analysis on differences created solely by the relative capabilities of the two financial technologies. Since X and ε are statistically independent, $E(X\varepsilon) = E(X)E(\varepsilon) = 0$.

Through exercising their greater monitoring and control capabilities, intermediaries can alter a nonfinancial firm's payoff distribution[26] to $H \equiv X - \alpha$. That is, the intermediary removes the noise from market agents' information by paying a constant marginal cost α per screened project.[27] Nevertheless, a time 1 realization of X continues to be driven by the same common factor $X \equiv X(f_1)$ as before.[28] For convenience we assume throughout that $E(H) = E(X) - \alpha > 0$.

None of the economies studied has any taxes. Borrowing at the riskless rate is not permitted, and there is no short selling of the risky securities.[29] Nonfinancial firms raise their funds through equity issues. New equity issues are sold only to market agents in the type M economy, only to intermediaries in the type H economy. In the type MH economy, nonfinancial firms can seek either type of financing, but any given firm is restricted to using the single financing source it initially approaches. Market agents purchase securities from nonfinancial firms at time 0 for price $S_M{}^0$ in the type M economy and for $S_M{}^*$ in the MH economy. Intermediaries purchase securities from nonfinancial firms at time 0 for price $S_H{}^0$ in the type H economy and $S_H{}^*$ in the MH economy.

The impacts of the different technologies are manifest through investor returns distributions. Investor returns on securities purchased from market agents are determined from returns $M \equiv X + \varepsilon$ and the time 0 price of securities S_M. Investor returns on securities purchased from an intermediary

---

[26] It would also be possible to rank financial technologies by a parameter γ, such that the payoff distribution is represented by $X + (1 - \gamma)\varepsilon$. However for simplicity we do not introduce this refinement.

[27] We assume the private information obtained by the intermediary cannot be transmitted to market agents.

[28] Our model represents the results of the signal extraction process. Details of the process itself are discussed, for example, in Marschak and Radner (1972).

[29] We later determine parameter values that rule out any possibility of short selling.

are determined from returns $H \equiv X - \alpha$ and the time 0 price S_H. Investors hold only securities purchased from market agents if the economy is type M, only securities purchased from the intermediary if the economy is type H, and a portfolio of both types if the economy is type MH.

Investor Preferences

There are N investors, all with identical time 0 wealth positions, expectations, and preferences. Hence all investors make identical decisions. Investor preferences are reflected by a negative exponential utility function, and investors maximize the expected utility of time 1 wealth W:

$$E\{u(W)\} = E\{-\exp -(\beta W)\} \qquad (6A.1)$$

where W is assumed to be normally distributed. The coefficient β is the investor's index of (constant) absolute risk aversion. For a negative exponential utility and normally distributed wealth it is well-known that

$$E\{u(W)\} = -\exp -\beta\{E(W) - (1/2)\beta\sigma^2(W)\} \qquad (6A.2)$$

See Huang and Litzenberger (1988). The sequel refers to the wealth position

$$E(W) - (1/2)\beta\sigma^2(W) \qquad (6A.3)$$

as the certainty equivalent value of investor wealth.

An Economy with Two Financial Technologies

Investors in an MH economy are permitted to implement one or both technologies and to invest in the riskless asset. They will implement both technologies so long as their combined set-up cost, for comparison's sake assumed to be the sum of the individual set-up costs, falls below a critical value.[30] If technology costs exceed this critical value, investors forgo setting up the technologies and purchase only the riskless security. We next analyze the risky securities purchases under the assumption that set-up costs fall below the critical value. The critical value itself will be found later.

Earnings on the risky securities are described by the normal distributions M and H, respectively. The securities' prices, denoted S_M and S_H, are

---

[30] The critical value will be specified later in the appendix.

temporarily taken as given. The model is closed and equilibrium prices are found later. Since[31] $M \equiv X + \varepsilon$ and $H \equiv X - \alpha$, the expected payoffs on the securities are

$$E(M) = E(X)$$
$$E(H) = E(X) - \alpha$$

and the payoff variances are

$$\sigma^2(M) = \sigma^2(X) + \sigma^2(\varepsilon)$$
$$\sigma^2(H) = \sigma^2(X)$$

Finally, the covariance and correlation between payoffs are respectively

$$\text{cov}(M, H) = \sigma^2(X);$$
$$\text{corr}(M, H) = \text{cov}(M, H)/\sigma(X)[\sigma^2(X) + \sigma^2(\varepsilon)]^{1/2} \qquad (6A.4)$$
$$= \sigma(X)/[\sigma^2(X) + \sigma^2(\varepsilon)]^{1/2}$$

Assuming the fixed technology costs are paid at the outset, investor wealth is the normally distributed variate

$$W = [w - (\theta_H S_H + \theta_M S_M) - (\lambda_M + \lambda_H)/N](1 + r) + \theta_H H + \theta_M M$$
$$= [w - (\lambda_M + \lambda_H)/N](1 + r) + \theta_H[X - \alpha - S_H(1 + r)]$$
$$+ \theta_M[X + \varepsilon - S_M(1 + r)]$$

$$(6A.5)$$

where w is initial wealth and $(\lambda_M + \lambda_H)/N$ represents each investor's share of the fixed costs. The first two moments of W are

$$E(W) = [w - (\lambda_M + \lambda_H)/N](1 + r) + \theta_H[E(X) - \alpha - S_H(1 + r)]$$
$$+ \theta_M[E(X) - S_M(1 + r)]$$

and

$$\sigma^2(W) = \theta_H^2 \sigma^2(H) + 2\theta_H \theta_M \text{cov}(H, M) + \theta_M^2 \sigma^2(M)$$
$$= \theta_H^2 \sigma^2(X) + 2\theta_H \theta_M \sigma^2(X) + \theta_M^2[\sigma^2(X) + \sigma^2(\varepsilon)]. \qquad (6A.6)$$

As is well-known the above assumptions imply a mean-variance utility maximization problem whose optimal solution trades off mean payoff

---

[31] Note that $a > 0$ is necessary to rule out second degree stochastic dominance of M by H.

against a risk premium attributable to payoff variance. The details are presented formally in Appendix 6B.

Securities Demands and Prices

The optimality conditions (6A.5), stated in Appendix II, can be rewritten explicitly as:

$$
\begin{aligned}
S_M(1+r) &= E(X) - \beta\{\theta_H\sigma^2(X) + \theta_M[\sigma^2(X) + \sigma^2(\varepsilon)]\} \\
S_H(1+r) &= E(X) - \alpha - \beta\{\theta_H\sigma^2(X) + \theta_M\sigma^2(X)\}
\end{aligned}
\tag{6A.7}
$$

The securities demand functions can then be written

$$
\begin{aligned}
\theta_M{}^* &= [(S_H - S_M)(1+r) + \alpha]/\beta\sigma^2(\varepsilon) \\
\theta_H{}^* &= \{[E(X) - S_H(1+r) - \alpha]/\beta\sigma^2(X)\} - \theta_M{}^*
\end{aligned}
\tag{6A.8}
$$

Market clearing requires that the fixed supply of securities be taken up:

$$
(\theta_M{}^* + \theta_H{}^*) = K/N
$$

Consistent with the assumption of market clearing, henceforth we write

$$
\begin{aligned}
\theta_M{}^* &\equiv (1-\delta)(K/N) \\
\theta_H{}^* &\equiv \delta K/N \\
&\delta\varepsilon[0,1]
\end{aligned}
\tag{6A.9}
$$

Using equation (6A.9) allows rewriting equation (6A.7) as

$$
\begin{aligned}
S_M{}^*(1+r) &= E(X) - \beta(K/N)\sigma^2(X) - (1-\delta)\beta(K/N)\sigma^2(\varepsilon) \\
S_H{}^*(1+r) &= E(X) - \beta(K/N)\sigma^2(X) - \alpha
\end{aligned}
\tag{6A.10}
$$

Securities prices will be positive if, as we assume, $E(X)$ is sufficiently large in relation to the remaining terms of the two equations in equation (6A.10).

The two suppliers of capital bid for the same securities, and assuming they vie for business in a perfectly competitive capital market, equilibrium requires they offer the same securities prices. Equations (6A.10) are consistent with a competitive securities market equilibrium in which $S_M{}^* = S_H{}^*$ if and only if

$$
\alpha = (1-\delta)\beta K\sigma^2(\varepsilon)/N
\tag{6A.11}
$$

that is, if and only if the intermediary's greater marginal cost is just offset by the greater risk premium required by investors who purchase securities from market agents.

Critical Values for Adopting Both Technologies   If the investors purchased only riskless securities, their time 1 certainty equivalent wealth would be $w(1 + r)$. On the other hand, if investment returns are large enough to compensate for the fixed costs of adopting the two financial technologies, the MH economy's certainty equivalent wealth is

$$
[w - (\lambda_M + \lambda_H)/N](1 + r) + (\beta/2)(K/N)^2[\sigma^2(X) \\
+ (1 - \delta)^2\sigma^2(\varepsilon)] \tag{6A.12}
$$

Since expected utility is monotonic in certainty equivalent wealth, investors will implement the MH economy's financing arrangements if and only if

$$
(1 + r)(\lambda_H + \lambda_M)/N \le (\beta/2)(K/N)^2[\sigma^2(X) + (1 - \delta)^2\sigma^2(\varepsilon)] \tag{6A.13}
$$

Although equation (6A.13) might only be satisfied for sufficiently large values[32] of δ, whenever the inequality is satisfied long positions are taken in both risky securities. In these cases the MH economy supports both market and intermediary technologies.

Economies with One Financial Technology

Solutions for implementing only one financial technology can be obtained by specializing the derivations of the previous section. As before, we first assume that long positions are taken in the available securities, then find conditions that imply this result. Specializing the results in this appendix, the securities price in a single technology economy is

$$
S_Z{}^0(1 + r) = E(Z) - \theta_Z{}^0\beta\sigma^2(Z) \\
Z\varepsilon\{M, H\} \tag{6A.14}
$$

Since market clearing requires $K \equiv N\theta_Z{}^0$, equation (6A.14) can be rewritten as

$$
S_Z{}^0(1 + r) = E(Z) - \beta K\sigma^2(Z)/N
$$

$$
Z\varepsilon\{M, H\}
$$

---

[32] Since $\sigma^2(\varepsilon) < \sigma^2(X)$.

Hence for the type M and type H economies, respectively,

$$S_M^0(1+r) = E(X) - \beta(K/N)\sigma^2(X) - \beta(K/N)\sigma^2(\varepsilon X)$$

and

$$S_H^0(1+r) = E(X) - \beta(K/N)\sigma^2(X) - \alpha \tag{6A.15}$$

The conditions are, of course, analogous to the MH economy conditions (6A.10).

Critical Values   Again from this appendix, the certainty equivalent wealth of each investor is

$$
\begin{aligned}
&[w - (\lambda_Z/N)](1+r) + (\beta/2)[E(Z) - S_Z^0(1+r)]^2/\sigma^2(Z) \\
&= [w - (\lambda_Z/N)](1+r) + (\beta/2)[K/N]^2\sigma^2(Z) \\
&Z\varepsilon\{M, H\}
\end{aligned}
\tag{6A.16}
$$

where S_Z^0 is the market clearing price consistent with a fixed supply of securities.[33] In either economy, the single governance structure will be adopted if by so doing each investor's certainty equivalent wealth can be increased relative to the status quo. That is,

$$
\begin{aligned}
(1+r)\lambda_M/N &\le (\beta/2)[K/N]^2[\sigma^2(X) + \sigma^2(\varepsilon)] \\
(1+r)\lambda_H/N &\le (\beta/2)[K/N]^2\sigma^2(X)
\end{aligned}
\tag{6A.17}
$$

Note from equations (6A.13) and (6A.17) that the type M economy can establish a viable financing mechanism at a higher setup cost than either the type MH or the type H economy.

Price-Elastic Securities Supply   Note from equations (6A.12) and (6A.16) that certainty equivalent wealth is an increasing function of the portfolio variance. This property is a consequence of the assumption that the fixed supply of securities is fully taken up at whatever price investors offer. Certainty equivalent wealth and consequently expected utility could be decreasing functions of $\sigma^2(Z)$ if the supply of securities were sufficiently price elastic. For example, taking K to be an increasing function of S_Z means it is also a decreasing function of $\sigma^2(Z)$. If the decrease in K were sufficiently rapid, certainty equivalent wealth would also be a decreasing function of

---

[33] Note that $S_M^0 > 0$ if and only if $E(M) > K\beta\sigma^2(M)/N$, a restriction we assume throughout the rest of the section.

$\sigma^2(Z)$. More generally than in the present model, the effect on investor utility of optimal portfolio choice will be a function of the price elasticities of both securities demand and securities supply.

APPENDIX 6B: FORMAL STATEMENT OF PROBLEM

Assuming investors implement the available technologies, their certainty equivalent wealth is defined by

$$
\begin{aligned}
W^* &\equiv [w - (\lambda_M + \lambda_H)/N](1 + r) + \max_\theta \{c'\theta - (1/2)\beta\,\theta'A\theta\} \\
&= [w - (\lambda_M + \lambda_H)/N](1 + r) + (1/2)\beta c'Ac
\end{aligned}
\tag{6B.1}
$$

where

$$
\begin{aligned}
c' &\equiv E' - S'(1 + r) \equiv (E(X) - \alpha - S_H(1 + r),\ E(M) - S_M(1 + r)) \\
\theta' &\equiv (\theta_H, \theta_M)
\end{aligned}
\tag{6B.2}
$$

and

$$
A \equiv
\begin{bmatrix}
\sigma^2(X) & \sigma^2(X) \\
\sigma^2(X) & \sigma^2(X) + \sigma^2(\varepsilon)
\end{bmatrix}
\tag{6B.3}
$$

Given the monotonicity of the negative exponential, the utility-maximizing portfolio is found by maximizing (6B.1). Since the necessary conditions for a maximum of (6B.1) are also sufficient, taking partial derivatives with respect to θ and setting the results equal to zero gives the optimal demand functions for the risky securities:

$$
\begin{aligned}
c - \beta\, A\theta &= 0 \\
\theta^* &= (1/\beta)A^{-1}c = (1/\beta)A^{-1}(E - S(1 + r))
\end{aligned}
\tag{6B.4}
$$

Given our assumption of a constant absolute risk-averse utility, the utility maximizing portfolio is independent of initial wealth, as confirmed by equation (6B.4).

Suppose the supplies of the two securities are fixed,[34] that is, $K' \equiv K(\delta, 1 - \delta)' > 0$. Then with N identical investors market clearing implies:

$$
K/N = (1/\beta)A^{-1}c = (1/\beta)A^{-1}(E - S(1 + r))
\tag{6B.5}
$$

---

[34] The securities supply functions and the assumption that they are perfectly inelastic will be analyzed later.

and equilibrium securities prices can be found immediately from the right-hand side of equation (6B.5). Note moreover that equation (6B.5) can be rewritten as

$$\mathbf{c} = (\beta/N)\,\mathbf{AK} \tag{6B.6}$$

The investor's optimal certainty equivalent wealth is found by substituting equation (6B.6) into (6B.1) and noting the symmetry of $\mathbf{A}$:

$$\begin{aligned}
W^* &\equiv [w - (\lambda_M + \lambda_H)/N](1+r) + (1/2\beta)\,\mathbf{c}'\mathbf{A}^{-1}\mathbf{c} \\
&= [w - (\lambda_M + \lambda_H)/N](1+r) + (1/2\beta)(\beta/N)^2\mathbf{K}'\mathbf{AK}
\end{aligned} \tag{6B.7}$$

It is evident from equation (6B.7) that, other things being equal, certainty equivalent wealth and consequently investor utility increases in either $\sigma^2(X)$ or $\sigma^2(\varepsilon)$. This result is a consequence of (1) the fact that the equilibrium price of a security decreases in its variance; and (2) the assumption that securities supply is perfectly inelastic with respect to price. The result in equation (6B.7) does not necessarily obtain if the securities supply function is price elastic.

Finally, the adoption of both technologies will increase certainty equivalent wealth and consequently investor utility if and only if

$$(1+r)(\lambda_M + \lambda_H)/N \le (\beta/2N^2)\mathbf{K}'\mathbf{AK} \tag{6B.8}$$

Appendix 6A and the main text interpret equation (6B.8) further.

CHAPTER 7

Terms of Deals

This chapter explains how the terms of a deal can fine tune the capabilities utilized in its governance. In particular, the informational conditions under which a deal is originated, and the likely evolution of that information, have important implications for selecting deal terms. When deals are arranged under risk, they can be formulated as complete contracts. In addition, when they are arranged under conditions of symmetric information, it is relatively easy to select appropriate terms. However, if the deals are arranged under conditions of information asymmetry, they usually present potential complications of moral hazard and adverse selection. Each can be governed effectively, but at the expense of incurring additional costs. Finally, when deals are arranged under uncertainty the contracts are necessarily incomplete, and as a result their governance requires different methods and terms. Although a few exceptions are noted, in almost every instance the terms examined in this chapter are likely to be implemented by an intermediary or internally rather than a market agent, illustrating how the details of nonarm's-length governance differ from the governance provided by market agents.

This chapter also examines how deal terms are used to fine tune agreements between financier and client. The discussion emphasizes the financier's perspective, since he or she usually proposes a standard set of terms to be negotiated. If the applicant finds the terms generally acceptable, she may propose additional negotiation to resolve any remaining differences. As negotiations proceed, the financier may also propose additional conditions intended to enhance the deal's safety, profitability, or both. Finally, if both parties are agreed on the conditions, the deal will be struck and the financing extended.

COSTS OF DEALS

Deals with differing attributes will usually be arranged at differing interest rates in order to compensate for the risk or uncertainty involved. The difference between the effective interest rate[1] charged to a client and the interest cost of funds to the financier will vary according to the deal's particular attributes, the governance capabilities of the financier, and the competitiveness of the environment in which the financing is arranged. For example, a market exchange of bonds is usually a risky deal based on information publicly available to both parties. In such a transaction the difference between financiers' total interest cost and the effective rate paid by the client will not usually be large, especially if the market is competitive. On the other hand, financing a new business venture represents a deal under uncertainty, and the parties are likely to have quite different information about possible payoffs. The interest premium for facing uncertainty, and for incurring transactions and information processing costs, is therefore likely to be greater—in some cases very much greater—than in the bond deal. Moreover, the markets for financing business ventures are not as likely to be competitive, meaning that financier profit margins will likely be higher than in the first example.

Transactions Costs

From the client's point of view, transactions costs include both direct and indirect costs. Direct costs are those the client pays to the financier. Indirect costs are those paid to others, but the outlays still comprise part of the client's expenses. For example, the owner of a small business might look long and hard to find someone interested in investing long-term capital in his business, and would have to bear the costs of continuing to search for an accommodating financier until one is found.

From the financier's point of view, a deal's costs include the financier's costs of raising the funds, the marginal costs of assessing the deal, a contribution to the financier's fixed costs, and an allowance for a profit margin. The magnitude of the charges depends on the financier's efficiency, the competitiveness of the market she serves, and the kind of deal information she must obtain, both at the outset when the deal is being negotiated (ex ante information obtained by screening) and subsequently as the deal is being worked through (ex post information obtained from monitoring). If a

---

[1]Although some of the charges may actually be specified as lump sums, for comparative purposes it is usually convenient to convert them to effective interest rates.

financier is to stay in business over the longer term, she must recover all costs, whether through interest charges, explicit fees, or a combination of the two.

Screening and Monitoring Costs

Screening costs are the ex ante costs a financier incurs to assess a funding proposal, while monitoring costs are the ex post costs involved in the deal's continuing governance. Since screening costs are usually the sum of a fixed set-up cost and an ex ante variable cost, the average cost of screening individual deals can be expected to decline as the number of deals screened increases. The same is likely to be true of monitoring costs.

The average cost of administering a deal is the sum of its screening and monitoring cost, along with the cost of making any adjustments that monitoring indicates would be desirable. While scale economies explain why this average cost function will likely decline with transaction volume, other factors can affect the function's position and how it is likely to shift. First, the position of the screening cost function will be higher for deals with greater informational differences between clients and financier. Second, the screening cost function may shift downward as financiers gain experience with a particular type of deal and, thereby, learn how to screen it more efficiently. Monitoring costs differ according to the kinds of information differences involved, and a monitoring cost function can also shift as a result of learning. Finally, as shown in both this chapter and particularly in Chapter 10, both screening and monitoring costs can be greater in deals where it is necessary to manage the effects of asymmetric information.

The potential volume of a given deal type is determined by the intersection of the demand and supply curves for the financing type. If client demand is relatively great many deals are likely to be completed, and per deal screening costs will be low because financiers can take advantage of both scale economies and learning effects. However, the economics of screening can work to deter the entry of a new supplier to a market, especially if the cost function shifts downward as the number of completed deals increases. In such circumstances the financier who first enters a market can gain a first mover advantage over subsequent entrants, particularly if the skills the financier acquires are experiential and therefore difficult to communicate.[2] Potential new entrants may not be willing to set up innovative financing arrangements because they see existing financiers as having entrenched advantages that are difficult to overcome.

---

[2]Practical knowledge—"know-how"—can be more difficult to transmit than theoretical knowledge—"know-why."

The economics of screening can also work to inhibit the viability of new deals. First, financiers have to incur costs to determine whether the deal is viable. Moreover, financiers' perceptions of economic viability depend in part on the skills they have already acquired. To illustrate, there are high fixed costs to setting up venture capital firms, both because the personnel in a new firm need to learn how to screen prospects, and because any one person can only supervise a limited number of venture investments. Even if a venture firm has some personnel with screening experience, their skills are acquired principally through experience rather than in a classroom setting. As a result any new employees have to gain similar experience, and at any given time existing firms may not be able to accommodate the entire market's demands for financing. Nevertheless, unless there is enough unsatisfied demand to cover the fixed costs of setting up a new firm, the supply deficiency may persist.

INFORMATIONAL CONDITIONS

The information available to a financier affects his estimate of a deal's profitability and determines the kinds of reports he will require from the client. When financiers take on familiar deals they are likely to treat the transactions routinely, especially in the absence of informational asymmetries. For example, the purchaser of a government Treasury bill has access to almost all potentially relevant information when the purchase is made. On the other hand, the venture capitalist investing in a growing firm has much less precise ex ante information, particularly when the firm's principal asset is the talent of its owner-manager. Moreover, the venture capitalist is much more likely to refine her ex post estimates of the client's potential profitability over the life of her investment than is the purchaser of a Treasury bill.

If a financier has less information than her client, she will try to determine whether it is cost-effective to obtain more details. If she thinks it would be, she may incorporate her informational requirements in the terms of the deal, as illustrated by the model in the subsection "Renegotiating a Bank Loan" later in this chapter. Some information may be available ex ante while other information may only be obtainable ex post. For example, a retail client borrowing against accounts receivable might be asked to submit quarterly statements of accounts receivable outstanding, thus keeping fresh the lender's information about the quality of the security.

Information and Contract Types

As Table 7.1 indicates, financiers select governance mechanisms according to each deal's informational conditions. Deals arranged under risk are easier

TABLE 7.1 Deal Attributes and Governance Structures

Informational Attribute	Governance Mechanism
Risk	Complete contract. Rule based; little or no provision for monitoring and subsequent control.
Uncertainty	Incomplete contract. Structure allows for discretionary governance. Details of monitoring and control are typically negotiated.

to govern than deals under uncertainty, because they present situations in which complete contracting is possible. The terms of deals arranged under uncertainty cannot usually be specified quantitatively. For example, if the relevant states of nature are observable but not verifiable, it will not be possible to write a complete contract. In still more complex situations it may not even be possible to define the relevant states of nature.

Financings arranged under uncertainty usually provide for the exercise of discretion to compensate for contract incompleteness. For example, the arrangements may provide for relatively intensive monitoring over the deal's life, as well as for flexibility of response to evolving information. If an unforeseen contingency does occur, it may not have been possible to specify in advance what the appropriate adjustments would be.[3] For this reason, many incomplete contracts are expressed in terms of the principles to be followed in making adjustments if and when the need for them becomes apparent. Hart (2001) observes that one way of coping with such eventualities is through different forms of financial structure. For example, equity gives shareholders decision rights if the firm is solvent, but debt gives creditors those decision rights if the firm is insolvent.

Another possibility is that whatever financial instrument is used, a preamble to the contract may state principles for renegotiation under certain general conditions that by necessity cannot be well specified in advance since the future is "simply too unclear" (Hart 2001, 1,083). The possibility of renegotiation implies that financiers' governance costs will increase, and the increased costs will only be warranted if financiers believe they can reduce possible losses at least commensurately. Financiers will also seek larger interest rate premiums for bearing what they perceive to be greater degrees of uncertainty, and will attempt to recover these costs and premiums from clients. As a result, the client presenting a highly risky deal can expect to pay a higher effective interest rate than a client presenting a less risky deal,

---

[3]As a practical problem, it may be difficult to detect whether or not a contract is incomplete, since it can be difficult to determine whether unanticipated contingencies have arisen.

and a client presenting a deal under uncertainty can expect to pay a higher effective interest rate than a client presenting a deal under risk.

Informational Asymmetries

While informational asymmetries are not unknown in public market transactions, they have greater importance in private market and in intermediated transactions, mainly because they are more difficult to resolve in the absence of active market trading. Indeed, in intermediated transactions informational differences may persist even after intensive screening. First, financier and client may differ in their estimates of a deal's profitability, in part because they have different information processing capabilities. Second, the parties may have the same ex ante information about a deal, but their ability to keep informed about its progress may differ. Finally, financiers are well aware that clients sometimes provide biased information in attempts to improve the financing terms they can obtain.

It is much more difficult to reach a satisfactory agreement when financier and client differ greatly over a project's viability than when they share the same view. If the asymmetries are great enough, it may only be possible to do the deal at nonmarket interest rates. In other cases, it may not be possible to reach agreement at any interest rate. For example, in the early 1980s opinion regarding the value of the troubled Continental Illinois Bank's loan portfolio varied so greatly that counterparties found it difficult to agree on a mutually satisfactory price for the bank's shares. As a second example, the parties attempting to exchange CMOs backed by subprime loan portfolios in 2007 and 2008 found that, as the instruments became increasingly illiquid, getting any estimate of the securities' value was difficult.

Sufi and Mian (2007) explore some of the ways that information asymmetry influences loan syndicate structure and membership. First, lead bank and borrower reputation mitigates, but does not eliminate information asymmetry problems. Moreover and consistent with moral hazard in monitoring, the syndicate's lead bank both retains a larger share of the loan and invites fewer other syndicate members when the borrower requires more intense monitoring. When information asymmetry is potentially severe, accommodating lenders are likely closer to the borrower, both geographically and in terms of previous lending relationships. The models presented in the rest of this chapter further illustrate some of the ways financiers attempt to cope with the effects of informational asymmetries.

Third-Party Information

Financiers can sometimes reduce information costs through purchasing information rather than producing it in-house. Deal information will be provided by third parties if they can turn a profit doing so. For example, rating agencies like Moody's and Standard & Poor's monitor the creditworthiness of public companies' debt issues and publish their ratings. Companies seeking funds will pay to be rated if by so doing they can reduce their financing costs more than commensurately. Benson (1979) argues that by producing bond rating information and then finding clients interested in purchasing the bonds, underwriters can reduce financing costs to less than they would be if buyers produced the information individually. In the United States, municipal bond insuring agencies serve as another type of information producer (Fabozzi, Modigliani, and Ferri 2001, 345–346).

Even though information is collected and used privately by the insurers, other members of the investing public may interpret the issuance of an insurance policy as a signal regarding the municipality's creditworthiness. Similarly, Fama (1985) argues that short-term bank lending may signal a borrowing firm's quality, and that a bank's willingness to extend short-term financing may reduce the firm's total financing costs. As still another example, when a portfolio of loans is securitized (see Chapters 5 and 15) it is quite common for a third party to insure the securities issued against such events as default on their principal amount. In effect, the insurance amounts to a third party rating of the default risk in the loan portfolio backing the issuance of the new instruments.

Asymmetries and Financing Choice: Debt versus Equity

Many writers have addressed the question of why firms use both debt and equity financing. The famous Modigliani-Miller (MM) theorem establishes conditions under which there is no advantage to using one rather than the other. MM argue that if there are no taxes or bankruptcy costs to defaulting on debt, then financing with a combination of debt and equity rather than with equity alone adds nothing to the value of the firm. In the circumstances envisioned by MM, debt and equity are merely ways of dividing up cash flows and different ratios of debt to equity financing neither create nor destroy firm value. However, subsequent research recognizes that taxes, bankruptcy costs, and other forms of market imperfection can explain why corporate treasurers are not indifferent to the manner in which they raise long-term finance. That is, the costs of long-term finance can be affected by differing ratios of debt to equity when taxes, bankruptcy costs, and other market imperfections are recognized as elements of the financing picture.

Ross (1977) notes that firms used both debt and equity financing even before corporate taxes were levied. Ross suggests that different levels of the debt-equity ratio can reflect management attempts to signal the quality of their firms, and that managers can be motivated to signal truthfully so long

TABLE 7.2 Outcomes and Probabilities

	Firm Earnings	Probability Estimates of Optimistic Owner	Probability Estimates of Pessimistic Financier
Scenario 1	8	0.25	0.00
Scenario 2	7	0.25	0.25
Scenario 3	6	0.25	0.25
Scenario 4	5	0.25	0.25
Scenario 5	4	0.00	0.25

as they face appropriate incentives. He shows that debt with a fixed face value and a bankruptcy penalty[4] is the optimal contract for maximizing a risk-neutral entrepreneur's expected return, given a minimum expected return to lenders. The Ross explanation is persuasive if management has personal resources to pay the bankruptcy penalties, but such a situation is not typical of an entrepreneur who has invested all available assets in his firm. In addition to Ross' explanation, debt-equity ratios can have value implications because they convey different control possibilities. Hart (2001) points out that shareholders have decision rights so long as a firm is solvent, but those decision rights pass to creditors when the firm is insolvent.

The next example shows still another effect, this time due to informational asymmetries: If financiers and entrepreneurs disagree regarding a firm's prospects, debt can come closer than equity to resolving their differences. The result is first demonstrated numerically and then considered a little more formally. Suppose both owners and financiers are risk neutral, and that interest rates are zero. Suppose also that the owners of a firm are optimistic, while financiers are pessimistic, in the sense reflected in Table 7.2. Owners expect firm earnings to be higher than do financiers; indeed owners do not expect earnings of 4 can occur at all, and attach equal positive probability to the remaining four scenarios. Financiers do not expect that earnings of 8 are possible, but attach equal positive probability to the other remaining scenarios.

Next consider the value of the equity in the firm, as viewed by the owner and the financier, respectively. The owner values the equity at $(8 + 7 + 6 + 5)/4 = 6.5$, while the financier's value is $(7 + 6 + 5 + 4)/4 = 5.5$. Nevertheless, both parties would agree that the firm's promise to pay 4 can be met all of the time and, therefore, both parties would place the same

---

[4]The penalty, borne by management, must be at least as great as any shortfall in the debt payment.

time 0 value on debt[5] promising to pay 4 at time 1. That is, even though they do not agree on the firm's prospects, the two parties can agree on the value of at least this limited amount of debt.

Now suppose the firm needs to raise 5, and that financiers have the power to set the terms on which they will purchase securities. If financiers were to purchase equity that they regard as being worth 5, they would demand 5.0/5.5 or 10/11 of the shares. However the owners regard 10/11 of the shares as having a value of (6.5)(10/11), or 5.91. Thus to the owners, equity financing carries a high implicit rate of return, even in the present case where interest rates have been assumed to be zero.

Alternatively, suppose financiers propose a debt issue that promises to pay off 5.5 if the firm has the funds, or whatever funds are available if the firm does not generate cash flows at least equal to 5.5. Financiers would value this debt at (4.0 + 5.0 + 5.5 + 5.5)/4 = 5.00. The owners, who regard the debt as worth (5.0 + 5.5 + 5.5 + 5.5)/4 = 5.38, would still think they were paying too much for funds. However they would also agree that the cost of debt financing was less than the cost of equity financing, since to them the value of the equity that would have to be surrendered is 5.91. Thus while financiers and owners do not always agree on what the securities are worth, they may still be able to agree that debt reduces the differences in their valuations more than equity. As the example suggests, entrepreneurs will prefer debt to equity if the choice of instrument affects their perceptions of financing costs.

To establish the difference between debt and equity a little more formally, suppose both financiers and entrepreneurs believe the firm can generate one of two possible cash flows. Let the financiers' estimates of these flows be y_H and y_L, while entrepreneurs' are $y_H + a$ and $y_L + a, a > 0$. To keep the symbolism to a minimum, suppose that financiers and entrepreneurs both believe either outcome can occur with equal probability. Financiers set the price of the instruments, but allow the entrepreneur to choose either the debt or the equity. In addition, suppose that if debt is used, financiers stipulate a repayment amount

$$y_H > R > y_L$$

It will simplify the analysis to assume in addition that

$$R > y_L > (y_H - y_L)/2 \qquad (7.1)$$

---

[5]This possibility is also discussed in Hart (2001, 1,087).

The second inequality in equation (7.1) implies that $y_H < 3y_L$, that is, for purposes of the present analysis the difference between high and low payoffs is limited.

Continuing to assume that financiers accept an interest rate of zero, financiers value the debt instrument at $(y_L + R)/2$. Financiers are also willing to provide equity financing, so long as the proportion of the equity they can obtain has a current market value equal to that of the debt with promised repayment R. In order to have the same value as the debt, the proportion of equity issued, α, must satisfy

$$(y_L + R)/2 = \alpha(y_L + y_H)/2$$

Solving the last equation for α gives

$$\alpha \equiv (y_L + R)/(y_L + y_H) \tag{7.2}$$

Using equation (7.1), equation (7.2) implies

$$\alpha(y_L + y_H)/2 = (y_L + R)/2 > y_L/2 + (y_H - y_L)/4 = (y_L + y_H)/4 \tag{7.3}$$

so that $\alpha > 1/2$. Then for any repayment $R < y_H$ the borrower's valuation of the debt is less than the borrower's valuation of the equity, as shown by

$$\begin{aligned} (y_L + R + a)/2 &= \alpha(y_L + y_H)/2 + a/2 < \alpha(y_L + y_H)/2 + 2\alpha a/2 \\ &= \alpha(y_L + y_H + 2a)/2 \end{aligned} \tag{7.4}$$

Since financiers will advance the same amount of funds whether debt or equity is offered, the borrower will prefer to use debt, since from the borrower's point of view it lowers financing costs. The argument can be generalized to more outcomes, different probabilities, and more complex differences in the payoff distribution, but for present purposes the simple assumptions used above are sufficient to illustrate the point.

While in the last example the client is assumed to have more information than the financier, the opposite can sometimes be true. Axelson (2007) studies security design when investors rather than managers have private information about the firm, and argues that in such cases it can be optimal to issue equity. A "folklore proposition of debt" from traditional signaling models says that the firm should issue the least information-sensitive security possible, that is, standard debt. However Axelson finds this proposition is valid only if the firm can vary the face value of the debt with investor demand. If a firm has several assets, debt backed by a pool of the assets is more beneficial for the firm when the degree of competition among investors is low, but equity backed by individual assets is more beneficial when competition is high.

MORAL HAZARD[6]

Moral hazard, a classic consequence of informational asymmetries, frequently affects relations between a financier and an individual client.[7] For example, if a financier does not take appropriate precautions, a client may use the proceeds of a debt issue to substitute a riskier project for the one originally proposed to the financier. The incentive to substitute a riskier project arises from the fact that, unless detected, shareholders of the firm would receive greater benefits from the substitution while debt holders would bear greater risk. The following model of moral hazard analyzes a complete contract drawn up under conditions of risk.

Avoiding Moral Hazard

Consider a situation in which a borrower might substitute a bad project for a good one unless the lender takes steps to prevent it. Suppose that without any preventive measures the lender who advances the single unit of capital needed to implement a project has no further control over the type of project actually chosen. Suppose there is a good project that pays off either G with probability p_G; or zero with probability $(1 - p_G)$. There is also a bad project that pays off B with probability p_B or zero with probability $(1 - p_B)$. Suppose in addition that $p_G G > 1 > p_B B$, so that the good project has the higher expected value. Assume also that the interest rate is zero, the expected present value of the good project positive, and that of the bad

---

[6]The section "Moral Hazard," and those that follow, "Complete Contracts," and "Incomplete Contracts," are based on models developed in Freixas and Rochet (1997). Arrow (1974) observes that moral hazard is present in nearly all types of insurance contracts, and suggests that direct control over the actions of the insured and co-insurance are possible ways of mitigating its effects.

[7]In contrast, the adverse selection problem discussed in Chapter 10 affects dealings between a financier and an entire class of clients.

project negative. Suppose finally that $B > G$, so that the owners of the firm could benefit from adopting the riskier project. The foregoing assumptions imply $p_G > p_B$. Depending on the size of the repayment, the owners of the firm may find themselves better off by choosing the bad project. They may be able to reap large rewards if the bad project succeeds, and it will be the financiers who suffer if it does not succeed.

The owners of the firm only face an incentive to choose the good project if they will be better off doing so after taking the size of the loan repayment into account. That is, the firm will choose the good project if

$$p_G(G - R) > p_B(B - R)$$

This last, incentive, condition defines a critical value for the amount of repayment

$$R < R_C \equiv [p_G G - p_B B]/(p_G - p_B)$$

Note that since $G < B$, the last line also implies that $R_C < G$: The financier cannot demand too high a repayment (i.e., too high an effective interest rate) without creating the possibility that the firm will substitute the bad project for the good one. Figure 7.1 indicates the situation from

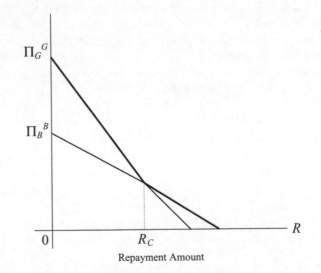

Repayment Amount

FIGURE 7.1   Repayment Amount
Note: $0 - R_C$: region in which borrower has an incentive to choose the good project.

the firm's point of view. Of course, the repayment that the lender can charge must also be high enough for the lender to profit in an expected value sense. If not, the lender will decline the financing application.[8]

Incentives to Repay

Some financiers recognize that gradual revelation of information can be used to their advantage. For example, moral hazard problems can be mitigated if firms with good repayment records can obtain additional funds at lower cost. John and Nachman (1985) show that when a firm has to return repeatedly to the market for financing, it will benefit from considering the effects of its repayment choices on both current and future securities prices.

If the contingencies can be defined in advance, they can be incorporated in the original, complete contract. To illustrate, suppose that firms and financiers are both risk neutral, that the interest rate is zero, and that firms have no initial resources. In each period a firm adopting an investment project will generate a random income y, and the possible realizations of y are respectively y_G and y_B. If a lender cannot observe the cash flow, the most it will lend in an unsecured single period arrangement is y_B. If it were to lend more, the borrower could claim he had only earned y_B, and consequently repay only that amount.

Now consider a contract which the lender agrees to renew for a second period whenever the borrower makes a payment of more than y_B at the end of the first. However if only y_B is paid at the end of the first period, the arrangement will be terminated immediately. Assuming there are only two periods, the firm has no incentive to maintain a good reputation after time 1 has passed. Thus if it has the cash flow to do so, the firm will make a payment larger than y_B at time 1, but not at time 2. The arrangement is detailed in the two parts of Table 7.3.

The lender's expected profit from this arrangement is

$$\pi = -L + (1 - p_G)y_B + p_G(R + y_B - L) \tag{7.5}$$

as may be determined from the preceding table. Equation (7.5) can be rewritten as

$$\pi = -L + y_B + p_G(R - L) \tag{7.6}$$

---

[8]Other models can be developed in which the bank can use costly monitoring to ensure that firms do not adopt the bad technology.

TABLE 7.3 Firm Cash Flows

A. Time 1 Cash Flows and Payments to Financier

Time 0	Time 1 Realized Cash Flow	Time 1 Payments to Financier
L advanced	y_B	y_B—Arrangement terminated at the end of time 1 since first scheduled repayment not made in full.
	y_G	R—A second amount L is advanced since first scheduled repayment made in full.

B. Times 1 and 2 Cash Flows and Payments to Financier

Time 1 and Time 2 Realized Cash Flows	Time 1 and Time 2 Payments to Financier
(y_B, y_B)	$(y_B, 0)$
(y_B, y_G)	$(y_B, 0)$
(y_G, y_B)	(R, y_B)
(y_G, y_G)	(R, y_B)

The lender will profit if R is large enough to ensure that $\pi \geq 0$. The entrepreneur will enter the arrangement if R is small enough that she makes a profit when things turn out well for the firm at time 1; that is, if

$$-R + p_G(y_G - y_B) \geq -y_B \qquad (7.7)$$

which is equivalent to

$$R \leq y_B + p_G(y_G - y_B) = E(Y) \qquad (7.8)$$

Any repayment that satisfies both the lender's profit condition and the borrower's incentive conditions will constitute a viable arrangement.

Collateral as a Screening Device

Contracts providing for collateral can be used as screening devices to mitigate the effects of informational asymmetries. Suppose loan contracts take the form (C_k, R_k) where C_k is the amount of collateral required, R_k is the corresponding repayment, and k is the type of firm entering the contract, k

$\varepsilon \{G, B\}$. The symbols G and B refer to firms with good and bad quality projects, respectively. The good project pays off y with a relatively high success probability p_G, or 0 with probability $1 - p_G$. The riskier, bad project B pays off y with a relatively low success probability p_B or 0 with probability $1 - p_B$. The risk of the project is defined by its success probability, and borrowers know which type of project they have.

In all except the first instance examined below, lenders do not know which type of project the borrower has selected. All the bargaining power, that is, the power to set terms, is assumed to reside with the lender. The amount the borrower will be required to repay depends on the amount of collateral taken: $R_k = R_k (C_k)$. If the project succeeds, the realized cash flow is y, the lender is repaid R_k, and the borrower keeps $y - R_k$. If the project fails, the realized cash flow is zero, the borrower loses the posted collateral C_k, and the financier realizes δC_k, $0 < \delta < 1$.

If the lender could observe the success probability p_k, she would set the repayment amount and collateral so that the borrower's remaining income would just be

$$p_k(y - R_k) - (1 - p_k)C_k = \pi_{k, \min} \tag{7.9}$$

where $\pi_{k, \min}$ is the minimum amount the borrower must earn in order to undertake the project. Assume that the repayment amount is enough to make the deal attractive to the lender as well. If the lender could not observe p_k, the best she could do is to earn an average profit dependent on the proportion of good and bad borrowers who might apply. The proportion will depend on the repayment required. If the repayment amount were sufficiently high, only the bad borrowers would find it worthwhile to apply for financing.

Lender profits can be improved by setting up a contract that will both induce good borrowers to post collateral and induce bad borrowers not to misrepresent themselves as good borrowers. In order for a contract to provide the correct incentives, it must specify repayments R_G, R_B, and collateral C_G, such that it pays type B (high risk) borrowers to declare themselves honestly as high risk:

$$p_B(y - R_B) \geq p_B(y - R_G) - (1 - p_B)C_G \tag{7.10}$$

At the same time the terms must be such that type G borrowers find it worth their while to declare themselves low risk and post the collateral to back up their declaration:

$$p_G(y - R_G) - (1 - p_G)C_G \geq \pi_{G, \min} \tag{7.11}$$

Inequality (7.11) indicates that the amounts realized by a borrower must exceed her opportunity cost $\pi_{G,\min}$. The repayment R_G required of borrowers declaring themselves to be of good quality will be less than the repayment R_B, which means the low risk borrowers pay a lower effective interest rate. In essence, low risk borrowers bet they will not fail, post collateral to indicate their confidence, and thereby qualify for a lower interest rate than that paid by high risk borrowers. High risk borrowers do not take the same arrangement because to do so they would have to post collateral that, according to their private information, they have a high probability of losing.

COMPLETE CONTRACTS

Qian and Strahan (2007) find that in countries with strong creditor protection, bank loans have more concentrated ownership, longer maturities, and lower interest rates. The authors argue that more credit can be extended and on more generous terms when lenders have more credible threats in the event of default. Similar research shows a wide variety in choices of loan terms, but a complete discussion of variations is beyond the scope of this survey. Instead, this section illustrates two elementary choices based on complete contracts. The succeeding companion section provides similar illustrations for incomplete contracts.

Costly Verification

Suppose financiers cannot directly observe the firm's cash flow. As a result, financiers must either accept the realized cash flow value as reported by the firm, or conduct a costly audit. It will be worthwhile for financiers to conduct the audit if that costs less than the benefits expected to be gained from the verification. For example, suppose the borrower could report a cash flow y_R even though she actually realized $y > y_R$. The financier could detect a propensity to report falsely by stipulating a repayment function and by designing an audit rule. If the firm's cash flow report is audited, the financier incurs a fixed cost γ; otherwise auditing costs are zero. Clearly, an audit rule cannot be efficient unless it minimizes expected audit costs. A first requirement for managing audit costs is to conduct an audit only if repayment is not made in full. A second requirement is to minimize expected auditing costs by writing the contract for a fixed repayment, and setting the repayment size so as to minimize the probability of having to conduct an audit. If both parties are risk neutral, such a debt contract will be both incentive compatible and efficient so long as the firm is required to pay all reportedly available cash flows whenever the announcement is less than the full amount of scheduled debt repayment (see Freixas and Rochet 2008).

Incentives to Report Honestly

Financiers can also try to design incentives for the borrower to report cash flows honestly. Suppose the borrower can be penalized for false reporting, using the penalty function

$$c(y, y_R) = \gamma |y - y_R| \tag{7.12}$$

where y is the actual cash flow, y_R the reported cash flow, and γ the proportional cost the borrower incurs if she does not report truthfully.[9] If $0 < \gamma < 1$, the borrower receives the realized cash flow, less the repayment (based on the reported cash flow) and less any penalty for not reporting truthfully:

$$\pi_B = y - R(y_R) - \gamma |y - y_R| \tag{7.13}$$

The function $R(y_R)$ represents the repayment to the lender. This mechanism is falsification proof if it is maximized at $y_R = y$, a situation that will occur if and only if

$$-\gamma \le R(y) \le \gamma \tag{7.14}$$

That is, the borrower faces an incentive to report truthfully if the amount by which repayment increases in y is less than the amount by which the penalty increases in y. By limited liability, $R(0) = 0$, which along with equation (7.14) means

$$R(y) \le \gamma y \tag{7.15}$$

In turn equation (7.15) means the lender cannot expect to be repaid more than $\gamma E(y)$. Then if L is the original amount lent and r the interest rate, the lender must also ensure that

$$(1 + r)L \le \gamma E(y)$$

---

[9]The model assumes the penalty will be paid if the borrower reports falsely. However, it does not stipulate how false reporting is detected, or how the penalty is actually collected.

If the borrower is risk averse and the lender risk neutral the optimal form of repayment is a call option[10] on the cash flow:

$$R(y) = \max(0, \ \gamma y - \alpha)$$

where α is some positive constant. This contract provides incentives for truthful reporting and can be shown to minimize the probability that it will be necessary to audit the firm if the financier is to receive the expected value of the contract. For example, an audit will only be conducted if $\gamma_R \leq \alpha/\gamma$; that is, if the borrower does not make the loan payment in full and the financier assumes control of the firm. If $y > \alpha/\gamma$, it is in the borrower's interest to make the scheduled repayment, since that maximize the amount of the proceeds he can retain.

INCOMPLETE CONTRACTS: INTRODUCTION

Diamond (2004) stresses that lenders can face difficulties in legal systems with ineffective enforcement, but if lenders do not attempt to collect from defaulting borrowers, the borrowers have greater incentives to default. Diamond argues that bank lenders would be more prone to enforce penalties if news about defaulting borrowers were to cause bank runs. In other words, tough collection schemes can help banks to retain depositor confidence. This section provides models of such schemes. It first shows how renegotiation can improve bondholder payoffs when cash flows are unverifiable, and how an incomplete contract can overcome what would otherwise be market failure. Another form of incomplete contract allows a bank to renegotiate a deal and extract a greater expected profit from it than could bondholders without the same freedom to renegotiate.

Bondholder Threat to Liquidate

A credible threat can improve bondholders' expected payoffs if they were to receive less than a scheduled repayment. The threat may even be effective enough to make viable an otherwise unviable transaction. Assume both the firm and bondholders are risk neutral, and that the interest rate is zero. The firm seeks one unit of money at time 0 in order to finance a project that generates cash flows at both times 1 and 2. At both time 1 and time 2 there are two possible cash flow realizations: y_H with probability p or y_L

---

[10]If $\alpha = 0$, the call option has the same payoff as a proportion of the firm's equity.

with probability $(1 - p)$; $y_H > y_L$. Thus the four possible cash flow patterns over two periods are (H, H), (H, L), (L, H) and (L, L), and they occur with probabilities p^2, $p(1 - p)$, $(1 - p)p$ and $(1 - p)^2$, respectively.

The firm operates for two periods unless bondholders shut it down early. The two-period profile of cash flows is assumed to be completely determined at time 1, but the realized values of the flows are assumed not to be verifiable by either party, or even by both parties acting together. Therefore no lender can write a complete contract contingent on the realized cash flow.[11]

Since interest rates are zero, the present (and the future) value of the firm equals the sum of the realized cash flows in the two periods, less the scheduled loan repayments. The realized cash flow at time 2 is zero if the firm is put out of business, and either y_H or y_L if the firm is allowed to continue operating in the second period. Bondholders can shut down operations after time 1 if they do not receive the full amount of the time 1 scheduled repayment. However if they do receive the time 1 repayment in full, bondholders permit the firm to continue operating for the second period.

In the event of liquidation the bondholders receive the larger of the cash flow y_L or the time 1 liquidation value A_1. The time 2 liquidation value is assumed to be $A_2 = 0$, so that the maximal amount a lender can realize at time 2 is just y_L. Since the bondholders cannot verify the firm's cash flow, the firm would never repay y_H at time 2. If $A_1 < y_L$ a liquidation threat is not credible, since the firm cannot be forced to repay more than y_L. In this case the bondholders can never expect repayment of more than $2y_L$. Since bondholders must advance 1 to finance the project, and since interest rates are assumed to be zero, the market will fail if $2y_L < 1$. The details are given in Table 7.4.

If $A_1 > y_L$ the liquidation threat is credible. Assuming that bondholders have no powers to renegotiate existing arrangements, they will shut down the firm if a scheduled time 1 payment is not made in full. In what follows we shall assume that the liquidation value is A_1, such that $2y_L < A_1 < y_L + R$. A firm that is shut down at time 1 cannot earn any income at time 2. Therefore, a firm that knows its cash flows will be (H, H) (remember they learn this at time 1) will want to continue operating, and will therefore make the time 1 scheduled repayment. A firm knowing its cash flows to be (H, L) will not default. If the firm were to default it would get nothing whereas if it pays R the firm gets to keep $y_H - R$ from the first period, but nothing from

---

[11] However, it would also be possible to stipulate that the firm would be liquidated if a contracted payment were not made at time 1. In the situation illustrated a complete contract could be written contingent on the size of the repayment received.

TABLE 7.4 Cash Flows and Their Distribution

	Cash Flows	Time 1 Repayments to Bondholders, Firm	Time 2 Repayments to Bondholders, Firm	Total Paid to Bondholders	Total Retained by Firm
NO CREDIBLE THREAT					
Firm always operates	yH, yH	$yL, yH - yL$	$yL, yH - yL$	$2yL$	$2(yH - yL)$
Firm always operates	yH, yL	$yL, yH - yL$	$yL, 0$	$2yL$	$yH - yL$
Firm always operates	yL, yH	$yL, 0$	$yL, yH - yL$	$2yL$	$yH - yL$
Firm always operates	yL, yL	$yL, 0$	$yL, 0$	$2yL$	0
CREDIBLE THREAT					
Let firm operate	yH, yH	$R, yH - R$	$yL, yH - yL$	$R + yL$	$2yH - R - yL$
Shut firm down		$A1, 0$	$0, 0$	$A1$	0
Let firm operate	yH, yL	$R, yH - R$	$yL, 0$	$R + yL$	$yH - R$
Shut firm down		$A1, 0$	$0, 0$	$A1$	0
Shut firm down	yL, yH	$A1, 0$	$0, 0$	$A1$	0
Shut firm down	yL, yL	$A1, 0$	$0, 0$	$A1$	0

Assume: $2yL \leq A1 \leq R + yL$

the second period. When the firm cannot offer more than y_L at time 1, the bondholders will shut it down and keep A_1.

The ability to threaten closure means that from the lender's point of view the financing will be viable whenever

$$p(R + y_L) + (1 - p)A_1 > 1 \qquad (7.16)$$

Condition (7.16) can be satisfied for sufficiently large values of both R and A_1 even if $2y_L < 1$, creating the possibility of market failure in the absence of a credible threat. For example, if $y_L = 1/6$ and $A_1 > 2/6$ then any value of $R > A_1 - 1/6$ will satisfy condition (7.16). Thus the threat to

TABLE 7.5 Timing of Contract, Renegotiation Decision, and Payoffs

Time 0	Time 1	Time 2
Contract is signed; R_0 determined	z is observed and parties decide whether to renegotiate	Action G or B is chosen, return obtained, and shared between lender and firm

liquidate can sometimes make market financing viable even if inability to invoke a credible threat would imply market failure.

Renegotiating a Bank Loan

Gorton and Kahn (1993) model how a bank might renegotiate with a borrower.[12] Essentially, depending on how the borrower's business evolves, the bank stipulates a right to renegotiate the loan contract, thus permitting it to contemplate a variety of outcomes ranging from full repayment, through extension, to completely forgiving the loan. In the following model, the bank will renegotiate rather than liquidate if the net present value of its loan repayments can be increased through restructured financing.[13]

The model has three times: 0, 1, and 2. The firm is assumed to borrow 1 at time 0, and agrees to repay R_0 at time 2. At time 1, both the borrower and the bank observe a (nonverifiable) signal z.[14] At that time a bank with a credible threat to liquidate can force renegotiation, thereby providing the firm with the incentive to choose a good investment project at time 2, and thus improve the prospects of both firm and bank. The timing is shown in Table 7.5.

The firm can choose between two investment projects. Project G has the returns distribution:

$$zy_G + A_2 \text{ with probability } p_G$$
$$A_2 \text{ with probability } (1 - p_G)$$

---

[12] This presentation is adapted from the simplified Gorton-Kahn model developed in Freixas and Rochet (1997, 114–118).

[13] This model illustrates one form of continued monitoring, a capability cited throughout the book as characteristic of bank governance.

[14] If they knew a signal would be available, most lenders would insist on receiving it before agreeing to the loan. The model may therefore be more suitably applied to situations in which lenders and their clients are surprised by the arrival of new information.

Project B has the returns distribution:

$$zy_B + A_2 \text{ with probability } p_B$$
$$A_2 \text{ with probability } (1 - p_B)$$

The assumptions $p_G y_G > p_B y_B$ and $y_G < y_B$ present the moral hazard problems discussed in 7.4.1. If lenders are to avoid the consequences of moral hazard, they must stipulate a repayment R_0, such that

$$p_G(zy_G + A_2 - R_0) \geq p_B(zy_B + A_2 - R_0) \tag{7.17}$$

Note that R_0 cannot be made too large without violating condition (7.17). As described in the subsection "Costly Verification," management must be motivated to choose the good project rather than the bad one. If the project fails, management gets nothing since the model assumes $R_0 > A_2$, meaning that financiers claim the entire amount A_2.

Condition (7.17) can be satisfied if z is known at the time of setting R_0. However, in the assumed circumstances z is not known when R_0 is set, and if the realized value of z is small enough then at time 1, then condition (7.17) will turn out to be violated for the given value of R_0. That is, for any given value of R_0 there is a critical value of $z^* = z^*(R_0)$, such that if $z < z^*$ management has an incentive to adopt the bad project. Given R_0, z^* is defined as the value of z that makes condition (7.17) an equality.

If the realized value of z is such that $z < z^*$, there is a potential for the bank to mitigate moral hazard by renegotiating the contract. Let the project have liquidation values A_1 and A_2 at times 1 and 2, respectively; $A_1 > A_2$. Suppose the possible realizations of z have a minimum value z_0 and suppose $p_B z_0 y_B \geq R_0 > A_2$ so that if the firm is allowed to continue until time 2 the lender will be repaid in full if the project succeeds, but not if it fails. The payments to both parties are illustrated for the case $z < z^*$ in Table 7.6.

TABLE 7.6 $z < z^*$, But Firm Continues until Time 2

$z < z^*$	Project Success	Project Failure
Payoff to lender	R_0	A_2
Payoff to borrower	$zy_B + A_2 - R_0$	0
Total payoff	$zy_B + A_2$	A_2

Suppose it is time 1 and the bank has no credible threat. In this case the lender cannot renegotiate, and her expected return is

$$\text{Prob}\{z > z^*\}[p_G R_0 + (1 - p_G)A_2] + \text{Prob}\{z < z^*\}[p_B R_0 + (1 - p_B)A_2] \tag{7.18}$$

The value of renegotiation lies in its potential to increase the lender's payoff, but in order for the bank to be able to force renegotiation, it must have a credible threat.[15] There is no credible threat if $z > z^*$, but if $z < z^*$, the threat is credible if also

$$A_1 > p_B R_0 + (1 - p_B)A_2 \tag{7.19}$$

Consider what would happen if equation (7.19) were satisfied. The bank's problem is to decide whether to liquidate early or to reset R_0 to a smaller value R_1 and allow the firm to continue in business. However, R_1 cannot be too large without again incurring moral hazard. The optimal decision is defined to be one that maximizes the bank's expected return,[16] taking account of the moral hazard possibility.

Continue to assume equation (7.19) and suppose the bank has all the negotiating power. Under these assumptions the bank can alter the repayment terms as it sees fit. The bank will liquidate the firm if that offers a higher expected value than other alternatives. However, if continuation has the higher expected value the bank can maximize its return by providing the borrower with an incentive to pick the better project. Suppose there is some value $R_1 < R_0$, such that

$$p_G R_1 + (1 - p_G)A_2 \geq A_1 > p_B R_0 + (1 - p_B)A_2 \tag{7.20}$$

Suppose, for a given value of z, that $R_1 = R_1(z)$ satisfies both equations (7.17) and (7.20). Then the bank will choose renegotiation rather than liquidation, because that increases the expected return of both the bank and the firm. For instance, if the bank sets

$$R_1 < (p_G z y_G - p_B z y_B)/(p_G - p_B) + A_2 \tag{7.21}$$

---

[15] As a practical alternative to finding a credible threat strategy, a contract might simply provide for renegotiation if the borrower has violated some of the original terms. The effectiveness of the threat is then the effectiveness of imposing legal sanctions.

[16] Although for simplicity the procedure is not developed here, the value of R_1 can be determined optimally using backward induction.

TABLE 7.7a $z < z^*$; before Renegotiation

	Project Success	Project Failure
Payoff to lender	R_0	A_2
Payoff to borrower	$zy_B + A_2 - R_0$	0
Total payoff	$zy_B + A_2$	A_2

TABLE 7.7b $z < z^*$; after Renegotiation

	Project Success	Project Failure
Payoff to lender	R_1	A_2
Payoff to borrower	$zy_G + A_2 - R_1$	0
Total payoff	$zy_G + A_2$	A_2

then equation (7.17) holds and the firm is motivated to choose the better project. The payoffs to both parties are shown in the two parts of Table 7.6.

The bank will profit from the renegotiation if

$$p_G R_1 + (1 - p_G)A_2 > p_B R_0 + (1 - p_B)A_2 \qquad (7.22)$$

INCOMPLETE CONTRACTS: FURTHER COMMENTS

This section further examines deals under uncertainty. In contrast to the previous section where cash flows were known but not verifiable, we now consider deals in which it is not possible to establish cash flow magnitudes using a probability distribution that is sufficiently precise to be useful. In some cases parties to the deal are aware that even though they cannot specify future contingencies exactly, the contingencies can still affect the deal's payoffs (see Hart 2001, 1,083). To complete such deals, financiers write contracts providing for adjustments to be made according to guidelines based on certain principles.

Uncertainty and Governance

A deal's payoff uncertainty can arise from a variety of sources, including client actions, third party actions, or changes in the economic environment. The different possible sources of uncertainty can affect financier responses. As one example, financiers may try to negotiate with different parties to absorb possible adverse impacts. In natural gas pipeline construction financiers may request their clients to obtain an advance ruling from the regulatory authorities, permitting the pipeline company to pass on any construction cost increases to consumers by increasing the cost of gas. The advance ruling has the effect of reducing the uncertainty that the project will be able to turn a profit large enough to repay the financiers.

Financiers may interpret management actions as signals indicating the possible gravity of different uncertainties. For example, management's willingness to join an endeavor likely evinces belief in the project's success, particularly if management personnel invest in the project. Equally, of course, resignation of key personnel could be taken as indicating management's lack of faith in project prospects.

Rating agencies are unlikely to play prominent information production roles under uncertainty, since their main function is to refine estimates of risks at relatively low cost.[17] However, consultants or other experts—observers with specialized knowledge—may be able to determine key implications of a deal's uncertainties. For example, market research experts might offer clients estimates of a product's likely sales volumes under different economic circumstances. This information could in turn affect the phasing of a business' product offerings and ultimately its profitability.

Ex Post Adjustment

All contracts involve client—financier interdependence, but the degree of interdependence is greater with an incomplete contract. For an uncertain deal to reach a successful conclusion, financier and client depend on each other to reveal information and to cooperate more fully than with a complete contract. This interdependence is usually reflected in arrangements that provide for greater flexibility in governance as and when originally unforeseen events occur. For example, the arrangements may include using equity in place of debt in order to obtain voting rights on the client's board rather than imposing contractual obligations such as maintaining a given working capital ratio.

---

[17]In the subprime meltdown of 2007–2008, it became clear that rating agencies had failed to assign appropriate ratings to complex CMOs and CDOs until relatively late in the subprime lending boom. Although the rating agencies might not have faced uncertainty initially, they clearly did so after investors lost confidence in CMOs and CDOs. After the loss of confidence market prices for the instruments sometimes exhibited large discounts attributable at least as much to investor fears as to objective changes in the underlying security.

Ex post adjustments can sometimes benefit both financier and client, as the preceding models of risky deals have indicated. Under uncertainty, ex post adjustments can be based on learning about the key profitability features of a deal and how to manage those features effectively. They may also allow clients to learn how to operate the firm more profitably, or to enhance the probability of its long-run survival. For example, some developing countries have found their financiers willing to accept equity in exchange for debt previously issued. The country obtains the advantage of more flexible repayment terms, while the financier may find the value of the existing investment increased. From the client's perspective, equity financing eliminates the technical possibility of default and its attendant renegotiation costs, an important consideration when debt carries fixed interest payments that might become too great for the debtor to bear. On the other hand, debt renegotiation subsequent to a default can be cumbersome and lengthy because it can mean obtaining agreement from a relatively large number of lenders who may not agree on the terms of the renegotiation.

A given set of terms does not necessarily offer net benefits in every possible outcome state; compare Hart (2001). A contract that does not provide for unforeseeable contingencies can be finely tuned to work perfectly under one set of circumstances, but can work badly if other circumstances are encountered. A more flexible contract that contains provisions for unforeseeable contingencies may not work perfectly under any set of circumstances, but there may be a considerable variety of different circumstances under which it works relatively well. The parties to a deal do not always recognize that their agreement constitutes an incomplete contract. Moreover, a failure of this type can weaken the financiers' ability to profit from the deal. If and when the incompleteness is recognized, financiers will then try to devise adjustments, but they will be in a weaker position than if they had originally foreseen the need for adjustments.[18]

Bypassing Uncertainty

One obvious way of dealing with uncertainty is to pass its effects on to another party, say the client. For example a few Japanese banks, concerned in the later 1980s about the possibility of eventual peaking in the then

---

[18] The credit crunch of 2007–2008 offers numerous examples. For instance, banks have found themselves forced, for reputational reasons, to take back the default risk on instruments they previously regarded as having been sold. As a second example, credit default swaps that were originally thought to be safe hedges came to be questioned as the issuing insurance companies' capital dwindled and could not be replaced.

rapidly rising Japanese real estate prices, were able to securitize some of their property loans using equity instruments. This strategy passed the risk of capital loss on to the purchasers of the equities. Of course, since it also passed on any future capital gains, it may well have been that the sellers placed a lower expected value on possible capital gains than did the purchasers.

Collateral can also be used to bypass the effects of uncertainties, since financing can be secured by the market value of the collateral rather than by the firm's uncertain cash flows, as discussed earlier in this chapter. Still further, various forms of guarantees might also be used for the same purposes. For example, governments frequently provide export credit insurance to businesses engaged in foreign trade. Export credit insurance cannot always be obtained from the private sector, because it may involve insuring shipments against risks that neither the financier nor the client can control, such as losses from acts of war. As a second example, clients can be bonded to cover financiers against losses arising from fraud or malfeasance. As a third example, financings may be insured against such eventualities as death of key management personnel.

Research Findings

Davydenko and Strebulaev (2007) examine an aspect of uncertainty in asking whether the strategic actions of borrowers and lenders can affect corporate debt values. The authors find higher bond spreads for firms that have the capability to renegotiate debt contracts relatively easily: The firm's threat of strategic default depresses bond values ex ante. Moreover, the effect of strategic action is greater when lenders are vulnerable to threats, as might occur in the cases of relatively large proportions of managerial shareholding, simple debt structures, and high liquidation costs.

REFERENCES

Arrow, Kenneth J. 1974. *Essays on the theory of risk-bearing*. Amsterdam: North-Holland.

Axelson, Ulf. 2007. Security design with investor private information. *Journal of Finance* 62: 2,587–2,632.

Benson, E.D. 1979. "The search for information by underwriters and its impact on municipal interest cost." *Journal of Finance* 34: 871–885.

Davydenko, Sergei A., and Ilya A. Strebulaev. 2007. Strategic actions and credit spreads. *Journal of Finance* 62: 2,633–2,671.

Diamond, Douglas W. 2004. Committing to commit: Short-term debt when enforcement is costly. *Journal of Finance* 59: 1,447–1,479.

Fabozzi, Frank J., Franco Modigliani, and Michael G. Ferri. 2001. *Foundations of financial markets and institutions*. Upper Saddle River, N.J.: Prentice-Hall.

Fabozzi, Frank J., Franco Modigliani and Michael G. Ferri. 2001. *Foundations of Financial Markets and Institutions*, Upper Saddle River, NJ: Prentice-Hall.

Fama, Eugene F. 1985. What's different about banks? *Journal of Monetary Economics* 15: 29–39.

Freixas, Xavier and Jean-Charles Rochet. 1997. *Microeconomics of Banking*. Cambridge, MA: MIT Press.

Freixas, Xavier, and Jean-Charles Rochet. 2008. *Microeconomics of Banking*, 2nd ed. Cambridge, MA: MIT Press.

Gorton, G., and J. Kahn. 1993. The design of bank loan contracts, collateral, and renegotiation. Working Paper 1–93, Rodney L. White Center for Financial Research, Wharton School, University of Pennsylvania.

Hart, Oliver. 2001. Financial contracting. *Journal of Economic Literature* 39: 1,079–1,100.

Hart, Oliver D. and J. Moore. 1998. Default and renegotiation: A dynamic model of debt. *Quarterly Journal of Economics* 113: 1–41.

John, Kose, and David C. Nachman. 1985. Risky debt, investment incentives, and reputation in a sequential equilibrium. *Journal of Finance* 40: 863–878.

Kaplan, Steven N., and Per Stromberg. 2004. Characteristics, contracts, and actions: evidence from venture capitalist analyses. *Journal of Finance* 59: 2,177–2,210.

Qian, Jun, and Philip E. Strahan. 2007. How laws and institutions shape financial contracts: the case of bank loans. *Journal of Finance* 62: 2,803–2,834.

Ross, Stephen A. 1977. The determination of financial structure: The incentive-signalling approach. *Bell Journal of Economics* 7: 23–40.

Sufi, Amir, and Atif R. Mian. 2007. The consequences of mortgage credit expansion: Evidence from the 2007 mortgage default crisis. NBER Working Paper No. W13936.

Three

Asset Prices and Market Relations

Financiers and investors spend much of their time establishing the values of financial instruments. For example, a financier needs to assess the value of a loan contract in order to determine the extent to which funds can profitably be advanced against it, and a trader needs an estimate of what a security might be worth before she bids to acquire it. Since risks can vary greatly across instruments, it is important to determine how risk and value are related. It would be even more important to have systematic ways of recognizing how uncertainty affects an instrument's valuation, but this part of financial theory is still relatively underdeveloped, partly because the effects of uncertainty are largely unquantifiable.

CHAPTER 8

Pricing Stocks and Bonds

This chapter focuses on methods for valuing financial instruments under risk, in markets where all opportunities for arbitrage have been taken up. This review provides a point of departure for studying securities price relations in practice. Some highly active markets exhibit price relations that conform closely to the results of financial theory, while other markets exhibit large and persistent deviations from theoretical predictions. Hence after summarizing the principal results of asset pricing theory, the chapter attempts to assess the pricing implications of various market imperfections. While financial research is actively concerned with assessing the pricing effects of influences like informational differences, a practical explanation of asset price relations in different markets is still far from being fully realized. Nevertheless, it is possible to present some qualitative guidelines for valuing instruments in practice.

Perhaps the most straightforward way of pricing a security is to compare its price to those of other similar securities when trading profit opportunities have been eliminated. Thus, Chapter 8 reviews the pricing of corporate securities in the assumed absence of arbitrage opportunities. Conveniently, arbitrage-free prices are related to each other by an underlying measure known as a risk-neutral probability. The chapter shows both how risk-neutral probabilities can be found, and how the values of securities with different risks can be calculated using the risk-neutral probabilities. In particular, the chapter shows how debt and equity can be used to divide up the risks of earnings generated by a given asset, and how the instruments' values are related to the value of the underlying asset. In addition, the chapter shows how the same risk-neutral probabilities can be used to address some of the valuation problems presented by bonds.

This chapter and Chapter 9 review how securities are priced under the neoclassical paradigm. This chapter studies the pricing of corporate securities and the next chapter the pricing of derivative securities, both under the assumptions of no arbitrage opportunities. These two chapters provide benchmarks that are used throughout the rest of the book to assess how such effects as institutional rigidities, transactions costs, and behavioral influences can cause observed prices to deviate from the neoclassical predictions.

PROFIT-SEEKING ELIMINATES ARBITRAGE OPPORTUNITIES

A financial asset's value is based on the timing and the probability distribution of the payments it promises. Financial theory establishes that payments to be received in the future can be converted to their present value using appropriate discount factors. For example, the appropriate interest rate for discounting payments to be received with certainty is the riskless rate.[1] In a market where agents are risk-averse, the appropriate discount factors for risky payments use interest rates greater than the riskless rate.[2] This chapter begins by showing how asset values are related to each other when no arbitrage possibilities remain, and how differing risks of receiving payments are reflected in the risk premiums.

To calculate asset prices under the assumption of no arbitrage opportunities, the neoclassical paradigm inquires how they would be related at equilibrium. For example, suppose there are two assets with identical payment streams, streams known either with certainty or to have identical probability distributions. Since there are no differences between the two payments streams the two assets should both have the same market value,[3] and this result must hold at equilibrium in a competitive market with no transactions costs. If it did not, profit-seekers would buy the cheaper asset and sell the

---

[1]The riskless interest rate may change from period to period, as some of the later calculations in the chapter recognize.

[2]Differences between rates are referred to as "risk premiums."

[3]The assumption of identical probability distributions means equality of such concepts as market risk and default risk, as will later be shown.

dearer, thereby earning arbitrage profits. Such profit opportunities could not persist indefinitely, but neither would arbitrage-based trading end before the instruments' prices converged. In other words, profit-oriented trading will eliminate arbitrage opportunities when there are no impediments to trading the assets in question.[4]

Financial market efficiency can lead to an absence of arbitrage opportunities, but efficiency is actually a different concept because it examines value in relation to underlying information about the assets' payoffs. Since underlying information will not necessarily be distributed evenly among all market participants, possible differences are described as leading to strong, semistrong, or weak forms of efficiency. Stock prices in a strongly efficient market fully reflect all available information, both public and private. The efficient market hypothesis based on strong form efficiency states that any investment strategy based on available information cannot outperform the market, because all available information is accounted for in prevailing stock prices. In particular, neither technical nor fundamental analysis will lead to strategies that can outperform a stongly efficient market.

Stock prices in a semistrong, efficient market reflect all available public information, while stock prices in a weakly efficient market reflect only the influence of past prices. If the market is weak form efficient, then investors cannot earn abnormal returns by trading on the information embodied in past prices, since that information is already reflected in current prices. On the other hand, weak form efficiency does not rule out the possibility that fundamental analysis can be used to identify undervalued and overvalued stocks. Therefore, profits can be earned by keen investors looking for profitable companies through researching the financial statements. Although practitioners and scholars subscribe to a wide range of viewpoints as to how market efficiency varies across markets, a considerable body of empirical evidence indicates that markets are at least weak form efficient. Additionally, the more liquid the market, the more active the trading in it, and the more homogenous the instruments traded, the stronger the form of market efficiency that is likely to prevail.

---

[4]Arbitraging in its technical sense means profiting from trades without taking any risk. In practice, the financial markets witness both the riskless arbitrage opportunities discussed in this chapter and transactions commonly known as "risk arbitrage." The latter phrase, used in practice but not in theoretical discussions, describes such transactions as purchasing shares of a potential takeover target in the hope of making a profit.

PRICING SECURITIES RELATIVE TO EACH OTHER

The absence of arbitrage opportunities is a necessary condition[5] for market equilibrium. If any arbitrage opportunities were to remain, trading would continue and prices would keep adjusting until the opportunities were eliminated. Thus at market equilibrium the prices of different instruments offering the same promised payments with the same probability distributions will have the same value, at least as long as any instrument can be exchanged for any other without payment of transactions costs. As will be shown shortly, this observation has important implications: The absence of arbitrage opportunities makes it possible to calculate the value of any security from any other, so long as the relations between the security's promised payments can be described exactly. To illustrate the usefulness of these results, we first consider some simple examples and then show how financial theory can be used, still in the absence of arbitrage, to calculate prices for all securities.

Consider first whether there are any practical differences between $5 in coins and a $5 bill. If it is only total buying power that matters, there are no practical differences between the two: The coins should exchange freely for the $5 bill and vice versa. On the other hand, any impediments to free exchange of the coins for the bill, or vice versa, can frustrate the principle's workings. For example, if you have $50 worth of pennies, a bank will not likely exchange them for a $50 bill. Rather, they are likely to impose a service charge for making the exchange. You will see the same thing in supermarket machines that accept your coins in exchange for paper currency. Usually the machine is programmed to deduct a fee for making the exchange.[6]

As a second example, consider assets with risky payoffs. Suppose you have made a bet with someone that involves paying them $10 if a fair coin comes up tails, and their paying you $10 if the fair coin comes up heads. Compare this with a second bet, on which you will get $10 if the first roll of a balanced die comes up 1, 2, or 3, and will lose $10 if the first roll comes up 4, 5, or 6. In either case it is assumed that both you and your companion

---

[5]Most of the time, we shall simply assume the absence of arbitrage opportunities and not specify whether or not an equilibrium exists.

[6]As an example of a puzzle, Scottish bank notes can be used or redeemed at par in London, but if one presents Scottish bank notes to a currency dealer outside the United Kingdom, they are sometimes bought at a discount relative to British pounds. The ability to exchange these notes at par in London denies the existence of a risk premium in the United Kingdom. Thus currency dealers in other countries either have different expectations from London banks or face less demand for Scottish bank notes and find it more costly to take them into inventory.

TABLE 8.1 The Risky Assets S and Y

	S_1: Payoff at Time 1	Y_1: Payoff at Time 1	Probability
Good scenario	100.00	200.00	p
Bad scenario	95.00	190.00	$1 - p$
Time 0 values	$S_0 = Y_0/2$	$Y_0 = 2S_0$	

will honor the arrangement as stated. The probability of winning (or losing) is then one-half, whichever one of the two bets you take. The principle of valuation in the absence of arbitrage opportunities says that either bet has the same value to you, because either offers exactly the same payoffs with the same probability distribution, and there are no impediments to substituting one bet for the other.

As a third and final example, suppose one security promises to pay the amounts specified by the risky asset S_1 whose payoffs are shown in Table 8.1. Suppose that a second security Y_1, also shown in Table 8.1, promises exactly twice the amounts specified by S_1. That is, each outcome is twice as large, but occurs with the same probabilities as for the original asset. In the absence of arbitrage opportunities the second instrument must then have a value that is exactly twice that of the original risky asset. The payments from holding $2S_1$ are exactly the same as the payments from holding Y_1, regardless of which outcome is actually realized. Substituting $2S_1$ for Y_1 leaves the asset holder's position unchanged, and since the positions are the same, the value the asset holder places on either of them is also the same. A further implication of this conclusion is that the time 0 price of the asset, S_0, must equal $Y_0/2$.

It is possible to utilize the same ideas for assets that are related in more complicated ways. However, in order to establish the possibility, it is convenient to define some tools that will help the discussion to proceed.

CALCULATING RISK-NEUTRAL PROBABILITY MEASURES[7]

The absence of arbitrage opportunities can be used to organize valuation calculations in an especially convenient way. The procedure involves defining new quantities called *risk-neutral probabilities*. Despite the name

---

[7]For a full discussion of the relations between no arbitrage opportunities, the absence of dominant trading strategies, and the law of one price, see Pliska (1997, 4–10).

risk-neutral probabilities, the method actually takes risk into account, because risk premiums are embodied in the securities prices used to calculate the probabilities. Formally, a risk-neutral probability distribution is defined so that the expected value of an asset's payments, when discounted at the risk-free rate, equals the asset's current market value.[8] Moreover, if that current market value is determined in a risk-averse market, it incorporates a risk premium.

The calculations involve the following ideas. Begin with a security's value at the current time, here denoted time 0, and assume a value for the risk-free interest rate between time 0 and time 1, the time at which securities' payoffs will be realized. For any given security when viewed from the perspective of time 0, the time 1 payoffs are assumed to be describable by a probability distribution. For example, suppose a security whose time 0 value is $S_0 = 92.00$, might pay off either 95.00 or 105.00 at time 1. Only one of the payoffs will actually be realized, but from the time 0 perspective no one knows which it will be. Suppose also that the riskless interest rate between time 0 and time 1 is 5%, so that if we discount time 1 payoffs at the riskless rate to find their time 0 value, we arrive at 95.00/1.05 for the smaller possible payoff and 105.00/1.05 for the larger.

If we now assume that the price S_0 is a price that admits no arbitrage opportunities,[9] the risk-neutral probabilities q and $1 - q$ are defined to satisfy[10]

$$92.00 = q(105.00/1.05) + (1 - q)(95.00/1.05)$$

Consequently, $q = [92.00(1.05) - 95.00]/[105.00 - 95.00] = 0.16$ satisfies the above condition, as does $1 - q = 0.84$. Shortly, we will

---

[8]If the asset has only two possible outcomes, its time 00 value and time 1 payoffs are sufficient for determining the risk-adjusted probability distribution whenever the risk-free interest rate is known. If assets have three outcomes, the values of two instruments will be needed to find the risk-adjusted probability distribution, and so on. More formal details of the approach are given in the next section, "Using Risk-Neutral Probabilities for Securities Valuation."

[9]The no arbitrage condition means that all securities traded in the market have prices that admit no arbitrage opportunities. After showing how a risk-neutral probability is calculated, we will use it to price other securities, and at that point the usefulness of the no arbitrage opportunities assumption will become clearer.

[10]If there are two possible payoffs we say there are two possible future states of the world. In this case there are two risk-neutral probabilities, one for each state. Moreover since there are only two states, one of them must actually be realized at time 1, and so the probabilities for the two states must add to unity.

show how the same risk-neutral probabilities can be used to value other securities.[11]

Formally, when there are only two possible future states of the world, finding the risk-neutral probabilities means finding a vector

$$\mathbf{Q} \equiv (q, 1 - q)'$$

whose components are both positive and satisfy the value calculation

$$S_0 = E_Q[S_1/(1 + r)|\Im_0] \tag{8.1}$$

The right-hand side of equation (8.1) means "take the expectation, under the risk-neutral probability, of the discounted value of the time 1 pay-offs." The effect of riskless interest accumulation from time 0 to time 1 is described by $1 + r$, so that the riskless discount factor is $1/(1 + r)$. The symbol $\Im_t$ means the expectation is to be taken conditionally on the basis of what is known at time t, and in the present example $t = 0$.

To see how risk-neutral probabilities are used to value securities, suppose q, $1 - q$, and the riskless rate are all given. In the absence of arbitrage opportunities, it would be correct to use these data to calculate the value of S_0. The calculations look exactly like discounted expected value calculations.[12] Since $1 + r = 1.05$,

$$S_0 = [105.00q + 95.00(1 - q)]/1.05$$

Substituting the value of q into the last line

$$S_0 = \{105.00(0.16) + 95.00(0.84)\}/1.05 = 92.00$$

Of course, the calculations must lead to the time 0 value of the asset, because the risk-neutral probabilities were defined to give that result. But the importance of risk-neutral probabilities is that once they have been

---

[11] The theoretical rationale for making the calculations in this way is developed in such works as Pliska (1997).

[12] It is important to reiterate that risk-neutral valuation does not mean that interest rates on risky assets have no risk premium. Risk-neutral probabilities incorporate a risk adjustment whenever the market is risk-averse. If the market were risk-neutral the asset price S_0 would be $100.00/1.10$ rather than $97.90/1.10$. Moreover the risk-neutral probabilities would then equal the underlying objective probabilities, assumed to be $1/2$.

obtained, they can also be used to value other related instruments—so long as the instruments' prices admit no arbitrage opportunities.

One way to see that risk-neutral probabilities can be used to value different instruments (other validity checks will be presented later) is to recalculate the value by which S_0 exceeds the 95.00/1.05; that is, the amount a bank would lend against the asset at the riskless interest rate of 5%. If the asset has a high time 1 payoff, there will be $10.00 = 105.00 - 95.00$ left over after the debt repayment has been made. However if the asset has a low time 1 payoff, there will be just enough to pay the bank; nothing will be left over for the asset's owners. Thus according to the risk-neutral probability calculation the value of the asset over and above the time 0 value of the debt, $95.00/1.05 = 90.48$, is

$$[q(105.00 - 95.00)/1.05]$$
$$= [0.16(10.00) + (0.84)0.00]/1.05$$
$$= 1.60/1.05 = 1.52$$

Finally, adding up the values of the debt and the equity gives

$$90.48 + 1.52 = 92.00$$

exactly the total asset value, verifying the manner in which the 1.52 was obtained.

USING RISK-NEUTRAL PROBABILITIES FOR SECURITIES VALUATION

It can be shown by advanced methods (see Huang and Litzenberger 1988, Pliska 1997) that if at a given time the prices for all securities traded in a market admit no arbitrage opportunities, then the risk-neutral probabilities defined above will exist and can be used to value any risky asset.[13] To give an elementary demonstration of how the risk-neutral probabilities are used for securities valuation, we record some conventions. Suppose as before that there are only two time points, the present time 0 and a future time 1. Securities values are found at time 0 by taking the expected present value

---

[13] If one does not assume the absence of arbitrage opportunities, then risk-neutral probabilities need not exist, and if they do, they are not necessarily unique. For a full discussion of these issues, see Pliska (1997).

of their time 1 payoffs in different states of the world, with the expectation being calculated under the risk-neutral probability measure. Suppose there are K states of the world, described by

$$\{s_1, \ldots, s_K\}$$

and that $N \geq K$ securities are traded. Exactly K of these securities are assumed to have linearly independent time 1 payoffs, which means that if you construct a portfolio of the K securities you will have an asset that will pay off some positive amount in each of the K states. Finally, suppose the market is in equilibrium so that each of the N securities has a given time 0 market value S_{0n}; $n = 1, \ldots, N$. Transactions costs are assumed to be zero, and therefore have no impact on securities price relations.

Let $S_{n,k}$ be the (time 1) payoff to security n in state k. Then the time 1 payoffs discounted at the riskless rate are

$$S^*_{n,k} = S_{n,k}/B_1$$

where $B_1 \equiv 1/(1+r)$ is a discount factor reflecting the riskless rate of interest over the time period in question. Now consider the system of equations $S_1^*Q = S_0$, where S_1^* is an $N \times K$ matrix of the securities payoffs S_{nk}^*, discounted at the riskless interest rate, Q is a $K \times 1$ vector of risk-neutral probabilities, and S_0 is an N-vector of time 0 securities prices. The values of S_1^*, S_0, and the riskless discount factor $1/B_1$ are all assumed to be given. Since the matrix S_1^* contains K linearly independent rows, it is possible to find Q by solving[14] the system $S_1^*Q = S_0$; that is $Q = (S^*_1)^{-1}S_0$; where $(S^*_1)^{-1}$ is the inverse of S^*_1. In the example of section 8.3, $K = 2$ and the solution is $Q = (0.29, 0.71)'$.

Risk-neutral probabilities can be further interpreted by regarding any security as a package of fundamental instruments called *unit contingent claims*. A unit contingent claim has a payoff of exactly one unit in a given state, say state k, and zero in all other states. In each state, the payoff to the package of claims exactly equals the payoff the security offers in that state. Using the values of Q, it is then possible to find the value of the discounted payoff to any contingent claim. This time 0 value is equal to q_k/B_1, where q_k is the risk-neutral probability associated with state k. If security j pays off S_{jk} dollars in state k, then that payoff must be worth $S_{jk}q_k/B_1$ at time 0.

---

[14] Each component of Q must be positive and the sum of the components must equal unity if the risk-neutral measure is to value securities according to the law of one price; see, for example, Pliska (1997).

Adding up these quantities over all possible states gives the value of the security at time 0.

For example, suppose there are four states of the world and the values of Q for the four states are respectively 0.15, 0.20, 0.35, and 0.30. If the riskless interest rate is 0.03, then the time 0 value of a contingent claim on state 1 is 0.15(1.00)/1.03. If you have a security that offers a time 1 payoff distribution of 3.00, 7.00, 0.00, and 2.00 in the four states, then the time 0 value of that security will be [3.00(0.15) + 7.00(0.20) + 0.00(0.35) + 2.00(0.30)]/1.03 = 2.45/1.03 = 2.38. Note that if state 2 is realized, the value of your security at time 1 will be 7.00, but if state 3 is realized, the value of your security at time 1 will be zero—the example is that of a risky investment whose payoffs vary according to an underlying probability distribution.[15]

DEBT VERSUS EQUITY

Financial instruments of different sorts present different kinds of risks, but under the absence of arbitrage opportunities their values can still be related to each other using risk-neutral probability calculations. For example, the payoffs to risky assets can be divided using debt and equity, and the two instruments have payoffs with different risk characteristics. [16]

How Are Risks Divided with Debt and Equity?

Let us now interpret the asset payoffs S_1, introduced in the section "Calculating Risk-Neutral Probability Measures," as cash flows generated by a firm (e.g., the net earnings from its operations). Suppose that a bank lender (or purchaser of a bond issued by the firm[17]) believes the firm's realized earnings will either be $105.00 or $95.00 as before. Also, suppose the current market value of the firm's assets is 89.00. If the loan is to be repaid from the realized cash flow, there is a maximum amount the banker will lend on a risk-free basis. Assuming the risk-free rate of interest to be 10%,

---

[15] Unless all agents in the market are risk-neutral, the objective probabilities of the possible payoffs will be different from the risk-neutral probabilities. This issue is examined further in the following examples.

[16] Note, however, that whatever the risks, they are all defined according to the same set of underlying events, known as a state description.

[17] For simplicity both bonds and bank loans are assumed to perform the same function in this example. But recall that Chapter 6 showed that bank loans differ from bond investments in that the bank typically has greater governance capability than the bond investor.

TABLE 8.2 Valuing Debt and Equity

	S_1(Firm)	D_1(Debt)	E_1(Equity)
Time 1 High Payoffs	105.00	95.00	10.00
Time 1 Low Payoffs	95.00	95.00	00.00
Time 0 Values	97.90/1.10 =89.00	95.00/1.10 = 86.36	2.90/1.10 = 2.64

that maximal amount is 95.00/1.10. (If the principal and interest to be re-paid one year from now are exactly 95.00, the proceeds are valued today at 95.00/1.10 = 86.36.) Given the assumed distribution, by advancing no more than 95.00/1.10, the lender is assured of getting back 95.00 at time 1 whether the firm does well or badly. With such a deal the lender is assured of earning 10% without risk. A loan for more than 95.00/1.10 could not be always paid in full from the firm's cash flows, because in the less favorable scenario the firm will only have a cash flow of 95.00. In other words, loans with a promised repayment of more than \$95.00 are subject to default risk.

Assuming the firm does raise 95.00/1.10 on a risk-free basis, consider what happens one year later when the firm's cash flows are realized and the loan is due to be repaid. The promised 95.00 principal and interest will be paid to the lenders, and any cash flows in excess of 95.00 will be available as a return to the firm's shareholders. Symbolically, this division of payoffs into debt and equity can be written $S_1 \equiv D + E$, where S_1 represents the asset's payoffs, D the principal and interest payments to debt holders, and E the payments to shareholders, all at time 1. The data for the present example are shown in Table 8.2.

The column headings of Table 8.2 indicate the available funds and the amounts paid to the two classes of security holders for the two possible asset values. Each of the first two rows represents a scenario, the first showing the payoffs to be received if the firm does well, the second if it does badly. By summing across a row of Table 8.2, it can be seen that the combined payoffs to debt and equity exactly equal the payoffs to the firm as a whole. However, note also that the payments to the debt holders are the same whether the firm does well or badly. Thus the debt in the current example has a riskless payoff, but the equity does not. Instruments with different risk characteristics will command different expected rates of return, as we shall see when we apply the risk-neutral probabilities to their valuation.

Valuing Debt and Equity

The principle of determining prices in the absence of arbitrage opportunities can be used to value the debt and equity payoffs defined above. First, the fact that the row payoffs in columns D and E sum to the row payoff in column S_1 means that in the absence of arbitrage opportunities the time 0 values in columns D and E must also add to the time 0 value in column E. That is, you only have to know two of the columns' time 0 values to determine the third—so long as the assumption of pricing in the absence of arbitrage opportunities is maintained. Continuing to assume the riskless interest rate is 10%, the market value of a riskless investment in the firm is 95.00/1.10. Assuming further that the market value of the whole firm continues to be 89.00, it follows from the absence of arbitrage opportunities[18] that the value of the equity in the project must equal the difference between the value of the whole firm and the value of its debt. That is, the equity is worth

$$E_Q[S_1/B_1|\mathfrak{I}_0] - D_1/B_1 = 89.00 - 95.00/1.10$$
$$= [97.90 - 95.00]/1.10 = 2.90/1.10 = 2.64$$

Table 8.2 verifies the following observations. The 89.00 at the bottom of column S_1 is given by assumption, and the value 86.36 at the bottom of column D must be the value of the riskless debt if interest rates are 10%. (The debt is riskless because it has the same payoff whether the firm does well or badly.) It can be seen that under either the high or the low payoff scenario, the payoffs to the equity are exactly the same as the payoffs to the whole firm minus the payoffs to the debtholders. It follows that, in the absence of arbitrage opportunities, the value of the equity equals the value of the whole firm less the value of the debt.

Risky Debt

Now suppose the firm issues debt with a promised repayment of more than 95.00. It is clear from the total payoff distribution shown in Table 8.2 that the firm will not always be able to redeem such a promise in full. For example, suppose the firm issued debt that nominally promised to pay 99.00 in principal and interest at time 1. Assuming the firm has no other resources, and that there are no additional costs of default, the payoffs to the security holders would be as shown in Table 8.3.

In this case the debt is not riskless. The amount that can be repaid is 99.00 if the firm does well, but is only 95.00 if earnings turn out badly. The value displayed for the debt, 87.42, will be calculated shortly.

Since the two possible realized outcomes are assumed to be equally likely in the present example, the expected discounted value of the time 1

---

[18] Known, famously in this context, as the Modigliani-Miller theorem.

TABLE 8.3 Valuing Debt and Equity When Debt Promises to Pay 99.00

	S_1 (Firm)	D_1 (Debt)	E_1 (Equity)
Time 1 High Payoffs	105.00	99.00	6.00
Time 1 Low Payoffs	95.00	95.00	0.00
Time 0 Values	89.00	87.42	1.58

payments to the debt holders is

$$E[D_1/B_1|\Im_0] = [(99.00) + (95.00)]/1.10 = 97.00/1.10 = 88.18$$

where E means "take the expected value," in this case using the objective rather than the risk-neutral probabilities. In the absence of arbitrage opportunities, the time 0 value of the debt must be less than $97.00/1.10 = 88.18$, since discounting an expected value at the riskless rate is not sufficient to adjust for the debt being risky.

To put the matter another way, the firm cannot become worth more just because it has changed the amount it promises to pay debt holders. Investors look at what the firm can earn, and will value its securities in relation to those earnings, no matter what the nominal promises made by the firm are. Thus, to obtain the value of the debt, it is only necessary to value the equity and subtract that amount from the value of the firm. Given the two payoffs of 105.00 and 95.00, the riskless interest rate of 10%, and the current market value of the firm as 89.00, the risk-neutral probabilities, calculated as in section 8.3, are respectively $q = 0.29$ and $1 - q = 0.71$. Hence the value of the equity is

$$E_Q[E_1/B_1|\Im_0] = (0.29)[6.00]/1.10 = 1.58$$

as shown in the lower right-hand corner of Table 8.3. It then follows immediately that the value of the debt must be $89.00 - 1.58 = 87.42$. Continuing to suppose that the two earnings scenarios are equally probable, the expected debt repayment is

$$E[D_1|\Im_0] = (1/2)[(99.00) + (1/2)(95.00)] = 97.00$$

Therefore, the discount rate applied to the debt is

$$(97.00 - 87.42)/87.42 = 0.1096$$

or 10.96%. Since the riskless rate has been assumed to be 10.00%, the risk premium on this particular debt issue is 0.96%.

The Risk-Adjusted Cost of Financial Distress

Almeida and Philippon (2007) consider implications of risk premiums changing over time in response to changing market and economic conditions. They argue that financial distress is more likely to happen in bad times, and that the present value of financial distress depends on the current size of risk premiums. The authors estimate this value using risk-adjusted probabilities of default, derived from corporate bond spreads. For a firm rated BBB, its benchmark calculations show that the NPV of distress is 4.5% of predistress value. In contrast, a valuation that ignores risk premiums generates an NPV of only 1.4%. Thus the authors conclude that marginal distress costs can be as large as the marginal tax benefits of debt, meaning that changing risk premiums can help explain why firms appear to use debt more conservatively than has been suggested by other previous studies.

APPLICATION: BOND VALUATION AND MARKET RISK

Although in practice bonds are regarded as low-risk securities, this does not mean they are completely riskless. First, many corporate bonds and even some government bonds are subject to default, meaning that they might not be redeemed in full with interest. Second, even if the issuer of a bond has such an impeccable credit rating that for all practical purposes the bond can be regarded as default free, bond returns can still vary randomly if the risk-free discount rate varies, or if it is affected by changes in price levels. These types of risk are forms of market risk, and will be examined in this chapter. Valuing bonds subject to default risk is discussed in Chapter 11.

Valuation with Risk-Neutral Probabilities

Changes in interest rates can create market risk in bond values, even if the bonds have no default risk. The following example, based on Pliska (1997), shows how stochastic evolution of the risk-free interest rate can create this form of market risk. The example also indicates how risk-neutral probabilities can be used to determine the bond values.[19] While the valuation

---

[19] For a more extended discussion of the methods involved see Pliska (1997, Chapter 6).

TABLE 8.4 Interest Rates and Probabilities

r_{01}	r_{12}	Risk-Neutral Probabilities of the Time 1–2 Rates
	0.09	0.3000
0.06	0.06	0.3000
	0.03	0.4000

procedure is not conceptually different from that of the previous section, it is now applied to random changes in interest rates rather than directly to changes in payoff as before.

Suppose there are two zero-coupon bonds,[20] each promising to repay a principal amount of 1, the first at time 1 and the second at time 2. The present time is zero, and the riskless interest rates that are assumed to prevail between times 0–1 as well as between times 1–2 are shown in Table 8.4. The 0–1 interest rate is assumed to be known with certainty at time 0, but the 1–2 interest rate is known only probabilistically at time 0, and will not become known with certainty until time 1. The risk-neutral probabilities for the rates between times 1 and 2, assumed to have been calculated at time 0, are shown in column 3.

Now consider how a zero-coupon bond, issued at time 0 and maturing at time 1, will be valued. At time 1 it will be redeemed for the principal amount, 1, and at time 0 it will be worth the present value of the time 1 payment, discounted at the 6% interest rate certain to prevail from time 0 to time 1. (Because the relevant interest rate is known with certainty, the 6% interest rate is treated as occurring with a risk-neutral probability of 1.0000.) Thus, as shown in Table 8.5, the time 0 value of the one-period bond is 0.9434.

Now consider valuing a two-period bond. At time 2 it is worth the promised payment of 1, no matter what the prevailing interest rate is. If the interest rate r_{12} could be known with certainty at time 1, the bond value at time 1 would then be the time 2 value discounted by the known rate. However, at time 1 (just before the realized rate r_{12} becomes known), the time 1 market value is the sum of the three possible values associated with the three possible interest rate outcomes, each multiplied by its respective risk-neutral probability. The calculations are shown in column 2, Table 8.6. The time 0 value of the bond is its time 1 value discounted by 1.06, as shown

---

[20]Using zero-coupon bonds simplifies the example. The calculations for a bond with a coupon can be set up as a valuation for a zero-coupon bond representing the principal and another bond (or bonds) representing the coupon payment(s).

TABLE 8.5 Values of a Zero-Coupon Bond Maturing at Time 1

Time 0	Time 1
1.00/1.06 = 0.9434	1.00

TABLE 8.6 Values of a Zero-Coupon Bond Maturing at Time 2

Time 0	Time 1	Time 2
	$(1.0000/1.09) \times 0.3000 = 0.2752$	1.0000
	$(1.0000/1.06) \times 0.3000 = 0.2830$	1.0000
	$(1.0000/1.03) \times 0.4000 = 0.3883$	1.0000
Time 0 Value	Time 1 market value just before r_{12}	
= 0.9465/1.06 = 0.8929	becomes known = 0.9465	

in the bottom line of column 1. Note the example shows that if you buy a two-period bond and resell it at time 1, the bond will be subject to a price risk, determined by the value of the time 1–2 interest rate that obtains when you sell the bond.

Bond Prices and Inflation

Bonds exhibit market risk for another reason as well: Their prices can be affected by inflation. Whatever the underlying pattern of real interest rates (rates adjusted to allow for changes in purchasing power), nominal interest rates can be affected by changes in the expected rate of inflation. This second sort of change may or may not be predictable. For example, a sudden burst of inflation can disturb normal interest rate patterns because it can take time to be fully reflected in nominal rates. In particular, nominal rates may change sluggishly with the result that following on a burst of inflation, posted real rates of interest may become negative for a time. However, once the adjustment of nominal rates is complete, real rates should and usually do revert to more customary levels.[21]

To illustrate the effect of inflation on nominal interest rates, suppose for simplicity that the real interest rate is known with certainty and remains unchanged. Suppose also that an investor buys a three-year bond and intends to hold it to maturity. The bond is assumed to pay no interest over its lifetime,

---

[21] The process may be lengthy in some economies. For example, Japan witnessed lengthy periods of negative real interest rates in the late 1990s and the 2000s.

and to be redeemable for the lump sum of 1,000.00 at the end of the three years. If it were known that inflation would be zero and that the risk-free rate would remain unchanged at 4% over each of the next three years, the bond would sell at time 0 for $1,000.00/1.04^3 = 889.00$. An investor purchasing the bond for 889.00 would earn a real interest rate of 4%, compounded annually, if he held it to maturity.

Now suppose that even though price levels have not been expected to increase, the expected inflation rate actually does increase by 1% per annum, compounded annually. This means in turn that, if nominal interest rates are used for discounting purposes, they will be affected by the inflation. Consequently the investor who did not anticipate the inflation and paid the purchase price of 889.00 would earn substantially less than a real interest rate of 4% on his investment. In terms of purchasing power the investor will only be repaid $1,000.00/1.01^3$ when the bond matures. Since the unanticipated inflation was not taken into account, the real interest rate realized on the investment is found by solving the following equation for r:

$$889.00(1 + r)^3 = 1,000.00/(1.01)^3$$
$$[1,000.00/1.04^3](1 + r)^3 = 1,000.00/(1.01)^3$$

That is,

$$(1 + r) = (1.04)/(1.01)$$

so that $r = 2.9703\%$. The real interest rate on the bond has been decreased by the unexpected change in inflation.

The preceding example shows that a bond's real interest earnings can be affected by unanticipated changes in the rate of inflation. Moreover, an investor cannot escape this risk by selling the bond as and when expectations regarding inflation are revised. For as soon as expectations are revised,[22] bond prices will change accordingly, at least in a liquid market. Suppose that in the previous example, the inflation forecast changes from 0% to 1% just after our investor has purchased the bond. When the change is reflected in the market, the bond price will fall from its original

$$1,000.00/(1.04)^3 = 889.00$$

to

$$1,000.00/(1.01)^3(1.04)^3 = 862.85$$

---

[22] As mentioned above, revisions can sometimes be subject to lags.

that is, by 2.94% of its original capital value! And once bond prices have changed, it is too late for the investor to sell the bond without suffering the capital loss illustrated in the last calculation.

Index-Linked Bonds

Index-linked bonds adjust payments of interest and principal by current price level indexes so that the purchasing power of the payments is maintained, at least approximately. Thus, by purchasing index-linked bonds investors can assure themselves that their funds will earn something close to the real rate of interest, the degree of closeness depending on how well the index chosen to inflate the bond principal and interest payments reflects the actual impact of inflation. Index-linked bonds both make it easier for investors to hedge against inflation risk, and display less market risk than bonds without index linking.

Index-linked bonds also make it possible to test the validity of a relation between nominal and real interest rates, known as the Fisher effect (see Sack, 2000). Before the advent of index-linked bonds, tests of the Fisher effect were hampered by the difficulty of finding an appropriate proxy for the expected rate of inflation. Bond yields are expressed in nominal terms and it is not usually easy to infer the market expectations of future inflation, and hence the level of real interest rates, from these yields. However, by taking an index-linked bond and by assuming that the index used to increase the bond payments mirrors inflation rates relatively well, the observed rates of return on the indexed bonds are close to the real rates of interest. The data on Canadian bonds in Table 8.7 give an approximate indication of the Fisher effect for bonds of a 10-year maturity. Note that the fourth column, which roughly indicates the market's expectation of the inflation premium over the life of the bond, varies from 0.98% per annum in January 1999 to 2.66% in January 2006.

Expected rates of inflation can be calculated if the index used to increase the linked bond's interest and principal payments is a good proxy for inflation and if the index-linked bond can be compared with another, nominal interest rate bond of about the same risk and same maturity. Such information can be quite informative. For example, Francis Breedon (1995) finds that while inflation expectations are volatile, they are also reasonably good leading indicators of price level increases.

Nominal Rates and Yield Curves

For the reasons just developed, a bond's nominal interest earnings are risky. Unless an investor intends to hold a bond until maturity, she cannot

TABLE 8.7 Real and Nominal Canadian Long-Term Interest Rates, January 1998–2008

Year	Nominal	Real	Difference
1998	5.63	4.11	1.52
1999	5.08	4.10	0.98
2000	6.36	4.02	2.34
2001	5.71	3.36	2.35
2002	5.72	3.73	1.99
2003	5.45	3.22	2.23
2004	5.15	2.57	2.58
2005	4.69	2.03	2.66
2006	4.22	1.54	2.68
2007	4.23	1.79	2.44
2008	4.17	1.98	2.19

Note: Nominal rate is on Government of Canada bonds of 10 years and over to maturity. Real rate is on Government of Canada 10-year inflation-adjusted bonds. Data for U.S. Treasury Inflation-Protected Securities are available at www.federalreserve.gov/releases/h15/data.
Source: Bank of Canada.

be certain of the interest rate she will realize on it.[23] If market conditions change, her realized rate of return may be less than she expected. For example, suppose that after purchasing the bond, our investor finds that real interest rates have risen above the original 4%. She will then wish she had been able to purchase the bond for less, because she will see that other investors just now coming into the market can earn more than the 4% for which she has arranged.

Recognizing that interest rates can change and hence contribute to bonds' market risk, investors may attempt to compensate by requiring higher returns.[24] For instance, if they believe that long-term bonds carry greater earnings risks than short-term ones, they will demand higher interest rates on the longer bonds. Thus, for example, in the case of the three-year bond just discussed, investors might expect real interest rates to be 4% in each year if they forecast zero inflation in each of the next three years. However, they

---

[23] Moreover, even if she decides to hold the bond until maturity, there is still an opportunity risk to take into account. She might, for example, find herself holding a bond with a relatively low yield to maturity in an environment where interest rates had risen substantially. Unless she changes her investment strategy, this would mean continuing to hold a low-yielding asset in a higher-interest-rate environment.

[24] In later chapters, we consider hedging against different types of interest rate change.

might still add liquidity premiums[25] to future expected rates in order to compensate for what they regard as an increasingly greater risk that the inflation forecast might change. They might, for example, price the bond using

$$1,000.00/R_3 = 1,000.00/(1.04)(1.05)(1.06) = 863.92$$

where the terms 1.04, 1.05, and 1.06, respectively, reflect investors' using interest rates of 4%, 5%, and 6% in years one, two and three. They might do this even though their expectations of the rate in the next three years are currently an unchanging 4%. The example assumes that although investors add no liquidity premium to the expected interest rate in the first year, they do add a liquidity premium of 1% to the interest rate expected to prevail in the second year, and a liquidity premium of 2% in the third year, to compensate them, both for the possibility that the expected 4% might change, and also that change might become more likely over longer time horizons. Under these assumptions, the average yield to maturity on the three-year bond is

$$R_3^{1/3} - 1 = [(1.04)(1.05)(1.06)]^{1/3} - 1 = 4.9968\%$$

Holding bonds of different maturities presents different risk patterns. The realized return on a two-year bond can be calculated with certainty if the investor is sure to hold the two-year bond until its maturity. However, the return over the first two years from holding a three-year bond can only be calculated from expectations regarding the bond's value at the end of the first two years, and if the expectations are not realized, the return on the bond will change as illustrated in the subsection "How Are Risks Divided with Debt and Equity?"

To provide a second example, consider how an investor would value a two-year zero-coupon bond using forecast interest rates of 4% over the first year and 5% over the second year. A 1,000.00 two-year bond would be worth

$$1,000.00/(1.04)(1.05)$$

and would have an average yield to maturity of

$$[(1.04)(1.05)]^{1/2} - 1 = 4.4988\%$$

---

[25] Estimates of liquidity premiums appear to increase quite rapidly during the first year or two, then relatively slowly in successive years.

The last calculation can be made because the two-year bond is assumed to be default-free and will hence be redeemed for a certainty amount of 1,000.00 at the end of two years.

However, at the end of two years the value of a three-year bond will be determined by the interest rate and inflation expectations in force over the last year of its life. For example, consider a three-year bond in an environment where the interest expectations are the same as in the previous example for the first two years, and 7.12% in the third year, say, because expectations of inflation have changed. Accordingly, the three-year bond will be worth

$$1,000.00/(1.0712) = 933.53$$

at time 2. An investor selling the bond at time 2 for the new market price of 933.53 will realize a different annual average yield over the first two years of her investment than she would if the third-year interest rate were 7% because in that case the value of the bond at time 2 would be

$$1,000.00/(1.07) = 934.58$$

The relations between interest rates on bonds with different terms to maturity are displayed using graphs known as yield curves. A yield curve drawn on a given date shows the average interest rates calculated as of that day on bonds having different maturities but comparable default risk. Most published yield curves display the average yields to maturity on government securities. Government yield curves are popular choices because government bonds are usually priced as zero-default-risk securities, meaning their yields reflect riskless interest rates (i.e., rates including no default premium).

Yield curves can be calculated using either coupon bonds or the pure discount (zero-coupon) bonds employed in the above examples. Calculating a yield curve using coupon bonds is only slightly more complex than calculating a yield curve for pure discount bonds, because each of the coupons on a coupon bond can itself be regarded as a pure discount bond, as can the principal payment. Thus the yield to maturity on a coupon bond is a value-weighted average of the yield on the principal amount and on the different coupon payments. An example of the yield curve for Canadian government zero-coupon bonds calculated on January 3, 2008 is displayed in Figure 8.1.

Even though they hold default risk constant, yield curves reflect the differing degrees of interest rate risk to which investors in different bond

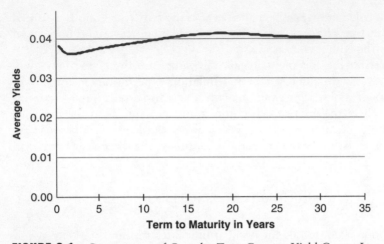

FIGURE 8.1 Government of Canada, Zero-Coupon Yield Curve, January 3, 2008
Source: Bank of Canada.

maturities are exposed. The longer a bond's maturity, the greater the percentage fluctuation in its capital value due to changes in expectations. Table 8.8 compares the prices of a 1- and a 10-year bond under two interest rate scenarios. The scenarios envision either that annual rates are expected to be 4% in each successive year, or 5% in each successive year. An increase from 4% to 5% causes the price of the 1-year bond to fall by $9.15 or 0.95%, whereas the price of the 10-year bond falls by $61.65 or 9.13%. Of course, in the first case it is only the one-year rate that is assumed to fall, whereas in the second case the one-year rate in each of 10 successive years is assumed to fall.

The assumption that rates will change by an equal amount in all future years will not always be valid. (Indeed, it corresponds to a parallel shift

TABLE 8.8 Comparisons of Changes in Bond Prices

Interest Rates	1,000.00 Bond Maturing in 1 Year	1,000.00 Bond Maturing in 10 Years
4%	961.53	675.56
5%	952.38	613.91
Ratio of value at 5% to value at 4%	0.9905	0.9087

in the entire yield curve, but empirically yield curves vary over a wider range for short maturities than for longer ones.) If the scenario is altered, the foregoing conclusions must also be amended. For example, if next year's rate is expected to rise to 5% but all subsequent rates are expected to remain at 4%, the value of the one-year bond remains as shown in the second row, first column, but the value of the 10-year bond becomes

$$\$675.56 \times 1.04/1.05 = \$669.13$$

since the rate change from 4% to 5% is now assumed to occur only in the second year. In this scenario the ratio of $669.13 to $675.56 is 0.9905, the same as the relative change shown in the first column for the one-year bond.

REFERENCES

Almeida, Heitor, and Thomas Philippon. 2007. The risk-adjusted cost of financial distress. *Journal of Finance* 62: 2,557–2,586.

Breedon, Francis. 1995. Bond prices and market expectations of inflation. *Bank of England Quarterly Bulletin* 35 (May): 160–165.

Huang, Chi-Fu, and Robert H. Litzenberger. 1988. *Foundations for Financial Economics.* New York: North-Holland.

Pliska, Stanley R. 1997. *Introduction to Mathematical Finance.* Malden, MA: Blackwell.

Sack, Brian. 2000. Deriving inflation expectations from nominal and inflation-indexed treasury yields. *Journal of Fixed Income* 10: 1–12.

TERMS

Fisher effect   An approximation to the relation between real and nominal interest rates, taking the form Nominal interest rate = Real interest rate plus anticipated inflation rate. The approximation holds closely for relatively low real interest rates and relative low inflation rates. Since the exact calculation of the Fisher effect is (1 + Nominal interest rate) = (1 + Real interest rate)(1 + Anticipated inflation), it can be seen that the approximation ignores the cross term (Real interest rate)(Anticipated inflation) in the second equation. As both the real interest rate and anticipated inflation increase, the approximation becomes less exact.

risk-neutral probability   A measure found in the absence of arbitrage opportunities that permits security prices to be calculated by taking the expectation, under the risk-neutral probability measure of the security's discounted payoffs. In a risk-averse market, risk-neutral probabilities actually take risk into account because they are calculated from market values that are influenced by risk aversion.

unit contingent claim   A security, like a lottery ticket, that has a payoff of exactly one unit in a given state, say state k, and zero in all other states. Also known as "Arrow-Debreu securities" and as "state claims."

Pricing Derivatives by Arbitrage

Chapter 9 analyzes how derivative securities are priced in the absence of arbitrage opportunities. It examines and values forward contracts, options, and futures contracts. The chapter emphasizes how the different instruments represent different ways of dividing and trading underlying asset risk. Relations among debt, equity, and options are also reviewed in order both to emphasize the risk management implications of using different instruments and to relate the risk in debt and equity to the risks in options.

This chapter continues Chapter 8's development of securities pricing in the absence of arbitrage. Here, we see how forwards, options, and futures can be used for dividing up and pricing risks. While the discussion does not intend to make you an expert in using or valuing derivative securities, it will show you how the different instruments are composed of the same building blocks. The chapter also shows how different contracts can be valued using the principles of pricing by arbitrage. The chapter begins by examining forward contracts. It next examines options, and then follows with a discussion of relations between debt, equity, and options. The nature and uses of futures contracts are outlined. Finally, the chapter values two futures contracts and a credit default swap.

This chapter also reviews how different contracts can be used in practice. This part will help you understand subsequent chapters that discuss the instruments' uses in greater detail. For instance, the present material is used in Chapter 12 to describe how derivatives are traded on organized exchanges, and why derivatives trading has virtually exploded since the 1970s, even though the instruments had been around for years. Similarly, Chapter 14 shows how portfolio administrators can use derivatives for risk management.

INTRODUCTION

Options, forwards and futures are all used for risk management. The instruments are generically referred to as derivatives because their payoffs derive from the value of the assets against which they are written. Derivatives can be written against almost any kind of asset, but the most frequently chosen underlying assets are actively traded financial instruments or commodities such as crude oil, agricultural products, and gold.

Although there are close conceptual relations between derivatives and such traditional instruments as debt and equity, the two classes of instruments are used differently: debt and equity are used primarily for raising funds from investors,[1] while derivatives are primarily used for dividing up and trading risks.[2] Moreover, debt and equity are direct claims against a firm's assets, while derivative instruments are usually claims on a third party. A derivative's value depends on the value of the underlying asset, but the instrument itself represents a claim on the issuer of the derivative.[3]

FORWARDS

Forward contracts are one of the simplest forms of instruments used for trading an asset's future price risk. In essence, a forward contract specifies that an asset can be bought or sold at a given future date for a stipulated price. Since the asset's cash price will likely be different from the contracted forward price when the contract matures, the instrument serves to separate the risk of price change from the forward price stipulated in the contract.

---

[1]In practice, raising funds may involve tailoring the firm's securities issues to the preferences of particular financiers. In the perfectly competitive markets of this chapter, tailoring securities issues will affect neither their prices nor the firm's cost of funds. However, when a firm has to negotiate its financings in imperfectly competitive markets tailoring can influence the cost of funds. These matters are discussed in Chapter 6 and also in Chapter 22.

[2]There are, however, exceptions. Some debt issues are accompanied by option-like instruments, called "warrants," designed to improve the marketability of the debt. Other debt issues are convertible, meaning they have a built-in option to exchange the debt for equity.

[3]Since derivatives are obligations of their issuers, they carry credit risk. As will be discussed further in this chapter, exchange-traded derivatives are often guaranteed to be honored as written, meaning that an instrumentality of the exchange assumes the credit risk.

What Is a Forward Contract?

A forward contract is an agreement under which an investor assumes an obligation to trade a specified asset, at a given time, and for a given price. Taking a long position in a forward contract means assuming an obligation to purchase a specified asset at a fixed price, to be paid on the future date specified in the contract. This date is called the delivery date. Similarly, taking a short position in a forward contract means assuming an obligation to sell the specified asset, again at a forward price that is originally specified when the contract is drawn up. The principal purpose of taking a position in a forward contract is to trade the risk of price changes between the time the contract is originated and its delivery date. The parties entering the contract may or may not own the asset when the contract is originated, and they may or may not intend to take physical possession of the asset on the delivery date. These practical issues will be discussed further in Chapter 12.

The gross profits or losses on a forward contract, and consequently the contract's value, depend on the relation between the forward price specified by the contract and the asset's actual cash price on that date. A long position in a forward contract conveys an opportunity to profit if the asset's cash price turns out to be more than the forward price. For example, if a party to a forward contract has agreed to buy an asset for $100.00, and if the asset actually turns out to be worth $111.00 on the delivery date, the holder of the long position can turn an immediate gross profit[4] of $11.00 by purchasing the asset according to the terms of the forward contract, and then reselling it in what is known as the cash market. By the same token, taking a long position incurs a loss if the asset's future cash price turns out to be less than the forward price. For example, if the holder of a forward contract has agreed to buy an asset for $100.00, and if the asset turns out to be worth only $91.00 on that date, the holder loses $9.00. Since a short position is the reverse of a long position, the gross profits or losses to a party with a short position are exactly the opposite of those realized by the party with the offsetting long position.

How Is a Forward Contract Valued?

A forward contract is written to separate trading profits or losses from the current expectation of the asset's price. In order to trade this risk of price change, the parties must strike a contract that is acceptable to them both. To see conceptually how such a contract might be set up, consider again the payoffs to a risky asset discussed in Chapter 8. (See Table 9.1.)

---

[4]That is, a profit calculated without taking account of transactions costs.

TABLE 9.1   Payoffs to a Forward Contract

S_1: Possible Market Value (Cash Price) at Time 1	Objective Probability of Realizing This Price
105.00	0.5
95.00	0.5

TABLE 9.2   Profits or Losses on a Forward Contract with Forward Price of $100.00 (forward price is to be paid at time 1)

	S_1 (Asset Payoff)	O_1 (Forward Price)	$S_1 - O_1$ (Gross Gains or Losses)
Time 1 High Price	$S_1 = 105.00$	$O_1 = 100.00$	$S_1 - O_1 = 5.00$
Time 1 Low Price	$S_1 = 95.00$	$O_1 = 100.00$	$S_1 - O_1 = -5.00$
Time 0 Values	$S_0 = 89.00$	$O_1/B_1 = 90.91$	$S_0 - O_1/B_1 = -1.91$

In Table 9.2, S_1 is assumed to represent the distribution of the asset's possible market values at time 1, and the objective probabilities shown in the previous table indicate that either outcome is equally likely.[5] Suppose you have taken a long position in a forward contract at time 0, specifying that you will buy the asset at time 1, and that your forward contract specifies a forward price of $100.00. The first question about such a contract is what gains or losses does it represent to you? A second question is what are these potential gains or losses worth to you now?

Although industry practice is to create contracts whose initial value is zero, it is useful to begin by showing that the present contract starts out with a nonzero market value. The third column of Table 9.2 shows the gross profits or losses that your long position will realize at time 1. The time 1 payoffs represented by S_1 refers to quantities whose value will only be realized at time 1. However, the forward price O_1 is set at time 0 and is a known quantity from that moment on. (The time 1 subscript indicates the time the payment is to be made, not the time the contract is written.) In this example the riskless interest rate is assumed to be 10%, so the riskless discount factor $1/B_1 = 0.9091$.

If you take a long position in the forward contract at time 0, you agree to pay $100.00 for the asset at time 1. This means you will be $5.00 ahead if the asset price turns out to be high, but $5.00 out of pocket if it

---

[5]The probabilities used for valuation purposes are the risk-neutral probabilities and differ from the objective probabilities as described later in the chater.

is low. In essence, Table 9.1 says that a forward contract divides the risky payoffs represented by S_1 into a sure payment O_1 and a random profit or loss $(S_1 - O_1)$. Symbolically, this division of the original risk can be expressed as:

$$S_1 \equiv O_1 + (S_1 - O_1)$$

where S_1 represents the asset payoffs, O_1 the forward price, and $S_1 - O_1$ the gross gains or losses to the (long) forward position. Adding the symbols corresponds to adding across each row of Table 9.2. In effect, the equation summarizes the information in the table: The forward contract represents a division of payoffs no matter which value of the asset is actually realized. The holder of the long position agrees to pays a fixed price, and the counterparty assumes the profits or losses (calculated between times 0 and 1) to any price change between the specified forward price and the cash price.

What will be the time 0 value of assuming the price risk? The answer clearly depends on the forward price. In the present example, taking a long position in the contract means you will pay $100.00 for the asset, come what may. In the absence of any arbitrage opportunities, the time 0 value of the forward contract must equal the difference between the time 0 value of the asset and the time 0 value of the certainty payment,[6] $100.00. Suppose as before that the asset has a time 0 value of $89.00. Also suppose that the riskless interest rate is 10%, implying that a certainty payment of $100.00 has a time 0 value of $90.91. Therefore, in the absence of arbitrage opportunities it follows that the payoffs to the forward contract in Table 9.1 must have a time 0 value of

$$\$89.00 - \$90.91 = -\$1.91$$

This negative value means that, given the asset price of $89.00 and the riskless rate of 10%, the counterparty will have to pay you $1.91 at time 0 to induce you to enter into this forward contract.[7] The value calculations are summarized in the last row of Table 9.2.

---

[6]The example ignores any possibility of defaulting on the $100.00 payment.
[7]The price of $1.91 that you require is determined under the assumption the individual promising to buy the asset will not default. If there were some possibility the contracting individual might default on her obligation to you, you would require more to enter the contract.

How Is a Forward Price Determined?

Almost always, forward contracts specify a forward price that gives the contract a value of zero at the time it is written. In the present example, the forward price will have to be less than $100.00 if the contract is to have a market value of zero at time 0. Since the asset is worth $89.00 today, its certainty equivalent value must be $89.00(1.10) = 97.90$ one year from now. If the forward contract stipulates paying this amount one year from now, the present value of the payment is $89.00, the same as the current market value of the asset. That is, with a forward price of $97.90, the contract has a present value of zero.

As shown in Table 9.3, this contract yields gains of $7.10 if the asset price turns out to be high, and losses of $2.90 if the asset price turns out to be low. If the underlying asset has a market price today of $89.00, and if the riskless interest rate is 10%, the time 1 payments in the third column must have a time 0 market value of zero. As we have already determined, the forward price that makes the contract worth zero at time 0 is today's price, accumulated at the riskless interest rate, that is, $89.00(1.10) = 97.90$. The value calculations are summarized in the last row of Table 9.3.

The risk-neutral probabilities found in Chapter 8, $q = 0.29$ and $1 - q = 0.71$, can be used to check that the new forward contract indeed has a present value of zero:

$$E_Q[(S_1 - O_1)/B_1 \,|\, \Im_0]$$
$$= (0.29)(7.10)/1.10 - (0.71)(2.90)/1.10 = 0.00$$

It is now time to generalize the insights of the previous example. In writing forward contracts, standard practice stipulates a forward price that implies the contract has an initial value of zero. Let the contract origination time be denoted time 0, and the contract delivery date time T. Let O_T be the forward price (to be paid at time T, but set at time 0). Let S_T be the price of the underlying asset at time T, and let B_T be the value of $1 accumulated at

TABLE 9.3   Valuing a Contract with a Forward Price of $97.90

	S_1	O_1	$S_1 - O_1$
Time 1 High Payoffs	105.00	97.90	7.10
Time 1 Low Payoffs	95.00	97.90	-2.90
Time 0 Values	89.00	89.00	0.00

the riskless interest rate from time 0 to time T. In the absence of arbitrage opportunities, the forward price must be such that

$$E_Q[(S_T - O_T)/B_T \mid \Im_0] = 0 \tag{9.1}$$

where Q is the risk-neutral probability measure, and $\Im_0$ means the risk-neutral probability measure is established using information available at time 0. From the time 0 perspective, the forward price O_T is known with certainty, while the asset price S_T is a random variable. The riskless interest rate effect represented by B_T is assumed to be known with certainty.[8] Rewriting equation (9.1) gives

$$E_Q[S_T/B_T|\Im_0] = O_T E_Q[(1/B_T)|\Im_0] = S_0 \tag{9.2}$$

The forward price can be taken outside the expectation sign because it is assumed to be a deterministic value at time 0.

Rewriting equation (9.2), the calculations for the forward price on a contract with delivery date T can be expressed as

$$O_T = S_0/E_Q[(1/B_T)|\Im_0] \tag{9.3}$$

Equation (9.3) says that if interest rates are random, the forward price equals the current asset price accumulated at the expected interest rate, where the expectation is taken under the risk-neutral probability. Notice that the interest effects are calculated by taking the expectation of the discount factors, which is not the same thing as taking the expectation of the interest rates themselves. Nor is it the same thing as the reciprocal of the expected interest rate.

If interest rates are deterministic as currently assumed, B_T can be taken outside the expectation sign and equation (9.3) reduces to

$$O_T = S_0/B_T \tag{9.4}$$

With a deterministic interest rate, the expression for the forward price is straightforward: It is the current asset price, accumulated at the deterministic

---

[8]Although we generally assume the riskless interest rate is deterministic, we show shortly how this assumption can be relaxed without inordinately complicating the valuation exercise.

interest rate until the delivery date. Since the interest rate in the example is deterministic, (2.4) can be used to calculate

$$O_T = S_0/(1/B_1) = 89.00/(1 \div 11/10)$$
$$= 89.00 \div 10/11 = 89.00 \times 11/10 = 97.90$$

the value found before.

OPTIONS

An option is a contract that permits its holder to trade some asset at a fixed price, should the holder elect to do so. A contract that permits you to purchase an asset is known as a call option; one that permits you to sell it is known as a put option. Options can be written either to permit exercise on a given date or over a given time interval. Instruments that can only be exercised on a given date are called European options, those that can be exercised any time within a given interval are called American options.[9]

What Are Options Contracts?

This chapter discusses and values European options, while Chapter 12 shows how the methods can be extended to value American options. A European call option allows its holder to purchase an underlying asset[10] at a fixed purchase price and fixed future point in time, should the holder wish to exercise the option. A European put option is a similar security that allows its owner to sell a specified asset at a fixed price and at a fixed point in time, should he wish to do so.

Like forwards, options offer a way of dividing up the payoffs to risky assets. A forward contract requires you to trade whether asset prices increase or decrease, while an options contract permits you to trade should you elect to do so. Options are exercised at the discretion of the holder, meaning the holder need only exercise the option when it is profitable to do so. Exercising a call will be profitable if the underlying asset price rises above the call exercise price, exercising a put will be profitable if the underlying asset price falls below the put exercise price.

---

[9]There are other types of options, called exotics, not referred to in this introduction. For example, Asian options have payoffs determined relative to the underlying asset's average price rather than its current price. For further discussion, the interested reader should consult such standard references as Jarrow and Turnbull (1996) or Hull (2008).

[10]The underlying asset is usually a security, but options can also be written on such real assets as, say, property.

TABLE 9.4 Options with Exercise Price of $100.00

	S_1 (Asset)	K_1 (Exercise Price, Set at Time 0)	C_1 (Call Position)	$-P_1$ (Short Put Position)
Time 1 High Payoffs	105.00	100.00	5.00	0.00
Time 1 Low Payoffs	95.00	100.00	0.00	−5.00
Time 0 Values	89.00	90.91	1.32	−3.23

In effect, options split up the gains or losses that are realized on a forward contract. That is, with options the potential gains or losses are represented by two contract positions—a long call and a short put, respectively, both written at the same exercise price. Recall the asset payoffs given at the beginning of the chapter. Since options are very often written against shares, assume for purposes of discussion that the asset now represents one share. As before, the possible time 1 values that the asset can reach are either $105.00 or $95.00. Suppose a European call option with an exercise price of $K_1 = \$100.00$ has been written against the share. The call conveys to its owner the right to purchase the share for $100.00 at time 1. As listed in column C_1 of Table 9.4, the call will have a payoff of $5.00 at time 1 if the share price is $105.00, since the option holder can use his option to buy the share for only $100.00 and then resell it for $105.00. If instead the share price is $95.00, the option is valueless. Since there is no profit to buying something for $100.00 and immediately reselling it for $95.00, the holder will instead discard it.

Now consider a put option, also written with an exercise price $K_1 = \$100.00$. If you own this option, it allows you to sell the share to someone else for $100.00. Clearly, you would want to do this when the market value of the share was $95.00, but not when it was $105.00. The put option is therefore worth $5.00 to its holder if the share value turns out to be $95.00, zero if it turns out to be $105.00.

Now consider the payments you might have to make under the put option if you are the person who writes it. You lose $5.00 to the put's purchaser when the share price is $95.00, because in that case the holder of the put will require you to buy the share, worth only $95.00, for a contracted price of $100.00. However, you lose nothing when the share price is $105.00, because in that case the holder of the put discards it without exercise. The gross profits or losses to you, as issuer of the option, are shown in the column headed $-P_1$, where the negative sign indicates that the column adopts the viewpoint of the put writer. Column C_1, with its implied positive sign, adopts the viewpoint of the call purchaser.

We can now see that the combination of a call and a short put position give the same payoffs as does the previously discussed forward contract. In either row of Table 9.4, the algebraic sum taken across the last two columns equals the corresponding amount in column F of Table 9.2. Recall that symbolically the payoffs to the forward contract could be written

$$S_1 \equiv O_1 + (S_1 - O_1)$$

Comparing Tables 9.2 and 9.4 indicates that

$$(S_1 - O_1) = (S_1 - K_1) \equiv C_1 - P_1$$

When the forward price equals the common exercise price of the two options, we can write

$$S_1 \equiv K_1 + C_1 - P_1 \tag{9.5}$$

You can now verify equation (9.5). In any row, the sum of the payoffs in columns K_1, C_1, and $-P_1$ equals the corresponding amount in column S_1, no matter which share price is realized. In other words, the distribution of asset payoffs S_1 can be divided up into the payoffs to a sure thing, the positive payoffs represented by the long call position, and the negative payoffs represented by the short put position. This is the sense in which options permit a finer division of payoffs than does a forward contract.

Since a forward contract has exactly the same payoffs as a properly constructed portfolio of a call and a short put, the question of why market agents would trade both kinds of instruments arises. A quick answer is that in practice forward and options contracts are not the same, because they trade on different exchanges, possibly at different transactions costs, are typically used by different kinds of risk traders, and may help to overcome different kinds of market imperfections. It is also possible that at some time one of the instruments may be available at a disequilibrium price, but you should be able to explain why this will be unlikely in markets with active arbitraging.[11] Practical reasons for preferring one kind of instrument to another will be examined further in Chapter 12. For the present, we continue to develop theoretical relations between the instruments, remembering that they are all used for risk trading.

---

[11] If there were never any disequilibrium prices, there would never be any opportunity for arbitrageurs to make profits, and hence arbitraging would not be carried out. The practical difficulty for most traders is finding disequilibrium prices before arbitrageurs locate and eliminate them.

Note that equation (9.5) shows there are at least two ways of getting the payoffs in column S_1 of Table 9.5. One way is to hold the share. Another way is to hold the instruments in columns K_1 and C_1 while simultaneously issuing the instrument in column $-P_1$. This portfolio offers the same payoff distribution as does S_1. Another way of expressing equation (9.5) is to note that S can always be written as

$$S_1 \equiv K_1 + \max(S_1 - K_1,\ 0) - \max(K_1 - S_1,\ 0)$$

The last line says you can divide any risky payoff distribution such as S_1 into a certainty part, a positive part representing payoffs to a call, and a negative part representing payoffs to a short put position.

Although Table 9.5 conceptually defines an instrument with a certainty payoff $K_1 = \$100.00$—regardless of whether the asset does well or badly—we know the asset is not always worth \$100.00. Thus Table 9.5 needs to be interpreted rather carefully. The table means that if you own the asset (i.e., the payoffs in column S_1), then you are in the same position as if you held a portfolio of the securities in columns K_1, C_1, and $-P_1$. In other words, owning the whole asset is conceptually the same thing as having a portfolio composed of all three securities. This idea can be used to find the individual values of the put and the call, as shown in the next section.

Method of Riskless Hedge[12]

Options were first valued using by constructing a riskless portfolio. There are several ways to construct a riskless portfolio, one of them being to combine a long position in the stock with a short position in a call on the stock.[13] The value of this portfolio was then used, along with knowledge of the riskless interest rate and the stock price, to infer the value of the call. The riskless hedge method is both of historical interest and helpful to the student looking for alternative ways of deriving option values. The idea is straightforward, but calculating the riskless hedge can look a little tricky at first. Let us begin with the underlying idea, and then perform the calculations.

First, if we know the riskless interest rate, we can value a riskless portfolio by discounting its payoff. Now suppose we also know the current

---

[12] The most popular options pricing model, developed using riskless hedge arguments, is the continuous time model originally developed by Black and Scholes (1973). Detailed discussions of the Black-Scholes model can be found in, for example, Cox and Rubinstein (1985), Hull (1989), or Jarrow and Turnbull (1995).
[13] A riskless portfolio can also be constructed with the stock and a put.

TABLE 9.5 Valuing the Call by the Riskless Hedge Method

	$S_1/2$	$-C_1$	$S_1/2 - C_1$
Time 1 High Payoffs	$105.00/2 = 52.50$	-5.00	47.50
Time 1 Low Payoffs	$95.00/2 = 47.50$	-0.00	47.50
Time 0 Values	$89.00/2 = 44.50$	$-1.45/1.10$	$47.50/1.10$
		$= -1.32$	$= 43.18$

(time 0) price of an asset, say a stock, and the two[14] possible payoffs to be received from investing in the stock and holding it over some fixed period. (A year is used in the following example.) Then, if we could make up a portfolio consisting of a position in the stock and a call option, taking care to structure the portfolio so that it had the same payoff in either state of the world (i.e., a riskless payoff), we could derive the time 0 value of the option using the other, known values. If we make up a portfolio of a stock with a known value and an option with an unknown value, and if the portfolio is riskless so that we can value it using the riskless rate, we can then infer the value of the option. Let us turn to an example.

The present example continues to be based on S_1, now representing the payoffs to a firm financed entirely by equity. (You can continue to think of the asset as one share if you wish.) As before, there is a difference in call payoffs according to whether the value of the equity turns out to be $105.00 or $95.00. Assuming the call is written on the whole of the firm's equity, that the call has an exercise price of $100.00, and that the firm's payoff distribution is the same as at the beginning of the chapter, the difference in call payoffs is

$$\$5.00 - \$0.00 = \$5.00$$

The difference in the payoffs to the equity position, assumed to consist of a single share, is

$$\$105.00 - 95.00 = \$10.00$$

Accordingly, the difference in payoffs to one-half of a share can be used to offset exactly the difference in payoffs to a short call position. That is, the payoff to $S_1/2 - C_1$ is a sure $47.50, as shown in Table 9.4.

---

[14] If there are more than two payoffs, more assets will be needed to construct the riskless hedge.

Under the assumption of arbitrage free prices, a portfolio having the time 1 payoffs

$$S_1/2 - C_1$$

must have a time 0 value

$$\$89.00/2 - C_0 = 44.50 - C_0$$

where C_0 is the time 0 value of the call. Also, since $S_1/2 - C_1$ represents a certainty payoff of \$47.50 at time 1, it must have a time 0 value of $\$47.50/1.10 = \$43.18$. Equating the two expressions,

$$(\$44.50 - C_0) = \$47.50/(1.10)$$
$$C_0(1.10) = \$44.50(1.10) - \$47.50 = \$48.95 - \$47.50 \qquad (9.6)$$
$$C_0 = [\$48.95 - \$47.50]/1.10 = \$1.45/1.10 = \$1.32$$

As shown in Table 9.5, the time 1 payoffs in each row add to the total time 1 payoffs. Accordingly, by the absence of arbitrage opportunities the time 0 values of the equity position, \$44.50, and the short call position, –\$1.32, must add up to the time 0 value of the portfolio, \$43.18.

Risk-Neutral Probabilities and the Riskless Hedge

Recall that the subsection, "How Is a Forward Contract Valued?" used the risk-neutral probability $q = 0.29$ to value payoffs realized when the firm does well, and $1 - q = 0.71$ to value payoffs realized when the firm does badly. For the payoffs to the call of the previous section, the risk-neutral probability calculation gives a value of

$$C_0 = E_Q[C_1/B_1|\Im_0] = [(0.29)\$5.00 + (0.71)\$0.00]/1.10$$
$$= (0.29)\$5.00/1.10 = \$1.45/1.10 = \$1.32$$

the same as before. (The \$1.32 is preceded by a minus sign in Table 9.5 because there it represents the value of a short position.)

The reason the risk-neutral probabilities give the same value as the riskless hedge method is that, when rearranged, the numbers in the riskless hedge calculation actually define the risk-neutral probability q. To verify this observation, notice that equation (9.6) can be written

$$(\$89.00/2 - C_0)(1.10) = \$105.00/2 - \$5.00$$

That is,

$$C_0(1.10) = \$5.00 + \$97.90/2 - \$105.00/2$$
$$C_0(1.10) = \$5.00 - [\$105.00 - \$97.90]/2$$
$$C_0(1.10) = \$5.00\{1 - [\$105.00 - \$97.90]/\$10.00\}$$
$$C_0(1.10) = \$5.00\{1 - [\$105.00 - \$97.90]/[\$105.00 - \$95.00]\}$$
$$C_0(1.10) = \$5.00\{[\$97.90 - \$95.00]/[\$105.00 - \$95.00]\}$$

and the expression in the braces of the last line is the value for q.

Put-Call Parity

Even though the discussion of this section is at a conceptual level, it has practical application. To illustrate, suppose you own the firm and want to keep its expected payoff of $100.00, but without assuming any risk at all. (You realize, of course, that you will have to pay something to induce another party to assume the risk that the payoff will differ from its expected value. The principle is the same as buying insurance.) The key is to think of actually trading the options whose payoffs are listed in Table 9.5. Could you add other securities to your holdings of the stock in such a way as to eliminate the risk of changes in the payoffs you would receive? Recall from Table 9.5 that when you wrote a put, you did badly if the share price fell. On the other hand, as the owner of a call, you did well when the share price rose. So, if you own shares and want to eliminate the risk of changes in value, one way to do so would involve selling or taking a short position in a call, and buying or taking a long position in a put, as shown in Table 9.6.

Now, the portfolio in the three right-hand columns consists of an investment in the firm, a short call and a long put position. It has a payoff of exactly $100.00 whether the firm payoff is high or low. This relationship between the shares of a firm, options on the shares, and a riskless investment with certainty payoffs is a well-known one in options pricing theory, and is referred to as put-call parity.[15] At this point you can see that the present

---

[15] In many discussions of options values put-call parity is discussed mainly in terms of market values at time 0, and the put-call parity relationship itself is usually specified in terms of time 0 values. Note that here we usually begin with payoff distributions at time 1, and derive time 0 values when appropriate.

TABLE 9.6 Devising a Portfolio with a Certainty Payoff: Illustration of Put-Call Parity

	K_1 (Certainty Payoffs)	S_1 (Long Position in Firm or Shares of Firm)	$-C_1$ (Short Call Position)	P_1 (Long Put Position)
Time 1 High Payoffs to Firm	100.00	105.00	−5.00	0.00
Time 1 Low Payoffs to Firm	100.00	95.00	0.00	5.00
Time 0 Values	90.91	89.00	−1.32	3.23

interpretation of put-call parity shows how to devise an insurance policy to offload certain kinds of investment risks.

Symbolically, the payoffs defining the put-call parity relation derived above can be expressed in terms of time 1 values as

$$K_1 \equiv S_1 - C_1 + P_1 \qquad (9.7)$$

(An expression in terms of time 0 values will be developed shortly.) Equation (9.7) is algebraically the same expression as equation (9.6), but with K_1 rather than S_1 on the left-hand side. Since the two equations are the same, equation (9.6) and (9.7) show formally that the put-call parity relation uses the same idea of dividing up risks that were used in the earlier discussion.

We can also use the risk-neutral probabilities to verify the put-call parity relationship stated in equation (9.7). For example, the value of the put position in Table 9.6 is

$$E_Q[P_1/B_1|\Im_0] = (1 - q)\$5.00/1.10 = 0.71(\$5.00)/1.10$$
$$= \$3.55/1.10 = \$3.23$$

Similarly, the value of the short call position in Table 9.6 is

$$-E_Q[C_1/B_1|\Im_0] = (-\$5.00/1.10)q = (-\$5.00/1.10)(0.29)$$
$$= -\$1.45/1.10 = -\$1.32$$

Symbolically, the valuation relations corresponding to the payoffs can be written

$$K_1/B_1 = E_Q[S_1/B_1|\Im_0] - E_Q[C_1/B_1|\Im_0] + E_Q[P_1/B_1|\Im_0] \qquad (9.8)$$

TABLE 9.7 Finding a Put and a Call with the Same Value

	S_1	$K_1{}^*$	C_1	$-P_1$
Time 1 High Payoffs	105.00	97.90	7.10	0.00
Time 1 Low Payoffs	95.00	97.90	0.00	-2.90
Time 0 Values	89.00	89.00	1.87	-1.87

Finally, substituting the values obtained above into equation (9.8), along with the previously determined value of the firm, we can verify that the left-hand side

$$K_1/B_1 = \$100.00/1.10 = \$90.91$$

is just equal to the value of the right-hand side,

$$E_Q[S_1/B_1|\Im_0] - E_Q[C_1/B_1|\Im_0] + E_Q[P_1/B_1|\Im_0] \\ = (\$97.90 - 1.45 + 3.55)/1.10 = \$90.91 \tag{9.9}$$

completing the verification.

If you look at equation (9.9) carefully, you might guess that there would be a special value of the exercise price K_1, say $K_1{}^*$, such that a call and a put written with exercise price $K_1{}^*$ would have exactly equal values. Table 9.7 shows how to verify that such an exercise price $K_1{}^*$ can be found.

The time 0 values at the bottoms of columns C_1 and $-P_1$ can be checked using the method of risk-neutral probabilities. They are given respectively by

$$E_Q[C_1/B_1|\Im_0] = (0.29)(\$7.10)/1.10 = \$1.87$$

and

$$-E_Q[P_1/B_1|\Im_0] = -(0.71)(\$2.90)/1.10 = -\$1.87$$

Conceptually, Table 9.7 shows that the value of a risky asset can be divided, using options, into the value of a sure thing, the value of its upside potential and the value of its downside risk. Moreover, when the size of the exercise price (equal to the size of the certainty payoff) is chosen to equate the values of the call and the short put position, the value of the upside potential is exactly equal to the value of the downside risk. (The possible payoff on the upside is greater than the payoff on the downside because the market agents valuing the options are assumed to be risk-averse.)

This same idea is used in writing forward contracts whose time 0 value is itself equal to zero. If you go back to Table 9.3, you will see that the price that gave the forward contract an originating value of zero is the same as the $97.90 exercise price that equated the value of the put and the call. Since the forward contract can be interpreted as a long call and a short put, the equality of values verifies once again that in the absence of arbitrage opportunities the value of the forward contract must equal the value of a long call and a short put, when the exercise prices of the options are both equal to the forward price specified in the forward contract.

Changes in Volatility

In a risk-averse market, an increase in volatility will decrease the price of an underlying asset even as it increases the value of derivative contracts written on the asset. To understand the effects, consider the data in Table 9.8, which shows an asset with a larger high payoff and a smaller low payoff than the asset in Table 9.7. It is easy to check that the payoffs have a higher standard deviation, or volatility, than those in Table 9.7. Suppose the new asset value, lower because the increase in volatility is treated by the market as an increase in asset risk, is $88.00. For simplicity, suppose the riskless rate remains 10%. Then the recalculated risk-neutral probabilities are $q = 0.23$ and $1 - q = 0.77$, as may be verified by examining

$$S_0 = [106.00(0.23) + 94.00(0.77)]/1.10 = 88.00$$

The exercise price of the options is set to $88.00(1.10) = 96.80$. The call and the short positions then have the respective values 1.95 and −1.95. Even though the risk-neutral probabilities have changed, Table 9.8 illustrates that the increase in volatility means both option values are greater than those in Table 9.7, and that this occurs even though the value of the underlying asset has decreased.

TABLE 9.8 Finding a Put and a Call with the Same Value: Increased Volatility

	S_1	$K_1{}^*$	C_1	$-P_1$
Time 1 High Payoffs	106.00	96.80	9.20	0.00
Time 1 Low Payoffs	94.00	96.80	0.00	−2.80
Time 0 Values	88.00	88.00	1.95	−1.95

DEBT, EQUITY, AND OPTIONS

You might suspect that the payoffs to debt and equity could somehow be related to the payoffs to option contracts. If so, your suspicions would be correct, and this section shows how the relations can be determined. Recall the example of risky debt discussed in Chapter 8. The numbers are repeated in Table 9.9, which shows a firm that has issued two classes of securities—debt and equity. Table 9.10 shows the related option positions. Comparing the two tables shows that the payoffs to the debt are the same as the payoffs to a sure thing and a short position in a put option: For any row in Table 9.9, the payoffs to the debt are actually equal to the algebraic sum of the payoffs to K_1, regarded as a certainty payment, and the short put position in Table 9.10. In other words, holders of risky debt are in the same position as investors who hold riskless debt and have also written a put option whose exercise price is the promised amount of debt repayment. The short position represents the risk that the debt holders will not be repaid in full.

TABLE 9.9   Payoffs When Risky Debt with Principal and Interest Payment of $99.00 Is Issued

	S_1 (Firm)	D_1 (Debt)	E_1 (Equity)[16]
Time 1 High Payoffs	105.00	99.00	6.00
Time 1 Low Payoffs	95.00	95.00	0.00
Time 0 Values	89.00	87.42	1.58

TABLE 9.10   Options with Exercise Price of $99.00

	S_1	K_1	C_1	$-P_1$
Time 1 High Payoffs	105.00	99.00	6.00	0.00
Time 1 Low Payoffs	95.00	99.00	0.00	−4.00
Time 0 Values	89.00	90.00	1.58	−2.58

As before, the securities in Tables 9.9 and 9.10 can be valued using risk-neutral probabilities. The value of the debt in Table 9.9 is

$$E_Q[D_1/B_1|\mathfrak{I}_0] = [(0.29)(99.00) + (0.71)(95.00)]/1.10 = \$87.42$$

---

[16] Although E is used both to denote an expectation operation and an equity position, the differences in usage should be clear from the respective contexts.

and the value of the equity is

$$E_Q[E_1/B_1|\Im_0] = [(0.29)(6.00)]/1.10 = \$1.58$$

Note that the sum of the instruments' values equals \$89.00, the value of the firm. In the case of Table 9.10, the same kinds of calculations show that the value of the risky debt, \$87.42, is just equal to the time 0 value of a sure payment of \$99.00 less the time 0 value of a put with an exercise price of \$99.00. Comparison of Tables 9.9 and 9.10 shows that risky debt implicitly creates a short put position which reduces the value of the debt from what it would be if the promise were riskless.

FUTURES

This section examines futures contracts. It discusses how and why futures and forward contracts are different and then shows how the futures contract can be valued. Valuing a futures contract is a more complex exercise than valuing a forward contract because the delivery prices on a futures contract can change stochastically during its life, and because the contract provides for periodic payment of capital gains or losses realized during the life of the contract.

What Is a Futures Contract?

A futures contract is like a forward contract, but with the additional feature that it provides for interim settlement of any realized capital gains or losses. Like forwards, futures can be written against many different kinds of assets. Also like forwards, futures can post either capital gains or capital losses. Unlike forwards, the capital gains or losses on a futures contract are realized at the end of each trading period (usually the business day) rather than just on the delivery date. When a futures contract is first issued, the usual practice is to set the futures price so that the contract's initial value is zero. The contract value typically changes each trading day as the value of the underlying asset changes. The change in asset value produces a capital gain or loss for the holder of the futures contract, and at the end of each trading day, this gain or loss must be settled with the broker arranging the contract. After the gain or loss is settled, the futures contract is "marked to market" by resetting the futures price so that the contract once again has a value of zero.

The principal reason for settling capital gains or losses each day is to limit the possible losses arising from contract default. There is always a possibility that a forward contract will be defaulted upon by the losing

TABLE 9.11 Forward and Futures Contracts

	Time 0	Time 1	Time 2
Cash Flow from Forward Contract	0	0	$S_2 - O_{02}$
Cash Flows from Futures Contract	0	$U_{12} - U_{02}$	$S_2 - U_{12}$

party, either before or at maturity. The default risk of a futures contract is lower than that of a forward contract, because capital gains or losses must be settled every trading day instead of being permitted to mount up.

Relations between Futures and Forward Prices

To value a futures contract, one must take into account the possibility that the futures price embodied in the instrument will be changed as realized capital gains or losses are credited to the parties' trading accounts. Although a complete investigation of the issues in valuation is a complex subject beyond the scope of this text, the following example shows (1) how to compare forward and futures prices and (2) the principal differences between the two types of contract. As will become evident, the principal technical difference between the two is that futures contracts create cash flows from the marking to market process. This technical difference reduces the possible costs of default, and also has particular valuation effects if interest rates are uncertain.

First, compare the cash flows from going long in either a forward or a futures contract when the two contracts will remain outstanding for two periods.[17] The futures contract will be revalued at time 1, while the terms of the analogous forward contract remain unchanged at that point. The cash flows from the two contracts are shown symbolically in Table 9.11.

In the table, O_{02} is the forward (fOrward) price, set at time 0 and referring to delivery at time 2. Similarly, U_{02} is the futures (fUtures) price,[18] set at time 0 and referring to delivery at time 2. In addition, U_{12} is the futures price after the contract, still specifying delivery at time 2, has been marked to market at time 1. Finally, S_2 refers to the price of the asset at time 2.

As is evident from Table 9.11, the difference between the long positions in the two contracts is the cash flow (positive or negative) on the futures contract, which results from its being marked to market at time 1. If the cash

---

[17] We could consider more periods, but to do so would mean having to repeat similar calculations without adding further insights.

[18] The futures price has two subscripts because, even for a contract with fixed maturity, the price itself changes from one period to the next.

flow is positive, we assume it can be invested at the then prevailing riskless interest rate, while if it is negative, we assume funds can be borrowed at the riskless rate.

Let $B_1 = (1 + r_{01})$, where r_{01} is the interest rate between time 0 and time 1. Similarly $B_2 = (1 + r_{01})(1 + r_{12})$, so that the interest rate between time 1 and time 2 is $(B_2/B_1) - 1 = r_{12}$. The discount factors between times 0 and 1 is then $1/B_1$, and B_1/B_2 is the discount factor between times 1 and 2. At time 0, we assume the interest rate between time 0 and 1 is known with certainty, but the interest rate between times 1 and 2 is known only as a random variable[19] until time 1. The assumed randomness of B_2/B_1 means that the time 1 cash flow is random when viewed from a time 0 perspective.

Table 9.11 shows why the two contracts have different risks when they are regarded from the perspective of time 0. If the spot price at time 2 were known, the cash flows from the forward contract could be stated with certainty at time 0. However, the time 0 value of the time 2 cash flows from the futures contract could not be stated with certainty even if the spot price were known, because the present value of the cash flows would still depend on a random interest rate.

Finding Futures Prices Using Risk-Neutral Probabilities

The relations determining futures prices, and the differences between forward and futures prices, can be developed further using the ideas of arbitrage free securities prices and risk-neutral probabilities. Suppose that the contracts call for delivery of one unit of some underlying security. In any such contract, the amount to be paid on delivery date T is the value of the security at the time. Suppose also that the security does not pay a dividend between the present time 0 and the delivery date T. Repeating equation (9.4) for convenience, recall that the forward price set at time 0 on a contract with delivery date T is[20]

$$O_{0T} = S_0 / E_Q[1/B_T | \Im_0]$$

---

[19] The interest rate is called riskless because it is the market rate of interest on a bond with no default risk. Nevertheless, such a rate can also change randomly from time to time. Our assumptions regarding when the riskless rate becomes known with certainty mean we are treating it as a predictable process; see Pliska (1997).

[20] For comparison purposes, we now give the forward price two subscripts, reflecting both the date of origination and the delivery date, when the forward price is to be paid.

and may be rewritten as

$$O_{0T} = E_Q[(S_T/B_T)|\Im_0]/E_Q[1/B_T|\Im_0] \tag{9.10}$$

We next show that the futures price is

$$U_{0T} = E_Q[S_T|\Im_0] \tag{9.11}$$

First, at time 0, standard market practice is to set the futures prices so that the cash flows from a two-period contract are valued at zero:

$$E_Q[(U_{12} - U_{02})/B_1 + (U_{22} - U_{12})/B_2|\Im_0] = 0$$

However, marking to market also means that at time 1:

$$E_Q[(U_{22} - U_{12})B_1/B_2|\Im_1] = 0 \tag{9.12}$$

If the contract allows for no substitutions in the asset to be delivered,[21] $U_{22} = S_2$. But equation (9.12) means that

$$U_{12} = E_Q[U_{22}|\Im_1] = E_Q[S_2|\Im_1] \tag{9.13}$$

since U_{12}, B_1, and B_2 are all known at time 1. Then substituting equation (9.13) in equation (9.12) gives

$$E_Q[(U_{12} - U_{02})B_1 + 0|\Im_0] = 0 \tag{9.14}$$

and since B_1 is also known at time 0, equation (9.14) can be rewritten as

$$E_Q[(U_{12} - U_{02})|\Im_0] = 0$$

It then follows immediately that

$$\begin{aligned} U_{02} &= E_Q[U_{12}|\Im_0] = E_Q\{E_Q[U_{22}|\Im_1]|\Im_0\} \\ &= E_Q[U_{22}|\Im_0] = E_Q[S_2|\Im_0] \end{aligned} \tag{9.15}$$

establishing equation (9.11).

---

[21] Some futures contracts do allow such substitutions, making their valuation more complex than shown here.

TABLE 9.12 Security Prices

Time 0	Time 1	Risk-Neutral Probability
5	8	$q = 7/18$
5	4	$1 - q = 11/18$

If interest rates are random, the values of B_T, $T > 1$, are random when viewed from the perspective of time 0. However if interest rates are deterministic, the value of B_T is deterministic also. In the latter case, the value of B_T can be taken outside the expectation operator and we obtain

$$O_{02} = E_Q[(S_T/B_T)|\Im_0]/E_Q[1/B_T|\Im_0] = E_Q[S_T|\Im_0] = U_{02} \qquad (9.16)$$

the last equality following from equation (9.14). That is, time 0 forward and futures prices are equal in a world of deterministic interest rates.

Note from equation (9.16) that when interest rates are random the expression for forward prices contains interest terms, but the corresponding expression (9.15) for futures prices does not. You can see why by comparing equation (9.16)with equation (9.14)and equation (9.15). Under a futures contract capital gains or losses are received or paid each period, and thus do not need to be equated between time points. Finally, if there is only one time period remaining before the delivery date, the forward price and the futures price[22] are equal, because the two contracts represent the same outcomes at this point in time.

Examples

This section presents two examples of relations between forward and futures prices, both due to Pliska (1997). The first is a one-period example with deterministic interest rates. It verifies that a forward and a futures contract are the same in this context, and also displays the differences between the forward and futures price formulae. Moreover, it shows that despite the differences in the formulae, the same value is obtained in the present restricted context. Suppose a security has a time 0 market value of 5 and pays off either 8 or 4 at time 1 as shown in Table 9.12.

---

[22] After the futures contract has been marked to market at that point in time.

Suppose also that $B_1 = 10/9$, a statement equivalent to saying that the riskless interest rate is 1/9. Assuming the absence of arbitrage opportunities, the risk-neutral probabilities can be found using

$$S_o = E_Q[S_1/B_1|\Im_0]$$

Applying the last line to the present example means solving

$$5 = q \times 8 \times (9/10) + (1-q) \times 4 \times (9/10)$$

for q. The value of the solution is shown in the first line, third column of Table 9.12. The time 0 determined forward price, to be paid at time 1, is given by

$$O_{01} = S_0 \times B_1 = 5 \times (10/9) = 50/9$$

The futures price is given by

$$U_{01} = E_Q[S_1|\Im_0] = 8 \times (7/18) + 4 \times (11/18) = 100/18 = 50/9$$

As already mentioned, these calculations show the essential similarity of one-period forward and futures contracts, and also show that with deterministic interest rates the forward and futures prices are the same.

The second of Pliska's examples (1997, 146) has two time intervals and random interest rates between times 1 and 2. Each row of Table 9.13 shows a possible evolution of security prices from time 0, through time 1, to time 2.

Bond prices are 1 at time 0, 1 at time 1, and either 17/16 or 9/8 at time 2. The price of 17/16 is associated with the events in the first two rows of the preceding table, and the price of 9/8 is associated with the events in the second two rows. Thus the interest rate from time 0 to time 1 is zero, while the interest rate from time 1 to time 2 is either 1/16 or 1/9, according to whether the security price has risen or fallen by time 1. The values of the

TABLE 9.13 Security Prices

Time 0	Time 1	Time 2	Risk-Neutral Probability
5	8	9	5/24
5	8	6	1/24
5	4	6	9/24
5	4	3	9/24

risk-neutral probability measure, consistent with the assumption of arbitrage free prices, are here taken as given.

The futures price at time 1 takes on two values, corresponding to the two possible securities prices. If the securities price is 8 at time 1, one knows the security price must either be 9 or 6 in the next period. The conditional risk-neutral probabilities that reflect these events are respectively $(5/24)/(6/24) = 5/6$ and $(1/24)/(6/24) = 1/6$. In that event, the time 1 futures price can be found using (5.6):

$$(U_{12}|S_1 = 8) = E_Q[S_2|\Im_1] = 9(5/6) + 6(1/6) = 51/6 = 17/2$$

If the securities price is 4, the conditional risk-neutral probabilities are both equal to 1/2 and the futures price is

$$(U_{12}|S_1 = 4) = E_Q[S_2|\Im_1] = 6(1/2) + 3(1/2) = 9/2$$

Finally, the futures price at time 0 is given by

$$(U_{02}) = E_Q[S_2|\Im_0] = 9(5/24) + 6(1/24) + 6(9/24) + 3(9/24)$$
$$= 132/24 = 11/2$$

The futures price at time 0 can also be computed as a conditional expectation, under the risk-neutral probability measure, of the previously calculated time 1 futures prices. Using equation (9.11),

$$U_{02} = E_Q[U_{12}|\Im_0] = (17/2)(1/4) + (9/2)(3/4) = 11/2$$

On the other hand, the forward price at time 0^{23} is found from equation (9.1):

$$O_2 = 5/[(16/17)(6/24) + (8/9)(18/24)] = 5/[46/51] = 255/46$$

In keeping with the discussion following equation (9.1), the expected discount rates in the previous calculation are

$$E_Q[(1/B_1)|\Im_0] = (16/17)(1/4) + (8/9)(3/4) = 46/51$$

That is, the forward price is the current asset price accumulated at the expected interest rate.

---

[23] It is possible to calculate forward values at time 1, but the contract does not permit delivery at that time.

VALUING A CREDIT DEFAULT SWAP

This section shows how to value a one-year credit default swap using the method of risk-neutral probabilities.[24] In essence, the example shows that value is determined using the risk-neutral probabilities and discounting at the riskless interest rate, just as in the previous examples of this chapter. The differences between the previous examples and the present one are differences in the nature of the instrument used, its purposes, and the conditions under which payments are made.

Suppose a bank buys one-year default protection from a counterparty, whose exposure to defaults is to be determined by defaults in a specified reference portfolio. That is, the counterparty's payments on the swap will be made if a default occurs in the reference portfolio. For simplicity, suppose there can be one or more reference portfolio events. An event means one or more defaults can occur, at the end of six months, at the end of a year, or at both times. If a default in the reference portfolio occurs at the end of six months, the counterparty agrees to pay the bank an amount F at that time, and the counterparty liability is extinguished. However, if there are no defaults in the first six months, a liability of F can still be incurred by the counterparty at time 1 if one or more defaults in the reference portfolio occur then. The valuation question we address is: If the bank makes a single payment at time 0 for the protection,[25] how much should it pay?

We model the situation by referring to the present time as time 0, the time six months from now as time 1, and the time one year from now as time 2. Table 9.14(A) shows the riskless discount factors applicable to payments received at time 1 and at time 2 respectively. Table 9.14(B) displays the event tree and the risk-neutral conditional probabilities that are assumed to be applicable to the different possible outcomes. Table 9.14(C) displays the value calculations, including the discount factors used to equate the time 0 values of the payments.

Hence the time 0 value of the contract, arrived under the assumption of an absence of arbitrage opportunities, is 0.07965 per dollar, times the total liability of F dollars.

---

[24]The example is adapted from Jarrow and Turnbull (1996, 583–586).

[25]Industry practice may call for more than a single payment, say in the present example one at the outset and a second payment after six months. Of course, the present value of the series of payments should equal the present value of a single payment made at the outset.

TABLE 9.14 Security Price

A. Riskless Interest Rate Data

	Time 0	Time 1	Time 2
One-year bond	0.9749	1.0000	
Two-year bond	0.9496 = 0.9741 × 0.9749	0.9741	1.0000

B. Event Tree

Time 0	Time 1	Time 2
Default swap arranged	No default RNP = 0.95922	No default, no payment, liability terminates. RNP = 0.95913
Default swap arranged	No default RNP = 0.95922	Default. F Paid, liability terminates. RNP = 0.04087
Default swap arranged	Default: F paid, Liability terminates. RNP = 0.04078	

C. Value Calculations under Risk-Neutral Probability

	Time 0	Time 1	Time 2
Time 0 expected value, no default	0	0	0
Time 0 expected value, default at time 2	F × 0.04087 × 0.95922 × 0.9741 × 0.9749	F × 0.04087 × 0.95922 × 0.9741	F × 0.04087
Time 0 expected value, default at time 1	F × 0.04078 × 0.9749	F × 0.04078	
Sum of time 0 values, equal to the value of the default swap	F × 0.07695		

REFERENCES

Black, Fischer, and Myron Scholes. 1973. "The pricing of options and corporate liabilities." *Journal of Political Economy* 81: 637–654.

Cox, John C., and Mark Rubinstein. 1985. *Options Markets*. Englewood Cliffs, NJ: Prentice-Hall.

Hull, John C. 2008. *Options, Futures and Other Derivatives*, 7th ed. Upper Saddle River, NJ: Prentice-Hall.

Jarrow, Robert A., and Stuart M. Turnbull. 1996. *Derivative securities*. Cincinnati: South-Western Publishing Company.

Pliska, Stanley R. 1997. *Introduction to Mathematical Finance*. Malden, MA: Blackwell.

Markets with Impediments to Arbitrage

Chapter 10 explores market relations when there are impediments to arbitrage. It begins by explaining how markets differ in providing liquidity. If all markets were perfectly liquid and there were no transactions costs, prices would be related as in the no arbitrage world. However, with differing degrees of information, of liquidity, and in the presence of transactions costs, asset price relations become very much less well defined. Furthermore, these same market imperfections can lead to such phenomena as credit rationing equilibriums, market segmentation, market failure, and financial system externalities.

In an arbitrage-free world, securities are always liquid, all market transactions are linked by arbitrage, and externalities and market failures are assumed away. The assumptions are valuable both in their own right and for analyzing some of the complications arising when the assumptions are relaxed. Market imperfections can imply that market prices are no longer completely linked to each other, that securities' liquidity can vary, and that externalities or third-party effects may influence prices. Sometimes equilibrium prices may not be attainable, and in other cases market failure can occur.

Despite the foregoing complications, the prices determined in arbitrage-free markets can still serve as a guide to value, although depending on circumstances the guide can range from being helpful to being unreliable. This chapter attempts to trace some of the ways in which the benchmarks' reliability can be affected by different forms of imperfections. The chapter begins by examining market liquidity and its determinants, and then examines market linkages and market segmentation, financial system externalities, credit rationing equilibriums, and market failure.

SECURITIES MARKETS AND LIQUIDITY

The role of the stock exchange specialist was first examined by Baumol (1965) and by Demsetz (1968). Their work indicates that making a market involves assembling information regarding both the company whose shares are being traded and its business environment. Agents using a market maker's services do not need to acquire information themselves, but can pay the market maker to do so for them. To Demsetz, one of the main roles of the market maker is to supply immediacy of trading. Since the market maker holds an inventory of the security, in effect he provides a form of insurance against temporary order imbalances. The market maker also insures a potential trader against entering the market without success—at least so long as the agent is ready to trade at or near the current market price. The market maker or specialist buys at a price below the market and sells at a price higher than the market. The price spread covers the specialist's costs of providing trade immediacy services, as well as any other operating costs.

One of the most important risks faced by a market maker is the risk of inventory price change. Since market makers have limited capital, they can be quite sensitive to these risks. Baumol argues that when market makers infer from order imbalances and other information that conditions may be changing, they change prices more frequently and reduce their price quotations to the minimum amounts of trading allowed in order to limit their inventory risks. Market makers also face the risk of trading with better-informed parties, in which case they suffer the effects of adverse selection. On average, market makers will lose when trading with better-informed parties, and will have to cover those losses through the bid-ask spreads they set when trading with uninformed parties.

Liquidity differences among markets depend on such factors as differences in market structure, the nature of the instruments traded, and the kinds of obligations the instruments represent. This section, based on Grossman and Miller (1988), considers how the economics of dealing in a market-place can influence the number of active market makers whose presence contributes to liquidity. Grossman and Miller explain why liquidity differs among markets and show that the number of active market makers can be used to measure market liquidity. To do so, the model links the observed presence of market specialists to the profits they can expect to earn in different markets. For example, making a market for Treasury bonds can prove profitable while making a market for residential housing will likely not be.

The model considers a group of market makers and a group of outside customers trading in a single stock. If customers wish to sell their stock, they can either sell immediately to market makers, or wait until later to determine if additional potential buyers might respond with a more favorable offer. Selling immediately brings a certainty price, typically lower than the price customers might expect to realize from waiting. On the other hand, waiting for a possibly higher price also means bearing a risk of adverse price change. Grossman and Miller refer to customers' willingness to sell at once as their demand for immediacy, and postulate that the demand for immediacy depends on both the volatility of the stock price and any possibilities that the customers might be able to diversify against price moves.

Market makers who stand ready to buy are said to supply immediacy services, and their supply function is determined by the economics of market making. Gross returns from market making must cover both the costs and risks of holding an inventory and the opportunity costs of standing ready to buy whenever sellers demand their services.[1] First, making a market means assuming a price risk, described analytically by its variance. From a market maker's point of view, an increase in price variance increases both the risk of holding an inventory and the possibility of earning trading profits. Second, market makers must cover their operating costs. As compensation, market makers will buy at prices lower than the prices they expect to realize when reselling the inventory.

Differences in the supply of and demand for immediacy jointly determine market liquidity. The greater the demand for immediacy, and the lower the market makers' costs, the larger will be the proportion of transactions channeled through market makers. The larger the proportion of transactions so channeled, the greater will be the degree of market liquidity.

Liquidity Differences in Practice

Successful futures markets offer an example of markets where both the demand for immediacy and the supply of market-making services are relatively great, and consequently these markets exhibit a relatively high degree of liquidity. The futures markets' demands for immediacy stem from the fact that delaying futures trades can be highly risky, especially when a trade is part of a portfolio adjustment strategy. Since futures markets also stimulate hedging, Grossman and Miller argue that the demand for immediacy is both urgent and sustained (1988, 619). At the same time, the supply of market-making services is relatively great because market makers' costs and inventory risks are relatively low.

On the other hand, markets for retail transactions in residential housing are highly illiquid. Sellers of individual homes are less concerned with immediacy than with making sure that all potential buyers (i.e., the largest possible

---

[1]Inventory risk may be a more important factor in the short run; opportunity cost a more important factor in the longer run.

set it is economic to inform) are notified of the intended sale. Moreover, the supply of market-making services is limited both by the opportunity costs of maintaining a presence in a thin market and by a very high degree of inventory risk. The inventory risk can also be affected by moral hazard if the seller has adverse private information about the property's condition. In consequence, almost all residential housing is traded by brokers (who do not take inventory positions) rather than by market makers.

Stock markets lie between the two extremes just outlined. For a few widely held and very actively traded stocks, the NYSE[2] comes close to the futures markets in providing a high degree of liquidity, and for much the same reasons. However the same is not true for NYSE-listed stocks that are less actively traded. For these stocks, a specialist trader is granted a trading monopoly in exchange for an obligation to stand ready to buy or sell during exchange business hours, at least if the proposed orders are relatively small.[3] For larger transactions the specialist can, with the permission of the exchange, suspend trading while searching for counterparties. This search will likely involve participants in the upstairs market, discussed next.

The upstairs market is an institutional market for block trades. The upstairs market originally emerged in the 1960s as a facility aimed at finding institutional traders whose spreads were lower than the commissions then charged by exchange specialists. Since the late 1960s upstairs market participants have taken increasingly larger inventory positions, thereby increasing the liquidity of the market. Since the early 1980s, upstairs market participants have been able to sell off some of their inventory risks by using futures and index options, offsetting some of the previously assumed inventory risks. As a result market making has become more economic, and upstairs market liquidity has increased still further.

When they were originally set up, OTC markets handled stocks whose trading was too thin to merit listing, even on a regional exchange. At the outset OTC markets functioned mainly as bulletin boards on which market makers could list price quotes valid for minimum order amounts. For at least some stocks, lower computing and communications costs have changed the supply of market-making services, stimulating the emergence of more market makers. At the same time, and particularly in the late 1990s with the emergence of electronic computer networks, both the number of OTC participants and the demand for liquidity services have increased.

---

[2]Now NYSE Euronext. However, the two markets still maintain separate trading facilities, known as the NYSE and Euronext respectively.
[3]While the specialist's position creates a potential for the exercise of monopoly power, stock exchange regulations are designed to limit the potential for exploiting the monopoly.

As a result, the OTC markets are now more liquid than previously,[4] and some large stocks that formerly traded on organized exchanges now trade OTC.

A Model of Market Liquidity

The Grossman-Miller model (1988) assumes that both outside customers and market makers maximize the expected utility of their wealth as at time 2. Their terminal wealth positions are affected by trading that place at times 0 and 1. Agents can trade both a riskless asset and a risky security. The price of the riskless asset is certain, while the price of the risky security is stochastic. Risky security prices are affected both by changes in effective demand and by revisions of the information reaching the market.

At time 0 a group of outside customers experience a liquidity event, following which they become net sellers of the risky security. The model assumes another group of outside customers arrive at time 1 with an exactly offsetting endowment of the risky security. Thus at time 0 the first group of outsiders can anticipate selling to the second group at time 1, but at a price that is known only stochastically at time 0.[5] Alternatively outside consumers may sell immediately at time 0 to market makers and obtain a deterministic price.[6]

The holders of the risky security, either the first group of outside customers or the market makers, bear its price risk between times 0 and 1. The model studies the allocation of this price risk between the two groups. Assume that both outside customers and market makers have a negative exponential utility defined on terminal wealth, and that stock prices P_t are distributed normally at each of the three times, $t = 0, 1, 2$. As in Chapter 5, these assumptions mean that agents can be modeled as maximizing

$$E[W_2|\Im_0] - \rho\sigma^2[W_2|\Im_0]/2 \qquad (10.1)$$

---

[4]The same comment can be made regarding the electronic markets known as Alternative Trading Systems. Although the literature does not usually so describe them, the OTC markets can be regarded as constituting the first ATSs. Moreover, the largest and best known of the original OTC markets, the Nasdaq, is now large enough and liquid enough to qualify as another exchange.

[5]As will be seen later, if both groups have the same risk-averse utilities and the same price expectations, at equilibrium they will all hold a zero position in the risky stock.

[6]In a world where future prices were deterministic and constant market makers could, if interest rates were zero, resell the inventory to the second group for neither a loss nor a gain. Indeed, market makers would be unnecessary since the first group would neither gain nor lose by selling directly to the second group.

where $E(W_2|\Im_0)$ is expected time 2 wealth viewed from the perspective of time 0, $\sigma^2(W_2|\Im_0)$ its variance, and ρ is a measure of risk aversion. The symbol $\Im_t$ refers to information available at time t; $t = 0$, 1, or 2.

To examine solution properties, consider an investor using a time 1 perspective. The investor desires to determine the optimal combination of the riskless and the risky securities, assessed in terms of the expected utility of her wealth position as at time 2. If the riskless security has a zero return and the stock pays no dividend, stock returns between time 1 and 2 are given by $(P_2 - P_1)/P_1$. Then the investor's time 1 problem is to maximize the certainty equivalent value of time 2 wealth, that is,

$$E[(W_1 + X_1(P_2 - P_1)|\Im_1] - \rho\sigma^2(X_1 P_2^2|\Im_1)/2 \tag{10.2}$$

where W_1 is investor wealth at the beginning of period 1, and X_1 is the risky security position after trading at the beginning of period 1. Finally P_t is the price that obtains at time t, $t = 0$, 1, 2. Using the methods of Chapter 6, the optimal investment in the risky security is

$$X_1^* = [E(P_2|\Im_1) - P_1]/\rho\sigma^2(P_2|\Im_1) \tag{10.3}$$

This generic form of solution will be used a number of times later.

Now consider the problem as it appears from the perspective of time 0, before trading occurs. Outside customers still choose their security holdings to maximize

$$EU(W_2|\Im_0) \equiv E(W_2|\Im_0) - \rho\sigma^2(W_2|\Im_0)/2$$

but the maximization is determined with respect to possible trades at both times 0 and 1. The maximization is subject to

$$\begin{aligned} W_2 &= b_1 + P_2 X_1 \\ W_1 &= b_1 + P_1 X_1 = b_0 + P_1 X_0 \\ W_0 &= b_0 + P_0 X_0 = (P_0)\, i + W_e \end{aligned} \tag{10.4}$$

where i and W_e are the customer's initial endowments of the risky security and wealth respectively. The symbol b_t represents both the position and the value of the riskless asset after trading at time t. The customer's total wealth at time t is indicated by W_t, $t = 0$, 1, 2. In equation (10.4) the value of the riskless asset does not change between time 0 and time 1 because the interest rate is assumed to be zero.

It is now convenient to eliminate b_0 and b_1 from the expression for time 2 wealth. From the first and second lines of equation (10.4),

$$W_2 = (W_1 - P_1 X_1) + P_2 X_1 = W_1 + (P_2 - P_1) X_1 \qquad (10.5)$$

Similarly from the second and third lines of equation (10.4)

$$\begin{aligned} W_1 &= (W_0 - P_0 X_0) + P_1 X_0 = W_0 + (P_1 - P_0) X_0 \\ &= W_e + (P_1 - P_0) X_0 + (P_0)i \end{aligned} \qquad (10.6)$$

Rewriting equation (10.6) gives

$$W_1 = W_e + (P_1 - P_0) X_0 + P_0 i = W_e + (P_1 - P_0)(X_0 - i) + (P_1)I \quad (10.7)$$

Then substituting equation (10.7) in equation (10.5) gives

$$\begin{aligned} W_2 &= W_e + (P_1 - P_0)(X_0 - i) + P_1 i + (P_2 - P_1) X_1 \\ &= W_e + (P_1 - P_0)(X_0 - i) + (P_2 - P_1)(X_1 - i) + (P_2)i \quad (10.8) \\ &= W_e + (P_1 - P_0) Y_0 + (P_2 - P_1) Y_1 + (P_2)i \end{aligned}$$

In equation (10.8), the terms $X_t - i \equiv Y_t$ represent the time t excess demand for the security. In general, excess demands can be either positive or negative, but as already mentioned they are assumed to be negative for the group of outside customers with orders at time 0, because they are treated as net sellers.

Using equation (10.8), at time 0 outside customers face the problem of maximizing

$$EU(W_2|\mathfrak{I}_0) = EU[(W_e + (P_1 - P_0)Y_0 + (P_2 - P_1)Y_1 + P_2 i)|\mathfrak{I}_0] \quad (10.9)$$

Problem (10.9) is solved by first determining an optimal value for Y_1, then working backwards to obtain an optimal value for Y_0. From the perspective of time 1, P_0 and P_1 are known and the problem is to maximize, with respect to $X_1 \equiv Y_1 + i$,

$$\begin{aligned} &EU[(W_1 - P_1 i + (P_2 - P_1)Y_1 + P_2 i)|\mathfrak{I}_1] \qquad (10.10) \\ &\equiv EU[(W_1 + (P_2 - P_1)(Y_1 + i)|\mathfrak{I}_1] \end{aligned}$$

In equation (10.10), equation (10.7) is used to rewrite the argument of equation (10.9). The solution to equation (10.10) has the same form as equation (10.3):

$$Y_1^* + i = \{[E(P_2) - P_1]/\rho\sigma^2(P_2)|\Im_1\} \tag{10.11}$$

There can be many identical outside customers, but for simplicity Grossman and Miller use equation (10.11) to express both individual and aggregate demand.

Let Z_t be the excess demand of a single market maker, and suppose there are m such agents. Each market maker is assumed to have $W_e = i = 0$. The optimal excess demand of the group of market makers can then be written

$$mZ_1^* = m\{[E(P_2|\Im_1) - P_1]/\rho\sigma^2(P_2|\Im_1)\} \tag{10.12}$$

Next, assume that at time 1 new outside customers arrive with an initial security endowment $-i$, that is, exactly the negative of the first group. Then the market clearing conditions at time 1 are

$$[\{[E(P_2|\Im_1) - P_1]/\rho\sigma^2(P_2|\Im_1) - i + m[E(P_2|\Im_1) - P_1]/\rho\sigma^2(P_2|\Im_1)$$
$$+ [E(P_2|\Im_1) - P_1]/\rho\sigma^2(P_2|\Im_1) + i\}] = 0 \tag{10.13}$$

Market clearing implies that all trades in the stock must sum to zero at time 1, and since the initial security endowments are offsetting they do not affect the price relations in equation (10.13). The only role played by P_2 is to value security holdings after trading is completed, and equation (10.13) can only be zero if $E(P_2|\Im_1) = P_1$, that is, if the expected time 2 price just equals the current price.

Given that prices are not expected to change, equation (10.11) implies $Y_1^* = -i$. Moreover, since $Y_1^* \equiv X_1^* - i$, it also follows that $X_1^* = 0$; the optimal portfolios of the original outside customers contain none of the risky security at time 1. (And nor do those of the second group, since at their optimum they purchase the supply of the first group.)

Using the foregoing observations, it is now possible to find the outside customers' time 0 demand for the risky security. The time 0 problem is to maximize

$$EU\{(W_e + [(EP_2 - P_0)Y_0 + E(P_2)i]|\Im_1)|\Im_0\} \tag{10.14}$$

with respect to $Y_0 + i$. The solution to equation (10.14) is

$$Y_0^* + i = [E\{E(P_2|\Im_1)|\Im_0\} - P_0]/\rho\sigma^2(P_2|\Im_0)$$
$$= [E(P_2|\Im_0) - P_0]/\rho\sigma^2(P_2|\Im_0) \tag{10.15}$$

A probability law known as the law of iterated expectations is used to obtain the second line of equation (10.15). As before, the demand of the individual consumer is treated as the aggregate demand.

Using similar reasoning, the solution to each market maker's problem at time 0 is

$$Z_0^* = [E(P_2|\Im_0) - P_0]/\rho\sigma^2(P_2|\Im_0) \qquad (10.16)$$

Finally, market clearing at time 0 requires

$$mZ_0^* + Y_0^* = 0 \qquad (10.17)$$

Combining equations (10.15), (10.16), and (10.17) gives

$$Z_0^* = [E(P_2|\Im_0) - P_0]/\rho\sigma^2(P_2|\Im_0) = i/(1+m) \qquad (10.18)$$

Let $r \equiv P_1/P_0 - 1$ be the market maker's return on inventory between times 0 and 1. Then from equation (10.14)

$$E(r|\Im_0) = [(P_0)i/(1+m)]/\rho\sigma^2(r|\Im_0) \qquad (10.19)$$

Since the value of the inventory held by a typical market maker is

$$P_0 Z_0^* = (P_0)i/(1+m) \qquad (10.20)$$

it can be seen from (10.19) that the larger this inventory value the higher must be the market maker's expected return in order to compensate for bearing additional inventory risk.

A market maker who pays a fixed cost c to enter the market must compare his or her expected utility of wealth from having done so with the status quo. Using (10.15), the market maker is indifferent between entering or not entering if

$$c = [E(P_1|\Im_0) - P_0]^2/2\rho\sigma^2(P_1|\Im_0) \qquad (10.21)$$

The quantity (10.21) is obtained by evaluating the criterion function at the optimal portfolio (see the discussion in the section "Consequences of Segmentation"). Equation (10.18) shows that for given c an increase in σ^2 will reduce each market maker's inventory position and will also mean an increase in the number of market makers. It also follows from equation (10.20) that

$$c = [E(P_1|\Im_0) - P_0]i/2(1 + m) \qquad (10.22)$$

Equation (10.22) shows that an increase in c will, other things being equal, imply a reduction in the number of market makers. If equation (10.22) holds with equality and the expected price increases, more market makers will enter the business.

Since equations (10.15), (10.16), and (10.17) imply that

$$Y_0^* = -mi/(1 + m) \qquad (10.23)$$

and since from the discussion following equation (10.13) $Y_1^* = -i$, it follows that

$$Y_1^* - Y_0^* = -i/(1 + m) \qquad (10.24)$$

Then equations (10.23) and (10.24) together imply that the fraction of total trade completed by market makers, Y_0^*, increases relative to the amount of deferred trade, $Y_1^* - Y_0^*$, as the number of market makers increases. In the absence of market makers, at time 0 the original outside consumers hold i of the risky security if there are no market makers while in the presence of m market makers they decrease their holdings to $i/(1 + m)$. That is, the market becomes more liquid as the number of market makers increases.[7] Of course, in either case outside customers further decrease their holdings to zero at time 1.

Further Aspects of Market Liquidity

Subsequent empirical and theoretical studies elaborate the picture conveyed by Grossman and Miller. Chordia, Roll, and Subrahmanyam (2001) study aggregate market spreads, depths, and trading activity for U.S. equities, covering more securities and over a longer time period than previously studies. Chordia et al. find that daily changes in average liquidity and trading activity are both highly volatile and negatively correlated over time. The authors observe that liquidity declines significantly in down markets, but the effect is asymmetric: Spreads increase dramatically in down markets, but decrease only marginally in up markets. The authors also find strong day-of-the-week effects: There is a significant decrease in trading activity

---

[7]Grossman and Miller point out that the bid-ask spread is a flawed measure of liquidity because it is not a measure of price differences at a given point in time.

and liquidity on Fridays, while Tuesdays display the opposite pattern. Long- and short-term interest rates both influence liquidity. Finally, market depth and trading activity increase just prior to macroeconomic announcements.

O'Hara (2003) examined the implications of market microstructure for asset pricing. O'Hara contends that standard asset pricing theory (as developed in Chapters 8 and 9) does not recognize that asset prices evolve in markets affecting established prices.[8] To O'Hara, symmetric information-based asset pricing models do not well describe market trading processes because they assume that the underlying problems of liquidity and price discovery have been solved. In contrast, O'Hara contends that the market processes actually provide liquidity and price discovery, implying that asset pricing models should incorporate varying degrees of liquidity, the changing transactions costs that varying liquidity implies, and the risks of price discovery.

O'Hara develops an asymmetric information asset pricing model along the foregoing lines. Her model explains that the equilibrium risk premium is higher for assets when a larger fraction of relevant valuation information is private rather than public. She also speculates that the equity premium puzzle—the fact that equity returns contain a higher risk premium than current models predict—may be due to the fact that equity returns also contain an information risk component. Finally, when information is asymmetrically distributed, uninformed investors will demand to be compensated for portfolio-induced risks that they cannot diversify.

Vayanos and Weill (2008) investigate the question of why "on-the-run" (just-issued) bonds trade at generally higher prices than similar "off-the-run" (previously issued) bonds. To do so, the authors propose a model in which assets with identical cash flows can trade at different prices. The model is based on infinitely lived agents who can establish long positions in a spot market, or short positions by first borrowing an asset in a repurchase market. In the model, short sellers concentrate in trading one asset because of search externalities and the constraint that they must deliver the asset they borrowed. That asset displays greater liquidity as measured by search times, carries a higher lending fee, and trades at a premium relative to no-arbitrage prices. The authors show that the model generates realistic sizes of on-the-run premiums.

Limits to Arbitrage

As Chapter 4 explained, financiers are usually described as seeking out profitable arbitrage opportunities, both within a given market and between

---

[8]In fact, equilibrium may never be reached because new information is continually becoming available.

markets. Through trading, financiers link securities prices to each other. The linkages are strengthened by market operators who strive to attract business through executing trades quickly and at the lowest possible charges. Market trading is at its most active when deal terms are standardized, when agents have ready access to the same information, and when transactions costs comprise a relatively small percentage of trades' values. For example, the traditional forms of commercial and finance company paper trade in markets whose interest rates are very closely related. Indeed, these two markets are often referred to as parts of a single money market, as described more fully in Chapter 11. Similarly, there is usually active arbitraging among government securities of different maturities.

Trading among complementary securities is usually less active than among close substitutes. For example, there is relatively little or no trading between government and corporate securities of similar maturities. Corporate securities are less liquid than governments, and there is usually less information regarding the creditworthiness of the corporations involved. Accordingly, interest rates on government and corporate securities markets are less closely related than interest rates on different maturities of government securities. In addition, some trading practices can impede arbitraging and frustrate efforts to attract order flow. For example, in attempts to minimize the adverse selection effects of trading large positions, some traders prefer to remain anonymous and to conceal the amounts they are ready to trade. As still another example, while it can be easy and cheap to switch between exchanges when trading stocks, it is not equally easy and cheap to switch between stock and futures exchanges. This difference means there are stronger linkages between markets for actively traded stocks than there are for actively traded futures contracts (Bookstaber 2007).

Shleifer and Vishny (1997) point out that while textbook arbitrage requires no capital and entails no risk, in practice arbitraging transactions almost always require capital and can entail varying degrees of risk, depending on the nature of the particular transaction. In addition, professional arbitrage is carried out by a relatively small number of agents, who must raise capital from investors to finance their activities. Moreover, professional arbitrageurs raise capital by demonstrating that their strategies have produced trading profits in the past. Hence professional arbitrageurs have an incentive to avoid positions that expose them to the possibility of liquidating the portfolio under pressure from investors in the fund. When professional arbitrageurs find it difficult to finance emerging arbitrage opportunities, they may avoid the opportunities as being too risky, and market pricing anomalies can persist.

Gabaix, Krishnamurthy, and Vigneron (2007) provide further evidence regarding the limits of arbitrage. Shleifer and Vishny argue that the marginal investor in a particular asset market is a specialized arbitrageur, and in confirmation, Gabaix et al. show that the risk of homeowner prepayment, which does not contribute to overall risk, is priced in the mortgage-backed securities (MBS) market. Moreover, the Gabaix et al. evidence shows that the covariance of prepayment risk with aggregate wealth has the wrong sign to explain the observed prices of prepayment risk on the basis of conventional theory. Rather, the price of prepayment risk is better explained by MBS marketwide specific risk, a finding consistent with the specialized arbitrageur hypothesis.

Since both incentives and impediments to trade differ in kind and degree among markets, at any point in time the financial system exhibits a complex mixture of market linkages. Where there are no impediments to trading or intermediation, effective interest rates on deals will be closely related. On the other hand, where trading or intermediation is impeded, the affected parts of the financial system are likely to be segmented to a degree that depends on the severity of the impediments.

MARKET SEGMENTATION

When trading is severely inhibited by market imperfections, the result is called market segmentation. Segmentation presents the possibility of carrying out the same transaction at different effective interest rates in different markets, after duly adjusting for such differences as risk, tax rates, and maturity. Segmentation is likely indicated when instruments representing the same risk persistently trade at different rates of interest[9] (see Vayanos and Weill 2008).

Segmentation occurs if neither arbitrageurs nor intermediaries discern profit opportunities to linking different transactions through trading, but the segmentation may not always be total. For example, transaction costs usually impede the search for arbitrage profits and thereby weaken linkages, but they do not necessarily destroy the relationships entirely. Indeed, much effort has been devoted to testing derivative securities pricing theories, and when transactions costs are taken into account the theories provide relatively good predictions of prices for the most actively traded derivatives. "The empirical evidence on the pricing efficiency of the stock options market suggests that, after considering transactions costs, the market appears to be efficient" (Fabozzi and Modigliani 1992, 291).

---

[9]At least if the anomalies cannot be explained on the basis of such institutional features as differing tax treatment or differing degrees of liquidity.

Nevertheless, price relationships among markets will not be maintained if existing opportunities are not perceived or if financiers do not have the technical knowledge to eliminate them. Trading can also be impeded if agents do not have access to the same information, if the counterparties are unknown to each other or if the instruments traded are not guaranteed by a third party and, therefore, require individual assessment of their credit risk. Finally, instruments representing incomplete contracts are much more difficult to trade than instruments representing complete contracts.

In some cases, transactions costs may frustrate profitable trading because financiers lack the technical knowledge needed to reduce the costs. If segmentation is due to a lack of technological knowledge, its effects may eventually be mitigated by learning, although the process can be lengthy. In some cases, information differences and transaction costs can remain high enough to affect price relationships more or less permanently. For example, trading can be impeded if the instruments in a given market are not all written according to an agreed standard, because then transactions costs are higher than they would be with standardized instruments.

Segmentation may also be observed in relatively small markets if the traders who would potentially enter the market cannot spread their fixed entry costs over a sufficiently large volume of deals. For example, if screening is subject to scale economies, intermediaries may not find it profitable to develop the screening capability needed to serve a small market.

In sum, markets are segmented when the types of services that traders offer differ from the types of services that clients demand. A particular market organization will serve some clients better than it serves others, and when the benefits from differentiation to some clients exceed the benefits from consolidation, markets tend to be linked less strongly. For example, some traders are impatient to trade, and are therefore willing to pay for liquidity as discussed in the first section. Other traders are patient and willing to wait until they can obtain what they regard as a fair market price for the asset in question.

In sophisticated and highly developed economies, strong and persistent examples of segmentation are difficult to find, especially in the markets for actively traded stocks. On the other hand, segmentation appears to arise more frequently, and to be relatively more important, in less developed countries. As one example, some Asian financial markets exhibited a very strong form of segmentation prior to the 1970s when it was not possible to raise funds for agricultural projects yielding annual returns in excess of 40%, while export businesses yielding returns of less than 6% were readily able to obtain financing. McKinnon (1973) argues that a combination of inadequate geographical diffusion of financial services and political conditions enabled well-connected exporters to obtain funds more easily than could agricultural borrowers. Governance considerations strengthened the effects of the segmentation. It was more difficult for banks to obtain credit information about rural borrowers than about well-known exporters, and the assets of the latter were usually more liquid than those of the former. As a result, potential agricultural investment projects faced more severe credit limitations than did such other businesses as the export trade.

Regulation can contribute to segmentation, at least temporarily, by restricting the kinds of businesses permitted.[10] On the other hand, financiers have strong incentives to find ways of circumventing regulations that limit profit opportunities. In the 1960s and 1970s the U.S. Federal Reserve Board's Regulation Q attempted to limit the maximum interest rates paid on deposits with U.S. banks, but the larger clients of these banks circumvented the regulation by placing funds in Eurodollar deposits, sometimes with overseas branches of U.S. banks. At the time these banks could offer higher rates in cities (e.g., London) outside the Fed's jurisdiction, but not within the United States.

CONSEQUENCES OF SEGMENTATION

Segmentation creates problems of allocative inefficiency. For example, the prices of less actively traded, smaller or neglected shares do not always conform to the predictions of asset pricing theory. The term "neglected shares" is used to refer to instruments whose price—earnings ratios are judged to be atypically low, given the degree of risk they represent. Such shares are likely to be issued by relatively small companies, and their low price-earnings ratios can be attributed in part to informational asymmetries stemming from a lack of institutional research (Arbel and Strebel 1983). Since it is uneconomic for larger institutions to trade smaller issues, it is also uneconomic for them to conduct research on small companies, and as a result the neglected share phenomenon is likely to persist.

At the same time, segmentation can contain the seeds of its own destruction. The very impediments that create segmentation present potential profit opportunities to financiers who can find profitable ways of overcoming the impediments. Such potential opportunities might be exploited by designing new securities issues or by developing new kinds of transactions. If profitable forms of deals can be found, funds will be moved from low-yield opportunities to higher-yield ones.[11] As and when these opportunities are discovered

---

[10] For example, Domowitz, Glen, and Madhavan find that "ownership restrictions effectively segment the equity market in Mexico" (1998, 190).

[11] Assume the comparison takes possible differences in risk into account.

existing forms of segmentation will weaken or disappear. For example, the junk bond market evolved as a way of mobilizing institutional funds for investment in high-risk bonds. In cases where the impediments cannot be overcome, markets remain segmented and effective interest differentials persist.

Some potential opportunities may exist for relatively long periods of time without being viewed as potentially profitable, while others are exploited soon after they are discovered. New means of exploiting opportunities can arise either from new sources of information or from technological change that increases net transaction revenue. As and when innovative agents can find such opportunities, they may well be able to earn above normal rates of return on them, at least temporarily. At the same time, the innovators' profit-making actions are quite likely to attract competition, and as a result the above normal rates of return will only persist until the original market segmentation is weakened or eliminated.

Should it not prove possible to realize profits on private transactions by moving funds between segmented markets, the segmentation will likely persist unless and until legislative action is taken to deal with it. However as Chapter 21 points out, public sector intervention to deal with segmentation is only rarely justified, and even when it is the form of intervention must be carefully designed to ensure its effectiveness.

INFORMATIONAL ASYMMETRIES AND CREDIT MARKET EQUILIBRIUMS

Informational asymmetries can have effects additional to those created by unavailed arbitrage opportunities. They can affect credit markets as well, and even lead to a credit rationing equilibrium; that is, an equilibrium in which only some potential clients can raise funds at market rates of interest. Other clients presenting the same risks, and seeking the same terms, cannot obtain credit.

While it is commonly believed that changes in interest rates will always equate supply with demand, there are circumstances under which the customarily expected adjustment will not take place. The situation occurs if potential clients take on increased risks when their financing costs are increased, and if intermediaries' profit maximization depends on both interest rate and average risk. There is no reason to suppose that the demand for credit at the profit maximizing interest rate will just equal the amount of credit supplied. If demand exceeds supply, intermediaries will lend to some but not to all borrowers, that is, intermediaries will ration credit. The issues are considered in the following three subsections.

TABLE 10.1 Repayment Terms and Client Reactions

States	Objective Probability	Risk-Neutral Probability	Asset Payoffs	Actual Debt Repayment	Payoff to Equity
1	0.50	0.45	H	R	H–R
2	0.50	0.55	L	L	0
Time 1 Expected Values			(H + L)/2	(R + L)/2	(H–R)/2
Time 0 Market Values			(0.45H + 0.55L)/ (1 + r)	(0.45R + 0.55L)/ (1 + r)	0.45(H–R)/ (1 + r)

Client Reactions to Terms

It is useful to begin a discussion of credit rationing with a model of client reactions to lender terms. The model shows that lenders can, in certain circumstances, create perverse results by proposing more stringent repayment schemes.

Consider the scenario shown in Table 10.1. It assumes that lenders advance the time 0 market values of the scheduled repayment R. The table further assumes $H > R > L$, so that in state 1 the borrower repays in full but in state 2 the borrower partially defaults and pays only L. Given these data along with the objective and risk-neutral probabilities shown, the proposed repayment scheme has an expected value of $(R + L)/2$. The market value of the payments is $(0.45H + 0.55L)/(1 + r)$, where r is the riskless interest rate. The owners' rewards are $H - R$ in state 1, zero in state 2, and have a time 0 market value of $0.45(H - R)/(1 + r)$. Assume these rewards are just equal to the owners' reservation level.[12]

The scenario in Table 10.2 assumes that the lenders propose a larger repayment $R + 1$ that would, unless compensated for, reduce the owners' rewards below their reservation level. Assume the owners can offset this possibility by increasing the variance of the asset payoffs, while holding the mean payoff constant.[13] The result of the combined actions is to decrease the market value of the assets, and the market value of the promised repayments to the lenders, but to maintain the value of the owners' position as shown next.

The net effect on the lenders' position depends on whether they are aware of the change in risk and if so, whether they adjust the amount they

---

[12] In states where firm payoffs do not permit full debt repayment, lenders receive the value of the firm and there is costless default of the remaining unpaid amount.

[13] For simplicity, we also assume the risk-neutral probabilities are unaffected by the change.

TABLE 10.2　Reactions to a Larger Proposed Repayment

States	Objective Probability	Risk-Neutral Probability	Asset Payoffs	Actual Debt Repayment	Payoff to Equity
1	0.50	0.45	$H + 1$	$R + 1$	$H–R$
2	0.50	0.55	$L – 1$	$L – 1$	0
Time 1 Expected Values			$(H + L)/2$	$(R + L)/2$	$(H–R)/2$
Time 0 Market Values			$(0.45H + 0.55$ $-0.10)/$ $(1 + r)$	$(0.45R + 0.55L$ $-0.10)/$ $(1 + r)$	$0.45(H–R)/$ $(1 + r)$

will lend. If they are not aware of the moral hazard problem presented by the owners' reaction, they might advance the same amount as in the first scenario. If so their expected earnings would be unchanged, but the market value of the repayments is decreased and consequently the value of the lenders' position is impaired.

In summary, the lender's attempt to extract a larger repayment can be frustrated by owners' reactions. As will be shown in the rest of this chapter, in these kinds of circumstances, the lender's profit-maximizing solution may involve credit rationing.

Adverse Selection and Backward Bending Supply

We can now employ the insights from the model in the previous subsection to investigate further the effects of borrowers' responding to more stringent repayment terms. For example, credit rationing can occur at equilibrium if the expected return on a bank loan for a given class of borrowers is not a monotonically increasing function of the nominal interest rate charged on the loan. The supply curve for credit can be backward bending if an increase in the required repayment (and in the effective interest rate charged) can lead the client to respond by taking greater risks. Thus the result of proposing an increase in repayments could mean that lenders end up advancing the same amount of funds to riskier borrowers (Stiglitz and Weiss 1981). In such circumstances there is no incentive for financiers to raise the interest rate, and a form of credit rationing may instead be used to equate demand with supply.

To illustrate the circumstances explicitly, suppose now that borrowers differ by a risk parameter θ. Borrowers know the value of their own θ, but financiers do not. Therefore, financiers offer all borrowers a standard debt contract based on an average value of θ and calling for all clients to repay R per unit amount of financing raised. If a client firm cannot make a scheduled repayment, its current cash flow y will be seized by the lender. On the basis of this contract, financiers advance a fixed amount to each client they accommodate. The realized value of the cash flow to the firm is thus

$$\pi(y) = \max(0, \ y - R) \tag{10.25}$$

Assuming that the owners use an expected value criterion, this model will exhibit adverse selection if the firm's expected profit

$$E(\pi(y|\theta)) \tag{10.26}$$

increases in θ. The assumption means that when firms take on riskier projects, the expected profits to them are increased. (In the example of the previous subsection, the expected profits to the firm's owners remained constant, but the market value decreased.) As a result there is at most one value of θ, say θ^*, that satisfies

$$E(\pi(y|\theta^*)) = \pi_{\min} \tag{10.27}$$

where $\pi_{\min}$ is the reservation level of profit that will induce the firm to adopt the project. If firms cannot take on a certain degree of risk, they cannot generate their reservation earnings, and do not operate.

The lending banks' expected profits depend on the contracted repayment R and on the quality distribution of firms applying for credit. Given that the amount advanced is fixed, an interest rate increase means R is increased. Then the firm's profit expectations for any given value of θ decrease, since for any given value of θ

$$E(\pi(y|\theta)) = E[(\max(0, \ y - R))|\theta] \tag{10.28}$$

is a decreasing function of R. To compensate for the decrease in expected profit, each firm will consider adopting riskier projects, that is, adopting projects with a larger value of θ. As a result the critical value θ^* defined in equation (10.27) increases, meaning that the population of firms now finding it worthwhile to seek credit bearing the new and more stringent repayment terms is riskier than before. Thus an increase in interest rates can decrease the demand for loans, but as the demand decreases the less risky firms drop out of the market. In these circumstances the increase in interest rates need not necessarily increase banks' expected profits, and to maximize profits banks may ration the amount of credit made available to the remaining clients.

TABLE 10.3 Example of Bank Profit Function and Associated Supply Curve

Credit Risk θ	$y(\theta)$	$p(\theta)$	R	Demand for Credit[a]	Expected Repayment[b]	Expected Return to Lending[c]	Supply of Deposits, Equal to Supply of Credit[d]
1	1	0.9	1	10	4.5	−0.55	0
2	2	0.8	2	9	7.2	−0.20	0
3	3	0.7	3	8	8.4	0.05	1
4	4	0.6	4	7	8.4	0.20	4
5	5	0.5	5	6	7.5	0.25	5
6	6	0.4	6	5	6.0	0.20	4
7	7	0.3	7	4	4.2	0.05	1
8	8	0.2	8	3	2.4	−0.20	0
9	9	0.1	9	2	0.9	−0.55	0
10	10	0.0	10	1	0.0	−1.00	0

[a]Suppose $R = 7$. Then only firms with $y(\theta)$ equal to 7, 8, 9, or 10 will go into operation.
[b]If $R = 7$, the lender will receive an expected payment of $7(0.3 + 0.2 + 0.1) = 4.2$.
[c]If $R = 7$, 4 loans of 1 are made, and $(4.2 − 4.0)/4.0 = 0.05$.
[d]The supply of deposits increases with the expected return to lending. Thus if $R = 7$ only one of the four borrowers applying can be accommodated.

Example Let the measure of credit risk be θ as indicated in the first column of Table 10.3. The second column shows the value of the cash flow $y(\theta)$ if the project is successful. An unsuccessful project brings in zero as discussed previously. The third column shows the probability $p(\theta)$ with which a positive cash flow $y(\theta)$ is realized. In accord with the previous discussion, $p(\theta)$ decreases as $y(\theta)$ increases in θ.

To keep the calculations simple, we suppose the firm's reservation profit is zero so that any firm required to make a payment $R \le y(\theta)$ will operate, but if $R > y(\theta)$ the firm has no incentive to operate. Any firm that commences operations seeks a loan equal to one unit of capital. Suppose for simplicity there is exactly one firm in each credit risk class. Then, setting repayments to the integral values as shown in the fourth column, the demand for credit as a function of R takes on the values shown in the fifth column. For example, if the required repayment is set to 7, only firms with credit risk of 7 or greater will apply for loans, so the demand for credit will be 4. The expected repayments are shown in the sixth column. For example, if the required repayment is 7, the applying firms have credit risks 7, 8, 9, and 10.

The firm in class 7 repays its loan of 1 with probability 0.3, the firm in class 8 with probability 0.2, and so on. The expected value of all positive repayments when the scheduled repayment amount is 7 thus becomes

$$7(0.30 + 0.20 + 0.10 + 0.00) = 4.20$$

as shown in the sixth column. For later use, note that the last calculation is exactly equal to a calculation using the total amount to be repaid and the average repayment probability:

$$(7 \times 4) \times \{(0.30 + 0.20 + 0.10 + 0.00)/4\}$$
$$= (28) \times \{0.15\} = 4.20$$

The expected return to lending is calculated in column 7. For example, if $R = 1$, the calculation is

$$(4.50 - 10.00)/10.00 = -0.55$$

Suppose the bank does not hold any cash reserves, operates at a zero profit, and can attract deposits according to a supply function that is linear in the expected interest rate on loans. An expected return of 0.5 brings in deposits totaling 1 unit of capital, a return of 0.20 brings in 4 units, and so on. Negative interest rates are assumed to bring in zero deposits.

The supply and demand functions for credit are shown in Figure 10.1. Since demand is greater than supply at all values of R, the supply and demand functions do not intersect. The bank will have to practice credit rationing,

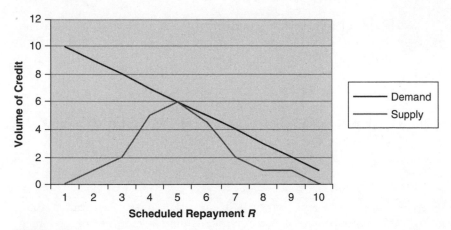

FIGURE 10.1 Demand and Supply of Credit

accommodating some borrowers but turning down others with exactly the same characteristics.

On the other hand if the function relating banks' expected cash flow to the scheduled repayment were always increasing, the effect would not occur. And nor would the effect occur if it were somehow possible for banks to sort out the quality of the different borrowers applying for credit.

Example (Stiglitz and Weiss 1981)   The model studied in this section depicts adverse selection, but in the next section it is also used to depict moral hazard. Suppose all firms are identical and have a choice of two projects, either of which requires financing in amount 1. If successful, the projects yield B and G respectively. Any project that is unsuccessful yields zero, regardless of its type. Suppose $B > G$ but the success probabilities are p_B and p_G respectively, with $p_B < p_G$. Thus project B is a riskier project than is G. The model depicts adverse selection if the announcement of lending terms is interpreted as meaning that only firms with project B will seek funding unless the repayment terms are set appropriately. This interpretation applies to an entire population of B and G firms, and it is supposed the selection occurs ex ante.

If a firm is indifferent between projects G and B at repayment R^*, then

$$(B - R^*)p_B = (G - R^*)p_G \qquad (10.29)$$

that is,

$$R^* \equiv (p_G G - p_B B)/(pG - p_B) \qquad (10.30)$$

Whenever equation (10.29) is satisfied, the return to the bank is not monotonic in R. If the return to the bank is $p_G R$ for $R \leq R^*$, then $p_B R$ for $R^* \leq R < B$. Thus the interest return increases for $R < R^*$, falls sharply when $R = R^*$, then increases again for $R^* < R \leq B$. For $R < R^*$ firms choose the safe project, while for $R \; \varepsilon \; (R^*, B)$ firms choose the risky project.

The maximum repayment the bank could require and still induce investment in project G is R^*. The maximum expected return to the bank also occurs at R^* if and only if

$$p_B B < p_G R^* \qquad (10.31)$$

where R^* is given in equation (10.30). Whether or not equation (10.31) holds, the nonmonotonicity of return means the bank chooses a repayment amount that will maximize its effective return. There is no reason to suppose the chosen repayment amount will equate demand with supply, and hence there may be credit rationing.

Moral Hazard and Backward Bending Supply

As already indicated, the moral hazard interpretation can use the same model as did the adverse selection discussion. However, now the individual firm is viewed as being able to switch clandestinely from project G to project B after obtaining a commitment for funds from the bank. Again financiers cannot observe which technology firms actually choose, and must therefore specify that all firms promise the same repayment R in order to borrow the single unit of capital needed to acquire the technology. Also assume

$$p_G G > p_B B \tag{10.32}$$

while $B > G$. In combination, these assumptions mean that

$$p_B < p_G \tag{10.33}$$

the bad technology is riskier than the good one. The firm will choose the good technology if and only if

$$p_G(G - R) \geq p_B(B - R) \tag{10.34}$$

that is, if and only if

$$R \leq (p_G G - p_B B)/(p_G - p_B)$$

As before there is a largest feasible repayment

$$R^0 \equiv (p_G G - p_B B)/(p_G - p_B) \tag{10.35}$$

and potential borrowers will only select the good project if $R \leq R^0$. If $R \leq R^0$ the expected return to the lender is $\pi_G R$, but if $R > R^0$ then the expected return to the lender is $\pi_B R$.

Suppose there is an infinitely elastic supply of funds at expected rate r; that is, any amount can be borrowed by paying the market interest rate. Then if

$$p_G R^0 > 1 + r > p_B R^0$$

there can be two different loan quantities at which the credit market clears. That is, there may be some $R^{00} > R^0$ such that $\pi_B R^{00} = 1 + r$. At the same time there may be some other repayment $R^{000} \leq R^0$ for which it is also true that $\pi_G R^{000} = 1 + r$.

On the other hand, if the supply of credit function attains only a local maximum at R^0 the credit market may not clear, just as in the adverse selection case (see subsection "Client Reactions to Terms"). Rationing will occur whenever the quantity of credit demanded at R^0 exceeds the quantity of credit supplied.

MARKET FAILURE

Informational differences can sometimes be extreme enough to lead beyond credit rationing to market failure. For example, if a newly appointed bank manager cannot distinguish good from bad clients, she may decide that it is profitable only to lend against collateral, in which case the market for unsecured loans in her business area can be said to have failed. As another example, it may be difficult to resell the shares of a small business at a price reflecting its value as a going concern, because the purchaser cannot verify the information on which a going concern value would be based.

FINANCIAL SYSTEM EXTERNALITIES

Financial system performance can be assessed from either a private or a societal point of view. The criteria of private cost and benefit are used to assess the private value of economic activity. A private optimum occurs when the activity is pursued to the point at which privately determined marginal costs, reflected in the prices of resources employed, rise to a point at which they are just equal to privately determined marginal benefits[14] (as reflected in output prices).

The criterion of social costs and benefits is used to reflect society's (possibly differing) assessment of the same activity. A social optimum occurs when an activity is pursued until marginal social costs rise to the point that they just equal marginal social benefits. It will not always be the case that marginal social benefits equal marginal social costs at the level of activity for which marginal private benefits equal marginal private costs.

---

[14] Assuming that only one optimum obtains.

The term "externality" refers to the impact of an economic activity whose market price, based on calculations of private cost and private benefit, does not fully reflect the activity's balance of social benefits and social costs.[15] For example, a market-determined price may not fully reflect the costs of resources used by the firms producing the good or service in question. Similarly, when a good or service is sold at a market-determined price, the private revenue firms realize they may not equal the social value of the goods produced.

While externalities are not ubiquitous, and while they are not always significant even when they do occur, there are circumstances in which they can be important enough to merit remedial attention. In financial markets the most important instances of externalities occur when social benefits go unrealized because the quantities of funds advanced are smaller than is socially optimal. The problem usually arises because it is unprofitable for private sector lenders to extend a socially optimal quantity of funds.[16]

In developed economies it is not usually easy to find instances where externalities are present. Moreover even if externalities are present it may not be possible to find cost-effective ways of securing the social benefits currently being forgone. However, export credit insurance offers one example of a situation where society may have benefited from intervention. Social benefits may well stem from the jobs created by expanding export-oriented businesses, but it is sometimes difficult or costly for an exporting firm privately to insure against possible default losses on international shipments made on credit. Exporters may need the credit to secure the business, and private sector insurance companies may regard it uneconomic to provide credit insurance. In these circumstances it may be worthwhile for the public sector to increase the amount of insurance provided and thus capture social benefits that would otherwise be forgone. In the turbulent markets of 2007–2008, a number of institutions have been rescued by U.S. federal authorities on the grounds that the institutions' failure would create severe externalities for the world's financial systems. As Chapter 21 discusses, in these circumstances it may be desirable to use public sector intervention to offset the negative externalities that would otherwise be suffered.

---

[15] The theoretical model of a competitive equilibrium has the desirable property that prices exactly cover both the social and the private costs of production.

[16] The point is not that the interest rate is somehow incorrect, but that it does not reflect the net social gain or cost to the transaction. The example of the export industry in the next paragraph argues that a bank's interest earnings on a loan to finance exports will not typically reflect such social benefits as the employment creation following on the growth of export business made possible by the bank lending.

REFERENCES

Arbel, A., and P. Strebel. 1983. "Pay attention to neglected firms." *Journal of Portfolio Management* 9: 37–42.

Baumol, William J. 1965. *The Stock Market and Economic Efficiency*. New York: Fordham University Press.

Bookstaber, Richard. 2007. *A Demon of Our Own Design*. New York and London, John Wiley & Sons.

Chordia, Tarun, Richard Roll, and Avanidhar Subrahmanyam. 2001. Market liquidity and trading activity. *Journal of Finance* 56: 501–530.

Demsetz, Harold. 1968. The cost of transacting. *Quarterly Journal of Economics* 82: 33–53.

Domowitz, Ian, and Benn Steil. 1999. Automation, trading costs, and the structure of the trading services industry. Brookings-Wharton Papers on Financial Services.

Domowitz, Ian, Jack D. Glen and Ananth Madhavan. 1998. Country and Currency Risk Premia in an Emerging Market. *Journal of Financial and Quantitative Analysis* 33: 189–216.

Fabozzi, Frank J., and Franco Modigliani. 1992. *Capital Markets: Institutions and Instruments*. Englewood Cliffs, NJ: Prentice-Hall.

Gabaix, Xavier, Arvind Krishnamurthy, and Olivier Vigneron. 2007. Limits of arbitrage: theory and evidence from the mortgage-backed securities market. *Journal of Finance* 62: 557–595.

Grossman, Sanford J., and Merton H. Miller. 1988. Liquidity and market structure. *Journal of Finance* 43: 617–637.

Harris, Lawrence. 1995. Consolidation, fragmentation, segmentation, and regulation. Chapter 18 in *Global Equity Markets: Technological, Competitive and Regulatory Challenges*, edited by Robert A. Schwartz. New York: New York University Salomon Center; Burr Ridge, IL: Irwin Professional Publishing.

O'Hara, Maureen. 2003. Liquidity and price discovery. *Journal of Finance* 58: 1,335–1,354.

Shleifer, Andrei, and Robert W. Vishny. 1997. The limits of arbitrage. *Journal of Finance* 52: 35–55.

Stiglitz, Joseph, and Andrew Weiss. 1981. Credit rationing in markets with imperfect information. *American Economic Review* 71: 393–410.

Vayanos, Dimitri, and Pierre-Olivier Weill. 2008. A search-based theory of the on-the-run phenomenon. *Journal of Finance* 63: 1,361–1,398.

Four

Applications: Market Activity

This part analyzes practical aspects of financial market activity. The discussion examines the differing capabilities of exchanges and over-the-counter markets, as well as those of broker and dealer markets. As the book's earlier theory holds, differences in kinds of markets can be explained by discriminating alignments: Particular transaction attributes are aligned with differing markets' capabilities on the basis of cost-effectiveness. Moreover, market organizations evolve with a view to enhancing market performance and are driven by changing economics.

CHAPTER 11

Securities, Bond, and Mortgage Markets

This chapter begins by summarizing the economic differences among markets, particularly differences in capabilities. The chapter then applies the ideas of capability differences to the money, equity, bond, and mortgage markets. The money markets discussion emphasizes the common attributes of money market instruments, and the market's consequently integrated nature. In comparison to the money market, equity markets exhibit a much greater range of governance capabilities and a correspondingly greater range of deal attributes. These ranges are illustrated by discussions of raising capital, the effects of institutional trading, program trading, and some market anomalies. The bond market discussion examines differences between stocks and bonds, determinants of interest rate spreads, trading in high yield bonds, and the use of restrictive covenants. The mortgage markets' discussion emphasizes the markets' importance and functions, with particular emphasis on securitization and trading the instruments created thereby.

ECONOMIC DIFFERENCES AMONG MARKETS

Chapter 5 maintained that from a resource allocation point of view the economically significant capabilities of markets include the degree of liquidity they exhibit, the degree to which the instruments traded are standardized, and the degree of homogeneity in market agents' trading information. Chapter 10 pointed out that markets range from being highly active and liquid to relatively inactive and illiquid. The differences depend on the numbers of potential participants, the volumes they normally trade, and on the markets' detailed structures. Markets that are liquid, have standardized instruments and homogeneous information usually have highly developed capabilities to execute trades quickly, at or near prevailing market prices. Greater numbers of participants and more frequent trading generally improve a market's execution capabilities, although specific forms of trading rules may sometimes reduce execution capabilities. The opposite is also true: An illiquid market trading nonstandardized instruments under conditions of informational asymmetry will generally have slow, negotiated completion of trades, at prices that can deviate substantially from each other.

Markets exhibit a rich variety of arrangements, and this chapter can only consider their major aspects. According to O'Hara (1995, 6–9, passim):

> *The process of exchange occurs in many ways. Buyers and sellers can contact each other directly. Traders can gather at a central setting or communicate through a computer screen. A single intermediary can arrange every trade, or there can be numerous individuals who meet to set prices. Whatever the setting, however, there are rules either explicit or implicit that govern the trading mechanism, and it is these rules that result in the formation and evolution of market prices.*
>
> *Any trading mechanism can be viewed as a type of trading game in which players meet (perhaps not physically) at some venue and act according to some rules. The players may involve a wide range of market participants, although not all types of players are found in every mechanism. First, of course, are customers who submit orders to buy or sell. These orders may be contingent on various outcomes, or they may be direct orders to transact immediately. . . . Second, there are brokers who transmit orders for customers. Brokers do not trade for their own account, but act merely as conduits for customer orders. These customers may be retail traders, or they may be other market participants such as dealers who simply wish to disguise their trading intentions. Third, there are dealers who trade for their own account. In some markets, dealers also facilitate customer orders and so are often known as broker/dealers. Fourth, there are specialists, or market makers. The market maker quotes prices to buy or sell the asset. Since the market maker generally takes a position in the security (if only for a short time while waiting for an offsetting order to arrive) the market maker also has a dealer function. The extent, however, to which the market maker acts as a dealer can vary dramatically between markets.*

In addition to exhibiting these rich varieties, financial markets are evolving rapidly.

The world of securities trading is changing. Advances in technology, combined with the dramatic decrease in the cost of information processing, have conspired to change the way that securities transactions occur. While broker-dealers, specialists and market makers still ply their trades, they are now joined by a host of new market participants such as robot traders and electronic limit order providers (Macey and O'Hara, 2005).

Up until the 1990s exchanges were the most common places for stock trading, but by the 2000s electronic communications networks were becoming very much more widespread. Some networks are organized to trade shares for retail clients, others for institutional clients. Still other networks are striving to establish computerized trading for futures contracts and other forms of derivative instruments. Bonds and foreign currencies now trade almost exclusively via electronic communication networks rather than in some central location.

MONEY MARKET

The most active and most liquid of all markets is the money market, a specialized market for trading short-term,[1] highly creditworthy, and highly liquid instruments in large amounts. When regarded from the perspective of the entire financial system, the instruments traded in the money market are very close substitutes. The instruments are either obligations of highly creditworthy issuers or are guaranteed by them, as in the case of bankers' acceptances. They are usually issued in bearer form, sold on a discount basis, and may be traded several times prior to their maturity.

The main participants in money market transactions are governments, businesses, financial institutions, and investment dealers. These groups, which include both domestic and foreign parties, use the money markets chiefly to invest or borrow over the short-term. Open market purchases or sales of the most prominent money market instrument, government Treasury bills, are the principal instrument used by the central bank to implement domestic monetary policy. Second, the money market provides agents both with short-term funds to finance working capital needs and investment outlets for those with surplus cash.

---

[1]Maturities typically range from one to 180 days, but maturities up to one year are not uncommon. Occasionally, government bonds with maturities up to three years are also classified as money market instruments.

In most financially developed countries, the money market has a relatively small number of dealers who are well-known to each other and who trade mainly using computer networks. Again, in most economies the money market is operationally and allocatively efficient. The value of money market instruments depends primarily on short-term risk-free interest rates, since the instruments' default risk is usually minimal. Since there is active arbitrage between instruments, any persistent interest differentials can usually be explained by differences in the size of the issue, the instruments' perceived default risk, or their tax status. The governance of money market transactions mainly involves deciding when to trade the instruments.

The value of corporate money market instruments depends on the same short-term interest rates, but a risk premium will usually be added to recognize that corporate instruments carry greater default risk. The size of the risk premium depends on the obligant. For example, a large corporation may be thought to have a relatively low default risk and hence carry a low risk premium, while a local and relatively small corporation would typically carry a higher risk premium.

The U.S. money market is probably the world's most highly developed, although those of Germany, Japan, the United Kingdom, and other sophisticated economies are very similar in nature. The instruments traded in the U.S. money market include U.S. Treasury bills, commercial paper, bankers' acceptances, negotiable certificates of deposit, repurchase agreements, and federal funds. Although they may be traded by both domestic and foreign parties, all these instruments are domestic: Short-term foreign currency instruments are traded in the foreign exchange markets examined in Chapter 12.

Types of Instruments

U.S. Treasury Bills   United States Treasury bills are government securities issued at a discount and maturing in one year or less from the date of issue. Treasury bills are the most liquid of the money market instruments and represent the greatest volume of money market trading. New issues of the bills are sold at auctions organized by the U.S. Department of the Treasury. The auctions are held at regular intervals and the issue is allocated among the highest bidders. In the event of tied bids, amounts are allocated proportionally. The Treasury uses a maximum or stop yield to determine the lowest price at which it will sell a given issue of bills. The U.S. Federal Reserve System may bid for a part of any issue, and those bids are deducted from the issue before it is offered to the money market dealers. Secondary market trades are carried out by private sector money market dealers, a category that includes large banks and investment banking firms.

Commercial Paper Nonfinancial corporations use short-term promissory notes called commercial paper to raise short-term funds.[2] For entities with strong credit ratings, issuing commercial paper is an alternative to borrowing directly from a bank or banks. For entities with sufficiently high credit ratings, commercial paper will frequently prove cheaper than direct borrowing from banks as a way of raising short-term funds. Commercial paper is also sometimes used as a form of bridge financing, that is, for raising funds temporarily until longer-term funding can be arranged.

Commercial paper is a close, but not a perfect, substitute for a Treasury bill. Interest rates on the two instruments follow the same time pattern, but there is a positive spread between them because of the greater default risk on commercial paper and because commercial paper is less liquid than Treasury bills. The size of the spread depends on both current volumes of trading and on the credit rating of the issuing corporation.

Since the U.S. Securities and Exchange Commission (SEC) requires registration of paper with more than 270 days to maturity, and since complying with registration requirements is costly, most U.S. issues are for maturities of 270 days or less. Some issuers of commercial paper use direct placements rather than selling the issue through a money market dealer. The emergence of direct issues has dramatically reduced the fees formerly charged by money market dealers.

Bankers' Acceptances Bankers' acceptances are short-term promissory notes issued and sold by a corporation on the strength of a bank guarantee. The guarantee, evidenced by a stamp on the instrument, enhances the note's marketability by substituting the credit rating of the accepting bank for that of the issuing corporation. The risk premium on an acceptance thus reflects the default risk of the accepting bank and not that of the issuing corporation. Bankers' acceptances are used in raising funds domestically, when a corporation's credit standing is not widely known. They are also used in foreign trade, where they may be more acceptable to an exporter than the unsecured note of a foreign importer. Both investment bankers and commercial banks usually act as dealers in the secondary markets for bankers' acceptances.

Negotiable CDs Negotiable certificates of deposit (CDs) are issued by banks or other depository institutions. Unlike ordinary deposits, they are payable

---

[2]Asset-backed commercial paper (ABCP) does not currently have the same kind of high credit rating as the instruments now being discussed. ABCP is examined in Chapter 14.

to the bearer. Thus if the original depositor of funds needs cash before a negotiable CD comes due, she can sell it in the money market rather than pay the issuing institution a penalty to redeem it. Negotiable CDs were first issued in the 1960s. Their greater convenience led to ready market acceptance, and the instruments became important for helping banks to raise additional money market funds. CDs are now issued on both fixed and floating rate terms, in both domestic and foreign money markets. The default risk on CDs is determined by the perceived creditworthiness of the issuing bank.

Negotiable CDs are advantageous to banks because unlike ordinary deposits, they are subject to low or no reserve requirements, meaning that nearly all of the funds raised are available for investing in higher-yield assets. On the other hand, negotiable CDs are not usually covered by deposit insurance, and thus present a credit risk to their holders. To compensate for this credit risk, the yield on an uninsured negotiable CD would be higher than the yield on a similar insured instrument. Similarly, a negotiable CD would be more liquid than a nonnegotiable CD whose terms (including the provision of insurance) were otherwise the same. In this case, at time of issue the negotiable CD could be expected to offer a lower effective rate than its nonnegotiable counterpart.

Repurchase Agreements A repurchase agreement is the sale of a security accompanied by a commitment from the seller to buy the security back at a specified price and on a specified date. A repurchase agreement is very similar to a collateralized loan, where the security serves as collateral. Although traditionally repurchase agreements have mainly made use of money market instruments, as practices have evolved other instruments, notably MBSs and CDOs, have also been used as collateral.[3]

Repurchase agreements are generally used by money market dealers for inventory financing purposes. The default risk on a repurchase agreement is not strictly that the seller will fail. Rather, it is that the seller will fail and the buyer of the securities will also take some loss because, in the event of default, proceeds from resale of the securities will not cover the amount originally advanced.

Federal Funds Market The Federal Funds market offers another venue in which banks can manage their liquid positions. As its name implies, the Federal Funds market is one in which banks borrow or lend reserve funds. The major money center banks are the typical users of Federal Funds, while banks

---

[3]Frank J. Fabozzi, personal communication, December 2008.

in other centers are suppliers. The default risk in the Federal Funds market is determined by the credit standing and capitalization of the issuing bank.

EQUITY MARKETS

The shares of public companies have traditionally traded in two principal types of equity markets: the organized exchanges and the *over-the-counter* (OTC) markets. Organized exchanges traditionally imposed more rigorous listing requirements than the OTC markets, and organized exchanges traditionally operated in specific locations while the main OTC markets operated as trading networks. However, both these historical differences are now diminishing. In addition, a third type of market based on Internet trading facilities and called *alternative trading systems* (ATSs), provided by privately organized firms, began to emerge[4] in the late 1990s and continued to grow in importance in the 2000s.

All equity markets offer both retail and wholesale trading. Individuals and their agents trade relatively small amounts in retail transactions; financial institutions trade relatively large amounts in wholesale ones.[5] Much of the wholesale trading on the stock exchanges is conducted in what is called the *upstairs market* where buyers and sellers negotiate trades and report the terms to the exchange floor after completing the transaction.

Exchange-listed shares all satisfy the standardized listing and reporting requirements of the exchange on which they are traded, but not all exchange-listed shares are equally liquid. The shares of the largest and most actively traded companies are highly liquid, but many smaller issues do not enjoy the same status. Most stock exchanges have a number of dealers, known as market makers, who take positions in stocks,[6] but even the activities of market makers are not sufficient to make all an exchange's stocks equally liquid. On the other hand, as network trading increases in popularity and many potential counterparties can contact each other

---

[4]Since traditional OTC markets offer alternatives to organized exchanges, they could also be regarded as alternative trading systems, but are seldom referred to in that manner.

[5]The first through fourth markets are respectively the exchange markets for listed stocks, the OTC markets for unlisted stocks, the dealer markets created for block trades by independent position houses, and the market for direct trading between institutions.

[6]Stock exchanges in the United States have specialists who are entitled to make a market in a given stock. In return for this privilege, specialists are required to purchase or sell stocks if they receive orders to be carried out at market prices.

readily, liquidity increases even in the absence of officially designated market makers.[7]

Importance and Functions

The first public marketplaces for securities trading were the stock exchanges. Exchanges have traditionally played, and still play, important roles in raising primary funds and in fostering secondary market trading. For example, McInish (2000, 161) observes that "As a percentage of GDP, stock market capitalization in Chile, Hong Kong, Malaysia and Singapore has been comparable to, or even exceeded, that of the United States and the United Kingdom. In many emerging markets, stock markets play a more important role in raising capital for industry than they do in industrialized countries."

As already mentioned, most stock exchanges have market makers whose primary function is to promote secondary market trading. U.S. stock exchanges normally have only one market maker (called a specialist) for a given share. A given specialist may deal in several stocks, some of which may be quite thinly traded.[8] A specialist is required by the rules of the exchange to complete orders by taking inventory positions in the stock or stocks for which he makes a market. Orders can arrive at the specialist's post from floor traders, from electronic systems, and from other exchanges. The specialist must clear submitted orders at currently quoted prices, but is free to announce changes in those prices at any time. All orders crossing an exchange are routed through the specialist, even if the specialist does not participate in the particular trade. In the OTC markets of the United States, as well as on exchanges in other countries, market agents themselves determine, through competing with each other for the business, whether they wish to act as dealers or as brokers.[9]

Firms usually prefer to list their shares on the largest and most active exchanges for which they can qualify, because an active secondary market means that emerging information regarding a company's business will be quickly valued. Moreover, company shares usually trade at relatively favorable prices in such an environment. On the other hand, listing requirements are at their most rigorous on the largest and most active exchanges, reflecting

---

[7]An OTC market, as indeed any form of ATS, may have either brokers or dealers trading a given stock, depending on the average volume of trading.

[8]Lindsay and Schaede (1990) report that specialists handle an average of 3.7 stocks (see O'Hara 1995, 9).

[9]Only a few markets use the specialist system. Most markets employ some form of the competitive dealer system.... Computerization has been quite consistent with the competitive dealer system (Fabozzi, Modigliani, and Ferri 1994).

attempts by the market's organizers to define minimum quality standards for the securities they agree to trade. Listing standards reduce investors' screening costs and increase trading activity thereby.[10]

In North America, primary issues are usually not sold on the exchanges, but are marketed separately in off-exchange transactions. The practice of floating new issues off-exchange was established to avoid the possibility that the issues' underwriters might try to manipulate secondary market prices during the flotation process. However, the argument is not persuasive to all exchange organizers, and primary issues are sold on exchanges in many other parts of the world.

Although they were formerly set up as associations of their members, most stock exchanges are now organized as public companies. To promote exchange trading, members are required to register all their trades in listed stocks with the exchange. Before commissions on trades became negotiable, members were also required to charge their clients minimum commissions. The development of institutional trading in the United States, and the minimum commission rules in force in that country prior to 1975, contributed to the development of the third and fourth markets, as will be discussed later. The competition provided by the third and fourth markets, and pressure from securities regulators, together resulted in the eventual abolition of minimum commissions.

Although the practice has largely been replaced by electronic trading, some exchanges in the United States as well as in other countries still use a method of trading known as *open outcry*. Traders wishing to buy or sell listed instruments gather around a post on the exchange floor, shouting out and otherwise signaling the kinds of orders they wish to complete. Supporters of open-outcry methods claim that screen trading is inferior to their older method, but the continuing adoption of computerized trading systems suggests that these objections to the newer methods are being surmounted. Eventually, all markets are likely to be organized around computer networks, and open-outcry methods will likely disappear completely.

The original function of the OTC markets was to trade the stocks of companies unable to meet exchange listing requirements. In North America other securities such as bonds are also traded in the OTC markets, but in the U.K. bonds are exchange traded. The main OTC market in the United States now uses an electronic price quotation service known as Nasdaq (National Association of Securities Dealers Automatic Quotation service). Nasdaq prices are quoted by dealers, and brokers can negotiate with dealers

---

[10] Since exchange members' incomes are directly related to the exchange's volume of trading, increases in trading also increase the income of exchange members.

on behalf of customers. While some OTC deals are still done over the telephone, Nasdaq mainly uses screen-based trading systems. Nasdaq provides strong competition for exchange trading, and a substantial proportion of listed stocks are now traded on Nasdaq as well. Some companies have even cancelled their exchange listings, and now trade their shares exclusively on the Nasdaq market.

Privately owned ATSs (also sometimes known as electronic communications networks, ECNs) are emerging, and seem likely to offer growing competition for both the exchanges and the OTC markets.[11] At present ATSs make markets mainly in retail trades. However, institutional crossing networks, which currently exist mainly to cross trades negotiated by institutions, may eventually begin to negotiate prices as well. As and when that development occurs, the ECNs are likely to pose severe threats to traditional exchanges' viability. ECNs started by feeding trades into existing markets, but have increasingly come to serve as alternative trading outlets. ECNs have brought tighter bid-ask spreads, greater depth, and less market concentration, thus improving Nasdaq liquidity (Weston, 2002). Recently, E*TRADE has experienced a resurgence of activity in online retail trading, and is offering enhanced services to attract additional customers.

The regulations affecting equity trading are essentially an outgrowth of how exchanges traditionally conducted business. Historically, stock exchanges attempted to insure that all market participants had equal access to any relevant information regarding the issuing company. The current U.S. regulatory authority, the Securities and Exchange Commission (SEC) requires all different types of markets to cross their orders on an exchange floor so as to create a central record of transactions.

With related purpose, the disclosure rules governing primary public issues require issuing a prospectus that provides all potential buyers with the same information concerning the deal. Typically, disclosure regulations require that the prospectus stipulate the securities' terms and state how the financing will be used. Thus the prospectus indicates key information about the issuing firm's business plans. Meeting disclosure requirements usually involves a relatively large fixed cost, and public issues are therefore only economic if they exceed a certain minimum size. Private market deals are not subject to disclosure requirements, and as a result fixed issue costs are typically lower. Some clients use private issues so that they can reveal information to their financiers while keeping the information from business competitors.

---

[11] McInish (2000) reports more than 50 private markets in the United States.

Institutional Trading

Since the 1960s, institutions have been the major participants in the securities markets, and market operations have evolved to accommodate their trading needs. Institutional trading is wholesale trading that involves either large numbers of shares of a given issue, simultaneous trading of many different share issues, or both. Many institutional trades, known as *block trades*, involve the exchange of 10,000 or more shares in a single deal. Block trades may originate either in the upstairs market or on an exchange floor. While Shapiro (1995, 32) reports that only about one-eighth of NYSE volume is facilitated by upstairs trading desks, upstairs trading plays a particularly important role for large trades of less active stocks.

Institutional trading involves a network of telephone and computer links, including independent systems designed for direct trading between institutions without using any intervening third party. Instinet, which originated as an interdealer trading facility, offers screen-based dealing systems with updated market information, automatic execution of deals up to 1,000 shares, and on-screen negotiation for larger deals. In 2008, Instinet quoted over 1,700 listed stocks, over 3,000 OTC stocks, and also some stock and currency options. Instinet also has automatic routings to stock exchanges. The Crossing Network conducts after-hours institutional trading facilitates trading after exchange closing hours, as well as when exchange trading in a given stock has been suspended.

Shapiro (1995, 31) argues that "the electronic layer that is used to access all of the various liquidity sources (NYSE, OTC, electronic trading and crossing systems) will gradually become the marketplace, rather than just serving as a gateway...." The principal appeals of ATSs are their lower transactions costs and more rapid execution of trades. Institutional users do not always need the immediate liquidity of the continuous-style NYSE market. Moreover, ATSs permit institutions to execute transactions without revealing their intentions to intermediaries such as the stock exchange specialists. In other words, ATSs allow institutions to control how much trading information they reveal to fellow institutions.

The third market has traditionally been a facility in which institutions trade blocks with each other. Third-market firms known as *position houses* are not members of the stock exchanges and do not therefore have to follow exchange rules in conducting trades. Since position houses trade blocks off-exchange, they constitute a source of competition for the stock exchanges. In order to attract trades, position houses are usually willing to assume large inventory positions.

Position houses emerged in the late 1960s and early 1970s. Since they were not exchange members, they were able to waive the minimum commissions that exchange members were then required to levy, even on very large trades. Minimum commissions were abolished in the United States in 1975, but position houses continued to flourish despite the change. Like the dealers in the Grossman-Miller model, position houses profit on the spreads they earn from institutional trading. Part of the position houses' current competitive strength derives from the fact that a stock exchange specialist's capital is not always sufficient to finance a block trade. The typically greater capital of a position house means it can more readily take some or all of a block into its inventory, and may therefore be able to offer faster execution at or near the prevailing market price.

The price of a block traded in the upstairs market can differ from the current exchange price for the same shares. For example, while a specialist on a U.S. stock exchange usually takes any amount offered to her (up to a certain prespecified limit) at the buying price she posts, a dealer in the upstairs market will typically negotiate the price at which a block is purchased. The same is, of course, true for sales. However, any such price differences normally persist for only a very short time. As would be expected in an allocatively efficient market, if the exchange prices established by the specialist and the prices at which institutions trade differ, arbitrage will occur until they are brought back into line.

Block traders in the U.S. upstairs market claim to smooth out price fluctuations that could occur when large amounts of shares are traded. On the other hand, market makers are said to prefer dealing in cities such as New York and London where institutional arrangements make it easier to negotiate without revealing the extent of their intentions (Fabozzi, Modigliani, and Ferri 1997, 393–394). Dealers on the London Stock Exchange who specialize in executing institutional trades claim it can be to their disadvantage to reveal the full size of an order.

According to Gemmill (1996), London dealers are "vehement" in their desire to delay the publication of prices for block trades, arguing that it is not in the London market makers' interest to encourage the development of a U.S.-like upstairs (auction) market. However, the importance of this argument is called into question by Gemmill's study of trading data from the London Stock Exchange. Gemmill finds that "delaying publication does not affect the time taken by prices to reach a new level, which is rapid under all regimes. Spreads differ across years, but their size relates more closely to market volatility than to speed of publication" (1996, 1,765). Moreover, the different forms of organizing the larger institutional trades do not appear to have significant effects on the markets' allocative efficiency: "The different market structures—upstairs trading of blocks on the New York Stock Exchange and competitive dealership on the London Stock Exchange—lead to surprisingly similar outcomes" (1996, 1,788).

Program Trading   Technology has both improved equity market efficiency and created new types of trading concerns. *Program trading*, which involves simultaneous institutional trading of many different types of shares and in high volumes, is a case in point. Some types of program trades are aimed at eliminating emerging arbitrage opportunities, and work well during normal business conditions. But during a crisis, program trades cannot always be executed quickly and at market prices. As a result program trading has the effect of both generating additional volume and possibly increasing the volatility of market prices. As discussed further below, program trading used for portfolio insurance purposes will trigger massive additional selling at times when stock prices are declining, and can thus exacerbate the decline. An additional possibility is that such trading creates informational cascades, in the sense that selling by one institution may be taken as a signal for other institutions also to sell.

Program trading is used to implement investment strategies, such as creating index portfolios, and to arbitrage between the stock and stock index futures markets. Program trading originally came into favor for theoretical reasons. In an allocatively efficient market, theory suggests it will be difficult for portfolio managers to outperform the investment returns on an index portfolio. Studies of portfolio performance confirm the theoretical predictions. For example, when well-diversified portfolios' returns are adjusted for risk and for transactions costs, they do not generally[12] outperform the market (Malkiel 1995).

Although it has frequently been suggested that program trading can contribute to volatility, both theory and empirical research call the observation into question during normal business conditions. On a theoretical basis, if program trading were to create predictable price differences between the stock and derivatives markets, it is highly likely that arbitraging would spring up and eliminate the patterns. If arbitraging were to diminish the possibility of emerging price differences, volatility should not increase. For example, Santoni (1987) finds little or no evidence of volatility increases from program trading.

On the other hand, since program trading largely involves synthetic portfolios, there is a possibility that it might inhibit information-based trading in the underlying securities, thus reducing information-based trading and possibly increasing volatility (Grossman 1988a, 1988b). If such effects were

---

[12] It is not impossible to find undervalued stocks and to earn above normal returns on them, but most portfolio managers seem unable to obtain returns in excess of the cost of finding them. On the other hand "evidence based on the activities of insiders has generally revealed that insiders consistently outperform the stock market" (Fabozzi and Modigliani 1992, 254).

systematic, it might be expected that arbitraging would eliminate them, at least when arbitrageurs are not limited by insufficient capital, as discussed in Chapter 10. Moreover, Grossman and Zhou (1996) point out that the existence of hedging instruments can affect market prices when there are many traders desiring to hedge a risk, but few traders willing to take the risk on. In addition, Bookstaber (2007) emphasizes that market dynamics can differ greatly over time, and in certain instances of high trading volumes markets can witness a preponderance of either sellers or buyers, and prices are influenced accordingly. Aspects of these issues are discussed further in Chapter 14.

Pricing Anomalies: New Issues

The shares of small firms, the shares of firms neglected by analysts, and shares with low price-earnings ratios all seem capable of outperforming the returns on shares of larger firms with comparable risks.[13] One possible explanation of these effects is that institutions only find it cost-effective to trade in the larger issues. To save on transactions costs, institutions typically buy or sell in large amounts, as already discussed. Institutions are less willing to invest in small issues, because blocks of small companies' shares are less liquid than those of larger companies. Since institutions screen only the issues they regard as potentially suitable for investment, there is more institutional research available regarding the performance of the larger companies. Thus the shares of larger companies are more likely to reflect fundamental value as revealed by research information. A second possible explanation of small firm effects is that investment strategies sometimes have a faddish component, and some firms may be unpopular for a time. The two explanations are not conflicting, but the first provides economic reasons for neglecting to analyze some firms, while the second does not.

New issues are usually sold by investment bankers, who provide a number of services: advising on the best type of security to issue, preparing the prospectus for a new issue, and distributing a newly issued security among institutional buyers. In many cases investment bankers underwrite the issue, acting as a residual buyer and thus insuring that the issuer will be able to raise a minimum amount of funds. This kind of contract, know as a "firm commitment," is contrasted with a "best efforts" contract in which the risk of raising the funds remains with the issuing firm. Whether or not this risk shifting will occur depends on the nature of the issuing firm, the likely liquidity of the new issue, the capital of the underwriter, and the size of the

---

[13] For a review of these effects, see Fabozzi and Modigliani (1992).

underwriting fees. A firm commitment contract is functionally equivalent to the investment banker's acting as a dealer, whereas a best efforts contract is functionally equivalent to the investment banker's acting as a broker.

Market Evolution

Since the late 1990s, many exchanges have reorganized themselves as private, for-profit companies. The private company organization gives exchanges a focus on profitability that they did not previously have, thereby resolving some conflicts of interest between members. A focus on profitability also makes it easier for exchange members to trade seats, increasing the liquidity of their investment in the exchange's operations. For similar reasons, several of the newly reorganized exchanges have acquired ATSs to enhance their ability to attract more trades.[14]

Despite the foregoing, independent ATSs have also been growing rapidly, and have been capturing increasing shares of trading business. Since 2007, regulations[15] in the United States and Europe have required that trades be sent to the venue offering best execution, moves that further increased ATSs' competitive capabilities. In the United States, the traditional exchanges' market share of trades fell[16] from 86% in April 2007 to 73% in April 2008. In many cases ATSs offer both faster and cheaper execution than traditional exchanges, advantages that are particularly important to hedge fund traders and some specialist brokers. Some ATSs even plan to become full exchanges in the future.

Still other sources of competition, for both the exchanges and the ATSs, are private crossing networks and "dark pools," operated by institutional traders and designed primarily for nonpublic exchanges of large blocks of shares.[17] In the United States these types of trades are expected to account for about 20% of all trading by 2011.[18] Although these types of institutional trading can fragment the market, arbitraging between individual crossing networks and dark pools is also springing up, relinking them using computer programs to search for profit opportunities.

---

[14] Although the stock exchanges compete vigorously for trading business, this is not as true of futures markets, and consequently members of the latter have greater incentives to organize as private for-profit companies (Lee 2000).

[15] Regulation NMS in the United States, and the MiFID directive in the European Union.

[16] The Battle of the Bourses, *The Economist*, May 31, 2008, 77.

[17] These arrangements are variants of what is traditionally known as the "upstairs market."

[18] The Battle of the Bourses, *The Economist*.

In competitive responses, Nasdaq and the NYSE are striking arrangements with the operators of some dark pools, reflecting similar earlier attempts to respond to threats of possible market fragmentation. In another competitive response the traditional exchanges are acquiring derivatives exchanges. As examples of the latter, Deutsche Börse and Nasdaq have both bought options exchanges, and NYSE Euronext has acquired LIFFE, the London International Financial Futures Exchange. The acquisitions have been motivated both by the scale economies of large market operations and by the possibility of realizing scope economies, particularly through acquiring the technology developed by successful competitors. Additionally, the moves are intended to make the market operators attractive to a wider public, that is, to realize positive externalities on the revenue side of operations.

BOND MARKETS

This section first discusses the conceptual differences between stocks and bonds. It then examines the nature and importance of the bond markets, and the interest rate spreads in them.

Importance and Functions

Bond markets include government and corporate submarkets. Government bond markets have relatively standardized instruments and relatively homogeneous information. Corporate bonds differ considerably in their terms, and the availability of information about different issues can differ greatly, as can the information itself. Government bonds are usually seen as posing little or no default risk, while some corporate bonds are regarded as having relatively high default risk. Mainly as a result of these differences, government bond markets are substantially more liquid than their corporate counterparts.

As with the money and stock markets, this book's discussion of the bond market is developed using the United States as an example. Bills and bonds are issued and sold by the U.S. Treasury in amounts reflecting the government's financing needs. Corporate bonds are sold both through private placements and through public offerings. Many issuing corporations prefer using the public bond markets rather than bank loans, because the former, particularly during the 2000s, have come to embody fewer restrictive covenants. Like U.S. Treasury securities, corporate bonds are traded over the counter in the United States. However, the corporate bond markets are not as active as the government securities markets, mainly because corporate bonds are issued in smaller amounts and vary considerably more widely in terms and in quality.[19]

The securities firms that conduct most bond trading usually act as dealers in government bonds, and as either dealers or brokers in corporate bonds. The choice between acting as a dealer or a broker is made according to the ratio of inventory risk to expected trading profits, as discussed in Chapter 10. While most bonds are bought by financial institutions, individuals can also be relatively important purchasers, especially of government issues. In most developed countries new issues of government bonds are sold mainly at auctions by a small number of firms known as primary dealers. Secondary market trading is conducted both by the primary market dealers and by others.

In order to enhance marketability, many companies pay to have their bond issues rated by an independent agency. Both Moody's and Standard & Poor's, the largest bond rating agencies in the United States, estimate creditworthiness in terms of how likely the firm is to default and the protection, if any, that creditors have in that event. Both agencies use letter grade systems to indicate their estimates of creditworthiness.[20] The markets for most bond issues are very much less active than are the money markets or the equity markets, in part because bonds offer a very much wider range of qualities than either short-term instruments or stocks. This wide range of qualities, plus the fact that new bond issues are often used to raise relatively small amounts of funds, implies that research into bond values is often uneconomic, and the resulting lack of available information further inhibits trading activity. However the informational situation is changing, as various companies now provide electronic access to information regarding current bond offerings, trading, and research.

Default Risk and Interest Spreads

Chapter 8 showed that bonds convey a priority claim on value, stocks a residual claim. The purpose of Table 11.1, presented next, is to show why bonds are normally regarded as less risky than stocks issued by the same firm. Table 11.1 describes, from the perspective of time 0, the possible values of a firm's securities at time 1. Suppose firm earnings available to pay off

---

[19] The proportion of funds raised through public bond offerings peaks at approximately the same time as the business cycle. The ratio of private placements to public offerings has increased since 1990 as a result of changes in the U.S. Securities and Exchange Commission's Rule 144a, which permits privately placed issues to be resold to institutions without registration of the primary issue.

[20] Standard & Poor's letter grades range from AAA (highest) to D (lowest), while Moody's range from Aaa (highest) to C (lowest).

TABLE 11.1 Claims of Bondholders and Stockholders: First Example

Possible Outcomes	Funds Available for Payment to Security Holders	To Bondholders (First Priority, Limited Claim of 8)	To Stockholders (Second Priority, All Remaining Funds)
High Earnings	30	8	22
Low Earnings	10	8	2

bondholders and stockholders could be one of two possible amounts as shown in the second column of Table 11.1. For simplicity, assume the firm is to be wound up after the time 1 earnings are received.

The first line of numbers represents best-case earnings, in which the cash available to pay all security holders is 30. The second line represents worst-case earnings in which available cash is only 10. Only one situation (one row) can actually obtain, but when agents contemplate the situation at time 0, either scenario might be realized.

The main difference between bonds and stocks is that bonds get first claim on funds up to the amount of the promised repayment (equal to 8 and representing both principal and interest in the example), while stockholders are entitled to the funds remaining after the debt holders are paid. In this sense you can think of bonds as being designed principally to avoid downside risk, stocks as being designed principally to take advantage of upside potential.

By changing Table 11.1 to reflect a different situation, it is also possible to show why bondholders sometimes ask for more equity (more shareholder investment) as a condition for buying the bonds. Suppose the firm issues debt, promising to pay 8, when the earnings distribution is as shown in Table 11.2. In this case bondholders cannot be assured that the promise will be redeemed in full.

If the cash available is only 6 it will be paid to the bondholders, but the remaining amount owing them will have to be written off because the firm has no other resources. Many bondholders would not find this arrangement attractive. They might, for example, find it difficult to assess the legal and other costs of not being fully repaid, in part because these costs include the time it might take to recover some of the promised funds. Potential bond buyers might instead prefer to avoid any consequences of a possible write-off by refusing to purchase any bond issue that promised a repayment of more than 6 (principal and interest). If the client asked for 8 as in the

TABLE 11.2 Claims of Bondholders and Stockholders: Second Example

Possible Outcomes	Funds Available for Payment to Security Holders	To Bondholders (First Priority, Limited Claim of 8)	To Stockholders (Second Priority, All Remaining Funds)
Best Case	30	8	22
Worst Case	6	6	0

first case, the potential bond purchasers might respond with a statement that "you need more equity." Their response would mean that they did not regard a proposal to lend against a promise to repay 8 as a riskless proposition like the one shown in the previous example. In this case the bondholders might be willing to lend the present value of 6, since they would be repaid 6 with certainty. If the bondholders' funding were to be limited in this way, the shareholders would then have to put up the rest of the funds.[21] Alternatively, prospective bondholders might propose terms that reflect higher risks, as examined in the next, extended example.

The principle of pricing by arbitrage establishes that interest rates on instruments of the same quality and terms will tend to be equalized. In a market with frequent and costless arbitraging transactions, any persistent interest rate differences between bond issues will likely be explained by differences in risk or in the details of issue terms. Insofar as risk is concerned, default risk is almost always greater for corporate than for government issues. The lower a corporate bond's quality rating, the greater is the likely spread between it and a comparable government issue.

Theoretically, the discount rate on risky debt is determined as shown in the following example. Suppose a firm's assets follow the value process shown in Table 11.3, and that the riskless rate is 1% between time 0 and time 1, as well as between time 1 and time 2. Assuming the absence of arbitrage opportunities, the risk-neutral probabilities are then found from

$$100.00 = q(120.00/1.05) + (1 - q)(83.33/1.01)$$

---

[21] In the absence of arbitrage opportunities, if the value of the firm was known it would be possible to estimate the value of both riskless and risky debt. The point being made here is that the principle of riskless arbitrage does not take into account all the features of financial distress that are relevant to potential bond purchasers.

TABLE 11.3 Asset Price Process

Time 0	Time 1	Time 2
		144.00
	120.00	
100.00		100.00
	83.33	
		69.44

with the solution $q = 0.4819$ and $(1 - q) = 0.5181$. Assuming the debt issue promises to pay \$100.00 at time 2, and that bankruptcy is costless, the actual debt payments are \$100.00 if the assets are worth \$121.00, \$100.00 if the assets are worth \$100.00, and \$69.44 if the assets are worth \$69.44. The time 0 value of this debt is thus

$$(q^2 + 2q(1 - q))(100.00/1.01^2) + (1 - q)^2(69.44/1.01^2) = 89.99$$

If we suppose that the four possible asset price paths are equally likely, the expected value of the debt repayments is

$$100.00(0.25 + 2 \times 0.25) + 69.44(0.25) = 92.36$$

Thus the discount rate applied to the debt is

$$(92.36 - 89.99)/89.99 = 0.0264$$

or 2.64% over the two periods; 1.31% over one period. Since the riskless rate of interest over one period has been assumed to be 1%, the risk premium on this particular debt issue is 0.31% over a single period.

Special Features

In practice, several other features also affect a bond's risk premium. Call risk refers to the possibility that a bond can be redeemed prior to maturity. The effective yield on a callable bond will be higher than the effective yield on a comparable noncallable bond because the firm has an option to redeem the bond if interest rates fall relative to the rate the issue promises. That is, a callable bond presents its purchasers with the possibility of facing a reinvestment risk as and when the issuing firm exercises the call privilege, and investors require to be compensated for the risk. If two bonds are issued on the same terms except that one has a call feature and the other does not, the effective yield on the callable bond is likely to be higher to compensate for the reinvestment risk.

Marketability risk refers to the possibility that traders do not find it economic to provide continuous quotes for an issue. This risk will be especially prominent in cases where bonds are partially redeemed prior to maturity; such as bonds subject to *serial redemption*. Still another form of risk, event risk, refers to possibilities such as industrial accidents or takeover attempts. The greater the probability of event risk, the greater the risk premium on the bond in question.

A corporation or junior government manager planning to retire a bond issue serially may set up a fund, called a *sinking fund*, to provide for repayment of the issue. The serial retirement feature will impair marketability, but the sinking fund provision may enhance the bond's quality. Quality may also be enhanced if the bond is not to be retired serially, but a sinking fund is still set up to funds for retiring the bonds at maturity.

In practice, corporations also issue hybrid instruments such as preferred shares. These securities represent a mix of the instruments already discussed rather than a completely new type of claim. For example, a corporation may issue bonds, common shares, and preferred shares. The preferred share is a hybrid of a bond and a stock, because it has a claim to income that is junior to the claim of ordinary bondholders but senior to that of ordinary common shares. Hybrids are used principally when different groups of potential investors seek securities tailored to their particular needs. Shareholders are usually more eager to purchase securities offering relatively large returns if the firm is successful, while bondholders are usually more eager to purchase securities offering relatively safe returns under most if not all operating conditions.

Speculative-Grade Bonds

The late 1980s boom in leveraged takeovers of public companies greatly increased the popularity of negotiated financings, especially those using high-yield, speculative-grade bonds (bonds whose quality ratings are Standard & Poor's BB or below; Moody's Ba or below). The amount of speculative-grade bonds outstanding in the United States increased from $20 billion in 1977 to about $240 billion in 1990 (Fabozzi, Modigliani, and Ferri 1997, 429). This huge increase in popularity reflects the importance of speculative-grade bonds as a financial innovation. Essentially, the bonds represented a new way of channeling institutional funds to corporations that otherwise relied on bank borrowing or privately negotiated financings. Institutions were willing to purchase speculative-grade bonds because studies suggested that the risk premium on a diversified portfolio of such bonds more than offset the increased risk of holding them.[22] Speculative-grade bond financing is cheaper than bank debt for some corporations, and is also typically longer-term than bank borrowings.

Like many other financial innovations, the speculative-grade bond market development had mixed effects. It presented profit opportunities for innovators and increased the financial markets' allocative efficiency, presenting an important new source of financing. For example, speculative-grade bonds provided the funding for many companies in the telecommunications industry. The rapid growth of this innovative financing practice also created a new set of problems. So much speculative-grade financing was used during the 1980s that firms became overlevered and vulnerable to default following on cyclical declines in their profitability. As default rates increased the bonds became very much less popular, and new issues declined precipitously. With the passage of time, a more balanced point of view has come to prevail—high-yield bonds present higher than normal risks, but when used judiciously they do not need to create extraordinary risks—and in the late 1990s speculative-grade bond activity was again on the increase. The private equity leveraged buyouts of the early- to mid-2000s used a similar tactic in that much of the financing took the form of relatively high-risk bonds. As with speculative-grade bonds, these issues have also been sharply curtailed during the market turmoil of 2007–2008.

Auction Rate Securities

This section describes a relatively short-term bubble in the U.S. bond markets. Although the idea of auction rate securities first appeared in the 1980, the market showed rapid growth from the early 2000s until it experienced a wave of failures in 2007 and 2008. Its growth and decline were both stimulated by an interaction of factors. In late 2002, the U.S. federal funds rate had been reduced to a low of 1%, and because of the historically low yields on high-quality, short-term bonds, investors were seeking higher-rate investment opportunities. At the same time long-term interest rates remained considerably higher, and long-term borrowers were seeking to reduce the interest rates they were paying. Investment bankers were seeking to profit from serving both types of client, and proposed auction rate securities as a

---

[22] Existing studies do not suggest that investing in portfolios of high-yield bonds offers exceptional value, but rather that they offer an increase in return commensurate with their higher risk (Fabozzi and Modigliani 1992, 497). However, the innovators in the market may have received, or at least believed they would receive, excess returns for establishing the new form of financing.

means of achieving their goals. During its early years the auction rate securities (ARS) market worked well, but was flawed because it represented an attempt to finance long-term assets through short-term borrowings. When it ultimately failed in 2007, several additional attempts to revive the market also failed.[23]

During the heyday of the scheme, investors were attracted to auction rate securities because they represented high-grade, short-term paper with a higher yield than Treasury bills. Long-term borrowers (municipalities, hospitals, utilities, port authorities, housing finance agencies, student loan authorities, and universities)—were attracted to the market because, for a time, auction rate securities allowed them to issue 20-year term debt at rates much lower than 20-year fixed rates.

The key to the market's success involved issuing bonds with long maturities, but with coupons that reset frequently, say every four or five weeks. The rates were reset at the end of each period through a Dutch auction establishing the lowest rate that would clear the securities then being sold. The basic difficulty with the scheme was that borrowers were using the short end of the market to finance long-term assets, and were therefore vulnerable to interest rate increases. However, borrowers could offset interest rate risk by using instruments like interest rate caps, and initially this type of insurance was not costly. At the same time, borrowers might be vulnerable to reduced credit ratings stemming from any cash flow problems that interest rate increases could bring. But this risk could be covered by default insurance, also not costly in the earlier stages of the market's development.

The scheme proved popular with both investment bankers and borrowers, and by early 2007 about $300 billion of auction rate securities had been issued. Even CDOs were sold in the ARS market to finance long-term (subprime) assets. When failures began to occur in mid-2007, it was suspected that many CDOs were backed by low-quality assets. At the same time, bond insurers were leveraged at triple-digit multiples of their capital and investors lost confidence in bond insurers' ability to redeem the liabilities created by the default insurance. As a result investor interest in the auctions fell sharply, and in some auctions there were no bids.[24] The dealers who were to provide

---

[23] For discussion of how similar forces were at work in the subprime mortgage market, see the subsection "Securitization and Trading" and Chapter 15. For a related discussion of asset-backed commercial paper, see Chapter 17.

[24] McConnell and Saretto (2008) attribute the failures to embedded interest rate caps that limited the returns on the bonds. At its peak in a sample of 793 bonds analyzed by McConnell and Saretto, the overall auction failure rate was 46%, and the authors produce evidence suggesting that in the failed auctions market clearing yields lay above the level of the embedded caps.

liquidity in the paper were unable to do so because of other difficulties they were facing, and the ARS market was frozen.

In later 2008, regulators in the United States began to negotiate with issuers to buy the paper back. UBS agreed to repurchase $19 billion, Merrill and Citigroup about another $20 billion. But the buyback arrangements reached at this writing cover just a little less than 15% of the $300 billion ARS outstanding, and at this writing (December 2008) the market itself remains frozen.

RESIDENTIAL MORTGAGE MARKETS[25]

This section discusses the importance and functions of both the primary residential mortgage markets and the underlying institutional markets where blocks of mortgages are traded. This chapter examines the normal operations of the U.S. mortgage lending industry, while the subprime market problems contributing to the 2007–2008 market turmoil are discussed in Chapter 15. Difficulties faced by U.S. thrift institutions in the 1970s and 1980s are discussed in Chapter 17.

Importance and Types of Loans

Most mortgage borrowing finances home investment. An equity position in a home is the largest investment most households have, and offers possibilities for sizeable capital gains or losses. Consumers often use mortgage loans to finance both new home construction and extensions or improvements to their primary residences. Some consumers borrow against their principal residence to finance the purchase of vacation homes, to invest in rental housing, or even to finance consumption. Finally, some consumers use reverse mortgages to generate an installment income by borrowing against the equity in a home.

The primary residential mortgage markets are venues for arranging individual mortgage loans between a lending intermediary and a client, frequently with the aid of a mortgage broker. The market has two subsectors—prime and subprime—based on the credit quality of the borrower. Prime loans are further classified as either conforming or nonconforming. Although made by private sector lenders, prime conforming loans satisfy the standards of one of the U.S. government mortgage agencies—Ginnie Mae, Fannie Mae,

---

[25]This section is greatly indebted to Fabozzi (2009).

or Freddie Mac.[26] Prime nonconforming loans meet agency borrower credit rating and first lien standards, but fall short in other ways. Subprime loans are nonconforming loans that are made to borrowers with an impaired credit rating, to borrowers arranging a second mortgage, or both.

Most lenders require residential mortgages to be insured against default. For example, one form of mortgage insurance pays off the outstanding principal if the borrower dies. Banks and near banks have historically been strong proponents of such insurance,[27] and in prosperous times have offered it at relatively low cost. The insurance both reduces the lender's risk and makes it easier to securitize a mortgage loan portfolio, as discussed below.

With regard to institutional markets, all types of mortgage loans can be and usually are securitized, but with different types of residential mortgage-backed securities (RMBSs). Agency mortgage-backed securities (MBSs) are backed by prime conforming loans, private label MBSs by prime nonconforming loans, and subprime MBSs by subprime loans.

Innovations

From the 1950s through the 1980s, the U.S. mortgage loan market saw banks and other depository institutions replace insurance companies as the principal providers of mortgage funds. Most of the mortgages granted in that period were fixed rate mortgages, and many of them also had a fixed term to maturity. Fixed rate mortgages are preferred by most borrowers when interest rates are relatively low. However during higher interest rate periods, such as the 1970s and 1980s, arranging a new fixed rate mortgage required relatively high installment repayments, and the higher the repayments, the more difficult it became for both new borrowers and any borrowers whose mortgages had to be renewed at higher interest rates to finance a home purchase. An indication of the difficulties is illustrated by Table 11.4.

Fixed rate mortgages also create problems for lenders who use short-term deposits as their main source of funding, because such lenders assume interest rate risk. Interest revenues on a portfolio of fixed rate mortgages are stable over the longer term, but if deposit costs rise with interest rates, fixed-rate lenders can face serious profitability problems. These problems became evident in the 1970s and early 1980s, since at that time most lenders

---

[26] Respectively the Government National Mortgage Association (GNMA), Federal National Mortgage Association (FNMA), and Federal Home Loan Mortgage Corporation (FHLMC). Each of the agencies facilitates secondary market financing of particular types of mortgage portfolios.

[27] Changing standards in the subprime market are discussed in Chapter 15.

TABLE 11.4 Interest Sensitivity of Level Payments on Mortgages

Principal Term	Interest	Rate	Monthly	Index of Payments
$100,000	5 yr	5%	$1887.12	(1.00)
$100,000	5 yr	10%	$2124.70	(1.13)
$100,000	5 yr	15%	$2378.99	(1.26)
$100,000	25 yr	5%	$584.59	(1.00)
$100,000	25 yr	10%	$908.70	(1.55)
$100,000	25 yr	15%	$1280.83	(2.19)

still retained most mortgages on their own books.[28] In later periods when increasingly large proportions of the loans were securitized, some of the interest rate risks were transferred to investors in any fixed-rate securities issued by the securitization entity.

Adjustable rate mortgages are one response to the problem with level payment mortgages. Adjustable interest rates stabilize financial institutions' net interest earnings, but pass interest rate risk on to the borrower, with the result that adjustable rate mortgages can create borrower cash flow problems similar to those illustrated by the data of Table 11.4. Graduated payment mortgages have been designed for use with adjustable rates to minimize the impact of borrower interest rate risk, and in some cases it has proved possible to extend adjustable rate mortgages enough to ease the impact of an interest rate increase on the borrower.

Innovations became even more important in the 1990s and early 2000s as a trend of rapidly rising house prices stimulated additional demand for homes and for new types of mortgages to finance the purchases. Some of the new forms of financing, such as low down payment financing interest-only mortgages, and extended-term mortgages offered additional incentives to borrowers. These kinds of financings looked particularly attractive during the low interest period of the later 1990s and early 2000s, probably because many borrowers did not look ahead to the situation they might face if interest rates were subsequently to rise. Subprime lending, particularly using adjustable rate mortgages offering low initial interest rates, swelled in response. With many of these arrangements there was little real possibility of eventual repayment, as became evident when interest rates began to rise in the later 2000s. As increasing numbers of adjustable rate mortgages began

---

[28] The 1970s and early 1980s issues with thrift institutions are discussed in Chapter 17.

to approach their reset dates, the specter of increased payments loomed. The adjustments increased the probability of default because the borrower's equity interest in the property was frequently minimal at the outset, was made more onerous by payment increases, and was subsequently worsened by declines in house prices. In a considerable number of cases borrowers ended up with negative equity, and defaults mounted rapidly. As Chapters 15 and 22 discuss further, policy moves in the late 2000s were geared to address the twin problems of increasingly onerous mortgage terms and increasing probabilities of default.[29]

Reverse mortgages offer a means of selling a house owned by a person who wishes to convert the value of the house into an income stream, usually for the remainder of his or her life. In effect, the reverse mortgage allows the owner of a house to sell off the equity piecemeal and obtain income while continuing to live in the house. Reverse mortgages may become increasingly popular as many countries' populations continue to increase in average age during the 2000s. Nevertheless, in the early 2000s the effective interest rates on these instruments still seemed to be atypically high in comparison to other mortgage loans, and there had not been much demand for them, even before the problems of 2007–2008.

Securitization and Trading

Growing areas frequently face demands for mortgage financing that exceed the local supply of savings to finance them. On the other hand, mature areas may have a supply of savings exceeding local demands for mortgage financing. Mortgage lenders facing supply-demand imbalance problems find them easier to resolve if well-functioning secondary mortgage markets can be used to transfer funds from savings-surplus to savings-deficit areas. These kinds of transactions, although originated by mortgage brokers, were greatly enhanced by securitization, as this section shows. In addition, smoothly working securitization helps to improve terms in the primary mortgage markets.[30]

As explained in Chapter 5, securitization creates a separate entity to hold an asset portfolio financed by issuing securities against it. The mortgage

---

[29] In most countries a defaulting mortgagor is liable for the amount owed on the mortgage, regardless of what the property is worth. In contrast, a mortgagor's liability in the United States is often limited to the value of the property, giving the borrower greater incentive to default if payments increase and house prices decline.
[30] The difficulties created by originating and securitizing subprime loans are discussed in Chapter 15.

securitization process involves the original lenders' selling loans to entities that create residential mortgage-backed securities (RMBSs). The RMBSs represent debt obligations issued against a mortgage pool and are backed by the cash flow the pool generates from mortgage repayments.[31] Prime conforming loans—loans that satisfy the underwriting standards of the agencies, Fannie Mae, Freddie Mac, and Ginnie Mae—are pooled to create a class of securities known as agency[32] MBSs. Nonagency MBSs are issued by private sector entities. They are further subclassified as either private label MBSs (using prime nonconforming loans as collateral) or subprime MBSs (using subprime loans as collateral).

The agency market is the largest part of the MBS market, and is also the largest sector of the U.S. investment-grade bond market.[33] Three types of securities are traded in the agency MBS market—agency mortgage pass-through securities, agency collateralized mortgage obligations (CMOs), and agency stripped MBSs.[34] A mortgage pass-through security is a type of MBS created by issuing certificates that entitle an investor to receive a pro rata share in the cash flows of the underlying pool of mortgage loans.[35] As discussed later, an agency CMO is a type of mortgage-backed security that creates separate pools of pass-through rates for different classes of bondholders with varying maturities, called tranches. A stripped MBS separates the principal and interest payments accruing to an MBS, allowing an investor to take separate positions in either expected prepayments or expected interest rates.[36]

Institutional investors regard pass-through certificates as attractive investments because they typically offer attractive interest rates, standardized

---

[31] Collection of the original mortgages usually remains with the original lender.

[32] Agency MBSs have either been issued by or guaranteed by a government or government-sponsored entity. Fannie Mae and Freddie Mac do not originate primary mortgage loans, but acquire pools of loans and securitize them. The two agencies, formerly private, were placed in conservatorship in September 2008 and are now government agencies. Ginnie Mae is also a U.S. government agency, but does not itself issue MBSs. Rather, it guarantees pass-through certificates that are issued by private sector approved lenders.

[33] The agency MBS market accounted for about 45% of that sector in 2008 (Fabozzi 2009).

[34] Since the latter two types are created from mortgage pass-through securities, they are usually referred to as derivative MBS products.

[35] If there is only one class of bondholder, the pass-throughs are referred to as single-class certificates.

[36] See Fabozzi (2005).

terms, and default guarantees. Pass-through certificates function as substitutes for long-term bonds if the underlying mortgages have mid- to long-term maturities and carry both a fixed term and a fixed rate of interest. Interest rates on such certificates should converge to long-term bond rates, since the principle of pricing by arbitrage predicts that rate differences not attributable to differences in risk will quickly be eliminated.

Many mortgages are not fixed term, and in this case the associated portfolios' pass-through certificates also have uncertain terms, since both cash flows and pool earnings are passed on proportionately to certificate investors. Thus investors face the risk that mortgages in the pool may be paid down either more rapidly or more slowly than as scheduled. The risk of rapid redemption, called contraction risk, is similar to the risk faced by the holder of a callable bond. It occurs when interest rates fall and holders of flexible term mortgages may pay them down more quickly than forecast. On the other hand repayments on adjustable term mortgages can become slower than forecast when interest rates rise, resulting in a diminution of cash flows known as extension risk. The combination of contraction and extension risks is referred to as prepayment risk.

Pass-through certificates can also be created for mortgages that do not bear an agency guarantee. In this case the certificates are usually covered by private sector default insurance to create the higher-quality bond ratings similar to those enjoyed by agency pass-throughs. For example, to create a market for funding portfolios of subprime mortgages, mortgage pool managers designed securities that attempted to minimize both investor risks and administrative costs.

As previously mentioned, mortgage lenders also use CMOs to fund loan originations. The practice allows mortgage lenders to raise additional funding, to transfer most or all of the risks of the mortgage loan portfolio to the administering special purpose entity (SPE), and to earn fees for issuing the CMOs. Administrative costs are minimized by leaving the actual collection of payments with the original lender. The SPE usually divides its issues into risk tranches subject to different loss provisions. For example, the most junior CMO may absorb all original mortgage defaults up to a given amount before more senior securities are required to absorb any defaults at all. Any cash flow not needed to meet the terms of CMOs is called the CMO residual and functions like equity. It is however, a form of equity that increases in value as interest rates increase.

Liquidity of CMO issues was not always regarded as important by the institutional investors buying the CMOs, and illiquidity became a feature contributing to investor losses in subprime CMOs when the underlying mortgages began to default. As the defaults mounted in 2007–2008, the portfolios fell in value, and their illiquidity made the declines considerably more pronounced. These matters are discussed more fully in Chapter 15.

REFERENCES

Bookstaber, Richard. 2007. *A Demon of Our Own Design*. Hoboken, NJ: John Wiley & Sons.

Fabozzi, Frank J., and Franco Modigliani. 1992. *Capital Markets: Institutions and Instruments*. Englewood Cliffs, NJ: Prentice-Hall.

Fabozzi, Frank J., ed. 2005. *The handbook of mortgage securities*. New York: McGraw-Hill.

Fabozzi, Frank J. 2009. *Bond Markets: Analysis and Strategies*, 6th ed. Upper Saddle River, NJ: Prentice-Hall.

Fabozzi, Frank J., Franco Modigliani, and Michael G. Ferri. 2001. *Foundations of Financial Markets and Institutions*. Upper Saddle River, NJ: Prentice-Hall.

Gemmill, Gordon. 1996. Transparency and liquidity: A study of block trades on the London Stock Exchange under different publication rules. *Journal of Finance* 51: 1,765–1,790.

Grossman, Sanford A. 1988a. An Analysis of the Implications for Stock and Futures Price Volatility of Program Trading and Dynamic Hedging Strategies. *Journal of Business* 61: 275–296.

Grossman, Sanford A. 1988b. Program trading and stock and futures price volatility. *Journal of Futures Markets* 8: 413–419.

Grossman, Sanford A. 1995. Dynamic asset allocation and the informational efficiency of markets. *Journal of Finance* 50: 773–785.

Grossman, Sanford J., and Zhongquan Zhou. 1996. Equilibrium analysis of portfolio insurance. *Journal of Finance* 51: 1,379–1,403.

Macey, Jonathan R., and Maureen O'Hara. 2005. From markets to venues: securities regulation in an evolving world. *Stanford Law Review* 58: 563–599.

Malkiel, Burton G. 1995. Returns from investing in equity mutual funds 1971 to 1991. *Journal of Finance* 49: 549–572.

McConnell, John J., and Alessio Saretto. 2008. "Auction failures and the market for auction rate securities." Working Paper, Krannert School of Management, Purdue University. Also available at ssrn.com abstract=1253002.

McInish, Thomas H. 2000. *Capital Markets: A Global Perspective*. Oxford: Blackwell.

O'Hara, Maureen. 1995. *Market Microstructure Theory*. Oxford: Blackwell.

Santoni, G. J. 1987. Has programmed trading made stock prices more volatile? *Federal Reserve Bank of St. Louis Review* 67: 18–29.

Shapiro, James E. 1995. U.S. equity markets: recent competitive developments. Chapter 1 in *Global equity markets: Technological, Competitive and Regulatory Challenges*, by Robert A. Schwartz. New York University Salomon Center, 1995.

Weston, James P. 2002. Electronic communication networks and liquidity on the Nasdaq. *Journal of Financial Services Research* 22: 125–139.

TERMS

alternative trading system Any market or network other than an organized stock exchange. In current usage, the term almost always refers to an electronic marketplace.

block trades Trades in large numbers of shares, usually defined as single trades of 10,000 or more shares.

open outcry A method of trading assets in which interested parties gather around a trading post to signal the terms on which they are willing to buy or sell. Much of the trading activity is carried out using hand and eye signals, often accompanied by a good deal of shouted communication.

over-the-counter (OTC) markets Historically, the most important markets for trading securities other than those listed on stock exchanges. In the OTC markets most transactions are carried out between clients and brokers over the telephone or electronically as opposed to at a physical location like the stock exchanges. Some OTC markets, such as Nasdaq in the United States, have trades, especially in the larger issues, conducted by dealers as well as by brokers.

pass-through securities Securities created when mortgage holders pool mortgages and sell shares or participation certificates in the pool.

position house (block positioner) Wholesale dealer in securities, specializing in institutional trading of large amounts.

program trading Using computers for automated portfolio trading. Usually large numbers of stocks are traded both simultaneously and frequently.

serial redemption bonds Bonds whose terms provide that a certain proportion of the issue will be redeemed at regular intervals. The bonds to be redeemed are either chosen by selecting their serial numbers in a lottery or simply by buying the bonds in the market.

sinking fund bonds Bonds issued on terms that provide for gradually building up a repayment fund, called a sinking fund, to finance the bonds' retirement. The issue may be retired either all at once or serially at several points in time.

upstairs market A network of trading arrangements between major securities firms and institutional investors, communicating with each other by telephone and electronic display systems, designed to facilitate trading in large amounts of individual shares and simultaneously to facilitate trading in large numbers of different shares.

CHAPTER 12

Markets for Trading Risks

This chapter begins by introducing the types and importance of risk trading activity, then examines how risk trading differs between the options and futures markets. Next, it examines several issues of market evolution, including the development of the markets for catastrophe bonds, market mergers, the convergence of financial and insurance markets, and developments in the over-the-counter markets.

INTRODUCTION

This chapter examines the markets for trading risks. Applying the ideas of governance developed in Chapters 5 and 6, along with the pricing theories developed in Chapters 8 and 9, the present chapter explains how and why risks are traded in practice. It examines the options and futures markets' economic similarities and differences, and explains why risk trading has grown at such phenomenal rates since the early 1970s. It also explains that intermediaries trade risks in the over-the-counter (OTC) markets, sometimes acting as principals and holding one side of the transaction on their own books, at other times acting only as agents (i.e., brokers). The last part of the chapter points out that markets for risk trading are continuing to evolve in a number of ways. New instruments continue to be created, risk trading by banks and insurance companies continue to converge, and clearing houses are being set up for the over-the-counter markets.

Why Risks Are Traded

In one form or another, risks are traded in virtually every economy. However, specialized markets for trading risks are primarily concentrated in the world's major financial centers, largely because risk trading requires both

TABLE 12.1 A Risky Investment Proposition

Value of Outcome	Probability	Sure Payoff (S)	Call Payoff (C)	Payoff to Short Put (−P)
25.00	1/3	50.00	0.00	−25.00
50.00	1/3	50.00	0.00	0.00
75.00	1/3	50.00	25.00	0.00

highly developed skills and highly developed facilities. Despite the concentration of facilities, however, risks themselves are globally distributed and trading them is an international activity.

Although press discussions sometimes create the impression that risk trading is mainly of importance to speculators, in reality the activity is of much greater economic importance, and to many different participants. First, risk trading creates value both by efficiently allocating risks and by enhancing the ways the risks can be divided up when they are traded. Second, risk trading establishes market prices for different kinds of risks, producing information about their economic significance. To take just one example, in the turbulent markets of 2008, much attention was paid to indexes reporting the changing prices of credit default swaps, the indexes being taken as indications of the risks assumed by many different institutions. Third, markets for risk trading enhance agents' ability to undertake new risks in much the same way that active trading in a stock can help with floating a new issue. That is, undertaking new and risky ventures is facilitated by the existence of active risk trading markets.

Agents trade risks for at least three reasons. Their attitudes toward a given risk may differ, they may estimate its distribution differently, or they may wish to tailor portfolio returns. Consider first how attitudes affect risk trading.[1] *Risk-averse* individuals are motivated to sell risks, either to less risk-averse agents or to *risk lovers*, as the following example shows. Suppose as in Table 12.1 three individuals are interested in an investment that offers three possible outcomes, each believed to be equally probable, so that the investment's expected value is $50.00.

The attitudes of different investors toward the investment can be illustrated by recalling the put-call parity condition from Chapter 9. Suppose for ease of illustration that the call and put options illustrated in Table 12.1 both have a strike price of $50.00 and that the riskless interest rate is zero. Then the investment can be decomposed into a sure payoff of $50.00, an upside

---

[1]Other reasons for trading risks include different portfolio positions and different estimates of probabilities. These motives are discussed in later chapters.

potential (represented by the call payoffs) and a downside risk (represented by the payoffs to the short put position) as shown in the last three columns of Table 12.1. The risk-neutral investor will place equal personal values on both the call and the put, and value the whole investment at $50.00, its expected value. The risk-averse investor, who weighs the possibility of downside risk relatively heavily, will value the same investment at something less than $50.00, thus placing a negative personal value on the put position greater than the positive value he places on the call. Finally, a risk lover will weigh the upside potential relatively heavily and value the investment at more than $50.00, thus placing a higher personal value on the call than on the put.

Agents also trade risks because they sometimes have different estimates of the payoff distribution. In the foregoing example, one risk-averse agent might be able to sell a put to another, equally risk-averse agent if the first thought the probability of a price decline in the underlying stock was lower than did the second. Finally, agents may trade risks for portfolio reasons. For example, Chapter 9 showed how a put could be used to limit the downside risk of investing in a given stock.

Only certain kinds of risk instruments can be traded profitably in a marketplace.[2] These instruments have readily ascertained payoffs and conform to agreed contract standards. While the instruments' value may change rapidly according to the value of the underlying asset, the contracts do not require continuous, intensive monitoring of their creditworthiness. Purchasing a put option written on a well-known stock is a typical example, at least so long as the put is traded on an options exchange that guarantees the contract will be honored as written.

Types of Risk Trading

Risk instruments are issued against many different types of assets. Currently, options are most often written against financial assets, although options on nonfinancial assets can also be found. Futures contracts were originally written on commodities, but financial futures became very popular during the late 1970s and 1980s and have continued to grow in importance since then. Trading in financial futures has continued to increase at rapid rates mainly because interest rates and foreign currency values have exhibited considerably greater volatility than was the case prior to the 1970s. Options and futures on stock market indices have also come into increasing favor since the mid-1970s, as have catastrophe-linked and weather derivatives.

---

[2]More heterogeneous forms of risk can be traded over the counter on a negotiated basis, as discussed later.

The latter instruments were invented principally in the 1980s to enhance market exchange of risks, such as hurricane damage, that individual firms found too large or too costly to bear. The growth of catastrophe-linked and weather derivatives is discussed later in this chapter.

Derivatives markets differ in their liquidity, the degree to which traded instruments are standardized, and the homogeneity of participants' information. Derivatives contracts are traded both on exchanges and over the counter (OTC), in the latter case principally by financial institutions trading either for their own account or for those of relatively large clients. As first pointed out by Telser (1981), the organizers of an exchange can increase demand for trading by providing timely and close-to-market prices, as well as by carrying out the trading efficiently; that is, at lowest possible cost. To decrease transaction costs, options and futures exchanges standardize the kinds of contracts they trade. In most cases exchanges also set up clearing houses that guarantee traded contracts will be honored as written. The guarantees, backed by the assets of the clearing house, eliminate the need for counterparties to investigate each others' probity and credit ratings, thus reducing screening costs for exchange clients.

As with the stock markets, derivatives trading is increasingly becoming electronic and international. Developments in the exchange markets are illustrated principally by mergers of exchanges in different locations as well as by mergers of different types of exchange. As mentioned in Chapter 11, Deutsche Börse and Nasdaq have both purchased options exchanges, and NYSE Euronext owns London's International Financial Futures Exchange. NYSE Euronext is itself a combination of the NYSE and a number of European Union exchanges.

Table 12.2 shows the amounts of derivative financial instruments traded on organized exchanges at the ends of 2005, 2006, and 2007. Over the three years, the table shows that derivatives trading continues to grow rapidly, extending a trend that has persisted at least since the early 1970s, when organized options exchanges were first established. Both futures and options trading are now worldwide activities, although the bulk of the trading is still

TABLE 12.2 Derivative Financial Instruments Traded on Organized Exchanges Principal (US$ billions)

Amounts Outstanding (Notional)	2005	2006	2007
Futures, all markets	21,600	25,683	28,080
Options, all markets	36,188	44,760	52,543

Source: Bank for International Settlements.

located in North America and Europe. For example, at the end of 2007, 51% of the futures outstanding were traded in North America, 32% in Europe, 14% in Asia, and 2% in other markets. The corresponding percentages for options were North America 56%, Europe 41%, Asia 2%, and other markets 1%.

OPTIONS MARKETS

Options markets have grown enormously since the early 1970s. Throughout the world, daily turnover in options is now measured in trillions of dollars, as Table 12.2 indicates. Several factors explain this phenomenal and continuing growth. Demand for risk trading of all types originally began to expand in the late 1960s and early 1970s because in comparison to earlier periods the financial environment became much more volatile, leading to substantial increases in the demand for hedging services. Other factors also favor trading risk instruments rather than the underlying assets. Less capital is required to trade in derivatives, and transactions charges can be proportionately lower.

On the supply side, options exchanges were set up to standardize contracts and thus reduce transactions costs. Trading activity was further enhanced as financiers learned to guarantee contract performance and thus eliminate the need for parties trading on an exchange to investigate counterparty risk. Third, financiers learned to create new instruments by combining basic forms as shown in Chapter 9. This learning was facilitated by many new theoretical results, including some that showed how options can be used to create synthetic securities at costs lower than the costs of trading the underlying assets. In addition, financial theorists have shown how options can be used, not just to hedge risks, but to tailor portfolio returns, a subject examined further in Chapter 14.

Importance and Functions

Options are written on individual shares, share indexes, bonds, money market securities, commodities, foreign currencies and even on such instruments as futures contracts. Traded options are presently used in such a large variety of risk management transactions that they cannot all be detailed here. For further discussion the reader is referred to such works as Cox and Rubinstein (1986), Hull (2008), or Jarrow and Turnbull (1996). The present discussion attempts only to outline the principal ideas that underlie option trading.

Options are used both for hedging and for assuming risks. For example, a call option may be purchased to ensure that, until the option's maturity, an underlying number of shares can be bought for no more than the exercise (or strike) price specified in the option contract. The call has value to its purchaser only if the shares' price rises above the exercise price, and in effect, the call purchaser pays an insurance premium to limit the losses he would suffer if the share price were to increase. Similarly, buying a put on a share is purchasing insurance against a price decline. If the price of the share remains above the exercise price of the put, the put will be worthless. However if the share price falls below the put exercise price, the purchaser can still sell the share, at the exercise price specified, to the writer of the put contract. With regard to assuming risks, some investors might assemble a portfolio of options rather than a portfolio of shares. Options are riskier than shares in the sense that, relative to the amounts invested, the price changes on the options are much larger than on the underlying shares. These properties mean that option betas, a measure discussed in Chapter 15 later, are higher than the betas for the underlying shares.

The options pricing model of Chapter 9 valued an option extending over two periods. As shown next, the same model can readily be extended to more time periods, thus allowing the analyst to examine how changes in the share price and in the option value are related over time. The extension also shows that the option value will usually fluctuate over a wider proportional range than the underlying price, thus confirming the property of the option's having a greater beta than that of the underlying asset. Table 12.3 values a European call option having an exercise price of $100.00 and maturing in four time periods. The evolution of share prices is shown by the first number in each cell, the evolution of option values by the second number.

The model assumes share prices evolve multiplicatively by an increase factor of 1.10 or a decrease factor of 1.10^{-1} as in Chapter 9. For example, if the share price starts at $100.00 at time 0, it can either rise to $110.00 or fall to $90.91 at time 1. If it is $90.91 at time 1, it can either rise back to $100.00 or fall to $82.64 at time 2. For simplicity of calculation it is also assumed that the risk-free interest rate is 0. Finally, some cells in Table 12.1 have no entries, indicating that only some time-price combinations are attainable. For example, when the share price is $100.00 at time 0, the only possible time 1 values are $110.00 or $90.91. In the process assumed here, the share price can return to its original value after two periods, but cannot remain the same from one period to the next.

At time 4, the option values are

$$\max (S_4 - 100.00, \ 0)$$

TABLE 12.3 Relations between Share and Call Prices

Time 0	Time 1	Time 2	Time 3	Time 4
				146.41
				46.41
			133.10	
			33.10	
		121.00		121.00
		21.00		21.00
	110.00		110.00	
	12.49		10.00	
100.00		100.00		100.00
7.14		4.76		0.00
	90.91		90.91	
	2.27		0.00	
		82.64		82.64
		0.00		0.00
			75.14	
			0.00	
				68.31
				0.00

where S_4 is the time 4 share price. That is, the option value is the larger of 0 or the difference between the share price and the assumed exercise price of $100.00. At time 3, the option values are computed for each share price using time 4 option values and the risk-neutral probability

$$q = (1.00 - 1.10^{-1})/(1.10 - 1.10^{-1})$$

found in Chapter 9. For example, if the time 3 share price is $133.10, the associated option value is

$$q(\$46.41) + (1 - q)(\$21.00)$$
$$= (0.4762)(46.41) + (0.5238)(\$21.00) = \$33.10$$

In this particular case, the option value is just $100.00 less than the current price, because the same exercise price has been deducted from both outcomes. Once all the time 3 option values have been found, the time 2 option values can be computed from them, and so on. In exactly the same way, the calculations can be continued backward in time to find the time 0 value of the European option.[3] To give another example, when at time 1 the share price is \$110.00, the option value of \$12.49 is found from

$$q(21.00) + (1 - q)(4.76)$$
$$= (0.4762)(21.00) + (0.5238)(4.76) = \$12.49$$

Table 12.3 displays two important properties of option prices. First, it shows that for a given share price, the longer the time to maturity, the more the option is worth. Second, it shows that for a fixed time to maturity, the value of a call increases as the share price increases. It can also be inferred from this second property that the value of a put increases as the share price decreases.

The effect of any new information is assumed to be reflected simultaneously in both share and option prices, because our pricing theory assumes there is active arbitraging between shares and options. In practice, information reaching one market is usually transmitted to the other market with a lag. However the lag may be very short, say on the order of a few minutes, in markets that are closely related by arbitraging.

Transactions Data

While options have been traded over the counter for many years, the first exchange trades were conducted on the Chicago Board Options Exchange in 1973. Options trading has virtually exploded since the 1970s and now market quotations for exchange traded options are obtainable from the Internet, the press, and from securities firms, in forms resembling Table 12.4. Table 12.4 shows data for the five most active options traded on June 3, 2008, as reported by finance.yahoo.com.

Options prices and the prices of the underlying assets are determined mutually as trading takes place. Conrad (1989) examines data from both the Chicago Board Options Exchange (CBOE) and the American Options Exchange for 1974–1980. These data indicate that issuing options means that the price of the stock increases permanently by about 2%, the variance of returns falls, but that the beta of the underlying stock is unaffected. Similar findings are obtained by DeTemple and Jorion (1990) and by Kim and Young (1991). Kim and Young also find an absence of significant price and volatility effects after 1982. Grossman and Zhou (1996) argue that the

---

[3]It is easy to value American options using the same framework. To recognize the early exercise feature, the expected values at times 1 through 3 are replaced with the maximum of the expected value or the payoff to intermediate exercise. Then the calculations are carried backward as in the illustration.

TABLE 12.4 Five Most Active Options, June 3, 2008

Rank	Stock	Option	Option Symbol	Close	Volume	Open Interest
1	QQQQ	JUN08 48 Put	QQQRV.X	0.56	92,584	383,241
2	QQQQ	JUN08 49 Put	QQQRW.X	0.89	90,618	191,206
3	BAC	JUN08 30 Call	BACFF.X	3.3	81,470	2,919
4	BAC	JUN08 27.5 Call	BACFA.X	5.8	81,126	2,931
5	GCI	JUN08 25 Call	GCIFE.X	3.7	80,926	2,958

Source: Data taken from Yahoo.com as of June 3, 2008 5:28 P.M. EDT. The BAC calls are options on Bank of America stock, and the GCI call is written on the stock of Gannett industries.

demand for hedging can affect asset prices differently at different times. In particular, when the demand for hedging is great and there are few agents willing to provide the hedging instruments, the cost of hedging increases and the value of the underlying assets decreases.

As mentioned earlier, option trading can convey price information about underlying risks. Ni, Pan, and Poteshman (2008) investigate the effects of option trading on stock volatility. The authors construct a nonmarket maker net demand for volatility from data for the trading volume of individual equity options. They find that their demand measure indicates future realizations of underlying stock price volatility, and also that the impact of volatility demand on option prices is positive. The price impact increases by some 40% as informational asymmetry about stock volatility intensifies in the days leading up to earnings announcements, but diminishes to its normal level as volatility uncertainty is resolved subsequent to the announcements.

FUTURES MARKETS

Although futures contracts were first written against physical commodities, a large proportion of the contracts currently traded are written against financial instruments. Actively traded financial futures contracts include interest rate futures, currency futures, and share index futures. Like the instruments discussed in Chapter 9, financial futures contracts are mainly used as risk management instruments. Also as Chapter 9 pointed out, futures contracts create obligations (not privileges as with options) for the holder to buy or sell a specified asset at a time and price written into the contract.

Futures contracts are written by both individuals and institutions, and most are traded on exchanges. Contract performance of exchange traded contracts is usually, but not always, guaranteed by an instrumentality of the exchange on which the contracts are traded. Most futures contracts are "marked to market," creating a difference between a forward and a futures contract that resembles the difference between holding a long maturity bond and rolling over a series of short maturity bonds. Marking to market means that futures contracts present smaller default risks than forwards because capital gains or losses are realized rather than remaining unrealized as with a forward contract.[4] The counterparty risks of exchange traded futures contracts are small because both seller and purchaser formally treat the exchange as the official counterparty to the contract, and performance under the contract is almost always guaranteed by the exchange's clearinghouse.[5]

Importance and Functions

Futures contracts are used in trading the risks of price change in the commodities or financial instruments against which they are written. Risks can be exchanged whenever the two parties can find mutually acceptable terms. Hedgers sell off risks, and risk bearers or speculators typically acquire the risks. For example, some portfolio investors find it cost-effective to use interest rate futures to reduce the interest rate risk of an investment position, as shown in the next subsection.

Financial futures are traded in many of the world's developed economies. Some of the larger futures markets include the International Monetary Market of the Chicago Mercantile Exchange, the New York Futures Exchange, and Euronext.liffe in the United Kingdom and Europe. These exchanges trade a large variety of instruments including government bill futures contracts, bond futures contracts, and Eurodollar CD Futures. Japanese government bond futures trade on the Tokyo Stock Exchange as well as on the Chicago Board of Trade Options Exchange.

Some U.S. futures exchanges still trade according to the open-outcry method, where members of the exchange are physically present in an area called the trading pit and complete their orders by a combination of shouting, hand, and eye signals. Screen trading is likely to become the universal

---

[4]Intermediary uses of forward contracts are discussed in Chapters 17 and 18. It should be noted that forward contracts may periodically be marked to market on the books of the institution holding them. But only futures contracts are marked to market by exchanges.

[5]Performance guarantees are not universally available. Following the stock market crash of October 19, 1987, some of the liabilities of contracts traded on the then Hong Kong Futures Exchange (since 2007 part of Hong Kong Exchanges) were temporarily left unpaid. Defaults were eventually avoided as market participants assembled an emergency fund to meet the obligations of failed or failing firms. Defaults also occurred on the London Metal Exchange about two years earlier, an exchange which does not guarantee performance of the contracts it trades.

method of the future, and indeed most exchanges had adopted it by the mid-2000s. Brokers both enter orders, and accept others' orders, by entering their transactions into a centralized computer. The computer displays outstanding orders and other information on members' screens.

Using Financial Futures

Interest rate futures are used frequently in the daily operations of lending intermediaries. Currency futures and share index futures are presently used by security dealers, insurance companies, trust companies, pension funds, and multinational firms to hedge against the kinds of price risks the contracts represent. Similarly, interest rate risk can be, and is, hedged using futures contracts on Treasury bills or bankers' acceptances.

As the conceptual discussion of Chapter 9 indicated, a long position in a Treasury bill futures contract (also called an interest rate futures contract) will increase in value as the underlying bill increases in value. However, the bill itself will decline in value if interest rates rise, so that a short position in bill futures is needed to generate a capital gain to offset any decline in the value of the bill. If there is an interest rate increase and if the short sale of Treasury bill futures is in the correct amount, the capital losses on the bill will be offset by a capital gain on the short position in the futures contracts. The reverse is true if there is an interest rate decrease: The bills increase in value but there is a capital loss on the short position in the futures contract. Thus the combination of Treasury bill and short position in bill futures creates a hedged investment. The cost of the hedging is not great: Treasury bill futures contracts usually require posting margins amounting to 5% to 10% of the value of the underlying bills, and competitive interest rates are usually paid on margin accounts.

To illustrate the mechanics of hedging a position with a futures contract, suppose that a bank has a floating rate asset funded by a fixed rate liability such as a time deposit. The net interest revenues on this transaction will increase if interest rates increase, and decrease if interest rates fall. Table 12.5 shows the qualitative gains or losses on both the loan and the futures contract depend on the interest rate environment. The revenue risk can be hedged using interest rate futures.

TABLE 12.5 Interest Hedging with a Futures Contract

Transaction	Rates Increase	Rates Decrease
Floating rate loan, fixed rate deposit	gain ($)	loss ($)
Buy interest rate futures	loss ($)	gain ($)

If a bank buys interest rate futures and rates rise, the bank gains on the original loan-deposit deal but loses on its interest rate futures position. If interest rates decline, the bank loses on its loan portfolio but makes compensating gains on the value of its futures contracts. If the appropriate size of futures transactions is arranged, the sum of gain and loss in either cell can be made equal to zero, and the income risk on the transaction will be completely hedged in an accounting sense.

Naik and Yadav (2003) investigate how bond dealers use interest rate futures contracts to manage their core business risks. The authors find that bond dealers both take directional bets and hedge changes in their spot exposure using futures. They find that dealers with longer (shorter) risk exposure sell (buy) larger amounts of exposure the next day, and that this form of risk control takes place via the futures market and not the spot market. The authors also examine the extent to which market prices for interest rate futures can be affected by bond dealers managing their risks selectively, and find that dealers' capital constraints create futures market price effects.

Transactions Data

Table 12.6 provides data for representative Eurodollar interest rate futures contracts as traded on the CME-Globex market.

To interpret Table 12.6, consider the September 2008 Eurodollar contract which closed at 97.21. The standard Eurodollar contract is for three months; that is, one-fourth of a year. Market quotations are given according to the formula:

$$\text{Quote} = 100.00 - \text{Per annum forward interest rate}$$

In the present example the quote implies

$$97.21 = 100.00 - 2.79$$

TABLE 12.6 CME Globex Quotes, as of June 2008, 09:04 A.M. (CST)

Strike	Open	High	Low	Last	Vol (Thousands)
JUN08	97.3225	97.3275	97.30	97.31	87
JLY08	97.305	97.31	97.27	97.285	1,523
AUG08	—	—	97.24	97.24	
SEP08	97.235	97.255	97.18	97.21	143
OCT08	—	97.145	97.105	97.11	
NOV08	—	97.09	97.04	97.05	
DEC08	97.04	97.07	96.975	97.015	208

that is, the annual interest rate implied by the contract price is 2.79%. This system of quotations is used for convenience and traders do not need to make any computations other than those shown to establish annual interest rates on an instrument. The method is also convenient because futures markets are very closely related to the money markets by arbitrage, and interest rates in the two markets follow very much the same pattern over time. The headings of the remaining columns in Table 12.6 are self-explanatory, except possibly for "Open," which stands for Open Interest. This term refers to the number of contracts outstanding on the date to which the table refers. It is not a good indicator of exposure to risk because the same party might hold offsetting contracts, some as long positions and others as shorts. For example, if there were only two contracts outstanding, the open interest would be two, even if each of the two parties holding them had exactly offsetting positions and therefore no net exposure.

MARKET EVOLUTION

As the financial system continues to evolve, markets change with a view to increasing trading volume, to trading additional instruments, and to further standardizing the instruments traded. These developments have occurred in the options, futures, and swap markets, and are currently occurring within both financial and insurance markets as the two latter markets begin to converge. The most notable development in terms of growth has been in the credit derivatives market. At the same time, other markets are being reorganized to reap advantages of scale and scope economies, as well as to remove existing impediments to trading, particularly the control of counterparty risk, through creating new forms of clearinghouses. This section provides examples of each such development.

From Intermediated to Market Transactions

Certain forms of risk trading have evolved from intermediated to market transactions. Some deals that were originally negotiated on an individual basis by intermediaries became so popular that their terms were standardized and the deals governed as market transactions. For example, options have only traded on organized exchanges since 1973, when standardization contributed to decreasing the cost of trading. A second reason for the migration of some deals from intermediaries to markets, also illustrated in the development of the options markets, is that contract guarantees make it cheaper for parties to trade without investigating each others' creditworthiness. Finally, the first theoretical model for pricing options was published in the same year (Black-Scholes 1973), helping to define relations between market and theoretical prices, and giving further impetus to trading activity.

Trading in the options and futures markets was standardized relatively early, largely because these instruments have long been used by securities firms accustomed to promoting market transactions. On the other hand, foreign exchange trading was mainly originated by banks and much of it is still conducted on an over-the-counter basis. Even today the larger foreign exchange deals are not always standardized. Moreover, since most large banks have at least a rough idea of other banks' credit risk, default risk is usually managed by restricting the quantity of orders placed with any single counterparty in a given day. As a result contract guarantees are not as important in promoting foreign exchange trade, at least between large international banks, as they are in promoting options and futures trades.[6]

The explosive development of the swap market is due to changes in both demand and supply. On the demand side, both financial and nonfinancial firms have learned to manage interest rate and currency risks using swap transactions. With the increasing number of participants, search costs have been reduced by the emerging prominence of some market agents. At the same time, transactions costs have been reduced by standardizing swap terms. On the supply side, although banks originated the use of both interest and currency swaps, investment banking firms are now also prominent in swap trading. Interest and currency swaps can presently be arranged most cheaply using the standardized terms agreed by the International Swaps and Derivatives Association,[7] an organization created by trading firms. As yet, swaps do not bear performance guarantees, but the economic value of guarantees seems likely to become clearer as market growth continues, as more small financial firms start to trade in the markets, and as counterparty risk has become a more pressing issue.

The evolution of some deals toward greater standardization and market governance provides examples of increasingly discriminating alignment of deal attributes and governance capabilities. The changes occur gradually because agents learn incrementally, and change the ways they do deals accordingly.

---

[6]But conditions can change with the times. In 2007–2008 banks, concerned with each others' capital positions, have been much less willing to assume certain counterparty risks.

[7]Originally the International Swap Dealers' Association.

Catastrophe Bonds and Weather Derivatives

The idea behind catastrophe futures and other catastrophe-linked derivatives is that insurance companies can trade some of their liability risk to other investors. The development of instruments for trading the risks of underwriting losses was greatly stimulated by the losses suffered by insurance companies after Florida's Hurricane Andrew in 1992 and California's Northridge earthquake in 1994. Although underwriting risks can also be sold off in the wholesale reinsurance markets, those markets do not have unlimited capacity and consequently greater diversification can be obtained by using other institutional markets as well. The success of these attempts is partly illustrated by the fact that underwriting losses from 2005's Hurricane Katrina were better diversified.[8]

Catastrophe (CAT) bonds promise investors to pay a given rate of interest until maturity. However, all or part of the promised principal might not be redeemed in the event the issuing insurance company suffers documented underwriting losses. Indeed, even large reinsurers sometimes issue CAT bonds to diversify some of the underwriting risks they might have in areas exposed to relatively large underwriting risks from natural disasters.

From an investor's point of view, the main advantages of CAT bonds are that they are not closely linked with the stock market or economic conditions and yet offer attractive yields to investors. Investors can usually obtain a higher yield with CAT bonds relative to alternative investments carrying the same degree of risk, since CAT bond returns show no correlation with equities or corporate bonds. As a result, CAT bonds provide investors with an attractive means of diversifying risks. Moreover, there is no credit risk to CAT bonds as funds are paid in at the time of the bonds' issue. The volume of CAT bonds outstanding has steadily increased from 1997 to a 2002 level of approximately \$3 billion. In the first eight months of 2003 the volume of new issues was \$910 million, nearly equal to the whole of 2002.

A similar instrument, also used to improve the efficiency of the reinsurance market, is a CAT swap, in which equal risks are exchanged between counterparties who have their peak risks in different geographical locations. Both parties benefit from risk diversification in a CAT swap. In contrast, a CAT bond protects the issuer against extreme natural catastrophes by

---

[8]Parts of the 2005 underwriting losses were also borne by a contingency fund organized by the State of Florida.

raising capital from institutional investors. In both cases risk is transferred to another party.

Similarly, weather derivatives offer payments based on observations such as temperature. For example, an orange crop can be damaged by lower-than-normal temperatures. The risk of incurring this type of loss can be partially offset by purchasing puts that can be exercised in the event of low temperatures' actually occurring.

Convergence of Financial and Insurance Markets

Financial and insurance markets are beginning to converge, and this development can be expected to continue for some time to come. Convergence is likely to create profit opportunities for financial services wholesalers, particularly investment banks and reinsurers. Investment bankers offer capabilities in securities design, underwriting, marketing, and trading, while reinsurers' capabilities are mainly in pricing, underwriting, and management of liabilities traditionally associated with insurance products. The supply of new risk instruments is enhanced by advances in computing, communications and modeling technologies. Corporations are demanding new forms of financial and insurance products as they increasingly adopt risk-management strategies for the entire enterprise. Demand is strengthened by the emergence of new risks, including those posed by terrorism and natural disasters.

Some of the new risk products will be custom designed and traded OTC, while others will become standardized, exchange-traded products. Some of the obstacles currently facing the exchange trading of insurance-linked derivatives include investor unfamiliarity, regulatory and accounting obstacles, the lack of acceptable indices, and the lack of acceptable valuation models. Eventually, experts foresee:

> a worldwide market in insurance-linked securities that will be highly liquid and permit the global diversification of catastrophic risk as well as other insurance-linked risks and risks of exotic underlyings such as noncatastrophic weather events. Significant potential also exists for new types of securitizations of insurance and reinsurance liability portfolios, permitting insurers and reinsurers to transfer more risks to capital markets and reduce the need for costly equity capital. Future developments in securitization have the potential to improve the efficiency of both investment markets and insurance markets. (Cummins, 2005)

Credit Derivatives

The credit derivatives market began with bankers selling specialized forms of credit derivatives both to assist clients and to manage their own risks. This innovation, which separated loans from their credit risks, gained its original impetus from banks seeking to hedge and diversify credit risks in ways similar to those already used for transferring interest rate and currency risks. Banks, insurance companies, and hedge funds all contributed to spectacularly successful market growth, mainly involving credit default swaps. The credit default swaps (CDS) market grew from a trading volume of $180 billion in 1997 to over $20 trillion in 2006, and almost doubled in notional value[9] from 2006 to 2007. Much of the growth between 2004 and the collapse of 2007–2008 was in index CDSs, with the reference entity containing as many as 125 corporate entities. But with the advent of the 2007–2008 market turmoil, volume virtually collapsed and it will likely be some time before recovery occurs.

Synthetic CDOs

As pointed out in Chapter 5, a synthetic CDO does not actually own the asset portfolio whose credit risk it bears, but rather incurs credit risk exposure by selling credit default swaps. In turn, the synthetic CDO buys protection from investors via the tranches defining its securities issues.[10] The reference portfolio in a synthetic CDO is made up of credit default swaps, and the synthetic CDO is usually classified as a credit derivative in statistical reports such as those published by the British Bankers' Association. Much of the risk transfer that takes place in the credit derivatives market is effected using CDOs, and the instruments can be valued using the same derivative valuation techniques as are used for interest-rate swaps.

The first synthetic CDOs, issued by banks in 1997, were used either to hedge credit risk, reduce regulatory capital, or both. Even though they simply rearrange the payment priorities of other credit risk instruments, CDOs originally made economic sense because of their ability to reduce regulatory capital, and also helped overcome market imperfections stemming from the illiquidity of the underlying bonds and loans. In particular "the rapid adoption of CDO technology by credit investors suggests that the cost of

---

[9]*The Economist*, August 7, 2008. "Derivatives."

[10]The tranches are responsible for credit losses in the reference portfolio that rise above a particular point called an attachment point. A given tranche's liabilities end at a specified detachment or exhaustion point (Lucas, Goodman, and Fabozzi 2007).

creating a CDO is less than the cost a credit investor would incur to assemble a portfolio of bonds and/or loans to meet the investor's diversification and risk-return targets" (Gibson 2004). The synthetic CDO market continued to grow until the market turmoil of 2007–2008, at which time new issues dropped sharply.

OTC Trading and Clearinghouses

Much of the trading in credit derivatives is OTC and takes place on an individually negotiated basis. OTC trading requires counterparties to investigate each others' credit risks, and further involves the potential for creating systemic risks, either if a number of counterparties were to default at the same time, or if an actively trading institution taking positions with many counterparties were to fail.[11] In response to these potential dangers, both industry members and regulators are considering ways to improve market functioning at the time this is being written. Some regulators urge simplifying and standardizing the trading of OTC instruments, thereby creating products that would be more liquid, easier to value, more transparent, and with less risk of creating legal difficulties between trading parties. At one extreme, some regulators favor forcing all trading onto exchanges. However, the theory of this book indicates that restricting trading could be counterproductive. OTC instruments are useful as hedges because they are not standardized or exchange traded, even though the contracts are not likely to trade widely in a secondary market.

This book's theory suggests that it is desirable to let exchange traded instruments compete with specialized instruments traded by banks. Most industry representatives do not favor exchange trading, although they do favor setting up better arrangements for OTC trading. Such better arrangements could include standardizing contract forms wherever possible, thus speeding up clearing processes and helping to minimize potential disputes. Regulators could also require banks to post more capital against contracts with greater counterparty risk.

Clearinghouses for the OTC market instruments are supported by both industry and regulators. For example the Financial Stability Forum (2008)

---

[11] During and since the market turmoil of 2008, trading in credit default swaps has almost entirely collapsed as market participants have become more cognizant of the risks involved. For example, CDSs would have been subject to huge counterparty risk if a dealer like Bear Stearns had been allowed to fail. As a second example, the effects would have been similarly widespread if AIG, one of the principal sellers of credit default swaps, had not been rescued through government loans in the fall of 2008.

pointed out that clearinghouses can reduce both credit and other counter-party risks. However, for clearinghouses to be effective, they must be able to cover losses from the failure of any participant,[12] and for this purpose they must be able to raise assets sufficient to cover the losses. In addition the Forum recommended that supervisors should ensure the clearinghouses adopt effective risk management safeguards, and that legal or regulatory barriers to the establishment of clearinghouses be removed wherever possible.

REFERENCES

Black, Fischer, and Myron Scholes. 1973. The pricing of options and corporate liabilities. *Journal of Political Economy* 81: 637–659.

Conrad, Jennifer. 1989. The price of option introduction. *Journal of Finance* 44: 487–498.

Cox, John C., and Mark Rubinstein. 1985. *Options Markets*. Englewood Cliffs, NJ: Prentice-Hall.

Cummins, J. David. 2005. Convergence of banking and insurance. In *Current Directions in Financial Regulation*, edited by F. Milne and E. H. Neave. Montreal: McGill-Queens University Press.

DeTemple, Jerome, and Philippe Jorion. 1990. Option listing and stock returns: An empirical analysis. *Journal of Banking and Finance* 14: 781–801.

Financial Stability Forum. 2008. *Report of the Financial Stability Forum on enhancing market and institutional resilience*, April 7 2008.

Gibson, Michael S. 2004. Understanding the risk of synthetic CDOs. Federal Reserve Board Working Paper.

Grossman, Sanford J., and Zhongquan Zhou. 1996. Equilibrium analysis of portfolio insurance. *Journal of Finance* 51: 1,379–1,403.

Hull, John C. 2008. *Options, Futures and Other Derivatives*, 7th ed. Upper Saddle River, NJ: Prentice-Hall.

Jarrow, Robert A., and Stuart M. Turnbull. 1996. *Derivative Securities*. Cincinnati: South-Western Publishing Company.

Kim, W. S., and C. M. Young. 1991. The effect of traded option introduction on shareholder wealth. *Journal of Financial Research* 14: 141–151.

Lucas, Douglas J., Laurie Goodman, and Frank J. Fabozzi. 2007. Collateralized debt obligations and credit risk transfer. *Journal of Financial Transformation* 20: 47–59.

Naik, Narayan Y., and Pradeep K. Yadav. 2003. Risk management with derivatives by dealers and market quality in government bond markets. *Journal of Finance* 58: 1,873–1,904.

---

[12] The importance of clearinghouse performance guarantees was first discussed in Chapter 9.

Ni, Sophie X., Jun Pan, and Allen M. Poteshman. 2008. Volatility information trading in the option market. *Journal of Finance* 63: 1,059–1,091.

Telser, Lester. 1981. Why there are organized futures markets. *Journal of Law and Economics* 24: 1–22.

TERMS

risk aversion   A preference for less rather than more risk. If two random variables have the same expected value, the one with the greater variance is usually regarded as the riskier.

risk loving   A preference for more rather than less risk when the expected return on an arrangement is kept constant.

CHAPTER 13

Exchange Rates and Markets

This chapter examines exchange rates, the markets in which exchange rates are established, and the institutions that affect those markets. Theoretical benchmarks for international price and interest rate relations are established mainly under assumptions of no arbitrage opportunities, that is, under the neoclassical paradigm. Hence the chapter begins by examining benchmarks for effective exchange rates, the Fisher relation, interest rate parity, purchasing power parity, and forward parity. The chapter next examines foreign exchange trading, including spot and forward transactions, the role of the dealing banks, covered interest arbitrage, and the carry trade. It also discusses management issues in managing foreign currency risk, including the use of currency and interest swaps, both short- and long-term, and the evolution of international risk trading. Finally, the chapter considers exchange rate management at the macroeconomic level, examining exchange rate systems, central bank intervention, the European Monetary System, the Euro, and the European Central Bank.

INTRODUCTION

Chapter 11 described securities markets, and Chapter 12 described markets for trading risks, noting that many of the transactions described are international in scope. This chapter considers additional international influences on asset pricing, both short- and long-term. It first considers the theory of exchange rate relationships, then the workings of the foreign exchange markets and exchange risk management. Finally, the chapter considers international institutions concerned with exchange rate management.

EXCHANGE RATE RELATIONS

This section explains how arbitrage-based trading tends to establish relations among different currencies. The Fisher relation, introduced in Chapter 6, is recalled here and related to the remaining three, known respectively as the interest parity, purchasing power parity, and forward parity theorems. The section also discusses why the theoretical predictions of these theorems cannot always be observed in practice.

Effective Exchange Rates and Arbitrage

The absence of arbitrage opportunities can be used to establish well-known interest rate relationships between instruments denominated in different currencies. These relationships are based on the assumption of perfectly competitive markets in which no transactions costs are incurred. In practice relations between countries' currencies are more complex than arbitraging arguments suggest, and deviations from theoretical values occur frequently. These deviations may be attributable to market imperfections, to expectations, or to central bank intervention. They can occur in both the short run and the long run. Indeed some deviations can last for periods measured in years, as will be discussed further below.

Fisher Relation

The Fisher relation is a consequence of lenders' trying to preserve the real rather than the nominal earnings on their loans or investments. To do so, lenders set interest rates according to

$$(1 + R_D) = (1 + r)(P_{D1})/(P_{D0}) \tag{13.1}$$

where: R_D = current nominal interest rate
  r = current real interest rate
  P_{D1} = expected domestic price level at time 1
  P_{D0} = domestic price level at time 0

Equation (13.1) restates the Fisher relation, first introduced in Chapter 6, in a form that can easily be related to the remaining relations studied in this chapter. Equation (13.1) says that lenders or investors attempt to charge nominal rates of interest that offset possible future declines in purchasing power. When interest rates and inflation rates are both relatively low, (13.1) can be approximated by

$$(1 + R_D) = (1 + r + i) \qquad (13.2)$$

where i represents expected inflation over the period and the other variables are defined as before. Theoretically, the Fisher relation should hold over both the long and the short run, but it is considerably more difficult to measure expected inflation over the long run.[1] Fama and Gibbons (1984) show that the Fisher relation provides an adequate description of how nominal interest rates on U.S. short-term money market instruments behave up to the early 1980s.

Interest Parity

According to the *interest parity theorem*, the ratio of forward to spot exchange rates will equal the ratio of foreign to domestic nominal interest rates:

$$(F/S) = (1 + R_F)/(1 + R_D) \qquad (13.3)$$

where: F = forward rate (foreign currency units per domestic unit)
S = spot rate (foreign currency units per domestic unit)
R_F = current foreign interest rate
R_D = current domestic interest rate

Since the interest parity theorem is established by arbitraging arguments, it says in effect that individuals will invest in a foreign country if their net return on foreign investments exceeds the net return on domestic investments. The interest parity theorem goes further to predict that if returns differ, then the short-term investment flows will continue until currency values, interest rates, or both adjust so that the two investment possibilities offer equal returns:

$$(1 + R_D) = S(1 + R_F)/F \qquad (13.4)$$

To illustrate the workings of interest rate parity theory, consider Table 13.1, which displays the three logical possibilities regarding two countries' interest rates. The table assumes all instruments mature in one year, and considers various kinds of actions whose profitability depends on the nature

---

[1] If expected inflation is assessed using index-linked bonds, then the Fisher effect holds by definition. For, the index-linked bond rate is taken to be the real rate of interest, and the difference between this and nominal rates is attributed to inflation.

TABLE 13.1 Interest Arbitrage Activities

Assumptions	Domestic = Foreign Interest Rate	Domestic > Foreign Interest Rate	Domestic < Foreign Interest Rate
	$R_D = R_F = 0.10$ $S = 0.75$	$R_D = 0.10$ $R_F = 0.09$ $S = 0.75$	$R_D = 0.09$ $R_F = 0.10$ $S = 0.75$
Predictions of equilibrium forward rate from interest parity theory	$1.10 =$ $0.75(1.10)/F$ $F = 0.75 = S$	$1.10 =$ $0.75(1.09)/F$ $F = 0.7432 < S$	$1.09 = 0.75(1.10)F$ $F = 0.7569 > S$
Interest arbitraging activity	If $F^* < 0.75$, Canadians should invest in the United States.	If $F^* < 0.7432$, Canadians find it profitable to invest in the United States on a covered basis.	If $F^* > 0.7569$, the United States investors find it profitable to invest in Canada on a covered basis.
	If $F^* > 0.75$, the United States citizens should invest in Canada.	The United States investors could invest at home, borrowing in Canada.	Canadians can invest at home, borrowing in the the United States.

of interest rates and forward exchange rates. A spot rate S of 0.75 means $1.00 Canadian buys U.S. $0.75. The three columns display three possible interest rate scenarios. In each column, the first group of figures lists assumptions, following which Equation 13.6 is used to calculate the equilibrium forward rate. Next, the equilibrium forward rate is compared to the assumed spot rate. Finally, if the actual forward rate F^* differs from the equilibrium forward rate F, actions to take profit advantage of the situation are listed.

Interest parity theory applies reasonably well to the most liquid financial instruments, but not to others. For example, the theory has been observed to hold relatively closely in the Eurocurrency markets (see Taylor 1987). On the other hand, interest parity theory did not well describe relations between the former European Currency Unit (ECU) bonds and their synthetic equivalents, where the latter were made up of individual countries' government bonds held in a portfolio duplicating the currency composition of the ECU.[2] In this case the observed deviations from interest rate parity seemed to be

---

[2] The ECU was a currency basket that served as a precursor to establishing the Euro.

attributable primarily to a lack of liquid instruments available for use in trade. If the absence of liquidity had been overcome and arbitrage between ECU bonds and their synthetic equivalents had been profitable, the observed deviations would likely have been reduced or eliminated.

Purchasing Power Parity

The *purchasing power parity theorem*, like the interest parity theorem, says that agents think in terms of buying power rather than in terms of local prices. Suppose there are two economies, in both of which a single consumption good[3] is traded. The Absolute Purchasing Power Parity theorem says that if exchange rates can adjust freely and if the consumption good can freely be moved between countries, it should be offered for sale in either country at the same price, after adjusting for exchange rate differences using the prevailing exchange rate. In other words, changes in the exchange rate offset differences in prices stated in local currencies.

Temporal adjustments to exchange rates can be expressed using a related concept, relative purchasing power parity, that compares changes in an exchange rate to differences in two economies' inflation rates. Formally,

$$S_1/S_0 = (P_{F1}/P_{F0})/(P_{D1}/P_{D0}) \qquad (13.5)$$

where: $S_1 =$ spot rate at time 1
$S_0 =$ spot rate at time 0
$P_{F1} =$ expected foreign price level at time 1
$P_{F0} =$ foreign price level at time 0
$P_{D1} =$ expected domestic price level at time 1
$P_{D0} =$ domestic price level at time 0

For example, if Canada has zero inflation and the U.S. experiences 10% inflation over some period, the U.S. dollar should fall 10% relative to the Canadian dollar. To illustrate, consider Equation 3.5 and assume all values at time zero are unity. Then the right side will equal 1.1, because of the 10% inflation differential. Therefore the ratio of spot rates will also equal 1.1, meaning that at time 1 a Canadian dollar will buy 10% more of the U.S. dollar, or that the U.S. dollar is expected to decline in value against the Canadian dollar by 10%. More generally, a currency will appreciate or depreciate in relation to another depending on whether the first country has a lower or a higher rate of inflation than the second.

---

[3] The theorem can, of course, be expressed in terms of a representative basket of consumer goods rather than just a single good.

Both the absolute and the relative purchasing power theorems have been tested. It might be expected that the tests would not strongly confirm either version of the theorem, because there are many impediments to the emergence of purchasing power parity in the short run. These impediments include costly information, shipping costs, the presence of differentiated goods, and trade barriers such as tariffs, quotas, and administrative delays. As an example of a crude test, the *Economist* surveys of purchasing power parity use the Big Mac hamburger as a proxy for a basket of goods. The observed prices of Big Macs vary widely between countries after adjusting for exchange rate differences, suggesting that absolute purchasing power parity does not hold closely with respect to this standard.

If price changes caused exchange rate changes and if purchasing power parity theory were a good predictor, one would expect that exchange rates would change slowly over time. In fact, however, exchange rates exhibit frequent, sudden, and relatively large changes. There are several reasons for such changes. First, since not all goods are traded among countries purchasing power considerations are only one of several influences affecting exchange rates. Second, international trading in goods takes place in relatively imperfect markets, and so arbitraging is only carried out incompletely. Third, purchasing power parity theory ignores the effects of financial transactions on exchange rates. Short-term exchange rate variation is caused by interest rate changes, by news about the relative state of the domestic and foreign economies, and even by changes in the prices of other assets (Sercu and Uppal 1995, 367). A survey conducted by Rogoff (1996) concludes there are large deviations from purchasing power parity that die out at the rate of about 15% per year. Rogoff observes that the frictions preventing faster adjustment probably include "transportation costs, threatened or actual tariffs, nontariff barriers, information costs, (and) lack of labor mobility" (1996, 664). Culver and Papell (1999) also present evidence that over the long run, currencies reflect purchasing power parity.

Forward Parity

The Fisher effect, interest parity theorem, and purchasing power theorem together imply a fourth result: the *forward parity theorem*. The first three effects together imply that arbitraging tends to equalize real rates of interest between countries. The forward parity theorem then says that the forward exchange rate must equal the future spot rate. Recall the conditions:

$$
\begin{aligned}
(1 + R_D) &= (1 + r)(P_{D1})/(P_{D0}) \\
(1 + R_F) &= (1 + r)(P_{F1})/(P_{F0}) \\
(F_0/S_0) &= (1 + R_F)/(1 + R_D) \\
(S_1/S_0) &= (P_{F1}/P_{F0})/(P_{D1}/P_{D0})
\end{aligned}
\tag{13.6}
$$

The first two state the Fisher effect for domestic and foreign countries, respectively, using the notation defined earlier in this chapter. The third states the interest parity result, using notation indicating that the forward/spot relation is being considered at time 0. The fourth is the purchasing power parity condition. The ratio of the last two equations is

$$(F_0/S_1) = [(1 + R_F)/(1 + R_D)]/[(P_{F1}/P_{F0})/(P_{D1}/P_{D0})] = \\ [(1 + R_F)(P_{D1}/P_{D0})]/[(1 + R_D)(P_{F1}/P_{F0})] = \tag{13.7}$$

$$(1 + r)/(1 + r) = 1 \tag{13.8}$$

using (13.3) and (13.4) to eliminate $(1 + R_D)$ and $(1 + R_F)$. That is, $F_0 = S_1$ as claimed. As stated here, forward parity is derived under an assumption of certainty that does not recognize the importance of risk premiums, which may in practice also be incorporated in estimates of future interest rates.

Real gains or losses can be made in foreign investments if the actual spot rate at time 1 differs from its time 0 expected value. (The two values are the same under the certainty assumptions made above.) If S_{R1} (the realized spot rate at time 1) differs from S_1 (its expected value calculated at time 0) real gains or losses would be made according to

$$(1 + g) = S_{R1}/S_1 \tag{13.9}$$

where g measures the real gain or loss from investing in foreign rather than domestic assets. By equation (13.8) the time 1 spot rate is anticipated by the time 0 forward rate, that is, $S_1 = F_0$. We therefore have

$$(1 + g) = S_{R1}/F_0 \tag{13.10}$$

This result assumes the two countries' real interest rates are equal and shows only the excess earnings resulting from unanticipated changes in the spot rate. It says an investor should take a long position in a foreign currency if he expects the realized spot rate to rise above that predicted by the current forward rate. He should take a short position if he expects the realized spot rate to fall below the value predicted by the current forward rate.

For example, referring to Table 13.3, if the investor believes that the U.S. dollar will fall by more than is implied by $F = 0.75$, say $S_{R1} = 0.76$, the forward speculator will take a long position. That is, he will buy Canadian dollars forward at 0.75, and on maturity sell the contract in the spot market at 0.76, making 0.01 per dollar traded if things turn out as he expects. On the other hand, if he believes the U.S. dollar will revalue more than is implied by $F = 0.75$ (say $S_{R1} = 0.74$), the forward speculator will take a short position. That is, he will sell Canadian dollar forward contracts at 0.75, with the intention of buying spot at 0.74 when the contract matures. If he turns out to be right, he will make a profit of 0.01 per dollar traded.

FOREIGN EXCHANGE MARKETS

Foreign exchange transactions are used to settle accounts arising from trade as well as to conduct both investment and speculative transactions. Short-maturity instruments in major currencies trade actively, and as a result prices on different foreign exchange instruments are closely related to each other by arbitraging. For example, interest arbitraging takes advantage of emerging short-term interest differentials among countries, and currency arbitraging follows a similar rationale. The chief arbitrageurs are the world's dealing banks, hedge funds, multinational firms, and speculators.

Foreign exchange markets have traditionally been multiple dealer markets. By 2001, about 90% of the trading was done electronically, although some trades between large corporations and foreign exchange dealers were still done by telephone. CLS Bank was set up in late 2002 to provide continuous linked settlement of foreign-exchange transactions among the world's 50 or 60 largest banks. CLS Bank nets all transactions among banks and makes payments during the business day, eliminating a form of settlement risk. The development of CLS Bank had been under discussion since the 1974 failure of Bank Herstatt during the (North American) business day. It can be regarded as an early version of current attempts to improve the management of counterparty risk.

Spot, Forward, and Swap Transactions

Spot and forward foreign exchange transactions are referred to using a somewhat peculiar terminology. A *spot transaction* is a deal that calls for immediate delivery of foreign currency,[4] while a *forward transaction* is a deal providing for delivery at some later time. The most common interest arbitraging transaction involves a combination of a spot and a forward contract called a swap transaction. This terminology seems to have evolved because dealers make crude profit calculations using the difference between buying and selling rates, a difference known as the number of swap points. On the other hand, since to traders a forward transaction by itself is

---

[4] Technically, a spot transaction in U.S. dollars provides for delivery in one day. In most other currencies delivery is in two days.

relatively unusual, it is called an outright forward or just an outright, drawing attention to its uncommon nature.

Forward transactions are settled on the day the contract matures. In its 2007 survey of the London foreign exchange market, the Bank of England reported that swap trades were the fastest growing category of transactions, accounting for 66% of total U.K. foreign exchange activity in April 2007, compared with 57% in April 2004.

Covered Interest Arbitrage

Transactions intended to take advantage of interest rate differences, and hedged against the foreign exchange risk, are called *covered interest arbitrage* transactions. When covered interest arbitrage transactions can be arranged, any difference between countries' interest rates (hedged against the foreign exchange risk) is likely to be offset by an adjustment in currency values. The country with the higher interest rate will have a currency that is declining in value relative to the country with the lower rate. Indeed, higher interest rates can be used, if other circumstances between countries are equal, as a predictor of a subsequent decline in currency values.

As an example of the workings of covered transactions, consider how you might approach the question of whether to invest at home or abroad. Suppose funds can be transferred freely between countries, at least for short-term investments. Then, if any risk of change in the value of foreign currencies can be eliminated, pricing by arbitrage suggests that you invest in the country whose securities give you the higher rate of return. However, the principle of pricing by arbitrage actually goes further to argue that since all investors will make this calculation, the same effective interest rate should be earned in either of two countries, even though the countries' securities appear to offer different interest rates.

A forward foreign exchange contract can be used to eliminate risk on investments in other currencies, because it allows the investor to calculate both the cost and the proceeds in terms of his domestic currency. If the investment involves purchasing foreign government obligations with no (or little) default risk, a covered foreign investment's risk is not much different from the risk of investing in a domestic government bond. If the two risks are regarded as identical, then in the absence of arbitrage opportunities the two different ways of investing should yield the same interest rate in domestic terms.

To illustrate, suppose that today US$1.00 will buy A$1.08, that is, exactly 1.08 Australian dollars. In foreign exchange terminology, the

Australian dollar spot rate[5] is assumed to be US$1.08. Suppose further that U.S. Treasury bills can be purchased to yield 6% over one year, while similar Australian bills yield 11%. In the absence of arbitrage opportunities, the hedged Australian investment should yield the same 6% in U.S. dollar terms as the U.S. domestic investment. Under this assumption, the Australian dollar must be expected to fall relative to the U.S. dollar. That is, one year from now the U.S. dollar must be expected to buy more than A$1.08.

Denote the forward exchange rate for Australian dollars (expressed in U.S. dollar terms) by F. By assumption, a $1.00 investment in U.S. Treasury bills returns US$1.06 after one year. Thus if there are no arbitrage opportunities US$1.00 invested in Australian bills and hedged against changes in the value of the Australian dollar will also yield 6% to the U.S. investor. The deal involves purchasing Australian dollars in the spot market and using them to purchase the Australian dollar denominated securities. It is hedged by simultaneously selling the Australian dollar proceeds forward.

In the absence of arbitrage opportunities, either deal should earn the same 6% for the U.S. investor. That is, in U.S. terms

$$US\$1.00(1.06) = A\$1.08(1.11)/F \qquad (13.11)$$

or $F = 1.11(1.08)/1.06 = 1.1309$, which means that US$1.00 will sell A$1.1309 forward, for delivery one year from now. In other words, the Australian dollar one-year forward price, in terms of U.S. dollars, is 1.1309 if there are no arbitrage opportunities between the two countries. This means the Australian dollar is expected to fall, since US$1.00 will buy only A$1.08 in the spot market, but A$1.1309 in the forward market.

The above example illustrates the Interest Parity theorem developed above. Recall the theorem states that the ratio of the forward to the spot price of a foreign currency is equal to the return on an investment in the foreign country divided by the return on a similar investment in the home country. Symbolically

$$F/S = (1 + r_f)/(1 + r_d)$$

You should be able to work out the derivation of the formula from the interest arbitraging example just given.

---

[5] This form of spot rate quotation, number of foreign currency units per unit of domestic currency, is used in the United Kingdom and is sometimes called the indirect or left quote. In Europe a spot rate is usually quoted as number of domestic currency units per unit of foreign currency. This form of quotation, called the direct or right quote, is the reciprocal of the first.

Now, returning to the question of where you should invest, we have an answer, given the circumstances assumed previously, to the question of whether it should be in the United States or in Australia. If you can carry out the Australian investment on terms that allow you to exchange A$ forward at a better rate 1.1309 per U.S. dollar (for example, if you can get U.S. dollars for a forward price of A$1.10, meaning you have to surrender fewer A$ to get the same number of U.S. dollars), you should do so! By so doing, you would be one of the investors who were actually helping to establish the interest rate parity theorem in this particular case. (Incidentally if there are transactions costs, you need to take them into account before deciding whether the deal is still profitable.)

The Carry Trade

As the interest parity discussion showed, a currency with a high yield should theoretically compensate investors for the risk of a currency decline due to higher inflation in the country concerned. Although arguments relying on the absence of arbitrage opportunities suggest that a trader should only be able to earn small short-term profits by moving funds between currencies, in practice currency values can deviate from uncovered interest parity predictions for periods long enough to permit realizing more than a minimal profit.

Transactions taking advantage of these circumstances, known as examples of the *carry trade*, involve borrowing low-yield currencies to buy high-yield currencies. According to Frankel (2008) several surveys,[6] starting as early as 1977, show that "one can expect to make money on average by going short in the low interest currency (the one selling at a forward premium) and by going long in the high interest currency (the one selling at a forward discount)."

Markets do not appear to adjust as quickly to the theoretical predictions of the neoclassical paradigm as arguments based on arbitraging might suggest. Capital is not necessarily mobile, in part because some investors have a home bias and do not participate in foreign transactions. Second, investors without a home bias may be constrained regarding the amount of capital they can move between currencies. Third, carry trade transactions may create illiquid investments that are not always easy to unwind. Capital constraints and illiquidity can mean that the risk of carry trade transactions is sometimes underestimated, and that what appear to be profitable opportunities are in fact due to the presence of a risk premium

---

[6] Frankel (2008) remarks further that most such studies refer to the existence of a "forward discount bias," and that popular commentary does not always identify "carry trade" with the former phrase.

(see Brunnermeier, Nagel, and Pedersen 2008). Still further, central banks sometimes intervene in the currency markets, and they have historically been more effective at preventing rises in currency value than at preventing devaluation. Fifth, investor expectations of inflation may have been higher than central bank inflation targeting actually led them to be, implying that the high yields offered by some currencies have not been eroded by rising prices.

The principal risk in a carry trade is the uncertainty of exchange rates: If currencies show an increase in volatility, carry trade positions start to look less attractive. For example, if a trader borrowed in yen to invest in U.S. dollars, the trader would lose if the U.S. dollar fell relative to the yen. Moreover, since carry trade transactions are often highly levered, a small movement in exchange rates can result in large losses unless the deals are appropriately hedged.[7] In particular Brunnermeier, Nagel, and Pedersen (2008) find evidence that the exchange-rate risk is negatively skewed for high-interest-rate (investment) currencies, implying that traders are subject to crash risk.

EXCHANGE RISK MANAGEMENT

Exchange risks can be managed through currency and interest rate swaps or through hedging. Swaps are usually arranged by banks and investment banks known as swap dealers, as discussed in the next section. Some risks can be hedged in markets, but others can only be hedged through over-the-counter trades with counterparties. Still others, such as country risk, cannot usually be hedged through either market or OTC transactions, and it is necessary to manage them internally. For example, some exposures can be hedged by generating earnings in the same currency as the obligation.

Whether a given transaction can be arranged as a market or a nonmarket transaction depends on its attributes, as discussed in Part I of this book and as illustrated in Chapter 12. Active markets exist only for hedging short-term risks, because the expected returns relative to risk are uneconomic for longer maturity forward and futures transactions. For example, in the early 2000s an established market existed in U.S. dollars, Canadian dollars, and pounds sterling up to 10 years, in Australian dollars up to approximately two years, and in Spanish pesetas up to 12 months. Within each of the foregoing markets, the bulk of the trading is for instruments of one year or less to maturity. Beyond the time bands for established markets, swaps can frequently be arranged OTC by banking and investment banking companies in such major financial centers as New York, London, and Tokyo.

---

[7] Of course, the costs of hedging reduce the profitability of a carry trade transaction.

Short-Term Currency and Interest Swaps

The growth of swap transactions began in the early 1970s. Interest rate swaps were the first to be arranged, but currency swaps followed not long afterward. Originally, swaps were individually negotiated between the contracting parties. As transactions became more frequent, and as agents became more familiar with swap techniques, the cost and informational conditions under which they could be completed also changed. Standardized forms of transactions were worked out and agreed upon through an organization now known as the International Swaps and Derivatives Association (ISDA).[8] These simpler and more standard forms of swaps are now arranged and traded in a highly active OTC market. More complex forms of swaps are also traded, but less actively.

Interest rate swaps are frequently combined with currency swaps, and the transactions have helped forge stronger arbitrage links among markets. As one example, in 1990 it became profitable for British investors to borrow British pounds at floating rates in London (LIBOR) and to use the funds for purchasing Italian government fixed rate ECU bonds.[9] An interest income swap from fixed to floating was used to stabilize the interest earnings, and a swap of pounds for ECU's was used to stabilize the foreign exchange risk of the British investor. The currency swap meant the British investor exchanged pounds for ECUs when making the investment and ECUs for pounds when disinvesting. The net result of this deal, after transaction costs, was a profit of about 0.80% (80 basis points) per annum on the funds invested. As such transactions became increasingly commonplace, the effects of arbitraging discussed in Chapters 6 and 7 reduced their profit potential to competitive levels. However, less standard, negotiated swaps still exist, and in these transactions arbitraging does not always reduce the profits to the same extent as in the more active markets.

Exchange-traded currency futures and options are also extensively used for risk management purposes. Many such deals are pure market transactions, standardized according to terms set by the exchanges on which they trade. These kinds of options and futures market trading have some characteristics of retail trading, because the amounts involved are typically smaller, and because the contracts are often shorter-term. Both banks and investment banking firms act as agents in these markets.

---

[8] As mentioned earlier, the organization was originally known as the International Swap Dealers Association.

[9] The European Currency Unit, ECU, derived its value from a basket of national currencies. The ECU was the forerunner of the Euro.

Long-Term Swaps

Most foreign exchange transactions have short maturities, as already mentioned. In longer-term transactions, the inventory risk is large in relation to customary returns,[10] and to arrange such a hedge it is usually necessary to find a bank that will act as a broker in locating an offsetting transaction of approximately equal maturity between the same two countries. This kind of swap arrangement involves an exchange of funds at the outset, and one or more reversing transactions at time(s) of payment. For example, suppose Alcan, a Canadian firm, has a need for pounds while Imperial Chemical Industries (ICI), a British firm, has a similar need for Canadian dollars. Today the parties exchange $10 million Canadian for £4.5 million. They agree that 10 years hence they will reexchange at today's exchange rate. In the meantime ICI pays Alcan the difference in the 10-year interest rates minus a concession fee. Both firms eliminate foreign exchange risk in this transaction. Although the example assumes a fixed interest rate spread, arrangements with a floating spread are also possible. A long-term swap protects creditors by establishing a legally enforceable contract. Different formal arrangements may be used to alter the credit risk borne by the contracting parties.

EXCHANGE RATE MANAGEMENT

This section considers exchange rate management at the macroeconomic level. It examines a number of international arrangements, beginning with the differences between fixed and flexible exchange rate systems. It then addresses the potential for and the limitations to central bank intervention in foreign exchange markets. Finally, it discusses how the European community came to adopt a fixed exchange rate regime, first through the European Monetary System and then through the Euro.

Exchange Rate Systems

The value of a country's currency is affected by both international trade and international financing transactions. The adjustments to a currency's value can be quite rapid if the currency is managed under a floating rate system, since in that case the major determinants of value are the international currency markets' supplies of and demands for the currency. However, some countries' exchange rates are fixed,[11] and there are in fact

---

[10] See Chapter 10 for a theoretical discussion of inventory risk-return relations.

[11] Even under a fixed exchange rate system, currency values cannot be kept fixed for very long if the financial markets reach a consensus that the values do not reflect underlying economic reality.

several kinds of fixed rate systems. Considering one such example, the gold standard, illustrates the kinds of adjustments that take place under a fixed exchange rate system.

Under the gold standard, exchange rates are fixed in relation to gold by international agreement. To maintain its obligations under the gold standard, a country must limit its total currency issue to a prespecified multiple of its gold reserves. The country faces a credibility problem if it tries to exceed the agreed ratio of currency to gold reserves, since market agents may not believe the country can maintain the currency's value in relation to gold. Holders of the currency may then try to exchange their holdings for gold before others come to the same belief. The combined actions of agents with these beliefs can cause a speculative run on the currency.

Assuming that the amount of currency in circulation is at or near the maximal levels permitted by its gold stock, a country with a trade deficit must surrender an amount of gold equal in value to the excess of its imports over its exports.[12] Since the amount of currency outstanding is assumed to be at or near its permissible maximum in relation to gold reserves, and since agreements with other countries prevent the value of the currency from falling, the amount of currency outstanding must be reduced as gold reserves are surrendered.

Adhering to a gold standard means that an automatic adjustment mechanism is called into action if a country's price levels increase faster than those of other countries. To illustrate the adjustment, suppose the country in question has a current account deficit. Then as domestic price levels increase the deficit will also increase, as buyers throughout the world substitute cheaper foreign goods or services for the more expensive domestic goods or services. Gold shipments will increase to compensate for the increased trade deficit, and as the country's gold reserves are reduced, the outstanding amount of its currency will also have to be reduced. The effect of reducing the amount of currency outstanding is to curtail economic activity, which in turn limits imports and as a result reduces the current account deficit. While the chain of events is lengthy and requires macroeconomic analysis, the reduction in imports comes about because curtailing economic activity reduces national income, and imports are regarded as an increasing function of national income. Then, if imports fall faster than exports, the deficit on current account is reduced.

In the event of a current account surplus the adjustments are similar. In this case adhering to the gold standard means that the surplus will lead to an increase in gold imports, followed by an increase in the domestic money supply, and that will in turn increase domestic prices. The increase in

---

[12] Assuming that no long-term borrowing has been arranged.

domestic prices then leads to a chain of adjustments with an effect opposite to those already discussed. In particular, if exports become more expensive on world markets, the current account surplus is likely to be reduced.

The purpose of a gold standard is to stabilize currency values in relation to gold, and hence in relation to each other. This stability serves both to reduce foreign exchange risk and to encourage trading among countries. On the other hand, adhering to the gold standard limits the amount of currency outstanding. Implementing the gold standard therefore means that the value of transactions in a given period cannot exceed a certain maximum—the product of the currency outstanding and the rate at which it is exchanged between parties. Thus the gold standard can encourage trade by making a country's announced values of their currencies credible, but at the price of restraining economic growth. The trade-off between stable currency values and growth is known as the Triffin Dilemma, after Professor Robert Triffin who first pointed it out in the 1960s. The Triffin Dilemma is faced not only by countries on the gold standard, but also under any form of fixed exchange rate system. Its relevance to the establishment of the Euro will be discussed later in the chapter.

A flexible exchange rate system loosens the linkages between current account imbalances and adjustments to national income. A flexible exchange rate offers a country greater freedom in choosing economic policy, because its policymakers can allow the burdens of adjustment to fall either on the exchange rate or on the growth of national income, thus escaping some of the rigors of the Triffin Dilemma. Some observers believe that flexible exchange rates can impair trade by creating uncertainty about relative currency values. However these risks may have diminished, at least to some extent, as the growth of derivatives and currency trading has made hedging foreign exchange transactions easier and cheaper than formerly.

With flexible exchange rates, the value of a currency is determined by market forces rather than by agreement, and changes in the currency's value can occur independently of changes in the amount of currency outstanding. Moreover, a current account deficit can be eliminated by currency values falling on the international markets, at least so long as the decline in the currency leads to exports rising relative to imports. However if countries employ tariffs, duties, quotas, and domestic price controls, adjustments can be impeded and exchange rate flexibility may be translated, at least partially, into changes in real output.

Central Bank Intervention

Attempts by authorities to alter exchange rates away from their market determined levels can affect a currency's value for a time, but international financial markets are so large that trading can overcome attempts by even the largest central bank to maintain an exchange rate at a nonmarket level. When a central bank intervenes, it does not usually intend to resist fundamental changes in the value of the currency, but rather to smooth temporary changes. The central bank monitors potential supplies and demands in the market in attempts to offset short-term price changes, and also influences the currency indirectly by changing interest rate policies. For example, to offset downward pressures on its currency, a central bank will restrict monetary growth to keep interest rates somewhat higher than they would otherwise be.[13]

As the world's financial system becomes increasingly integrated, changing expectations are becoming increasingly important to explaining the volatility of currency and securities values, making central bank intervention even less influential than formerly. For example, in the mid-1990s a weakening of the Mexican peso created a similar weakening in the Canadian dollar. Even though the two countries' economic fundamentals were quite different, expectations for the two countries' currencies seemed to be related in the eyes of some of the world's currency traders.

The European Monetary System

One criticism of a flexible exchange rate regime is that it does not impose sufficient discipline on a country to keep its domestic costs in line with the rest of the world. With a flexible exchange rate system a country can tolerate large wage increases and yet offset most of the effects on export prices by devaluing its currency. Even with devaluations, however, in an environment of continued wage increases a country's costs can rise faster than those of its international competitors, weakening the country's ability to compete for a share of world trade. A second criticism of a flexible exchange rate is that it makes calculation of returns on foreign long-term investment difficult to calculate, and as already mentioned long-term foreign exchange hedges are difficult and costly to arrange.

Essentially, these concerns underlay the European countries' willingness to join the European Monetary System (EMS). While a full discussion of the advantages and disadvantages of the EMS is beyond the scope of this book, the principal issues are relevant to understanding the differences between

---

[13] As a point of interest, the monetary authorities in the United States rarely intervene in the markets for U.S. dollars, and did not do so at all between 1973 and 1985. However, in September 1985 when a major realignment of currencies was desired, the Federal Reserve System did attempt to influence the exchange rate.

fixed and flexible exchange rate regimes. Until the beginning of 1999,[14] each member of the EMS agreed to restrict the fluctuations in the value of its currency relative to those of other members. The so-called managed float made it difficult for special interest groups in any one country to obtain increases in income over and above those obtained by counterparts in other countries. Thus the EMS promoted anti-inflationary, pro-competitive conditions that individual countries sometimes found politically difficult to create on their own. During the years 1979 to 1992 the EMS worked relatively well, largely because member countries grew at about the same rate and had roughly the same rates of inflation. The necessary adjustments following on differences in growth rates and in inflation were made using relatively frequent, but small, realignments of currency values.

Strains began to show in September 1992 when Finland, which had uni-laterally pegged the Finnmark to the ECU, had to abandon its link and lower the value of its currency. The Swedish Krona was next to forgo its link to the ECU, and subsequently Spain devalued the peseta. In late September 1992 both Italy and Great Britain dropped out of the EMS. Spain, Portugal and Ireland imposed controls on the international movement of capital. Despite all these actions, France and Germany were able to maintain a fixed French franc/deutsche mark exchange rate, and the EMS continued to function in relatively quiet markets until the summer of 1993.

At that time the economic pressures of German reunification tested the EMS much more severely. To aid the East during reunification, the German federal government incurred relatively large deficits, and Germany's attempts to offset the inflationary effects of such a policy caused serious policy disagreements among EMS members. In order to resist inflationary pressures in Germany, the Bundesbank wanted to restrict monetary growth, largely by keeping interest rates high. The relatively high German interest rates meant that in order to maintain the values of their currencies relative to the deutsche mark, other EMS members were also under pressure to raise interest rates. However, the German policy conflicted with the preferences of other countries for promoting economic growth through lower interest rate policies. In particular, as France indicated a preference for not letting interest rates rise too sharply, the policy disagreements with Germany became serious enough that market agents began to speculate on a deval-uation of the French franc. Despite official attempts to stabilize currency values, speculation continued and the EMS intervention band had to be raised from its former 2.25% to 15%, in effect suspending the workings of the EMS.

---

[14] At that time the Euro was established, as discussed in the next subsecton.

The Euro and the European Central Bank

Despite the earlier difficulties faced by the EMS, pressures to fix exchange rates within the European Community continued to exert themselves. At the beginning of 1999 the members of Europe's Economic and Monetary Union took the first move to establish a common currency, the Euro. At that time, 11 countries[15] fixed the values of their respective currencies relative to the Euro, and thus relative to each other as well. National currencies remained in general circulation until the end of 2001, after which the Euro became the common currency for all transactions in the participating countries.

The move to a fixed exchange rate is based on an assessment of political and economic benefits. The political benefits are mainly those of unifying the countries' political and economic systems. The economic benefits are to remove the uncertainty attendant on investment in foreign countries and to reduce the transactions costs of international shorter-term transactions. The economic costs of maintaining a fixed exchange rate system include the costs attendant on the Triffin Dilemma, introduced above. They also include the political difficulties of ensuring that the monetary policy followed by the European Central Bank does not create undue hardship for member countries whose economies are growing more slowly than average. Some of the likely difficulties are suggested by the early 1990s history of the European Monetary System, as discussed previously.

REFERENCES

Brunnermeier, Markus K., Stefan Nagel, and Lasse H. Pedersen. 2009. Carry trades and currency crashes. In *National Bureau of Economic Research Macroeconomics Annual 2008*, vol. 23, edited by Daron Acemoglu, Kenneth Rogoff, and Michael Woodford. Chicago: University of Chicago Press.

Culver, S. E., and D. H. Papell. 1999. Long-run purchasing power parity with short-run data: Evidence with a null hypothesis of stationarity. *Journal of International Money and Finance* 18: 751–768.

Fama, Eugene F., and M. R. Gibbons. 1984. "A comparison of inflation forecasts." *Journal of Monetary Economics* 13: 327–348.

Frankel, Jeffrey. 2008. Getting carried away: How the carry trade and its potential unwinding can explain movements in international financial markets. *Milken Institute Review* 10 (January): 38–45.

Rogoff, Kenneth. 1996. The purchasing power parity puzzle. *Journal of Economic Literature* 34: 647–668.

---

[15] Austria, Belgium, Finland, France, Germany, Ireland, Italy, Luxembourg Netherlands, Portugal, and Spain. At that time the nonparticipating countries were the United Kingdom, Denmark, Greece, and Sweden.

Sercu, Piet, and Raman Uppal. 1995. *International Financial Markets and the Firm.* Cincinnati: South-Western.

Taylor, M. P. 1987. "Covered interest parity: A high frequency, high quality data study." *Economica* 54: 429–438.

TERMS

carry trade The borrowing of low-yield currencies to buy high-yield currencies.

covered interest arbitrage A transaction in which a resident in one country invests short term in another country, covering the foreign exchange risk of the transaction through a forward sale of the investment returns.

forward parity theorem Says that the forward exchange rate must equal the future spot rate.

forward transaction A transaction in which parties agree to exchange currencies at some future date.

interest parity theory A theory explaining that arbitrage is likely to remove differences between real interest rates obtainable on investments of the same risk but in different currencies.

purchasing power parity theory A theory explaining that arbitrage is likely to remove differences between prices payable in different currencies. For example, the price of a bottle of champagne, expressed in U.S. dollars, equals the price of a bottle of champagne, expressed in Euros and converted to their U.S. dollar equivalent.

spot transaction A foreign exchange transaction in which immediate delivery is specified. Also known as "benchmark rates," "straightforward rates," and "outright rates," spot rates represent the price that a buyer expects to pay for a foreign currency in another currency.The term "immediate" means "at once" for small amounts of currency, but with a delay of two or fewer working days in the case of larger electronic funds transfers. For example, in Canada, large amounts of U.S. dollars purchased in the spot market are usually delivered on the following working day. In the United States, large amounts of, say, French francs are usually delivered on the second working day after a deal is done.

swap transaction A transaction that involves the exchange of principal and interest in one currency for the same in another currency.

Five

Applications: Pooled Investments

This part covers portfolio governance. Chapter 14 shows how the Capital Asset Pricing and Arbitrage Pricing Theories explain why marketable securities portfolios are diversified, and how securities are priced relative to those diversified portfolios. When the assumptions of the neoclassical paradigm are satisfied, portfolio management is viewed by these theories as a task of balancing risk against return. While there are both static and dynamic versions of the CAPT and the APT, this chapter examines only the static theories. However, the also chapter deals with dynamic aspects of risk management by discussing the construction of synthetic portfolios and portfolio insurance. As in previous chapters, the theories help to provide additional benchmarks for applications. Chapter 14 examines applications to mutual funds, exchange traded funds, and hedge funds. It also considers the risk measure known as Value at Risk (VaR).

Chapter 15 examines portfolios composed mainly of nonmarketable, relatively illiquid securities. Since such portfolios cannot be managed effectively through market transactions, governance techniques focus on other means of influencing portfolio risk and return, mainly by portfolio restructuring and by trading derivative securities. Most such techniques work well under normal market conditions, when transactions can be described as risky. However, when portfolio values can be affected by Knightian uncertainty, the techniques offer much more limited scope, as the chapter's last part explains.

Marketable Securities Portfolios

Chapter 14 considers managing portfolios consisting mainly of publicly traded securities. The chapter develops the essentials of the capital asset pricing theory (CAPT) and of the arbitrage pricing theory (APT), then uses the theories to provide static benchmark valuations for both portfolios and the securities the portfolios contain. The chapter also examines dynamic aspects of portfolio management, using earlier discussions of derivatives pricing to illustrate the basics of dynamic hedging theory and the construction of insured portfolios. In applications, the chapter considers why small investors buy mutual funds and exchange-traded funds, as well as the popularity of hedge funds. Finally, it discusses the measure known as Value at Risk (VaR).

INTRODUCTION

Portfolio governance tasks depend on the kind of portfolio being held. A relatively liquid portfolio (i.e., one that mostly contains marketable securities) presents the tasks of acquiring securities with desirable risk-return trade-offs, monitoring the securities' performance, and selling them if their performance does not live up to expectations. Governance of a marketable securities portfolio begins with developing and screening a list of candidate securities from which the portfolio will be assembled. Portfolio managers will usually begin by selecting securities intended to generate a favorable risk-return trade-off, largely along lines suggested by the CAPT and the APT. After purchasing securities, the portfolio manager will continue to monitor their expected contributions to portfolio earnings and risk, tasks that involve forecasting expected earnings and earnings risk.

Under normal trading conditions, most marketable securities are relatively liquid.[1] Investments proving to be unsatisfactory can usually be sold in the marketplace, although perhaps at some discount from the prevailing price, when their performance does not meet expectations. A portfolio manager must also reinvest funds deriving from security sales, dividend receipts, and maturing securities. Finally, governance involves tailoring the resulting portfolio's risk and return by using risk management tools such as derivative securities.

Since liquidity problems arise only rarely in portfolios of marketable securities, the portfolios' managers do not usually participate actively in the operations of firms in which they have invested. However there are two circumstances in which active participation can become important.[2] First, a particular security may suddenly become wholly unsalable, say because the issuing firm experiences large losses or goes bankrupt without much advance warning. Second, when individual investments are relatively large, it may not be possible to sell out a position quickly. If the attempt to sell a large block of securities is interpreted by the marketplace as conveying unfavorable news, any securities sold may be discounted substantially from the prevailing price. In these cases of relatively large holdings, portfolio managers are likely to use procedures similar to those discussed in Chapter 15.[3]

Diversification: Portfolio Theory

The principal management problems addressed by portfolio theory are estimating probability distributions of returns on individual securities and determining how different combinations of those securities will affect portfolio risk. Portfolio theory explains that diversification can help reduce the risk of earning a given expected return. Let us begin by defining portfolio risk as the variance of its return,[4] and assume that investors prefer the

---

[1] The situation can be different for a control block. When a relatively large proportion of a securities issue is held by a single investor, disposing of the block may be taken as a signal of nonconfidence and adversely affect the securities price. In such cases, the control block can be regarded as illiquid to some degree.

[2] Private equity investments are considered in Chapter 15.

[3] Asset-backed commercial paper and structured investment vehicles dependent on returns from subprime mortgages are examples of securities that became suddenly illiquid in 2007 and 2008. These developments are discussed in Chapter 15.

[4] In later discussing the capital asset pricing model, it will also be convenient to describe risk using the standard deviation of return, i.e. the square root of the variance. As will be shown, the two measures convey essentially the same information. Orthodox portfolio selection theory does not distinguish between income and default

TABLE 14.1 Joint Probabilities of Returns

r_X/r_Y	4%	7%	10%
1%	1/9	1/9	1/9
3%	1/9	1/9	1/9
5%	1/9	1/9	1/9

smallest attainable variance for a given expected return. Portfolio theory shows how to achieve this goal by judiciously combining securities with different statistical characteristics. Portfolios composed of securities whose returns are not perfectly correlated can exhibit a lower risk-return trade-off than the component securities.[5]

To see how diversification can lower risk in relation to return, consider investing in just two securities, X and Y. Denoting realized returns on the securities by r_X and r_Y, Table 14.1 shows the joint probabilities, estimated at time 0, with which the returns might be realized one period later. For example, the joint outcome $r_X = 1\%$, $r_y = 10\%$ is assumed to occur with probability 1/9, as are all the other combinations shown in the table.

The expected return on either security in Table 14.1 is given by the sum of the outcomes multiplied by the probability of realizing each possible outcome. The probabilities of the outcomes of r_X are given by the row sums of the joint probabilities, while the probabilities of the outcomes of r_Y are given by the column sums of the joint probabilities. Thus

$$E(r_X) = (1/3)(0.01) + (1/3)(0.03) + (1/3)(0.05) = 0.03$$

and

$$E(r_Y) = 0.07$$

The variance of returns, and its square root the standard deviation, are both measures of how "spread out" returns can be—the greater the spread,

---

risks, since for the theory's purposes both concepts can be incorporated satisfactorily in return distributions. As a practical matter, default risk becomes more important in the case of nonmarketable investments, as discussed later.

[5] Portfolio theory recognizes that not all asset combinations reduce risk. Indeed, it is possible to construct portfolios whose risk exceeds that of its individual components. For example leveraging, say through purchasing a security on margin, increases portfolio risk, even if the margin loan carries a riskless rate of interest.

the greater the variance and hence also the standard deviation. The variance is defined as the expected value of the square of the differences between outcomes and their mean:

$$\text{VAR}(r_X) = \sigma^2(r_X) = E[r_X - E(r_X)]^2$$

For example, letting $\sigma^2(r_X)$ denote the variance of return on security X,

$$\begin{aligned} \sigma^2(r_X) &= E[r_X - E(r_X)]^2 \\ &= (1/3)[0.01 - 0.03]^2 + (1/3)[0.03 - 0.03]^2 + (1/3)[0.05 - 0.03]^2 \\ &= (2/3)(0.02)^2 = 0.000267 \end{aligned}$$

For subsequent use, note that the standard deviation of return on security X is $\sigma(r_X) = (0.000267)^{1/2}$. Similar calculations show that $\sigma(r_Y) = (0.0006)^{1/2}$.

Since the two securities offer expected returns of 0.03 and 0.07 respectively, any portfolio combining them will have an expected return equal to the weighted average of the two. For example, a portfolio assembled by investing half the available funds in each of the two securities has an expected return equal to

$$(1/2)[E(r_X) + E(r_Y)] = 0.05$$

The variance of return for a portfolio composed of the two risky securities is given by the formula

$$\sigma^2(w_X r_X + w_Y r_Y) = (w_X)^2 \sigma^2(r_X) + 2w_X w_Y \text{ cov }(r_X, r_Y) + (w_Y)^2 \sigma^2(r_Y)$$

where $\sigma^2(r_X)$ is the variance of return on security X, $\sigma^2(r_Y)$ the variance of return on security Y, w_X is the proportion of funds invested in security X, and $w_Y = 1 - w_X$ the proportion invested in security Y. Finally $\text{cov}(r_X, r_Y)$, known as the covariance between r_X and r_Y, is a measure of the statistical association between the two securities' returns. Covariance is defined as

$$\text{cov}(r_X, r_Y) = E(r_X, r_Y) - E(r_X)E(r_Y)$$

In the present example this covariance is equal to zero because the two securities' returns are distributed independently. You can see the returns are statistically independent by noting that regardless of which outcome you consider for r_X, the probabilities of the three outcomes for r_y are all equal.[6]

Correlation (a standardized covariance) is also used to describe statistical relations between securities. The correlation between the two securities' returns is defined as

$$\text{corr}(r_X, \ r_Y) = \text{cov}(r_X, \ r_Y)/\sigma(r_X) \ \sigma(r_Y)$$

In the present example this correlation is equal to zero because the covariance is zero. More generally and as a consequence of its definition, the correlation coefficient always lies between -1 and 1. When the correlation between securities returns equals 1 (or -1), the returns are said to be perfectly positively (negatively) correlated. When correlation lies strictly between -1 and 1, the returns are imperfectly (positively or negatively) correlated.

In the example, if equal proportions are invested in the two securities the variance of portfolio return is

$$
\begin{aligned}
\sigma^2(r_X/2 + r_Y/2) &= \sigma^2(r_X)/4 + 2 \ \text{cov}(r_X, \ r_Y)/4 + \sigma^2(r_Y)/4 \\
&= 0.000267/4 + 0 + 0.0006/4 \qquad\qquad (14.1) \\
&= 0.000217
\end{aligned}
$$

The example illustrates a special case of the fact that when two securities have imperfectly correlated returns, assembling them into a portfolio can reduce the variance of return. Equally, since it is the square root of the variance, the standard deviation of return is also reduced, and it is convenient to use this measure in looking at the example graphically. All the combinations of expected return and standard deviation that can be obtained with just the two securities are shown in Figure 14.1. Each point on the curve in Figure 14.1 represents a portfolio in which the two securities X and Y have different weights.

Of course, where the curve reaches the point $\sigma(r_X)$, $E(r_X)$, the portfolio is composed entirely of security X, and where the curve reaches $\sigma(r_Y)$, $E(r_Y)$ the portfolio is composed entirely of security Y. The portfolios that can be found along the northwest frontier of Figure 14.1 are called efficient portfolios, because they give the highest available expected return for a given standard deviation, or risk. In contrast, the combinations lying within the elliptical curve are inefficient, as are combinations lying along the southwest frontier.

---

[6] For statistical independence it would only be necessary that the conditional probabilities have the same ratio to each other.

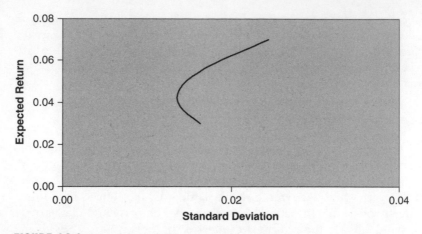

FIGURE 14.1   Portfolio Means and Standard Deviations

Portfolio theory can be applied to any number of securities, and in such cases the diversification principle establishes that combining securities whose returns are imperfectly correlated (whether positively or negatively) can offer potential for reducing risk relative to return. In all such cases, a semi-elliptical figure displaying combinations of mean return and standard deviation, resembling Figure 14.1, can be drawn.

Even more dramatically, if two securities are perfectly negatively correlated, a portfolio whose returns have zero standard deviation can be constructed; that is, a portfolio with a riskless return can be found. In this case the figure describing mean-standard deviation combinations would be triangular. One side joins the two securities' expected returns and standard deviations; the remaining two sides are drawn from the points just mentioned to a point on the vertical axis; that is, to a point with a given expected return and a standard deviation of zero.

If there is a risk-free security, the efficient portfolios lie along a straight line joining the riskless interest rate and the risk-return combination defined by a point where the straight line is just tangent to the northwest boundary of the portfolios of risky securities. All these portfolios offer better combinations of risk and return than do any other portfolios to the southeast of them, and hence all the portfolios on the line[7] are efficient combinations of the riskless security and the risky security portfolio represented by the tangency point M in Figure 14.2. The risk-free rate R_F is shown on the vertical axis.

---

[7] The line only extends to the right beyond the point of tangency with the frontier of risk portfolios if it is possible to borrow at the risk-free rate.

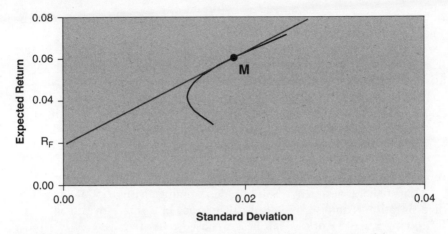

FIGURE 14.2 Combinations of Riskless Security and a Market Portfolio

Portfolio theory also recognizes that not all asset combinations reduce risk. Indeed, it is possible to construct portfolios whose risk exceeds that of its individual components. For example, a levered position such as the combination of a purchased security and the margin loan used to finance the purchase has greater risk than the security itself, even if the margin loan carries a riskless rate of interest. Similarly, either a call or a put option on a security has a higher standard deviation of return than does the security itself.

Diversification: Practical Aspects

In practice, the number of different securities used to diversify portfolio risk is determined by cost-benefit analysis. Including more securities in a portfolio can reduce portfolio risk if the securities' returns are imperfectly correlated, but investing in larger numbers of securities also means incurring larger transactions costs, both absolutely and proportionally. Nevertheless, since both costs and benefits are relatively easy to define, a satisfactory combination of risk and return can be found by comparing the marginal costs of buying additional securities to the marginal reductions in portfolio risk including the additional securities would bring about.

In addition, it is costly to search for candidate securities that might be included in a portfolio. However search costs are largely fixed, i.e. they are independent of the amounts invested in different securities. Since portfolio managers can spread their fixed search costs over whatever amounts they invest, a large portfolio's expected return is less affected by a given search cost than is a smaller portfolio. The costs of monitoring securities holdings are also largely fixed, and therefore unit costs of monitoring also tend to be smaller for larger portfolios.

On the other hand, managers of larger portfolios also face certain cost disadvantages. It is only cost-effective to place large amounts of funds in relatively large securities issues, because a large investment in a small issue can sometimes create adverse price effects, both when securities are purchased and when they are sold. Moreover, investment possibilities are limited by the financier's knowledge: A financier cannot invest in securities of which he is unaware. Hence the manager's search for additional new securities may be limited by a belief that additional search costs may not be recoverable through finding profitable new investments.

For smaller investment portfolios, determining an appropriate degree of diversification requires a modified calculation. In a small investment portfolio, only a few securities can be purchased cost-effectively. While most authorities suggest that a portfolio of 15 to 20 securities will give a risk-return combination close to that of a market index, small investors may not find it cost-effective to acquire even this number.

Capital Asset Pricing Theory

The idea that diversification can reduce risk relative to return has led to two theories of securities valuation: capital asset pricing theory, developed by William F. Sharpe and others in the late 1960s, and arbitrage pricing theory, developed by Steven Ross in the 1970s. Each of these theories recognizes that investors are concerned with risk at the portfolio level rather than with the risk of individual securities. Hence, theory values securities in relation to an underlying reference portfolio. Moreover, since both theories assume markets in which costless arbitrage is possible, the only aspect of a security's risk that enters into determining its expected return is the part of the risk that cannot be diversified away.[8]

The principal tenets of capital asset pricing theory are:

1. All investors use the same information, capital markets are in equilibrium, and trading involves no transactions costs.
2. Investors require to be compensated for risk, where risk is measured as the variance (or its square root, the standard deviation) of a portfolio's return.

---

[8] The CAPT was developed prior to arbitrage pricing theory, but it can be regarded as a special case of the APT. However, the CAPT actually specifies the nature of the risk factor, while the APT holds that relevant risk factors can be determined empirically.

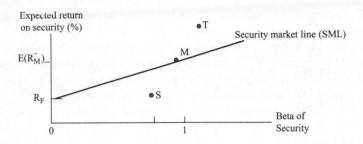

FIGURE 14.3 The Security Market Line
Note: The expected return on a security with a beta of 0 is equal to the risk-free rate, indicated by R_F. The expected return on a security with a beta of 1 is equal to the expected return on the market portfolio, indicated by $E(R_M)$.

3. Investors assess the risk of any security by its contribution to the risk of a reference or market portfolio.

When investors conform to the foregoing assumptions, the capital asset pricing theory provides an equilibrium theory of asset pricing. The theory argues that a security's risk premium is determined by the way investors define risks and by the compensation they demand for taking those risks. The theory further argues that since investors with homogeneous expectations[9] will all purchase the same diversified reference portfolio (called the "market portfolio") the risks of individual securities can and should be assessed in terms of their contribution to the risk of the market portfolio. Assuming there is also a riskless security traded in the market, the market portfolio is determined as the tangency point of a straight line drawn from the riskless rate to the efficient frontier of risky securities. The relations are shown in Figure 14.3.

The capital asset pricing model (CAPM), a formula derived from the relations depicted in Figure 14.3, states that the market required rate of return on a given security X is

$$E(r_X) = r_f + \beta_X[E(r_M) - r_f] \tag{14.2}$$

where $E(r_X)$ is the expected return on the security in question, r_f is the risk-free rate, $E(r_M)$ is the expected return on the market portfolio, and

---

[9] They can have some variation in the types of preferences they exhibit. For example, if security return distributions are unrestricted, investors can have quadratic utilities with different risk aversion coefficients.

β_X is a measure of the riskiness of asset X. In Figure 14.3, point M is the market portfolio, point S represents an overpriced security (its return is lower than the market return for its risk), and point T represents an underpriced security. In equation (14.2), the term $E(r_M) - r_f$ is identified as the market price per unit of risk. Intuitively, β_X measures the sensitivity of changes in the security's expected return to changes in the market portfolio's expected return. Capital asset pricing theory further establishes that

$$\beta_X = \text{cov}(r_X, r_M)/\sigma^2(r_M) \tag{14.3}$$

where r_X is the rate of return on asset X, r_M is the rate of return on the market portfolio, and $\text{cov}(r_X, r_M)$ is the covariance between the returns on X and M respectively. Finally $\sigma^2(r_M)$ is the variance of returns on the market portfolio. As already mentioned the CAPT assumes that the only risk that matters to an investor is risk that cannot be diversified away, and that is why the measure of risk β_X depends solely on how security returns covary with the returns on the market portfolio.

In essence, equation (14.3) states that the risk of security X is measured by its contribution to the risk of the market portfolio. For example, if we assume that $E(r_M) = 12.00\%$, that the risk-free rate is 10%, and the expected return on security X is 12.36%, then equation (14.2) takes the form

$$E(r_X) = 10.00 + \beta_X(12.00 - 10.00) = 12.36 \tag{14.4}$$

In equation (14.4), the 2.36% risk premium is the product of the risk measure β_X and the market price of risk. In the example, the market price of risk is the expected return on the market portfolio less the risk free rate of interest; that is, $12\% - 10\% = 2\%$. Then since $12.36 - 10.00 = 2.36 = \beta_X(2.00)$, it follows that the security in question has an equilibrium return if $\beta_X = 1.18$.

Similarly, an instrument with $\beta_X = 0.75$ will have an equilibrium market required rate of return equal to

$$E(r_X) = 10.00 + (0.75)(12.00 - 10.00) = 11.50\%$$

The risk-return relationship defined in equation (14.2) is often written in a form called the security market line (SML) as was shown in Figure 14.3. Capital asset pricing theory argues that if a security offers a risk-return combination that does not plot on the security market line, trading will occur until the anomaly is eliminated. Suppose, for example, a security is underpriced and yields a higher rate of return than other instruments with the same risk. Market agents will buy the underpriced security, bidding its price up until the excess return is eliminated. Similarly, an overpriced security offers too low a return and is subject to selling pressures until its price declines. In other words, if the CAPM correctly describes capital market equilibrium, profit-motivated trading will ensure that securities are priced so their risk-return combinations plot on the security market line.

Tests of the CAPM are difficult to conduct, and existing empirical findings are regarded as somewhat inconclusive. First, Roll (1977) argues that while the CAPM is testable in principle, it is unlikely that a definitive test of the model can be conducted. Roll demonstrates that the only potentially testable hypothesis of the CAPM is whether the market portfolio is mean-variance efficient, and that for a proper test the market portfolio should contain all assets sold worldwide. Cheng and Grauer (1980) designed a test that circumvents the need to identify a market portfolio, but their results actually comprise a joint test of the CAPM and of the returns distribution they assume. Stambaugh (1992) shows that changing the proxy for the market portfolio does not much affect the results of tests aimed at validating the CAPM. However, Stambaugh uses only a restricted set of assets in his tests and the results therefore do not address the criticism that the CAPM defines the market portfolio as consisting of worldwide assets.

Black-Litterman Portfolio Selection[10]

In practice applying the CAPM to market data does not lead to selecting optimal portfolios with sensible characteristics, largely because historical asset return data produce poor predictions of future asset returns. Portfolios chosen according to the CAPM and based on historical market data may exhibit inordinately large positive or negative weights for some securities. Even portfolios restricted as to the amount of permissible short selling may still have weights that seem unrealistic, particularly if the restrictions rule out what would seem to be sensible securities purchases if recent historical data could somehow be ignored.

The Black-Litterman approach to selecting an optimal portfolio reverses the idea of using historical data to predict the future. Rather, it assumes that investors begin with an optimal benchmark portfolio chosen from a given universe of securities. The assumption this portfolio is optimal can then be used, with the CAPM, to generate a set of benchmark expected returns. These returns can be interpreted as reflecting the market's information about the future returns on securities in the benchmark portfolio. If the investor does not regard some of the generated returns as indicative of what she

---

[10] This section follows Simon Benninga (2008) Chapter 13.

expected the future to bring, she can amend them and adjust the composition of the benchmark portfolio to reflect her expectations.

In other words, the Black-Litterman approach infers market expected returns using the Capital Asset Pricing Model, and then amends these returns where necessary to reflect any differences from market expected returns that the investor's own information indicates. As a practical matter, the approach both generates sensible portfolios and provides means to adjust market expectations data where they do not conform to individual investor expectations.

Arbitrage Pricing Theory

Like the CAPT, the arbitrage pricing theory (Ross 1976) argues that investors are concerned with portfolio risk and not the risk on individual securities, because some of the latter can be diversified away. The APT argues that equilibrium expected returns on marketable securities are jointly determined by trading that eliminates arbitrage opportunities. Unlike the CAPT, the APT argues that the risk of an individual security is measured relative to a number of underlying risk factors.[11] When all arbitrage opportunities have been taken up, the APT predicts that the market required return on any security will be determined by the manner the underlying risk factors affect that return. The APT does not explicitly define the risk factors entering into prices, but argues that both their definition and their number can be determined empirically.

The APT argues that $E(r_X)$, the expected return on an asset X, is determined as

$$E(r_X) = r_f + \beta_1 F_1 + \beta_2 F_2 + \cdots + \beta_I F_I \qquad (14.5)$$

where r_f is the risk free rate, F_i is the risk premium associated with factor i, and β_i is the sensitivity of the share returns to the i'th factor; $i = 1, 2, \ldots, I$. Equation (14.5) is established using arbitrage arguments, and is an equilibrium relation. For example, if the riskless rate is 10% as before, and if the expected return on a security X is 12.36%, the APT explains that the 2.36% risk premium is a weighted combination of premiums attached to individual risk factors:

$$12.36 = 10.00 + \beta_1 F_1 + \beta_2 F_2 + \cdots + \beta_I F_I \qquad (14.6)$$

---

[11] The single risk factor used in the CAPT is a security's β, which measures the security's contribution to the risk of the market portfolio.

If the security's return were only dependent on the first two factors, example values that would satisfy the equation are $\beta_1 = 1.08$, $\beta_2 = 0.64$, $F_1 = 1.00$, $F_2 = 2.00$, giving the calculation:

$$12.36 = 10.00 + 1.08(1.00) + 0.64(2.00) \qquad (14.7)$$

From a practical point of view, the APT can be tested by empirically identifying risk factors, their number, and their influence on securities' prices. For example, Chen, Roll, and Ross (1986) identify four risk factors. They are unanticipated changes in: an index of industrial production, the spread between high- and low-grade bonds, interest rates, and inflation.

MANAGING PORTFOLIO RETURN

The original version of the CAPT, presented previously, deals with risk-return relationships at a point in time. The original version of the APT also offers a static explanation of portfolio selection. While it is possible to elaborate the static CAPT to predict how risk-return relationships might evolve through time, and how they might be managed by changing portfolio composition, the theoretical approach is relatively complex and beyond the scope of this book. Similarly, dynamic versions of the APT can be explored, but these versions involve the use of econometric methods beyond the scope of this book.

Instead this section asks how a portfolio's evolving risk-return relations might be influenced with the use of risk management instruments. This section uses the earlier part of the book's theory to present two static ways of hedging portfolio payoffs, first with a put option, then synthetically using a bond and a call option. It then provides a related example that illustrates the basic aspects of dynamic portfolio hedging. After the examples, the section examines practical aspects of hedging portfolio payoffs.

Hedging Portfolio Payoffs

The options and futures contracts introduced in Chapter 7 can be and are used to tailor portfolio risk-return trade-offs.[12] Moreover, portfolio managers often prefer to use derivatives rather than the underlying securities,

---

[12] As an example of using options to increase risk, buying and holding stock options rather than the stocks themselves can be used to create a portfolio with both higher expected returns and a higher risk of achieving these return.

TABLE 14.2 Stock Price Process

Time 0	Time 1	Time 2
		121.00
	110.00	
100.00		100.00
	90.91	
		82.64

either because the investments involved are smaller, the transactions costs are lower, or both.

As an elementary example, consider how possible declines in portfolio value can be hedged at a point in time, in this first case by using a put option. Suppose a financial institution holds a single stock currently trading for $100.00. The institution wishes to ensure that the value of the portfolio will not fall below $100.00 two periods hence. Of course, obtaining the insurance will not be costless, and one of the tasks of the portfolio manager is to balance the cost of the insurance against the risk reduction achieved. The present example considers how this trade-off can be assessed.

The example begins by specifying the stock price process. Suppose the stock can either rise or fall in value by a multiplicative factor of 1.10 in each period, that either event is equally likely, and that the time 0 stock price is $100.00. At the end of two periods the stock will be sold for cash. To make computations simple, suppose (1) that risk-neutral probabilities can be used for valuation purposes,[13] and (2) that the risk-free interest rate is zero.

The calculations in Table 14.2 use the methods of risk-neutral probabilities first introduced in Chapter 8. Given that the stock is worth $100.00 today, the table shows that the stock can assume one of the two possible values − $110.00 or $90.91 − one period hence, and one of the three possible values − $121.00, 100.00, or $82.64 − at the end of time 2.

Next, since the riskless interest rate is assumed to be 0, in either period 1 or 2 an upward movement of the stock can be valued using the risk-neutral probability

$$q = (1.00 - 1.10^{-1})/(1.10 - 1.10^{-1}) = 0.4762$$

Similarly, a downward movement of the stock price can be valued using $1 - q = 0.5238$. Two successive upward movements can be valued using q^2,

---

[13] The conditions under which a risk-neutral probability exists are discussed in Chapter 8.

TABLE 14.3 Insured Portfolio

Time 2 Scenarios	Risk-Neutral Probability	Stock Price	Payoff to European Put	Portfolio Value
Scenario *uu*	q^2	$121.00	$ 0.00	$121.00
Scenario *ud* or *du*	$2q(1 - q)$	$100.00	$ 0.00	$100.00
Scenario *dd*	$(1 - q)^2$	$ 82.64	$17.36	$100.00
Time 0 value		$100.00	$ 4.76	$104.76

two successive downward movements using $(1 - q)^2$, and either an upward movement followed by a downward movement, or a downward movement followed by an upward movement, using $q(1 - q)$.

At time 0, the insurance can be arranged by purchasing a European put to expire two periods hence. The combination of stock and a put with a strike price of $100.00 has the time 2 payoffs shown in Table 14.3. The scenario *uu* means the stock increases in price both periods, the scenarios *ud* and *du* refer respectively to an increase followed by a decrease or vice versa, and *dd* means the stock decreases in price both periods. The last line of Table 14.3 shows that the cost of insuring against capital losses is the purchase price of the put. Using the risk-neutral probability, this purchase price is

$$(1 - q)^2(\$17.36) = (0.5238)^2(\$17.36) = \$4.76$$

Now consider the portfolio values at the intervening time 1, when the stock price can either be $110.00 or $90.91. If the stock price reaches $110.00 at time 1, the portfolio cannot fall below $100.00 by time 2, and the holder of the originally purchased European put might think of selling it to reduce insurance costs. But, making a sale implies finding a willing buyer, and the put maturing at time 2 cannot be sold for a positive price to anyone having the same price expectations as those used in the analysis. Under the price expectations used in the analysis the put is worthless if the price has reached $110.00 at time 1, because in that event it will not be possible for the price to fall below $100.00 by time 2. On the other hand if the time 1 price is $90.91, the investor should continue to hold the put purchased at time 0. He will discard the put if the price returns to $100.00 at time 2, but will exercise it if the price falls a second time to reach $82.64.

In the present example, once the problem has been stated and none of the parameters or the amount of required insurance changes, the original put purchase provides the desired insurance of time 2 portfolio value. If as assumed in the foregoing example, expectations do not change and the only purpose is to insure the portfolio's capital value at a fixed point in time, the same hedge can be maintained without any change at time 1 (see Huang and Litzenberger 1988). That is, the present example illustrates that the need for readjustment would only arise if expectations were to change from one period to the next, or if expectations remained fixed but for some reason the investor wished to change the amount of insurance.

Static Hedging with a Synthetic Portfolio

The put-call parity relationship developed in Chapter 9 can be used both to illustrate the concept behind the hedge just discussed and to suggest a second way of devising the same insured portfolio. One reason for learning more than one way to achieve the same end is that in practice, observed prices may offer arbitrage opportunities, and hence one way of constructing a hedge may be cheaper than another. Recall that the put-call parity relationship expressed in terms of payoff distributions states that the value of a certainty payment equal to the exercise price of a put and a call equals the value of the security, less the value of the call, plus the value of the put:

$$v(S) \equiv v(X) - v(C) + v(P) \tag{14.8}$$

Rearranging equation (14.8),

$$v(X) + v(P) \equiv v(S) + v(C) \tag{14.9}$$

an insured portfolio can be created by purchasing either the combination of the stock and a put, as in the above example, or the combination of an asset with a certainty payoff of S and a call. In practice the second alternative may be cheaper, because Treasury bills are a good proxy for a sure asset and typically sell for relatively low commissions. Similarly, call options may sell for lower transactions costs than would the stock itself. The right-hand side of equation 14.9 gives the values of what is normally called a synthetic insured portfolio, an example of which is given in Table 14.4.

Since a comparison of Tables 14.3 and 14.4 shows that the payoffs to the two portfolios are the same in every scenario, you know that if there are no arbitrage opportunities the two portfolios should have the same value at equilibrium in perfectly competitive markets. In practice, if the two possibilities were available at different prices, or if they involved different

TABLE 14.4 Synthetic Insured Portfolio

Time 2 Scenarios	Sure Asset	Call	Portfolio
Scenario *uu*	$100.00	$21.00	$121.00
Scenario *ud* or *du*	$100.00	$ 0.00	$100.00
Scenario *dd*	$100.00	$ 0.00	$100.00
Time 0 value	$100.00	$ 4.76	$104.76

transaction costs, you would choose the cheaper, thus helping to bring about the price relationships predicted by the absence of arbitrage opportunities.

Dynamic Readjustment

The effects of trading to maintain portfolio insurance dynamically are illustrated by the next example. This example constructs a synthetic put option by using bonds (whose principal accumulates at an assumed riskless rate of zero) and a short position in a stock.[14] Table 14.5 depicts a security price process and the trades needed to maintain the values of the put. It depicts three time points, at each of which the data are organized according to the scheme shown in Table 14.6. For comparability, this example depicts the same price process and put as used earlier. The difference is that the present example shows how to create the put synthetically by rebalancing positions in the bond and the stock. (To create the same insured portfolio as before, the transactions creating the put have to be combined with the share position originally held; this part of the previous example is omitted to focus on how the synthetic put is created.)

Begin at time 0, with the numbers on the left-hand side of the first panel in Table 14.5. The stock has an initial value of $100.00, and we assume the investor begins with $4.76 in bonds, the value of the put at time 0. The portfolio is rebalanced at time 0 to create a synthetic put, composed of a $52.38 long position in a bond, and a short position of 47.62 shares of stock. Given that the price of the bond is unity in the assumed environment with a riskless interest rate of zero, and that the price of the stock is $100.00 at time 0, the cost of this position is the value of the put in the first example, that is, $52.38 - 47.62 = 4.76$. This investment position is now carried forward

---

[14]Constructing a synthetic put is more complex than buying an ordinary put. But it can be a useful technique if either ordinary puts are mispriced, or if one is trying to insure an asset on which no puts are traded. In contrast to the first two examples, this one generates just the put payoffs themselves, thus focusing on the transactions needed to create the synthetic put.

TABLE 14.5 Values of Synthetic Put

Time 2	121.00
0.0000	0.00
0.0000	0.00
	0.00
End	

Time 1	110.00
0.5238	52.38
−0.4762	−52.38
	0.00
0.0000	0.00
0.0000	0.00
	0.00

Time 0	100.00
0.0476	4.76
0.0000	0.00
	4.76
0.5238	52.38
−0.4762	−47.62
	4.76

Time 2	100.00
0.0000	52.38
0.0000	−52.38
	0.00
End	

Time 1	90.91
0.5238	52.38
−0.4762	−43.29
	9.09
1.0000	100.00
−1.0000	−90.91
	9.09

Time 2	82.64
1.0000	100.00
−1.0000	−82.64
	17.36
End	

to time 1, when it is to be rebalanced. Consider the two possible time 1 situations.

Suppose first that the price rises at time 1 to $110.00. There is no longer any need to have downside protection between times 1 and 2, because the value of the stock cannot fall below the target of $100.00. Therefore, to cover the short position, 47.62 shares of stock are purchased at $110.00 per share, for a cost of $52.38, which is just equal to the value of the long bond position. At this point, then, the amount invested in the synthetic put is equal to zero, and of course that value will be obtained at time 2 whether the stock price rises further or falls back to $100.00.

TABLE 14.6 Key to Security Positions at Each Time Point

Time, Share price		
Before rebalancing	Number of bonds	Value of bonds
Before rebalancing	Number of shares	Value of shares
		Value of synthetic put
After rebalancing	Number of bonds	Value of bonds
After rebalancing	Number of shares	Value of shares
		Value of synthetic put

Now suppose instead the stock price falls to $90.91 at time 1. The original position now has a value of $52.38 − .4762($90.91) = $52.38 − $43.29 = $9.09. Then the investor wants the synthetic put to provide value at time 2 if the stock were to fall further still, and to do that the investor increases his short position to one share of the stock, using the proceeds of the short sale to increase his bond holdings to 1. The investor achieves this by selling 0.5238 shares of stock to realize 0.5238($90.91) = $47.62, and adds this amount to his bond holdings. Then if the stock price rises to $100.00 at time 2, the put position is worth nothing, but if the stock falls to $82.64, his cost of covering the short position is $82.64, and he realizes $100.00 from selling the bonds, for a net profit of $17.36. Thus with this synthetic arrangement he obtains the same insurance against downside risk as with the original put purchase illustrated earlier.

Portfolio Insurance: Practice

The most important practical feature illustrated by the last example is that if at time 1 stock prices rise, the put position is adjusted by purchasing more stock, while if at time 1 stock prices fall, maintaining the put requires additional short selling. Moreover, maintaining the synthetic put position assumes that the investor can trade immediately, without transactions costs, at the market prices assumed. In practice trading immediately at the assumed price may not be possible, particularly if many portfolio insurers are trying to sell at the same time and depressing prices as a result. In other words, maintaining portfolio insurance in practice will be less than wholly successful unless the assumptions of the underlying theory are satisfied. But these assumptions essentially assume perfect markets, and in practice markets may not satisfy those assumptions. For example, prior to the stock market declines of October 19, 1987, advocates of portfolio insurance did not always contemplate situations in which turbulent market conditions would impede trading securities at or near their theoretical values, and therefore had not worked out contingency plans to deal with such situations.[15]

As a further comment on practice, a portfolio manager will usually employ derivatives such as stock index futures to insure a portfolio. Index futures are used in place of the puts discussed previously because the markets in which index futures are traded are larger, subject to fewer limits, have longer maturities, and are less costly than puts (Fabozzi and Modigliani 1992, 318). But despite these advantages, the theoretical benefits of insured portfolios can only be approximated in practice because it is not always possible to trade instantaneously at market prices. Indeed, portfolio insurance schemes work better under normal trading conditions than when markets are turbulent. When securities markets exhibit rapid price change and atypically high trading volumes, market prices for options and futures can deviate substantially from their theoretically predicted values, making it difficult or impossible to trade quickly at or near those values.

On the other hand, the more efficient markets become the smaller the deviations between actual and theoretical prices are likely to be. In an increasingly efficient market, arbitrage works increasingly well and increasingly faster. Hence, if impediments to efficient market trading can be removed or lessened, portfolio insurance schemes' actual performance will more closely approximate theoretical predictions. Some of the impediments—constraints on trading capacity, slow settlement procedures, and separate settlement procedures for each exchange—are being ameliorated as exchanges expand their capacity to handle high volumes of trading and as they change settlement procedures and interexchange arrangements.

At the same time, there can also be other complications. Portfolio risks might change unpredictably subsequent to setting up the trading plan. Market volatility can change quite rapidly through time, and the changes may even be exacerbated by risk management tactics. For example, as predictions of volatility change a portfolio insurer may take a larger position in options to protect himself against risk, in a transaction known as "delta hedging." The difficulty with such transactions is shown by the following argument. Suppose that asset prices fall. The hedger then increases purchases of puts, increasing the cost of the insurance represented by the put. These increased costs may in turn place more downward pressure on the asset price. These pressures would not exist if markets were sufficiently liquid. However, in

---

[15] As discussed at later points in this book, the credit crisis of 2007–2008 also violates the perfect markets assumptions, and the results to this writing have been highly disruptive.

some cases there may not be enough traders on one side of the market—say, the side willing to sell puts—to offset the transactions offered by the other side of the market—the side trying to hedge the risks by buying puts. The situation is further complicated if agents view the price process as being affected by other traders whose actions they cannot predict (see Bookstaber 2007, Caballero and Krishnamurthy 2008).

MUTUAL FUNDS

Mutual funds (investment companies in the United Kingdom and some other countries) are financial intermediaries that sell shares to the public and invest the proceeds in diversified securities portfolios. From the viewpoint of small investors, their principal advantage is to provide the kinds of diversification service explained by the CAPT and APT at lower costs than individuals could achieve on their own.

Characteristics

There are three main types of mutual fund: open-end, closed-end, and unit trusts. The shares of open-end funds are sold to the public on a continuing basis, while a closed-end fund has fixed capitalization. *Open-end funds* operate according to two fee bases: load funds for which investors pay a commission to acquire the shares, and no-load funds for which there is no sales commission. In order to cover their operating costs,[16] no-load funds usually charge a higher annual administration fee than load funds. *Closed-end funds* issue nonredeemable shares that are generally traded on the over-the-counter market, although some are listed on stock exchanges. A unit trust is set up for a fixed period of time, issues trust units to the public, and typically holds the same security portfolio for its lifetime. It is like a form of closed-end fund whose portfolio is not actively changed and whose shares do not trade.

The shares of open-end funds trade at a price determined by their net asset value per share. Open-end funds usually make a market in their own shares, selling them to the public on a continuing basis and buying them back at prices determined by the net asset value per share. The shares of closed-end funds trade either on exchanges or in the over-the-counter market. Typically,

---

[16] Saunders (2000, 68) states that U.S. load funds charge no annual administration fee, while no-load funds charge sales fees that are sometimes as high as 8.5%.

the shares of closed-end funds sell at a discount from their net asset value, but as the price is determined by investor demand relative to the existing supply, the shares can and sometimes do sell at a premium over net asset value. The shares of unit trusts do not usually trade, but are retained by their original purchasers until the fund is wound up.

Mutual funds pursue a variety of goals. Some emphasize growth stocks, others mixed portfolios of bonds and stocks, still others just bonds. The principal advantage offered by any investment fund is that it can be a low-cost way to invest in a diversified portfolio. However, many studies show that mutual funds usually earn a return, after adjusting for administration expenses, no greater than that on a comparable market index portfolio. Nevertheless, investors are attracted to funds that offer the prospect of relatively lucrative returns. For example, in the late 1980s and early 1990s sales of mutual funds were exceptionally large. While new sales fell off and redemptions increased in the early 1990s, subsequently new sales strengthened and during the latter 1990s mutual funds became an increasingly popular vehicle for household savings. Sales rose in the early to mid-2000s, but have declined in 2007–2008.

Why Small Investors Buy Mutual Funds

Small investors purchase mutual funds because it can be cheaper than investing on their own, in part because mutual funds can realize scale economies both in research and in trading costs. To see the influence of both these factors, consider the following model.

Assume there are no taxes or marginal transactions costs, and that borrowing and short selling are both unrestricted. Investors choose between a riskless security numbered 0 and a risky security numbered 1. The riskless security offers a sure return r. The risky security is assumed to have returns that follow

$$R_1 = E(R_1) + b_1 Y$$

where $E(Y) = 0$ and $\sigma^2(Y) = 1$. Security 1 thus offers an expected return $E(R_1)$ with variance $\sigma^2(R_1) = b_1{}^2$. The riskless security can be interepreted as a government bond, the risky security as either a single security or a market index portfolio.[17]

---

[17] The model can easily be expanded to incorporate many securities, but one risky security will display the principles involved.

Each investor selects a portfolio that maximizes a Markowitz-Tobin mean-variance function of end-period wealth

$$U = E(RW) - \delta VAR(RW)/2W \qquad (14.10)$$

where W denotes the (common) value of each investor's initial wealth, R is the return per dollar on an investor's portfolio, and the risk aversion parameter is δ, $\delta > 0$. Investor choice is limited to securities 0 and 1.

Let w_1 denote the fraction of investor wealth allocated to security 1. Portfolio return is

$$R_I = r + w_1(E(R_1) - r) + w_1 b_1 Y \qquad (14.11)$$

where I refers to an investor-purchased portfolio combining the riskless and risky securities. The risk factor Y is scaled so that $E(Y) = 0$ and $\sigma^2(Y) = 1$. Since there are only two securities, the weights of the two investments add up to the amount of wealth which can be placed in the portfolio, that is, $w_0 + w_1 = 1$. Then

$$\sigma^2(R_I) = w_1^2 b_1^2$$

and

$$E(R_I) = r + w_1[E(R_1 - r)]. \qquad (14.12)$$

The investor's portfolio problem can thus be written

$$\max_w \{E(R_I) - \delta\sigma^2(R_I)/2\}$$

subject to

$$w_0 + w_1 = 1$$

The necessary optimality condition is

$$0 = [E(R_I) - r] - \delta w_1^1 b_1^2 \qquad (14.13)$$

where w_1^I indicates the optimal investment in security 1, given that only securities 0 and 1 are available to be purchased. The individual investor's demand for risky investment is

$$W w_1^I = W[E(R_1) - r]/\delta b_1^2 \qquad (14.14)$$

and her demand for the riskless investment is $W(1 - w_1{}^I)$. Substituting (3.5) into (3.4) gives the investor's derived utility

$$U(W) \equiv W\{r + [(E(R_1) - r)^2/2\delta b_1{}^2]\} \equiv WR_I > Wr \qquad (14.15)$$

Suppose an investor proceeding on his own must pay a fixed cost to buy the risky security. Since there is no cost to buying the riskless security, an investor with wealth W faces the choice of either investing W in the riskless security, or $W - \lambda$ in a utility maximizing portfolio composed of securities 0 and 1. If the investor purchases only security 0, her derived utility is WR. If she purchases securities 0 and 1, from (3.5) her derived utility is

$$U(W) = (W - \lambda)w_1^I = (W - \lambda)R_I > (W - \lambda)r$$

If the setup costs are paid, the derived utility remains linear in wealth, but has a steeper slope than the derived utility for investment in just the riskless security.

Suppose the alternative to purchasing the portfolio on one's own is to purchase a mutual fund. The mutual fund is available without paying any setup cost, but its expected return is diminished by a transaction cost c, representing an administration charge. The administration charge will change the weights of the risky and the riskless securities, and the derived utility for the mutual fund investment is the following version of equation (14.15):

$$U(W) \equiv W\{r + [(E(R_1) - c - r)^2/2\delta b_1{}^2]\} \equiv WR_M < WR_I$$

The investor must now compare $(W - \lambda)R_I$ with WR_M. It is easily seen that the two values are equal when W satisfies:

$$WR_M = (W - \lambda)R_I$$

or

$$W^* = \lambda R_I/(R_I - R_M)$$

Now for $W < W^*$ the mutual fund will be cheaper, while for $W \geq W^*$ the investor will be better off paying the lump sum charge λ. That is, an investor can save on fixed investment costs if she is not purchasing a large portfolio, but will be able to save more on administration charges by looking after her own portfolio if her invested wealth is sufficiently great.

In practice, investors are also influenced in their mutual fund purchases by marketing efforts. Sirri and Tufano (1998) find that consumers use prior performance information in making fund purchases. They do so asymmetrically in that they make relatively large proportionate purchases of funds that have done well in the past. Search costs are also an important determinant of investment decisions, in that consumers are influenced by favorable financial press coverage and by marketing efforts. In addition, consumers are likely to invest in funds belonging to well-known large groups of funds.

Exchange-Traded Funds

An exchange-traded fund (ETF) offers the advantages of a mutual fund but trades like a stock. That is, an ETF represents a basket of stocks that reflect an index such as the S&P 500. Unlike a mutual fund whose net-asset value is calculated at the end of each trading day, an ETF's price changes throughout the day, fluctuating with supply and demand. An ETF thus combines the diversification of an index fund with the flexibility of a stock. In particular, ETFs can be purchased in small quantities, sold short, and bought on margin. Those who prefer to use ETFs as investment vehicles argue that many mutual funds' administrative charges are greater than any returns that the fund can generate over and above a market index. While exchange-traded funds do not charge administration fees, transactions costs comparable to brokers' fees are charged for purchases or sales.

Exchange-traded funds thus appeal to investors who seek returns similar to those of market indexes and who prefer not to pay the administration charges levied by most mutual funds. According to a survey of investment professionals a majority of respondents called ETF "the most innovative investment vehicle" of the period 1988–2008, and also reported that ETFs have "fundamentally changed" the way they assemble their investment portfolios.[18]

In essence, when comparing a mutual fund with an exchange-traded fund, an investor compares a marginal administration charge on each dollar invested with a fixed cost of purchasing (and subsequently selling) an exchange-traded fund.[19] Clearly, the advantages of exchange-traded funds

---

[18] "ETFs Changing the Way Advisors Do Business, According to State Street and Wharton Study," *BusinessWire.com,* June 10, 2008.

[19] The comparison is most straightforward if the mutual fund is a no-load fund. If it also charges a loading fee, then it is the mutual fund's combination of fixed and variable cost that must be compared with the fixed transactions charges of the exchange-traded fund.

relative to mutual funds depend on the amount invested. Assuming the returns on the two funds are comparable, an investor with a small amount of funds may find it advantageous to incur the marginal costs of a mutual fund, while an investor with a large amount of funds may find it advantageous to incur the fixed costs of purchasing an exchange-traded fund.

The comparison between an index and an exchange-traded fund is not necessarily exact, however. Cherry (2004) points out that ETFs consistently trade away from their net asset value. Cherry finds further that ETFs are about 17% more volatile than their underlying assets, and that about 70% of this excess volatility can be explained by proxies for transaction and holding costs that limit successful arbitrage. In other words, the anomalies reported by Cherry are to a considerable extent explained by the recognition that arbitrage is not usually without cost.

HEDGE FUNDS

Hedge funds are pooled investment vehicles that invest in publicly traded securities. A hedge fund's managers are rewarded for improving fund performance, and thus face greater incentives to earn profits than do the managers of many mutual funds. Moreover, the managers of a hedge fund are typically substantial investors in the fund, and the fund itself is often organized as a limited partnership or limited liability company. As a result hedge fund managers are motivated to use leverage more aggressively than other portfolio managers, and for the most part follow relatively short-term investment strategies. Investors can withdraw their capital, but in many funds withdrawals are subject to lock-up periods and notice requirements, meaning that fund liquidity can be a key concern for investors.

Pure arbitrage hedge funds attempt to exploit observed price anomalies in a riskless fashion. For example, recall the payoff identity

$$\mathbf{X} \equiv \mathbf{k} + (\mathbf{X} - \mathbf{k})^+ - \mathbf{P}(\mathbf{X}, \ \mathbf{k})^+$$

and, in the absence of arbitrage opportunities, the corresponding value identity

$$v(X) \equiv k/(1 + r) + C(\mathbf{X}, \ k) - P(\mathbf{X}, \ k)$$

Ignoring bid-ask spreads and other market imperfections for the sake of simplicity, the classical hedge fund transaction would trade on value discrepancies. For example, if the stock and a put can be purchased for less than the sure payment and a call, the arbitrageur would buy the former and sell the latter. The price difference would create an immediate profit, and the position would be self-liquidating on maturity of the instruments.

Since observable price inefficiencies tend to be quite small, pure arbitrage requires large, usually leveraged investments and high turnover. Moreover, if an arbitrage strategy is successful, it gets duplicated and its profitability gradually disappears. In practice, hedge funds' trading strategies are more complex and riskier than pure arbitrage. For example, convertible arbitrage entails buying a corporate convertible bond, which can be converted into common shares, while simultaneously selling short the common stock of the same company that issued the bond. The arbitrageur hopes to profit from the bond if the rises in price, and to profit from the short sale if the stock declines. However, as the convertible bond and the stock can move independently, the arbitrageur can lose on both the bond and the stock, which means the position carries risk.

A hedge fund's capital consists of equity supplied by the partners and possibly some long-term debt financing that can be relied on in times of crisis. Most funds raise their capital through private offerings, in which case they need not be registered as investment companies. A hedge fund does not usually issue long-term unsecured bonds, but larger funds may obtain medium-term bank loans or lines of credit, and by the mid-2000s some funds had begun to issue combinations of bonds and permanent equity.

Larger investment bankers offer a special group of services, known as prime brokerage services, to hedge funds and other special clients.[20] The main source of leverage for hedge funds is collateralized borrowing from prime brokers. A hedge fund with a long position in shares can borrow against the shares but must also put up some of its own capital, the margin requirement, and margin requirements differ according to market conditions. A hedge fund must also provide some of its own capital in a short sale (it has to borrow the security), and even positions in exchange traded options must be backed by a certain amount of capital. The terms of these financings are subject to negotiation and hidden to outsiders. Hedge fund positions are marked to market and margins may have to be adjusted in the event the value of the position declines. The margin requirements themselves are negotiated between hedge funds and their brokers in a way that makes broker loans almost risk-free.

Brunnermeier and Nagel (2004) investigate hedge fund trading during the technology bubble of the late 1990s and early 2000s. The authors conclude that hedge funds did not exert a correcting force on stock prices during

---

[20] Hedge funds have been the principal impetus for providing prime brokerage services, mainly because they place large trades that frequently need special attention.

that time, but rather were heavily invested in technology stocks. Hedge funds were apparently aware of the bubble, since they captured the upturn, and by reducing their positions in stocks that were about to decline, avoided much of the downturn. The authors conclude that their findings question the efficient markets notion that rational speculators stabilize prices. Rather, their findings support the notion that rational investors ride bubbles because of predictable investor sentiment and limits to arbitrage.

Fung, Hsieh, Naik, and Ramadorai (2008) use a comprehensive data set of funds-of-funds to investigate performance, risk, and capital formation in the hedge fund industry from 1995 to 2004. While the average fund-of-funds delivered excess returns only in the period between October 1998 and March 2000, a subset consistently delivers excess returns. Such funds are less likely to liquidate than those delivering no excess returns, and experience far greater and steadier capital inflows. On the other hand, the capital inflows attenuate the ability of the funds to continue delivering excess returns.

Hedge funds are not usually regulated with respect to registration, investment positions, liquidity, and fee structure, nor are they typically registered with bodies such as the SEC. They can usually avoid registration by limiting the number of investors and requiring that the investors be accredited, which means they meet an income or net worth standard. On the other hand, many jurisdictions do regulate how hedge funds can market their investments and solicit participations. Cumming and Que (2008) analyze the flow-performance relationship for hedge funds, finding that such regulations as restrictions on distribution channels mitigate the impact of performance on fund flows, while distribution channels via investment managers and fund distribution companies enhance the impact. Funds registered in countries with larger minimum capitalization requirements for funds have higher levels of capital flows, and funds registered in countries that restrict the location of key service providers have lower levels. The data also suggest that tax factors influence fund flows.

VALUE AT RISK

Value at risk (VaR) is a measure of market risk originally developed by JPMorgan in the 1980s. Since the 1980s VaR has been widely used by both portfolio managers and banks as a measure of the risks they are facing during business-as-usual periods.[21] VaR attempts to reflect the maximum amount

---

[21] Moreover, VaR is a part of the new Basel II regime on bank capital adequacy, as discussed in Chapter 22.

of money a portfolio manager can expect to lose with a given probability, say maximum losses all but 1% of the time. However, the important losses faced by any portfolio manager occur during that 1% of the time, a time whose probability is often called the "long tail" of risk. VaR calculations typically use data from the preceding three or four years of business, and thus tend to reflect less risk as business operates smoothly for longer periods. That is, VaR measures based on loss experience during past business-as-usual periods are not particularly useful for predicting future losses if the economic environment has changed.

Portfolio managers have sometimes taken inappropriate comfort in VaR measures and have failed to ask where losses might be hidden if the assumptions of their VaR calculations were to change. That is, VaR helps create a belief that once risks have been quantified, they can be managed. In addition, VaR can contribute to dynamic instability. Episodes of volatility increase VaR, which in turn triggers moves to sell, creating still further volatility. Fair-value accounting, which requires assets to be valued at current market prices, also accentuates price movements because marking assets down to lower market prices can stimulate further selling. Recent difficulties in the CDO market have displayed exactly these characteristics (Bookstaber 2007).

REFERENCES

Benninga, Simon. 2008. *Financial Modeling*, 3rd ed. Cambridge, MA: MIT Press.

Bookstaber, Richard. 2007. *A Demon of Our Own Design*. Hoboken, NJ: John Wiley & Sons.

Brunnermeier, Markus K., and Stefan Nagel. 2004. Hedge funds and the technology bubble. *Journal of Finance* 59: 2,013–2,040.

Caballero, Ricardo, and Arvind Krishnamurthy. 2008. Collective risk management in a flight to quality episode. *Journal of Finance* 61: 2,195–2,230.

Cheng, Pao L., and Robert Grauer. 1980. An alternative test of the capital asset pricing model. *American Economic Review* 70: 660–671.

Chen, Nai-Fu, Richard Roll, Stephen Ross (1986). "Economic Forces and the Stock Market." *Journal of Business* 59 (3): 383–403.

Cherry, Josh. 2004. The limits of arbitrage: Evidence from exchange traded funds. Working Paper, University of California, Berkeley, Department of Economics.

Cumming, Douglas, and Li Que. 2008. Capital flows and hedge fund regulation. Paper delivered to the International Finance Conference, Queen's University.

Fabozzi, Frank J., and Franco Modigliani. 1992. *Capital Markets: Institutions and Instruments*. Englewood Cliffs, NJ: Prentice-Hall.

Fung, William, David A. Hsieh, Narayan Y. Naik, and Tarun Ramadorai. 2008. "Hedge funds: Performance, risk, and capital formation." *Journal of Finance* 63: 1,777–1,804.

Huang, Chi-Fu, and Robert H. Litzenberger. 1988. *Foundations for Financial Economics*. New York: North-Holland.

McInish, Thomas H. 2000. *Capital Markets: A Global Perspective*. Oxford: Blackwell.

Roll, Richard. 1977. A critique of the asset pricing theory: Part I. On the past and potential testability of the theory. *Journal of Financial Economics* 4: 129–176.

Ross, Stephen A. 1976. The arbitrage theory of asset pricing. *Journal of Economic Theory* 13. 341–360.

Saunders, Anthony M. 2000. *Financial Institutions Management*, third edition. Boston, MA. Irwin McGraw-Hill.

Sirri, Erik R., and Peter Tufano. 1998. Costly search and mutual fund flows. *Journal of Finance* 53: 1,589–1,622.

Stambaugh, Robert F. 1982. On the exclusion of assets from tests of the two-parameter model. *Journal of Financial Economics* 10: 237–268.

TERMS

closed-end fund   A mutual fund with a fixed capitalization. The shares of a closed-end fund may trade either on an exchange or in the over-the-counter market.

open-end fund   A mutual fund or investment company that continuously issues shares in response to demand for them. An open-end fund will also redeem shares at the current market value of the investment.

Nonmarketable Securities Portfolios

For portfolios of nonmarketable assets, governance presents all the tasks discussed in Chapter 14 except active trading, which is supplanted by a need for relatively more intense monitoring. In addition, there is a greater need for control and adjustment: If monitoring indicates some investment is presenting potential difficulty, the portfolio manager may find it necessary to influence operations of the firms in question. Still further, forward-looking governance of illiquid assets involves planning how to avoid liquidity crises and hence avoid the need to sell assets under pressure. Chapter 15 begins by explaining the importance of distinguishing market and default risk. It then discusses how governance of nonmarketable securities uses techniques for managing portfolio income and portfolio risk. The evolution of securitization is discussed, including the changing nature of mortgage pools. Finally default insurance, the use of credit derivatives and credit default swaps are discussed.

CHARACTERISTICS OF ILLIQUID PORTFOLIOS

Managing portfolios of nonmarketable securities involves governing illiquid investments that cannot readily be traded at prices close to their estimated value. The governance tasks differ according to whether the illiquid instruments are assets or liabilities: Governance of an insurance company portfolio containing mostly liquid assets and illiquid liabilities differs considerably from governance of a bank with mostly illiquid assets and liquid liabilities.[1]

---

[1]While most bank deposits are not market-traded instruments, the interest rates on them may change regularly with market conditions.

One of the major concerns for the insurance company is to assess the probability distributions of the liabilities it writes, while a major concern for the bank is to assess the default risk of the loans it makes. Moreover, banks raise large proportions of their funds as short-term deposit liabilities, and can thus face short-term funding problems that insurance companies are much less likely to encounter. Since the present chapter is concerned mainly with investment portfolios, it focuses on acquiring and governing asset positions. In this context portfolio governance mainly involves ex ante screening of assets, funding their acquisition, supervising the resulting holdings, and, as far as possible, tailoring the resulting portfolio income. Governance further involves ex post monitoring, and can involve adjusting the operations of firms whose assets are showing declines in quality. Issues related to managing liabilities will be considered further in Chapters 16 through 18.

Market Risk versus Default Risk

Managing an illiquid asset portfolio involves making a practical distinction between market risk and default risk. *Market risk* refers to the probability that securities values will change as markets adjust to new information and as trading conditions change,[2] while *default risk* refers to the possibility of suffering capital losses on investments held. Under normal trading conditions market risk refers to relatively small changes in value stemming from fluctuations in business as usual, while default risk refers to relatively larger loss possibilities stemming from longer-term changes in assets' income generating capabilities. Changes in market risk usually exhibit frequent changes over the short term while changes in default risk are more likely to be recognized only episodically.

Market and default risk reflect differences in degree of a security's liquidity: Liquid securities are principally subject to market risk since any change in information regarding asset value is usually reflected quickly in the securities' prices.[3] On the other hand, when securities are illiquid there is no reliable market price to reflect changes in expected earnings or changes in creditworthiness. For example, the loans or investments held by intermediaries are typically recorded at their nominal values unless and until it appears they are likely to default, at which time they may be sharply reduced in value or even written off entirely.

---

[2]As already mentioned, changes in market risk can be abrupt and significant during times of market crises.

[3]The issue is more than one of just failing to update the books to reflect changes in value. In some cases the intermediary can be unaware of any changes in potential value until default is imminent.

Financiers do not usually possess capabilities for assessing both market risk and default risk equally well, and the differences are quite frequently illustrated in practice.[4] The capabilities of commercial bankers have historically been greater with respect to assessing default risks, while the capabilities of investment bankers have historically been greater with respect to assessing market risk. The governance structures appropriate for managing market risk are not as useful for performing the screening, monitoring, and subsequent adjustment tasks of managing default risk. Governance of portfolios subject to default risk requires monitoring and control capabilities, that is, capabilities for valuing future earnings prospects and for influencing them where possible.

Investment bankers sometimes use their own capital to take longer-term positions in shares, and in doing so assume default risks with which they are unfamiliar. In the 1980s and even more notably in the later 2000s, substantial losses were incurred by investment bankers taking what they intended to be temporary positions. One factor contributing to their exposure was competing for merger and acquisition business, which usually brings very lucrative fees. In arranging a merger, the acquiring company needs funds to purchase the shares of the target company. Temporary or bridging finance may be provided by an investment banker who purchases the acquiring company's shares. These investment bankers expect to help the acquirer arrange longer-term financing which can then be used to redeem the investment bankers' investment. However, raising the longer-term financing sometimes proves difficult, and the investment bankers in effect become longer-term investors in the firm. A second factor contributing to unusual exposures stemmed from trading CDOs, CMOs, and other structured investments in the early and mid-2000s. Investment bankers acquired large inventories of these instruments with the intent of trading them at or near their then market values. However when the securities became illiquid in the later 2000s they were unable to do so without suffering heavy trading losses.

Governance

Investments perceived to be illiquid have historically been subjected to more intense ex ante screening than have their more liquid counterparts. Large portfolios of nonmarketable assets have historically been assembled by lending intermediaries. Unlike investors in marketable securities, lending intermediaries usually intend to hold the assets until the deal is paid off, not

---

[4]See, for example, "Confessions of a Risk Manager," *The Economist*, August 9, 2008.

only because the assets are difficult and costly to trade, but also because they require continuing close governance.[5] To illustrate the governance issues involved, consider the differences between a government bond and a residential mortgage loan. A bond whose return is evolving unfavorably can usually be sold (although possibly at a capital loss) and the proceeds reinvested. On the other hand, a mortgage loan is both less liquid and on a proportional basis presents a wider range of loss possibilities. After origination a mortgage loan presenting repayment difficulties cannot generally be sold off, but will rather present problems of collecting payments or of selling the underlying property.[6] With regard to differences in risk, the return distributions on two mortgage loans will typically differ more from each other than will the return distributions on two government bonds. As a result, mortgage loans require more intensive and specialized ex ante monitoring after they have been placed on an intermediary's books.

Diversification

Even though some of their individual loans or investments may be proportionately large, intermediaries still try to diversify their default risks, but diversifying illiquid assets is more difficult than diversifying their liquid counterparts. The examples of Chapter 14 show theoretically that a portfolio of statistically independent risks has a lower risk-return ratio than do the individual risks.[7] In practice intermediaries mainly place their funds in small loans of heterogeneous quality that are usually positively correlated rather than statistically independent or negatively correlated, meaning that diversification possibilities can be fairly limited. Moreover, since most assets

---

[5]As discussed later, the practice of securitizing nonmarketable assets is becoming widespread, as is the practice of obtaining default insurance on them. Recent experience, discussed in this chapter, suggests that both securitization and the use of default insurance attenuate the incentives to conduct close governance, and these changes have led to some serious adverse selection problems that have contributed to increases in default risk.

[6]Many residential mortgage loans in the United States are nonrecourse loans, which means the householder's obligation is limited to the lesser of the amount owed or the value of the mortgaged property. In most other countries, householder obligations extend to the amount of the outstanding mortgage, even if that is greater than the value of the property. Clearly, there is a greater default risk to a nonrecourse loan: If the value of the property falls below the unpaid mortgage balance, the householder has strong incentives to default.

[7]Theoretical analyses do not usually distinguish income from default risk, nor do they distinguish market risk from default risk.

are held until maturity, portfolio risk is heavily influenced by the ways assets are screened in making initial loan decisions.

Thus intermediaries seek the benefits of diversification through managing loan origination rather than by trading marketable securities. One way of doing so is to limit the amounts invested in particular asset categories. For example, intermediaries who specialize in real estate lending within a given region can face severe solvency problems if they lend only in that region and if real estate values then decline. Intermediaries also have another traditional means of diversifying—that of syndicating larger loans. In effect, syndication means arranging for loans to be made by several intermediaries rather than by just one. However, this tactic is not available in the cases of small individual loans that, because of fixed transactions costs, cannot economically be divided and resold.[8] Similarly, insurance companies diversify certain kinds of nonmarket liabilities by limiting the amounts of insurance they will write against different events, such as hurricane damage.

MANAGING EARNINGS RISK

Intermediaries[9] also attempt to manage portfolio earnings risks. They manage the interest terms of individual deals, such as whether the interest rate on a loan will be fixed or floating. At the portfolio level intermediaries use *asset-liability matching* (a form of internal hedging), interest-rate swaps, futures contracts, and *credit derivatives*. Interest-rate terms, asset-liability matching, and interest-rate derivatives are used principally for income management, while credit derivatives and *credit default swaps* are mainly used to transfer default risk to third parties. Asset-liability matching and some swap transactions are wholesale, involving transactions in the whole of the portfolio and are either managed on the intermediary's books or arranged by negotiation. Other techniques, such as market trading of derivatives as discussed in Chapters 7 and 14, are more likely to be used in smaller volumes, as in managing part of a portfolio or in individual transactions with clients.

---

[8]Portfolios of these loans can be securitized, as discussed later. Whether securitization can diversify default risk depends essentially on the instruments used for securitization. Securitized loans may also be covered by default insurance, in which case the transfer of risks depends on the instruments used. Finally, in some cases intermediaries have had to take back risks they thought they had transferred. All of these effects are discussed at later points in this chapter.

[9]Managers of marketable securities portfolios may also use some of the techniques now being discussed, but for brevity those applications are only sketched here.

Asset-Liability Matching

Risk-return trade-offs can be assessed for an asset-liability portfolio, an asset portfolio, or a liability portfolio. Consider an intermediary asset-liability portfolio. Its income risk can be reduced if assets' interest-rate earnings are positively correlated with liabilities' interest-rate costs.[10] Indeed, the resulting income stream can be close to riskless if the correlation is close to being perfectly positive, because in this case fluctuations in earnings are mostly offset by fluctuations in costs.

Asset-liability matching is one way of realizing the positive correlation just mentioned. Matching refers to borrowing and lending on essentially the same interest-rate terms. It does not typically involve market trading of the original assets or liabilities, nor does it typically involve derivatives transactions. Matching practices are commonplace in both domestic and international banking transactions. For example, intermediaries use asset-liability matching when funding a floating rate loan with floating rate deposits. If asset-liability matching is to be completely effective, the amounts of assets and liabilities having the same interest terms must be equal. If the amounts are unequal, say because of differing market conditions on the asset and on the liability side of the balance sheet, then a residual risk will remain. In some cases intermediaries simply assume the residual risk, particularly if they believe a short-term trend in interest rates will work in their favor. In other cases, the residual risks will be hedged using interest rate swaps or by trading derivative securities.

Interest-Rate Swaps

Interest rate swaps may either be market-traded or individually negotiated between banks and other institutions. Market-traded swaps are standard contracts that trade in an institutional (OTC) market rather than on an exchange. Larger, less standard transactions are usually negotiated between counterparties. [11]

To understand how income risks can be hedged using a swap, consider two future patterns of interest earnings, both as viewed from the perspective of time 0. Suppose Bank A has fixed rate loans and floating rate deposits, both in the amount of $100.00, while Bank B has floating rate loans and

---

[10] A perfect positive correlation between interest revenues and interest costs has the same effect as a perfect negative correlation between earnings on two different securities.

[11] Whether such transactions are privately negotiated or arranged in markets depends on transaction features discussed in Chapter 3.

TABLE 15.1 Net Earnings of Two Banks, before Swap

Rate Scenario	Bank A		Bank B	
(Time 1, Time 2)	Time 1	Time 2	Time 1	Time 2
High, High	$3.00	$3.00	$5.00	$5.00
High, Low	$3.00	$5.00	$5.00	$3.00
Low, High	$5.00	$3.00	$3.00	$5.00
Low, Low	$5.00	$5.00	$3.00	$3.00

fixed rate deposits, also both in the amount of $100.00. Suppose the average deposit rate is 6%, while the average loan rate is 10%. Fixed rate arrangements remain in force for the two periods, but floating interest rates can change randomly from one time period to the next. Suppose, to keep the example simple, that floating interest rates can be either high or low in each of the two periods, where high means 1% above the average, and low means 1% below the average. The floating rates on the deposits of Bank A and on the loans of Bank B are assumed to be perfectly positively correlated, being high together or low together. The earnings on the two banks' portfolios, when interest rates follow the patterns indicated, are shown in Table 15.1.

Assuming for simplicity that all rate scenarios are equally likely, expected net earnings will be $4.00 per period for either bank. Inspection of Table 15.1 also shows that when one bank's net earnings are low, the others are high, and vice versa. Clearly, if Bank A were to pay Bank B $1.00 when the earnings of Bank A were high, and if Bank B were to pay Bank A when the earnings of Bank B were high, both could report steady earnings of $4.00 in each time period. Note that if the four scenarios are equally likely, the expected value of the payments in either direction is zero, so that one bank would not gain an advantage for which a compensating payment was required. The advantage of the swap is that it stabilizes the net interest earnings of both institutions, and reports of stable earnings may be regarded favorably by investors.[12]

As Table 15.2 indicates, an interest rate swap makes use of both a reference interest rate and a reference amount, the latter being called the notional principal.

---

[12] Proponents of perfect markets theory might object that since risks can be diversified in the financial markets, there is no advantage to using the swap contract just mentioned. Recall, however, that the neoclassical paradigm provides benchmark guides to practice. Not all markets are perfect, and consequently not all risks can be diversified by market trading.

TABLE 15.2 Swap Payments from Bank B to Bank A (+), from Bank A to Bank B (−)

Rate Scenario	Time 1	Time 2
High, High	$1.00	$1.00
High, Low	$1.00	−$1.00
Low, High	−$1.00	$1.00
Low, Low	−$1.00	−$1.00

A swap contract can be interpreted as a package of forward contracts with different delivery dates, that is, different maturities. Consider the payment position of Bank A at time 1, which involves receipts when its interest revenues are high, and payments when its interest revenues are low. By interpreting the net revenues of Bank A as the cash price of an asset, and supposing A has a long position in a forward contract to buy the asset at a forward price of $4.00, the time 1 payments in Table 15.1 are seen to be exactly the profit or loss on a one-period forward contract. Similarly, the payments to Bank A at time 2 are exactly the profit or loss on a two-period forward contract written on the same terms. In other words, the maturities of the two forward contracts match the times that payments are contracted under the swap.

Since swaps are not performance-guaranteed by a third party, they carry a default risk. Under scenario HL, Bank A would have no incentive to default at time 1, but would have an incentive to default before making the contracted time 2 payment to Bank B. The reader can assess the circumstances in which Bank B would have an incentive to default. The present assumption that the swap can be valued at its expected value both assumes the parties are risk neutral and ignores any possibility of default in either direction.

Interest-Rate Futures

Financial intermediaries and other agents can also trade risks in the interest futures markets. As a management technique for dealing with earnings risks, hedging through interest-rate futures can only be effected for maturities up to about a year, and for relatively small amounts of funds. It is possible to use futures contracts to hedge risks on transactions in hundreds of millions of dollars, but not in tens of billions of dollars. As a result, many common transactions of this type hedge the risk of individual deals.

For example, a financier can reduce the earnings risk of a fixed interest rate loan by balancing expected interest gains or losses against capital losses or gains on interest-rate futures. Treasury bills have market values that are negatively correlated with changes in interest rates. Similarly, futures contracts written against Treasury bills have payments streams that are negatively correlated with interest rates. Thus, a short position in Treasury bill futures has earnings that rise as interest rates rise and fall as rates fall. Hence the combination of a fixed-rate loan and a short futures position of an appropriate size behaves like a floating-rate loan. If the arrangement is funded by floating-rate deposits, the intermediary effectively matches a floating-rate loan with a floating-rate deposit. The position can be maintained up to the delivery date of the futures contract. If the delivery date is earlier than the loan's maturity, it will need to be replaced by a second contract to maintain the hedge.

Interest-rate options and options on futures contracts can also be used to hedge interest rate risks. At present in the United States, the contracts traded include Treasury bill futures, Treasury bond and note futures, Eurodollar CD futures, and futures on the bond buyer municipal bond index. Financial institutions also use the foregoing instruments to create synthetic put options and to enhance returns when futures are mispriced. Options on futures contracts, and especially over-the-counter options on futures contracts, are a preferred vehicle for implementing some investment strategies.

Other Techniques

Financial institutions use risk management instruments both on their own account and on behalf of clients. Interest rate agreements are widely used to hedge both short-term domestic and foreign currency denominated interest rate risk, and most agreements can be arranged with either investment banks or commercial banks. Typical agreements provide that in exchange for an up-front premium, one party will compensate the other if a reference rate differs from a predetermined level called the strike rate. If payment is to be made when the reference rate exceeds the strike rate, the contract is called a "cap," and if payment is to be made when the reference falls below the strike rate, it is called a "floor."[13] Still other, more exotic instruments can also be found. They include options on swap contracts (swaptions), on caps (captions) and on floors (flotions). For example, a corporate treasurer can use an interest rate cap to fix the maximum interest cost of a loan, while a collar can be used to maintain interest costs within a given band, say the current prime rate plus or minus 2%. Naturally, the selling bank or investment banker assuming the risk charges a fee for arranging the transaction.

---

[13] A collar is a combination of a cap and a floor.

MANAGING CLOSELY HELD INVESTMENTS

Some financial holding companies assemble specialized asset portfolios, as do private equity investors. Both types of investor usually make relatively small numbers of large, illiquid investments. When they purchase public issues of securities, financial holding companies usually attempt to acquire control blocks, and private equity firms typically acquire all the outstanding shares. Managing closely held investments mainly involves acquiring capabilities to govern the investments' attributes while recognizing that the investments are illiquid. The requisite capabilities include ex ante screening, monitoring the evolution of the subject firms' businesses, deciding when adjustments to operations are needed, and choosing ways to effect the adjustments. Realizing returns on the investments involves determining when and how to sell off the illiquid investment position.

Incomplete Contracting

Financiers who specialize in administering large, closely held investments often invest under uncertainty, in which case the financiers' contracts with their clients are necessarily incomplete. For example, financing a new venture—especially if it uses unproven technology—may present a spectrum of financing and operating problems that were not anticipated when the original financing was arranged. Contract incompleteness calls for a governance structure that permits making flexible responses to changing conditions. Holding a control block is one way of dealing with the incompleteness, since it permits exercising a relatively intensive form of monitoring and adjustment capabilities through attending board meetings and voting on significant decisions regarding the venture's future.

However, even a control position will not always provide the flexibility necessary to adjust to unforeseen contingencies. For example, an effective control position might be upset by a takeover bid from a third party who acquires a sufficient number of voting shares. In order to guard against such a possibility, the financier should have at least a contingency plan for the actions to be taken if a third party were to begin assembling shares in anticipation of a possible takeover bid. Complete ownership of the firm through a private equity investment is another way of managing such possibilities.

Governance Responses

The managers of large, closely held investments may be willing to experiment with unfamiliar forms of financing if they have the capability to effect subsequent contract adjustments. For example, a conglomerate financier might invest in a new kind of asset with returns that seem unrelated to those of other investments, and thus gain information as to whether additional investments of the new type could be profitable over the long run. The conglomerate financier using a governance structure capable of adjusting to originally unforeseen events may regard an uncertain investment as offering better risk-return trade-offs than it would if the funds were provided by standard forms of public financing.[14]

Nonarm's-length governance is likely to be more costly than market governance, and these greater costs should be recognized in assessing financial system efficiency. For example, consider the difference between a deal using a cheap, low-capability governance structure and one using an expensive, high-capability structure. Suppose that once the costs of the differing governance structures are recognized, the estimated risks and returns from the two transactions are the same from the perspective of public investors. Even though public investors obtain the same risk-return trade-off, the effective interest rates paid by the two firms differs since the second type of governance is assumed to be more costly. It would be easy, in such a case, to compare the clients' effective interest costs with the risk-return earnings profiles of the two financiers and conclude that the system was either operationally or allocatively inefficient. But given the circumstances assumed, neither such conclusion would be correct.

Financial Conglomerates and Private Equity

Financial conglomerates and private equity investments represent variations of closely held portfolios, both aimed at increasing the governance capabilities of the investors. The conglomerate most closely resembles joint-liability intermediation and is best suited to low-quality/high-risk projects. Stein (1997) suggests an increase in investment productivity can be created by nonmarket resource allocations of internally generated information. However, different organizational structures have different potentials for generating information about investment projects and allocating capital to projects.

---

[14] High-capability governance structures are not incompatible with an issue of marketable securities so long as the investor holds enough shares to be able to influence board decisions. In the case of venture investments taking the form of public equity issues, the public does not exercise high-capability governance. However, the venture capitalist doing the financing prior to the firm's going public probably did resort to higher-capability governance. At the time the firm goes public, there might also be some overestimation of its worth on the part of the new purchasers of the equity. The firm would, of course, want to take advantage of any overpricing of its equity because that lowers its cost of funds.

Small, single-manager firms are likely to be attractive organizational structures when information is soft, difficult to transmit credibly. Hierarchies may perform better when information is hard, easy to transmit within the firm (Stein, 2002).

"Private equity" refers to equity investment in a firm that is not publicly traded. The essence of a private equity investment is to create value through making a public firm private, provide nonarm's-length governance for a period of time, and then realize that value by taking the acquired company public once again. The invested capital for private equity is typically used to enhance operations in some way that will, given the nonarm's-length governance, secure additional value in the acquired company. One difference with a private equity investment is that dissident investors have less capability to disrupt management plans than they would if the same investment were financed through a combination of conglomerate and public market investment.

Private equity investors either invest directly in private companies or buy out public companies and delist the shares. Since private equity investment can take a long time for value creation to take place and be realized, most private equity investors are institutions or individuals who can commit large sums of money for those long periods. The amounts raised will sometimes come from a group of institutional investors who pool funds together to take very large public companies private. For example, there were several private equity purchases in excess of $30 billion during 2006 and 2007 alone.

SECURITIZATION AND GOVERNANCE

This section continues the discussion of securitization introduced in Chapters 2, 5, and 11 by considering how securitization of the illiquid assets that banks and other lenders originally acquire affects the assets' need for governance. As securitization spread throughout the world, its success frequently led to the suggestion that the practice might eventually replace the traditional model of financing through intermediaries. The view was apparently buttressed by the fact that in the earlier 2000s banks were able to make extensive use of "originate and distribute" lending, in which securitization effected the sale of the loans to a special purpose entity (SPE) and the transfer of most or all of the portfolio risks to investors in SPE-issued securities.[15] As banks relaxed their screening and monitoring activities during some of the securitizations, neither the SPEs nor the investors in SPE securities

---

[15] See the Chapter 5 discussion of CDOs and CMOs.

assumed those roles. But the theory of Chapter 3 explains that public market financings and bank financing are complementary activities requiring different forms of governance,[16] and that the different forms of governance all play valuable economic roles for different kinds of funding activities.

The problems that can arise when more intensive governance is relaxed became especially evident during the market turmoil of 2007–2008. The events showed that institutional investors' willingness to purchase SPE issues ultimately depends on confidence in the originating lender's screening and monitoring functions.[17] Obviously, ex ante screening determines the quality of the portfolio held by the SPE. Moreover, governance includes continued monitoring of the individual transactions in the underlying asset portfolio, as well as pursuing defaulters. Securitization is not a substitute for screening, monitoring, and the pursuit of defaulters, and unless those governance functions are performed loan portfolios will exhibit declining quality and increasing default risks. Therefore, securitization is no more a threat to these bank-like activities than is reinsurance a threat to the insurance company selling policies to the public.[18] If the loans are sold outright, and if the monitoring and pursuit functions are not as rigorously performed, losses on the portfolio will increase from their previous levels.

MORTGAGE POOLS

Securities issued against pools of mortgage provide a case study of the evolution of securitization, showing both its advantages and its disadvantages.

Historical Development

The U.S. residential mortgage market consists of some $10 trillion worth of mortgage loans. Approximately 75% are securitized, mainly by the

---

[16] Corporations that consistently use both public market and bank financing reflect the statically complementary roles played by the two types. If the proportions of bank and public market financing are changing, the replacement of the former by the latter reflects dynamic complementarity.

[17] Even if the default risk is insured, the insurance company will set premiums on the default risk insurance according to its estimates of how screening and monitoring are being performed.

[18] While some instruments used in securitizing are guaranteed as to principal, this does not obviate performing the screening and monitoring functions, either. The cost of the insurance depends on confidence in the intermediary's capabilities to perform its role.

government-sponsored mortgage agencies that focus on mortgage credit, Fannie Mae and Freddie Mac.[19] Most of this market involves little risk, either to the original lenders or to subsequent investors in the mortgage pools the lender creates. The original lenders face relatively minimal default risks because two-thirds of conventional mortgage borrowers enjoy good credit, have arranged a fixed interest rate mortgage, and can depend on the value of their houses remaining substantially greater than their borrowings. When mortgages are securitized, default risk may remain either the responsibility of the original lender or the specialized trust to which the mortgages are sold, depending on the terms of the arrangement. Unless the original lender continues to carry a substantial proportion of the default risk, there are few incentives to incur the costs of ex post monitoring. Even the incentives to screen the mortgages in the first place are attenuated if the original mortgages carry borrower default insurance or if the loans are to be sold on without recourse.

Institutional and other investors depend on both the high quality of the underlying mortgages and on default insurance covering the instruments they purchase. Purchasers of mortgage pool securities are not directly concerned with the original mortgages' default risk because pool-issued securities are usually tailored using different risk tranches, subject to credit ratings, and often backed by default insurance. Partly, the monitoring incentives faced by institutional investors are attenuated because they are only exposed to the percentage of default risk borne by the tranche of securities they buy. When an insurer bears most or all of the default costs, the incentives of institutional investors are further attenuated.[20] Yet the securities the institutional investors purchase may still be subject to losses if (1) the particular mortgage pool absorbs enough mortgage defaults to jeopardize the pool's solvency; (2) the particular tranche is structured to absorb some of that residual risk; and (3) any insurance guarantees are called into question.

Investors in mortgage pool securities such as *collateralized mortgage obligations* (CMOs) are less familiar with the default risks in the mortgage pool than they are with a variety of other risks. In addition to the prepayment risk discussed in Chapter 11, investors face price risk on portfolios of fixed rate (or slowly adjusting flexible rate) mortgages as interest rates increase. Moreover, investors face liquidity risk since the instruments they purchase tend to be thinly traded in secondary markets.

Indeed, the secondary market for CMOs offers examples of instruments for which detailed negotiations may become a prerequisite to consummating

---

[19] The agencies acquire the mortgages from the original lenders, form portfolios, and issue the securitization instruments against the portfolios.

[20] When the original lender sells the mortgages to a specialized trust, the incentives to monitor the portfolio are further weakened.

any trades at all.[21] Negotiations are necessary because potential counterparties have important differences of opinion regarding the value of any securities offered for trade, and there are usually few such counterparties. Trading is relatively inactive and the prices of the instruments traded are likely to exhibit significant variation around prevailing market levels. Differences in the degree of active trading affect the degree to which current prices reflect available information. For example, there may be several CMOs outstanding at the same time, but a potential investor may not find it easy to determine a competitive interest rate in that market, because the CMOs have been issued in tranches to particular investors who do not actively trade them.

The Subprime Mortgage Market

The subprime mortgage market reflects a rather extreme evolution of securitization practices that, beginning in 2007, encountered serious difficulties. Essentially, the evolving subprime market business appears to have lost sight of the need for traditional loan governance in its fervor for doing increasing amounts of business. Yet it could be argued that since the subprime market is a market for higher-risk mortgage loans, the need for governance is actually greater than in such safer traditional markets as government-sponsored FHA loans. The complete picture involves a number of details, mainly having to do with the incentives facing the various parties to the business.

Johnson and Neave (2008) attribute subprime market difficulties to an evolving mismatch between loan quality, as measured by default risk, and the loans' governance as measured by the combined risk control capabilities of lenders and investors. The market situation was exacerbated still further by dynamically increasing risks, stemming first from responses to competitive pressures, and second from adjustable rate mortgages' being reset to require higher payments. The difficulties were further compounded by the use of default insurance and risk transfers, as discussed in the next section.

The subprime market grew rapidly with the advent of credit scoring techniques, but the problems are not simply consequences of using a new technology. Indeed, technological change in the form of credit scoring had been known to lenders since at least 1980, but was first implemented in the subprime market during the late 1990s. There its application contributed to a boom, mainly because combining scoring technology with online investigation of potential borrowers' credit ratings sharply reduced mortgage application processing costs, and the profitability of placing new mortgages

---

[21] On the other hand, some are fairly liquid, and some tranches trade more actively than corporate bonds (F. J. Fabozzi, private correspondence, January 2, 2009).

therefore soared. Increased profitability led to greater competition for new placements and, as competition heightened, both mortgage brokers and mortgage lenders relaxed their approval standards in attempts to maintain newly established profit rates.

Mortgage brokers were usually paid commissions to originate loans, an arrangement that gave them little incentive to conduct ex ante screening. Mortgage lenders then granted the loans, but usually sold the portfolios of new loans to a trust. The trust acquired both the principal amounts and the default risk of the portfolio. Thus the mortgage lenders did not face strong incentives to perform ex ante loan screenings, either. Nor did they face incentives for continued monitoring of the loans. Lender fee income from securities placements rose rapidly even as the need for greater risk control at the level of the original mortgages was obscured. Compounding the problem, expanding mortgage volumes and increasingly slack approval procedures meant default risks, originally relative, were also growing.

The lender-sponsored trusts then financed their acquisitions of mortgages, principally through issuing CMOs. The CMOs were issued in tranches to tailor investors' risk-return exposure, making it more difficult for institutional investors to ascertain the exact nature of the risks they were taking on. And the same investors were particularly eager to buy what they regarded as high-quality debt instruments with attractive interest rates. Still further, default insurance on the CMOs attenuated investor incentives to assess their credit risks. Moreover, some insurers eager for business underpriced the default insurance they sold.[22] Finally, the CMOs received high quality ratings from the rating agencies. Although the rating agencies followed established procedures, their methodologies apparently overestimated the qualities of the underlying loan portfolios. [23]

The governance theory of this book implies that as a business' riskiness increases, especially if it occurs during a time of unusually rapid loan growth, risk control capabilities should also be increased. If not, subsequent defaults are likely to be greater and longer-lasting than popular opinion believes. Ironically, risk control of subprime mortgage portfolios, both new and existing, actually decreased even as loan volumes were increasing and loan quality was decreasing.

---

[22] This has not been wholly true with all insurers. For example, the monolines MBIA and Ambac were thought in 2007 to have very little subprime exposure, and to be highly conservative in issuing liabilities. In particular, they had little exposure to the largest 2007 failure, New Century (*The Economist*, July 28, 2007). However, later reports suggest that even these monolines were facing relatively large subprime-related claims by mid-2008 (*The Economist*, June 5, 2008).

[23] CDOs were also used to purchase some of the riskier CMO tranches, and these CDOs typically also received high credit ratings.

As mortgage brokers responded avidly to attractive placement profits, lenders reduced standards in order to attract additional business and thus enhance the brokers' and their own incomes. As brokers and lenders publicized their relaxed standards, they also offered teaser loans that made the loans look unusually attractive to borrowers. The teaser loans had initially low but subsequently adjustable interest rates that further exacerbated adverse selection problems when interest rates began to rise and borrowers began to default.

There are clear warning signs when a form of lending, new or traditional, grows rapidly. The signs include growing competition for new loans, relaxation of quality screening, and underemphasis of residual risks. All these warning signs are familiar to lenders, but in the subprime markets they were overlooked or ignored by nearly all the participants—mortgage brokers, mortgage lenders, the mortgage pools they created, and the institutions from which the pools raised their funds. In part the risks were overlooked because, in different ways, each of the concerned parties faced incentives to do so. In addition existing regulatory jurisdictions were slow to issue cautionary commentary, and hampered by jurisdictional considerations in their ability to control the evolving problems.

The problems were attributable not to a defect of securitization per se, but rather to a misplaced confidence in the quality of the original loans and the securities used to finance the loan portfolios. In essence, the problems arose from failing to realize that the quality of a loan portfolio is only as good as the quality and the governance of the individual loans in it. If loans and default risks are both transferred, it is important, as stressed in the previous section, that governance of default risk not be attenuated. If governance of default risk is attenuated, both the original loan portfolio and securities issued against it are likely to deteriorate in quality just as happened in the subprime market.

DEFAULT INSURANCE

Credit default insurance involves the use of a financial agreement to mitigate the risk of default loss, that is, it allows for the transfer of credit risk without the transfer of an underlying asset. Credit derivatives emerged around 1993 or 1994, and form a part of the OTC derivatives markets. A credit derivative transfers a defined credit risk to a counterparty, normally the seller of the derivative.[24] Credit derivatives are most frequently purchased by lenders who wish to insure all or parts of a loan portfolio against default risk. Since

---

[24] In some cases credit risk may be transferred as a by-product of securitization.

its inception, the credit derivatives market has grown very rapidly, but that very growth presents a problem of attenuating incentives to monitor and control default probabilities, as described in the previous section. Since the market allows lenders to sell off the default risks in a loan portfolio to a third party, its existence can also reduce the incentives of the original lender diligently to pursue defaulting parties.

Currently the most widely used type of credit derivative is a credit default swap.[25] In its historical form, a CDS was designed to transfer default risk from the holder of a fixed income security to an insurer—the seller of the swap. The buyer receives credit protection, whereas the seller guarantees the creditworthiness of the product. For example, should the bond default in its coupon payments, the buyer of a credit swap is entitled to receive the par value of the bond from the seller. Since its inception, the market has developed rapidly and CDSs are now actively traded by parties who may not have any investment in the underlying securities. In effect, CDSs constitute a market for trading default risk without actually participating in the underlying bond instrument. Indexes of the credit default swaps prices report the current costs of trading the instruments.

REFERENCES

Bookstaber, Richard. 2007. *A Demon of Our Own Design.* Hoboken, NJ: John Wiley & Sons.

Fabozzi, Frank J., and Franco Modigliani. 1992. *Capital Markets: Institutions and Instruments.* Englewood Cliffs, NJ: Prentice-Hall.

Johnson, Lewis D., and Edwin H. Neave. 2008. The subprime mortgage market: Familiar lessons in a new context. *Management Research News* 31: 12–26.

Stein, Jeremy C. 1997. Internal capital markets and the competition for corporate resources. *Journal of Finance* 52: 111–133.

Stein, Jeremy C. 2002. Information production and capital allocation: Decentralized versus hierarchical firms. *Journal of Finance* 57: 1,899–2,002.

TERMS

asset-liability matching   Borrowing and lending on the same interest rate terms as assessed with respect to the points in time at which rates can change.

---

[25] An instrument designed to transfer credit risk but not interest rate risk. Total return swaps transfer both credit and interest rate risk.

collateralized debt obligations (CDOs)   Securities sold by banks or their agencies and secured by an underlying debt portfolio. A CDO is similar in structure to a CMO (see next entry). Either issues securities that represent different types of debt and credit risk, with the types being referred to as "tranches." Each tranche can have a different maturity and a different risk associated with it. The higher the risk, the higher the required yield on the securities representing the tranche.

collateralized mortgage obligations (CMOs)   Securities sold by banks or their agencies and secured by an underlying portfolio of residential mortgages.

credit derivative   An instrument offering a payoff to its holder in the event of a third party experiencing a default, or credit event.

credit default swap (CDS)   A credit derivative contract between two counterparties, in which the buyer makes periodic payments to the seller in exchange for a payoff if there is a default by a third party (reference entity). A CDS resembles an insurance policy, as it can be used by a debt holder to hedge against a default under the debt instrument. However, since there is no requirement to actually hold any asset, a credit default swap can also be used for speculative purposes and it is not generally considered insurance for regulatory purposes.

default risk   The risk that an obligor will be unable or unwilling to repay a loan, or to redeem an investment.

interest-rate swap   A financial instrument specifying how one party to the swap will exchange a pattern of interest earnings or costs with a second party.

market risk   The risk of fluctuations in market price due to changes in demand-supply conditions.

securitization   The practice of issuing new securities, designed to appeal to investors, against an asset portfolio of illiquid securities.

part Six

Applications: Intermediation

This part examines the economics of intermediary operations and the main policy issues faced by intermediary management. It first provides a model treating domestic intermediation as a portfolio problem solved subject to capital and reserve constraints, then considers applications—first to domestic and second to international intermediaries.

CHAPTER 16

Principles of Intermediation

Theories of financial intermediation stress that intermediaries both produce information and create liquidity. Parts One and Two of this book introduced the idea that intermediaries produce information relevant for governance of their asset portfolios, and in this part we look more closely at the economics of operating intermediaries.

INTRODUCTION

This chapter models domestic intermediation as a portfolio problem subject to regulatory and liquidity constraints. The chapter studies risk-return trade-offs, the theory of bank capital, determinants of intermediary size, and the economics of intermediary information processing. The model is then applied to such domestic operating issues as gap management, the evolution of interest rate risk management, default risk management, liquidity management, and capital management.

A STRATEGIC MANAGEMENT MODEL

A financial intermediary can be regarded as an investment portfolio operated to generate income for the owners of its common equity (Pyle 1971, Hart-Jaffee 1974). The portfolio theory introduced in Chapter 14 argues that investors strive to generate as large a return as possible for a given degree of risk. Accordingly, this chapter examines the effects of portfolio composition and portfolio trading strategies on the risk-return trade-offs generated by an intermediary.

In applying portfolio theory to analyzing intermediary operations, it must be recognized that most financial intermediaries' assets are not marketable securities, nor are large proportions of their liabilities. Since intermediary positions are not as liquid as positions in marketable securities, measures of their correlation may be difficult to obtain, and consequently portfolio theory's application to analyzing financial intermediary activities is primarily at the conceptual rather than the practical level. Nevertheless, a portfolio theoretic model still provides a useful framework for analyzing many of the strategic and operating issues associated with domestic intermediation. While the analysis is most directly applicable to value maximizing firms, it is also conceptually relevant to the other types of intermediary, such as cooperative credit societies. By offering guidelines indicating what the wealth maximizing firm would do, and how it would be affected by regulatory constraints, the model provides a standard of comparison for all firms, even those choosing not to maximize value.

Mean-Variance Version

Consider a skeleton form of financial intermediary, whose assets at a given point in time are cash reserves R and loans L. Its liabilities are interest-bearing deposits D, and it is capitalized by an amount C, representing owners' equity. The intermediary's operations involve raising funds through deposits and equity and then investing the proceeds in loans, the only earning asset. Some cash is also held, but for simplicity are assumed to earn no interest.

Operations are managed with a view to maximizing expected earnings for a given degree of risk, as measured here by variance of income. Operations are subject to constraints that can be interpreted either as regulatory or as policy limitations. Insofar as regulatory constraints are concerned, many jurisdictions require intermediaries to hold a specified proportion of their liabilities in the form of cash reserves, and even intermediaries that are not subject to reserve requirements usually hold some reserves voluntarily.[1] Similarly, many intermediaries are required by domestic regulation and the Basel agreements to hold certain proportions of capital, as discussed more fully in Chapter 22. Even unregulated intermediaries usually adopt a target capital ratio voluntarily. Simple versions of both liquidity and capital constraints are used in the model, leaving the details of current practice to be discussed further after the model's properties have been explored.

The intermediary's assets and liabilities satisfy

$$R + L = D + C = A \tag{16.1}$$

---

[1]International banks are not required to hold reserves against Eurodollar deposits. Moreover, some countries like the United Kingdom and Canada have adopted policies of zero required reserves. Nevertheless, even banks that face a zero required reserve requirement are likely to hold reserves (called "desired reserves") to meet the possibilities of cash losses.

where A represents total assets. The regulatory constraints are reflected by

$$C \geq bA \tag{16.2}$$

$$R \geq kD \tag{16.3}$$

where b is the minimum capital ratio and k is the minimum reserve ratio. We assume that, as a policy choice, the intermediary holds only the minimum required cash reserves and maintains only the minimum required capital position, thus allowing the inequalities in equations (16.2) and (16.3) to be treated as equalities. Thus the assets can be rewritten as

$$R + L = kD + L = A \tag{16.4}$$

while the liabilities and net worth become

$$D + C = D + bA = A \tag{16.5}$$

Solving equations (16.4) and (16.5) simultaneously for L and D gives

$$D = (1 - b)A \equiv dA \tag{16.6}$$

$$L = [(1 - k(1 - b)]A \equiv lA \tag{16.7}$$

Assume for the present there are no operating expenses,[2] and recall that the return on cash is zero. The intermediary's net interest income is given by

$$E(\pi) = E(r)L - E(c)D \tag{16.8}$$

Rewriting equation (16.8) using equations (16.6) and (16.7),

$$E[\pi(A)] = [E(r)l - E(c)d]A \tag{16.9}$$

Note that since owners' equity $C = bA$, the ratio of net interest income to equity will be a constant proportion, irrespective of intermediary size. In other words, in this model growth may be sought to increase absolute income, but it will not be sought to increase return to equity unless the intermediary's cost function is such that it can generate increasing returns to scale. Finally, although operating costs are not included in equation (16.9), it is relatively easy to see their effect. For example, if operating cost were regarded as unchanged by changes in lending or deposit operations, they

---

[2]Their effects will be discussed shortly.

would in effect create a breakeven value for asset size: Unless the intermediary could attain an asset size that would cover its fixed operating costs, it would not be viable. Alternatively, if the intermediary were modeled as enjoying operating economies to scale, that would provide another reason for expansion of its asset size.

Suppose intermediary risk is measured by the variance of its portfolio income:

$$\sigma^2(\pi(A)) = A^2\{l^2\sigma^2(r) + d^2\sigma^2(c) - 2\,l\,d\rho\sigma(r)\sigma(c)\} \qquad (16.10)$$

where $\rho = \rho(r, c)$ is the correlation between the interest rates r and c[3]. Assume the criterion function used by the intermediary is the now familiar

$$\max\nolimits_A\{E(\pi) - (\beta/2)\sigma^2(\pi)\} \qquad (16.11)$$

where β is a coefficient of risk aversion. Substituting equations (16.9) and (16.10) in equation (16.11), taking the first derivative with respect to A and setting the result equal to zero defines the intermediary's optimally chosen asset level as

$$A^* = \{E(r)l - E(c)d\}/\beta\{l^2\sigma^2(r) + d^2\sigma^2(c) - 2\,l\,d\rho\sigma(r)\sigma(c)\} \qquad (16.12)$$

Note from equation (16.12) that if

$$E(\pi)/A = [E(r)l - E(c)d] > 0 \qquad (16.13)$$

the intermediary's optimal asset size will increase as β decreases. Moreover, if

$$\sigma^2(\pi)/A^2 = l^2\sigma^2(r) + d^2\sigma^2(c) - 2\,l\,d\rho\sigma(r)\sigma(c) \qquad (16.14)$$

decreases, then again the intermediary's optimally chosen asset size will increase. Finally, equation (16.14) decreases as ρ increases; that is, as the intermediary becomes more closely hedged against interest rate risk.

Model Interpretation

For any given value of the risk aversion coefficient β, the optimal size of the intermediary is highly sensitive to its ability to hedge interest-rate risk, that

---

[3]The condition $\rho(r, c) > 0$ is sufficient for loans and deposits to have the correct signs in an unconstrained model and we make that assumption throughout.

TABLE 16.1 Optimal Asset Size

ρ	Total Assets
.99	2,081,165
.97	746,129
.95	454,545
.93	326,824
.91	255,135

is, to changes in ρ as ρ approaches unity, as shown in Table 16.1. Table 16.1 verifies the idea that the *gap* management (asset-liability matching) policies discussed in (16.4) are aimed at reducing risk relative to return.

An intermediary's risk-return trade-off is further affected by the types of assets and liabilities it holds, as well as by its proportions of reserves and capital. While these effects can be derived from the partial derivatives of equation (16.12), most readers will probably prefer a less formal exploration. Table 16.2 numerically illustrates the workings of two effects. Reading down the columns of the table shows that $E(\pi)/C$ decreases as b increases and k is held constant. That is, increases in required capitalization result in a lowered value of a common performance measure—return to equity—other parameters being held constant. Similarly, reading across the rows shows that $E(\pi)/C$ decreases as k increases and b is held constant. Other effects being held constant, increases in liquid assets result in a lower return to equity.

Second, equations (16.13) and (16.7) together imply that $E(\pi)/C$ decreases with k, which means the intermediary has a profit incentive to minimize its reserve holdings. The reason is clear: Cash reserves earn no interest, while loans do. The effects are confirmed by reading across the rows of Table 16.2. Similarly, equations (16.13) and (16.6) show that $E(\pi)/C$ increases as b (required capital) decreases, at least as long as interest earnings net of reserve requirements exceed the cost of funds. Hence the intermediary faces an incentive to minimize the proportion of equity capitalization. Again, the reason is clear: The more earnings that can be supported by a given amount of equity investment, the greater the return to equity will be.[4] The effects are confirmed by reading down the columns of Table 16.2.

To assess how risk affects the return on equity, consider the effects of different possible interest rate patterns on $\sigma^2(\pi)/C^2$. First as already noted,

---

[4]This will increase market value, at least as long as the risk is not viewed by the market as increasing too much. In normal circumstances, the market does not change its estimate of intermediary earnings risk very often or very much.

TABLE 16.2 Effect of Liquidity and
Capital Requirements on $E(\pi)/C =$
$\{E(r)[1 - k(1 - b)]/b\} - \{E(c)(1 - b)/b\}$

	k = 0.04	k = 0.10
b = 0.04	0.965	0.792
b = 0.10	0.437	0.372

Note: Assume $E(r) = 0.12$, $E(c) = 0.08$.

$\sigma^2(\pi)/C^2$ decreases as ρ increases from 0. That is, the closer a bank comes to matching its pattern of interest earnings with its pattern of interest costs, the lower its earnings risk. Table 16.3 shows how increasing the correlation between r and c creates this effect. In the table, suppose there are three possible values that can be taken on by r and c, as shown by the table's row and column headings. For each possible combination of r and c, the value of net interest earnings, $rl - cd$, is shown in the body of Table 16.3. Now suppose that only the entries on the table's main diagonal can occur with positive probability; that is, suppose that r and c are perfectly positively correlated. In this case the table entries show that earnings hardly change, which in turn means that their variance is also relatively low. That is, an intermediary with high positive correlation between loan revenues and deposit costs minimizes the effects on profits of changing interest rates, and that a less well matched one faces more interest rate risk. In contrast, consider one of the Table 16.3's rows. In this case the interest rate on loans is a deterministic quantity, correlation between r and c is zero, and the variance of the realized net interest earnings is substantially larger than in the case of perfect positive correlation. For example, the variance of the three terms along the main diagonal is .000072, and the variance of the three terms in the first

TABLE 16.3 Effects of Interest Rates Patterns on Return to Equity and Its Variance

	Possible Values of c		
Possible Values of r	c = 0.0600	c = 0.0800	c = 0.1000
r = 0.0800	0.3384	–0.0416	–0.4216
r = 0.1000	0.7080	0.3280	–0.0520
r = 0.1200	1.0776	0.6976	0.3176

Note: Assume $k = .08$ and $b = .05$ throughout. Numbers in the body of the table represent return relative to capital, that is, $E(\pi)/C$.

TABLE 16.4 Effect of b and k on Earnings and Earning Variance

	$k = 0.04$	$k = 0.10$
b = 0.04	0.965, 0.115	0.792, 0.109
b = 0.10	0.437, 0.017	0.372, 0.016

Note: Assume $r = 0.12$ and $c = 0.08$. Also, $\rho = 0$, and $\sigma^2(r) = \sigma^2(c) = .0001$. Entries in the body of the table are $E(\pi)/C$ and $\sigma^2(\pi)/C^2$, respectively.

row is .0962667. Similar effects can be derived for fixed deposit costs and variable loan interest rates.

To assess the effects of regulatory policy on risk-return combinations, consider Table 16.4. The entries in the body of this table are return and risk respectively. Reading down the columns of Table 16.4 shows that, under the assumptions of the model, increasing b—the proportion of equity capital—decreases both earnings and earnings risk. Reading across the rows of the table shows that increasing reserve requirements k decreases both earnings and earnings risk, but that the effect is proportionately smaller than the effect of changing capital requirements.

Liquidity Management

The problem of liquidity management is to ensure the intermediary holds enough liquid assets, usually short-term government securities,[5] to meet operating cash needs. Day-to-day cash losses result mainly from checks drawn on clients' deposit balances, and presented to the intermediary through the clearings. If the intermediary holds too little in the way of liquid assets, it must meet cash outflows by selling off other, less liquid assets at a possible loss. On the other hand, since government securities are both low risk and low return, the intermediary forgoes earnings if it holds too large a proportion of liquid assets. The model of the previous section shows both that greater reserve requirements reduce profitability and also, by reducing the variance of income, provide a somewhat greater measure of safety.[6]

---

[5]Usually some cash will also be held, but since cash yields no return while short-term government securities yield at least a low interest rate, the proportion of cash to government securities will be kept as low as possible.

[6]This chapter's appendix shows a similar result in the context of a more traditional form of liquidity management model.

Managing Capital Positions

The role of capital in a financial intermediary is to absorb losses, either from operations or from loan defaults. If an intermediary's capital is not sufficient to cover losses, it will be insolvent. Losses can result either from changes in net interest earnings or from defaulted loans. Losses arising from changes in net interest revenue are primarily cyclical, whereas losses from defaulted loans can increase gradually over several years if unsound lending policies have been followed in the past. While capital regulations may reduce solvency risk to a degree, the capital account is actually an accounting provision to absorb losses as they occur, and its size does not in itself guarantee that an intermediary would have liquid assets available for use in an emergency. Thus the surest protection against insolvency involves sound lending policies and maintaining adequate liquidity. If these strategies can credibly be communicated to investors, they will enhance the capacity of the intermediary to raise additional funds as and when the need arises.[7]

Diamond and Rajan (2000) regard banks and other similar intermediaries as creators of liquidity. The authors argue that liquidity is created as intermediaries accept deposits and relend the funds to borrowers who would otherwise be less liquid. But, since the intermediaries are primarily invested in illiquid assets, they cannot meet the claims of all depositors quickly in times of financing stringency, making them fragile and prone to runs.[8] Moreover, the greater the uncertainty that depositors will withdraw their funds, the more fragile becomes the deposit base.

As the model shows, greater proportional amounts of capital can be used to reduce the probability of an intermediary's suffering financial distress, but those greater amounts of capital also reduce liquidity creation. The proportion of intermediary capital held also influences the amount that banks can induce borrowers to pay. The more soundly capitalized the intermediary, the less likely there will be interruption of service to borrowers, and the more likely the intermediary will be able to collect from its borrowers. Thus optimal capital structure trades off effects on liquidity creation, costs of distress, and the ability to force borrower repayment.

In practice, capital ratios vary widely between intermediaries: from about 1:45 for certain depository intermediaries in some countries to about 1:8 for some lending intermediaries. Obviously, if all intermediaries earned the same rate of return on total assets and if their risks were the same, the more highly levered intermediaries would earn much higher returns on their

---

[7]The capacity to raise additional funds is also related to the intermediary's ability to make profitable loans.

[8]Models of bank runs are presented in Chapter 20.

shares. But different asset portfolios generate both different average incomes and different income risks, as shown later in this chapter.

The proportion of capital to assets is not regulated for all financial intermediaries, but most jurisdictions do regulate the ratios for banks, and many jurisdictions also apply capital requirements to near banks. With regard to bank capital, most countries adhere to standards developed by the Basel Committee under the sponsorship of the Bank for International Settlements. According to the 1988 Basel agreements, banks in signatory countries were expected to achieve a minimum target ratio of total capital to risk weighted assets of 8%, of which at least 4% must be in the form of common equity. The risk weightings reflect different kinds of business; for example, corporate loans have a weighting of 100%, while government securities have a weighting of 0%. In many banks, the risk weightings mean that capital is about 5% of the assets held on the books. The 1988 agreements gave banks an incentive to make lower- rather than higher-quality corporate loans, since both types carried the same capital requirements. Moreover, the agreements provided no recognition that capital might be reduced by diversifying loan portfolio risks. Both these incentive effects have created substantial amounts of regulatory risk arbitrage; that is, trading risks between banks (Altman and Saunders 2002).

In recognition of the existing difficulties the Bank for International Settlements has released reform proposals known as Basel II. For present purposes, the most important change in the agreements is to replaces the 100% risk weighting on all corporate loans by weightings based on the external credit rating agency of the borrower. Eventually, this system is to be replaced by banks' own internal loan rating systems, and at a still later date, banks should be able to use their own internal models to calculate their capital requirements (Altman and Saunders 2002). As of this writing, the changes have now come into effect in some countries, and are scheduled to be adopted by most other countries over the next several years.

ECONOMICS OF INTERMEDIATION

The evolution of domestic intermediation is driven principally by the changing economics of raising funds and relending them. Intermediary management tries to lead or at least keep abreast of economic changes in order to operate as profitably as possible, and meeting these challenges in a rapidly changing financial system means that intermediaries must continuously adapt their businesses to emerging opportunities. As one example, intermediaries still perform their traditional role of raising funds through deposits and repackaging the funds as loans, but they are increasingly also acting as agents for financings they do not retain on their own books.

Traditionally, intermediary activities have focused on gathering up small amounts of funds for lending in larger amounts, an activity called denomination intermediation. Intermediaries also employ maturity intermediation when they use short-term liabilities (such as funds deposited in checking and savings accounts) to finance medium-term loans. Since the beginning of the 1980s, intermediaries have grown rapidly through mergers and have also become much more sophisticated technologically. Growth into the 2010s is likely to be more modest. The subprime crisis of 2007–2008 will see revenues from fixed-income securitization much lower, even when securitization returns to the market. On the other hand, an aging population such as that to be found in many developed countries offers opportunities for wealth accumulation, and retail banking is likely to profit from the management of that wealth.

Intermediation also transforms risk: The depositing client of an intermediary does not face the same default risk as she would if she were to lend funds directly to one of the intermediary's clients. The depositor's risk is related to the diversified risk of the intermediary's asset portfolio rather than to the credit risk of individual borrowing clients. However, despite the advantages of diversification, the uninsured depositor can still face default risk if an intermediary's lending practices endanger its solvency. Indeed, when deciding where to place their short-term funds, large depositors do take intermediary default risk into account. On the other hand, small depositors do not face default risk if their funds are protected by deposit insurance.[9] From the point of view of an investor, risk can sometimes be transformed when portfolios of intermediary loans are securitized, as discussed in the "Securitization and Governance" section of Chapter 15.

Economies of Scale and of Scope

Scale economies provide intermediaries with reasons to expand asset size. For example, there are usually fixed costs to setting up a screening facility for a particular type of loan application, meaning that the unit cost of this type of screening will decrease as the number of screenings increases. Most intermediaries also enjoy scale economies in both loan and deposit administration. Moreover, mergers of large banks' data processing operations suggest that scale economies are realized in accounting for payments as well as in the administration of their asset portfolios. Empirical studies show that

---

[9]According to the jurisdiction and the type of intermediary business (bank, savings intermediary, securities firm, insurance company) client insurance against losses may be provided either by public or private sector agencies.

small intermediaries realize scale economies through asset growth, and there is little or no evidence showing that large financial intermediaries encounter scale diseconomies.[10]

Intermediaries can also realize scope economies by placing related types of deals on their books. Scope economies (cost complementarities) stem principally from sharing inputs across transactions that are not too different in type. For example, the skills needed to lend operating funds to medium-sized businesses may be partially transferable to a consumer lending division. Similarly, economies of scope might be realized from cross-selling agreements between banks and securities dealers or between banks and insurance companies. If they prove to reduce costs significantly, and if the product markets are sufficiently competitive, cross-selling agreements could also have significant impacts on product prices. In the same manner, securities firms might realize scope economies by offering cash management accounts or term deposit facilities.

Scope economies do not necessarily extend to all combinations of transactions, especially transactions that differ considerably. There may, for instance, be scope economies in combining the sale of fire and property insurance, but these economies would probably not extend to offering both insurance products and venture investments within the same business unit. As a second example of limits to scope economies, a life insurance representative may not initially be qualified to sell such financial products as registered retirement savings plans (RRSPs) and mutual fund shares or guaranteed investment certificates, and perhaps can only do so after relatively costly on the job training. Nevertheless the development of expert systems which take the form of computer programs used to guide the marketing efforts of intermediary personnel could change this picture, so that cross-selling of presently dissimilar products may eventually become more cost-effective than is now the case.

Information Processing and Screening

All intermediaries screen proposed loans or investments to determine which are acceptable. Screening costs differ by type of deal, but screening operations usually exhibit both a relatively large fixed cost and a relatively small marginal cost component. As a result, unit screening costs usually decrease with the volume of deals screened. A screening cost function can shift

---

[10] The lack of evidence for scale or scope diseconomies may simply mean that management is aware of when diseconomies start to manifest themselves and either prevent the intermediary from reaching such a size, or spin off divisions when they have been found not to contribute to the overall organization's profitability.

downward as intermediary personnel learn additional skills or acquire additional experience with a new type of deal.[11] For example, it takes about five years to train an investment officer in the venture capital industry. A reasonably experienced officer has the capacity to govern six to eight active investments, and to conduct some additional deal generation and screening activities. Intermediaries evolve different screening capabilities as a result of differing business experience. These different capabilities affect both their current screening costs and their likely future evolution—financial firms are more likely to enter lines of business related to their current expertise rather than businesses with which they have no experience. To the extent an intermediary has lower costs that result from learning by doing, it has an effective barrier to the entry of new competitors. The barriers are particularly effective if a market is small and potential entrants are therefore unsure whether they would be able to recover their fixed costs.

Intermediary Size

The most profitable size for an intermediary depends on both its operating economics and the markets it serves. Intermediaries expand until they exhaust their sources of operating economies, at least if the markets they serve are large enough to permit the expansion. Economies of scale and scope may provide firms with competitive advantages, but the evidence suggests the economies are restricted to specific activities. It seems likely that bank mergers can create efficiency gains, but there is little evidence that merged banks have reaped any economies of scale or scope in terms of returns on asset portfolios. Rather, most of the gains appear to be achieved through cost reduction, and most of the value created accrues to shareholders (Berger and Humphrey 1991, 1992). For example, new technologies can yield both scale and scope economies, particularly through making it possible to offer remote delivery of financial services and to develop common accounting schemes for different financial products. These possibilities are widely recognized, and the world's largest intermediaries all rely heavily on investments in technology.

Walter (2004) has assessed the factors that appear to be driving the structural reconfiguration of the financial services industry, and concludes that the financial services industry appears to be able to accommodate a

---

[11] Skills that can be taught in the classroom become an employment requirement in a competitive industry. For example, the skills needed to make working capital loans against the security of accounts receivable are easily taught, and new personnel might be expected to absorb them quickly. On the other hand, some of the skills needed to identify good prospects for mergers or promising venture capital opportunities are difficult to teach in a classroom setting and are usually gained from experience.

variety of firm sizes at equilibrium. DeLong and DeYoung (2004) argue that bank mergers do create value once banks have learned to integrate their businesses, a task that is characterized as learning by doing. Diseconomies of scope can arise from the workings of complexity and conflicts of interest.

Size can affect portfolio risk because large intermediaries usually have greater opportunities for geographical diversification than their smaller counterparts. Financial system observers also argue that large intermediaries are sometimes "too big to fail." That is, because the failure of large intermediaries could have widespread effects, such firms may be able to muster government support if and when they encounter financial difficulty. In recognition of both possibilities, larger intermediaries are perceived to be less risky than smaller ones, allowing them to benefit from lower overall costs of funding.

Why Intermediaries Specialize

Small specialized intermediaries flourish in most financial systems. Small firms usually have specialized skills that allow them to serve small markets effectively. They may also be more flexible than their larger counterparts, and thus able to adapt more rapidly and more cheaply to changing market conditions. Finally, some small firms may be able to gain cost advantages by incorporating under less burdensome regulation than their larger counterparts. No intermediary can attain a large size if it serves only one or a few small markets, but niche firms can survive by retaining cost advantages, at least so long as they are not vulnerable to takeover by larger firms. However, even a specialized intermediary incurs fixed setup costs, and if these setup costs are sufficiently large, some markets may not be served at all.

Bond (2004) argues that banks, conglomerates, and trade credit can all be regarded as instances of specialized financial intermediation: Institutions differ in the types of projects they fund, the types of claims they issue to investors, and the ways financed projects absorb intermediary risk. Bond examines the matching of borrower attributes and financier capabilities, particularly emphasizing the importance of the borrower's position if and when the intermediary runs into financial trouble. By so doing, Bond establishes the viability of intermediation without assuming that the probability of intermediary default is low.[12]

Bond assumes that information sharing is a costly activity.[13] With costly information sharing in mind, Bond views intermediaries like banks as

---

[12] In Diamond and Dybvig (1983) intermediary income is known with (near) certainty.

[13] Bond models information sharing as an exercise in costly state verification: An agent's output is private information unless a verification cost is incurred to disclose it to another agent.

funding low-risk/high-quality projects. This asset mix allows banks to issue low-risk liabilities, and also implies that there is little potential advantage to information sharing. Accordingly, borrowers from banks do not gain from absorbing each others' risks. Rather, it is efficient for bank investors to absorb project financing losses. Since banks are the kinds of low-risk intermediaries that are funded by many investors, specialized forms of banks can prove cost-effective. In contrast, intermediaries like conglomerates finance high-risk/low-quality projects and themselves issue high-risk liabilities to investors. In these situations there can be advantages to information sharing, and investors respond by arranging for funded projects to absorb some of other projects' cash flow fluctuations.

Intermediation lets the entrepreneur avoid disclosing information to multiple agents, but introduces the agency problem of keeping the intermediary honest. Diversification is the key to establishing that only limited disclosure is necessary, and consequently overall disclosure costs are lower. In a bond intermediary, income can fluctuate and, for that reason, devices to manage the fluctuations' impacts are needed. Bond concludes that intermediation can be more cost-effective than individually negotiated arrangements even when intermediaries default with positive probability.

At the same time, the existence and type of an intermediary is tied to the risk profile of the claims it must issue to raise financing. Specialized financial institutions emerge when they are more efficient at handling information disclosure. Trade credit comes about because monitoring/disclosure costs can be lower between trading partners.

OPERATING ISSUES

The operating issues of concern to intermediary management include managing the bank's balance sheet composition and choosing the technologies to drive day-to-day activities. Managing the balance sheet's composition is aimed mainly at achieving desired risk, liquidity, and capital positions, while management of technological change is intended to achieve efficiency in information processing and data delivering services.

Gap Management

In the 1950s and 1960s, the typical intermediary borrowed short and lent long (that is, had a balance sheet consisting chiefly of floating rate liabilities and fixed rate assets). The strategy of borrowing in short-term markets and lending in longer-term ones is called "straddling" the term structure. The policy generated relatively steady profits when the yield curve remained, year after year, in essentially the same position. However, as underlying economic conditions change, short-term interest rates can be much more variable than their long-term counterparts. Moreover, the traditional yield curve relation—that short rates will be lower than longer rates—will not necessarily obtain throughout the economic cycle, and sometimes an intermediary that is borrowing short and lending long can suffer net interest losses. This kind of interest rate risk is said to result from a mismatch of assets against liabilities. This risk was first clearly recognized in the 1970s and 1980s as interest rates become more variable. Recognition of the income risks to straddling the term structure led to the strategy of gap management, aimed at stabilizing net interest earnings in widely different economic environments.

Recalling the strategic management model of described earlier in this chapter, a gap management strategy attempts to manage interest rate risk by matching floating rate liabilities against floating rate assets. In the 1970s, banks and other intermediaries implemented gap management strategies by changing the interest terms of intermediary assets to match those on intermediary liabilities. In particular, long-term, fixed rate loans were changed to floating rate loans, so that interest revenues responded to market conditions in a pattern similar to the response of interest costs.[14]

For example, at one time mortgages were written at interest rates fixed for the life of the arrangement, but now the more common practice is for the interest rate to be renegotiable at regular intervals. The intervals can be as long as one to five years, as short as three months or even one month. These kinds of floating rate (or adjustable rate) mortgages reduce the lender's interest rate risk by transferring it to the borrower.

Evolution of Interest-Rate Risk Management

In practice, risk management involves both gap management and using derivative products to achieve a more desirable balance of portfolio return and risk. Insofar as gap management is concerned, changing from fixed to floating rate loans represents an important risk management decision for any institution that funds a large proportion of its loans with short-term deposits. To the extent that intermediaries still offer fixed rate loans, they

---

[14] Gap management is a practical technique using accounting concepts to stabilize earnings. Gap management does not necessarily ensure that maximization of the present value of the intermediary's cash flows as economic theory would advocate. Even in the early 2000s banks have not fully worked out practical ways of reconciling the two approaches, although the models of this section suggest the outlines of an approach.

attempt to fund them with fixed rate deposits. Since it is not always possible to change the terms of products to achieve perfect matching, interest rate swaps or other means of hedging the interest-rate risk are frequently used, as discussed in Chapter 12.

To understand intermediaries' rapidly growing demand for swaps, consider a mortgage lending institution that makes fixed rate loans and has only one source of funds—floating rate deposits. It is, of course, vulnerable to fluctuations in the cost of funds. But it might be able to find a bank in another country (Japan proved to be a good source in the 1970s and early 1980s) that has borrowed using long-term fixed rate notes and has relent the money as variable rate commercial loans. The swap means each takes on the other's interest obligations, and consequently each has a more closely matched pattern of interest revenues and interest costs after the swap has been arranged.

Intermediaries also use forward commitments to offer their clients a risk management service by guaranteeing the interest rate a client will pay on a loan. For example, if a forward commitment specifies a fixed interest rate, the issuing intermediary assumes the risk that rates might rise after giving the undertaking. The intermediary does not assume the interest-rate risk if it only agrees to provide a line of credit at the market interest rate prevailing when the loan is actually drawn down, but competitive pressures might dictate prespecifying the rate. In this case the intermediary may wish to hedge the risk in the futures markets.

Over the shorter term, intermediaries also use other strategies aimed at increasing their interest earnings, reducing the risk of those earnings, or both. For example, over an interest-rate cycle the typical intermediary may attempt to shorten the maturities of assets relative to liabilities when rates are rising, and to reverse this pattern when interest rates are falling. Finally, as financial markets have increased in size and sophistication, banks have been able to make greater use of trading interest-rate derivatives as another way of managing interest-rate risk.

Default Risk Management

Managing default risk requires an intermediary both to exercise suitable governance techniques and to choose the interest-risk premium to be charged on a loan. The latter requires the use of a benchmark, and this section introduces the theory of default risk management to show conceptually how risk premiums can be calculated. We first find the notional market value of a debt instrument and then show how an interest-rate risk premium can be calculated. Additional aspects of managing default risk were examined in Chapter 15 and are revisited in Chapter 17.

TABLE 16.5 Valuing Debt and Equity When Debt Promises to Pay 99.00

	S_1 (Firm)	D_1 (Debt)	E_1 (Equity)
Time 1 High Payoffs	105.00	99.00	6.00
Time 1 Low Payoffs	95.00	95.00	0.00
Time 0 Values	89.00	87.42	1.58

Theoretically, the default risk of a bank loan can be determined using the options pricing approach introduced earlier. Recall the example of Chapter 9, repeated here for convenience. (See Table 16.5.)

Since the example assumes the riskless interest rate is 10%, if the debt were to pay 99.00 with certainty it would be worth $99.00/1.10 = 90.00$. Thus one can conclude immediately that the value of the implicit put in the risky debt is $2.58, as shown in Chapter 9. The expected return on the risky debt is defined in the customary way as

$$[E(D_1) - D_0]/D_0 = [(1/2)(99.00 + 97.00) - 87.42]/87.42 = 0.1096$$

Since the assumed return on riskless debt is 0.10, it follows immediately that the risk premium on this particular risky debt issue is 0.0096.

The options approach offers a number of advantages over more traditional approaches for valuing risky debt. First, the approach recognizes that the probability of failure depends on the size of the debt, as the examples in Chapter 9 made clear. Second, using risk-neutral probabilities to determine the debt value means that market pricing of risk is taken into account. Third, the liquidation value of the firm is recognized in that even in cases when the debt is defaulted, the options approach takes account of whatever payment is available to debt holders. Since risky debt carries a higher effective interest rate than riskless debt, the example presented verified that more indebted firms pay higher interest rates.[15] It is also easy, using the options pricing approach, to show that the risk premium on risky debt will increase with asset volatility. Finally, although the present examples are only single-period ones, multiperiod examples also show that the risk premium increases with the maturity of the loan. On the other hand, the options pricing approach is premised on an assumed absence of arbitrage opportunities. But since bank

---

[15] At least as long as the increase in indebtedness means the debt is increasingly risky. Obviously, if a firm issues different amounts of riskless debt those securities will be priced to yield the riskless rate.

loans are not traded instruments, the assumption of no arbitrage opportunities may not be defensible, and hence the options pricing approach can only provide a rough guide to the actual risk premium on a nontraded, and usually nontradeable, loan. [16]

There are several additional aspects to managing default risk. Some intermediaries require borrowers to maintain compensating deposit balances, thus reducing the amount actually lent and at the same time increasing the effective interest rate on the loan. Chapter 6 examined the role of collateral in reducing risk. Third party guarantees, credit insurance, and loan covenants, are other examples of terms used to reduce default risk. In addition, credit derivatives are finding increasing favor as a means of selling off default risk to a third party, as discussed in Chapter 15. In the example just provided, it would only be necessary to sell the implicit put to achieve this transfer of risk. However in practice pricing credit derivatives is a relatively complex matter. The underlying instruments are not actively traded, making it difficult to find counterparties. In addition, assessing the instruments' risks is relatively difficult.

Technological Change

In finance as in many other service industries, the cost of human resources relative to technology has risen steadily since as early as the 1960s and is likely to continue doing at least into the 2010s: The trend begun by the proliferation of automatic banking machines and their electronic linkages will continue for some time. Changing relative costs mean that financial institutions will continue to substitute relatively cheap machines for relatively expensive labor. Various forms of communications media, including telephone and cable television facilities, will enhance future access to financial services, and it is likely that most routine financial transactions will eventually be effected using communications devices in almost any location.[17] These changes, along with the use of electronic networks for more efficient distribution of financial products, have changed the role of financial intermediaries at the same time as they have increased the intermediaries' efficiency. Mishkin and Strahan (1999) suggest that technological change will continue

---

[16] Even if the assumptions establishing the existence of risk-neutral probabilities are not satisfied, the use of estimated or subjected risk-neutral probabilities helps to calculate a benchmark. Sensitivity analysis can then be used to determine how the benchmark values change as assumptions regarding the environment are varied (see Benninga 2008).

[17] At the time of this writing, cell phone connections to the financial system are starting to become available in a number of countries.

to make it easier for borrowers to raise funds in financial markets, and that institutions will continue to become better at unbundling risks.[18]

Technology has brought impressive productivity gains to routine operations, and there are more to be realized. It is now possible to use debit cards in retail establishments to pay for goods electronically, eliminating the necessity for paper checks. Direct debit terminals have met with some resistance in the United States because the client loses checkbook float, but eventually higher charges on check and credit card transactions will alter the current attitudes. In Canada, debit card transactions accounted for more than half of all noncash retail transactions by 2007. In some countries, some automated banking machines can now dispense traveler's cheques, different forms of ticketing, information on savings products and on loans, and can even serve as convenient communications points for institutions offering tax preparation services. More prosaically, when transactions are conducted using automated banking machines or electronic communications media, the accounting for them is completed automatically once the transaction data have been entered and verified.

As routine financial transactions are increasingly automated, intermediary personnel will spend more time selling products and providing clients with advice. Management by exception will become the rule as most human activities come to focus on less readily programmed activities, such as generating some kinds of new business and supervising the nonroutine collection of slow-paying loans. Industrialized forms of providing services will likely emerge as one way of realizing scale economies in computing and communications technologies. Financial services franchise operations will probably use commercially available computer programs to realize economies in routine financial applications, both personal and corporate. For example, production-line financial services, operated on the same principles as fast-food outlets, are becoming more common. The total number of offices will also decline as more and more of the financial system disappears into communications and information processing infrastructures.

As technological applications continue to spread, financial firms will likely centralize some activities, decentralize others. Client information is increasingly being centralized in a bank's computers. However, the information is readily available for use by different divisions, as well as by the clients themselves. Interdivisional communications using a common client base mean that combinations of different centers' services can be provided to the same client. In another technological application, some institutions are now able to determine unit profitability more precisely than has been

---

[18] Recall that unbundling risks does not remove the need for governance of the assets.

possible heretofore, and their services are increasingly being priced to reflect their true costs.

REFERENCES

Altman, Edward I., and Anthony Saunders. 2002. An analysis and critique of the BIS proposal on capital adequacy and ratings. In *Risk Management: The State of the Art*, edited by Stephen Figlewski and Richard M. Levich. Boston: Kluwer.

Benninga, Simon. 2008. Financial modeling, 3rd ed. Cambridge, MA: MIT Press.

Berger, Allen N., and David B. Humphrey. 1991. The dominance of inefficiencies over scale and product mix economies in banking. *Journal of Monetary Economics* 28: 117–148.

Berger, Allen N., and David B. Humphrey. 1992. Megamergers in banking and the use of cost efficiency as an antitrust defense. *Antitrust Bulletin* 37: 541–600.

Bond, Philip. 2004. Bank and nonbank financial intermediation. *Journal of Finance* 59: 2,489–2,529.

DeLong, Gayle, and Robert DeYoung. 2004. The value-added from observing bank mergers. In *Current Directions in Financial Regulation*, edited by Frank Milne and Edwin H. Neave. John Deutsch Institute Policy Forum Series No. 40, Queen's University, 2004.

Diamond, Douglas W., and Philip Dybvig. 1983. Bank runs, deposit insurance, and liquidity. *Journal of Political Economy* 91: 401–419.

Diamond, Douglas W., and Raghuram G. Rajan. 2000. A theory of bank capital. *Journal of Finance* 55: 2,431–2,466.

Hart, Oliver D., and Dwight Jaffee. 1974. On the application of portfolio theory to depository financial intermediaries. *Review of Economic Studies* 41: 129–147.

Mishkin, Frederic, and Philip E. Strahan. 1999. What will technology do to financial structure?" NBER Working Paper 6892.

Pyle, David. 1971. On the theory of financial intermediation. *Journal of Finance* 26: 737–747.

Walter, Ingo. 2004. Regulatory targeting: Financial services strategies across borders and sectors. In *Current Directions in Financial Regulation*, edited by Frank Milne and Edwin H. Neave. John Deutsch Institute Policy Forum Series No. 40, Queen's University, 2004.

TERMS

gap   The difference between an intermediary's floating rate assets and its floating rate liabilities. An intermediary with more floating rate assets than liabilities is said to have a positive gap, and one with more floating rate liabilities than assets is said to have a negative gap.

APPENDIX: TRADITIONAL MODEL OF LIQUIDITY MANAGEMENT

While the problem of liquidity management can be addressed by considering the effects on earnings relative to capital described already in the subsection "Intermediary Size," it may also be helpful to consider a less comprehensive version that regards liquidity management as one of balancing two kinds of costs: the cost of having to sell illiquid assets when unexpected demands for cash must be met, and the opportunity cost of holding too much in cash or short-term assets bearing low rates of return. In principle, the liquidity management problem is resolved by choosing a level of cash that minimizes the expected value of the two costs. Liquidity management problems cannot usually be addressed effectively by attempting to forecast future interest rates, largely because such forecasts can be highly imprecise, even over relatively short time periods.

Define the earnings from managing liquid assets to be

$$\pi(R) = r_L(D - R) + r R - r_P E[\text{Max}(0, X - R)] \qquad (16A.1)$$

where: $R =$ cash reserves
$D =$ deposits
$X =$ random withdrawals
$r_L =$ return on loans
$r_P =$ penalty rate on cash shortages
$r =$ riskless rate

The amount of reserves that will maximize equation (A.1) can be found by differentiating equation (16A.1) with respect to R. Setting the derivative equal to zero gives

$$\pi'(R) = -r_L + r + r_P Pr\{X \geq R\} = 0 \qquad (16A.2)$$

Solving equaton (A.2) for R^* gives

$$Pr\{X \geq R^*\} = (r_L - r)/r_p$$

In other words, the optimal reserve position takes into account the cost differences between having either too large or too small a reserve position.

Management Practice

Domestic Institutions

Chapter 17 compares and contrasts the principal businesses conducted by the larger domestic financial firms found in many economies. The chapter surveys the composition and governance of the asset-liability portfolios of banks, investment banks, near-banks, insurance companies, pension funds, lending intermediaries, financial conglomerates, and venture capital companies. Its principal purpose is to explain how the different intermediary portfolios reflect differences in the economic environments in which each operates.

BANKS

Chapter 16 modeled intermediaries as profit-maximizing organizations, and the ideas behind that model are helpful in considering the practical aspects of banking evolution. Over the longer term, banks' businesses evolve as they search for new profit sources, sources deriving from the changing economic environment and its impact on banks' operating economics. In the 1920s and 1930s, banks mainly focused on accepting deposits from commercial enterprises and on using the funds to make commercial loans. In the 1930s and 1940s, banks gradually began to discover that it was also profitable to accept retail deposits from individuals. At that time the funds raised from both forms of deposits were principally lent to businesses, usually in the form of working capital loans.

In the 1950s, North American banks began to offer both consumer and residential mortgage loans. The banks first discovered that consumer credit was a relatively low risk business that they could conduct profitably even while charging lower interest rates than their competitors, the finance companies. Banks' costs of funds are typically lower than those of their competitors because banks raise a substantial proportion of their funds through low-cost deposits. For example, finance companies raise most of their funds either through higher-cost money market borrowings or through bank lines of credit. Deposits are lower-cost sources of funds despite their being subject to cash reserves requirements[1] and the costs of providing some free services to depositors. The banks also found that mortgage lending could be profitable, and once having made this discovery, pursued the business even in the face of regulatory obstacles. For example, in some jurisdictions where banks were hampered from making mortgage loans directly, they set up nonbanking subsidiaries to carry out the business.

Beginning in the 1970s, banks faced increased competition for both consumer and commercial business, competition stemming both from various forms of retail financial intermediaries and from investment bankers. In addition they faced increased competition for the corporate financing business, and from the 1970s through the mid-1990s bank portfolios show a declining percentage of assets held as business loans as corporations made greater use of the money and securities markets for their funding needs. At the same time banks' holdings of mortgages continued to increase. In the United States, the banks gained still larger shares of the mortgage market due to the difficulties faced by the thrift institutions[2] during the 1970s and 1980s. In the later 1980s and 1990s, banks continued to increase their mortgage lending, funding the loans through securitization. From the later 1990s into the 2000s, they developed another practice: that of selling mortgage loans, whether originated by mortgage brokers or by the banks themselves, to conduits. Selling loans to conduits kept the mortgages off the banks' balance sheets and reduced the capital charges imposed by the Basel agreements of 1988; see Chapter 22.

While banks have historically focused attention on their asset portfolios, in the late 1960s, they also began actively to manage their liabilities. Liability management was later carried beyond aggressively seeking term deposit funds to raising funds in both domestic and foreign markets, especially money markets. The practice of writing loan commitments and then raising deposits to fund the commitments also became increasingly important. As traditional forms of deposit growth slowed and interest rate patterns became more variable in the late 1960s and early 1970s, banks shifted their emphasis from demand to time deposits in attempts to sustain loan growth.[3] These

---

[1] Banks may hold both required reserves and additional desired reserves as discussed in Chapter 16, and both types of reserves add to the costs of deposit funds.

[2] See the "Near-Banks" section in this chapter.

[3] Even so, traditional forms of deposits continue to remain an important source of funds, particularly for retail banks. For example, as December 1993, U.K. retail

practices, combined with a more volatile economic environment, meant that banks' funding sources became both more costly and more volatile in a process that has continued up to this writing. For example, during the credit crunch beginning in 2007, the banks' ability to obtain financing for their conduits was seriously impaired, as discussed further in Chapter 21.

During the 1950s, 1960s, and 1970s, North American banks developed extensive domestic branch networks wherever legislation permitted.[4] Branching was mainly aimed at capturing larger market shares of retail deposit and lending business. In the 1980s branch profitability began falling, and from then into the 1990s many branches were reduced in size or eliminated as banks made greater use of automated banking machines and relied more heavily on electronic communications to carry out routine transactions. In the mid-2000s, some banks are once again beginning to emphasize their branch networks.

During the 1980s, banks began acquiring such other intermediaries such as trust companies, insurance companies, and securities firms.[5] At the retail level, combinations such as banking and insurance offer scope economies in selling services to customers. At the corporate level, banks entered the securities business both because they hope to realize scope economies from the combination and because they wish to retain corporate fee business, particularly in securitization, that might otherwise be lost to market agents.

Historically, when banks concentrated on short-term commercial loans, consumer loans, and mortgage loans,[6] their default risks remained relatively low. However, in the 1960s and 1970s competition for bank loans increased, and the products offered in response included term financing, project financing, and specialized loans to particular industries. As they moved into new types of lending, the banks' default risks and their operating costs both increased, leading them to search for still other sources of profit. The search led many of the world's largest banks to develop international lending businesses during the 1970s and 1980s, and also to move into active trading. These international aspects of banking developments are discussed in Chapter 18. In further domestic responses, banks emphasized revenue generating business, culminating in the 2000s with such activities as selling securities

---

banks attracted 64% of their funds in the form of sterling deposits, about half of which—known as "sight deposits" in the United Kingdom—are payable on demand.
[4]Although U.S. legislation technically prevented interstate banking, bank holding companies surmounted the legislative barriers.
[5]The practices vary according to jurisdiction, but the trend toward combining several financial businesses in a single organization is worldwide.
[6]Consumer loans are often secured by chattel mortgages against such assets as automobiles. Mortgage loans are secured by a mortgage against the borrower's residence.

issued by their conduits. They also increased their leverage in the 2000s, in part directly by reducing their capital to assets ratios and in part indirectly by conducting business off-balance-sheet to avoid capital charges, as mentioned earlier.

The ability of banks to sell their loans has changed the banks' incentives to screen and monitor credit risk, and has also led to a lowering of lending standards, at least in some markets. As one example, since the early 2000s U.S. mortgage lenders have advanced funds to needy borrowers with poor credit records in the subprime market. As a second example, in the early to mid-2000s, banks became more willing to lend to private-equity firms with few covenants, thus surrendering much of their usual power to intervene if the loans were to deteriorate.

Parlour and Plantin (2008) examine aspects of relationship banking and loan sales. They note that firms raise money from both banks and the bond market, and also that banks sell loans either to recycle their funds or to trade on private information.[7] The private information is likely to be developed in the context of relationship banking, in which banks deal with firms over a relatively long period and acquire expert knowledge about the firms' prospects.

Parlour and Plantin argue that liquidity in a secondary loan market depends on the reasons banks are selling or securitizing loans, and that secondary loan market liquidity has the potential to affect the complementarity between public and intermediary financing: Relationship banking can influence the degree to which some corporations find it easy to raise funds. The authors' models suggest there will be excessive trade in highly rated securities, and insufficient liquidity in riskier bonds.

Revenues from long-term relations with borrowers are especially important to banks. Dahiya, Saunders, and Srinivasan (2003) examine the wealth effects on lead lending banks when their *syndicated loans* have been made to borrowers suffering financial distress. The authors find a significant and negative return for the lead lending bank when a major corporate borrower announces default or bankruptcy. In addition, banks with higher exposure to the distressed firm have larger negative announcement-period returns. A bank that has a long-term lending relationship with a distressed firm experiences larger wealth declines for bank shareholders, presumably on the grounds that long-term relationships are value creating, and financial distress signals a reduction in or termination of rents previously enjoyed.

---

[7]Up until about the beginning of the 1990s, loans were usually securitized rather than directly sold to conduits. Subsequently, relatively large proportions of loans were sold to conduits, both to reduce capital charges, as mentioned earlier in this chapter, and to increase revenues from securities sales.

During the 1990s banks emphasized mergers and a continuing emphasis on acquiring computing and communications technologies. These changes were manifest throughout the world's developed financial system. Theoretically, mergers can be rationalized as being driven both by a search for new sources of scale and scope economies, and for additional sources of revenue from offering new products. Competing for international business is also easier for larger, well-capitalized institutions, and some mergers are rationalized on these grounds. At the same time, other mergers have involved efficient institutions acquiring their less efficient counterparts in attempts to create value.

Karceski, Ongena, and Smith (2005) consider how mergers have affected commercial borrower welfare, finding from a sample of Norwegian banks that mergers affect the nature of bank-customer relationships. Merger-induced increases in relationship termination rates suggest that firms with low switching costs switch banks, while those with higher switching costs are locked in. After a merger, borrowers of target banks lose about 0.8% of their equity value, while borrowers of acquiring banks earn positive abnormal returns.

Technology investments require such massive amounts of funds that only the largest banks can finance their undertaking, but these investments also typically yield increasing returns to scale. Technology has changed the nature of financial system products and services, and has also changed the nature of access to the financial system. These impacts of technology continue to change even as they are increasingly documented. For example, Petersen and Rajan (2002) find that with the increasing use of financial technology the distance between small firms and their lenders is increasing, and that bank-borrower communications are becoming more impersonal. Moreover, distant firms no longer have to be the highest quality credits, indicating they have greater access to credit. Peterson and Rajan argue that the changes do not arise from small firms locating differently or from consolidation in the banking industry. Rather, improvements in lender productivity appear to explain the findings. The changes in small business lending appear principally to be due to greater use of techniques such as credit scoring. When necessary, banks can still monitor and counsel firms individually, but they are likely to detect difficulties through technological means first, then to intervene in a more personal way.

INVESTMENT BANKS

Although the securities industry is comprised of a relatively large number of firms, the industry is dominated by a few of the larger investment banks.

Historically, some firms specialized in certain areas, such as underwriting on the one hand, providing investment management services and advice to retail clients on the other. However, by the mid-2000s, the largest investment banks mainly operated as full-service firms, combining securities underwriting, securities sales, trading, and wealth management.[8] Trading is conducted both on the firm's own account and on behalf of clients, and includes sales of investment products that have either been developed by or are sold on a licensed basis by the firm. The larger investment banks are also prominent in arranging mergers and acquisitions.

Investment banks' activities in raising public market financing comprise advising, administration, underwriting, and distribution of securities. In their advisory functions, most investment bankers offer clients information on raising finance, providing them with details of alternative financing methods, likely costs, and other advantages and disadvantages. Administrative functions primarily cover the legal and accounting services associated with new securities issues. Investment bankers underwrite new securities issues in several different ways. They may buy an entire issue outright (known as a *bought deal*), they may offer a guaranteed price a few days before the securities are issued, or they may offer a best-efforts distribution in which they attempt to raise as much money as possible from the security sale. The range of alternatives depends on the financial status of the issuing company, the state of the securities markets, and the details of the issue. The strongest issues—that is, the one easiest to market—may qualify for treatment as bought deals, while a fixed price arrangement is the most common. Weaker securities are more likely to be sold on a best-efforts basis.

Many securities firms underwrite both public and private market transactions, but set up different specialist groups within the firm to do so. When they can, clients choose between public and private market deals on the basis of cost and funding availability.[9] The costs of a public market issue are mainly placement costs, including underwriting commissions and the costs of information distribution, that is, preparing, registering, and distributing a prospectus. Subsequent secondary market trading enhances the issue's liquidity, and can therefore make it easier to sell the securities in the first place. In part, this is because a public issue of securities will subsequently trade in the secondary market. Active trading in turn means that new information

---

[8]The later 2008 changes in the investment banking industry are mentioned at the end of this section.

[9]The economics of the choice involves considering the costs and benefits of different forms of static complementarity, and is similar in concept to the economics of considering bank versus market financing.

about the issuing firm is valued in the marketplace as it becomes publicly available.

In the United States, the lines between commercial banking and investment banking became increasingly blurred during the 1970s, 1980s, and 1990s as commercial banks and investment banks became active competitors in some areas. From its passage in 1933 and until the late 1990s the provisions of the Glass-Steagall Act legally separated commercial and investment banking. Historically, commercial banks were the most important participants in the credit markets, while investment banks were the most important participants in selling new issues of debt or equity in the primary securities markets, as well as making secondary markets for the securities. During the period of increasing competition, the large money center and regional commercial banks saw their largest and most profitable customers increasingly switching from bank loans to direct issues of securities. At the same time money market accounts and similar investment products represented new securities industry competition for commercial banks' savings deposits.

In the face of the increasing competition both types of firms, but particularly the large commercial banks, sought to break down the barriers posed by the Glass-Steagall Act. The efforts resulted in the act's ultimately being replaced by passage of the Financial Services Modernization Act (1999), which created financial holding companies that can own commercial banking, securities, and insurance affiliates.[10] The Financial Services Modernization Act also gave investment banks greater opportunity to engage in commercial banking activities, and these possibilities were the basis of extensive investment banking changes in late 2008, as discussed in this section.

Mergers in the securities industry are common, as member firms continue to adapt to their changing economic environment. Mergers represent both attempts to realize scale and scope economies, and attempts to diversify earnings sources in a search for greater earnings stability. Profits in the investment banking industry are cyclical, and one of the main reasons for forming full-service firms has been to provide diversified income sources. The picture changed still further in 2008.

Beginning with the acquisition of Bear Sterns by JPMorgan Chase in mid-2008, the four remaining four large investment banks in the United States all were either sold or converted to bank holding companies during the market turmoil of 2008. Lehman Brothers failed in September of that

---

[10] Most European countries allow universal banks: institutions that can accept deposits, make loans, underwrite securities, and sell and manufacture other financial services such as insurance.

year and some divisions of the firm were acquired by other financial institutions. Shortly thereafter, Merrill Lynch announced its acquisition by Bank of America. Subsequently, but still in September 2008, both the Goldman Sachs group and Morgan Stanley announced they were becoming bank holding companies. The investment banks' capital had been seriously affected by losses stemming both from the subprime markets and from credit default swaps, and one of the principal driving forces behind the restructurings was to secure access to additional capital (some provided from government sources as discussed in Chapter 22). A second reason was ultimately to utilize deposits as additional stable sources of longer-term funding.

NEAR-BANKS

Other depository intermediaries, very often called "near-banks," closely resemble banks that specialize in the retail business. In most countries near-banks have operated almost exclusively in domestic markets, although since the 1980s some have begun to participate in syndicated lending. Near-banks mainly raise funds through savings deposits and relend the monies in the form of mortgage and consumer loans. Some near-banks emphasize their role as savings institutions, others stress their lending activities. In both cases, liabilities are mainly savings and term deposits with maturities ranging from a few months to as long as five years.

The near-banks' proportion of mortgages to consumer loans is frequently large. In the past, many regulatory jurisdictions restricted investments to mortgages and government bonds. If other assets were permitted, the proportions were usually limited. However, since the 1980s, most jurisdictions have increasingly granted near-banks greater freedoms and as a result many are evolving toward full service retail financial institutions.

Asset management in near-banks has mainly involved increasing the flexibility of terms on what had traditionally been fixed rate level payment mortgage loans. As interest rates on deposits became increasingly variable in the 1970s and 1980s, near-banks began to offer adjustable rate mortgages, allowing them better to match interest revenues against interest costs over changing market conditions.[11] They also began to use graduated rather than level payment mortgages in order to address the problem of borrowers' cash flows being adversely affected by increases in interest rates, as discussed in Chapter 11.

---

[11] Adjustable rate mortgages can also create problems for both borrowers and lenders, as discussed in the subprime mortgages section of Chapter 11.

Liability management mainly emphasizes attempts to raise longer-term deposits with the intent of providing a better match for interest revenues. But, since most consumers prefer short-term deposits, the attempt to raise long-term fixed-rate funds has not been very successful, and most interest-bearing deposits carry floating rates. Most near-banks now also offer checkable deposit accounts, some of which are interest bearing.

In North America the near-banks form one of the main links between deposit and loan markets. The near-bank industry has been highly innovative, perhaps even more so than the banking industry. For example, near-banks developed flexible mortgages and various forms of retirement savings plans, and were early to introduce daily interest savings accounts. On the other hand, few near-banks have experimented with reverse mortgages, an instrument designed to provide income to retired persons by making loans against equity in the person's residence. Such loans are liquidated by the sale of assets at the time of the person's death. The lack of aggressiveness in marketing this instrument is rather curious, since the near-banks are so familiar with mortgage lending and since the percentage of retired persons continues to increase in many countries.

Portfolio theory must be modified to apply to organizations other than publicly owned firms. For example, a mutually owned intermediary might try to maximize its market value, but a maximizing criterion might not be clearly defined. Moreover, the management of a mutually owned intermediary might not even be motivated to pursue the goal of market value maximization. In particular, since the mutually owned firm's management does not face the possibility of being ousted through a takeover bid, management can pay somewhat less heed to public acceptance of its decisions than can the management of a publicly owned, for-profit company. Since mutual firms have no publicly traded stock, resolving the conflict between stakeholder groups is not easy. Management cannot usually look to industry standards for assistance, because the same goals may be given different weights in different institutions. Other intermediaries may also deviate from a maximizing criterion. A goal such as providing cheap loans subsidizes some clients at the expense of others, but it may still be chosen by, say, some credit unions.

U.S. Thrift Institutions

The model of Chapter 16 can be used to explain the principal operational problems encountered by the U.S. thrifts. Until the early 1970s, U.S. thrifts financed fixed rate mortgages with floating rate deposit liabilities, which meant the correlation between interest revenues and interest costs was close to zero. With a correlation close to zero, a thrift's potential profit risk was relatively high, as can be verified by reading across a row or down a column of Table 16.2 in the previous chapter and noting that the return varies more than it does when reading down the table's main diagonal. However, until the early 1970s, the interest rate environment was relatively stable and the potential risks went unrecognized.

Although U.S. thrifts had been prosperous since about 1900, they began to experience operating difficulties in the mid-1960s as short-term interest rates began to rise. At that time the thrifts' principal investments were fixed rate mortgages, and rises in interest rates presented the possibility that formerly positive interest rate spreads would turn negative. During the 1970s, costs continued to rise while revenues remained largely fixed, and the possibility of losses became a reality.

The first attempt to keep the U.S. thrifts profitable was to stabilize their costs by imposing legislated ceilings on the rates they and banks could pay on savings accounts. However, savers then withdrew their funds from savings accounts in a process referred to as *disintermediation*, which meant taking deposits from intermediaries and investing them in more lucrative forms of assets, such as marketable securities.[12] After being found unworkable, the interest rate ceilings were removed, and the thrifts' potential profitability problems became real ones. The profitability problems were then further exacerbated by increases in interest rate volatility that faced the thrifts with variable as well as rising costs of funds.

A thrift institution can reduce its risk by increasing the correlation between its interest earnings and its interest costs, a change that could be brought about by using flexible rather than fixed rate mortgages. Eventually, following on changes in regulation that removed constraints from the kinds of liabilities the thrifts could issue and that also permitted them to offer floating rate mortgages, the thrifts began to restructure their portfolios. Attempts to stabilize accounting profits were the main reason why thrifts and other similar mortgage lenders began to offer floating rate mortgages in the 1970s and 1980s. During this restructuring period, however, the thrifts' profitability problems worsened and many firms became insolvent. The insolvencies were further exacerbated by fixed rate deposit insurance that created a moral hazard problem to which many thrift institutions succumbed. Deposit insurance allowed any thrift, no matter how risky, to compete equally with other, safer institutions for saver's funds. But the thrifts also faced strong incentives to improve profitability by acquiring highly risky earning assets. Since many were already near insolvency, their shareholders had little to lose if the risks did not pay off, much to gain if they did. These moral hazard problems with fixed rate deposit insurance are further examined in Chapter 20.

---

[12] Thus some of the competition between depository institutions and investment banks was actually stimulated by the interest rate ceilings.

Thrift depositors also faced strong incentives to direct their deposits toward the riskiest thrifts, because these institutions offered the highest interest rates. Since high-yield deposits carried the same deposit insurance as lower-yield ones, thrift clients did not face additional risks. Effectively, the depositors held a put option written by an agency of the U.S. government. If the thrift failed, the deposit insurance corporation (in this case the Federal Savings and Loan Insurance Corporation, FSLIC) paid off the depositor losses. Deposit insurance losses and recognition of the moral hazard problem led to further legislation, revision of deposit insurance schemes, restructuring of the FSLIC, and strengthening of thrifts' capital requirements. By the mid-1990s, the thrifts began to return to profitability, but the process of adjusting their portfolios to achieve floating rate earnings was a long, painful, and costly one. The costs attributed to the crisis amounted to some 3.7% of U.S. GDP (Laeven and Valencia 2008).

INSURANCE COMPANIES

Insurance companies constitute a significant class of financial intermediaries for several reasons. First, in many countries the assets of insurance firms are at least as large as those of banks. Second, insurance companies assume and trade risks at both wholesale and retail levels. Third, since the beginning of the 2000s banking and insurance functions have increasingly been combined within the same firms. Fourth, banking and insurance are related in concept, as this book has already noted in its discussion of the similarities between the risk pooling carried out by banks and the risks assumed by insurance companies.

Insurance companies are financial intermediaries because they collect premiums that remain invested until the funds are paid out in claims or transferred to earnings. Life insurance companies insure against policyholder death or loss of income, while property and casualty companies underwrite such events as fire or hurricane damage to a building. Insurance companies strive to profit from the premiums they charge for assuming risks. In effect, insurance companies write put options on insured parties' assets and sell the puts to their clients. The insurance policy premiums are, in effect, put option premiums. Most insurance policies are written for one year or more and arranged by individual negotiation with the client.

Life Insurance Companies

Some life policies offer both insurance and a form of savings, and industry growth depends on offering liabilities with a continuing appeal to savers. The industry has not always been successful in this regard. From the 1960s through the 1980s life insurance captured a declining proportion of North American savings, largely because many policies did not pay competitive interest rates on the savings portion of the contract. In attempts to recover lost ground, new products such as universal life insurance were developed to provide savers with rates of return commensurate with those on other forms of savings. To compensate the insurance company, premiums paid for life protection are usually subject to increases when higher interest rates are paid on policyholders' investments. Equally, premiums can decline when interest rates are lower.

The actuarial values of life insurance companies' liabilities can generally be calculated with considerable precision. As a result, life insurance companies hold relatively small proportions of liquid assets. On the other hand, since it is important to earn predictable returns on their long-run investments, life insurance companies invest mainly in long-term bonds and hold them to maturity. This investment policy allows life companies to fix a minimum rate of return on invested funds, and thus ensure that premiums plus investment income will be actuarially sufficient to cover claims on their policies.

Regulations applying to life insurance companies chiefly restrict the kinds of investments they can hold. In addition, investments must meet earnings and dividend tests similar to those faced by pension funds.

Property and Casualty Insurance Companies

Property and casualty insurance companies write policies whose claims are less predictable than those of life insurance policies. As a result, property and casualty insurance companies' investment portfolios are more liquid than those of life companies. For example, in the United States property and casualty insurance companies are the most important purchasers of municipal bonds because interest on the bonds is not regarded as a part of their taxable incomes.

The property and casualty insurance businesses are cyclical; several years of profits are likely to be followed by several years of losses. This phenomenon occurs primarily because profits attract new entrants to the business and these new entrants typically acquire business at lower premiums than those currently being charged, leading to periodic industry overcapacity.

In an attempt to diversify their underwriting risks geographically, some insurance companies establish regional underwriting limits. If the demand for insurance in a particular period exceeds the regional underwriting limits, insurance companies will stop writing policies for the rest of that period. Underwriting limits thus create financial market imperfections, and it is not clear why the insurance companies do not adopt the alternative of charging higher premiums. They may wish to avoid political or public relations difficulties that might result from charging discriminatory rates to similar clients in different locations or at different times of the year.

Monoline Insurance Companies

A monoline insurance company provides guarantees to issuers of bonds and other securities, often in the form of enhancements intended to support the issuer's credit. The companies, which must be highly rated by the rating agencies, guarantee payment of the debt of lower-rated bond issuers in exchange for a premium. Issuers will often use the services of monolines either to boost the rating of one of their debt issues or to ensure that a debt issue does not become downgraded. The ratings of debt issues so supported often reflect the monoline's credit rating. In this way a monoline can reduce an issuer's interest cost of debt by an amount greater than the premium paid for the guarantee.

Insurance company regulations prohibit life insurance companies, property and casualty insurance companies, and multiline insurance companies from issuing such guarantees. Monoline insurance companies first began providing enhancements for municipal bond issues, but their business has evolved to provide similar support for other types of bonds, such as mortgage-backed securities and collateralized debt obligations.

Monoline insurers first began business in 1971, and conducted a profitable business until 2006, reaching a total of more than three trillion dollars by the end of 2006. At the beginning of 2007, housing market declines led to losses on some structured products, and the underwriting business suffered as a consequence. By January 2008, most monolines had been subjected to reductions in their credit ratings, and many insured bonds were trading at interest rates little different from the rates on similar uninsured bonds. Since that time the monoline business has declined, although new insurers such as Berkshire Hathaway entered the market in late 2008.

Risk Diversification

Insurers provide risk diversification for both personal and business clients. They are thus motivated from a core business perspective to maintain a diversified pool of clients, as well as to seek more global diversification of their liabilities through purchasing reinsurance. During the 1970s and 1980s, the reinsurance business, in which international companies purchase large proportions of policies originated by small companies, began to grow rapidly. For example, in 1985, when issuing $900 million worth of default insurance on Citicorp's loans to less developed countries, CIGNA Corporation resold most of the liabilities in the reinsurance market. Growth of the reinsurance business has continued to the present writing, but the extent to which the growth allows offsetting cyclical profit risks (at least for the reinsurance companies if not for the smaller originating companies) does not yet seem to have been explored.

There are at least two alternatives to reinsurance: exchange trading of the original risks and the use of other instruments to spread risks. Insurance exchanges are markets in which newly originated risks can be traded. The most famous exchange is Lloyd's of London, but there are similar exchanges in New York, Chicago, and Miami. As to other instruments for spreading risks, the U.S. securities industry has created both catastrophe futures and catastrophe bonds—bonds whose payoffs depend on whether underwriting losses are incurred as a result of catastrophic events. Catastrophe bonds, sold by insurance companies to investors, are only redeemed if the issuing company does not face more than a given amount of claims resulting from such events as hurricane damage. Futures contracts are also used as a means of diversifying and trading the risks associated with large-scale storm, flood, and earthquake damage. They offer an increased payoff to insurance companies in the event of industry losses due to natural disasters.

Industry Change

As financial services become increasingly integrated, insurance companies are experimenting with new distribution systems, and selling such additional products as trust company deposits and mutual fund shares. Banks are beginning to sell insurance by making sales and distribution agreements with existing life companies. Banks have for some time utilized affiliated insurance companies to write life insurance against various kinds of personal loans they offer. U.S. insurance companies are attempting to obtain regulatory permission to sell their products through banks. In Canada, insurance products are now sold through credit unions, trust companies, banks, and some investment dealers.

Several life companies are selling each others' products and some trust companies sell life annuities through insurance agents. Large national retailers offer life insurance on credit purchases and there are sales of general insurance, financial counseling services, mutual and money market funds and securities brokerage. Some life companies also offer deposit accounts, focusing mainly on accounts with electronic access. Insurance companies are merging with each other and with banks, and both these trends can be expected to continue.

Technological change in insurance companies was rapid when computers first came into use around 1960, but since then the rate of change has slowed. The insurance companies attribute slow adjustment to technological change to the cost and indivisibility of computer systems as well as to a shortage of skilled personnel, but other financial companies have not found these factors as limiting. Insurance companies will probably need to acquire state-of-the-art technology to cope successfully with increased competition in the 2000s.

Cummins, Rubio-Misas, and Zi (2004) examine the wholesale services opportunities that arise from the convergence of the banking and insurance businesses. The authors argue that markets sort organizational forms into segments where the different business forms have comparative advantages. In particular, the authors show that joint stock and mutual insurance companies operate on different efficiency frontiers and thus represent distinct technologies. Their evidence shows that in cost and revenue efficiency, stock companies of all sizes dominate mutual companies in the production of stock output vectors, and smaller mutual companies dominate stock companies in the production of mutual output vectors. Larger mutuals neither dominate nor are dominated by stocks, and consequently these companies appear to be vulnerable to competition from stock insurers. The overall results are consistent with the conclusion that, as a result of market forces, insurers in different market segments adopt organizational forms that have comparative advantages.

In late September 2008, American International Group (AIG) obtained an $85 billion two-year loan, at a penalty rate, from the Federal Reserve System in what has become known as the rescue of one of the world's biggest insurers. In exchange for providing the facility, the Fed obtained a 79.9% stake in the company. The rescue was arranged because the investment banking business of AIG posed a systemic risk stemming from its credit default swap (CDS) business. The investment bank built up a notional exposure of $441 billion by June 2008, with the instruments covering both losses on subprime securities and losses on instruments written by banks in both the United States and Europe.

The arrangement is explained as forestalling a liquidity crisis. As subprime losses mounted, AIG had to put up more collateral with its counterparties, in turn prompting credit-rating downgrades, which in turn triggered more margin calls. The facility is intended to buy time for AIG to improve its liquidity and avoid a technical bankruptcy that could force the unwinding of many CDSs.

PENSION FUNDS

A private-sector pension fund represents employee savings accumulated to finance payment of retirement benefits. Pension funds have gained an increasing proportion of North American savings flows since the 1950s. Society's increasing wealth, and increases in the proportions of persons attaining retirement age are both contributory factors. At the end of 2005, U.S. private and public pension funds together held approximately $7.2 trillion in assets, an amount almost equal to the $9.2 trillion held by commercial banks as deposits.

Pension fund investment portfolios are financed by contributions from both employers and employees. The funds are usually invested by a board of trustees, chosen by the employer but acting on behalf of the employees. Employees cannot use their pension fund assets, even as collateral for a loan, until they retire. The success of this illiquid form of saving seems to be due to a combination of factors: Contributions are tax-exempt, and pension fund membership is a condition of employment with many large firms. In addition, persons who find it difficult to save voluntarily may regard it advantageous to enroll in compulsory forms of savings plans.

A pension fund may be organized either as a *defined benefit plan*, in which case a payout formula is specified in the pension contract, or as a defined contribution plan, in which case the contributions are specified and payouts depend on investment returns. Defined benefit plans whose payouts are guaranteed by insurance products are known as insured plans; others are called non-insured plans. Some insurance companies offer standard plans for small firms. Although many plans were initially formed as defined benefit plans, their increasing costs led many companies to wind up existing plans, replacing them in some cases with defined contribution plans and with incentives for individuals to invest funds personally to provide additional retirement benefits. Since most pension funds operate as nonprofit organizations, their investment returns are not usually subject to income taxation, although pension payments are usually taxed when they are received as income by the employee.

Pension funds are important buyers of corporate stocks and bonds, but the larger funds view capital market securities as only temporary outlets for their investments. They also invest directly in real estate, mortgages, and oil and gas development projects. Some pension funds have even entered merchant banking activity, helping finance corporate mergers and acquisitions. In the early to mid-2000s some pension funds were also active providers of private equity. Many funds are managed by advisory firms. Pension advisory firms are usually independent, although some trust and insurance companies have investment counseling subsidiaries.

Many individuals have a considerable proportion of their life savings invested in a pension fund, and some jurisdictions supervise the administration of pension assets quite closely. For example, in the U.S. pension funds are governed by the Employee Retirement Income Security Act (ERISA, 1974). This act requires that assets be sufficient to meet (all or a proportion of) each fund's actuarially calculated liabilities, a provision known as a minimum funding standard. Each fund is to be governed by trustees who are legally responsible for the prudent investment of assets. Minimum vesting standards are established, meaning that the contributions of both employer and employee belong to the employee after a minimum number of years service with the employed.

During the 1990s, individuals have increasingly turned to private savings as a way of supplementing future pension incomes. This private saving takes the form of mutual fund purchases, bond purchases, and bank deposits. In some jurisdictions all or portions of the contributions can be made out of pre-tax income, with taxes to be collected when the funds are paid out as pension income.

Although the large amounts of funds invested in pension funds are reason enough for their regulation, there are also other justifications for supervision. Pension fund managers strive to achieve high rates of return on pension investments, since higher returns reduce employer contribution costs. But higher return investments carry higher risks, and risk-taking is by definition not always successful. Thus the managers of weaker pension funds can be tempted to take relatively large risks with employees' savings.[13] In addition, some private sector funds hold relatively large amounts of their own firm's stock, so that the security of employees' pension assets is tied to the fortunes of the firm. Finally, some pension funds have become heavily involved in private equity investments, meaning their portfolio returns are increasingly dependent on the abilities of their private equity managers to overcome the operating problems of their acquisitions, to sell the acquisitions at a subsequent profit, and thereby create returns to their investments.

The ERISA also establishes the U.S. Pension Benefit Guaranty Corporation to make payments in the event a fund falls into bankruptcy, but not all jurisdictions treat pension assets with equal care. Canada has no federal pension plan insurance corporation, although Ontario insures funds established under its provincial legislation. As long as insurance premiums

---

[13] This is, of course, a variant of the same moral hazard problem faced by the U.S. thrifts, discussed earlier in this chapter.

risc with risk, an insurance plan will create fewer perverse incentives for its managers.[14]

LENDING INTERMEDIARIES

Lending intermediaries are institutions with specialized loan portfolios. For example, they may finance vehicle and equipment purchases, act as factors, provide export trade finance, or venture capital financing. Typically, lending intermediaries raise their funds by issuing money market instruments and by borrowing from other financial institutions. Their main funds are issues of short-term financial paper, long-term debt, bank loans, loans from affiliates, and owners' equity. They raise only small proportions of their funds by soliciting deposits from the public. In many cases a lending intermediary's principal role is that of an agent. For example, a loan initially made by a lending intermediary may ultimately be placed with a long-term investor such as a pension fund. Carey, Post, and Sharpe find that lending intermediaries specialize, both in attempts to establish a reputation and to satisfy regulatory requirements. The evidence produced by Carey et al. suggests that "lender reputation plays a role in solving private debt contracting problems" (1998, 876).

Term Lenders

A term lender's chief purpose is to provide medium-term loans to medium-sized businesses. Term lenders are often specialized bank affiliates, because most regular branch personnel do not possess the skills needed for successful term lending. Indeed many of the necessary lending skills, both screening capabilities and the art of ex post governance, are acquired on an experiential (learning-by-doing) basis. Term lenders specialize partly because they can realize scale economies in their governance activities. In addition, some lending intermediaries serve relatively small markets and cannot readily extend their skills to other markets. Term lenders are also skilled in raising funds from institutional investors such as pension funds or life insurance companies.

Other term lenders raise funds from financial institutions with a view to investing them in portfolios of residential and commercial mortgages originated by still other institutions. These firms, known as real estate investment trusts and mortgage investment companies, channel funds raised

---

[14] Nevertheless, some experts emphasize that risk-adjusted premiums alone are not sufficient to dampen the animal spirits of achievement-oriented investment managers. These experts argue that regulation and supervision are also necessary.

by institutions such as pension funds and life insurance companies into mortgage investments. In some jurisdictions they have had tax advantages not available to other kinds of businesses, but by the time of this writing these advantages have been attenuated and the activity has lessened.

Finance Companies

Finance companies mainly provide credit to consumers and to wholesale businesses engaged in selling consumer durables. To a lesser extent, finance companies also provide credit to wholesalers of industrial durable goods. Frequently the two activities are combined within the same finance company, suggesting the presence of scope economies to the two types of transaction. Acceptance companies mainly finance conditional sales contracts generated by retail or wholesale businesses. They can be subdivided into retailers, car and truck manufacturers, and farm equipment manufacturers, some of which also provide term loans and financial leases to their clients. General acceptance corporations also purchase installment finance contracts, but are not tied to one organization.

Finance companies generally fund their operations through money market instruments and bank borrowing. Finance companies usually have high costs of funds because they do not have access to retail deposit markets. Their asset-equity ratios are usually lower than those of the banks, and their ability to generate a return on equity can also be lower. In some cases, these features of finance company operations have led finance companies to restructure their operations as banks.

Financial Leasing Companies

Financial leasing companies mainly finance fixed capital equipment, offering advantageous terms to some companies, particularly companies that cannot use their depreciation allowances as tax shields. A leasing company can obtain depreciation tax shields not available to the lessee firm either because the prospective lessee's income is not taxable or because its income is not large enough to create a tax liability. Apart from possible tax advantages, financial lease contracts really offer an alternative to debt or term financing. For some firms, financial leasing is an important alternative to borrowing. Financial leasing companies in the United States, such as GE Capital Services, Associates Commercial Corporation, AT&T Capital Corporation, IBM Credit Corporation, and others are very fast-growing parts of the financial services industry. These firms provide strong competition for banks in some areas of corporate finance, especially areas where relatively complex financial structuring is required.

Asset-Backed Commercial Paper Programs (ABCPs)

An asset-backed commercial paper program (ABCP) essentially involves forming a conduit to issue commercial paper, and using the proceeds of the commercial paper sale either to acquire various types of assets or to make secured loans to third party purchasers. An ABCP program includes parties that perform various services for the conduit such as credit enhancement to provide a form of loss protection, and liquidity facilities that can be drawn upon to assist in timely redemption of commercial paper.

The repayment of outstanding commercial paper depends on the cash generated by the conduit's underlying asset portfolio and its ability to issue new commercial paper. The main risks faced by an ABCP are asset deterioration in the underlying portfolio, potential timing mismatches between portfolio cash generation, and the repayment of maturing commercial paper, the conduit's inability to issue new commercial paper, and risks associated with the financial institutions servicing the assets. Some protection against these risks is provided through credit enhancement, liquidity support, commercial paper stop-issuance arrangements and wind-down triggers.

However, the essential risk is the same as in banking: An ABCP funds long-term assets with short-term liabilities, and in the event of a liquidity crunch the ability to wind down such a portfolio without suffering losses can be severely compromised. These events occurred during the market turmoil of 2007–2008, when the ability of ABCP programs to raise short-term funds was severely curtailed, and many programs' paper was frozen. At this writing (January 2009), it is questionable whether ABCP programs will experience a revival.

VENTURE CAPITAL COMPANIES

Venture capital companies offer another example of intermediaries serving specialized markets. While they usually extend higher risk forms of financing than lending intermediaries, most venture investors fund existing rather than new businesses. Principally, venture capital companies provide medium-term loan and investment capital to selected firms with relatively high earnings growth prospects. Typically they accept about one per cent of the applications they consider. Venture capital companies seek high rates of return on their investments—on the order of 50% per annum—but realized returns are lower, since a substantial proportion of a venture firm's investments are unsuccessful and do not yield the target returns.

There are relatively high set-up costs to screening potential investments if the necessary screening skills are acquired experientially, and these experientially acquired skills are usually too expensive to be employed in more traditional types of lending. On the other hand, many venture capital firms need to show annual profits on their investments in order to satisfy the demands of the institutions funding them. Consequently such firms cannot invest entirely in investments with very long-run payoffs, even if the investments are likely to prove relatively rewarding. The typical venture investment is only likely to show profits after several years of operation, and therefore a judicious balancing of portfolio returns is necessitated if management is to appeal to investors.[15]

Venture financings involve negotiations between entrepreneur and financier, negotiations focusing both on how the client firm will be controlled and on the cost of financing. Entrepreneurs can derive private non-pecuniary benefits from having some control over a firm. In particular, the entrepreneur may be able to extract relatively high rents by taking advantage of asymmetric information; compare Kirilenko (2001). To reduce these entrepreneurial benefits, the venture capitalist may demand relatively high control rights. The entrepreneur is compensated for loss of control through better financing terms and improved risk sharing.

Cassamatta (2003) argues that the terms of venture financing arrangements depend on the relative expertise of the entrepreneur and the financier. Typically, outside financiers can enhance project value by supplementing the entrepreneur's expertise. A common stock position is often desired by a venture capitalist, but in cases where the entrepreneur must be strongly motivated, a financier may accept convertible bonds. Common stocks are likely to be preferred by financiers when the amount of external financing is small, while convertible bonds are more likely to be used when the amount of financing is large. Convertible bonds offer the advantage of providing for payment of interest that will allow generating a regular return for the institutional investors funding the venture capitalist.

Ueda (2004) notes that since venture capitalists specialize in gathering project information, entrepreneurs try to guard against the possibility that financiers will use their specialized knowledge to expropriate project earnings. On the other hand, Dessein (2005) argues that an entrepreneur may relinquish control to an investor to signal the congruence of their preferences. The more favorable the private information of the entrepreneur, the more formal control rights he may be willing to relinquish.

---

[15] Venture firms operating as agents or divisions of banks may not need to demonstrate annual profits on their investments, but can rather invest their funds with a view to generating longer-term earnings.

Kaplan and Stromberg (2004) examine 67 portfolio investments of 11 venture capital firms. They consider the allocation of cash flow rights, contingencies and control rights, and liquidation rights. They find that attempts to resolve agency and hold-up problems are important dimensions of contract design, but that risk-sharing is not. However, it is not clear from the paper whether risk-sharing is handled implicitly through the instruments employed in designing the contract.

Lindsey (2008) documents a new value-added role for venture capitalists by viewing strategic alliances as relational contracts that blur firm boundaries. Lindsey finds that alliances are more frequent among companies that share a common venture capitalist, and particularly if the companies' contracting problems are more pronounced. Lindsey's findings are consistent both with venture capitalists' utilizing informational advantages in providing resources, and with alliances' improving the probability of exit for venture-backed firms.

EVOLUTION

The financial institutions of the future will continue to perform the six main functions introduced in Chapter 2, as well as the many sub-functions discussed in the present chapter. However, the way in which the functions are performed will continue to change as technology continues to evolve, and the organizations that perform them will also likely change. For example as outlined in Chapters 6 and 7, risk management instruments permit firms to divide and trade risks in ways different from their principal nonfinancial businesses. In a risk trading environment, financial intermediaries will survive partly on their ability to assume and to unbundle different kinds of risks. The decision to sell risks, or to keep them, will depend largely on the economics of combining information and decisions, as examined in Chapter 3. Although experiments with different forms of governance will likely take place, it should be recalled that unless bank-like governance is provided to portfolios of individual loans, the write-offs from the portfolios have historically been shown to mount sharply. If derivatives are used to trade risks, the incentive effects on the management of the underlying risky assets need to be understood clearly if the risk management function is not to be attenuated.

REFERENCES

Carey, Mark, Mitch Post, and Steven A. Sharpe. 1998. Does corporate lending by banks and finance companies differ? Evidence on specialization in private debt contracting. *Journal of Finance* 53: 845–878.

Cassamatta, Catherine. 2003. Financing and advising: Optimal financial contracts with venture capitalists. *Journal of Finance* 58: 2,059–2,086.

Cummins, J. David, Maria Rubio-Misas, and Hongmin Zi. 2004. The effect of organizational structure on efficiency: Evidence from the Spanish insurance industry. *Journal of Banking and Finance* 28: 3,113–3,150.

Dahiya, Sandeep, Anthony Saunders, and Anand Srinivasan. 2003. Financial distress and bank lending relationships. *Journal of Finance* 58: 375–400.

Dessein, Wouter. 2005. Information and control in ventures and alliances. *Journal of Finance* 60: 2,513–2,549.

Kaplan, Steven N., and Per Stromberg. 2004. Characteristics, contracts, and actions: evidence from venture capitalist analyses. *Journal of Finance* 59: 2,177–2,210.

Karceski, Jason, Steven Ongena, and David C. Smith. 2005. The impact of bank consolidation on commercial borrower welfare. *Journal of Finance* 60: 2,043–2,082.

Kirilenko Andrei G. 2001. Valuation and control in venture financing. *Journal of Finance* 56: 565–587.

Laeven, Luc, and Fabian Valencia. 2008. Systemic banking crises: A new database. IMF Working Paper WP/08/224.

Lindsey, Laura. 2008. Blurring firm boundaries: The role of venture capital in strategic alliances. *Journal of Finance* 63: 1,137–1,168.

Parlour, Christine A., and Guillaume Plantin. 2008. Loan sales and relationship banking. *Journal of Finance* 63: 1,291–1,314.

Petersen, Mitchell A., and Raghuram G. Rajan. 2002. Does distance still matter? The information revolution in small business lending. *Journal of Finance* 57: 2,533–2,570.

Ueda, Masako. 2004. Banks versus venture capital: Project evaluation, screening, and expropriation. *Journal of Finance* 59: 601–621.

TERMS

bought deal　An outright purchase of a new issue of securities, which are then distributed from inventory by the securities firm arranging the deal.

defined benefit plan　A pension plan with specified payouts. It is contrasted with a *defined contribution plan* that specifies only the contributions into the fund.

disintermediation　The process of removing funds from depository intermediaries and placing them in securities.

syndicated loans　Loans to a given client, arranged by a lead bank and provided by a number of banks. The lead bank usually receives a commission for arranging the entire transaction and earns interest on its own portion of the loan. Other members of the syndicate may choose either to screen the loan themselves or delegate that function to the lead bank.

International Banking and Banking Markets

Chapter 18 focuses on international intermediaries and related institutions. It considers the similarities and differences among international banks, investment banks, and financial conglomerates. It also discusses reasons for the emergence of a truly international group of markets—the Euromarkets.

INTERNATIONAL BANKING

While there was little international banking activity between the 1930s and the late 1950s, burgeoning international trade in the 1960s stimulated a resurgence that has been ongoing up to the credit crunch of 2007–2008. The first forays into international banking took the form of banks following their nonfinancial clients into new markets as a way of protecting existing connections. The continuing growth of multinational firms contributed to more growth in both financial and nonfinancial international business, and from those beginnings, international finance and risk management have grown into today's integrated global activity.

Overview

International banks sometimes enjoy comparative advantages in being able profitably to make loans or investments that domestic banks do not find profitable. In smaller markets the average costs of an international bank can be lower than those of an indigenous bank because of scale economies, since the international bank has a larger volume of business over which to spread the fixed costs of entering new markets. Citigroup, with some 300,000 employees, is one of the best-known examples of an international bank, and is also one that has developed an important investment banking business in the 1990s and 2000s. Citigroup grew to its current size by a series of mergers and acquisitions, the largest of which was the $140 billion merger of Citicorp and Travelers in 1998. Citigroup provides financial services in national markets worldwide as well as in the Euromarkets. As another example, HSBC, which terms itself the world's local bank, is headquartered in London. HSBC is one of the largest banking and financial services organizations in the world, with some 9,500 offices in 85 countries and territories in Europe, the Asia-Pacific region, the Americas, the Middle East and Africa. HSBC provides personal financial services, commercial, corporate, investment, and private banking, and trading services.

As with the examples of Citibank and HKBC, many large international banks are known as universal banks, a term indicating they offer both banking and investment banking services. Kanatas and Qi (2003) argue that universal banks offering both lending and underwriting services can enjoy informational scope economies that give them an advantage in retaining their clients' business over the longer term. The universal banks' resulting market power may reduce their incentives to undertake costly underwriting efforts, and in confirmation of this point, universal banks have been observed to be less successful than specialized investment banks in selling their clients' securities. Kanatas and Qi thus conclude that an integrated financial services market can be less innovative than one with specialized intermediaries. At the same time, they find that universal banks are unlikely to emerge as a dominant form, because they offer advantages only in limited circumstances. For example, in thin markets universal banks are likely to offer marketing advantages in issuing new securities, but when markets are better developed specialized institutions are likely to have an advantage. The observation illustrates once again the book's principle that as volume increases and transactions become more specialized, specialized institutions are likely to emerge to carry them out.

Ferreira and Matos (2008) study the importance of connections between banks and firms in the global syndicated loan market, focusing on the lead banks' choices and loan pricing. The authors classify banks as insiders if they have a position on the borrower firm's board of directors or if they hold equity stakes in the borrower, either directly or through an affiliated money manager. Insider connections are found to have a positive and significant effect on a firm's choice of lead bank. In addition, insider banks charge higher interest spreads and face less ex post credit risk. The authors suggest that the influence of banks over firms seems to accrue mostly to the banks' benefit, and that there may be a conflict of interest between the role of lender and the role of firm insider. However as Chapter 3 stressed, nonarm's-length lending offers advantages in both acquiring information and controlling operations ex post, and these advantages can reduce the risk of a financing arrangement. In other words, while a potential conflict of interest may exist, it can be part of a tradeoff that also sees more discriminating types of financing being made available, and possibly on more favorable terms than would otherwise be available.

Trading Activities

International banks trade many different kinds of currency and risk instruments, as well as securities.[1] Banks and investment banks compete actively for business in the wholesale and negotiated parts of the foreign currency and risk management markets. While many wholesale transactions are handled on a standardized basis, very large transactions may be negotiated individually. (Some smaller but less standard transactions are also negotiated individually.)

Today's international trading business evolved from foreign exchange trading and the growth of the Euromarkets, described further below. Active participants in the foreign currency markets usually take positions in the currencies they trade and are known as dealing banks. A dealing bank's foreign exchange traders are responsible for managing their bank's foreign currency positions, and much of the traders' work involves trying to offset positions the bank assumes in its dealings with clients. For example, spot purchases are usually offset by spot sales as quickly as possible. Forward transactions may first be offset in the spot market and only later in the appropriate forward maturity, particularly if trading in spot markets is more active than in the forward markets. The strategy of offsetting a forward position with a spot position permits reducing some of the position risk while waiting for an appropriate forward transaction to present itself.

For example, suppose a dealing bank buys U.S. dollars three months forward. If it is unable immediately to sell U.S. dollars three months forward, it will sell them spot. The sale reduces the risk of the position, since the unhedged forward position is subject to fluctuation in the value of the currency, while the forward-spot combination is only subject to fluctuation in value differences between spot and forward contracts in the same currency. This latter, smaller risk is known as interest rate risk. When it becomes possible later to sell U.S. dollars three months forward, they will be bought back on the spot market, thereby netting out the initial spot position. Large orders in some lesser-traded currencies may take several days, or even possibly weeks, to offset completely.

---

[1]Smaller and more common transactions are also handled by domestic retail banking operations or by foreign exchange dealers.

Traders who speculate on their inventory positions place their employers at some risk, and as a result trading positions are usually subject to several kinds of limits. First, traders must end the day with a limited position in each foreign currency, so that the bank will not be exposed to undue foreign exchange risk overnight. Second, the amount of forward exposure in a given currency is also constrained, in this case with a view to managing the interest rate risk associated with differences between spot and forward rates. There are customary differentials between bid and ask rates in both spot and forward markets, but these differentials can widen or narrow as time goes by and various kinds of news regarding a currency's value are announced. For example, in the event of a major expected change in a currency's value, the forward markets first show a widening bid-ask spread, and, if the uncertainty continues to mount, may cease functioning for a time. Third, the total amount of transactions that a trader can enter with any given bank is constrained to manage what is known as settlement risk, that is, the risk that the other bank will not pay for the transactions as arranged. Finally, banks themselves are limited by regulations governing their allowable exposures to foreign exchange risk.

Since the 1980s, the world's largest banks have continued to increase the volume and complexity of the financial instruments they trade. As noted in Chapter 15, banks now purchase credit derivatives when they wish to sell off default risk from their own books. Second, when banks either sell or securitize loans, they may also sell credit derivatives to the investors, creating a source of revenue at the possible cost of having subsequently to bear defaults. Third, banks have come to be active traders of credit default swaps.

The resulting explosion of trading also means that rating agencies have come to play an important role in establishing the quality of loan and credit risk sales. Banks were once the experts who had inside knowledge of their borrowers, but now that banks sell their loans, they have passed some of the credit risk assessment responsibility on to outside rating agencies such as Moody's, Standard & Poor's, and Fitch. These agencies have profited substantially from the new business, but they do not have the same knowledge of borrowers as bank credit officers formerly had. Ultimately, it can be expected that the banks' governance capabilities will once again be seen as playing a valuable role that cannot readily be performed by arm's-length rating agencies.

INVESTMENT BANKING

Based mainly in London, New York, and Tokyo, international investment bankers advise businesses and governments on how to raise capital, guarantee the sale of new bonds and shares, and distribute new securities issues. They also help arrange mergers and acquisitions, effect corporate divestitures, and effect privatization of government owned firms. As international capital markets continue to become more closely integrated, banks' and securities firms' businesses are also becoming more closely integrated. The closer integration has led both to mergers and to unbundling some of the services investment banks offer to clients. Both mergers and unbundling result from reevaluating the changing economics of different transaction types.

The 1990s and early 2000s have witnessed many types of mergers—of the world's securities firms with each other, of securities firms with banks, and of banks with insurance companies. All these mergers can be explained at least partially in terms of the institutions' operating economics. The merging firms seek to penetrate new markets, to provide their corporate clients with a wider range of services, to securitize assets, and to reduce profit risk through diversification. Some other mergers appear to be based on the need to have large amounts of capital to fund underwriting and to provide bridging finance for client mergers and acquisitions. For example, the relatively large capital base provided by a parent bank can give a securities firm a competitive advantage in acting as lead underwriter for a new issue, or in arranging a bought deal.

Technological change has attracted investment banks to strongly innovative forms of financial engineering. The financial principles are not new: Parallels have been drawn between the spectacular growth of credit derivatives in recent years and the introduction of wheat futures in the United States in the mid-nineteenth century. But thanks to computing power the products have become much more diverse than they were historically. Some products are designed to appear complex and impenetrable, but they are not patented, and staff turnover across the investment-banking industry means that ideas can travel quickly among firms. Products that can be commoditized are likely to be sold in highly competitive markets, and to reduce costs and yet retain some profit margin such products are likely to be unbundled.

Investment banks operate complex businesses and their earnings are both volatile and cyclical. Since mid-2007, it has become very much harder for investment banks to finance their own asset inventories, leading to the kinds of restructuring of U.S. investment banks discussed in Chapter 17. Innovative investment banking has led to diversifying risks among a much wider group of parties, but credit risk has not become more evenly spread. Thanks to the current forms of deals between financial institutions, as and when liquidity dries up, risks that the banks or investment banks think they have outsourced to hedge funds, insurance companies and pension funds might and sometimes do return onto their books. Even in cases where the banks or investment banks are not formally liable for the risks, they sometimes assume them for reputational reasons. The result is a highly cyclical form of activity, which Bookstaber (2007) attributes to a combination of complexity and interconnectedness. The uncertainties created by not knowing which parties ultimately bear the risks mean the system may be prone to less frequent, but more violent shocks. In particular, uncertainty about value can lead to many parties deserting parts of the market until a form of stability returns (see Caballero and Krishnamurthy 2008).

The kinds of instabilities exhibited in the United States have spread to other parts of the world as the credit crisis has increased in scope. As of September 2008, financial institutions in, among other countries, Belgium, France, Germany, Iceland, Ireland, the Netherlands, Sweden, and the United Kingdom have faced the same kinds of pressures as did the U.S. financial industry before the liquidity crisis of AIG and the investment banks' absorption or conversion to universal banks (see Chapter 17). The principal reasons for the difficulties are losses on lending and on credit default swaps, and the principal cures are to obtain new sources of capital. The most likely possibilities are loans of last resort, the government purchase of troubled assets, and infusions of equity by governments or their agencies. The possibilities offer different combinations of advantages and incentives, as discussed in Chapter 20.

FINANCIAL CONGLOMERATES

Financial conglomerates combine financial and nonfinancial operations. They fund some of their investments through an internal capital market rather than through external market agents or intermediaries. The internal capital market's effectiveness stems from the conglomerate's ability to use both intensive initial screening and intensive governance of investments over their lifetimes. The theory of financial conglomerates was developed in Chapter 6, which argued that internal capital markets can be more productive than alternative forms of financing when clients are subject to limits on the amount of external financing they can raise.

Khanna and Tice (2001) study internal capital markets by examining the capital expenditure decisions of discount firms in response to Wal-Mart's entry into their markets. Before Wal-Mart's entry, focused incumbents and discount divisions of diversified incumbents were similar in size, geographic dispersion, and firm debt levels, but the discount divisions of diversified firms were significantly more productive. After Wal-Mart's entry, diversified firms either left the discount business or began to compete more vigorously. Capital expenditures became more sensitive to the productivity of the discount businesses, and internal capital markets transferred funds away from the worsening divisions. Thus it appears that diversified firms with internal capital markets were able to make better investment decisions than counterparts using only external finance.

Stein (2002) finds that different organizational structures exhibit performance differences in generating information about investment projects and in allocating capital to the projects. Small, single-manager firms are likely to be attractive organizational structures when information is soft, difficult to transmit credibly. Conglomerates may perform better when information is hard, easy to transmit within the firm.[2] Stein's arguments appear to refer to internal information that is different from the kinds of information produced by market transactions.

De Motta (2003) studies how capital budgeting is carried out in multidivisional firms. The size of the capital budget depends both on external financiers' assessments of the whole firm and on headquarters' assessment of the divisions. While corporate headquarters can create value by directly monitoring divisions, the external assessment of the firm becomes known to division managers who are then tempted to free ride. As the number of divisions increases, the free-rider problem is aggravated, and internal capital markets substitute for external capital markets as a means of controlling the free riders. De Motta thus finds that the value of internal capital market transactions depends in a complex fashion on the characteristics of the firm, the industry, and the external capital market.

Desai, Foley, and Hines (2004) suggest that internal capital markets give multinational firms significant advantages over local firms in countries with poorly developed credit markets. Local firms that borrow from external sources face high costs of debt in those countries. The same weak credit markets reduce external borrowing by multinational firms, but multinational affiliates are able to compensate by borrowing more from parent companies. The use of internal capital markets to attenuate the impact of adverse local economic conditions also appears when host countries impose capital controls.

EUROMARKET ACTIVITY

Many financial deals are carried out in international markets known as the "Euromarkets." The distinguishing feature of a Euromarket transaction is

---

[2]This idea also applies to the documented tendency for merged banks to stop lending to previously profitable small business clients.

that it is denominated in a national currency, booked in a foreign city, and is not subject to the domestic regulations of either the originating country or the country in which the city is located.[3] The term "offshore markets" is sometimes used in referring to Euromarkets. Euromarket transactions reduce the costs of complying with domestic regulations, and represent forms of regulatory arbitrage. While originally most Euro-transactions were short-term U.S. dollar transactions booked in London, now a number of major currencies are traded offshore, the deals can be booked in a number of the world's major cities, and both money and capital market transactions take place.

What Are Eurocurrencies?

The first Eurocurrency, the Eurodollar, appeared in the late 1950s. The innovation in creating Eurocurrencies was not the use of dollar deposits outside the United States, since U.S. dollar deposits first appeared in Canada as early as 1860. Rather, the distinguishing feature of Eurodollar transactions was their profitable placement and active trading in non-U.S. cities with relatively unrestricted regulatory environments.

When Eurodollar transactions were first originated many countries controlled foreign exchange transactions in order to maintain the fixed exchange rate system initiated by the Bretton Woods agreements established in 1945.[4] Some of the first Eurodollar deals, in the 1950s, were arranged to circumvent U.K. government restrictions on using pounds sterling[5] to finance foreign trade. British banks substituted U.S. dollar for sterling trade credits, increasing sharply the demand for offshore dollars in Europe. The British banks raised some of the necessary deposits from the Moscow Narodny Bank, which for geopolitical reasons did not wish to place U.S. funds in domestic U.S. banks. In the 2000s the regulations applying to Eurocurrency deposits still continue to be less stringent than those applying to domestic deposits, a feature that remains an important contributor to the market's continuing growth.

Other institutional arrangements also stimulated the market's development. In the 1950s, the supply of offshore U.S. dollar deposits was increased by U.S. balance of payments deficits. Moreover, restrictions on the interest

---

[3]Cities compete for international financial business, and one way of doing so is to offer appropriately qualified clients, usually sophisticated wholesale clients, freedom from domestic regulation.

[4]The agreements remained in force until 1972 when the United States effectively moved to a flexible currency regime.

[5]Now more commonly referred to as "British pounds," or just "pounds."

rates payable on U.S. dollar deposits booked in the United States provided another reason for depositing the funds outside the United States whenever interest rates were higher abroad. Finally, since there were no compulsory reserve requirements on offshore deposits, their effective cost to financial intermediaries was lower[6] than for domestic deposits, since the banks' desired reserves were usually lower than reserve requirements.

Once the market came into existence, transactions between banks effectively expanded the supply of Eurodollars in circulation, just as the domestic banking system can create a multiple expansion of reserves that are lent and relent even as the funds are redeposited within the banking system as a whole.[7] However, the extent to which Eurobanks could create a multiple expansion of currencies was affected in two ways. On the one hand, lower reserve holdings meant the total banking system's multiplier was increased from what it had previously been. On the other hand, the extent of the expansion depended on whether the Eurobanks faced independent demands for credit. If a Eurobank loan merely replaced what had formerly been a domestic loan, less expansion would be possible than if the demand for Eurobank loans was an addition to preexisting demand for domestic loans (Friedman 1969).

The emergence of the Eurocurrency markets was one of the most important developments in post–World War II international banking. Originally serving as a source of short-term funds for trade financing, the markets expanded to facilitate banks' foreign exchange transactions and to provide money market trading facilities. Not long after the first transactions occurred, the Eurocurrency market became the central mechanism for channeling international funds flows among banks, and the *London interbank offer rate* (LIBOR) became one of the best known and most important international interest rates. Now most Eurocurrency transactions are priced in terms of LIBOR plus a premium reflecting the risk of the arrangement, just as domestic loans are priced in relation to domestic banks' prime rates. At the end of 1997, more than 80% of international banking transactions took place in the Eurocurrency markets, while prior to the 1960s almost all foreign banking was done in domestic markets. Universal banks, commercial banks, investment banks, and merchant banks are all involved in the Euromarkets. Their clients include multinational corporations, government

---

[6]But not zero. Even in the absence of regulatory requirements, banks hold some reserves for their own business reasons.

[7]If funds are lent by, say, a capital corporation, and the loan proceeds are not redeposited within another capital corporation, the velocity of the existing money supply is increased, but there is no multiple expansion of deposits.

agencies, OPEC countries, and also the governments and central banks of less-developed countries.

How Are Eurocurrencies Created?

Consider a U.S. dollar–denominated bank deposit placed outside the United States. The deposit might be placed in a foreign branch of a U.S. bank, or in a non–U.S. bank. Any such deposit involves a transfer of ownership on the books of banks in the United States, say from the account of a U.S. citizen living in the United States to the account of a foreign bank. On the foreign bank's books the same transaction is recorded as both an asset—the bank's deposit with the U.S. bank—and a liability to the depositing client. If the funds on deposit are repeatedly lent out and redeposited in other foreign banks, the original amount of funds can theoretically be multiplied many times.[8] Nevertheless, there are practical limits to such an expansion, as discussed previously.

The center of the Eurocurrency markets is a group of banks that bid for deposits and relend the funds to other banks or to non-financial businesses. Most transactions are wholesale and involve a number of banks rather than a single bank, as is usual with a retail transaction. Most loans take the form of syndicated Eurocredits: bank loans managed by a lead member of a syndicate of banks. These syndicated arrangements split up the risk of a given credit among the participating banks. Since many banks can be involved in a given transaction, the system of banks can also create a relatively important maturity transformation even though any individual bank may not lend on a much longer term than that on which it borrows.

Eurosecurity Markets

Eurosecurity markets include the Eurobond market, international equities markets, the Eurocommercial paper market and Eurocurrency futures markets. All these markets are organized as international markets in order to avoid the costs of national regulatory restrictions. Since most of the market transactions are wholesale, it can be argued that the transacting parties are sophisticated and do not need regulatory protection.

Like the Eurocurrency markets, the Eurobond market is an international long-term bond market that came into being because of regulatory restrictions. One of the first restrictions avoided by issuers of Eurobonds was the

---

[8]The limit on the amount of funds created depends on the amount customarily retained for reserves, just as in the domestic economy the customary reserve ratio implies a theoretical limit to the money multiplier.

U.S. Interest Equalization Tax (IET), levied against non-residents who borrowed funds in the United States. Even after the removal of the IET in 1974, the Eurobond market continued to flourish because of other restrictions on domestic bond issues. For example, in the United States registration of foreign bonds involves meeting stringent SEC requirements, and there are similar requirements in other countries.

Eurobonds are not floated in a domestic capital market. Rather they are issued in the international Euromarket[9] and underwritten by an international banking syndicate not subject to any one country's laws. Much of the placement and trading activity actually occurs in London. Because Eurobond issues need not satisfy any country's regulatory requirements, it is usually possible to market an issue more quickly and cheaply in the Eurobond market than in a domestic capital market. Eurobonds may be denominated in an individual currency such as U.S. dollars or Euros. Before the Euro was adopted on January 1, 1999, many Eurobond issues were denominated in European Currency Units on the grounds that ECUs had a more stable value than individual currency issues.

Eurobonds are popular because their net costs are lower than those of domestic issues. Of the Eurobond issues, the most important currency used is the U.S. dollar, which accounts for one-third to one-half of the amounts raised in most recent years. The Euro, the yen, the British pound, and the Canadian dollar are of about equal importance, accounting for some 5% of amounts raised. Insofar as international bonds are concerned, the most important issuing country is Switzerland, which accounts for 40% to 50% of the total amounts raised. Borrowers will usually refrain from issuing long bonds when they judge interest rates to be unusually high. Thus as in domestic bond markets, primary Eurobond issues increase (decrease) when interest rates decline (increase). The Eurobond market has another characteristic similar to that of domestic markets. It began like most fledgling markets as a primary market, but following on primary market successes, secondary market trading increased significantly. In contrast to primary transactions, secondary market trading takes place within domestic capital markets because it is not usually subject to the same regulations as primary trading.

International equity markets are not as well developed as the bond markets just described. International trading in equities is hampered by international differences in trading and price setting methods, and by difficulties in obtaining information regarding the issues. Even with the growing trend

---

[9]This Euromarket is, of course, physically located in some country, but the laws of the country treat the transactions as if they took place offshore.

toward setting up international stock exchanges, companies interested in attracting shareholders worldwide may still have to list their shares in several markets. Thus trading in the international equities markets essentially involves a few hundred large, well-known companies.

Since the 1980s, the Euromarkets have also witnessed the emergence of trading in short-term instruments, including commercial paper, promissory notes, and longer-term instruments referred to simply as notes. Commercial paper and promissory notes are typical money market securities, are issued on a discount basis, and have maturities up to one year. Notes are medium term paper having maturities from one to seven years, and usually bear coupons. Euronote facilities can be regarded as blurring the traditional boundaries between banking and securities operations; compare Lewis (1999). Banks also issue Eurocurrency certificates of deposit that, apart from being issued and traded in an international market, are just like the domestic certificates of deposit discussed in Chapter 12.

The first Eurocurrency futures contract was a Eurodollar contract traded on the International Money Market of the Chicago Mercantile Exchange. Eurodollar futures are currently also traded in London and in Singapore. Nearly all Eurocurrency contracts are used to manage interest rate risk, and the contracts trade according to the principles discussed in Chapters 7 and 12. Many developed countries also have contracts written in their own currencies on the local interbank interest rate.

Eurocredits

Eurocredits are medium- or long-term bank loans with floating interest rates tied to short-term Eurodollar rates. Since they are usually in large amounts and provided to foreign borrowers, Eurocredits are often arranged with a syndicate of international banks. In addition to setting interest rates in terms of a spread over LIBOR, the syndicate's managing or lead bank usually charges a management fee, a participation fee, and a commitment fee. Facility and negotiation fees may also be added. Because of the fees, a borrower can effectively pay a relatively large spread over LIBOR, but the announced interest rate on the loan may be only a few basis points in excess of LIBOR. In part, this arrangement is struck to bolster the prestige of borrowers by making it technically possible for them to announce that they have obtained international loans at relatively low rates of interest.

Floating rate Eurocredits emerged in the 1970s, a period of volatile interest rates when banks were reluctant to make medium- or long-term commitments at fixed rates. A loan whose rate is specified as a spread over LIBOR eliminates the profit risk a bank faces due to changing interest rates. There are several types of credit lines called euro-facilities, among which the most important is Euro-commercial paper, similar to domestically issued commercial paper.

Like larger domestic loans, Euroloans are often written as a package that includes options on interest rates. The options may be caps, floors, or more exotic combinations of these instruments. In addition, there are forward contracts on interest rates, taking the form either of a forward forward (FF) contract or of a forward rate agreement (FRA). The first, FF contract, merely fixes an interest rate today for a loan or deposit starting at some future time and extending over some, usually fixed, maturity. A forward rate agreement stipulates an interest rate to be paid or charged at the time a loan or investment is originated, and thus offers a means of either speculating on or hedging against interest rate change. For example, a borrower wishing to arrange a loan for three months hence could fix the interest rate on the loan using an FRA. Like a swap, the FRA is based on a notional amount. Its worth is determined by the difference between a contracted interest rate of, say, a deposit of fixed maturity, and the actual rate prevailing on that deposit when the contract expires. The deposit is not actually made, and settlement of the instrument is in cash at the time specified in the contract.

FRAs are used mainly to help financial institutions manage maturity mismatches. According to Sercu and Uppal (1995) they offer the following advantages over financial futures. First, they are not marked to market by an exchange, and as a result do not nominally carry the interest-rate risk associated with a futures contract.[10] Second, when there is no marking to market, there are no intermediate cash flow problems associated with the instrument. Third, again when there is no marking to market, there is an exact arbitrage relationship between spot and forward rates that is easy to calculate. Finally FRAs are tailormade and can therefore suit two parties' interests more closely than can standard futures contracts. On the other hand, the absence of a clearing corporation can mean the holder of the FRA is presented with a more significant default risk, and one that can also be harder to estimate. In sum, since FRAs have the advantages of non-standard, negotiated arrangements, they are more suitable for use in intermediated rather than in market transactions; compare the distinctions in Chapter 3.

---

[10] While many argue that OTC instruments offer an advantage over exchange-traded products in not being marked to market, they may still be marked to market on the owner's books, depending on the credit of the counterparties (F. J. Fabozzi, private correspondence, January 2, 2009). Moreover, there is still an opportunity risk, as discussed in Chapter 6.

REFERENCES

Bookstaber, Richard. 2007. *A Demon of Our Own Design*. New York and London, Wiley.

Caballero, Ricardo, and Arvind Krishnamurthy. 2008. Collective risk management in a flight to quality episode. *Journal of Finance* 61: 2,195–2,230.

DeMotta, Adolfo. 2003. "Managerial incentives and internal capital markets." *Journal of Finance* 58: 1193–1220.

Desai, Mihir A., C. Fritz Foley, and James R. Hines Jr. 2004. A multinational perspective on capital structure choice and internal capital markets. *Journal of Finance* 59: 2,451–2,487.

Ferreira, Miguel A., and Pedro Matos. 2008. When banks are insiders: evidence from the global syndicated loan market. Presented to International Finance Conference, Queen's University, May.

Kanatas, George, and Jianping Qi. 2003. Integration of lending and underwriting: Implications of scope economies. *Journal of Finance* 58: 1,167–1,191.

Khanna, T., and S. Tice. 2001. "The bright side of internal capital markets." *Journal of Finance* 56: 1489–1531.

Lewis, Mervyn King, ed. 1995. *Financial Intermediaries*. Aldershot: Elgar.

Sercu, Piet, and Raman Uppal. 1995. *International Financial Markets and the Firm*. Cincinnati: South-Western.

Stein, Jeremy C. 2002. "Information Production and Capital Allocation: Decentralized versus Hierarchical Firms." *Journal of Finance* 57: 1899–2002.

TERMS

commitment fee   The fee charged by an international bank for agreeing to provide funds to a borrower under a syndicated loan arrangement.

LIBOR   The London interbank offered rate for short-term Eurocurrency loans. The LIBOR is the most responsive money market price in the world, changing quickly in response to changing supplies or demands. LIBB, the London Interbank Bid Rate, is offered to market participants for large deposits.

management fee   Fee for performing the administrative work of arranging a syndicated loan.

participation fee   The fee charged by an international bank for actually providing some of the funds to a borrower under a syndicated loan arrangement.

PART Seven

Industry Organization and Regulation

This part examines system issues at an aggregate level. First, Chapter 19 examines models of banking market structure and empirical research findings. Chapter 20 turns to the topics of bank runs and systemic risk. Chapter 21 examines macroeconomic impacts of financial activity, and Chapter 22 surveys financial regulation.

Banking Market Structure

Models and Empirical Research

This chapter first examines how market conditions influence financial intermediaries' interest rates, whether charged on loans or paid on deposits. These topics are part of a larger question: how a financial intermediary's profitability is affected by its economic environment. Early banking theory explained that the size of the banking system was determined mechanically as a fixed multiple of available cash reserves. This original explanation was enriched substantially when Gurley and Shaw (1960) and Tobin (1956) emphasized that financial institutions' portfolios are determined by profitability considerations. Following the lead of Gurley-Shaw and of Tobin, the theory presented in this chapter argues that financial intermediaries of most types—banks, insurance companies, mutual funds, and other financial services providers—manage their operations in attempts to maximize profitability.[1] After examining some equilibrium models of banking markets, the chapter considers recent empirical studies and their relations to existing theory.

While the analytical and empirical issues considered in this chapter are variations on the theme of profit maximization, their details vary according to the type of intermediary. In the case of a bank, one principal question is whether the bank can increase its profitability by raising additional funds and relending them. In the case of an insurance company that seeks to expand its insurance business lines, the main questions revolve around whether these companies can sell their liabilities to the public at a profit after taking into account actuarially estimated underwriting costs, interest earned on

---

[1]Most of the literature's models do not attempt to analyze risk-return tradeoffs explicitly; see Chapter 15 for a discussion.

premiums collected in advance, and operating expenses. In the case of a mutual fund, the profit maximization question is whether the administration fees collected from unit-holders cover the costs of assembling the securities portfolio, trading securities, conducting securities research, and so on. In the case of merging organizations such as banks and insurance companies, the questions are those of whether the combined activities can be delivered more profitably if they are organized within a single firm rather than being carried out by separate firms.

BANKING UNDER PERFECT COMPETITION

So far, most financial industry theory examines just one type of business. For example, in a neoclassical microeconomic setting, the models next presented determine equilibrium interest rates in banking markets under varying market structures.[2] Consider first an industry of perfectly competitive banks. Each bank has features similar to the bank modeled in Chapter 16, except that in the equilibrium models presented here interest rates are deterministic and risk is not taken into account. The lending and deposit taking behavior of any bank in a competitive industry is assumed to be determined by profit maximization. Since the bank takes loan, deposit, and money market interest rates as given, its profit function can be written

$$\pi = r_L L + r M - r_D D - c(D, L) \tag{19.1}$$

where r_L is the average rate the bank earns on loans
r is the riskless rate, paid or earned on money market investments
r_D is the average rate paid on deposits
L is the loan balance carried by the bank
D is the balance of deposit liabilities issued by the bank
M is the balance of money market transactions (positive or negative) entered by the bank
$c(D, L)$ represents the bank's cost function, dependent on deposits and loans

The bank is assumed to sets loan and deposit levels with a view to maximizing the profit function (19.1). As in Chapter 16, the bank's

---

[2]The models in the next three sections are based on the presentation in Freixas and Rochet (1997, 2008).

TABLE 19.1 Bank Investing Funds in Money Market

Assets		Liabilities	
Reserves	R	Deposits	D
Loans	L		
Money Market	M		
Total Assets		**Total Liabilities**	

operations are constrained by a reserve requirement represented as a fraction of deposits:

$$R = kD \qquad (19.2)$$

Cash reserves are assumed to earn no interest. Once the reserve requirements have been set aside, the bank will lend or borrow in the money markets to balance any difference between the funds it raises and the funds it uses:

$$M = (1 - k)D - L \qquad (19.3)$$

Tables 19.1 and 19.2 show the balance sheet entries that give rise to equation (19.3).

Substituting equations (19.3) and (19.2) into (19.1) permits rewriting the profit function as

$$\pi(D, L) = (r_L - r)L + [r(1 - k) - r_D]D - c(D, L) \qquad (19.4)$$

Under perfect competition, the bank maximizes its profits by selecting optimal quantities of loans and deposits, taking interest rates as given. The necessary (and assumed to be sufficient) optimality conditions are found by setting the partial derivatives of (19.4), denoted π_L and π_D, respectively, to zero:

$$\pi_L = (r_L - r) - c_L(D, L) = 0 \qquad (19.5)$$

$$\pi_D = [r(1 - k) - r_D]D - c_D(D, L) = 0$$

TABLE 19.2 Bank Borrowing Funds from Money Market

Assets		Liabilities	
Reserves	R	Deposits	D
Loans	L		
		Money Market	M
Total Assets		**Total Liabilities**	

Conditions (19.5) say that the profit-maximizing intermediary sets loan and deposit quantities to equate its interest margins on lending and deposit taking with their respective marginal costs of operation. The second condition includes a term that adjusts the interest margin on deposit taking to account for required holdings of cash reserves.

Since competition ensures that marginal costs of funds are just equal to the marginal revenues a bank can earn on those funds, it provides a standard with which bank decisions under different market structures can be compared. Conditions (19.5) also show that loan and deposit decisions are independent of each other if the cross partial derivative $c_{LD} = 0$. If $c_{LD} < 0$, then an increase in L decreases the marginal cost of deposits; a form of scope economies. Finally, if $c_{LD} > 0$ then an increase in L increases the marginal cost of deposits, a form of scope diseconomies.

BANKING UNDER OLIGOPOLY

All banks take market interest rates as given in the perfectly competitive model of the previous section. However, if the market is oligopolistic, each firm's deposit taking and lending activities can affect market interest rates. This section studies a Cournot oligopoly, one in which intermediaries act as if they can select loan and deposit quantities optimally while other intermediaries' chosen quantities remain constant.

Suppose there are N banks, each with the profit function

$$\pi(D_i, L_i; D, L) = [r_L(L) - r]L_i + [r(1 - k) - r_D(D)]D_i - [\gamma_D D_i + \gamma_L L_i]$$

$$(19.6)$$

The profit function (19.6) differs from (19.1) in the following ways. First, the index i refers to the activities of a particular bank: $i = 1, \ldots,$ N. Next, each bank recognizes that its interest revenues are dependent on its own lending decision L_i and on the aggregate lending decisions of all banks L. Similarly, a bank's interest costs are dependent both on its own deposit taking activities D_i and on the aggregate deposit taking activities of all banks D. That is, an individual bank's profit function depends on both its own decisions and the reactions of other banks in the industry. Money market interest rates are assumed to be competitively determined, and are therefore regarded as unaffected by individual banks' decisions. Finally, for ease of subsequent analysis each bank's operating cost function is assumed to be linear in deposits and in loans. Recall from the section "Banking under Perfect Competition" that the assumption of linear costs in lending and in deposit taking means that banks realize neither scope economies nor scope diseconomies.

The optimality conditions become

$$\pi_L = r'_L(L) + (r_L - r) - \gamma_L = 0$$
$$\pi_D = -r'_D(D) + [r(1-k) - r_D] - \gamma_D = 0 \qquad (19.7)$$

where the prime indicates a (partial) derivative taken with respect either to L_i or D_i under the assumption that the other banks' decisions remain constant. Since each intermediary is identical, the Cournot assumption means that at equilibrium each intermediary will have optimal values of loans and deposits that are just $(1/N)$th of the deposit or loan totals. As a result, the optimality conditions can be written

$$\pi_L = r'_L(L) \cdot (L/N) + (r_L - r)\gamma_L = 0$$
$$\pi_D = -r'_D(D) \cdot (D/N) + [r(1-k) - r_D] - \gamma_D = 0 \qquad (19.8)$$

and it is no longer necessary to index the individual bank decisions by i since the opitmality conditions are identical for each bank. The percentage changes in quantities lent or raised following on a small change in interest rates are functions known as elasticities, and are defined as follows:

$$\varepsilon_L = -r_L L'(r_L)/L(r_L) = -r_L/r'_L(L) \cdot L > 0$$
$$\varepsilon_D = -r_D D'(r_D)/D(r_D) = r_D/r'_D(D) \cdot D > 0 \qquad (19.9)$$

The right-hand terms in equation (19.9) use the fact that the derivative of an inverse function is the reciprocal of the original function's derivative. Using the right-hand terms in equation (19.9), conditions (19.8) can be rewritten as

$$(r_L - r + \gamma_L)/r_L = 1/N\varepsilon_L$$
$$(r(1-k) - \gamma_D)/r_D = 1/N\varepsilon_D \qquad (19.10)$$

Equations (19.10) say that under imperfect competition intermediation margins are set equal to marginal operating costs as in section 1. However, since now each intermediary is large in relation to the whole market, the effect of its own decision on interest rates must be recognized. That is, equations (19.10) show that a bank's market power drives a wedge between the interest rate it charges on loans and the marginal cost of funds; and between the interest rate it pays on deposits and the marginal revenue from using those funds. Conditions (19.10) also show that the smaller the number of banks, the greater is the wedge.

More formally, the intermediation margins' Lerner indices (the right-hand sides of equation (19.10)), defined as (Price less cost)/Price) are set equal to the reciprocal of the relevant elasticity, scaled by the number of banks N. The smaller is N, the greater is market power. However, market power and margins can both be reduced if substitutes to banking products appear. The appearance of substitutes has the same effect as that of increasing N. It can also be shown that the oligopoly model reduces to a monopoly if $N = 1$ and to the previously examined competitive case if $N = \infty$.

Although it is sometimes believed that a ceiling on deposit rates will reduce loan rates,[3] the linear cost function assumed in this section imposing a ceiling on deposit rates will have no effect on loan rates, since there is no interaction between the marginal revenues on loans and the marginal costs of deposits. Indeed, there would only be a beneficial effect for borrowers if the cost function were such that $C_{LD} > 0$, that is, if there were scope diseconomies. Empirically, the presence of scope diseconomies is probably less likely than that of scope economies or an absence of either economies or diseconomies.

MONOPOLISTIC COMPETITION AND THE NUMBER OF BANKS

In the previous models banks did not offer differentiated products. However, one way in which banks can readily differentiate themselves is through choice of convenient location. A model due to Salop (1979) considers how monopolistic competition for location can affect the total cost of providing banking services.

For ease of analysis, Salop's stylized model assumes there are N banks located at equidistant points on a circle. The banks are assumed to collect deposits from the public and invest them in riskless loans with return r_L. Depositors differentiate among banks on the basis of their transportation costs αx, where α measures depositor transportation cost per unit distance and x is the distance to the bank each depositor chooses. Suppose there are many small depositors distributed uniformly around the circle. The total

---

[3]This idea was the rationale behind the Federal Home Loan Bank Board's limiting the interest rates that U.S. savings and loans companies, or thrifts, could offer on deposits. The Federal Reserve Board applied similar interest rate caps on bank deposits. Both were found unworkable and were abandoned in the 1970s.

amount of their deposits is D, and the circumference of the circle is assumed to be 1.

No depositor will have to travel a distance greater than $N/2$ to reach the nearest bank, and each depositor chooses to make his or her deposits in the nearest bank. The total of all depositors' transportation costs can then be calculated as

$$2N \int_0^{1/2N} \alpha \, xDdx = \alpha D/4N \qquad (19.11)$$

where N is the number of banks. The costs measured by equation (19.11) are multiplied by a factor of 2 because depositors can travel to a given bank from points on the circle that lie to either side of the bank.

Suppose the unit cost of setting up a bank is F, and that efficiency means finding the number of banks N to minimize the total of bank operating costs and depositors' transportation costs.[4] That is, N must satisfy

$$\text{Min}\{NF + \alpha D/4N\} \qquad (19.12)$$

The solution to equation (19.12) is given by

$$N^* = (1/2)(\alpha D/F)^{1/2} \qquad (19.13)$$

Now compare the cost minimizing solution (19.13) with the number of banks that would emerge if there were completely free competition, with no entry restrictions and no rate regulations. Let N banks enter, locate uniformly on the circle, and set deposit rates $r_{D1}, \ldots r_{Dn}$. A depositor will be indifferent between going to bank i or bank $i+1$; $i = 1, \ldots N - 1$, for a distance x_i^*, such that

$$r_{D, i} - \alpha x_i^* = r_{D, i+1} - \alpha[(1/N) - x_i^*] \qquad (19.14)$$

Condition (19.14) has a solution

$$x_i^* = (1/2N) + [r_{D, i} - r_{D, i+1}]/2\alpha$$

---

[4]Implicitly, the function assumes that operating costs and transportation costs can be reduced to commensurate quantities, even though transportation costs might actually be measured in such terms as depositor convenience.

and the total volume of deposits attracted by bank i is

$$D_i = D\{(1/n) + [2r_{D,\,i} - r_{D,\,i+1} - r_{D,\,i-1}]/2\alpha\}$$

The profit of bank i is

$$\pi_i = D_i(r_L - r_{Di})$$
$$= D\{(1/n) + [2r_{D,\,i} - r_{D,\,i+1} - r_{D,\,i-1}]/2\alpha\} \qquad (19.15)$$

Consider a Cournot equilibrium in which the ith bank maximizes its profits with respect to r_{Di} subject to the restriction that the other banks hold their interest rates constant. Differentiating equation (19.15) with respect to bank i's interest rate gives, after a little simplification,

$$r_L - r_{Di} = \alpha/N + [2r_{D,\,i} - r_{D,\,i+1} - r_{D,\,i-1}] \qquad (19.16)$$

By symmetry, all banks will offer the same rates and hence the right-hand term in (19.16) will be zero. This means the solution for every bank is the same,

$$r_{Di} = r_L - \alpha/N; \; i = 1, \, 2, \, \ldots, \, N \qquad (19.17)$$

Profit is also the same for all banks

$$\pi_i = [r_L - (r_L - \alpha/N)] \cdot D/N = \alpha D/N^2; \; i = 1, \, 2, \, \ldots, \, N$$

Competitive equilibrium occurs at the point where profit equals setup cost F, which gives

$$F = \alpha D/N^2 \qquad (19.18)$$

and (19.18) has solution

$$N^{**} = (\alpha D/F)^{1/2}$$

Note that $N^{**} = 2N^*$, where N^* minimizes the costs of operating the banking system. The solution N^{**} is more costly, and therefore in that sense less efficient, than the solution N^*. Some authors advocate deposit rate regulation as a remedy for what they regard as this inefficient equilibrium (see Freixas and Rochet 1997, 69–73). But deposit rate regulation should not be advocated simply on the narrow efficiency grounds of the model in this section, since the model ignores several pertinent effects. As a general matter, interest rate regulation can have both multiple and profound dysfunctional effects, as shown in the discussion of the U.S. savings and loan industry in Chapter 17 as well as in other parts of this book.

EMPIRICAL ASPECTS OF BANKING COMPETITION

Hughes and Mester (1993) investigate empirically the connection between bank size and interest paid on deposits, holding bank asset quality and default risk constant. Among the largest banks, increases in asset size lower significantly the interest rates paid on uninsured funds. Although the authors attribute this to a "too big to fail doctrine," it is also consistent with depositor beliefs that larger banks are safer banks. Even in the absence of a "too big to fail doctrine," it is at least possible that market participants will regard large banks as safer than their smaller counterparts.

The nature of interbank competition can be affected if there are costs to switching between banks. Suppose that consumers deal with banks for two consecutive periods. If consumers select their bank at the beginning of the first period, during the second period they can be locked in by switching costs and firms can change their prices to supra-competitive levels. The same argument applies to services. If there are switching costs and services can only be learned about through dealing with a bank, then in a two-period model (depositors are assumed to live for only two periods) depositors will not switch between unit banks after learning in the first period that services are bad. However, if there were branch banking and some depositors moved between cities, service would be better in order to offset the switching that would otherwise take place (Gale 1993).

MARKET STRUCTURE AND COMPETITION

Much of the financial system literature, as well as much practical commentary, suggests that banks choose riskier portfolios when they are confronted with increased competition. These beliefs may even be shared by central bankers and regulators. However, in a review of empirical literature Boyd and de Nicolo (2005) find there are mixed impacts to increased competition—sometimes greater competition leads to riskier portfolios and sometimes it does not. Moreover, existing theoretical analyses are fragile in the sense that some models predict banks will become more risky as their markets become less competitive. Consequently, current beliefs holding that competition always increases risk-taking receive little support from the literature. Which models apply, and in which circumstances, require more detailed analysis than they have so far received.

Weinstein and Yafeh (1998) find that when access to capital markets is limited, close bank-firm ties increase the availability of capital to borrowing firms, but the firms do not then post higher profitability or growth. The cost of capital of firms with close bank ties is higher than that of their peers, indicating that the benefits from these relationships go mostly to banks.[5] Slow growth rates of bank clients suggest that banks discourage firms from investing in risky, profitable projects. On the other hand, liberalization of financial markets reduces the banks' market power.

Cetorelli and Gambera (2001) show that bank concentration promotes growth of industrial sectors that depend heavily on external finance, and that it does so by facilitating credit access to younger firms. However, concentration also has an overall effect of depressing growth rates. In another model (Cerasi 1995) deregulation can increase competition in the short run, but may also lead to the exit of unprofitable banks, thereby increasing concentration in the longer run.

Guiso, Sapienza, and Zingales (2003) study the effects of differences in local financial development within an integrated financial market. They construct a new indicator showing that financial development increases the probability of an individual starting his own business. Development also favors entry, increases competition, and promotes growth of firms. As predicted by the theory of this book, the effects are weaker for larger firms, which can more easily raise funds outside of the local area. The authors find the effects to be present even when their indicator accounts for local banking market structure in 1936. For regulatory reasons, the 1936 market structure affected the supply of credit for the next 50 years or so. The authors' results suggest that local financial development is an important determinant of the economic success of an area even in an economy which presents few frictions to capital movements.[6]

Cetorelli and Strahan (2006) explore how competition might influence firm entry and mature firms' access to bank credit. They find that in markets with concentrated banking, potential entrants face greater difficulty in obtaining credit than in more competitive markets. Again as might be expected from the theory of this book, changes in bank competition have little or no effect on the largest firms, but they do have effects on smaller firms.

---

[5]Unless the loans made by banks with close ties are riskier and require more expensive governance, in which case returns could be expected to be greater.
[6]The authors refer to regulatory obstacles. Local markets might still overcome informational restrictions that would otherwise affect bank-client relations.

di Patti and Gobbi (2007) investigate the effects of banking consolidation on corporate borrowers in Italy. Some of the firms in the sample faced relationship termination, while others did not. Adverse effects were experienced after the mergers, particularly by firms whose relationships were terminated. The negative effects persisted for approximately three years, after which the firms appeared to be able to compensate.

Bertrand, Schoar, and Thesmar (2007) examine the effects of banking deregulation and changing industry structure on banks' lending behavior. They find that following deregulation of the French banking industry in the 1980s, banks became less willing to finance poorly performing firms, and firms in the more bank-dependent sectors became more likely to restructure. At the industry level, banking reforms led to an increase in assets and to job reallocations, an improvement in allocative efficiency across firms, and a decline in concentration.

REFERENCES

Bertrand, Marianne, Antoinette Schoar, and David Thesmar. 2007. "Banking deregulation and industry structure: evidence from the French banking reforms of 1985." *Journal of Finance* 62, 597–628.

Boyd, John H., and Gianni de Nicolo. 2005. "The theory of bank risk-taking and competition revisited." *Journal of Finance* 60: 1329–1344.

Cerasi, Vittoria. 1995. A model of retail banking competition. Working Paper, London School of Economics.

Cetorelli, Nicola, and Philip E. Strahan. 2006. Finance as a barrier to entry: Bank competition and industry structure in local US markets. *Journal of Finance* 61: 437–461.

Cetorelli, Nicola, and Michel Gambera. 2001. "Banking market structure, financial dependence, and growth." *Journal of Finance* 56: 617–648.

di Patti, Emilia Bonaccorsi, and Giorgio Gobbi. 2007. "Winners or losers? The effects of banking consolidation on corporate borrowers." *Journal of Finance* 62, 669–695.

Freixas, Xavier, and Jean-Charles Rochet. 1997. *Microeconomics of Banking*, 1st ed. Cambridge, MA: MIT Press.

Freixas, Xavier, and Jean-Charles Rochet. 2008. *Microeconomics of Banking*, 2nd ed. Cambridge, MA: MIT Press.

Gale, Douglas. 1993. Informational capacity and financial collapse. In *Financial Intermediation in the Reconstruction of Europe*, edited by C. Mayer and X.Vives. London: Centre for Economic Policy Research.

Guiso, Luigi, Paola Sapienza, and Luigi Zingales. 2003. Does local financial development matter?" CRSP Working Paper 538.

Gurley, John G., and Edward S. Shaw. 1960. *Money in a Theory of Finance*. Washington, D.C.: Brookings Institution.

Hughes, Joseph P., and Loretta J. Mester. 1993. A quality and risk-adjusted function for banks: Evidence on the too-big-to-fail doctrine. *Journal of Productivity Analysis* 4: 293–315.

Salop, Steven C. 1979. Monopolistic competition with outside goods. *Bell Journal of Economics* 10: 141–156.

Tobin, James. 1956. The interest elasticity of the demand for cash. *Review of Economics and Statistics* 38: 241–247.

Weinstein, David E., and Yishay Yafeh. 1998. "On the costs of a bank-centred financial system: Evidence from changing main bank relations in Japan." *Journal of Finance* 53: 635–672.

CHAPTER 20

Bank Runs and Systemic Risk

This chapter examines performance and stability issues associated with bank operations. It first shows how bank portfolio structures pose a trade-off for both bank and system stability. It next considers policies for reducing the likelihood of speculative bank runs, examining the roles of lender of last resort, deposit insurance, and information production. Finally, the chapter considers how system risks differ from the risk of individual bank operations, and sketches policies for dealing with them.

This chapter discusses why bank runs and bank failures occur, and the risks that these phenomena can present. The chapter also considers how simultaneous runs on several banks can amount to a bank panic, examines the system risks that a panic can present, and offers some comments for dealing with system risks.[1]

Financial history reports episodes of banking instability in several countries, indicating that bank runs and bank failures are not uncommon features of a financial system. For example, England witnessed many bank failures before the Bank of England was established as a state bank[2] in 1946. Similarly, there were almost 100 failures of United States banks in the late 1930s and early 1940s, although between the 1940s and the 1980s failures[3] were relatively rare. The difference in U.S. failure rates was attributed to both a changed environment and a stronger regulatory framework. However U.S. regulatory revisions did not prove adequate to the task, and another spate of nearly 250 failures occurred between the late 1980s and early 1990s. In yet another series of examples, bank runs

---

[1]This chapter is partly based on Freixas and Rochet (1997).
[2]The Bank of England was founded as a private organization in 1694.
[3]As discussed in Chapter 17, problems with the U.S. thrift industry began to appear in the 1970s.

and bank failures occurred in several Asian countries during the late 1990s. The problems began with individual banks, but eventually spread throughout the banking system and ultimately affected the creditworthiness of the countries themselves. Similarly, the credit crisis of 2007–2008 began with U.S. banks and U.S. investment banks, and later spread to financial institutions in many other parts of the world.

Despite failures in many countries, however, banking instability is not universal. For example, Scotland has never had a bank run, although its banking history extends over more than 300 years, beginning with the formation of the Bank of Scotland in the late 1600s. Bank shareholders faced unlimited liability during the earlier years of Scottish banking history, but even after changing to limited liability ownership the Scottish banking system exhibited no instabilities. Similarly, Switzerland reports no bank runs over its lengthy banking history. At least part of the explanation for such differences appears to lie in countries' political differences. Both Allen and Gale (2007) and Rochet (2008) argue that political interference can play an important role in creating difficulties.

A bank run is a loss of confidence in an individual bank, and can be a proximate cause of bank failure, although the fundamental reasons for bank failure are operating or loan losses.[4] To reflect these differences, many authors distinguish between speculative and fundamental bank runs. Speculative bank runs are those in which depositors withdraw a disproportionate amount of funds from a solvent bank, while fundamental bank runs occur when depositors attempt to recover their funds from an insolvent bank. As we show later, one difficulty with this definition is that of distinguishing between a solvent and an insolvent bank.

One bank's failure can create an atmosphere in which depositors lose confidence in other banks, possibly causing them to fail as well. If several failures do occur, the situation can develop into a bank panic, in which depositors lose confidence in a country's entire banking system. A loss of confidence in some banks, or a panic affecting all banks, can develop from either speculative runs or fundamental failures. The possibilities present real dangers, as the 2007–2008 worldwide credit crisis vividly demonstrates. Nevertheless, and also as shown later, bank runs or bank panics are less

---

[4]A crippling loss of confidence is particularly likely in the absence of deposit insurance or other safety net arrangements.

likely when credible safety net provisions such as deposit insurance schemes or lender of last resort facilities have been set up. Similarly, restoration of confidence in a system experiencing difficulties has historically been brought about by combinations of private sector and government support.

LIQUIDITY PROVISION AND SYSTEM STABILITY

Banks provide liquidity services by issuing liquid claims that are backed mainly by illiquid assets. Chapter 6 showed that banking operations can increase consumer welfare if they provide a liquidity service that would otherwise be unavailable to depositors.[5] Banks provide liquidity both by agreeing to redeem deposits when depositors request withdrawals, and by lending funds to their borrowing clients. Since deposits are mainly available on demand and since most loans are repaid in installments over time, the combination means that the liquid assets held by the system's banks are typically only a fraction of their short-term (i.e., liquid) liabilities. In such a fractional reserve system, only banks' liquid assets are immediately available to meet a sudden increase in withdrawals, and consequently banking systems are subject to instability problems.

The extent and severity of the instability problems that can be created by a fractional reserve system depends critically on both institutional arrangements and the attitudes of banking clients, as will be shown in greater detail later. Nevertheless, the speculative runs to which a fractional banking system can prove vulnerable are really a proximate rather than a fundamental cause of bank failure. The fundamental cause of bank failure is not a run on its deposits, but the fear that led to the run. That fear is one of being unable to redeem one's deposits if the bank were to suffer sufficiently large losses, especially in its lending business. The possibility of such losses can be either real or imagined, but once that fear lodges in the minds of the public, a run on a bank becomes much more likely.

The fact that insurance companies also fail from time to time strengthens the conclusion that a run on deposits is not the fundamental cause of a financial intermediary's failure. Insurers cannot be subject to runs on deposits, since (at least up until the time of this writing) most insurance companies have not offered extensive deposit services.[6] Rather, insurance companies

---

[5]Similarly, banks create liquidity for their borrowing customers, and that liquidity leaves borrowers better off.

[6]In the future, insurance companies may well undertake a depository intermediary role.

fail because they incur unanticipated losses, either on their underwriting business or on their investments.[7]

The Diamond-Dybvig Model

Diamond and Dybvig (1983) explain how speculative runs can stem from a loss of depositor confidence in a given bank. The model assumes a fractional reserve banking system in which banks raise funds from deposits and place the funds in long-term investments. In the event of unanticipated liquidity demands, the bank may have to liquidate some of its long-term investments at a cost. If it has to liquidate large amounts of long-term investments, and if the cost of doing so is sufficiently great, the solvency of the bank can be endangered.

The situation can be modeled along the following lines. Suppose depositors have identical preferences and wealth positions, and that each depositor places a deposit of 1 with a bank at time 0. In exchange for her initial deposit of 1, each depositor receives a demand deposit contract that promises to pay either C_1 at time 1 or C_2 at time 2, but not both.[8] Some of the depositors will face liquidity demands that require them to withdraw deposit funds at time 1, while other depositors will be able to leave their funds on deposit until time 2. We assume that at time 1 each depositor learns whether she needs liquidity immediately or can leave her funds on deposit until time 2.

Suppose that competing banks all offer the same contract, denoted by (C_1, C_2), and that the contract maximizes depositors' expected utility. Each bank will set aside some funds to redeem the deposits of clients with liquidity needs at time 1. If the bank knows the proportion of clients likely to face liquidity needs, and if those are the only clients who actually seek to redeem their deposits at time 1, all parties' expectations can be fulfilled and the bank can operate without difficulty. If they remain confident of the bank's solvency, other clients will be content to wait until time 2 and obtain a larger return than they could by withdrawing the funds at time 1 and reinvesting on their own.

However, the amount of funds set aside by the bank to meet aggregate liquidity demands may not be enough to meet requested time 1 withdrawals. First, the bank might not anticipate liquidity needs correctly. Second, clients might change their plans. For example, suppose a client who would normally

---

[7]In many countries, the insurance industry maintains contingency funds to ensure that policyholders do not suffer losses from such failures.

[8]The arrangement now contemplated differs from the model of Chapter 5 because the depositor has the option of deciding when to withdraw the funds.

wait until time 2 to withdraw comes to believe that she could realize greater gains, or minimize expected losses, by withdrawing her deposit at time 1 and investing it on her own. Actions of this type would not be a problem if they were confined to a small number of clients, but could easily become a problem if the number of clients who change their plans is large enough.

Worse yet, if still other clients interpret the first group's actions as indicating a loss of confidence in the bank, they, too, may decide it is best to withdraw their funds at time 1. These remaining clients might well reason that the bank could suffer losses by having to liquidate long-term investments to meet unusually large time 1 demands for cash, and might even fail as a result. If these depositors are to recover their funds, then they must act quickly before the failure occurs. The greater the loss of confidence, and the greater the number of depositors who rush to withdraw their funds at time 1, the greater the amount of long-term investments the bank has to liquidate. In turn, this means the greater the losses from liquidation, and the greater the likelihood the bank will fail. That is, a lack of confidence can become a self-fulfilling prophecy under the institutional arrangements now assumed.[9]

Table 20.1 displays a situation in which it is assumed that all of the bank's clients are originally thought to be clients who will not withdraw before time 2. On this assumption, the bank has placed all its funds in long-term investments. For each unit of funds invested in long-term assets at time 0, the bank will realize $R_2 > 1$ if it can leave the funds invested until time 2. However, it will only realize $L_1 < 1$ if it has to redeem one investment unit early. Now, contrary to the bank's assumptions regarding depositor behavior, suppose m of the n original depositors do decide to withdraw funds at time 1. (Their deposit contract formally permits them to do so, even though the bank did not anticipate this event.)

Using the conventions of Chapter 6, the bank would have to redeem $j = mC_1/L_1$ of its investments to meet withdrawals at time 1. Assume that $L_1 < C_1$, as would be the case if the bank had not structured its deposits to avoid early liquidation problems, $j > m$. The situation can clearly become unstable. For example, if $R_2 = C_2$ the bank will be insolvent, because scheduled deposit redemptions at time 2 are then $(n-m)R_2 > (n-j)R_2$ since $j > m$ as already observed. Indeed the value of the bank will be decreasing in m, as shown in the bottom right-hand corner of Table 20.1. Moreover, if at or before time 1 the initially patient clients come to expect that the bank might face a liquidity crisis, they will rush to withdraw funds at the time 1 opening of

---

[9]Some commentators have likened the short selling of bank stocks in September 2008 to the kind of run being described here. In other words, a bank can lose the confidence of different kinds of clients, and in each case their support of the bank is then likely to be withdrawn.

TABLE 20.1   Position of Bank if $m > 0$

	Time 0	Time 1	Time 2
Cash from Deposits	n	$-mC_1$	$-(n-m)C_2$
Long-Term Investment	$-n$	$+jL_1$	$+(n-j)R_2$
Net Cash Position	0	0	$(n-j)R_2 - (n-m)C_2$

The net cash position is
   negative if $R_2 = C_2$.

business, since only the first few clients to do so may be able to recover their funds before the bank becomes insolvent.

To compare the Diamond-Dybvig model to the Edgeworth model of Chapter 6, recall that in Chapter 6 depositors held independently and normally distributed balances, each with a mean of \$100.00 and a standard deviation of \$4.00. During a crisis of confidence, depositor's balances would likely have a lower mean, a higher standard deviation, and become positively correlated as well. All these changes would mean that the Edgeworth reserve positions would be much less safe than they were judged to be under the assumptions of Chapter 6. To demonstrate just part of the effect, if two depositors' balances are perfectly positively correlated but have the same individual mean and standard deviation as in Chapter 6, the average total balance is still \$200.00, but the standard deviation is now 8.00 rather than the previous $(32.00)^{0.5}$. The reserve positions would have to be greater still if the mean balances were to reduce, the standard deviations of individual balances were to increase, or both.

Reducing Incentives for Speculative Bank Runs

Since the incentive for depositors to withdraw early depends heavily on institutional arrangements, changes in those arrangements can mitigate the potential instability shown in Table 20.1. The insight of the next model is not that instabilities can be ruled out, but that their causes can be more delicate, and their occurrence better managed, than is suggested by the classic Diamond-Dybvig model.[10] Moreover, the possibility of difficulty depends on

---

[10] Indeed, recognizing that banks have some freedom to structure the terms of the deposits they accept shows more clearly that the most likely fundamental reason for bank failure is losses due to bad lending or other forms of asset mismanagement. If a bank's asset quality is called into question, and clients fear that the bank is potentially insolvent, the probability of a run on the bank increases.

TABLE 20.2 Position of Bank if $m < e$

	Time 0	Time 1	Time 2
Cash from Deposits	n	$-m$	$-(n-m)C_2$
Cash from Equity	e		
Long-Term Investment	$-n$		nR_2
Net Cash Position	e	$e - m > 0$	$(e-m) + nR_2 - (n-m)C_2$

the probability that many depositors will withdraw funds all at once. That is to say, the risk of a run can be described using a probability distribution of depositor behavior (see the discussion of Goldstein and Pauzner 2005) in this chapter).

To begin examining the effects of institutional arrangements, assume the bank continues to provide liquidity services as before, continues to hold few or no reserves, but amends the deposit contract to $(1, C_2)$.[11] That is, depositors who withdraw at time 1 just receive their initial deposit without interest.[12] Since the allocation represents an improvement over the autarkic allocations examined in Chapter 6, it could be attractive to consumers[13] under the conditions of Chapter 6. As in Table 20.2, suppose there are n consumers, m of whom face liquidity needs and must withdraw early. Suppose also the bank has raised equity capital e, paid in as cash at time 0 and held as cash until needed.

It is evident from Table 20.2 that if $e > m$ the bank can meet the liquidity-motivated demand for initially unanticipated withdrawals. Moreover, the bank will still return a net profit to capital if $R_2 \geq C_2$, and can even do so if $R_2 < C_2$ but $nR_2 - (n-m)C_2 \geq 0$. Indeed, the return to shareholders could even increase as depositors withdraw funds early, because those depositors are required to sacrifice a share of their promised returns in order to satisfy their liquidity needs. Thus the crisis of confidence that affected the bank in the first section would not necessarily arise under the present assumptions. It is, of course, up to the bank's management to find investment opportunities and to set deposit interest rates in such a way that the return to capital is

---

[11] A competitive bank could offer such a contract so long as the implicit rate of interest was at least as great as depositors' opportunity costs.

[12] A small positive interest payment could be paid without affecting the solution materially. We assume zero interest for ease of discussion.

[13] However, it may not allow consumers to attain an expected utility maximum.

at least equal to a market return. In other words, an incentive compatibility constraint such as

$$e(1 + r) \leq (e - m) + nR_2 - (n - m)C_2$$

where r is an appropriate measure of investor opportunity cost, must also be satisfied.[14]

Lender of Last Resort

Financial difficulty can stem from either liquidity or solvency problems. Although it can be practically difficult to distinguish between liquidity and solvency problems, it is worth examining the differences conceptually. Liquidity problems arise when entities (financial institutions, countries, non-financial companies like real estate developers) that hold mainly illiquid assets face unanticipated short-term cash outflows. Examples include the 1998 difficulties of Long-Term Capital Management, the 1980s difficulties of real estate developers such as Olympia and York, runs on banks prior to the advent of deposit insurance, and many others. The subprime crisis and the auction rate securities crisis, both beginning in mid-2007, also posed liquidity problems for a number of institutions that depended on short-term financing of their longer-term investments. Canada's asset-backed commercial paper crisis beginning in 2008 is still another example.

Solvency problems arise when the market value of assets is not great enough to cover all liabilities. In the model presented in the previous subsection, it was easy to see that the institution would be solvent. But, as noted by Goodhart (1995), the distinction between liquidity and solvency can be practically difficult or even impossible to make.[15] Nevertheless, Goodhart also argues that it can be important to rescue failing banks because of the negative externalities the failures could generate if they were allowed to occur.

Borrowing in the interbank market or from a lender of last resort can cushion individual banks against idiosyncratic liquidity shocks, as has long been recognized. Bagehot (1973) suggested that a lender of last resort should lend to illiquid but solvent institutions. Bagehot also argued that loans of last resort should be granted at a penalty rate to discourage their being

---

[14] The reader may wish to consider how the model applies to the capital support provided by Warren Buffett to the newly formed Goldman Sachs bank holding corporation in September 2008.

[15] Liquidity problems can turn into solvency problems if the former are important enough and protracted enough, as the discussions of the Diamond-Dybvig and subsequent models show.

TABLE 20.3 Position of Bank if $m > e$

	Time 0	Time 1	Time 2
Cash from Deposits	n	$-m$	$-(n-m)C_2$
Cash from Equity	e		
Long-Term Investment	$-n$		nR_2
Net Cash Position		$e-m > 0$	$e-m+nR_2-(n-m)C_2$

used inappropriately. Moreover, loans of last resort should only be made available against good collateral (albeit valued at prepanic prices). Finally, to induce system stability, the lender of last resort would have to make clear its willingness to lend to any institution that meets its criteria.

Providing lender of last resort facilities can also present a disadvantage. Many analysts note that a lender of last resort facility can create a moral hazard problem: The loans' availability may encourage banks to take risks they would not otherwise assume. Despite this disadvantage, however, lender of last resort facilities can create net benefits if they offset the possibility of negative externalities.[16]

The next model shows how individual banks' liquidity problems can be ameliorated with either interbank loans or advances from a lender of last resort. Thus a lender of last resort facility can reduce the possibility of speculative runs. Indeed, the problem can now be mitigated[17] even if m exceeds e in Table 20.2. Table 20.3 shows that the bank remains solvent so long as $R_2 \geq \max \{C_2, R_L\}$, where R_L is one plus the interest rate charged on the emergency loans that are granted at time 1. It is, of course, incumbent on bank management to find sufficiently lucrative investment opportunities R_2; the net return to capital must still exceed an appropriate measure of opportunity cost.[18]

---

[16] During the 2008 crisis, both Joseph Stiglitz and George Soros argued for capital infusions to be provided through preferred shares accompanied by warrants. The difference between this form of support and a loan of last resort is that the Stiglitz-Soros proposals probably reduce the moral hazard that the bankers will take risks on the assumption that the authorities will rescue them if the risks fail. For, if the bankers do ultimately prosper, the warrants mean the emergency supporters will be able to buy bank equity at prespecified prices and, thereby, share in any profits from the risk taking.

[17] On the other hand, a lender of last resort does not rule out the possibility that a bank might fail because of bad lending practices.

[18] Note that while C_2 and R_2 determine effective interest rates over two periods, the model assumes that emergency liquidity, if needed, is provided for only one period. Therefore R_L determines a one-period effective interest rate.

It is easy to amend the previous examples to show that forbidding early withdrawals is another way of possibly achieving stability. However, this attempt to provide stability can be flawed, since most banks issue a mixture of demand and notice deposits. In the face of a loss of confidence, a bank's asking for more time to redeem notice deposits is not likely to reassure depositors, and such attempts could eventually prove damaging to the banking industry. The action might be less problematic if regulators were to suspend convertibility of deposits into cash, and especially if the regulators could credibly guarantee that depositors would receive the returns they had originally anticipated.

Still another way of working toward stability is to require a bank to hold 100% cash reserves against its deposits. A related way is to require banks only to invest in government securities.[19] However, either the 100% cash reserve policy or the policy of investing in government securities is less satisfactory than a lender of last resort facility because either constrains the bank's investment decisions more tightly. Moreover if banks can earn economies of scope by extending illiquid loans that are financed by demand deposits, a 100% reserve policy could prevent them from adopting a profit-maximizing organizational structure.

Yet another solution is to make the deposits claims like equity. Making deposits like equity claims is in one sense similar to allowing depositors to trade their deposits at time 1, since market prices could be established at values less than the nominal amount of the claim.[20] Equity claims are necessarily immune to bank runs, because the worth of the shares depends on the market value of the bank's net assets. For example, if the deposits were treated as equity rather than as fixed liabilities, the holders of the bank's liabilities would be in exactly the same position as is now the case with persons who are unit-holders in mutual funds.

However, not all depositors want to purchase equity claims, for reasons given in the Chapter 6 discussion of differences between debt and equity. In essence, the main difficulty with the equity solution is that some depositors want to hold claims whose redemption amount is fixed. A second difficulty is that equity claims are not immune to being sold off early at sacrifice prices, since the assets on which their value is based are not easy to value. In contrast to the marketable assets of a mutual fund, the value of a bank's assets can be subject to sharp and sudden changes, because the assets are difficult for the marketplace to value.

---

[19] As shown in Chapter 5 this requirement can reduce to a market solution, at least in the circumstances discussed there.

[20] Since tradable deposits represent a fixed promise, they are more like risky debt than like equity.

Diamond (2004) further considers the effects on bank runs of loan contracts that may not easily be enforceable. Lenders can find it difficult to collect debts in legal systems with ineffective contract enforcement. But if lenders do not enforce, borrowers will misbehave. Lenders will be more prone to enforce if bad news subjects them to runs. An alternative is for lenders and borrowers to be able to renegotiate and share the risks differently upon receipt of bad news.

Goldstein and Pauzner (2005) note that the original Diamond-Dybvig analysis does not provide tools to determine the probability of an equilibrium in which there is a run on the banks, and it is consequently difficult to assess whether banks can increase overall welfare. In contrast, Goldstein and Pauzner offer a modified model that can compute the ex ante probability of bank runs. They then find conditions under which banks increase overall welfare. They also construct a demand deposit contract that trades off the benefits of liquidity creation against the costs of runs.

DEPOSIT INSURANCE

As already suggested, deposit insurance is another way of reducing the possibility of speculative runs. Suppose a bank with no initial equity investment faces the following planning problem at time 0. The bank, to be wound up at time 1, acquires assets whose time 1 realized values are random when viewed from a time 0 perspective. To simplify the situation, suppose the bank can end up at time 1 with an asset value that is either $A_G > D$ or $A_B < D$. Assume a risk-neutral probability measure q exists and that interest rates are zero. Assuming the existence of a risk-neutral probability measure is equivalent to assuming the absence of arbitrage opportunities, which in the present case means that the time 0 value of bank deposits must equal the time 0 expected value of the assets, calculated under the risk-neutral probability:

$$q A_G + (1 - q) A_B = D \qquad (20.1)$$

At time 0 the bank is solvent in the sense that the market value of its assets is exactly equal to the market value of its liabilities.

Now consider the two possible asset values when the bank is wound up at time 1. If A_G is realized, shareholders will receive $A_G - D$ and depositors D. However if A_B is realized, the bank will also have to default partially on its obligations to depositors, and shareholders will receive nothing. If the default is costless, depositors receive $A_B < D$.

Given the possible asset values and payoffs, the time 0 value of the potential shareholder gains is $q(A_G - D)$. However, the potential shareholder gains stem from the assumption that depositors assume a liability[21] with a negative time 0 value

$$(1 - q)(A_B - D)$$

as may be seen by rewriting equation (20.1):

$$q(A_G - D) + (1 - q)(A_B - D) = 0 \qquad (20.2)$$

The problem with the foregoing reasoning is that depositors who made the preceding calculations would not place deposits on the terms just outlined. Indeed, since interest rates are zero depositors will only be willing to deal with the bank if they can be certain their entire deposit will be returned at time 1, whether the bank does well or badly.

A deposit insurance scheme could ensure that depositors do not suffer negative returns. If things were to turn out well, depositors would be paid an amount D from the value of the bank's assets A_G. If things were to turn out badly, depositors would receive A_B from the sale of bank assets and a payment of $D - A_B$ under the deposit insurance scheme. An insurer would provide such an arrangement for an actuarially fair premium, to be paid at time 0, of

$$(1 - q)(D - A_B)$$

If shareholders had to pay this premium to set up the bank, the value of their anticipated gains $q(A_G - D)$ would be just offset by the actuarially fair insurance premium costs, as shown in equation (20.2). With deposit insurance structured in this way, shareholders could not gain at the expense of depositors, nor vice versa.[22]

However, depending on the availability of information about bank management decisions, the solution just advanced could be subject to moral hazard. Suppose there is another possible strategy that gives asset values B_G and B_B, such that $B_G > A_G > D > A_B > B_B$ and also

$$qB_G + (1 - q)B_B = D \qquad (20.3)$$

If the insurance premium were to remained unchanged, either because the insurance scheme does not use risk-adjusted premiums or because

---

[21] Assuming depositors are willing to put up funds on the terms now specified. This question will be examined directly.

[22] The first theoretical paper to relate deposit insurance to options is Merton (1977).

management could substitute one strategy for another without the insurer's knowing, then the shareholders are better off by $q(B_G - A_G)$ and the insuring agency worse off by $(1 - q)(B_B - A_B)$. On the other hand, if the insurance premium were to be revised to $(1 - q)(D - B_B)$ then the bank would again have an initial value of equity equal to zero, because shareholders were prevented from profiting through increasing the risk of the bank.

The practice of "gambling for resurrection" is illustrated by the foregoing discussion. If management did not expect to be detected when substituting policy B for policy A, and if insurance premiums were not raised when the substitution was made, management's wealth position would be improved by taking greater risks. Chari and Jagannathan (1986) point out that the practice is a real possibility: Management can face an incentive to keep a bank open even when further operations imply a decrease in its net wealth. As suggested by the foregoing example, under limited liability gambling for resurrection can increase the value of the equity by shifting risk to such other parties as the deposit insurer. Buser, Chen, and Kane (1981) argue that regulatory authorities can sometimes implicitly increase insurance premiums by exerting extra regulatory control over certain institutions, thus mitigating the moral hazard problem to some extent.

From a depositor point of view, deposit insurance makes the liabilities of different financial institutions perfect substitutes. Deposit insurance therefore enhances competition by making it easier for small new intermediaries to compete for savers' funds. However as shown above, deposit insurance can also encourage moral hazard since intermediaries that have purchased deposit insurance may choose riskier investments than those without insurance cover. Indeed, Arrow (1974) observes that moral hazard is a major problem in providing insurance of any type. He suggests using coinsurance and direct control over the actions of the insured as ways of mitigating moral hazards' costs. In regulating financial intermediaries, the authorities try to reduce the possible effects of moral hazard by imposing the kinds of prudential regulation and capital adequacy requirements discussed above. In addition, they sometimes use risk-adjusted premiums as discussed next.

Although only a few deposit insurance agencies have adopted risk-adjusted premiums at this writing, an insurance scheme provides greater incentives for risk control if the insured who takes on greater risks must pay higher insurance premiums for doing so. Without risk-adjusted premiums, insurance effectively subsidizes the risk takers at the expense of less risky institutions. The model[23] outlined in Table 20.4 shows how the effects may be mitigated.

---

[23] The model is due to Freixas and Rochet (1997, 266–272).

TABLE 20.4 Level Premium Deposit Insurance and Moral Hazard

	Time 0	Time 1
Loans	L_0	L_1
Insurance (Premium/Payment)	P_0	$\text{Max}(0, D_1 - L_1)$
Deposits	$-D_0$	$-D_1$
Equity	$-E_0$	$-E_1$

Table 20.4 shows assets with a positive sign, liabilities with a negative sign. All time 0 values are deterministic, as is D_1. The other time 1 values (L_1 and E_1) are regarded as random variables when viewed from the perspective of time 0. Suppose also that regardless of the risk to the bank's portfolio the insurance premium P_0 is constant. Since assets equal liabilities, the sum of the entries in column 2 is zero. In other words, the value of the equity is a residual that maintains the equality between total assets on the one hand, the sum of liabilities and owners' equity on the other.

Although L_1 is a random variable when viewed from the perspective of time 0, its value is realized with certainty at time 1. If $D_1 < L_1$ or if $D_1 = L_1$, the intermediary is solvent. However if $D_1 > L_1$, equity is formally negative at time 1 and the intermediary is insolvent. With limited liability, negative equity means the shareholders get nothing. In this case the insurance scheme pays off the depositors taking the value of the bank's loans in partial compensation. Thus the time 1 value of the bank to shareholders is

$$E_1 = L_1 + P_1 - D_1 = L_1 - D_1 + \text{Max}(0,\ D_1 - L_1) \tag{20.4}$$

Assuming a zero interest rate, $D_1 = D_0 = L_0 + P_0 - E_0$. Then replacing D_1 in (1.1) gives

$$\pi \equiv E_1 - E_0 = (L_1 - L_0) + \text{Max}(0,\ D_1 - L_1) - P_0 \tag{20.5}$$

Equation (20.5) says the return to the shareholders is the profit on loans, plus any net gains or losses on the insurance contract. If the value of the insurance contract (the sum of the last two terms) is positive it represents an insurance subsidy, if negative an insurance penalty. Now suppose that L_1 can take on only two values: X with probability θ if the client's project is successful; 0 with probability $1 - \theta$ if it is not. Then the bank's expected return to shareholders $E(\pi)$ is

$$E(\pi) = \theta[(X - L_0) + 0 - P_0] + (1 - \theta)[(0 - L_0) + (D_1 - 0)] - P_0$$
$$= (\theta X - L_0) + (1 - \theta)D_1 - P_0 \qquad (20.6)$$

In the event of failure the insurance company will pay off the depositors, an action that creates value for the shareholders as recognized by the term $(1 - \theta)[(0 - L_0) + (D_1 - 0)] - P_0$ in equation (20.6). Now suppose that banks can choose among projects of varying riskiness subject to the condition that

$$(\theta X - L_0) = c \qquad (20.7)$$

a constant. Then equation (20.6) becomes

$$E(\pi) = c + (1 - \theta)D_1 - P_0 \qquad (20.8)$$

and banks will be motivated to choose projects with small values of θ; that is, with low success probabilities. Banks can benefit from increasing the risks they take because their expected returns are increased but the expected cost increases are borne by the insurance scheme. That is, if the risk does not pay off the deposit insurance scheme bears the loss. Of course, if the insurance premium were to change with any change in θ (i.e., if the insurance premium were properly risk-adjusted) shareholders would not face the same perverse incentives to take on greater risks at the expense of the insuring agency.

In theory, risk-related premiums can be calculated quite easily when there are no informational asymmetries and no arbitrage opportunities. In essence deposit insurance allows a bank to put its loan assets to the insuring agency for a strike price that is equal to the bank's deposit liabilities. If there are no arbitrage opportunities, a risk-neutral probability measure Q exists and the value of the put option can be calculated using

$$P_0 = E_Q\{\text{Max}[0, \ (D_1 - L_1)/B_1]\} \qquad (20.9)$$

As usual, the expectation is taken under Q, and B_1 is used to reflect discounting at the riskless rate. (When interest rates are zero as in the present example, $B_1 = 1$.) The right-hand side of (20.9) can be used to determine the actuarially fair premium to be charged for the put option, that is, P_0. Both the models of Chapter 9 and the model of this section show that if the volatility of the project increases, the insurance premium should be larger.

The situation is more complex if there are informational asymmetries among the stakeholders. While it is still possible to find an actuarially fair

TABLE 20.5 Unanticipated Changes in Information

Possible Range of Asset Values	Risk-Neutral Probabilities Estimated at Time 0	Risk-Neutral Probabilities Reestimated at Time 1
1,000	1/4	0
950	1/4	1/4
900	1/4	1/4
850	1/4	1/4
800	0	1/4

See note 24 below.

premium when there are informational asymmetries, some qualified observers question whether the necessary premium increases could ever be large enough to eliminate the moral hazard problem in a practical sense.

INFORMATION PRODUCTION

So far, this chapter has assumed that all interested parties can estimate the probability distribution of investment returns, and can also find the risk-neutral probabilities that value the investment returns. But one of the most important difficulties in banking is that a loan portfolio may turn out to be worth less than originally anticipated, that is, investment returns may be uncertain because the actual distribution of returns cannot be estimated cost-effectively. For example, if a bank's return on investment could never be publicly observed, the solutions advanced so far become much more difficult to implement.

The valuation problem next to be examined will not arise if depositors and investors can postulate the full range of possible performances ex ante. However, the problem will arise if depositors or other stakeholders revise their ex ante expectations because they receive unexpected information as shown in Table 20.5. Consider a model with three time points, 0, 1, and 2. As before, interest rates are zero. In this example the bank will be wound up at time 2, and as usual the planning problem is first examined from a time 0 perspective. However in this example unanticipated and surprising information becomes available to stakeholders at time 1, as reflected by two sets of risk-neutral probabilities shown in Table 20.5.[24]

---

[24] Technically, risk-neutral probabilities are required to be positive for all states that can be realized. This example presumes that the two parties use different personal sets

TABLE 20.6 Balance Sheet, Market Value Basis, Time 0

Assets		Liabilities and Owners Equity	
Cash (paid in by shareholders)	50	Deposits	975
Loans at market value	925	Market value of equity	0

Under the risk-neutral probabilities used at time 0, a bank with deposits of 975 and equity of 50 is solvent, because the time 0 value of the assets, assuming a riskless interest rate of zero, is 925. The 50 paid in by shareholders covers the difference between the deposit liabilities and the market value of the loans. The bank's balance sheet, prepared on a market value basis, using the information available at time 0, is shown in Table 20.6. As can be inferred from Table 20.5, there is a possibility that a bank in this situation will eventually turn out to be insolvent, but at time 0 the market valuation of these risks is such that the bank is still solvent.

Now suppose that new and previously unanticipated information about the bank's lending policy is released. For convenience, assume the new information comes at time 1, but that nothing else has changed. Under the new set of risk-neutral probabilities, assumed to be determined after the information release, the bank is now judged to be insolvent. It has assets with a market value of only 875, and it cannot therefore be expected to meet its deposit liabilities. As a result, it has a negative net worth of 50.

The revised balance sheet is shown in Table 20.7. In this circumstance there is still a chance the bank will eventually turn out to be solvent, but according to current market valuations it is presently insolvent. Clearly, this is another circumstance in which the management of the bank might be tempted to gamble for resurrection unless it is constrained by the regulators.

The foregoing examples illustrate that the efficient allocation of financial resources requires widely distributed, reliable, and timely information. It has long been recognized that efficiency in trading and pricing stocks, including the stocks of intermediaries, depends critically on a widely distributed information base and on good information processing. Yet it is only recently that research has begun to show how widely stock markets vary with respect to the quality of the information base on which trading takes place

---

of risk-neutral probabilities and that in each case they regard a particular state of the world as not being possible. If it were desired to use a common partition of the states along with different risk-neutral probabilities, it would only be necessary to attach a small positive risk-neutral probability to one state, and reduce the probabilities of other states accordingly. This change would not affect the essence of the example, but would complicate the discussion somewhat.

TABLE 20.7 Balance Sheet, Market Value Basis, Time 1

Assets		Liabilities and Owners Equity	
Cash (paid in by shareholders)	50	Deposits	975
Loans at market value	875	Market value of equity	−50

(Yu 1997, Bhattacharya 1998, Hong and Stein 1999). Insofar as intermediation is concerned, public release of asset quality information could improve the positions of depositors and other investors, financial institutions, and the regulators who supervise them.

SYSTEM RISKS AND CURRENT POLICY ISSUES

So far, this chapter has discussed risks from the standpoint of an individual bank. But bank panics affect an entire banking system, and thus present problems of a different scale from those discussed so far. A significant proportion of both bank depositors and bank borrowing clients may be affected by banking system difficulties, and in such circumstances both consumer spending and business capital formation may be reduced. For example, a bank panic might lead to a credit crunch, that is, circumstances in which it is difficult for businesses with viable projects to obtain financing. That is, the problem can affect an entire economy, as mentioned at the beginning of the chapter in relation to the late 1990s difficulties in Southeast Asia, and in relation to worldwide difficulties in 2007–2008. In the event of such system problems, emergency liquidity is not likely to be available from the interbank market, and even the resources of a supportive government may be strained.

Diamond and Rajan (2005) explore some of the reasons bank failures can be contagious. The authors argue that contagion can result as bank failures shrink the common pool of liquidity, creating or exacerbating aggregate liquidity shortages. Given the costs of a financial crisis, there is a possible role for government intervention, but liquidity and solvency problems interact and can cause each other, making it difficult to deal effectively with the crisis.

Information Release

As with market transactions, the allocative efficiency of intermediary operations depends critically on a widely distributed information base and on good information processing. If stakeholders are able to determine the probability distribution of future possible events then they can price the events appropriately and will not suffer from taking unanticipated risks. They may still suffer losses, but they are at least better able to evaluate the possibility of losses at the outset.

In practice, the public availability of asset quality information varies widely. Moreover, much of the relevant asset information is produced by intermediaries for their own use, and is therefore not publicly distributed. As a result, it is often difficult for either investors or regulators to obtain pertinent asset quality information. In recognition of this difficulty, Ross (1989) distinguishes between institutions whose asset portfolio quality is difficult to determine, or opaque, and institutions whose asset quality is transparent.

Measures to reduce institutional opacity could both improve the efficiency of the resource allocation process and enhance prudential regulation. Providing more and better information is not a panacea, but information release can play both proactive and retroactive roles in managing financial difficulties. Its value can even extend to helping manage the periodic recurrence of financial crises.

A solvency crisis can arise at the system level when a number of intermediaries or their stakeholders find that the values of intermediary assets are less than those of their liabilities. Systemic forms of solvency crises are very frequently created by fads in lending or investing. Such fads arise in many contexts, including the 1970s and 1980s sovereign loan mania, the 1980s real estate lending in both North America and Japan, the difficulties of Long-Term Capital Management in the late 1990s, and subprime lending in the mid-2000s. Lending or investing fads are almost always fueled by overoptimistic forecasts. One peculiar feature of these forecasts is that while they have nearly always been proven wrong in the past, in each new fad the managers who stand to profit essentially argue "this time is different." They do not seem to draw the obvious lessons from history, a matter considered further in Chapter 21. Further, incentives to lend or invest recklessly can also be fuelled by the prospect of generous bailout policies, as previously discussed.

Solvency crises cannot be overcome as easily as liquidity crises because the asset value needed to redeem liabilities simply does not exist. Indeed, to manage solvency crises effectively over the longer term, it becomes necessary to alter the incentives that contributed to creating the solvency problem in the first place. The main defense against overly optimistic managers is probably to bring contrarian thinking to bear on their statements. However, a policy that relies on critical thinking must by implication rely on the availability of credible asset valuations to support the thinking.

Regular, consistent, and early reporting of asset quality information seem to be a much more effective way of demonstrating soundness than does the current practice of only reporting problems when banks have clearly failed. A proactive approach could be used to help show problem institutions how they are likely to face difficulties if they persist in making weak loans, and could also make it clear to riskier institutions that they would have little prospect of being bailed out if they persisted in taking undue risks. That is, information release should provide at least some incentive for institutions to work on reducing portfolio risk. Even if the public opprobrium attendant on information release is insufficient to discourage risk-loving management, information release might still be of value. The release could make it easier for regulators to defend any "cease and desist" actions they might have to take in such circumstances.

Regulators sometimes argue that producing too much information can make it difficult for them to negotiate with troubled institutions. While this argument has some virtues, its benefits may be outweighed by the benefits to a policy of greater openness. Third, proactive management of potentially emerging solvency crises offers dynamic advantages discussed, for example, in Neave (1998) and in Neave and Milne (1998). The idea of information release is, of course, not new. One suggestion for developing better asset quality information is that banks might be able to rate each others' portfolios. The mutual supervision suggestion has much in common with the idea that institutions might from time to time sell off representative parts of their asset portfolios to permit better outside evaluations of asset quality. However both suggestions suffer from the difficulty that in the past some institutions have been demonstrably deficient in their policing activities, and it is not easy to see why they might do better in the future. Indeed, the prospect of large profits can blind even conservative bankers to the risks they might be taking. The contrarian thinking of regulators is needed to offset either kind of overoptimism, and regulatory judgments need to be published in a timely fashion to be effective.

The kinds of instabilities exhibited in the United States during the credit crisis of 2007–2008 have spread to other parts of the world as the crisis has increased in scope. As of September 2008, financial institutions in many countries of the European community and also in Asia have faced the same kinds of pressures as did the U.S. financial industry before the liquidity crisis of AIG and the investment banks' absorption or conversion to universal banks (see Chapter 17). As noted earlier, the principal reasons for the difficulties are losses on lending and on credit default swaps, and the principal cures are to obtain new sources of capital.

The most likely possibilities are loans of last resort, the government purchase of troubled assets, and infusions of equity by governments or their agencies. The best choice among the possible alternatives depends on regulators' and the markets' assessment of what best will restore confidence and how a given scheme will affect institutional incentives to resolve the difficulties. For example, providing more equity to banks gives the banks a greater incentive to collect bad loans than does a policy of purchasing the loans. Buying banks' preferred shares, issued with accompanying warrants, provides a capital infusion that leaves banks with the incentives to rectify their lending problems and at the same time means that government rescuers will share in the profits if the banks effect a successful recovery. These matters are discussed in Chapter 22.

REFERENCES

Allen, Franklin and Douglas Gale. 2007. *Understanding financial crisis*, Oxford University Press.

Arrow, Kenneth J. 1974. *Essays in the Theory of Risk-Bearing*. Amsterdam: North-Holland.

Bagehot, Walter. 1873. *Lombard Street: A Description of the Money Market*. London: Smith and Elder. 1910.

Bhattacharya, Utpal. 1998. When an event is not an event: The strange case of Mexico. Indiana University Working Paper.

Buser, Stephen A., Andrew H. Chen, and Edward J. Kane. 1981. Federal deposit insurance, regulatory policy, and optimal bank capital. *Journal of Finance* 35: 51–60.

Chari, V. V., and R. Jagannathan. 1986. Banking panics, information and rational expectations equilibrium. *Journal of Finance* 43: 749–761.

Diamond, Douglas W. 2004. Committing to commit: Short-term debt when enforcement is costly. *Journal of Finance* 59: 1,447–1,479.

Diamond, Douglas W., and Philip Dybvig. 1983. Bank runs, deposit insurance, and liquidity. *Journal of Political Economy* 91: 401–419.

Diamond, Douglas W., and Raghuram G. Rajan. 2005. Liquidity shortages and banking crises. *Journal of Finance* 60: 615–648.

Freixas, Xavier, and Jean-Charles Rochet. 1997. *Microeconomics of banking*, 1st ed. Cambridge, MA.: MIT Press.

Goldstein, Itay, and Ady Pauzner. 2005. Demand deposit contracts and the probability of bank runs. *Journal of Finance* 60: 1,293–1,327.

Goodhart, C. 1995. *The Central Bank and the Financial System*. Cambridge, MA: MIT Press.

Hong, Harrison, and Jeremy C. Stein. 1999. A unified theory of underreaction, momentum trading, and overreaction in asset markets. *Journal of Finance* 54: 2,143–2,184.

Merton, Robert C. 1977. An analytic derivation of the cost of deposit insurance and loan guarantees: An application of modern option pricing theory. *Journal of Banking and Finance* 1: 3–11.

Neave, Edwin H. 1998. *Financial Systems: Principles and Organisation*. London: Routledge.

Neave, Edwin H. and Frank Milne. 1998. Revising *Canada's Financial Regulation: Analyses and Recommendations*. Toronto: C. D. Howe Research Institute Commentary 101.

Rochet, Jean-Charles. 2008. *Why are there so many banking crises?* Princeton, NJ: Princeton University Press.

Ross, Stephen A. 1989. Institutional markets, financial marketing, and financial innovation. Journal of Finance 44: 541–556.

Yu, Wayne W. 1997. Essays on capital markets. Unpublished PhD Dissertation, Edmonton: University of Alberta.

APPENDIX 20A: SOLVENCY REGULATIONS

Recall the portfolio theoretic model of Chapter 16 where a constrained solution, subject to reserve and capital requirements, was obtained. Banks maximizing a criterion like that used in Chapter 16 will not necessarily choose the levels of capital and cash reserves they were constrained to choose there. To see the difference, suppose the bank is now free to select its loan and deposit amounts. Recall that if there are no operating expenses, the intermediary's expected net interest income is

$$E(\pi) = E(r)L + E(c)D \qquad (20A.1)$$

where r is the interest received on loans L, and c is the interest paid on deposits D. Since equation (20A.1) adds the interest income and interest expenses, and since both $E(r)$ and $E(c)$ are assumed to be positive, a solution will only be meaningful if $L > 0$ and $D < 0$.

Suppose intermediary risk is measured by the variance of income:

$$\sigma^2(\pi) = \{L^2\sigma^2(r) + D^2\sigma^2(c) + 2LD\rho\sigma(r)\sigma(c)\} \qquad (20A.2)$$

where $\rho = \rho(r, c)$ is the correlation between the interest rates r and c. Assume the criterion function used by the intermediary is[25]

$$\text{Max}_{L,D}\{E(\pi) - (\beta/2)\sigma^2(\pi)\} \qquad (20A.3)$$

where $\beta > 0$ is a coefficient of risk aversion. Substituting equations (20A.1) and (20A.2) in equation (20A.3), taking the first partial derivatives with respect to L and D, and setting the resulting equations equal to zero

---

[25] Criterion (20A.3) can be justified by assuming a negative exponential utility function and normally distributed random variables. It can also be justified by assuming a quadratic utility function.

defines the intermediary's optimally chosen asset and deposit levels as the solution to

$$E(r) - \beta\{L\sigma^2(r) + D\rho\sigma(r)\sigma(c)\} = 0$$
$$E(c) - \beta\{L\rho\sigma(r)\sigma(c) + D\sigma^2(c)\} = 0 \tag{20A.4}$$

Conditions (20A.4) can be solved using the method of determinants to obtain

$$L^* = [E(r)\sigma^2(c) - \rho\sigma(r)\sigma(c)\,E(c)]/\beta\Delta$$

and

$$D^* = [E(c)\sigma^2(r) - \rho\sigma(r)\sigma(c)E(r)]/\beta\Delta \tag{20A.5}$$

where

$$\Delta = \sigma^2(r)\sigma^2(c) - \rho^2\sigma^2(r)\sigma^2(c) \tag{20A.6}$$

Clearly, equation (20A.6) can only be nonzero if the necessary condition for an interior solution,

$$\rho\varepsilon(-1,\ 1)$$

is satisfied. Then further investigation of conditions (20A.5) shows that conditions for $L > 0$ and $D < 0$ are $\rho > 0$ and $\rho E(r)/\sigma(r) > E(c)/\sigma(c)$. That is to say, interest revenues and interest costs must be positively correlated if the solution is to be economically meaningful.

The following parameter values give a representative solution. Let

$\sigma^2(r) = 0.01$
$\sigma^2(c) = 0.01$
$\rho(r, c) = 0.98$
$\beta = 0.01$
$E(r) = 0.09$
$E(c) = 0.06$

With these parameters $L^* = 7,879$ and $D^* = -7,121$. In order to operate the bank needs a minimum equity investment of $E = 7,879 - 7,121 = 758$, and with E at that value cash reserves will be zero.

The main point of the exercise is to show that in the absence of regulatory constraints there is little reason to assume the bank would freely choose the levels of cash reserves and of equity deemed suitable by the regulators. Regulatory constraints will generally move a firm away from the optimal portfolio position established by its own criteria.

APPENDIX 20B: CLOSURE DECISIONS

Closure policies are not always credible, either because closure is costly in an absolute sense or appears more costly at a given time than it might be at some future date. Also, regulators may face incentives not to close institutions if they see the closure decisions as affecting their careers. Such regulators might want to leave a troubled bank open until their tenure has ended. Finally, if banks are tempted to invest in highly risky assets, the reputational benefits of avoiding those risks and not having to subject its portfolio to outside scrutiny may compensate for a lack of the rents it could have earned by taking on the greater risks.

Separation of ownership and control creates incentive problems when contracts are incomplete. The kinds of incentive problems that arise are those of insuring that management will exercise due diligence with respect to obtaining repayment of outstanding loans. The incentive problems can be particularly difficult to deal with in the case of incomplete contracts. When contracts are incomplete, some decisions cannot be prespecified, even in the form of decision rules contingent on some event.[26] That is, incomplete contracts are those for which the decision rules themselves cannot be worked out in advance, as Chapter 7 showed.

To examine the incentive problems attendant on closure decisions,[27] consider a bank that makes a loan at time 0, and arranges for repayments at times 1 and 2. The quality of loans can be improved through managerial effort, but since effort is unobservable regulators face a problem of how to motivate the managers. In the following situation it is assumed that management attempts to collect the time 1 repayment before learning whether the regulators will shut down the bank or not, and this uncertainty motivates management to make the loan quality as high as possible. If the firm is still operating at time 2, management is assumed to continue exerting effort then

---

[26] If decisions are specified as rules contingent on some event, they still constitute a complete contract in the sense of this book.

[27] This section is based on the Freixas and Rochet (1997, 281–286) discussion of a model developed by Dewatripont and Tirole. Some model features have been altered to facilitate presentation.

TABLE 20B.1 Sequence of Events

Time 0	Time 1 Action of Firm	Time 1 Regulatory Information and Action	Time 2 Action of Firm
L_0 is advanced	P_1. Management exerts effort to keep loan quality high.	$u = G$; operations allowed to continue.	P_{2G}. Management exerts further effort.
		$u = B$, operations shut down.	P_{2B}. Management exerts no further effort.

because there is a higher payoff from doing so. However, if the firm has been shut down management has no incentive to continue its efforts to improve loan quality, and therefore does not exert further effort. The effort management exerts at time 1 is assumed to be costless, while the effort management exerts at time 2 is assumed to cost K.

Table 20B.1 presents the sequence of events schematically. At time 1, regulators decide either to allow the bank to continue operations, or to shut it down. The optimal regulatory act at time 1 depends on the signal regarding future loan repayments, u. Define a difference in payoff functions

$$D(u) = E\{P_2|u, \ C\} - E\{P_2|u, \ S\}$$

If $D(u)$ is increasing in u, there is a critical value of u, say u^*, such that regulators allow the bank to continue operating if the signal $u \geq u^*$. Suppose the signal u can take on one of two values, $u = G$ or $u = B$, such that $G \geq u^* \geq B$. Thus the situation assumes the regulator will allow the bank to continue operations if the signal is G, but not if it is B.

However, the signal is not a perfect indicator. Following on a good signal, from the perspective of time 1 the actual loan repayment at time 2 might be either P_{2G} or P_{2B}. Since the particular value of the loan repayment only becomes known at time 2, the regulatory decision taken at time 1 is based on the expected value of the total loan repayments calculated as shown in Table 20B.2.

The conditional probabilities of the time two outcomes depend on the value of the signal as follows:

$$\text{Prob}\{P_2 = P_{2G}|u = G\} > \text{Prob}\{P_2 = P_{2B}|u = G\}$$

TABLE 20B.2 Expected and Realized Payoffs

Time 1	Time 2 Realized Values
$u = G$ and further effort exerted at cost K. Expected loan value at time 2 is $E\{P_1 + P_2 \vert u = G\} - K$.	$P_1 + P_{2G} \vert u = G$
	$P_1 + P_{2B} \vert u = G$
$u = B$ and no further effort exerted. Expected loan value at time 2 is $E\{P_1 + P_2 \vert u = B\}$.	$P_1 + P_{2G} \vert u = B$
	$P_1 + P_{2B} \vert u = B$
	$P_1 + P_{2B} \vert u = B$

and since there are only two possible values the foregoing also implies

$$\text{Prob}\{P_2 = P_{2G} \vert u = B\} < \text{Prob}\{P_2 = P_{2B} \vert u = B\}$$

Assume the expected values are $E\{P_1 + P_2 \mid u = G\} - K \geq 0$ and $E\{P_1 + P_2 \mid u = B\} < 0$, so that the regulator will keep the bank open if the signal is G but not if the signal is B. Moreover, if the signal is G, the managers are assumed to benefit from exerting effort, but not if the signal is B.

The signal u cannot be observable to managers if the contract is to be interpreted as an incomplete contract. If managers could observe the signal, they could work out the regulator's decision rule, and the contract would then be a complete, albeit contingent, contract. However, even a complete contract could be effective if management were to face appropriate incentives to exert effort whenever the bank is kept open.

CHAPTER 21

Financial Activity and Capital Formation

This chapter studies relations between credit conditions, financial structure, and real economic activity. The models presented later show that credit conditions, firms' financial conditions, and capital formation are all interdependent. While the models are informative, they are also elementary and explain only some of the links between finance and economic activity. However, as the chapter's last section shows, model development is currently an active research area and the links will come to be better understood as the research proceeds. In evidence, the chapter summarizes recent empirical work that supplements the insights developed from the models.

ADVERSE SELECTION AND CREDIT CONDITIONS

Adverse selection can contribute to financial system fragility through its effect on credit conditions. For example, if market interest rates on deposits increase, banks must earn greater returns on their loans to compensate. The attempt to increase loan returns can mean that credit terms become more stringent. A change in terms can alter the riskiness of a pool of borrowers, leading in turn to the possibility of a credit market collapse (Mankiw 1986).

To model the situation, suppose there are many risk-neutral borrowers, each of whom seeks one unit of money to finance a project that cannot be implemented without financing. Assume the project returns X, and that the realizations of X are either x/p with probability p or zero with probability $1 - p$. Project success probability p is private information, possessed only by the borrower. It cannot credibly be transmitted to financiers because the borrower has an incentive to misrepresent her ability to pay.

Banks are assumed to be risk-neutral, and unable to distinguish among borrowers with different success probabilities. Banks offer limited liability debt contracts that provide an advance of 1 at time 0 on the stipulation that R will be repaid at time 1 if the project is successful. If a project fails, the borrower is bankrupt and the bank receives nothing.

Suppose the value of x is constant across all borrowers.[1] Each borrower expects to earn

$$E_p(X) = p(x/p) + (1 - p)0 = x$$

A borrower will apply for credit only if her expected earnings exceed a pre-set minimum, here taken to be zero. Thus a borrower will seek funds only if the bank stipulates a repayment R, such that

$$x - pR > 0 \tag{21.1}$$

Condition (21.1) implicitly defines the individual's demand for credit.[2] Hence market demand for credit can be obtained by aggregating (1.1) across individuals. For example, if $R < x/p$ every borrower seeks funds. In this case the average probability of repayment is $E(p)$ and the amount of funds demanded equals the total number of borrowers in the population.

However if $R > x/p$, only borrowers with probability $p > x/R$ will seek funds and the average probability will be the expectation over p conditional on $p > x/R$. In this case the quantity of funds demanded equals the total number of borrowers whose success probability satisfies the last condition. The resulting aggregate demand for credit can be written implicitly as a function of the average probability of repayment

$$\pi(R) = E[p|x - pR > 0] \tag{21.2}$$

or

$$\pi(R) = E[p|p < x/R] \tag{21.3}$$

where the expectation is taken conditionally with respect to p as shown. It follows immediately from condition (21.3) that $\pi(R)$ is a non-increasing function[3] of R, since with the assumed constant value of x the upper limit on

---

[1] Mankiw (1986) allows x either to vary across borrowers or to be constant.
[2] The amount of credit obtained will be the present value of the repayment R.
[3] If x is not constant, Mankiw (1986) shows that $\pi(R)$ need not be monotonic.

the conditional expectation is decreasing in R. In other words, as R increases, individuals whose success probability p no longer satisfies condition (21.3) drop out of the market. As the best risks drop out, the average probability of repayment decreases.

For example, suppose p is distributed uniformly on $(0,1)$ and that $x > 1 + r$. Then the average success probability of borrowers who find the deal attractive depends on the size of R:

$$\pi(R) = 1/2; \quad R < x;$$
$$x/2R; \quad R > x \tag{21.4}$$

To see how equation (21.4) is determined, first consider $R < x$. In this case, the conditional expectation (21.3) is satisfied for all $p \, \varepsilon(0, 1)$ because all potential borrowers can expect to earn more than the riskless rate. Therefore, they will all undertake the project and their average success probability will be 1/2. On the other hand, if $R > x$ only borrowers whose success probability p does not exceed $p_{\max}$, where

$$p_{\max} = x/R < 1$$

will undertake the project. Given the uniform distribution of success probabilities, the average success probability in this case is $x/2R$.

Credit market equilibrium requires that the return to risk-neutral lenders equal the riskless return $1 + r$. That is, the expected value of the required repayment must equal $1 + r$:

$$\pi(R)R = 1 + r \tag{21.5}$$

Equation (1.5) implicitly defines the supply of credit function. When p is distributed uniformly, the slope of $\pi(R)\, R$ is 1/2 for $R < x$, and 0 for $R > x$. In more general cases, the supply of credit function can have a positive slope for small values of R, and a negative slope for larger values of R. (The example of credit rationing in Chapter 10 exhibits this behavior.)

If the demand for credit function (21.2) cuts the supply of credit function (21.4) from below,[4] an equilibrium will be attained. However, if the riskless interest rate were to increase from its equilibrium value, it is possible the

---

[4]If the demand for credit function (21.2) cuts the supply of credit function (21.4) from above, there may be an unstable equilibrium; see Mankiw (1986).

two curves would no longer meet. In this case there is no equilibrium[5] with a positive amount of lending and borrowing. Mankiw (1986) interprets this situation as a credit market collapse, brought about by an increased average risk of the borrower pool that is in turn attributable to the workings of adverse selection. The model illustrates the possibility that in normally functioning credit markets, an interest rate increase could cause the markets to collapse. As was shown in Chapter 10, another possibility is that credit rationing might emerge.

MORAL HAZARD

The financial conditions of borrowers and investors can also have an impact on capital formation when deals are subject to moral hazard. Bernanke and Gertler (1990) show that if firms suffer a decline in wealth, then the difficulties presented by moral hazard can induce lenders to cut back on the amount of credit they will extend. As a result, firms may have to curtail their capital investment.

Consider a setting in which an infinite number of agents face individual planning problems defined over two points in time. Entrepreneurs represent proportion μ of the agents while households represent the remaining $(1 - \mu)$. Both entrepreneurs and households are risk-neutral. There is a riskless technology that returns $1 + r$ at time 1 for each unit of capital invested at time 0. In addition, each entrepreneur owns a risky technology that yields either x at time 1 with probability p, or zero at time 1 with probability $(1 - p)$, again for each unit of capital invested at time 0. The project success probability p is initially unknown to the entrepreneurs, but they can determine its value by paying a screening cost C.

Internal Finance

The model is developed by first examining the case when entrepreneurs can finance their projects internally, then the case where entrepreneurs borrow funds from households. In the first case, every agent is assumed to have an endowment equal to one unit of capital. Accordingly, every agent has a choice between investing in the risky technology or in the riskless alternative. The sequence of events is shown in Table 21.1. Consider first the situation

---

[5]That is, there is no equilibrium of the usual sort, although as Chapter 10 showed there could be a credit rationing equilibrium. Such a credit rationing equilibrium can be interpreted as a form of credit market collapse.

TABLE 21.1 Sequence of Decisions and Events

Time 0		Time 1
Entrepreneur does not screen; chooses risk-free investment.		Entrepreneur realizes $1 + r$.
Entrepreneur screens[6] and learns value of p.	Probability below critical value. Project abandoned; entrepreneur chooses risk-free investment.	Entrepreneur realizes $1 + r$.
	Probability equal to or above critical value. Project adopted.	Project succeeds; entrepreneur gets x.
		Project fails; entrepreneur gets zero.

in which the entrepreneur chooses not to screen. In this case, the firm's expected profit is

$$\text{Max}[E(p)x, (1 + r)] \tag{21.6}$$

Without screening the entrepreneur will not gain any information about p, and the best she can do is to follow a fixed strategy: Always adopt the risky project, or always adopt the safe project. Henceforth, it will be assumed that the maximum of equation (21.6) is $1 + r$, that is, in the absence of screening the risky projects are not worth undertaking.

When an entrepreneur screens she first learns p. Then if p equals or exceeds a critical value (to be defined shortly) she will decide to adopt the risky project. If p falls below a critical value, she does not proceed with the project but rather invests in the safe asset. Thus with screening the firm's expected revenue will be

$$E_p\{\text{max}[px, (1 + r)]\} \tag{21.7}$$

Risky projects with a positive net present value

$$px > 1 + r \tag{21.8}$$

---

[6]Entrepreneurs will only screen if ω_e is greater than a critical value ω_c.

will be adopted, but projects for which

$$1 + r \geq px$$

will not. Thus a project will only be adopted if its success probability does not fall below

$$p_{\min} = (1 + r)/x \qquad (21.9)$$

In comparison to a fixed policy of always investing in the safe asset, the screening process creates an incremental value V that is equal to the value of a call option[7] with an exercise price of $(1 + r)$:

$$V \equiv E_p\{\max[px - (1 + r), 0]\} \qquad (21.10)$$

Projects will be screened if $V \geq C$, where C represents the screening cost. Henceforth, it will be assumed that $V \geq C$ is always satisfied, that is, screening is always worthwhile.

Allocation in the Absence of Credit Constraints

Let $H(p)$ be the distribution function of p, where p is the success probability determined through screening. Since entrepreneurs will only adopt projects with a positive net present value, the success probability must exceed the critical minimum given in equation (21.9). Then the first best levels of the per capita macroeconomic variables are investment

$$I^* = \mu[1 - H(p_{\min})]$$

(where it will be recalled that μ is the proportion of agents who are entrepreneurs) and output value

$$q^* = 1 + r + \mu(V - C) \qquad (21.11)$$

Equation (21.11) says, respectively, that total investment per capita and total output per capita depend on the distribution of projects, the proportion of entrepreneurs μ, and the relation between screening value and screening

---

[7]The expectation in equation (21.10) is taken with respect to p rather than a risk-neutral probability q because firms are assumed to be risk-neutral.

TABLE 21.2 Sequence of Events

Time 0		Time 1	
	Project abandoned.		
Entrepreneurs screen.[8]	Project financed; $1 - w_e$ lent by outside lender.	Project succeeds.	Lender gets R and entrepreneur gets (x-R).
		Project fails.	Both lender and entrepreneur get zero.
No screening. Risk-free investment chosen. Risk-free payoff obtained.			

costs. Firms invest their available funds either in acceptable risky projects or in the safe asset if their risky projects are not acceptable. Since firms have no need to borrow from households, the latter invest only in safe assets.

Credit Constraints and Limited Liability

Now suppose the average endowment of all agents continues to be 1, but that entrepreneurs' endowments are only $w_e < 1$. Entrepreneurs must therefore obtain financing from households if they wish to implement the risky project. Initial endowments are publicly observable, but as before only the entrepreneur can observe the project's success probability (see Table 21.2).

Household lenders contract to extend $(1 - w)$ at time 0 in exchange for being paid $R(w)$ at time 1 if the project succeeds. Entrepreneurs have limited liability and pay nothing if the project fails. The contract is signed after borrowers have learned p, but they cannot credibly communicate the value of p to lenders. As will be shown explicitly in equation (21.13), the entrepreneur must therefore invest a minimum amount in order to assure lenders the contract is not subject to moral hazard.

No entrepreneur will undertake a project unless she expects to earn the riskless rate of interest on it:

$$[x - R(w)]p(w) = (1 + r)w$$

---

[8]Entrepreneurs will only screen if ω_e is greater than a critical value ω_c.

Thus project and loan contract characteristics together determine a minimum probability $p_{min}(w_e)$ required by the entrepreneur to implement the project:

$$p^0{}_{min}(w) \leq w(1+r)/[x - R(w)] \tag{21.12}$$

Equation (21.12) defines a minimum probability different from (21.9). One reason for the difference is that with outside financing entrepreneurs do not retain all the cash flow if the project is successful. A second reason is that the repayment required by households will depend on the amount entrepreneurs invest in their own projects. Comparing (21.12) with (21.9) shows that

$$\begin{aligned} p^0{}_{min}(w) &< p_{min} \Leftrightarrow \\ w(1+r)/[x - R(w)] &< (1+r)/x \Leftrightarrow \\ wx &< x - R(w) \Leftrightarrow \\ R(w)/x &< (1 - w) \end{aligned} \tag{21.13}$$

that is whenever the required repayment does not demand a share of the proceeds greater than the share of the funds provided by financiers. Henceforth, for simplicity, $p^0{}_{min}(w)$ is written without qualifying sub- or superscripts as $p(w)$.

The lender's zero profit condition is

$$A[p(w)]R(w) = (1+r)(1-w) \tag{21.14}$$

where

$$A[p(w)] \equiv E\{p | p \geq p(w)\}$$

The quantity $A[p(w)]$ is the average probability of project success after screening, and $R(w)$ is the required repayment. Condition (21.14) says that lenders must expect to earn at least the riskless rate on the projects they finance. Conditions (21.12) and (21.14) together determine the equilibrium contract.

The levels of per capita macroeconomic variables are now investment by entrepreneurs

$$F^{**} = \mu w[1 - H(p(w))] \tag{21.15}$$

and investment by households

$$S^{**} = \mu(1 - w)[1 - H(p(w))] \tag{21.16}$$

Any remaining initial endowments, whether of firms or households, are placed in the riskless investment. Recall, for example, that a firm with a risky project whose present value is negative will purchase the safe investment. Finally, in comparison to the earlier solution, the option value of the screening technology is now

$$V(w) = E_p\{\max[p(x - R(w)) - (1 + r)w, 0]\} \qquad (21.17)$$

The model predicts that

- With credit constraints there is over-investment among screened projects in the sense that the relevant cutoff probability does not always ensure projects have positive net present value. The lower cutoff probability results from the workings of moral hazard (see equation (21.14).
- There is a critical value of entrepreneurial wealth, w_C, below which firms will not invest in projects. This value is defined implicitly by $V(w_C) = C$, where $V(w)$ is the value defined in equation (21.17). That is, if entrepreneurs do not have sufficient wealth they will eschew screening and simply invest in the safe project.
- The nominal interest rate $r(w) \equiv R(w)/(1 - w)$ is decreasing in w; the more entrepreneurs invest in their own projects the lower the effective interest rate they pay on additional financing.

Since household investment in the projects depends on the minimum adoption probability and the initial wealth positions (financial situations) of firms, it follows that aggregate investment depends on the same variables. That is, output depends on the expected value of screening, its costs, and on the financial situations of firms. In particular, if a relatively large number of firms suffered a decline in wealth they might all fall below the critical level for screening, undertake no investment, and produce no output.

Although there is nothing to prevent households from lending to an intermediary that passes the funds on to the borrowing firms, Bernanke and Gertler do not model the financial sector completely. In effect, the authors explain financial cycles by showing that firms' financial conditions can, through moral hazard, affect their ability to implement capital formation projects. The model does not address how financiers might improve productivity by selecting among projects to find the more promising ones.[9]

---

[9]The Milne-Neave model of Chapter 6 depicts financial intermediaries and markets with different screening capabilities, as does the Holmstrom-Tirole model presented in the next section, "Banks, Markets, and Economic Activity."

FINANCIAL CYCLES

Aspects of financial structure have been suggested as explanatory factors in longer-term economic cycles. This section first reviews an early model incorporating credit constraints and then surveys three newer models. The first and second examine how the interaction between banks and hedge funds can amplify cyclical effects, especially when hedge fund activity reaches a certain critical level. The third considers how news from several sources can contribute to rallies and crashes.

Kiyotaki and Moore Model

Kiyotaki and Moore (1995) assume that firms are credit constrained and must use their assets as collateral for borrowing. In this setting a decrease in the price of a productive asset can have a cyclical impact on investment through creating changes in firms' ability to obtain credit.

Assume there are many risk-neutral infinitely lived agents who maximize the present value of expected future consumption. The economy has a non-storable good used for both consumption and production. Another asset—real estate—can be used in any of three ways: in production, as collateral against loans, or in real estate developments. Entrepreneurs own the technology and the land, while lenders have endowments of the consumption good. Entrepreneurs borrow all the consumption good used in production. The technology in which entrepreneurs invest is a constant return to scale, fixed input proportions technology: One unit of the consumption good and λ units of land invested at time t yield X units of the consumption good at time $t + 1$.

All loans are for one period, and to ensure repayment lenders require loans to be fully collateralized. The debt principal and interest at time 1 are therefore restricted to be no greater than the forecast value of the land.

Let

k_t = the number units of land a borrower owns at time t

q_{t+1} = the future price of land, perfectly forecast by financiers

b_t = borrowers' liability at time t

The price of the consumption good is 1. Firms are assumed to borrow as much as they can against the value of the land:

$$b_t = k_t q_{t+1}/(1 + r) \tag{21.18}$$

where r is the riskless rate of interest. Alternatively, land can be leased for real estate development. The value of the rents is given by

$$h_t = h_t(A_t) = m \times (A_t + h_0) \tag{21.19}$$

where: h_t = the per period rental rate per unit of land
         A_t = the number of units of land used in production

The model determines both A_t and the equilibrium price of land q_t. Recall that production of a unit of output requires λ units of land and one unit of the consumption good. The consumption goods used in production are purchased from the proceeds of borrowing against the future value of the land. Let the total quantity of land be A, and suppose the next period price of land is q_{t+1}. Then the owners of the land can borrow $Aq_{t+1}/(1+r)$ against the land, and buy $Aq_{t+1}/(1+r)$ units of the consumption good at price 1. Since they use $Aq_{t+1}/(1+r)$ units of the consumption good in production, the fixed input proportions technology requires that they also use

$$A_t = \lambda A q_{t+1}/(1+r) \tag{21.20}$$

units of land in production.

Land can be used as an investment as well as in production. Thus in the absence of arbitrage opportunities the net return on the value of one unit of land must equal the riskless rate r:

$$\begin{aligned} q_t(1+r) &= q_{t+1} + [X - (1+r)][q_{t+1}/(1+r)] \\ &+ h_t[1 - (\lambda q_{t+1}/(1+r))] \end{aligned} \tag{21.21}$$

Starting with the left-hand side of equation (21.21), an investor with q_t units of money can obtain $q_t(1+r)$ one period later by purchasing the safe investment. This return must be equaled by the three uses of land described on the right-hand side of equation (21.21). The first term on the right-hand side indicates the next period value of land, q_{t+1}. The second period refers to the proceeds received from using consumption goods to the value $q_{t+1}/(1+r)$, along with $\lambda q_{t+1}/(1+r)$ units of land, in production. The third term refers to the rental income on the land not used in production.

Using equation (21.19) to replace h_t in equation (21.21) gives a quadratic equation in land prices of the form

$$q_t = a q_{t+1}^2 + b q_{t+1} + c \tag{21.22}$$

where

$$a = -\lambda^2 mA/(1+r)^3$$
$$b = [X + \lambda m(A - h_0)]/(1+r)^2 \tag{21.23}$$
$$c = mh_0/(1+r)$$

Equations (21.22) and (21.23) can generate cycles in both land prices q_t and the quantities of land used in production A_t. For example, consider equation (21.22) with $a = -0.75$, $b = 3.50$, and $c = 0.00$:

$$q_t = -.75q_{t+1}^2 + 3.5q_{t+1} \tag{21.24}$$

It is easy to check that $q_t = 2$, $q_{t+1} = 4$, and $q_t = 4$, $q_{t+1} = 2$ are both solutions to equation (21.24). That is, the equilibrium price of land is 2 and 4 in alternative periods. When the land price is 4, firms can borrow twice as much against their land as they can when the price is 2. Equally, investment projects double in value. Changes in the amount of land used in production can be determined using equation (21.20).

Other values of the coefficients in equation (21.22) will give different price and land use behavior. Prices can cycle explosively, grow monotonically and explosively, or diminish either cyclically or monotonically. In other words, in this model financial constraints can create both credit and investment cycles, and depending on the model's parameters the cycles can be regularly recurring.

Despite their demonstration that financial conditions can create cycles, Kiyotaki and Moore do not establish that the cycles are created by the details of the financial system. The factors causing cycles in the model are the assumed terms on which firms can borrow, rather than any endogenous properties of financial intermediaries. In contrast, the models next discussed indicate that at least some financial market cycles are created by a combination of exogenous and endogenous factors.

Models with Interacting Agents

Brunnermeier and Pedersen (2007) link asset market liquidity (the ease with which an asset is traded) to traders' funding liquidity (the ease with which they can obtain funding). Traders' ability to provide market liquidity depends on the funding available to them. Moreover, traders' ability to raise funds depends on both the margin requirements they face and on the asset markets' liquidity. Under certain conditions, changes in margin requirements can be destabilizing, market and funding illiquidity can be mutually reinforcing, and liquidity spirals can result. The model explains why market liquidity can suddenly dry up, why market liquidity has common features across securities, why it is related to volatility, why it is subject to "flight to quality" and why it co-moves with the market.

In recent unpublished work, Stefan Thurner and J. Doyne Farmer of the Santa Fe Institute, in work with economist John Geanakoplos of Yale, develop an agent model of the securities market that includes hedge funds, banks, and ordinary investors. The model's hedge funds try to identify momentarily mispriced securities, seeking to profit from buying or selling in the expectation that the price will return to a realistic value in the future. As in the real world, they finance their investments by borrowing from the banks. The simulations reveal that with no leverage, a hedge fund can only lose its own investors' money. However as leverage increases a hedge fund can also lose money borrowed from a bank, possibly putting that bank into difficulties. Moreover, increasing leverage begins to pose the threat of failures cascading through the market, and the risk of cascades does not increase gradually. Rather, trading proceeds smoothly until leverage reaches a certain threshold, at which point the model shows the market undergoing a sudden change.

Harras and Sornette (2008) use an agent-based model to study how the triggering factor of a crash or a rally might be related to the details of financial structure. Agents form opinions and invest, based on (1) public information (news), (2) information from a network of contacts, and (3) privately developed information. Agents use Bayesian learning to adapt their trading strategy based on observations showing the relevance of the three information sources. The authors find that rallies and crashes occur as amplifications of random lucky or unlucky streaks of news, the amplifications arising from feedback effects on agents' strategies. Bayesian learning and traders' imitating each create a positive feedback loop that results in rallies and crashes whose price sequences are qualitatively different from other price moves.

BANKS, MARKETS, AND ECONOMIC ACTIVITY

The next model, due to Holmstrom and Tirole (1997), provides a value creation role for financiers by assuming they act as monitors to reduce agency costs. Both entrepreneurs and financiers are assumed to be risk-neutral. Firms have to find external finance for an investment of fixed size I, but there is a moral hazard problem. Firms' managers may choose either a good project with a high probability of success p_G or a bad project with a low probability of success p_B. Either project has the same return y, but managers have an incentive to choose the bad project because it gives them a private benefit B. The good project pays no private benefit. A project, good or bad, that does not succeed has a payoff of zero. Suppose that only the good project has a positive expected net present value:

$$p_G y - (1 + r)I > 0 > p_B y + B - (1 + r)I \tag{21.25}$$

where r is the riskless rate of interest. Holmstrom and Tirole consider both direct lending and intermediary finance. The terms of direct lending can be used to manage the moral hazard problem in one way, and the terms used by intermediaries manage it differently. Direct lenders have no monitoring role, but intermediaries do. Consider each type of finance in turn.

Direct Borrowing from Uninformed Lenders

If the firm is to borrow from uninformed lenders the latter cannot demand too large a repayment R_u without creating the moral hazard problem of inducing the borrower to proceed with the bad project. To avoid such a possibility, R_u must satisfy:

$$p_G(y - R_u) \geq p_B(y - R_u) + B \tag{21.26}$$

or

$$y - B/(p_G - p_B) \geq R_u \tag{21.27}$$

But uninformed investors must also recover at least their opportunity costs r:

$$p_G R_u \geq I_u(1 + r) \tag{21.28}$$

Equations (21.27) and (21.28) together imply

$$p_G[y - B/(p_G - p_B)]/(1 + r) \geq p_G R_u/(1 + r) \geq I_u \tag{21.29}$$

The project can only be financed if the firm has enough assets of its own:

$$A + I_u \geq I \tag{21.30}$$

or using equation (21.29)

$$A \geq I - I_u \geq A^+(r) \equiv I - p_G[y - B/(p_G - p_B)]/(1 + r) \tag{21.31}$$

In other words, equation (21.31) defines the minimum level of assets the firm must have if it is to obtain external financing from uninformed investors. Firms can have different amounts of assets A, but the amounts are publicly observable.

Intermediary Finance

Suppose that by incurring a cost C, a bank can monitor a borrowing firm. To reflect the idea that an intermediary adds value by performing the monitoring, suppose monitoring reduces a borrowing firm's private benefit to b, where $b + C < B$. To resolve the moral hazard problem, the monitoring bank demands that a borrowing firm invest some of its own assets A in the project. If the firm is to borrow funds from both an external source that requires repayment R_u and from an intermediary that requires repayment R_m, the firm's incentive compatibility constraint must still be satisfied

$$p_G(y - R_u - R_m) \geq p_B(y - R_u - R_m) + b \tag{21.32}$$

Management now gets only a private benefit of b from the bad project because the intermediary will monitor, providing that the intermediary's incentive condition

$$p_G R_m - C \geq p_B R_m \tag{21.33}$$

is also satisfied.

Since scarce resources are used to carry out the monitoring, bank finance is assumed to be more expensive than direct finance. Hence the firm is assumed to borrow as little as possible from the bank. The repayment required by the bank must then also be as small as possible; that is, just enough to compensate for the additional cost of monitoring reflected in equation (21.33):

$$(p_G - p_B) R_m = C \tag{21.34}$$

If the bank's required return on loans is β, equation (21.34) means the proceeds of the loan will be

$$I_m(\beta) = [(p_G - p_B) R_m]/(1 + \beta) = C/(1 + \beta) \tag{21.35}$$

Next, rewrite equation (21.32) as

$$(p_G - p_B)(y - R_u - R_m) \geq b$$

Then using equation (21.34),

$$(p_G - p_B)(y - R_u) \geq b + C$$
$$y - R_u \geq (b + C)/(p_G - p_B) \tag{21.36}$$
$$[y - (b + C)/(p_G - p_B)] \geq R_u$$

Moreover, recalling equation (21.28), that is, $p_G R_u \geq I_u(1 + r)$, equation (21.36) can be written

$$p_G[y - (b + C)/(p_G - p_B)]/(1 + r) \geq p_G R_u/(1 + r) \geq I_u \tag{21.37}$$

Equation (21.37) means the firm must have assets of its own, such that

$$A \geq A - (\beta, r) \equiv I - I_m(\beta) - I_u$$
$$= I - I_m(\beta) - p_G[y - (b + C)/(p_G - p_B)]/(1 + r) \tag{21.38}$$

The patterns of finance are shown in Table 21.3.

Different patterns of finance can result from changes in r, β, or both. For example, Holmstrom and Tirole (1997) describe a credit crunch as a situation in which r decreases and β increases. Both the upper and the lower limits on financing types will decrease as a result of the decrease in r, but the lower limit on bank finance will to some extent be offset because the increase in β will increase the lower limit, while leaving the upper limit unchanged (see Table 21.4).

In other words, borrowers can partially offset the difficulties created by moral hazard through using some of their own limited capital. However, the need to use limited capital can affect production decisions, thus linking the financial and the real sectors.

The Holmstrom and Tirole model provides some details of financial structure in which a bank has a greater capability than other agents to

TABLE 21.3   Patterns of Finance

Assets Less than $A^-(\beta, r)$	Assets between A^- (β, R) and $A^+(r)$	Assets Greater than $A^+(r)$
No external finance	Bank finance only	Bank finance and direct finance, but bank finance minimized as far as possible

TABLE 21.4 Effects of Parameter Change

	$A^-(\beta, r))$	$A^+(r))$
Increase in r	Increase	Increase
Increase in β	Increase	No change

control the effects of moral hazard. On the other hand, the model does not ascribe a positive role to finance in the sense that banks might sometimes be able to generate better information than, say, market agents, and thus contribute to an increase in the value of the firm being financed.

EQUILIBRIUM, FINANCIAL STRUCTURE, AND ECONOMIC ACTIVITY

Biais and Cassamatta (1999) extend Holmstrom and Tirole (1997) to study the optimal financing of investment projects when moral hazard can take on the two dimensions of unobservable effort and unobservable risk-shifting. As with Holmstrom and Tirole, both entrepreneurs and financiers are assumed to be risk-neutral. Each entrepreneur is endowed with an investment of fixed size I. Each entrepreneur also has initial wealth $A \le I$, so that outside financing of $I - A$ is needed to implement the project. If $I - A$ can be raised, the project can be implemented and then returns R_J with probability p_J, $J \varepsilon \{G, M, B\}$. We assume $R_G > R_M > R_B$.

Managerial Choice

The manager can choose between two levels of effort, and two levels of risk. With no effort and a low level of risk, $p_J = 1/3$, $J \varepsilon \{G, M, B\}$. If the manager exerts effort, p_G is increased to $1/3 + \varepsilon$, while p_B is decreased to $1/3 - \varepsilon$. The cost of this effort (or equivalently, the manager's utility from shirking) is L. Assume that the projects have a non-positive expected value unless effort is exerted, that is,

$$V \equiv (1/3)R_G + (1/3)R_M + (1/3)R_B \le 0 \tag{21.39}$$

while with effort

$$V_L \equiv (1/3 + \varepsilon)R_G + (1/3)R_M + (1/3 - \varepsilon)R_B \tag{21.40}$$
$$= V + \varepsilon(R_G - R_B) > 0$$

TABLE 21.5   Effect of Managerial Actions on Probabilities

State	Probability without Effort	Probability with Effort	Probability with Effort and Risk-Shifting
G	1/3	$1/3 + \varepsilon$	$1/3 + \varepsilon + \alpha$
M	1/3	1/3	$1/3 - \alpha - \beta$
B	1/3	$1/3 - \varepsilon$	$1/3 - \varepsilon + \beta$

The effect of effort is shown by the difference between the first two probability columns of Table 21.5.

Now consider the effect of risk-shifting, shown in the third column of probabilities in Table 21.5. Entrepreneurs have an incentive to shift risks because it can improve their own positions. Although this risk-shifting could be analyzed whether or not the entrepreneur also exerts effort, we shall examine risk-shifting only after effort has been exerted. In this case risk-shifting further influences V_L by adding terms as follows:

$$V_{LR} = V_L + \alpha(R_G - R_M) - \beta(R_M - R_B)$$

We suppose further that

$$\alpha(R_G - R_M) < \beta(R_M - R_B) \tag{21.41}$$

Condition (21.41) implies the riskier distribution is less favorable for shareholders in the sense of second-degree dominance. In other words, the probability of receiving the state M payoff is decreased while the probabilities of receiving the state G or state B payoffs are both increased. Moreover, the changes are such that the distribution's mean is decreased.

Depending on their compensation scheme the riskier distribution can be better for managers, because the probability of receiving a reward in state G is increased. Condition (21.41) implies that if managers are to be given an incentive to avoid the riskier project, their compensation scheme must be designed to ensure that their expected earnings under the less risky distribution are greater than their expected earnings under the riskier distribution.

Effort is assumed to be socially optimal, that is,

$$V_L > V + L \tag{21.42}$$

an assumption that by equation (21.40) is equivalent to

$$R_B < R_G - L/\varepsilon \tag{21.43}$$

Next, rewrite equation (21.41) as

$$R_B < [(\alpha + \beta)R_M - \alpha R_G]/\beta \tag{21.44}$$

Notice that either equation (21.43) or (21.44) will generally be redundant. If the right-hand side of equation (21.43) is less than the right-hand side of equation (21.44), the effort problem presents the binding constraint. If the right-hand side of equation (21.43) were to be greater than the right-hand side of equation (21.44), the risk-shifting problem would present the binding constraint.

Financial Contracts

The contract between the manager and the investor specifies the reward each will receive under each state of the world. When the payoff is R_J, the amount $(1 - \delta_J)R_J$ is allocated to managers and $\delta_J R_J$ is allocated to investors. Managers' and investors' liabilities are limited, as reflected by the assumption that $\delta_J \varepsilon(0, 1)$ for all J.

To motivate the manager to work rather than to shirk, the rewards for working must be at least as great as those from shirking:

$$(1/3 + \varepsilon)(1 - \delta_G)R_G + (1/3)(1 - \delta_M)R_M + (1/3 - \varepsilon)(1 - \delta_B)R_B$$
$$\geq (1/3)(1 - \delta_G)R_G + (1/3)(1 - \delta_M)R_M + (1/3)(1 - \delta_B)R_B + L \tag{21.45}$$

For later use, it is convenient to rewrite equation (21.45) as

$$(1 - \delta_G)R_G - (1 - \delta_B)R_B \geq L/\varepsilon \tag{21.46}$$

To motivate the manager to avoid taking excessive risks, the rewards for adopting the safe project must be at least as great as the rewards from the riskier project:

$$(1/3 + \varepsilon)(1 - \delta_G)R_G + (1/3)(1 - \delta_M)R_M + (1/3 - \varepsilon)(1 - \delta_B)R_B$$
$$\geq (1/3 + \varepsilon + \alpha)(1 - \delta_G)R_G + (1/3 - \alpha - \beta)(1 - \delta_M)R_M$$
$$+ (1/3 - \varepsilon + \beta)(1 - \delta_B)R_B \tag{21.47}$$

Again for later use, it is convenient to rewrite (21.47) as

$$\alpha(1 - \delta_G)R_G + \beta(1 - \delta_B)R_B \leq (\alpha + \beta)(1 - \delta_M)R_M \tag{21.48}$$

If the cost of financing is r, investors can only be attracted to the project if they are promised an expected return on their investment that is at least equal to r:

$$(1/3 + \varepsilon)\delta_G R_G + (1/3)\delta_M R_M + (1/3 - \varepsilon)\delta_B R_B$$
$$\geq (I - A)(1 + r) \tag{21.49}$$

An optimal contract is defined as one that satisfies constraints (21.46), (21.48), and (21.49). Assuming there are no bankruptcy costs, debt financing with face value D, $R_B < D < R_M$, is represented by $\delta_B = 1$, $\delta_M = D/R_M$, and $\delta_G = D/R_G$. Similarly, outside equity financing is represented by $\delta_B = \delta_M = \delta_G = \delta$.

Biais and Cassamatta (1999, 1,298) establish that an optimal contract can be written, and the positive NPV project financed, if initial wealth A is large enough relative to the cost of effort L and the risk-shifting incentive α. The condition for existence of an optimal contract can be expressed in terms of problem parameters as

$$A(1 + r) \geq A_0(1 + r) \equiv I(1 + r) - \{V_L - (L/\varepsilon)[(1/3) + \varepsilon$$
$$+ \alpha/3(\alpha + \beta)]\} \tag{21.50}$$

Condition (21.50) states that a sufficiently large value of initial wealth serves to offset moral hazard problems in much the same way as in the Holmstrom and Tirole model discussed earlier.

While the Biais-Cassamatta results require a simultaneous algebraic examination of several inequalities, the intuition underlying (21.50) can readily be established as follows. Any set of project payoffs can be standardized as $R_B = 0$, $R_M = 1$, and $R_G > 1$ without affecting the algebraic or geometric relations studied, and the resulting inequalities are simpler to interpret. Given the standardization, the incentive to exert effort (21.46) can be written

$$\delta_G \leq 1 - L/R_G\varepsilon \tag{21.51}$$

while the incentive to avoid risks becomes

$$\delta_G \geq \alpha - [(\alpha + \beta)/R_G\varepsilon](1 - \delta_M) \tag{21.52}$$

Finally, the investors' minimum return requirement becomes

$$\delta_G \geq [3(I - A)(1 + r) - \delta_M]/(1 + 3\varepsilon)R_G \tag{21.53}$$

Depending on parameter values, a combination of debt, equity, and outside stock options may be needed to satisfy the three constraints simultaneously. Biais and Cassamatta show that the value A_0 in (21.50) satisfies $A_0 \leq A_1 \leq A_2$, where A_1 is the minimum initial wealth needed to implement the same projects if pure debt financing is used, and A_2 the minimum initial wealth if pure equity financing is used. Essentially, debt financing ensures the manager will exert effort, but it can create perverse incentives leading to risk-shifting. Equity can create the same problem, but a combination of debt, equity, and stock options can create both an incentive for the manager to exert effort and an incentive for the manager to avoid taking excessive risk.

Aggregate Investment and Equilibrium Cost of Capital

The previous section took individual entrepreneurs' cost of capital r as a given. This section shows how Biais and Cassamatta endogenously determine r within the context of a simple general equilibrium model.

Assume there is a unit mass continuum of agents living and consuming during two periods. Agents are risk-neutral and their time preference is represented by a discount rate ρ. Each agent faces the same two investment opportunities: a safe asset or a risky asset. However, potential entrepreneurs differ in terms of their initial wealth A. The population of entrepreneurs is described by density f and distribution function F, both defined over $(0, I)$. Revenues from different projects are assumed to be independent, implying there is no aggregate uncertainty.

Agents make consumption-investment decisions. In particular they can lend at the market rate r or invest in their own projects. An agent who invests in the market solves

$$\text{Max}_s\{(A - s) + \rho(s(1 + r))\} \tag{21.54}$$

where s is lent on the financial market, $(A - s)$ is first period consumption and $s(1 + r)$ is the second period consumption. If $\rho(1 + r) > 1$, the agent consumes only in second period, while if $\rho(1 + r) < 1$ the agent consumes everything in the first period. If $\rho(1 + r) = 1$, the agent is indifferent between consuming in the first or the second period.

If an agent invests in the safer of her two projects and exerts effort L she will earn

$$V_L - (I - A)(1 + r) - L \qquad (21.55)$$

Financial market demand stems from all agents who invest in their own projects, while financial market supply of funds stems from all agents who lend on the financial market. Suppose r_L satisfies

$$\rho(1 + r_L) = 1 \qquad (21.56)$$

and that

$$V_L - L > I(1 + r_L) \qquad (21.57)$$

that is, at rate r_L all projects have positive NPV. Note that when equation (21.56) holds, (21.57) is equivalent to

$$\rho(V_L - L) > I \qquad (21.58)$$

To determine a capital market equilibrium without moral hazard, suppose effort and risk choices are both observable. Since at r_L all agents desire to invest in their own project, the equilibrium return must be greater than r_L. Equilibrium return is such that investors are indifferent between lending on the market and investing in their own project to earn

$$(V_L - L - I)/I \equiv r^*$$

In this equilibrium all available wealth is invested in projects, that is, aggregate investment is equal to $E(A)$.

Suppose that at r^* the agents who lend are those with wealth below A^*, while the agents who borrow are those with wealth at least equal to A^*. Equilibrium is defined by the interest rate at which the quantity of funds demanded equals the quantity of funds supplied:

$$D(r^*) \equiv \int_{A^*}^{I} (I - A)dF(A) = \int_{0}^{A^*} AdF(A) \equiv S(r^*) \qquad (21.59)$$

To continue, recall that whenever some entrepreneurs must borrow at a rate r, only those with initial wealth $A \geq A_0(r)$ can obtain funds. The incentive compatible demand for funds is

$$D(r) = \int_{A_0(r)}^{I} (I - A)dF(A) \qquad (21.60)$$

Since $A_0(r)$ is increasing in r, $D(r)$ is decreasing in r.

Entrepreneurs with $A \leq A_0(r)$ face capital rationing in the sense they cannot borrow, although they can still choose to lend or to consume. If $r < r_L$, they will consume, and the aggregate supply of funds will be zero. If $r > r_L$, they will lend, and the aggregate supply of funds is given by

$$S(r) = \int_{0}^{A_0(r)} AdF(A) \qquad (21.61)$$

If $r = r_L$, they are indifferent between lending and consuming, and supply will be somewhere in the interval $[0, S(r)]$. One of two different possibilities can occur: an underinvestment or a full investment regime.

In the underinvestment regime, $A^* \leq A_0(r_L)$. If the inequality is strict, aggregate investment is below its first best level. Indeed, for all rates $r \geq r_L$, $D(r) \leq D(r_L)$, the first best demand defined in equation (5.6). Investment is correspondingly no greater than its first best level.

The full investment regime occurs when $A^* \geq A_0(r_L)$. In this case the equilibrium return is an interest rate r^*, such that $A^* = A_0(r^*)$. This interest rate gives the same as the first best solution, that is $D(r_L) = D(r^*)$, and investment is correspondingly equal to its first best level.

In summary, the equilibrium consequences of moral hazard are:

1. Some agents cannot invest because their wealth is too low. If there are enough such agents, aggregate investment is lower than in a first best equilibrium.
2. Since the incentive compatible demand for finance is lower when some agents cannot invest, the equilibrium cost of capital is also lower than in a first best equilibrium.
3. The remaining agents, those who can invest, earn more than in the first best equilibrium. Of course, the agents who cannot invest earn less.

The macroeconomic consequences of moral hazard are attendant on the consequences of capital rationing. First, the credit rationing bound increases as either α or E increases. If the worsening of moral hazard is such that

that $A_0(r_L)$ is raised above A^*, aggregate investment is reduced. Also, as moral hazard worsens, incentive-compatible demand decreases and so does the interest rate.

FINANCIAL STRUCTURE AND ECONOMIC ACTIVITY

This section summarizes recent research findings regarding the relations between financial structure and economic activity. It first considers cyclical effects, then longer-term impacts.

Impacts of Cyclical Activity

The models of cyclical activity presented previously address an empirically important phenomenon. Braun and Larrain (2005) examined relations between finance and the business cycle in more than 100 countries. By considering annual production growth rates for several manufacturing industries over approximately 40 years, the authors show that industries more dependent on external finance suffer greater reductions in borrowing during recessions. The difference in industry behavior appears to be larger if financial frictions are more prevalent. In particular credit-dependent industries are more strongly affected by recessions when they are located in countries whose regulators are less protective of financiers, and whose firms have few assets capable of being pledged as collateral.

Dell'Ariccia and Marquez (2006) discern a sequence of financial liberalization, lending booms, and banking crises typical of those observed in many markets. They examine how the informational structure of loan markets interacts with banks' lending standards, lending volumes, and the aggregate allocation of credit. The authors show that as banks obtain private information about borrowers, and as informational asymmetries across banks decrease, banks typically loosen their lending standards. The change in standards then leads to an equilibrium in which loan portfolios have lower quality, banks have lower profits, and aggregate credit is expanded. The lower standards are in turn associated with greater risk of financial instability.

Santos and Winton (2008) consider how bank loans and bond issues are related across the business cycle. They suggest that banks' private information about borrowers allows the banks to charge higher interest rates. If the banks' power to increase interest rates increases further with borrower risk, banks with private information should be able to raise their rates in recessions by more than a market risk premium. The authors test this hypothesis by comparing loan pricing for borrowers with access to public debt markets (after controlling for risk factors). They find that loan spreads rise in recessions, and also that firms with access to public securities markets face lower spreads, spreads that also rise significantly less in recessions.

Examining financial crises that include episodes from Finland, Japan, Norway, Spain, and Sweden, Reinhart and Rogoff (2008) conclude that crises can reduce output growth per person by an average of two percentage points. The authors find that output growth can fall by up to five percentage points from a peak, and that recovery can sometimes take more than three years. The authors observe that most historical crises have been preceded by financial liberalization, and that crises exhibit similar patterns of asset price increases, debt accumulation, economic growth, and current account deficits. In the case of the subprime crisis, liberalization involved growth by unregulated and lightly regulated financial institutions, reductions in transactions costs, and broadening of available financial instruments. More than a trillion dollars worth of funds, much provided by petroleum exporting countries, was recycled into the sub-prime mortgage market before the crisis occurred.

The effects of crises can be magnified by several factors that are illustrated by the subprime example. Standard & Poor's has estimated that financial institutions' total write-downs on asset-backed securities may reach nearly $300 billion, but only about half that amount represents projected losses on subprime mortgage lending. The remaining projected losses are on financial instruments that create asset exposures without actual ownership. For example, collateralized debt obligations (CDOs) contain synthetic exposures to subprime-asset-backed securities of some $75 billion.[10] Moreover, the notional values of exposures in the credit-default swaps market are also much greater than the value of the bonds outstanding. Still further, the use of market value accounting amplifies cyclical effects because it can cause overshooting of prices both as market activity expands and as it contracts. Finally, when downward price movements occur, they can trigger a fourth factor: the need to unwind investments, depressing prices still more.

Financial crises can saddle an economy with relatively large costs in forgone output and rescues of troubled financial institutions. Laeven and Valencia (2008) develop a data base that estimates the costs of financial crises in several affected countries over the period 1970–2007. A summary of their findings is given in Table 21.6.

---

[10] Confessions of a Risk Manager, *The Economist*, August 7, 2008.

TABLE 21.6 Costs of Financial Crises, Estimated from Data for 1970–2007

Country	Start of Crisis	Gross Fiscal Cost as Percent of GDP
United States	1988	3.7
Finland	1991	12.8
Sweden	1991	3.6
Mexico	1994	19.3
Japan	1997	24.0
South Korea	1997	31.2
United States	2007	5.8

Source: Laeven and Valencia, 2008. Data reported by *The Economist,* Sept. 25, 2008.

Longer-Term Effects

Chapter 1 reiterated a widely held belief that financial system structure can contribute to economic development over the longer term. In support of this view, King and Levine (1993) argue that there is a strong correlation between financial system development and economic development, but such findings do not establish causation. Theory supporting causation argues, as in Chapter 5, that financial intermediation increases the efficiency of the financial system and hence implies that financial structure contributes to economic development. Although most of the models presented in this book interpret financial activity as adding value through controlling the impacts of informational asymmetries and other market imperfections, there is a positive role for finance as well.

Some financiers may be better than others at extracting new information about the value of projects they finance, quite irrespective of the agency cost effects on which most models rely. For example, if intermediaries may have different capabilities for screening and monitoring projects, a variety of intermediary types is likely to increase possibilities for funding viable projects. When intermediaries can monitor continuously, projects that could not otherwise be financed may receive funding, and fewer projects may be unnecessarily liquidated.

For example, Demirguc-Kunt and Maksimovic (1998) find that differences in legal and financial systems affect the ability of firms to raise external finance. A greater proportion of firms use long-term external financing in countries whose legal systems are rated highly. Both an active stock market and an active banking sector are associated with externally financed growth. While the stock market need not be particularly large to play such a role, a larger banking sector appears to be more effective than a smaller one. Growing firms' economic rents are reduced by the availability of external finance since financiers share in the rents to some extent. The kinds of external finance vary sharply among countries, but government subsidies do not appear to increase the proportion of firms having access to external finance.

Moreover, developed financial markets can allocate financial resources effectively to at least some projects. Rajan and Zingales (1998) find that industrial sectors heavily dependent on external finance grow faster in economies with developed financial systems. Their empirical findings are based on the ideas that financial markets and institutions help firms overcome credit constraints stemming from moral hazard and adverse selection, and thus reduce the cost of firms' external financing. Financial development principally assists firms or industries that are most heavily dependent on external finance. Rajan and Zingales find that financial development stimulates the growth of new firms, and that it has almost twice the effect on growth in the number of establishments as on their average size.

Extending Rajan and Zingales' reasoning, Cetorelli and Gambera (2001) ask whether the market structure of the banking sector can affect economic growth. They hypothesize that market concentration might affect growth negatively by reducing credit availability, and also that concentration could give banks greater incentives to engage in relationship lending. Empirically, Cetorelli and Gambera find that bank concentration has a negative effect on the growth of all firms in all sectors. But at the same time, bank concentration creates a substantial positive effect through funding sectors more heavily dependent on external funds.

Fisman and Love (2003) document similar effects for the use of trade credit. They observe that implicit borrowing in the form of trade credit may provide an alternative source of funds for firms in poorly developed financial markets. They find that industries with higher dependence on trade credit financing exhibit higher rates of growth in countries with weaker financial institutions. In these cases, and consistent with barriers to trade credit access among young firms, most of the effect comes from growth in the size of previously established firms.

Claessens and Laeven (2003) find that in countries with more secure property rights, firms are likely to allocate resources better and to grow faster. The authors attribute the effects to greater protection for returns on different asset types, and find evidence consistent with this proposition. The findings show that the growth effect is as large as that attributable to greater financial development. Their results are robust across different samples and specifications, and include controls for growth opportunities.

Desai, Foley, and Hines (2004) analyze the internal capital markets of multinational corporations and the capital structures of foreign affiliates. The authors find that higher local tax rates are associated with higher proportions of external debt to assets, and also that internal borrowing is particularly sensitive to local tax rates. Multinational affiliates are financed with less external debt in countries with underdeveloped capital markets or weak creditor rights, and greater borrowing from parent companies substitutes for three-quarters of the reduction. Multinational firms appear to employ internal capital markets opportunistically to overcome imperfections in external capital markets.

Garmaise and Moskowitz (2006) investigate the social effects of credit market competition as manifest through bank mergers and acquisitions taking place in the 1990s. The authors find that neighborhoods experiencing more bank mergers also experienced higher interest rates, lower rates of local construction, lower prices, an increase in the proportion of poorer households, and subsequently higher property crime. The findings have been confirmed by using state branching deregulation as an indicator of bank competition.

Detragiache, Tressel, and Gupta (2008) examine how poor countries' financial sectors are affected by foreign bank penetration. The authors argue theoretically that when foreign banks are better than domestic banks at monitoring high end customers, entry benefits those customers but may damage others. Empirically, the authors find that a stronger foreign bank presence is associated with less credit to the private sector. In addition, more foreign bank penetration implies slower credit growth and less access to credit. The authors do not find similar adverse effects in more advanced countries.

REFERENCES

Bernanke, B., and M. Gertler. 1990. Financial fragility and economic performance. *Quarterly Journal of Economics* 105: 87–114.

Biais, Bruno, and Catherine Casamatta. 1999. "Optimal leverage and aggregate investment." *Journal of Finance* 54: 1291–1323.

Braun, Matias, and Borja Larrain. 2005. Finance and the business cycle: International, inter-industry evidence. *Journal of Finance* 60: 1,097–1,128.

Brunnermeier, Markus, and Lasse Pedersen. 2009. Market liquidity and funding liquidity. Forthcoming. *Review of Financial Studies*.

Cetorelli, Nicola, and Michel Gambera. 2001. "Banking market structure, financial dependence, and growth." *Journal of Finance* 56: 617–648.

Claessens, Stijn, and Luc Laeven. 2003. Financial development, property rights, and growth. *Journal of Finance* 58: 2,401–2,436.

Dell'Ariccia, Giovanni, and Robert Marquez. 2006. Lending booms and lending standards. *Journal of Finance* 61: 2,511–2,546.

Demirguc-Kunt, Asli, and V. Maksimovic. 1998. "Law, Finance, and Firm Growth." *Journal of Finance* 53: 2107–2137.

Desai, Mihir A., C. Fritz Foley, and James R. Hines Jr. 2004. A multinational perspective on capital structure choice and internal capital markets. *Journal of Finance* 59: 2,451–2,487.

Detragiache, Enrica, Thierry Tressel, and Poonam Gupta. 2008. Foreign banks in poor countries: Theory and evidence, *Journal of Finance* 63: 2,123–2,160.

di Patti, Emilia Bonaccorsi, and Giorgio Gobbi. 2007. Winners or losers? The effects of banking consolidation on corporate borrowers. *Journal of Finance* 62: 669–695.

Fisman, Raymond, and Inessa Love. 2004. Financial development and intersectoral allocation: A new approach. *Journal of Finance* 59: 2,785–2,807.

Garmaise, Mark J., and Tobias J. Moskowitz. 2006. Bank mergers and crime: The real and social effects of credit market competition. *Journal of Finance* 61: 495–538.

Holmstrom, Bengt, and Jean Tirole. 1997. Financial intermediation, loanable funds, and the real sector. *Quarterly Journal of Economics* 112: 663–691.

King, Robert G., and Ross Levine. 1993. Financial intermediation and economic development. In *Financial Intermediation in the Construction of Europe*, edited by Colin Mayer and Xavier Vives. London: Centre for Economic Policy Research.

Kiyotaki, Nobuhiro, and John Moore. 1995. Credit cycles, Discussion Paper 205, Financial Market Group, London School of Economics.

Laeven, Luc, and Fabian Valencia. 2008. "Systemic Banking Crises: A New Database," IMF Working Paper WP/08/224.

Mankiw, Gregory. 1986. The allocation of credit and financial collapse. *Quarterly Journal of Economics* 101: 455–470.

Rajan, Raghuram G., and Luigi Zingales. 1998. "Financial Dependence and Growth." *American Economic Review* 88: 559–586.

Reinhart, Carmen M., and Kenneth S. Rogoff. 2008. Is the 2007 US sub-prime financial crisis so different? An international historical comparison. Harvard University Working Paper.

Santos, Joao A. C., and Andrew Winton. 2008. "Bank Loans, Bonds, and Information Monopolies across the Business Cycle." *Journal of Finance* 63: 1315–1360.

CHAPTER 22

Financial Regulation

This chapter considers how regulation can help enhance financial system performance. The discussion begins by considering regulatory principles, the effectiveness of regulatory policy, and the approaches regulation can take. The next section compares and contrasts regulation of different institutions and markets, both domestic and international. In the last section, it considers how the market turmoil of 2007–2008 has stimulated recent corrective measures and proposals for future regulatory action.[1]

AIMS AND APPROACHES

Although regulation is aimed at improving system performance, its benefits are very often sought through imposing either restrictions or reporting requirements. These kinds of regulatory actions can both increase the cost of doing business and in some cases stifle innovation. At the same time, if regulation limits profitable business activity, a substantial proportion of managerial effort will likely be devoted to finding ways of avoiding the restrictions, frequently through innovation. Thus in at least some instances regulators face a choice of either trying to guide private sector initiatives or of restricting private sector initiatives and then attempting to deal with innovations aimed at avoiding the restrictions. In addition, successful innovations can create their own difficulties, such as the lowered lending and investment standards accompanying asset price bubbles. Regulators usually respond to such emerging difficulties through new restrictions,[2] with the

---

[1]The events leading up to the market turmoil are described in a Financial Stability Forum report included as an appendix to this chapter.

[2]As evidenced later, remedies may also include support measures, although the price for support measures may also be additional restriction.

result that regulatory change can fruitfully be regarded as a dynamic process of adaptation between the regulators and the regulated.

Regulation is most effective when it can harness economic forces at work within the system. However, the problems that regulators must address are numerous, and discussing them on an individual basis would be a very lengthy task. Therefore, this chapter considers broad questions relevant to enhancing financial system performance, both in the long run and over economic cycles. The questions include:

- How can regulation encourage the financial system to finance an economy's viable economic prospects?
- Are financiers faced with incentives to act as responsible custodians of others' funds? Are they faced with incentives to perform due diligence in assessing the risks of loans they extend?
- Is the public reasonably well-informed about the risks inherent in making different kinds of investments?
- Can public confidence in the financial system be strengthened, and if so, how?
- Can the existing regulatory framework detect interactions among financial system components? That is to say, can regulatory processes consider the possible impacts of macroeconomic shocks capable of affecting many institutions at once, and can they consider adequately the possibilities for effects created by contagion?
- What is the appropriate scope for a given kind of regulation? For example, can international banks be supervised adequately by national authorities, or is international oversight necessary? If so, to what matters should the supervisory authority attend?

When viewed in static terms, financial regulation is mainly justified by market failure or malfunction, either of which can stem from the difficulties posed by asymmetric information, the presence of externalities, or both. This section will consider the principles involved in devising a static regulatory framework, and the sections following will apply the principles to discussing current industry regulation. The chapter's last sections will consider both desirable structural reforms and regulation intended to respond to cyclical phenomena.

Overview

Regulatory change is sometimes advocated as an attempt to deal with the emergence of market power. While financial firms can sometimes gain market power, many financial markets are competitive enough that an increase in market power may only be temporary, particularly if new entrants are able to present new forms of competition relatively quickly. However, if a situation does arise in which financial firms appear to have more lasting sources of market power, some forms of regulatory intervention may be justified.

A second possible reason for regulating is to offset negative effects of informational asymmetries. Informational asymmetries are ubiquitous in financial deals, but private arrangements to remove them can be expected to spring up whenever profits can be earned from doing so. It is only when the effects of informational asymmetries are important and lasting, and their removal uneconomic from a private profit perspective, that regulatory intervention should be considered. One such argument for publicizing more information about banks' asset quality was examined in Chapter 20.

A third reason for regulating financial firms is that their failure can affect many different stakeholders, creating negative externalities in the process. Of course, the failure of any firm can create externalities, but those created by the failures of financial firms can have particularly widespread effects. For example, many uninsured depositors can lose funds in a bank failure. However, no single depositor is in a position to evaluate cost-effectively the financial soundness of the institutions with which he deals, and consequently a regulatory role of promulgating information can be justified. Borrowing clients' operations can also be disrupted by bank failure, and to offset this possibility support of banks in difficulty can sometimes be justified. Finally, there can be systemic effects. For example, if a number of banks reduce their lending activities at the same time, their combined actions can lead to a credit crunch with serious impacts on economic activity, as discussed later in this chapter.

Effectiveness

The ability of regulation to correct difficulties is limited. First, the conclusion that the benefits of new regulation will exceed their costs is difficult to establish empirically. Second, creating a safety net for financial institutions can create problems of moral hazard, as both Chapter 20 and later discussions in this chapter show. Moreover, regulation favoring the interests of client groups can create its own difficulties: If it restricts competition, regulation can both create economic rents for regulated firms[3] and stifle financial innovation.

Not all regulations achieve their intended effects. If legislation attempts to restrict financiers from doing profitable business, financiers may find

---

[3]In some cases restricting competition to create rents can accelerate economic development; see Hellman et al. (1996).

innovative ways to avoid the legislation. For example, the 1980s development of the U.S. money market fund stemmed in part from the Federal Reserve Board's Regulation Q interest rate ceilings imposed on banks and, through similar regulation, on such other savings institutions as thrifts. Originally intended to encourage mortgage lending by keeping the mortgage lenders' costs of funds low, the interest rate ceilings turned out to work perversely when market interest rates rose quickly to unexpected levels. Institutions could not retain deposits when market interest rates rose above the ceilings: At those times large amounts of deposits were withdrawn from banks and near-banks in a process known as *disintermediation*. These financial institutions therefore faced incentives to circumvent the interest ceilings. As these difficulties with interest rate ceilings emerged, the ineffectiveness of interest rate ceilings came to be better understood and most such restrictions were eliminated in the 1980s. As a second example, discussed in the section "Regulating International Activity," banks formed trusts and other structured investment vehicles to reduce the capital requirements they formerly faced under the 1988 Basel Accord.

Credit controls and foreign exchange controls are other examples of ineffective intervention. They may appear to be successful when financiers do not wish to carry out the transactions covered by the controls, but their lack of effectiveness quickly becomes evident if the transactions come to be seen as profitable. In such circumstances financial business will likely seek ways to frustrate or circumvent the controls.

Although many analysts have a bias against it, self-regulation can be quite effective in markets with small numbers of firms that stand to gain long-term benefits from policing themselves. For example, foreign exchange markets in many parts of the world were effectively self-regulated for several decades.[4] The major players compete actively for business, but they all have a large stake in maintaining confidence in the market's operations.[5] On the other hand, self-regulation will work poorly in an industry when new firms can enter easily, especially if they are likely to be present for relatively short periods of time. For example, stock promoters in the resource exploration industry are poor candidates for a self-regulatory organization.

---

[4]This is not to claim that small numbers of firms can never earn any oligopoly profits. It is only to observe that there have been no reported problems of fraud within the foreign exchange market, largely because it has been in the long run interests of a few large incumbents to maintain the market's good reputation. The question of whether profits are above competitive levels does not seem to have been studied empirically.
[5]As the 2008 difficulties experienced first by Bear Stearns and then by many other financial institutions showed, the possibility of negative externalities can change the picture. These issues are discussed in this chapter.

Regulatory Approaches

Justifying new regulations requires regulators to show, at least conceptually, that the new regime will secure benefits at least commensurate with its costs. The cost-benefit argument can be difficult to make, since the benefits are usually social and accrue to a broad segment of society, while the costs are largely private and affect a segment of the financial industry. Moreover, both benefits and costs are difficult to quantify, and establishing their magnitude is usually a matter of judgment. As a result, resistance to regulatory change can often prove more effective than arguments favoring it.

Most of the literature on regulation is pragmatic in its thrust, and deals primarily with positive rather than normative issues. This focus implies that regulatory analyses are usually concerned with assessing impacts of particular changes rather than with attempts to devise globally optimal regulatory schemes. Policy makers recognize that different regulatory methods—the use of detailed rules, broad guidelines, or self-regulation—can offer different benefits, and have different cost impacts. Broad guidelines can be applied more flexibly than can detailed rules, and a good principle is to avoid detailed regulations whenever it is possible to achieve the same results with broad guidelines. On the other hand, regulatory purposes cannot always be achieved by pronouncing broad principles, and in some cases detailed regulations must be imposed even though they are less flexible, as well as more costly to frame and implement.

INDUSTRIES

This section examines how regulation has historically differed between industries, particularly in the United States. The section first considers banking, then the securities business and investment banking.[6] It next considers reasons for regulating near-banks and related financial institutions, and closes with a discussion of whether rating agencies ought to be regulated.

Banking Regulation

Banking requires risk-taking, and the job of regulators is to ensure that the benefits of risk-taking are realized while simultaneously recognizing the

---

[6]At this writing all the large U.S. investment banks have either converted themselves to bank holding companies, been absorbed by banks, or broken up and sold. The reasons for treating banking and investment banking separately are therefore both to provide historical perspective and to indicate the kinds of regulation applying to remaining, smaller securities firms.

need to protect the public interest. To achieve these objectives, banks are usually supervised by a combination of a central bank, domestic bank regulators, and deposit insurance agencies. International bodies also exert an influence, as exemplified by the Basel agreements regarding minimum capital positions.

Managing the trade-offs between encouraging risk-taking and protecting the public interest is a complex undertaking. First, banks perform special functions in the economy, such as providing liquidity to both depositors and borrowers. Second, banks are frequently provided special privileges such as deposit insurance cover. Banks carry out this combination of special roles and special privileges in an environment subject to problems created by asymmetric information, particularly moral hazard and adverse selection. In particular, bank asset positions are opaque to outsiders' scrutiny and informational asymmetry arguments justify monitoring by a central authority rather than by individual depositors or other small claimants. Deposit insurance,[7] restrictions on bank asset holdings, and capital requirements are all intended to offset problems created by informational asymmetries.[8]

Safety and Soundness   The need for a financial sector safety net arises from the perceived need to treat deposit-taking institutions differently from other economic agents. In recognition, most countries have provided deposit insurance since the 1930s. The recent emergence of substitutes for bank deposits, along with the recent emergence of alternative payment mechanisms, both lead to the question of whether current developments in technology and deregulation are eroding the nature of what previously made banks special. With respect to deposits, nonfinancial institutions now offer deposit-taking facilities and payments facilities of various sorts, and banks are less special with regard to these products than formerly.

Loan transactions require the kind of specialized governance that has in the past been provided mainly by banks and some other lending institutions. While governance methods may change with technology, the need for

---

[7]Countries that provide deposit insurance usually do so up to some limit, which may apply to more than a single account. The insurance policy may also be partial, that is, require depositor coinsurance. In the United States, deposit insurance limits are $100,000 and there is no coinsurance. The limit is administered per account and a depositor may be able to insure a sum of more than $100,000 by appropriate structuring of accounts. The maximum value insured in the United Kingdom is 20,000 pounds and the percentage repaid is 75%.

[8]Since banks are a conduit for transmitting the effects of monetary policy, they are also regulated for this reason. However, topics in monetary policy are beyond the scope of this book.

effective nonmarket governance remains. Even with the widespread use of securitization, bank loans continue to require the attention of relationship bankers or other lenders with similar screening, monitoring, and adjustment capabilities. The cost of failing to provide appropriate forms of governance is a relaxation in lending standards and an eventual increase in default rates. Indeed, sufficiently lax loan governance can endanger banking solvency, as the events of 2007–2008, discussed later, have demonstrated.

In the past, legislation restricted the assets in which banks could invest. For example, portfolio restrictions were applied to banks on the grounds of mitigating conflicts of interest. Without the legislation separating commercial lending and trustee functions, trustees working for a bank could recommend, with impunity, that their clients invest in companies to which the bank was a lender. In this way the trustees might serve the bank's interests by increasing the capitalization of the client company. However, this policy would not serve the interests of the bank's trust clients, who could be induced to place funds in weak investments. Other restrictions have sometimes been imposed and defended as contributing to safety even though they had perverse effects. For example, when banks were restricted as to the percentage of conventional mortgages they could hold, the restriction limited the banks from competing effectively against other mortgage lenders.

Competition Policy Competition policy aims at ensuring access, efficient production, and fair pricing. Recent changes in the financial industry are making financial services more like other goods and services markets, and making financial markets more like nonfinancial markets. Financial innovation is increasingly becoming a function of the degree to which entry of both financial and nonfinancial companies is allowed, and this mixing of financial and nonfinancial activity makes competition policy even more important.

The main issues facing competition policy are what market definitions to use, what constitutes market power, what barriers to entry exist, and what ownership structures—vertical and horizontal—can be allowed within an industry. Are all providers of a financial service to be subject to the same competition policy? Although competition tests require a definition of a product and a market, the task is becoming more difficult as traditional financial services take on the characteristics of financial contracts and as new instruments like weather and energy derivatives blur the distinction between financial and nonfinancial arrangements. Similarly, the continuum from cash through stored value cards to point programs like AirMiles makes it difficult to define payment services or deposits with precision, and it is awkward to define barriers to entry when services cannot be well-defined. Moreover, both market sizes and delivery modes are changing as markets increasingly become globally rather than locally defined.

Consumer Protection   Consumer protection issues include security, privacy, transparency, and investor protection. The issues of setting standards of protection, their impact on market development, and defining the authorities best equipped to enforce the standards all arise. The rapid proliferation of delivery channels and institutions has allowed easier comparison of prices and financial products, especially for traded securities. On the other hand, a proliferation of products and the emergence of portals can work to reduce transparency. Regulatory solutions are thus faced with task of balancing the objectives of increased competition with access and fairness.

Some observers believe that increasing use of technology is likely to restrict banking access for the poor and the elderly. On the other hand, technology has extended the reach of the financial system in countries like South Africa, making it more accessible to poor and illiterate clients with relatively small amounts of financial business. It thus appears at least possible that improved forms of ATMs and debit cards can be developed to make access easier rather than more difficult.

Securities Markets and Investment Banking

Securities market and investment banking regulation has become particularly challenging since the 1990s, largely because the pace of technological change and the development of derivatives trading have influenced the organization of both securities markets and securities firms. To ensure the viability of the firms in the industry, securities regulators supervise the capital and liquidity positions of investment banking firms trading in risk management products. Regulators also seek to obtain full disclosure of pertinent information, both to reduce the possibilities for insider trading and self-dealing, and to publicize transaction information.

During the 1980s U.S. banks entered the securities business, often by acquiring discount brokerage firms. Up to that time, U.S. banking regulation had prevented banks from entering the securities business directly, and the discount brokerage acquisitions were attempts to test the regulations' legality. Canada has permitted banks to acquire securities firms' affiliates since the mid-1990s, but the United States was not as accommodating until the passage of the Financial Services Modernization Act (Gramm-Leach-Bliley) in 1999. In the future, closer business combinations will probably continue to be formed in both countries, since there appear to be economies of scope to combining securities sales and trading with domestic banking activity. In September 2008, large U.S. investment banks either converted to bank holding companies, were absorbed by banks, or failed and were sold to other institutions. It appeared that, as a result of the loss of confidence following of market turmoil, investment banks could no longer survive without access to the longer-term funding available to deposit-taking universal banks.

Nonbank Intermediaries

As with banks and investment banks, near-banks and nonbank intermediaries are regulated principally because problems of asymmetric information make it difficult for clients to assess the values of the institutions' asset portfolios. Nonbank intermediaries are supervised in much the same way as banks, but sometimes with additional restrictions. For example, thrift institutions' investments are restricted largely to residential mortgages and government bonds. Similarly, insurance companies and pension funds are only permitted to purchase the securities of companies that meet certain earnings and dividends standards. None of these restrictions has convincingly been shown to enhance safety, but they do reduce financial system adaptability and the profitability of the restricted firms.

As earlier chapters have shown, some kinds of commercial-industrial links make it possible to finance projects that could not otherwise obtain funds. On the other hand, commercial-industrial links can create conflicts of interest, particularly if the institutions are closely held. For example, a real estate developer with a controlling interest in a near-bank might be tempted to use depositors' funds to finance speculative real estate projects. She would have even more incentive to do so if her near-bank could obtain level premium deposit insurance, as discussed in Chapter 20. To balance the advantages and disadvantages of commercial-industrial links, it is probably better not to restrict them. Rather, regulation and enforcement should probably be aimed at intensive oversight of any closely held financial institutions that are likely to abuse the linkages.

Rating Agencies

Up to the time of this writing rating agencies have not been closely regulated. However in 2008 ratings companies downgraded thousands of mortgage-backed securities as delinquencies increased rapidly and home values fell. For example, from 2005 to the third quarter of 2007, S&P rated approximately $855 billion of AAA subprime, first-lien residential mortgage-backed securities. To November 2008, the company has downgraded about 18% of those securities, but company officials say that more than 94% of the currently outstanding issues still hold an investment-grade rating. The agencies have faced allegations both that their ratings may have been inflated by errors in computer models and that they succumbed to conflicts of interest, the latter arising because debt issuers rather than investors pay for credit ratings.

Many investors accepted ratings at face value, without conducting further checks of their own. Moreover, since banks are now required by Basel II to use the agencies' ratings, it seems likely that at least some investors will continue to accept them at face value.

In mid-2008 the three largest U.S. agencies, Standard & Poor's, Moody's, and Fitch, held discussions with the New York State attorney-general regarding their roles. In a July 2008 report the U.S. Securities and Exchange Commission (SEC) found that credit-rating companies improperly managed conflicts of interest and violated internal procedures in granting top rankings to mortgage bonds. In October 2008, House Oversight and Government Reform Committee Chairman Henry Waxman said that "The story of the credit-rating agencies is a story of colossal failure." Representative Stephen Lynch, a Massachusetts Democrat, said House Democrats are mulling legislation that would hold rating agencies legally liable for losses to investors. During the hearings, ratings company executives stated that while potential conflicts of interest are inherent in their business, their companies would not increase their ratings as a way of winning business from borrowers. They also claimed that the companies have refined their methodologies, increased the transparency of the analyses, and adopted revised policies to avoid conflicts of interest.

The Financial Stability Forum Report (2008) recommends that the credit rating agencies should implement a revised IOSCO code of conduct (see the subsection "Investment Banking and Securities Regulation" later in this chapter) to improve the rating of structured products and to manage conflicts of interest in the ratings process. The report further recommends that ratings on structured products should be treated differently from ratings on bonds. At this point, it appears that as events continue to unfold additional regulatory proposals, and intendedly remedial legislation, are both likely. Similar recommendations from the G20 November 2008 summit are mentioned in the subsection "International Measures" later in this chapter.

REGULATING INTERNATIONAL ACTIVITY

In today's global financial system regulatory issues have important international dimensions, and development of a framework to address them is very much an ongoing process. This section discusses regulatory initiatives regarding international banking and Basel II, investment banking and the securities business, and risk trading. Further recommendations from the G20 November 2008 summit are mentioned later in this chapter.

International Banking Regulation and Basel II

International coordination of banking regulation can be justified on several grounds. As the events of 2008 have dramatically shown, contagion is a serious problem: The failure of banks or stock market crashes in one country can contribute to a collapse of confidence throughout the world.[9] In addition to the 2008 emergencies, discussed separately in later sections, a number of other issues also present themselves. Benston (1998) proposes that branches of foreign banks be required to post collateral against their deposits if their home country capital requirements are not adequate. Second and as the Basel agreements recognize, without international cooperation the costs of regulation could differ importantly from country to country, and countries with the least costly regulatory environments are most likely to attract aggressively risk-taking businesses. Third, payments system risk cannot be contained without international harmonization. Regulators can help offset payments risks by providing information, but the main cure is to require banks to post collateral that will cover their potential clearing liabilities. Fourth, cooperation among regulators could make it easier to prosecute the fraudulent operators. Finally, standardized reporting could reduce the information costs of both regulatory authorities and investors.

Basel II constitutes the most important set of agreements regarding international banking. Evolving from the 1988 accord, Basel II seeks to align regulatory capital requirements more closely to the underlying risks that banks face. Basel II is based on three pillars, the first of which attempts to link the capital requirements for large, internationally active banks more closely to the portfolio risks they assume. It lays out calculations for the amount of capital that banks must set aside for credit risk, market risk, and operational risk. In its Pillar 1, Basel II specifies many categories of risks and their risk weights in a standardized approach, but also allows some sophisticated banks to use their own internal models of credit risk. Pillar 2 focuses on supervisory activity, emphasizing banks' quality of risk management and their procedures for determining capital requirements. Pillar 2 also covers reputational risk, and allows regulators to impose additional capital requirements if needed. Pillar 3 attempts to strengthen market discipline of banks by requiring more public disclosure of banks' lending activity, their risk management activities, and their reserves and capital.

---

[9]At this writing, the difficulties initially experienced by U.S. banks have led to a worldwide collapse in confidence that has led in turn to an international liquidity crisis.

The Basel II measures were implemented within the European Union at the beginning of 2008, and many European banks now report their capital adequacy ratios according to the new system. The accord will be implemented in the United States in 2009 and in most other countries over several succeeding years. The timetable stipulates that all signatory countries will comply with the accord by 2015.

One potential problem with Basel II, raised by Laeven and Levine (2007), is that some banks might actually take on greater risks in order to compensate for the effects of tougher capital requirements. Such responses might arise in banks whose owners have sufficiently large shareholdings to be able to exercise control over bank policy. However, Laeven and Levine also observe that capital requirements will usually reduce risk if the legal system is supportive of the regulation.

Investment Banking and Securities Regulation

At this writing international investment banks are nearly all organized either as *universal banks* or as *bancassurance* organizations. Universal banks combine both commercial banking and securities activity, while bancassurance combines these businesses with insurance as well. The U.S. investment banks, historically the main exceptions to the universal bank and bancassurance models, were reorganized during the credit, liquidity, and solvency crises of 2008. In September 2008 the four largest remaining U.S. investment banks either failed (Lehman Brothers), were absorbed (Merrill Lynch by Bank of America), or were reorganized as bank holding companies (Goldman Sachs, Morgan Stanley). Thus while the rest of this discussion continues to distinguish between commercial banking and investment banking, it does so primarily for historical reasons. For the foreseeable future, it appears the universal bank model will be the dominant form of organization, and that it will be supervised primarily under banking regulation.

While the banks and investment banks initially affected by the 2007–2008 market turmoil were domestic institutions, the difficulties have since spread to banks throughout the world. The Federal Reserve System assumed responsibility for dealing with one of the first major problems, the collapse of Bear Stearns, but the responsibilities were more diffuse in cases such as Belgium's universal bank, Fortis. Fortis had earlier acquired parts of its Dutch rival ABN Amro, increasing its leverage to do so. On October 3, as Fortis saw its wholesale funding sources disappear and retail investors threatened to quit in droves, the Dutch government and central bank took over Fortis's entire Dutch business. During the weekend of October 4–5 BNP Paribas acquired Fortis' Belgian banking and insurance business and its international banking operations.

Currently there is no formal framework for solving a cross-border crisis. Although bilateral relationships between home and host regulators have worked well under normal business conditions, the French and Dutch actions in the Fortis case have created some unrest in Belgium. In one attempt to address the complications that future crises might present, the Committee of European Banking Supervisors has been operating a project for cross-border banks in which the principal regulators share information and conduct joint inspections. However, crisis simulations involving a bank with a substantial market share in four Scandinavian countries suggest that coordination problems could be difficult to solve. For example, what combination of countries should save a troubled border-crossing bank? Would taxpayers in a bank's home country pay for the cost of rescuing its operations abroad? For the most part, the rescuers in the Fortis case were mainly motivated by national interests and did not face painful trade-offs between individual countries' interests. These complex issues are currently being discussed in a number of different venues, as discussed further in the next two sections.

The principal body concerned with international securities regulation is IOSCO—the International Organization of Securities Commissions. IOSCO works to resolve such issues as establishing international capital adequacy standards for securities firms. It also supervises international financial conglomerates, establishes international auditing standards, and is concerned with derivatives trading. IOSCO is also concerned with attempting to check money laundering, and with promoting transparency in international financial transactions.

IOSCO has long tried to adopt a uniform set of minimum accounting disclosure standards, but it has been difficult to obtain agreement among the commissioners because they differ on which standards are best applicable. In addition, IOSCO wants rating agencies to scrutinize their own models and to improve transparency by, for example, ensuring that ratings of structured products are differently labeled from those of less volatile bonds.

Risk Trading

Risk management activity grew at an explosive rate over the 1980s and 1990s, and continued to do so until the credit market turmoil of 2007–2008. At least two overriding issues arise in supervising derivatives trading. First, do the firms involved employ appropriate risk management technologies? Second, is there adequate international regulation of trading so that any externalities created by a single firm's failure could largely be confined to that firm?

The main regulatory issues were addressed in 2007 by an OTC Derivatives Oversight Committee with representation from the Securities and

Exchange Commission, the Commodities Futures Trading Corporation, and the United Kingdom's Financial Services Authority.[10] The agencies worked out standards addressing: the exchange of regulatory information for monitoring derivatives risks, netting arrangements, assessment of firms' capital adequacy and internal risk controls, customer protection, multilateral credit risks, and accounting standards.

Since 2007 considerable work has been done on designing a clearing house for such instruments as credit default swaps. The clearing house's assets, assembled from member contributions, would be used to absorb counterparty defaults, the principal concern underlying the U.S. rescue of Bear Stearns in early 2008. On November 14, 2008, the Federal Reserve, the Commodity Futures Trading Commission and the Securities and Exchange Commission announced an accord intended to enhance clearing procedures for the CDS market.[11] The memorandum of understanding establishes a framework for consultation and information sharing for newly established clearing houses that are being created to absorb the risk of widespread market losses when a CDS dealer fails.

In addition, U.S. regulators may require banks and insurers to disclose data about all credit-default swap trades to a central registry as a means of increasing transparency in the $47 trillion market. The regulators want information about nonstandard forms of credit-default swaps to be disclosed in a record of all trades. While information on about 70% of outstanding credit-default swaps is recorded by the Depository Trust & Clearing Corporation in a central registry, data have also been compiled by the International Swaps and Derivatives in periodic surveys.

TOWARD THE FUTURE

The difficulties with the U.S. subprime mortgage markets discussed in Chapter 15 led to a chain of events[12] that by later 2008 had raised serious questions about the adequacy of both domestic and international regulatory environments. The sequence of events began with a mortgage lending boom

---

[10] At the time the report was filed, the responsible part of the Financial Services Authority was known as the Securities and Investments Board.

[11] As evidence of the possibilities for obtaining improvement, institutions like CLS Bank, an agency set up in the early 2000s to provide continuous linked settlement of foreign-exchange transactions among the world's 50–60 biggest banks, have successfully reduced certain types of clearing risks.

[12] Details of the subprime lending crisis and some of its implications are described in detail in a *Report of the Financial Stability Forum*, included for reference in this chapter's appendix.

in the United States that started in the late 1990s. It was followed in the early and mid-2000s by a very rapid expansion of mortgage lending and an unprecedented relaxation of lending standards. The lending increases were accompanied by rapid expansion of securitization, especially through structured vehicles, and the equally rapid expansion of credit default swaps.[13] All these developments increased the leverage of banks and investment banks to abnormally high levels.[14] Moreover, the financing of the mortgage lending and the increases in leverage were supported by rating agencies that assigned high-quality ratings to virtually all of the securities being sold by banks and their agencies.

As loan losses and defaults on securitized instruments began to erode banks' capital positions, they began to seek additional equity funding. At the same time large proportions of the banks' short-term borrowings were coming due and refinancing them was becoming more difficult as concerns about the banks' capital positions mounted. At the same time, banks reduced their lending activity in an aim to conserve funds, but those actions also contributed to concerns about an emerging worldwide recession. Insurance companies that had written credit default swaps felt similar pressures as the possibility of defaults mounted rapidly and the adequacy of insurance company capital to meet the claims they had issued began to be questioned. By October 2008, the financial system faced a combination of liquidity and solvency crises that affected both banks and insurance companies throughout the world, leading to an almost total loss of confidence in the ability of financial institutions to solve their problems without emergency government help.

To indicate the seriousness of the situation, all of the following events occurred in the summer and fall of 2008, most of them during September. They began in the United States with the absorption of Bear Stearns as mentioned previously, but were followed by a number of other serious developments. The incidents included the need for Treasury support of Fannie Mae and Freddie Mac announced on September 7, 2008, the acquisition of Merrill Lynch by Bank of America, the subsequent failure of Lehman Brothers, the rescue of AIG, and the conversion of Morgan Stanley and Goldman Sachs to bank holding companies. By late September 2008, similar difficulties had been encountered by numerous banks and mortgage lenders throughout the world. Again, the difficulties began with loan losses that led to impairment of capital positions, the need to raise both new equity, the need to replace

---

[13] While various forms of credit derivatives had been used previously, the explosive expansion of default swaps in effect represented a new development.

[14] In early 2008, investment banks' leverage came closer to 30 times capital than the more traditional 20 times capital of earlier years.

short-term funding, and a loss of confidence that banks would be able to raise the necessary funds. All these events increased the urgency of discussions regarding both long-term regulatory reform and shorter-term rescue measures. Implications for future regulation are discussed in the rest of this section, while the details of the emergency rescue programs are examined in the section "Dealing with the Global Credit and Liquidity Crises."

Structural Prescriptions

With regard to structural issues, the current difficulties raise questions of where and how financial system externalities may have changed significantly, and the appropriate forms of regulatory response. The developments just mentioned have all increased the interconnectedness of the world's financial system and made it more vulnerable to declines in asset values. Consequently, the combination of changes and the speed with which they have occurred make harmonizing standards across borders an urgent concern for global public policy formation. One of the themes in the longer-term discussions now beginning is how to devise international agencies that can provide global regulation, thus managing emerging externalities in a more effective fashion. A second theme is whether regulatory reform should be based on rules or principles.[15] Regulation based on principles offers flexibility but leaves room for the regulated to evade obligations, while rules are inflexible, limit innovation, and in some circumstances can also be evaded. Probably a mix of rules and principles is needed for greatest effectiveness, since implementing any single corrective measure almost always creates some incentives for evasion.

International cooperation appears to be increasing as regulators become more aware of the global effects to changing system responses. First, Internet trading can create large international flows of short-term capital unless actions are carefully managed to minimize the incentives for creating such flows. Second, risks affecting the global system are created by the changing forms of financial activity, as shown earlier by the Long-Term Capital Management crisis of 1998 and most recently by the 2007–2008 credit and liquidity crises. Third, risks are no longer limited to the world's traditional capital markets. For example, in early 2008, Indian regulators were wrestling with the issue of how best to control the hedge fund trading that appeared

---

[15] At the time of this writing (November 2008) regulators are focused on emergency measures to deal with the combination of capital and liquidity crises faced throughout the finance system. It will probably be some time before they can return to longer-term issues.

to be affecting the value of the rupee. In later 2008, the same regulators were dealing with the effects of commodity price changes in international markets.

Further regulatory change is likely to emerge both from domestic initiatives and from recent instances of international regulatory cooperation. With respect to domestic initiatives in the United States, then Treasury Secretary Paulson presented an early 2008 plan to address the fragmented nature of the domestic U.S. system. Currently none of the half-dozen U.S. federal regulators has an overview of the entire financial system and consequently the present design does not always apply rules effectively. Industry regulators concentrated on their own agencies' problems, and missed the need to control such activity as that of mortgage brokers. Moreover, federal regulators have not always been given appropriate mandates: The SEC obtained oversight of investment banks in 2004 as part of a compromise following legal changes in Europe.

Former Secretary Paulson's short-term recommendations included creating a federal Mortgage Origination Commission designed to consolidate oversight of the mortgage business. The Commission is seen as a partial solution to the current difficulties with securitization, as it would grade the underwriting of mortgage loans going into pools. Paulson's longer-term plan proposed three agencies—a remodeled Federal Reserve with a responsibility to supervise market stability, a prudential regulator for banks and near-banks, and a business conduct agency that takes in much of the SEC's current oversight responsibilities. The proposed new Fed is the most important and most controversial element of the plan. Though the Fed would lose supervisory authority over large institutions such as Citigroup and JPMorgan Chase, its overall power would be greatly expanded, allowing it to investigate numerous possible sources of systemic risk, including those posed by the activities of hedge funds and investment banks.[16] Although plans of this nature are likely to receive further discussion in the more distant future, for the next two or three years regulatory authorities will likely be focusing mainly on offsetting effects of the 2007–2008 market turmoil rather than on the longer-term issues.

The Financial Stability Forum Report (2008) also offers pertinent recommendations. Its proposals include revising capital requirements, raising them for certain structured products and also providing extra charges for default and event risk in the trading books of banks and securities firms.

---

[16] Subsequently former Federal Reserve Chairman Alan Greenspan has argued that a separate agency should assume responsibility for dealing with failing institutions, thus attempting to ensure that the Federal Reserve System maintains as much political independence as possible.

In addition, capital requirements for providing liquidity facilities to off-balance-sheet conduits are to be strengthened. Both risk management practices and their supervision are to be strengthened. Disclosure practices are to be improved, and greater transparency in reporting structured products' risks is sought.[17]

Other countries are likely to implement changes based on the lessons emerging from the 2008 credit and liquidity crises. The UK and European banks' 2008 difficulties have provided strong impetus for the EU countries to develop more effective regimes for shutting down failing banks, to provide more robust deposit-insurance schemes, and to obtain greater co-operation between countries. In particular, government support of banks through equity investment was first initiated by the United Kingdom, and almost immediately followed by the United States, as discussed further in the next section, "Dealing with the Global Credit and Liquidity Crises."

Cyclical Prescriptions

The global financial system's current regulations create procyclical effects that future regulatory reform will likely attempt to offset. Measures of risk management at individual institutions do not fully reflect the individual institutions' risks. In the past, individual institutions assumed that their risk exposure reflected a static environment in which positions could quickly be closed out, and that closing the positions would not move market prices. In addition, the widespread use of Value at Risk leads to prescribing lower capital requirements when the data have shown a relatively long period of stability, and more capital when markets become volatile. Yet financial crises occur just after the top of the economic cycle, when VaR measures are likely to be at relatively low levels.

Given high leverage, procyclical risk management models and illiquid assets, the effect of many different institutions trying to reduce their individual risk at the end of an asset price bubble can increase systemic risk (see Bookstaber 2007). Regulators are therefore discussing whether they should implement additional capital requirements during cyclical upturns when risks are building, and to reduce them during cyclical downturns. Such an approach would help offset such existing procyclical forces as mark-to-market accounting of illiquid products (e.g. credit-default swaps) and to discourage speculative traders whose activities can sometimes accentuate cyclical movements.

---

[17] The theory of this book indicates that in many instances the goals of achieving greater transparency may well prove illusory.

Regulators also need to determine where risks are concentrated, when to attempt to reduce those risks, and how to respond to changing liquidity conditions. As an example of adaptations, previous regulation incorporated perverse incentives for concentrating some risks. Banks created off-balance-sheet vehicles because Basel I did not impose capital charges on the banks creating the vehicles. Moreover, even though they had sold the assets, subsequently banks felt a need to maintain their reputations by taking assets back onto their balance-sheets. To rectify this earlier situation Basel II charges banks for the risk exposures associated with such vehicles. In addition, regulators are now also emphasizing pillars 2 and 3 of Basel II. Pillar 2 covers reputational risk and allows regulators to impose additional capital requirements if needed, while Pillar 3 is designed to improve the quality of banks' disclosure on their risk profiles.

Spanish regulators have implemented two attempts to dampen cycles.[18] The first requires banks to set aside the same amount of capital against assets in off-balance-sheet vehicles as they would against on-balance-sheet assets. Despite Basel I, Spanish regulators regarded structured investment vehicles as a banking business that did not effectively transfer risk, and hence imposed the same capital requirements on them as on other forms of business. In addition, the Bank of Spain has operated a dynamic provisioning regime, where bank reserves increase when lending is growing quickly. Over the cycle the effect is designed to be neutral, but the timing of provisions has the potential to dampen both upturns and downturns.

Liquidity risk receives little mention in the Basel II Accord, largely because capital and liquidity have been viewed as separate matters. But the dependence of banks on wholesale market funding has left them increasingly vulnerable to liquidity crises, as urgently demonstrated by the events described previously. Earlier in 2008, the Financial Stability Forum promised an updated set of liquidity standards, but devising those standards is likely to prove difficult, not the least because liquidity positions are affected by existing schemes for deposit insurance and central-bank funding. The regulators may also have to recommend guidelines regarding maturity mismatches between banks' assets and liabilities, both on- and off-balance-sheet. In addition, regulators will also pay closer attention to how banks manage liquidity internally. Finally, questions about acceptable bank collateral will have to be addressed.

British Prime Minister Gordon Brown has pressed for regulatory revision to focus on the operations of world capital markets as opposed to

---

[18] This is not to argue that Spain has been immune from cyclical problems, but it is to point out that regulatory actions did help to reduce the potential problems.

individual countries' markets. The main points of Brown's program are: (1) fully disclosing critical bank information globally; (2) ending conflicts of interest such as those affecting the rating agencies; (3) holding board members fully responsible for their company's risks; (4) changing solvency and liquidity provisions to eliminate their procyclical aspects; and (5) creating a new international regulatory agency that will provide a global early warning system. In some senses, the ideas of regulatory integration worldwide are similar to Paulson's advocacy of regulatory integration for the United States: Both are aimed at reducing existing externalities.

DEALING WITH THE GLOBAL CREDIT AND LIQUIDITY CRISES

The U.S. credit crisis of 2007–2008 spread throughout the world as related financial difficulties were recognized in many countries. As of September 2008, financial institutions in the European community and also in Asia were facing the same problems of loan losses and capital adequacy as in the United States (see Chapter 17 and earlier comments in this chapter). Further, as concern over banks' solvency spread, the world suffered an international liquidity crisis as banks cut back on lending to each other. Contemporaneously, a credit crunch emerged as banks also cut back on lending to clients, in attempts to conserve their resources. Resolving the situation has been made extraordinarily difficult because a crippling loss of confidence in the financial industry has swept the world, exacerbating further both the shortages of capital and the emerging liquidity crisis. By November 2008, write-downs and losses at financial institutions totaled nearly US$1 trillion, leading to a surge in the cost of credit and to restrictions on lending to consumers and companies. The Euro area fell into its first recession in 15 years in the third quarter of 2008 and data suggests the United States, Japan, and United Kingdom have as well.

The urgency of the situation is starkly stated by Eichengreen and Baldwin (2008): "We are in the throes of what is certainly the most serious economic and financial crisis of our lifetimes. . . . The policy response needs to be decisive. It needs to be global. The stakes could not be higher." The most likely possibilities for remedial action are infusions of equity by governments or their agencies, the government purchase of troubled assets, loans of last resort, and provisions of emergency liquidity from central banks. Commentators frequently remark that all these types of remedial action are likely to be needed.

The choices among the possible alternatives depend on regulators' and the markets' assessments of what best will restore confidence and how a given scheme will affect institutional incentives to resolve the problems arising from their lending practices. For example, injecting capital into banks works more quickly than asset purchases and also gives the banks a greater incentive to collect bad loans. By requiring the banks to issue preferred shares with accompanying warrants, government rescuers can share in the profits if the banks effect a successful recovery. On the other hand, neither injections of capital nor governmental purchases of troubled assets will resolve liquidity crises, as the latter need to be addressed both by emergency liquidity provisions and by longer-term measures to restore confidence in the financial system. Moreover, questions of depositor and lender confidence need to be addressed, probably through coordinated guarantees of deposits and loans. In addition, the questions of whether and how to assist distressed mortgage borrowers in the United States and other countries also requires to be addressed. Details of some proposed actions are given below.

Troubled Asset Recovery Program

The U.S. Troubled Asset Recovery Program (TARP) provides a total of $700 billion to the Secretary of the Treasury either to fund the purchase of troubled assets from financial institutions or to provide them with capital injections.[19] It can be expected that most assets qualifying for purchase will be portfolios of subprime mortgages and related securities. Only strong banking firms will qualify for capital injections, as further detailed later.

If TARP purchases take place they are to make use of auctions, and details of both proposed and completed transactions are to be made transparent by publication on a web site. As a part of each transaction, the treasury secretary is required to obtain either warrants for common or preferred stock or senior debt instruments that entitle the Treasury an appropriate return in either equity appreciation or interest rate on the debt.[20] The senior executives of institutions participating in the TARP will be subject to compensation limits.

As another alternative to purchasing troubled assets, the secretary is required to create a guarantee program for troubled assets, and institutions may then choose between selling assets or purchasing insurance against their decline. Mark-to-market accounting of the securities involved may be suspended as the SEC determines it to be necessary or appropriate.

---

[19] The initial emphasis was on asset purchases, but following the lead of the United Kingdom the current emphasis is first to provide equity injections. Eichengreen and Baldwin (2008) forcefully recommend this approach.

[20] Note that asset purchases by the Treasury are more likely to face the Treasury with the costs of adverse selection than are capital injections that provide the banks with incentives to collect loans and report greater profits.

As the TARP approach has been adapted to changing market sentiment, the Treasury's first actions are focusing on purchases of up to $250 billion in senior preferred shares of a number of financial institutions. In any individual bank, the TARP assistance will be up to the lesser of $25 billion or 3% of a bank's risk-weighted assets. The program may later buy troubled assets, and also mortgages, the latter particularly from regional banks. Further, it will insure mortgage-backed securities and mortgages, so that banks and investors are protected if borrowers default. Finally, it will work out details of helping delinquent borrowers stay in their homes.[21]

Other U.S. Measures

By the end of November 2008, the Federal Reserve, the Federal Deposit Insurance Corporation (FDIC), and the Treasury had jointly announced financial system support of more than $7.76 trillion in the form of loans and loan guarantees. The total involvement was much larger than the TARP program, amounting to approximately one-half of U.S. annual GNP. At this writing some $3.18 trillion had been committed to assist financial institutions, including a Fed program to buy up to $2.4 trillion in commercial paper, and $1.4 trillion from FDIC to guarantee bank-to-bank loans. Another of the elements, put in place on November 23, guaranteed $306 billion of Citigroup Inc. debt, and the guarantee was provided at the same time as the Treasury injected $20 billion in bank capital.

Regulators hope the measures will encourage banks to lend, and thus offset the possibility of continuing the 2008 credit crunch. Several of the programs are administered by the New York Fed, whose rescue attempts began in December 2007 with the creation of the Term Auction Facility to allow lending to dealers for collateral. After Bear Stearns' collapse in March 2008, the Fed started making direct loans to securities firms at the same discount rate it charges commercial banks. The failure of Lehman Brothers Holdings Inc. in September 2008 led to the creation of the Commercial Paper Funding Facility and the Money Market Investor Funding Facility, or MMIFF. The two facilities, which have pledged $2.3 trillion, are designed to restore liquidity and hence to calm the money markets segments dealing in certificates of deposit, commercial paper, and Treasury bills.

---

[21] In this connection, Bank of America promised during the week of October 6 to alter the terms of 390,000 subprime mortgages. Since that time several other major banks, as well as Fannie Mae and Freddie Mac, have announced a similar willingness to renegotiate terms.

The FDIC has contributed about 20% of the total commitments. The FDIC's $1.4 trillion in guarantees will amount to a bank subsidy of as much as $54 billion over three years, because borrowers will pay a lower interest rate than they would on the open market. Congress and the Treasury have supplied some $892 billion in TARP and other funding, or 11.5%. The Federal Housing Administration was given the authority to guarantee $300 billion of mortgages, or about 4% of the total commitment, with a program designed to help distressed borrowers avoid foreclosure.

In late December 2008, General Motors Acceptance Corporation (GMAC) received permission to reorganize itself as a bank holding company, and was further promised a capital infusion of $5 billion from the TARP program. In addition, the Treasury agreed to add a new $1 billion to previously arranged auto industry loans of $17.4 billion to assist General Motors with an upcoming equity rights issue.

The GMAC conversion to a bank holding company is a new feature of the more systematic approach recently taken by the government for dealing with the current financial crisis. As part of the arrangements, both GM and Cerberus will have to reduce their equity stakes significantly, with the result that GMAC will no longer function as a captive finance subsidiary for GM. The reorganization follows on the severe solvency and liquidity pressures GMAC has recently faced because of sharp declines in the collateral valuations of its automobile and residential mortgage assets.

GMAC has been having difficulty raising funding, with the result that automotive credit has been restricted. Spreads on automotive loans widened considerably in the second half of 2008, and this contributed to the sharp downward decline in automotive sales that we have seen for several months. The arrangement will significantly improve GMAC's access to funding and ability to function as a financial intermediary. GMAC now has access to near zero-cost funds from the Federal Reserve, and the much higher level of capitalization should reduce GMAC's term borrowing costs. These developments will in turn ease the upward pressure on auto loan borrowing spreads, and provide greater access to auto loan credit for American households. Similarly, the FDIC arranged for $139 billion in loan guarantees for General Electric Company's finance unit. In early 2009 the extent of support was summarized in a speech by FRB Atlanta President Lockhart. Lockhart observed that

> *Initially, as the Fed responded to credit market strains, the focus was on interbank markets. But, as problems spread, the Fed introduced almost a dozen targeted credit and financial market facilities . . . [including] short-term credit programs for financial institutions, longer-term lending arrangements, direct asset purchases, and swap*

lines with foreign central banks. The Fed has intervened, for example, in the commercial paper market, the agency market, and the private asset-backed securities market. Programs have supported banks, nonbank financial institutions, money market mutual funds, and ... specific institutions deemed to be systematically critical. Among the programs in force is the direct purchase of agency (Fannie Mae, Freddie Mac, etc.) notes and mortgage-backed securities. (Lockhart 2009)

International Measures

The world's principal central banks announced a coordinated reduction of discount rates as of October 8, 2008. In a further and unprecedented move to inject liquidity into global markets, the Federal Reserve announced on October 13 that it will lend an unlimited amount of dollars[22] to the central banks of the United Kingdom, Switzerland, and the European Union.

The U.K. and European governments have also bought stakes in their banks and taken other steps similar to those taken in the United States. The leaders of 15 European nations agreed on October 12 to a wide-ranging plan both to invest in their financial institutions and to guarantee interbank lending.[23] For example, the British Exchequer announced on October 13 that it will invest $63 billion in the Royal Bank of Scotland, HBOS, and Lloyds. Other European countries have announced similar moves. In Belgium, the Netherlands, and France, nationalization of parts of Fortis, a bancassurer, was announced to provide that institution with capital. Another bank, Dexia, was also rescued in similar fashion.

The 15 European nations also said they would protect individual depositors' accounts by increasing deposit insurance coverage. Finally, they would move to ease accounting regulations that determine how assets are valued, removing a requirement that they be based on market prices—so-called "mark-to-market" accounting.

The leaders of the G20 countries held the first of a series of summits[24] in the United States on November 15. The G20 will hold additional meetings to

---

[22] At a fixed interest rate.

[23] In some instances precedents for the moves emanated from the British and European governments, after which the moves' political acceptability increased in the United States.

[24] The G20 countries are Argentina, Australia, Brazil, Canada, China, France, Germany, India, Indonesia, Italy, Japan, South Korea, Mexico, Russia, Saudi Arabia, South Africa, Turkey, the United States, the United Kingdom, and the European Union. The Netherlands and Spain also attended, as did representatives of the IMF, the World Bank, the Financial Stability Forum, and the United Nations.

deal with strengthening accounting standards, increasing the transparency of derivatives markets, and providing greater oversight of hedge funds and debt-rating agencies. The Group differed over the kinds of policies to be followed, advancing the case for detailed rules on the one hand and for regulation mainly according to principles on the other. In an attempt to reconcile the differences, the Group's closing statement recognized that regulation is "first and foremost" a national responsibility, while at the same time demanding "intensified international cooperation" to oversee financial firms whose operations and problems cross national borders. The leaders called for the creation of "supervisory colleges" for bank regulators around the world to better coordinate oversight and share information about activities and risk-taking of international banks.

The Group also advocated raising capital standards, particularly for banks' structured credit and securitization activities. The leaders directed their finance ministers to address enhancing financial disclosure by investors and institutions, including hedge funds. Debt rating agencies should be registered and oversight of their actions strengthened to ensure they provide unbiased information and avoid conflicts of interest. Accounting standards should be harmonized around the world, and regulators should consider whether current rules properly value securities, particularly complex, illiquid products, during times of stress.

The G20 leaders followed the earlier lead of the United States (see the previous section) and endorsed the use of clearinghouses for financial derivatives to back trades and absorb losses in case of a dealer failure. The first central clearinghouse for the $33 trillion credit-default swap market should be in operation by year-end in the United States, under an agreement signed last week by U.S. financial regulators. The G20 leaders recommended that credit default swaps should be traded on exchanges or electronic trading platforms, and more disclosure should be required for other derivatives traded over the counter.[25]

The G20 leaders said executive compensation should be managed to "avoid excessive risk-taking," but did not recommend any salary or bonus caps. Member governments are to review the "adequacy of resources" at the IMF and World Bank, and look for ways to increase them, as well as to buttress the role of smaller economies. Some emerging-market nations with large reserves have been reluctant to raise their IMF contributions unless they are granted greater voice in determining IMF policies.

---

[25] The Depository Trust and Clearing Corporation began releasing CDS trading data in the week leading up to the G20 meetings.

REFERENCES

Arrow, Kenneth J. 1974. *Essays in the Theory of Risk-Bearing*. Amsterdam: North-Holland.

Benston, George J. 1998. *Regulating Financial Markets: A critique and some proposals*. London, Institute of Economic Affairs.

Bookstaber, Richard. 2007. *A Demon of Our Own Design*. New York and London, Wiley.

Cecchetti, Stephen G. 1999. The future of financial intermediation and regulation: An overview. (Federal Reserve Bank of New York) *Current Issues in Economics and Finance 5*, no. 8: 1–7.

Courchene, Thomas J., and Edwin H. Neave, eds. 1995. *Financial Derivatives: Managing and Regulating Off-Balance Sheet Risks*. Kingston, Ont.: Queen's University, John Deutsch Institute for the Study of Economic Policy.

Dewatripont, Matthias, and Jean Tirole. 1994. *The Prudential Regulation of Banks*. Cambridge, MA: MIT Press.

Eichengreen, Barry, and Richard Baldwin. 2008. Rescuing our jobs and savings: What G7/8 leaders can do to solve the global credit crisis. London: Centre for Economic Policy Research.

Freixas, Xavier, and Jean-Charles Rochet. 1997. *Microeconomics of Banking*, 1st ed. Cambridge, MA: MIT Press.

Hellman, Thomas, Kevin Murdock, and Joseph Stiglitz. 1996. Deposit mobilisation through financial constraint. In *Financial Development and Economic Growth*, edited by Niels Hermes and Robert Lensink. London: Routledge.

Johnson, Lewis D., and Edwin H. Neave. 1994. Governance and comparative advantage. *Managerial Finance* 20: 54–68.

Laeven, Luc, and Ross Levine. 2007. Corporate governance, regulation and bank risk taking. Brown University Working Paper.

Lockhart, Dennis. 2009. Speech to the Atlanta Business Council. Federal Reserve Bank of Atlanta, January 12, 2009.

TERMS

bancassurance   Firms that combine a banking or universal banking business with insurance activities as well.

disintermediation   The process whereby depository institutions, unable to pay market rates of interest because of restrictive regulation, lost deposit funds to alternative sources of savings, such as government securities.

universal banks   Universal banks combine both commercial banking and securities activity.

APPENDIX: THE MARKET TURMOIL OF 2007–2008[26]

Factors Underlying the Market Turmoil

The turmoil that started in the summer of 2007 was the culmination of an exceptional boom in credit growth and leverage in the financial system. This boom was fed by a long period of benign economic and financial conditions, including historically low real interest rates and abundant liquidity. These conditions increased the amount of risk and leverage that borrowers, investors, and intermediaries were willing to take on. At the same time, a wave of financial innovation expanded the system's capacity to generate credit assets and leverage, but outpaced its capacity to manage the associated risks.

As the global trend of low-risk premiums and low expectations of future volatility gathered pace from 2003, the financial technology that produced the first collateralized debt obligations (CDOs) a decade earlier was extended dramatically. The pooling and tranching of credit assets generated complex structured products that appeared to meet the credit rating agencies' (CRAs') criteria for high ratings.[27] Credit enhancements by financial guarantors contributed further to the perception of unlimited high-quality investment opportunities. The growth of the credit default swap market and related index markets made credit risk easier to trade and to hedge, thus greatly increasing the perceived liquidity of credit instruments. For a time, easy credit availability and rising asset prices contributed to low default rates, reinforcing the low level of credit risk premiums.

Banks and other financial institutions enhanced this process by establishing off-balance-sheet funding and structure investment vehicles (SIVs). In many cases, the SIVs invested in highly rated structured credit products, in turn often largely backed by mortgage-backed securities (MBSs). The SIVS were not subject to the regulatory and accounting constraints applying to banks and operated with less capital than their organizers. They were often characterized by significant liquidity and maturity mismatches and their asset compositions were often misunderstood by investors. Both the

---

[26]This appendix is an edited version of events summarized in the Financial Stability Forum's *2008 Report of the Financial Stability Forum on Enhancing Market and Institutional Resilience*.

[27]In some cases the products were backed by many small independent mortgage assets. Issuers and investors both appeared to overlook the possibility that in the event of interest rate increases these assets were likely to default together, losing their properties of independence. See related discussions in Chapters 6 and 20.

originating banks and the rating agencies misjudged the liquidity and concentration risks that a deterioration in general economic conditions could
pose. Banks also misjudged the reputational risks arising from the sponsorship of the vehicles.

The demand for high-yield assets with low default rates also encouraged
a loosening of credit standards, most glaringly in the U.S. subprime mortgage
market, but more broadly in standards and terms of loans to households and
businesses, including loans for buy-outs by private equity firms. Here, too,
banks, investors, and credit rating agencies misjudged the level of such risks
as the instruments' common exposure to a weakening housing market or to
a fall in the market liquidity of high-yield corporate debt.

Worsening underwriting standards for subprime mortgages and a weakening in the U.S. housing market led to a steady rise in delinquencies
and, from early 2007 onward, sharply falling prices for indices based on
subprime-related assets. These problems led both to write-offs and to increased margin calls for leveraged holders of subprime backed products.
Moreover, the problems in the subprime market provided the trigger for a
broad reversal in market risk-taking. As credit rating agencies downgraded
structured subprime products, investors lost confidence in the ratings of a
wider range of structured assets. For example, in August 2007 investors in
asset-backed commercial paper (ABCP) refused to roll over investments in
bank-sponsored conduits and structured investment vehicles (SIVs) backed
by structured products.

As sponsoring banks moved to fund liquidity commitments to ABCP
conduits and SIVs, they sought to build up liquid resources and became
unwilling to provide term liquidity to others. In both the United States
and Europe, the resulting shortage of liquidity led to a severe contraction of
activity in the term interbank market, to a substantial rise in term premiums,
and to disruption of related short-term financial markets.

Just as low risk premiums, low-funding costs, and ample leverage had
fueled the earlier increase in credit and liquidity, the sharp reduction of
funding availability and leverage accentuated the subsequent contraction.
Fears of asset price declines both reinforced upward pressures on credit
spreads and, self-fulfillingly, led to valuation losses in many asset classes
across the quality spectrum. When primary and secondary market liquidity
for structured credit products evaporated, major banks faced increasing
challenges in valuing their own holdings, became less confident in their
credit risk assessments and in the capital strength of others.

The disruption to funding markets lasted longer than many banks'
contingency plans had allowed for. As large banks reabsorbed assets and
sustained large valuation losses, their balance sheets swelled, their capital
cushions shrank, and they tightened their lending conditions. Both bank

and capital market financings slowed, and new issues in securitization markets fell sharply. As the turmoil spread, increased risk aversion, reduced liquidity, market uncertainty about the soundness of major financial institutions, questions about the quality of structured credit products, and uncertainty about the macroeconomic outlook fed on each other.

In later 2008, deleveraging continues to pose significant challenges for large parts of the global financial system. Although some financial institutions and guarantors have moved to replenish capital, the system is burdened by market uncertainties about the health of key financial institutions. There are concerns about the large overhang of assets held by banks, SIVs, hedge funds, and other leveraged entities, as well as about the quality of those assets. The resulting financial system weaknesses have contributed to deteriorating prospects for the real economy, although to different degrees in different countries.

Underlying Weaknesses

Given the maturing of the credit cycle and the weakening in the U.S. housing market, a pullback in risk-taking of some kind was inevitable. However, because of accumulated weaknesses in risk management and underwriting standards, and the sheer scale of the required adjustments, attempts by individual institutions to contain their risk exposures have led to reinforcing dynamics in the system as a whole.

Poor Underwriting Standards The benign macroeconomic conditions gave rise to complacency among many market participants and led to an erosion of sound practices in important financial market segments. In a range of credit market segments, business volume grew much more quickly than did investments in the supporting infrastructure of controls and documentation. Misaligned incentives were most conspicuous in the poor underwriting and in some cases fraudulent practices that proliferated in the U.S. subprime mortgage sector, especially from late 2004. Many of the subprime loans underwritten during this time had multiple weaknesses: less creditworthy borrowers, high cumulative loan-to-value ratios, and limited or no verification of the borrower's income. The combination of weak incentives, an increasingly competitive environment, low interest rates, and rapidly rising house prices led originators and mortgage brokers to lower underwriting standards and to offer products to borrowers who often could not afford them or could not bear the associated risks. Weak government oversight of these entities contributed to the rise in unsound underwriting practices, especially by mortgage companies not affiliated with banks. Another segment that saw rapid growth in volume accompanied by a decline in standards was the corporate leveraged loan market, where lenders agreed to weakened loan covenants to obtain the business of private equity funds.

Shortcomings in Firms' Risk Management Practices   Some of the standard risk management tools used by financial firms are not suited to estimating the scale of potential losses in the adverse tail of risk distributions for structured credit products. The absence of a history of returns and correlations and the complexity of many products created high uncertainty in VaR measures and scenario-based estimates of risks. Market participants severely underestimated default risks, concentration risks, market risks, and liquidity risks, particularly for super-senior tranches of structured products. A number of banks had weak controls over balance sheet growth and over off-balance-sheet risks, as well as inadequate communication and aggregation across business lines and functions. Some firms retained large exposures to super-senior tranches of CDOs that far exceeded the firms' understanding of the risks inherent in such instruments, and failed to take appropriate steps to control or mitigate those risks. When the turbulence started, firms and investors misjudged or were unable to rapidly assess their exposures, particularly as liquidity evaporated and markets became unavailable.

Poor Investor Due Diligence   In parallel, many investors, including institutional ones with the capacity to undertake their own credit analysis, did not sufficiently examine the assets of underlying structured investments. They overlooked leverage and tail risks and did not question the source of high promised yields on purportedly safe assets. These weak due diligence practices further fueled the issuance of complex structured credit products. Many investors placed excessive reliance on credit ratings, neither questioning CRAs' methodologies nor fully understanding the information credit ratings do and do not transmit about the risk characteristics of rated products.

Poor Performance by the Rating Agencies' Treatment of Structured Credit Products   The sources of concerns about rating agencies' performance included: weaknesses in rating models and methodologies; inadequate due diligence of the quality of the collateral pools underlying rated securities; insufficient transparency about the assumptions, criteria and methodologies used in rating structured products; insufficient information provision about the meaning and risk characteristics of structured finance ratings; and insufficient attention to conflicts of interest in the rating process.

Incentive Distortions   The shortcomings in risk management, risk assessment, and underwriting standards reflected a variety of incentive distortions.
Originators, arrangers, distributors, and managers in the originate-to-distribute chain all faced insufficient incentives to generate and provide initial

and ongoing information on the quality and performance of underlying assets. High demand by investors for securitized products weakened the incentives of underwriters and sponsors to maintain adequate underwriting standards.

The pre-Basel II capital framework encouraged banks to securitize assets through instruments with low capital charges (such as 364-day liquidity facilities).

Compensation schemes in financial institutions encouraged disproportionate risk-taking with insufficient regard to longer-term risks. This risk-taking was not always subject to adequate checks and balances in firms' risk management systems.

Weaknesses in Disclosure   Weaknesses in public disclosures by financial institutions have damaged market confidence during the turmoil. Public disclosures that were required of financial institutions did not always make clear the type and magnitude of risks associated with their on- and off-balance-sheet exposures. There were also shortcomings in the other information firms provided about market and credit risk exposures, particularly as these related to structured products. Where information was disclosed, it was often not done in an easily accessible or usable way.

Feedback Effects between Valuation and Risk-Taking   The turbulence revealed the potential for adverse interactions between high leverage, market liquidity, valuation losses, and financial institutions' capital. For example, write-downs of assets for which markets were thin or buyers were lacking raised questions about the adequacy of capital buffers, leading to asset sales, deleveraging, and further pressure on asset prices.

Weaknesses in Regulatory Frameworks and Other Policies   Public authorities recognized some of the underlying vulnerabilities in the financial sector but failed to take effective countervailing action, partly because they may have overestimated the strength and resilience of the financial system. Limitations in regulatory arrangements, both international and domestic, contributed to the growth of unregulated exposures, excessive risk-taking, and weak liquidity risk management.

Underpinnings of the Originate-to-Distribute Model   Although securitization markets and the OTD model of intermediation have functioned well over many years, recent innovations greatly increased leverage and complexity and, as noted above, were accompanied by a reduction in credit standards for some asset classes.

When accompanied by adequate risk management and incentives, the OTD model offers a number of benefits to loan originators, investors, and borrowers. Originators can benefit from greater capital efficiency, enhanced funding availability, and lower earnings volatility since the OTD model disperses credit and interest rate risks to the capital markets. Investors can benefit from a greater choice of investments, allowing them to diversify and to match their investment profile more closely to their risk preferences. Borrowers can benefit from expanded credit availability and product choice, as well as lower borrowing costs.

However, these features of the OTD model progressively weakened in the years preceding the outburst of the turmoil. Aside from weakened underwriting standards, in some cases, risks that had been expected to be broadly dispersed turned out to have been concentrated in entities unable to bear them. For example:

- Some assets went into conduits and SIVs with substantial leverage and significant maturity and liquidity risk, making them vulnerable to a classic type of run.
- Banks ended up with significant direct and indirect exposure to many of these vehicles to which risk had apparently been transferred, through contingent credit lines, reputational links, revenue risks, and counter-party credit exposures.
- Financial institutions adopted a business model that assumed substantial ongoing access to funding liquidity and asset market liquidity to support the securitization process.
- Firms that pursued a strategy of actively packaging and selling their originated credit exposures retained increasingly large pipelines of these exposures, without adequately measuring and managing the risks that materialized when they could not be sold.

Although all market participants involved in the OTD chain had weaknesses in risk management, and nearly all ultimately needed to write down their structured product portfolios substantially, some firms seem to have handled these challenges better than others. This suggests that it is not the OTD model or securitization per se that are problematic. Rather, these problems, and the underlying weaknesses that gave rise to them, show that the underpinnings of the OTD model need to be strengthened.

Among the issues that need to be addressed are:

- Misaligned incentives along the securitization chain. As described earlier, these existed at originators, arrangers, managers, distributors, and CRAs, while investor oversight of these participants was weakened by complacency and the complexity of the instruments.

- Lack of transparency about the risks underlying securitized products and, in particular, the quality and potential correlations of the underlying assets.
- Poor management of the risks associated with the securitization business such as market, liquidity, concentration, and pipeline risks, including insufficient stress testing of these risks.
- The usefulness and transparency of credit ratings. Despite their central role in the OTD model, CRAs did not adequately review the data input underlying securitized transactions. This hindered investors in applying market discipline in the OTD model.

References

Aghion, Philippe, and Patrick Bolton. 1992. An incomplete contracts approach to financial contracting. *Review of Economic Studies* 59: 473–494.

Allen, Franklin D., and Douglas Gale. 2000. *Comparing Financial Systems*. Cambridge, MA: MIT Press.

Allen, Franklin and Douglas Gale. 2007. *Understanding Financial Crisis*. Oxford University Press.

Almeida, Heitor, and Thomas Philippon. 2007. The risk-adjusted cost of financial distress. *Journal of Finance* 62: 2,557–2,586.

Altman, Edward I., and Anthony Saunders. 2002. An analysis and critique of the bis proposal on capital adequacy and ratings. In *Risk Management: The State of the Art*, edited by Stephen Figlewski and Richard M. Levich. Boston: Kluwer.

Arbel, A., and P. Strebel. 1983. "Pay attention to neglected firms." *Journal of Portfolio Management* 9: 37–42.

Arrow, Kenneth J. 1974. *Essays on the Theory of Risk-Bearing*. Amsterdam: North-Holland.

Axelson, Ulf. 2007. Security design with investor private information. *Journal of Finance* 62: 2,587–2,632.

Bagehot, Walter. 1873. *Lombard Street: A Description of the Money Market*. London: Smith and Elder. 1910.

Baumol, William J. 1965. *The Stock Market and Economic Efficiency*. New York: Fordham University Press.

Benninga, Simon. 2008. *Financial Modeling*, 3rd ed. Cambridge, MA: MIT Press.

Benson, E. D. 1979. "The search for information by underwriters and its impact on municipal interest cost." *Journal of Finance* 34: 871–885.

Benston, George J. 1998. *Regulating Financial Markets: A Critique and Some Proposals*. London, Institute of Economic Affairs.

Berger, Allen N., and David B. Humphrey. 1991. The dominance of inefficiencies over scale and product mix economies in banking. *Journal of Monetary Economics* 28: 117–148.

Berger, Allen N., and David B. Humphrey. 1992. Megamergers in banking and the use of cost efficiency as an antitrust defense. *Antitrust Bulletin* 37: 541–600.

Bernanke, B., and M. Gertler. 1990. Financial fragility and economic performance, *Quarterly Journal of Economics* 105: 87–114.

Bertrand, Marianne, Antoinette Schoar, and David Thesmar. 2007. Banking Deregulation and Industry Structure: Evidence from the French Banking Reforms of 1985. *Journal of Finance* 62: 597–628.

Bhattacharya, Utpal. 1998. When an event is not an event: The strange case of Mexico. Indiana University Working Paper.

Biais, Bruno, and Catherine Casamatta. 1999. "Optimal leverage and aggregate investment." *Journal of Finance* 54: 1,291–1,323.

Black, Fischer, and Myron Scholes. 1973. "The pricing of options and corporate liabilities." *Journal of Political Economy* 81: 637–654.

Blanco, Roberto, Simon Brennan, and Ian W. Marsh. 2005. An empirical analysis of the dynamic relationship between investment grade bonds and credit default swaps. Bank of England Working Paper No. 211, Cass Business School Research Paper.

Bodie, Zvi, and Robert C. Merton. 2005. Design of financial systems: Towards a synthesis of function and structure. *Journal of Investment Management* 3: 1–23.

Bond, Philip. 2004. Bank and nonbank financial intermediation. *Journal of Finance* 59: 2,489–2,529.

Bookstaber, Richard. 2007. *A Demon of Our Own Design*. Hoboken, NJ: John Wiley & Sons.

Boot, Arnoud, and Anjan Thakor. 1993. Security design. *Journal of Finance* 48: 1,349–1,378.

Boyd, John H., and Gianni de Nicolo. 2005. The Theory of Bank Risk-Taking and Competition Revisited. *Journal of Finance* 60: 1,329–1,344.

Braun, Matias, and Borja Larrain. 2005. Finance and the business cycle: International, inter-industry evidence. *Journal of Finance* 60: 1,097–1,128.

Breedon, Francis. 1995. Bond prices and market expectations of inflation. *Bank of England Quarterly Bulletin* 35 (May): 160–165.

Brinson, Gary P., and Richard C. Carr. 1989. International equities and bonds. Chapter 19 in *Portfolio and Investment Analysis: State-of-the-art Research, Analysis and Strategies*, edited by Frank J. Fabozzi. Chicago: Probus Publishing.

Brunnermeier, Markus K., and Stefan Nagel. 2004. Hedge funds and the technology bubble. *Journal of Finance* 59: 2,013–2,040.

Brunnermeier, Markus, and Lasse Pedersen. 2009. Market liquidity and funding liquidity. Forthcoming. *Review of Financial Studies*.

Brunnermeier, Markus K., Stefan Nagel, and Lasse H. Pedersen. 2009. Carry trades and currency crashes. In National Bureau of Economic Research macroeconomics annual 2008, vol. 23, edited by Daron Acemoglu, Kenneth Rogoff, and Michael Woodford. Chicago: University of Chicago Press.

Buser, Stephen A., Andrew H. Chen, and Edward J. Kane. 1981. Federal deposit insurance, regulatory policy, and optimal bank capital. *Journal of Finance* 35: 51–60.

Caballero, Ricardo, and Arvind Krishnamurthy. 2008. Collective risk management in a flight to quality episode. *Journal of Finance* 61: 2,195–2,230.

Cai, Jun, Stephen Cheung, and Vidhan K. Goyal. 1999. "Bank monitoring and the maturity structure of Japanese debt issues." *Pacific-Basin Finance Journal* 7: 229–250.

Carey, Mark, Mitch Post, and Steven A. Sharpe. 1998. Does corporate lending by banks and finance companies differ? Evidence on specialization in private debt contracting. *Journal of Finance* 53: 845–878.

Cassamatta, Catherine. 2003. Financing and advising: Optimal financial contracts with venture capitalists. *Journal of Finance* 58: 2,059–2,086.

Cecchetti, Stephen G. 1999. The future of financial intermediation and regulation: An overview. (Federal Reserve Bank of New York) *Current Issues in Economics and Finance* 5, no. 8: 1–7.

Cerasi, Vittoria. 1995. A model of retail banking competition. Working Paper, London School of Economics.

Cetorelli, Nicola, and Michel Gambera. 2001. "Banking market structure, financial dependence, and growth." *Journal of Finance* 56: 617–648.

Cetorelli, Nicola, and Philip E. Strahan. 2006. Finance as a barrier to entry: Bank competition and industry structure in local US markets. *Journal of Finance* 61: 437–461.

Chari, V. V., and R. Jagannathan. 1986. Banking panics, information and rational expectations equilibrium. *Journal of Finance* 43: 749–761.

Chava, Sudheer, and Michael R. Roberts. 2008. How does financing impact investment? The role of debt covenants. *Journal of Finance* 63: 2,085–2,121.

Chen, Nai-fu, Richard Roll, and Stephen A. Ross. 1980. Economic forces and the stock market: Testing the APT and alternative asset pricing theories. *Journal of Business*, 383–403.

Cheng, Pao L., and Robert Grauer. 1980. An alternative test of the capital asset pricing model. *American Economic Review* 70: 660–671.

Cherry, Josh. 2004. The limits of arbitrage: Evidence from exchange traded funds. Working Paper, University of California, Berkeley, Department of Economics.

Chordia, Tarun, Richard Roll, and Avanidhar Subrahmanyam. 2001. Market liquidity and trading activity. *Journal of Finance* 56: 501–530.

Claessens, Stijn, and Luc Laeven. 2003. Financial development, Property rights, and growth. *Journal of Finance* 58: 2,401–2,436.

Conrad, Jennifer. 1989. The price of option introduction. *Journal of Finance* 44: 487–498.

Courchene, Thomas J., and Edwin H. Neave, eds. 1995. *Financial Derivatives: Managing and Regulating Off-Balance Sheet Risks*, Kingston, Ont.: Queen's University, John Deutsch Institute for the Study of Economic Policy.

Cox, John C., and Mark Rubinstein. 1985. *Options Markets*. Englewood Cliffs, NJ: Prentice-Hall.

Crane, Dwight B., Kenneth A. Froot, Scott P. Mason, Andre E. Perold, Robert C. Merton, Zvi Bodie, Erik R. Sirri, and Peter Tufano. 1995. *The Global Financial System: A Functional Perspective*. Boston: Harvard Business School Press.

Culver, S. E., and D. H. Papell. 1999. Long-run purchasing power parity with short-run data: Evidence with a null hypothesis of stationarity. *Journal of International Money and Finance* 18: 751–768.

Cumming, Douglas, and Li Que. 2008. Capital flows and hedge fund regulation. Paper delivered to the International Finance Conference, Queen's University, May.

Cummins, J. David. 2005. Convergence of banking and insurance. In *Current Directions in Financial Regulation*, edited by F. Milne and E. H. Neave. Montreal: McGill-Queens University Press.

Cummins, J. David, Maria Rubio-Misas, and Hongmin Zi. 2004. The effect of organizational structure on efficiency: Evidence from the Spanish insurance industry. *Journal of Banking and Finance* 28: 3,113–3,150.

Dahiya, Sandeep, Anthony Saunders, and Anand Srinivasan. 2003. Financial distress and bank lending relationships. *Journal of Finance* 58: 375–400.

Davydenko, Segei A., and Ilya A. Strebulaev. 2007. Strategic actions and credit spreads. *Journal of Finance* 62: 2,633–2,671.

Dell'Ariccia, Giovanni, and Robert Marquez. 2006. Lending booms and lending standards. *Journal of Finance* 61: 2,511–2,546.

DeLong, Bradford. 1991. Did J. P. Morgan's men add value? An economist's perspective on financial capitalism. In *Inside the Business Enterprise: Historical Perspectives on the Use of Information*, edited by Peter Temin. Chicago: University of Chicago Press.

DeLong, Gayle, and Robert DeYoung. 2004. The value-added from observing bank mergers. In *Current Directions in Financial Regulation*, edited by Frank Milne and Edwin H. Neave. John Deutsch Institute Policy Forum Series No. 40, Queen's University, 2004.

Demirguc-Kunt, Asli, and V. Maksimovic. 1998. Law, finance, and firm growth. *Journal of Finance* 53: 2,107–2,137.

DeMotta, Adolfo. 2003. "Managerial incentives and internal capital markets." *Journal of Finance* 58: 1,193–1,220.

Demsetz, Harold. 1968. The cost of transacting. *Quarterly Journal of Economics* 82: 33–53.

Desai, Mihir A., C. Fritz Foley, and James R. Hines Jr. 2004. A multinational perspective on capital structure choice and internal capital markets. *Journal of Finance* 59: 2,451–2,487.

Dessein, Wouter. 2005. Information and control in ventures and alliances. *Journal of Finance* 60: 2,513–2,549.

DeTemple, Jerome, and Philippe Jorion. 1990. Option listing and stock returns: An empirical analysis. *Journal of Banking and Finance* 14: 781–801.

Detragiache, Enrica, Thierry Tressel, and Poonam Gupta. 2008. Foreign banks in poor countries: Theory and evidence, *Journal of Finance* 63: 2,123–2,160.

Dewatripont, Matthias, and Jean Tirole. 1994. *The Prudential Regulation of Banks*. Cambridge, MA: MIT Press.

Diamond, Douglas. 1984. Financial intermediation and delegated monitoring. *Review of Economic Studies* 51: 393–414.

Diamond, Douglas W. 2004. Committing to Commit: Short-Term Debt when Enforcement is Costly. *Journal of Finance* 59: 1,447–1,479.

Diamond, Douglas W., and Philip Dybvig. 1983. Bank runs, deposit insurance, and liquidity. *Journal of Political Economy* 91: 401–419.

Diamond, Douglas W., and Raghuram G. Rajan. 2000. A theory of bank capital. *Journal of Finance* 55: 2,431–2,466.

Diamond, Douglas W., and Raghuram G. Rajan. 2005. Liquidity shortages and banking crises. *Journal of Finance* 60: 615–648.

di Patti, Emilia Bonaccorsi, and Giorgio Gobbi. 2007. Winners or losers? The effects of banking consolidation on corporate borrowers. *Journal of Finance* 62: 669–695.

Domowitz, Ian, and Benn Steil. 1999. Automation, trading costs, and the structure of the trading services industry. Brookings-Wharton Papers on Financial Services.

Edgeworth, F. Y. [1885] 1995. The mathematical theory of banking. Read to the British Association, September 1886. In Mervyn K. Lewis, *Financial Intermediaries*. Aldershot, U.K.: Elgar, 1995.

Eichengreen, Barry, and Richard Baldwin. 2008. Rescuing our jobs and savings: What G7/8 leaders can do to solve the global credit crisis. London: Centre for Economic Policy Research.

Fabozzi, Frank J., and Franco Modigliani. 1992. *Capital markets: Institutions and instruments*. Englewood Cliffs, NJ: Prentice-Hall.

Fabozzi, Frank J., Franco Modigliani, and Michael G. Ferri. 2001. *Foundations of Financial Markets and Institutions*. Upper Saddle River, NJ: Prentice-Hall.

Fabozzi, Frank J., ed. 2005. *The Handbook of Mortgage Securities*. New York: McGraw-Hill.

Fabozzi, Frank J., and Vinod Kothari. 2007. Securitization: The tool of financial transformation. *Journal of Financial Transformation* 20: 34–44.

Fabozzi, Frank J. 2009. *Bond Markets: Analysis and Strategies*, 6th ed. Upper Saddle River, NJ: Prentice-Hall.

Fama, Eugene F. 1985. What's different about banks? *Journal of Monetary Economics* 15: 29–39.

Fama, Eugene F., and M. R. Gibbons. 1984. "A comparison of inflation forecasts." *Journal of Monetary Economics* 13: 327–348.

Ferreira, Miguel A., and Pedro Matos. 2008. When banks are insiders: evidence from the global syndicated loan market. Presented to International Finance Conference, Queen's University, May.

Financial Stability Forum. 2008. *Report of the Financial Stability Forum on enhancing market and institutional resilience*, April 7, 2008.

Fisman, Raymond, and Inessa Love. 2004. Financial development and intersectoral allocation: A new approach. *Journal of Finance* 59: 2,785–2,807.

Frankel, Jeffrey. 2008. Getting carried away: How the carry trade and its potential unwinding can explain movements in international financial markets. *Milken Institute Review* 10 (January): 38–45.

Freixas, Xavier, and Jean-Charles Rochet. 1997. *Microeconomics of Banking*, 1st ed. Cambridge, MA: MIT Press.

Freixas, Xavier, and Jean-Charles Rochet. 2008. *Microeconomics of Banking*, 2nd ed. Cambridge, MA: MIT Press.

Fung, William, David A. Hsieh, Narayan Y. Naik, and Tarun Ramadorai. 2008. Hedge funds: Performance, risk, and capital formation. *Journal of Finance* 63: 1,777–1,804.

Gabaix, Xavier, Arvind Krishnamurthy, and Olivier Vigneron. 2007. Limits of arbitrage: theory and evidence from the mortgage-backed securities market. *Journal of Finance* 62: 557–595.

Gale, Douglas. 1993. Informational capacity and financial collapse. In *Financial Intermediation in the Reconstruction of Europe*, edited by C. Mayer and X. Vives. London: Centre for Economic Policy Research.

Garmaise, Mark J., and Tobias J. Moskowitz. 2006. Bank mergers and crime: The real and social effects of credit market competition. *Journal of Finance* 61: 495–538.

Gemmill, Gordon. 1996. Transparency and liquidity: A study of block trades on the London stock exchange under different publication rules. *Journal of Finance* 51: 1,765–1,790.

Gibson, Michael S. 2004. Understanding the risk of synthetic CDOs. Federal Reserve Board Working Paper.

Goldstein, Itay, and Ady Pauzner. 2005. Demand deposit contracts and the probability of bank runs. *Journal of Finance* 60: 1,293–1,327.

Goodhart, C. 1995. *The Central Bank and the Financial System*. Cambridge, MA: MIT Press.

Gorton, G., and J. Kahn. 1993. The design of bank loan contracts, collateral, and renegotiation. Working Paper 1–93, Rodney L. White Center for Financial Research, Wharton School, University of Pennsylvania.

Gorton, Gary, and James Kahn. 2000. The Design of Bank Loan Contracts. *Review of Financial Studies* 13: 331–364.

Grossman, Sanford A. 1988a. An analysis of the implications for stock and futures price volatility of program trading and dynamic hedging strategies. *Journal of Business* 61: 275–296.

Grossman, Sanford A. 1988b. Program trading and stock and futures price volatility. *The Journal of Futures Markets* 8: 413–419.

Grossman, Sanford A. 1995. Dynamic asset allocation and the informational efficiency of markets. *Journal of Finance* 50: 773–785.

Grossman, Sanford J., and Merton H. Miller. 1988. Liquidity and market structure. *Journal of Finance* 43: 617–637.

Grossman, Sanford J., and Zhongquan Zhou. 1996. Equilibrium analysis of portfolio insurance. *Journal of Finance* 51: 1,379–1,403.

Guiso, Luigi, Paola Sapienza, and Luigi Zingales. 2003. Does local financial development matter? CRSP Working Paper 538.

Gurley, John G., and Edward S. Shaw. 1960. *Money in a Theory of Finance*. Washington, D.C.: Brookings Institution.

Harras, Georges, and Didier Sornette. 2008. Endogenous versus exogenous origins of financial rallies and crashes in an agent-based model with Bayesian learning and imitation. Swiss Finance Institute Research Paper 08–16.

Harris, Lawrence. 1995. Consolidation, fragmentation, segmentation, and regulation. Chapter 18 in *Global Equity Markets: Technological, Competitive and Regulatory Challenges*, edited by Robert A. Schwartz. New York: New York University Salomon Center; Burr Ridge, IL: Irwin Professional Publishing.

Hart, Oliver. 2001. Financial contracting. *Journal of Economic Literature* 39: 1,079–1,100.

Hart, Oliver D., and Dwight Jaffee. 1974. On the application of portfolio theory to depository financial intermediaries. *Review of Economic Studies* 41: 129–147.

Hart, Oliver D., and J. Moore. 1998. Default and renegotiation: A dynamic model of debt. *Quarterly Journal of Economics* 113: 1–41.

Hellman, Thomas, Kevin Murdock, and Joseph Stiglitz. 1996. Deposit mobilisation through financial constraint. In *Financial Development and Economic Growth*, edited by Niels Hermes and Robert Lensink. London: Routledge.

Holmstrom, Bengt, and Jean Tirole. 1997. Financial Intermediation, loanable funds, and the real sector. *Quarterly Journal of Economics* 112: 663–691.

Hong, Harrison, and Jeremy C. Stein. 1999. A unified theory of underreaction, momentum trading, and overreaction in asset markets. *Journal of Finance* 54: 2,143–2,184.

Huang, Chi-Fu, and Robert H. Litzenberger. 1988. *Foundations for Financial Economics*. New York: North-Holland.

Hubbard, R. Glenn, and Darius Palia. 1999. A reexamination of the conglomerate merger wave in the 1960s: An internal capital markets view. *Journal of Finance* 54: 1,131–1,152.

Hughes, Joseph P., and Loretta J. Mester. 1993. A quality and risk-adjusted function for banks: Evidence on the too-big-to-fail doctrine. *Journal of Productivity Analysis* 4: 293–315.

Hull, John C. 2008. *Options, Futures and Other Derivatives*, 7th ed. Upper Saddle River, NJ: Prentice-Hall.

Jarrow, Robert A., and Stuart M. Turnbull. 1996. *Derivative Securities*. Cincinnati: South-Western Publishing Company.

Jensen, Michael C., and William Meckling. 1976. Theory of the firm: Managerial behavior, agency costs and ownership structure. *Journal of Financial Economics* 3: 305–360.

John, Kose, and David C. Nachman. 1985. Risky debt, investment incentives, and reputation in a sequential equilibrium. *Journal of Finance* 40: 863–878.

Johnson, Hazel J. 2000. *Global Financial Institutions and Markets*, Oxford, Blackwell.

Johnson, Lewis D., and Edwin H. Neave. 1994. Governance and comparative advantage. *Managerial Finance* 20: 54–68.

Johnson, Lewis D., and Edwin H. Neave. 1999. *Strategic Management of Canadian Financial Intermediaries*. Waterloo, Mutual Life Research Centre, Wilfrid Laurier University.

Johnson, Lewis D., and Edwin H. Neave. 2008. The subprime mortgage market: Familiar lessons in a new context. *Management Research News* 31: 12–26.

Kanatas, George, and Jianping Qi. 2003. Integration of lending and underwriting: Implications of scope economies. *Journal of Finance* 58: 1,167–1,191.

Kaplan, Steven N., and Per Stromberg. 2004. Characteristics, contracts, and actions: evidence from venture capitalist analyses. *Journal of Finance* 59: 2,177–2,210.

Karceski, Jason, Steven Ongena, and David C. Smith. 2005. The impact of bank consolidation on commercial borrower welfare. *Journal of Finance* 60: 2,043–2,082.

Khanna, T., and S. Tice. 2001. "The bright side of internal capital markets." *Journal of Finance* 56: 1,489–1,531.

Kim, W. S., and C. M. Young. 1991. The effect of traded option introduction on shareholder wealth. *Journal of Financial Research* 14: 141–151.

King, Robert G., and Ross Levine. 1993. Financial intermediation and economic development. In *Financial Intermediation in the Construction of Europe*, edited by Colin Mayer and Xavier Vives. London: Centre for Economic Policy Research.

Kirilenko, Andrei G. 2001. Valuation and control in venture financing. *Journal of Finance* 56: 565–587.

Kiyotaki, Nobuhiro and John Moore. 1995. Credit cycles, Discussion Paper 205, Financial Market Group, London School of Economics.

Knight, Frank H. [1933] 1971. *Risk, Uncertainty, and Profit*, Chicago: University of Chicago Press.

Laeven, Luc, and Ross Levine. 2007. Corporate Governance, Regulation and Bank Risk Taking. Brown University Working Paper.

Laeven, Luc, and Fabian Valencia. 2008. Systemic banking crises: A new database. IMF Working Paper WP/08/224.

Leland, Hayne, and David H. Pyle. 1977. Informational asymmetries, Financial structure, and financial intermediation. *Journal of Finance* 32: 371–387.

Lewis, Mervyn King, ed. 1995. *Financial Intermediaries*, Aldershot, U.K.: Elgar.

Li, Donghui, Fariborz Moshirian, Peter Kien Pham, and Jason Zein. 2006. When financial institutions are large shareholders: The role of macro corporate governance environments. *Journal of Finance* 61: 2,975–3,007.

Lindsey, Laura. 2008. Blurring firm boundaries: The role of venture capital in strategic alliances. *Journal of Finance* 63: 1,137–1,168.

Lockhart, Dennis. 2009. Speech to the Atlanta Business Council. Federal Reserve Bank of Atlanta, January 12, 2009.

Longstaff, Francis A., and Arvind Rajan. 2008. An empirical analysis of the pricing of collateralized debt obligations. *Journal of Finance* 63: 529–563.

Lucas, Douglas J., Laurie Goodman, and Frank J. Fabozzi. 2007. Collateralized debt obligations and credit risk transfer. *Journal of Financial Transformation*, 20: 47–59.

Macey, Jonathan R., and Maureen O'Hara. 2005. From markets to venues: Securities regulation in an evolving world. *Stanford Law Review* 58: 563–599.

Malkiel, Burton G. 1995. Returns from investing in equity mutual funds 1971 to 1991. *Journal of Finance* 49: 549–572.

Mankiw, Gregory. 1986. The allocation of credit and financial collapse. *Quarterly Journal of Economics* 101: 455–470.

Marschak, Jakob, and Roy A. Radner. 1972. *Economic Theory of Teams*. New Haven: Yale University Press.

McConnell, John J., and Alessio Saretto. 2008. Auction Failures and the Market for Auction Rate Securities. Working Paper, Krannert School of Management, Purdue University.

McInish, Thomas H. 2000. *Capital Markets: A Global Perspective*. Oxford: Blackwell.

Merton, Robert C. 1977. An analytic derivation of the cost of deposit insurance and loan guarantees: An application of modern option pricing theory. *Journal of Banking and Finance* 1: 3–11.

Mishkin, Frederic S. 2007. *The Economics of Money, Banking, and Financial Markets*, 8th ed. Boston: Pearson Addison-Wesley.

Mishkin, Frederic, and Philip E. Strahan. 1999. What will technology do to financial structure?" NBER Working Paper 6892.

Naik, Narayan Y., and Pradeep K. Yadav. 2003. Risk management with derivatives by dealers and market quality in government bond markets. *Journal of Finance* 58: 1,873–1,904.

Neave, Edwin H. 1991. *The Economic Organisation of a Financial System*. London: Routledge.

Neave, Edwin H. 1998. *Financial Systems: Principles and Organisation*. London: Routledge.

Ni, Sophie X., Jun Pan, and Allen M. Poteshman. 2008. Volatility information trading in the option market. *Journal of Finance* 63: 1,059–1,091.

O'Hara, Maureen. 1995. *Market Microstructure Theory*. Oxford: Blackwell.

O'Hara, Maureen. 2003. Liquidity and price discovery. *Journal of Finance* 58: 1,335–1,354.

Parlour, Christine A., and Guillaume Plantin. 2008. Loan sales and relationship banking. *Journal of Finance* 63: 1,291–1,314.

Petersen, Mitchell A., and Raghuram G. Rajan. 2002. Does distance still matter? The information revolution in small business lending. *Journal of Finance* 57: 2,533–2,570.

Pliska, Stanley R. 1997. *Introduction to Mathematical Finance*, Malden, MA: Blackwell.

Pyle, David. 1971. On the theory of financial intermediation. *Journal of Finance* 26: 737–747.

Qian, Jun, and Philip E. Strahan. 2007. How laws and institutions shape financial contracts: the case of bank loans. *Journal of Finance* 62: 2,803–2,834.

Rajan, Raghuram G., and Luigi Zingales. 1998. "Financial Dependence and Growth." *American Economic Review* 88: 559–586.

Ramirez, Carlos D. 1995. Did J. P. Morgan's men add liquidity? Corporate investment, cash flow, and financial structure at the turn of the century. *Journal of Finance* 50: 661–678.

Reinhart, Carmen M., and Kenneth S. Rogoff. 2008. Is the 2007 U.S. sub-prime financial crisis so different? An international historical comparison. Harvard University Working Paper.

Rochet, Jean-Charles. 2008. *Why are There So Many Banking Crises?* Princeton, NJ: Princeton University Press.

Rogoff, Kenneth. 1996. The purchasing power parity puzzle. *Journal of Economic Literature* 34: 647–668.

Roll, Richard. 1977. A critique of the asset pricing theory: Part I. On the past and potential testability of the theory. *Journal of Financial Economics* 4: 129–176.

Ross, Stephen A. 1977. The determination of financial structure: The incentive-signalling approach. *Bell Journal of Economics* 7: 23–40.

Ross, Stephen A. 1989. Institutional markets, financial marketing, and financial innovation. *Journal of Finance* 44: 541–556.

Sack, Brian. 2000. Deriving inflation expectations from nominal and inflation-indexed Treasury yields. *Journal of Fixed Income* 10: 1–12.

Salop, Steven C. 1979. Monopolistic competition with outside goods. *Bell Journal of Economics* 10: 141–156.

Santoni, G. J. 1987. Has programmed trading made stock prices more volatile? *Federal Reserve Bank of St. Louis Review* 67: 18–29.

Santos, Joao A. C., and Andrew Winton. 2008. Bank Loans, Bonds, and Information Monopolies across the Business Cycle. *Journal of Finance* 63: 1,315–1,360.

Savage, Leonard J. 1954. *The Foundations of Statistics*. New York: Wiley.

Sercu, Piet, and Raman Uppal. 1995. *International Financial Markets and the Firm*. Cincinnati: South-Western.

Shapiro, James E. 1995. U.S. equity markets: recent competitive developments. Chapter 1 in *Global Equity Markets: Technological, Competitive and Regulatory Challenges*, by Robert A. Schwartz. New York University Salomon Center, 1995.

Shleifer, Andrei, and Robert W. Vishny. 1997. The limits of arbitrage. *Journal of Finance* 52: 35–55.

Sirri, Erik R., and Peter Tufano. 1998. Costly search and mutual fund flows. *Journal of Finance* 53: 1,589–1,622.

Sorenson, Martin. 2007. How Smart is Smart Money? A Two-Sided Matching Model of Venture Capital. *Journal of Finance* 62: 2,725–2,762.

Stambaugh, Robert F. 1982. On the exclusion of assets from tests of the two-parameter model. *Journal of Financial Economics* 10: 237–268.

Stein, Jeremy C. 1997. Internal capital markets and the competition for corporate resources. *Journal of Finance* 52: 111–133.

Stein, Jeremy C. 2002. Information production and capital allocation: Decentralized versus hierarchical firms. *Journal of Finance* 57: 1,899–2,002.

Stiglitz, Joseph, and Andrew Weiss. 1981. Credit rationing in markets with imperfect information. *American Economic Review* 71: 393–410.

Sufi, Amir, and Atif R. Mian. 2007. The consequences of mortgage credit expansion: Evidence from the 2007 mortgage default crisis. NBER Working Paper No. W13936.

Taylor, M. P. 1987. "Covered interest parity: A high frequency, high quality data study." *Economica* 54: 429–438.

Telser, Lester. 1981. Why there are organized futures markets. *Journal of Law and Economics* 24: 1–22.

Tinic, Seha M., and Richard R. West. 1974. Marketability of common stocks in Canada and the USA: A comparison of agent versus dealer dominated markets. *Journal of Finance* 29: 729–749.

Tobin, James. 1956. The interest elasticity of the demand for cash. *Review of Economics and Statistics* 38: 241–247.

Tufano, Peter. 1989. Financial innovation and first-mover advantages. *Journal of Financial Economics* 25 (December): 213–240.

Ueda, Masako. 2004. Banks versus venture capital: Project evaluation, screening, and expropriation. *Journal of Finance* 59: 601–621.

Vayanos, Dimitri, and Pierre-Olivier Weill. 2008. A search-based theory of the on-the-run phenomenon. *Journal of Finance* 63: 1,361–1,398.

Walter, Ingo. 2004. Regulatory targeting: Financial services strategies across borders and sectors. In *Current Directions in Financial Regulation*, edited by Frank Milne and Edwin H. Neave. John Deutsch Institute Policy Forum Series No. 40, Queen's University, 2004.

Weinstein, David E., and Yishay Yafeh. 1998. "On the costs of a bank-centred financial system: Evidence from changing main bank relations in Japan." *Journal of Finance* 53: 635–672.

Weston, James P. 2002. Electronic communication networks and liquidity on the Nasdaq. *Journal of Financial Services Research* 22: 125–139.

Williamson, Oliver E. 1975. *Markets and Hierarchies: Analysis and Antitrust Implications*. New York: Free Press.

Williamson, Oliver E. 1985. *The Economic Institutions of Capitalism*. New York: Free Press.

Williamson, Oliver E. 1987. Transaction cost economics: The comparative contracting perspective. *Journal of Economic Behavior and Organization* 8: 617–625.

Williamson, Oliver E. 2002. "The theory of the firm as governance structure: From choice to contract." *Journal of Economic Perspectives* 16: 171–195.

Yu, Wayne W. 1997. *Essays on Capital Markets*, Unpublished PhD dissertation, Edmonton: University of Alberta.